979.

*Navajo and
Photography*

Navajo and Photography

*A Critical History of the Representation
of an American People*

James C. Faris

University of New Mexico Press
Albuquerque

979.004972 F228n

Faris, James C.

Navajo and photography

© 1996 by the University of New Mexico Press
All rights reserved.
First edition
Design by Mary Shapiro

Library of Congress Cataloging-in-Publication Data

Faris, James C.
Navajo and photography : a critical history of the representation of an American people /
James C. Faris. — 1st ed.
p. cm.
Includes bibliographical references and index.
ISBN 0-8263-1725-1 (cl.)
1. Navajo Indians—Pictorial works.
2. Photography in ethnology—Southwest, New—History.   I. Title.
E99.N3F384   1996
979'.004972—dc20   95-41781
                                              CIP

To all Navajo, past and present, subject to the West's lens

Contents

Illustrations ix
Preface and Acknowledgments xi

1. **The Gaze of Western Humanism** 11
   Photography as Enterprise 11
   Navajo, Photography, Anthropology 17
   Navajo History 21

2. **The Registers of Photography of Navajo** 31
   Method as Political Critique 31
   Valences in the Photography of Navajo 40

3. **A Historical Sketch of Nineteenth-Century Photography of Navajo** 53
   The First Photographers 53
   Photographers, 1870–1900 70

4. **The Vanishing Race: Edward S. Curtis** 107

5. **Photography of Navajo to Mid-Century: Saturated Fields of Visibility** 149
   The Settling of Tropes: The First Two Decades 149
   Photography of Navajo After 1920: Bureaucrats, Postal Cards, and Color Slides 188

6. **The Endearing Navajo: Laura Gilpin** 235

7. **Selling Navajo Images: Contemporary Picture Books and Photographic Modernism** 267

8. **Navajo Photographers** 291

9. **Conclusions** 301

Notes 311
Appendix 339
Chart 1. List of Photographers of Navajo 340
Chart 2. List of Color Slide Companies/Postal Card Companies/
    Stock Companies of Navajo Images 364
Chart 3. List of Navajo Photographers 366
Bibliography 369
Index 386

Illustrations

All illustrations are incorporated in relevant text, except for the following:

Portfolio I: The Machine   1
Portfolio II: Navajo Elected   25
Portfolio III: Avoidance   45
Portfolio IV: Navajo in Image, 1900–1950   93
Portfolio V: Church and State   123
Portfolio VI: Hands-on Social Relations   225
Portfolio VII: Loom   255
Portfolio VIII: Mimesis   287

Preface and Acknowledgments

Our God Tscorenci was our Father and created the sun, which is like a mirror. He sees us from up on high and makes photographs of our reflection. When we die the photograph disappears. Many have been lost.
Kenchori, an Asháninka from Peruvian Amazonia, when asked to tell a story concerning cameras. (From W. Baker, Backward: An Essay on Indians, Time, and Photography, *1983:266).*

This study is an examination of the photography of Navajo people of the American Southwest. It is thus first historical, an attempt to explore the range of photographs that exist over time and note changes in photographic practices, in the photographs themselves and their receptions, and in resistances of Navajo. I will endeavor to correct errors, to flesh out the historical material available, and to suggest further projects in a general commentary on a history of the representation of Navajo. Second, this is a critical volume. Photographs of a minority indigenous group were produced largely by a dominant, aggressive, and exploitative majority foreign culture with institutional trajectories and disciplines that emphasized vision and was oriented toward the consumption of images. Additionally, I offer some reflexive commentary on visualism in the West and the development of photography as a discursive enterprise. My purpose is also thus polemical—to counter the hegemonic discourses currently commanding analysis of photography of Navajo and to suggest alternatives.

This study was first stimulated from questions that occurred in the examination of specific photographic materials in earlier research efforts (cf. Faris,

Preface

1990) as well as from experiences with photography of minority peoples elsewhere (cf. Faris, 1972, 1988a, 1993a; Riefenstahl, 1976, 1987, 1992) and a general critical interest in the implications of photography (cf. Faris, 1992a, 1992b, 1993b). It became clear that an incredible number of photographs of Navajo existed, that the vast published corpus of photography of Navajo was very narrow in its range of forms and contents, and that some unpublished photographs stored in the larger archives differed from those published (especially noticeable in the cases of Edward Curtis and Laura Gilpin).

Because this is a study concerned with the limits and boundaries of representation and its technologies and discourses, it is important to specify something of the book's own borders and parameters. Work was systematically undertaken from the late 1980s until 1994, when it became clear I simply had to prepare the materials on hand, cease chasing down ever-narrowing historical leads, and stop trying to exhaust more minutely the forever-widening corpus of photographic sources that kept coming to my attention. I decided to confine the work largely to still photographs and not deal with the ciné materials, whose more complex and involved narrative issues are beyond the scope of this study. I do not mean to imply that still photographs are not narrative, but there are different orders involved (cf. Mulvey, 1989; Pinney, 1990a, 1990b). A systemic study of the ciné materials thus remains for another researcher. This project needs to be done, but there are over 1,000 videos alone in the Navajo Office of Broadcast Services and at least 50 documentary films on Navajo noted in Navajo Nation Library—and these are conservative numbers. There are many other sources of Navajo films in most standard film source guides, to say nothing of the great numbers of Hollywood films that have been made in Navajoland, nor the plethora of advertising photographs and videos depicting Navajo and Navajoland.

I have also not attempted to make any systematic survey of newspaper photographs. Though newspaper photographers have come to attention from their still photographs in other archives, I have not examined in detail newspapers of the region. I am aware of the lacunae, but this project is not simply a content analysis (though it may be complexly so). Newspaper photographs and photojournalism as such were not specific categories of reference that deviated from other general Western photography.

I am not a historian and have not attempted to assemble biographical information on photographers except where such issues might bear on an analysis of specific photographs. Moreover, most museums and archives attempt to maintain biographical information on those persons whose photographs they hold, and these may be consulted, as may published biographies and sketches. Thus, the charts of the Appendix are not intended to be more than minimally referential. Many readers will be able add entries, and certainly corrections are to be anticipated. These charts clearly do not stand as monuments to exhaustive research.

There are undoubtedly many historical details to be established or corrected (attributions, for example). I have not, then, attempted to historicize the photography of Navajo within the larger whole of American photography (where I am not competent). Rather, I have tried to critique representation of Navajo in basically subjective and political terms. Such history that emerges is particular to this task; I make no further claims.

It should be noted that the terms *West* and *Western* are used herein as special construct and disquisition, not geographical notion. They apply to a world that is usually European, European-American, and/or "white" (but not always, as sometimes today the Japanese [and Japan] are included in the West, as, of course, are non-Native American minorities located among the "white"). The West is usually capitalist (but not always, as the former USSR and its satellites could sometimes be [and today certainly are] included) and always institutionally and politically dominant. In other words, it is a locus of power and dominant discourse both within and without. It holds the camera. In this sense, *West* will always be capitalized (see Frankenberg, 1993, for discussion). A common English-language reference partially (but only partially) covering this category in Navajoland is *Anglo*, or the term *bilagáana*, coming from *American*. It is a set of assumptions, a way of doing things, a means of viewing.

Navajo is used without the definite article: There is no *the* Navajo. This peculiarity is an attempt to eliminate any hint of objectification, as well as to eliminate any claim to speak for or represent all Navajo. My intent is to give Navajo voice precedence over that of photography, to eliminate Navajo as object. Indeed, herein photography will be objectified.

I would almost preferred to have published this book with no photographs at all, especially given the polemic in the analysis. But that would have deprived readers of some very fine and generous photographs indeed, some illustrative materials that have not heretofore been seen, and images necessary to make the points in discussions and comparisons. I have tried, however, not to reproduce any photographs that might be demeaning, insulting, or invasive (they are plentiful in unpublished archives). There will be no prints of photographs of Navajo known to be intoxicated, ill, or not living at the time of the photograph, nor of still-living Navajo from whom permission has not been received. There are no prints of photographs of sacred materials or sandpaintings. I will provide references to sources in which such photographs can be found. Finally, I use as few previously published photographs as possible but where necessary make reference to their publication.

The University of Connecticut Research Foundation has been especially generous in providing grants for my research and for the printing of the photographs included here. In addition, I must thank the National Endowment for the Humanities for a Travel to Collections Grant.

I thank my editor at the University of New Mexico Press, Barbara Guth, who has had to labor with my syntax, vocabulary, and polemic now for years, and her hand and good cheer has made it a very much more comprehensible volume. (It has also made it a less expensive and smaller volume, and there was a struggle over each photograph included.) The remaining lack of clarity, arcane vocabulary, and rhetorical and inflammatory usages are due to my insistences. And thanks to the designer, Mary Shapiro, whose talent and forbearance with my sometimes stubborn requests and the constraints on paper and photographs have generated such a handsome volume. Thanks also to Andrew L. Christenson who prepared the index.

Chapters 4 and 6 have appeared in shortened versions elsewhere (see Faris, 1993c, 1993d), and several audiences have provided valuable feedback when I have read other portions of the manuscript. Dozens of archivists, photo historians, curators, photographers, and other scholars have been vital to this project. Indeed, none of the work could have been done without their cooperation. I know very well that many will not agree with the polemic and interpretations here, nor with the selections of photographs. But they and many others were generous to have assisted me in any case, and for their contributions I must sincerely thank the following: John Adair, Lana Babbij, Jonathan Batkin, Kathleen Baxter, Stephen Becker, Clarenda Begay, Richard N. Begay, Nate Benn, Bruce Bernstein, Pat Berrett, M. Guy Bishop, Jennifer Brathovde, David Brugge, Sina Brush, Ted Bundy, Carol Burke, Richard Buchen, Kristie Butler, John Cahoon, Cathy Cesario, Liz Clancy, A. D. Coleman, Dale Connely, Fr. Simon Conrad OFM, Charlotte Cornfield, John Craig, Sam Day III, Robert Dauner, Sharon Dean, Rose Díaz, Carol Downey, Rod Dresser, Edward Earle, K. R. Faris, Charles Fergus, Linda Fisk, Paula Fleming, Harris Francis, Karen Furth, Gretchen Garner, Diana Gaston, Jerri Glover, John W. Grassham, Bonnie Greer, Diane E. Grua, Janet Hall, Russell P. Hartman, Anselm Harvey, Heather Hatch, Helen R. Herzer, Louis Hieb, George Hight, Richard Hill, Elizabeth Hill, Raymond Holstein, Laura Holt, Dorothy House, Kathleen Hubenschmidt, Therese Thau Heyman, Ira Jacknis, Sandy Jarmillo-Macias, Roberta John, Alan Jutzi, Eunice Kahn, Thomas W. Kavanagh, Kenji

Preface

Kawano, Jerry Kearns, Klara Kelley, Charles Kline, Craig Klyver, Denise Kusel, Martha Labell, Mary Anne Laugharn, Stephen T. LeCuyer, Rebecca Lintz, Paul Long, Brita Mack, Janice Madhu, Pierre Mahaim, Charles Mann, Karen Marshall, Natasha Bonilla Martinez, Barbara Mathé, Roy McJunkin, Kathy M'Closky, Danyelle Means, Joseph M. Meehan, Lynette Miller, Lynn Marie Mitchell, Ron Montoya, Russ Morgan, Jonathan Morse, Laura Nash, Mark Nohl, Tamara Northern, Caroline Olin, Arthur Olivas, Susan Otto, Joan M. Pace, Mo Palmer, Peter Palmquist, Natalie Pattison, Richard Pearce-Moses, Michele M. Penhall, Joyce M. Peters, Alessando Pezzati, Helen Plummer, Willow Powers, Gene Prince, Bettina Raphael, Al Regensberg, Stella de Sá Rego, Seth Richardson, Marion Rodee, Monty Roessel, Steve Rogers, Hazel Romero, Meridel Rubenstein, Richard Rudisill, Paul Saavedra, Richard Salazar, Stefani Salkeld, David Scheinbaum, Joanna Scherer, Betty Sena, Tom Southall, Peter Steere, Paula Stewart, Joy Stickney, Laine Sutherland, Joel Sweiler, Dace Taube, Vyrtis Thomas, Barbara Thurber, Marcia Tiede, Alan Trachtenberg, T. K. Treadwell, Hulleah Tsinhnahjinnie, Stephanie Turnham, Michael Wagner, Henry Walt, Harry Walters, Dorothy Washburn, Jennifer Watts, Peter Welsh, Karen Whitehair, Lynette Williams, Michael Winey, Robert Wolfenstein, Yoshiko Miko Yamamoto, Steve Yates, and Alfred Yazzie.

Under formal agreement, any and all royalties resulting from the sale of this book accrue to the Navajo Nation Museum, Window Rock AZ.

James C. Faris
Connecticut, December 1994

Portfolio I
The Machine

Portfolio I

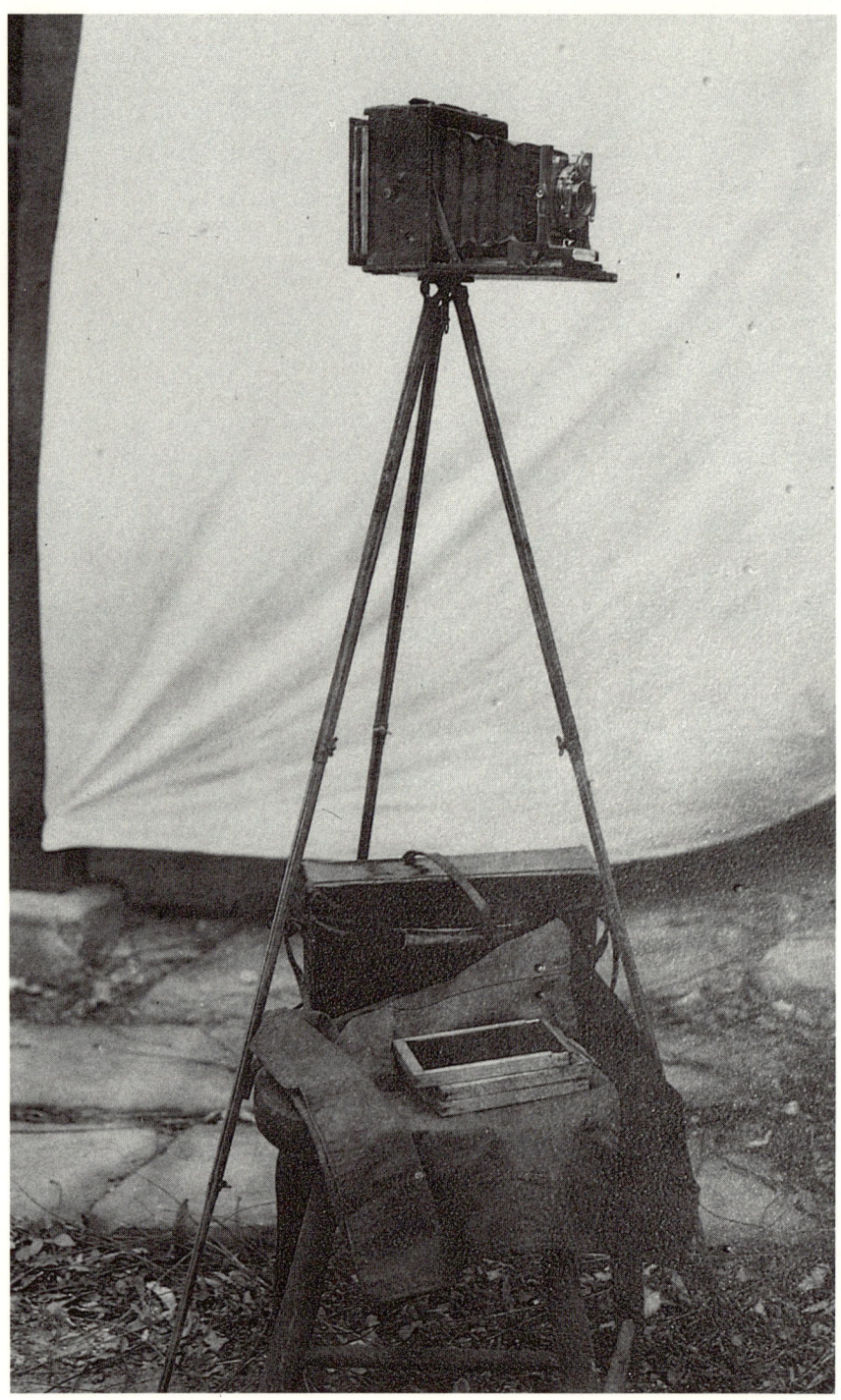

Figure 1

The Machine

Figure 1. "The 4x5 plate camera and telescope tripod that I used to photograph Indians when I was at Meadows Trading Post, on the San Juan River, New Mexico Territory, in August 1902. The Navajos were very superstitious about having their picture taken, and Meadows told me that they called this strange 'medicine' the 'Magic Black Box With the Evil Eye.' The tripod is the earliest type of telescope metal tripod. The sole leather case in which I carried it and six double plate holders, strapped to the side of the horn of my saddle is on the chair together with the focusing cloth and three plate holders are on the chair. This is a Tel-Photo Poco Camera, made by the Rochester Optical Company, Rochester, New York, a firm long out of business. This company had designed this style of plate camera to be carried on a bicycle." Earle R. Forrest, photographer, August 1902. Meadows Trading Post. Forrest sometimes used the sheet in the background as a backdrop but more frequently did not. Photograph courtesy Earle R. Forrest Collection, Museum of Northern Arizona. MS 9-143-5393. See also Samuel Barnett, MPM Neg. No. 122522, Milwaukee WI, for an early motion picture camera in Navajoland.

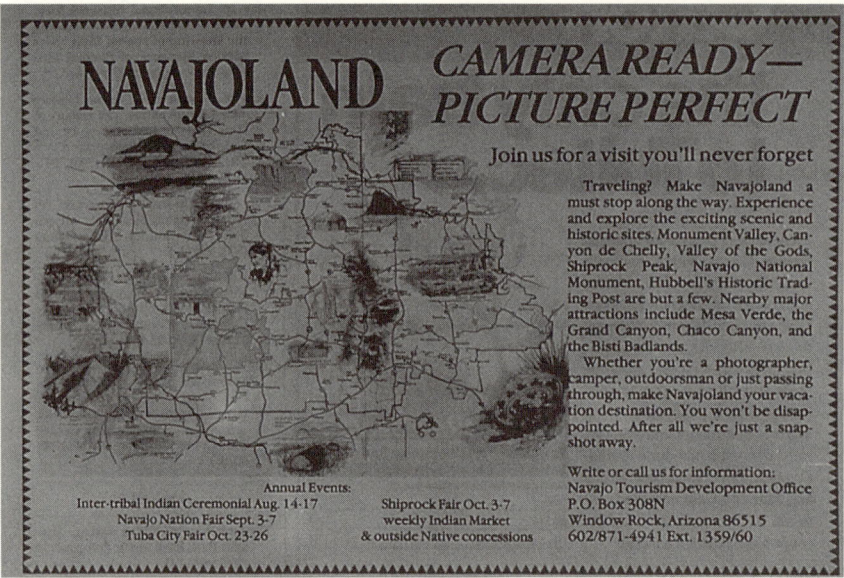

Figure 2

Figure 2. "Navajoland. Camera Ready—Picture Perfect." Advertisement, New Mexico Magazine, 64(5):9, 1986. Copy courtesy Navajo Tourism Development Office and New Mexico Magazine.

Figure 3. "Navajo children." Photographer unknown, ca. 1925. This may be a Clarkson photograph taken on an Indian Detours coach trip. The European-American attempts to photograph the children while the missionary student attempts to hide the young naked child. But the photographer here exposes everything. The children are distracted and so cannot avoid the photographer. Photograph courtesy Museum of New Mexico. Neg. No 53801.

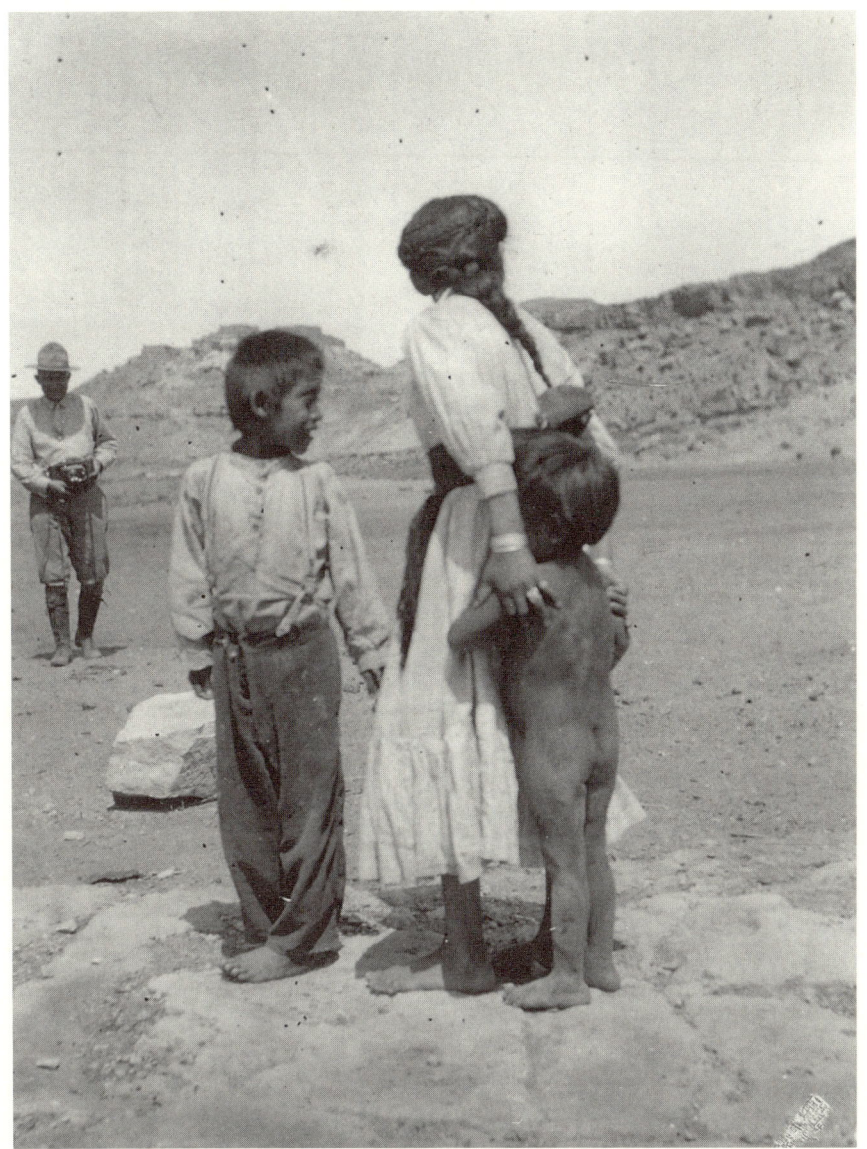

Figure 3

Portfolio I

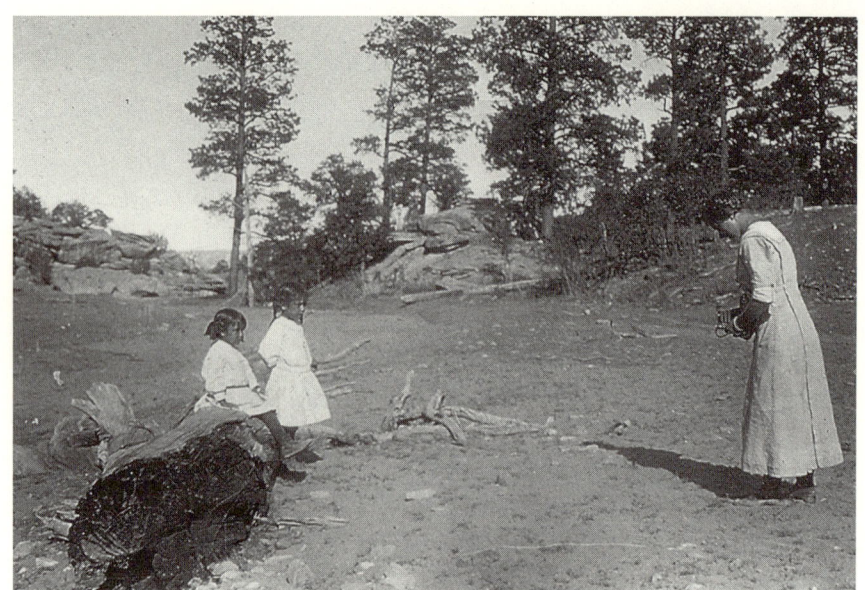

Figure 4

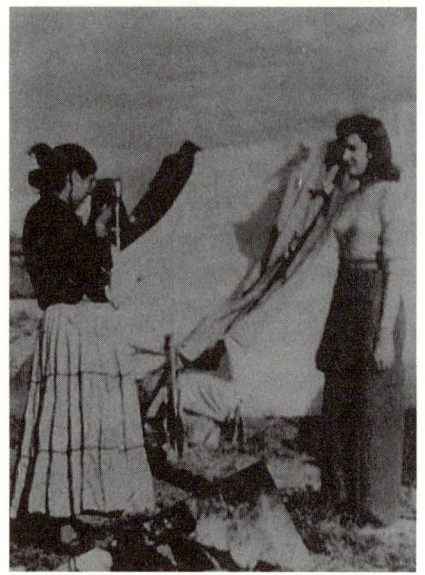

Figure 5

Figure 4. Navajo mission school girl photographing Navajo children in mission clothing, perhaps on the occasion of their first communion. Photographer unknown, n.d. This charming photograph is an early example of Navajo photography— very much like Western family photography. Indeed, in this circumstance, Navajo as Westerners. The little girls do not seem any more comfortable, however, with a Navajo photographer than with any other. The presence of the photographer here may add to their sense of unease. Photograph courtesy Museum of Northern Arizona and Franciscan Friars at St. Michaels AZ. MS 119-61-751.

Figure 5. Navajo woman photographing. Photographer unknown (probably Wyatt Davis), n.d. (before 1974). Of course, she is not taking a picture; she is holding the Argus C wrong, is nowhere near the shutter release, and is not looking through the viewfinder. This type of photograph was widespread at the time, presumably meant to be amusing. Instead of condemning such representations as racist, observers today commonly consider such images ironic and celebrate them (cf. McAuley, 1989). Photograph courtesy New Mexico Magazine (original now lost).

Portfolio I

Figure 6. "Little Navajo Girl." David Burnett, photographer, n.d. (1992??). Monument Valley. "The Native Americans have a cagey relationship with the camera, but they know the value of a good picture" (Nicholson and Burnett, 1993:31). Certainly it is important for Westerners to have these attitudes, as if Native Americans ultimately have much choice. Why is one of their only means of earning income locally held in such contempt, and why is contempt not extended to those who make such activity desirable? The little girl seems uncertain and appears to be seeking instruction or support from elsewhere. See below for more little girls in "costume," a favorite image of European-Americans. See Lippard, 1992:27, for a similar photograph. Despite the "reality" of the landscape, this photograph credits the thesis that Navajo are not aboriginal but only "adapters." Photograph courtesy David Burnett/Contact Press Images.

The Machine

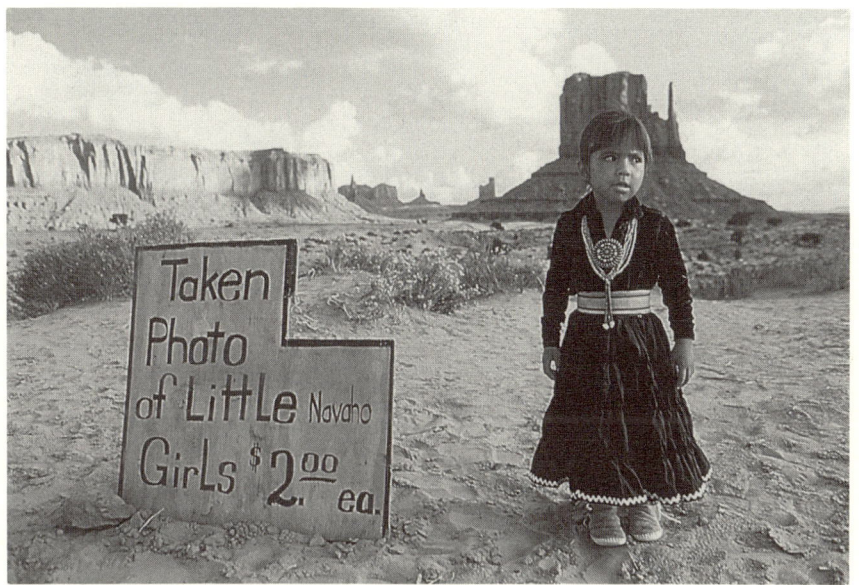

Figure 6

Chapter One

The Gaze of Western Humanism

I want to see, that's all. This is my life. I want to see.
   Leni Riefenstahl, on the occasion of her ninetieth
   birthday (Vanity Fair, *September 1992)*

Photography as Enterprise

There are broad circumstances that characterized the intellectual organization of the social forms in which photography developed. The West had long privileged scopic enterprises and visual modalities, and by the mid-nineteenth century an observational visualist hegemony became a persistent focus of modernism in social, scientific, and aesthetic endeavors—and certainly of anthropology.[1] More specifically, photography came into being at a time when the notion of observation itself was in change in the West, as a complex interaction of technology, emerging mass culture, surveilling state institutions, and associated intellectual ferment.[2] This transition entailed a wholesale shift in vision itself and the rise of an assertive observational and perspectival paradigm that was matched locally by the United States's conquest and aggressive expansion in Navajoland. These are the intellectual, institutional, and disciplinary settings in which and by which Navajo were photographed.

The history of photography, especially given the recent sesquicentennial celebrations of its invention, has generated an enormous literature. More recently, there has begun to appear a literature specifically on photographic encounters with non-Westerners, both critical and introspective (cf. Graham-Brown, 1988; Coombes, 1994; Lippard, 1992; Edwards, 1992 and references therein; and Baker, 1983, and Fergus, 1991, for recent literary treatments of

Chapter 1

the topic) and celebratory, art historical, and aesthetic (cf. Fleming and Luskey, 1993).

It is now increasingly accepted that photography's vision is peculiar and historical and can be divorced neither from specific developments in its history nor from the particularly Western milieu (a changing and sometimes contradictory one) in which it emerged. These considerations are compounded when photographic practices and discourses intersect with other cultural forms whose knowledges and practices are (or were) independent of photography and its history in the West. These encounters have been, of course, unequal, and conquest and oppression have usually warped the engagement. Photography evolved and matured in the same capitalist environment as did anthropology,[3] and both moved, with an expansionist West, into Navajoland at approximately the same time.

Navajo constitute both a generic as well as a unique and peculiar Other to photography's West and the West's photography. I will first consider photography as a practice of the West, then apply this analysis to the photography of Navajo. Much of what might be said about photography of Navajo can be said of the photography of all local minorities, but much is specific. I must echo some recent debate concerning photography and its limitations in order to outline some of the positions by which I will approach the photography of Navajo. Thus, in this chapter I discuss some of the possibilities and limitations, the framings and the exposures, of the depiction of Navajo by non-Navajo. After this initial commentary, I will examine specific photographic registers, modes and characters of representation, and concrete histories of photography in Navajoland.

Just what can be expected or understood from photographs? I will argue that, culturally, not very much can be understood about Navajo from photographs of them. But certainly something can be understood of photographers, of the various ways the West privileges photographs, and of the way Navajo photographically appear to the West. Photographs of Navajo mirror the West's desire and ambition, its obsession and pathology, and something of the specificity of social relations the West views as important (normal) and/or important for Navajo to have (marginal and/or normalized).[4] However, in addition to reading the West in its photography of Navajo, we also can read the limits and boundaries of how Navajo can appear in such representations and typical ways in which they do appear.

The focus became a black hole into which freedoms disappeared; frames become the limits and boundaries of representations. Photographs are gripping because they have boundaries and focus; the limits are clear, established.

Framing is a device for speaking (showing) truth. Parameters are as vital as the "frame" of an ethnography—the table of contents, with its categories presented in some hierarchy, priority, unity, or totality. Of course, the severity of its framing and editing greatly limited any interactive possibilities.

But what is not represented? What is outside the frame? What is not focused? What are the silences to be listened (watched) for? To ask this is to displace intention and the founded field of representation; it is to pose a question not of vision but of project. It is, indeed, to critique—to disrupt the closure, the framing, the representation—by noting within the representation that which cannot be represented (by the photograph, by the white man, by the texts available to viewers). It is to deconstruct (or to challenge without program) the conceptual space, the rule of being, the representation. It is to subvert desire (perhaps for another one). Framing is, then, in this sense, censoring. It is not, however, a simple aesthetic gesture, for an alternative power might rest in what does not appear.[5]

Photography exposes another rigidly limiting feature—the strange notion that, by freezing the moment, it transcends temporality (or that which we allow in conventional Western wisdom). But in fact, quite the opposite is true. Photography represents a shutter stop/closing, a deliberate avoidance of any and all other notions of time. Positioning in time and space to allow discourse, allowing speech to subjects, is impossible. Photography is thus an index in but a single tense, one voice, and one time.[6] Photography makes present; it appears to transcend time. But this appearance, this presence, in photography's rigidly fixed single dimension obviously cannot transcend time, particularly if such time involves (as it always does) the possibility of an alternative historical discourse, completely opaque or invisible to photography. As Benjamin (1969:226) noted, photographs "become standard evidence for historical occurrences, and acquire a hidden political significance. They demand a specific kind of approach; free-floating contemplation is not appropriate to them." Temporally, then, photography could only look back, could only be reactionary, and could only satisfy in terms of nostalgia, preservation, desire, and other nihilistic fixations from a single discursive view. The image exceeds both the photographer and the subject and is present in different time, open to different judgments and protocols. It no longer "represents" what might have been intended, and we are not sure what that might have been. We are not only *allowed* to read and assign meaning, we are required and forced to do so.

Through its ubiquitous extension as a mechanically reproduced commodity, photography soon succumbed to the gaze, as the world (especially the non-Western world) came to be an exhibition to silent consumers. Whereas "spectacles" (local events focused upon) once had specific audiences, they now became available to all individuals, though (ironically) increasingly privately, to the point of isolation. Photography made gazing upon events (thereby making them "spectacles") safe for voyeurs. This form of isolating and emphasizing events demanded an observational pacifism, and it was particularly important in photography's extension to distant peoples—now domesticated, made safe.[7] With the rise of hunting metaphors that dominated photographic production (the "shot," the "captured" image), photography thus became symbolic in the West's history of conquest, of defeat, of assimilation or disappearance, a force by which white men's power was validated. This aspect was particularly vital in photography that involved social relations with minorities and of subjugation. Such considerations give rise to a preservational motivation—things (cultures, peoples) only disappear as evidence of the West's own history. Nostalgic tendencies, so common in the repertoire of the photography of Native Americans, have come to signify desire for, at best, more liberal and generous white men and, at worst, the conqueror, the Indian fighter, the raw expansionist, the frontier tamer.

Photography introduced, as no other visual medium could, the "death effect," such that "the person who has been photographed is dead . . . dead for having been seen" (Metz, 1985:85)—dead for having been stopped from breathing, speaking. Photographs mute; they render speechless, "for every photograph of the Other is a visual reduction of the Other—both a distancing and a muting" (Owens, 1993:106). They do not speak; they are "worth a thousand words" only if there is nothing to say, if all communication has already taken place, if every possible sign is already shared—i.e., if all texts are already accepted. The photograph is transparent only if we allow it to be.[8] This transparency produces a curious alienation, a strange appearance of unarguable reality whose monuments are photographs. We can have little idea about, say, Navajo social relations from photographs of Navajo except those the photographer or the viewer (whose expectations are themselves constituted in part by photographs) brings.

I am suggesting that photography has no undeniable, necessary, or essential characteristics. Though it emerged in a historical setting, a prepared field, a way of seeing, a set of visualist discourses, a saturated domain in and by which it was accepted, utilized, extended, and allowed, these were and are ever-shifting fields. Moreover, consumers of photography changed over time, and just as there is no existential production, neither is there a monolithic, pan-historical observer. On the contrary, viewers and subjects were immersed in specific and changing social, political, and aesthetic relations that helped shape photography's development and future quite as much as photography imposed itself on them. This instability is perhaps an important reason to remain optimistic in the face of an otherwise somewhat inimical critique.

Of course, there have always been claims that photography was a "neutral technology," for it was but simply (or complexly) a photochemical process that somehow candidly reflected the world on the other side of the photographer (albeit with a cultural component, especially if the camera were in the hands of the Other,[9] excluding all ethical issues). These insistences were often heard loudest from anthropological photographic practitioners,[10] for they were important in expediting the discipline's emergence as a social *science*.

The emergence of anthropology as a distinct field of inquiry with an abstract methodology coincided very closely with photography's rise.[11] The earliest anthropological methodology primers mention the importance of photography,[12] and by the late nineteenth century photography of non-Westerners, of the exotic, was very popularly consumed.[13] At this time the great imperialist powers were extending across the globe, and the United States was pushing toward the Pacific. The West's authorizing signatures—rhetorics, disciplinary apparatuses (Western humanism), history, knowledges—were commonly expressed in photography, culminating in banal "Family of Man" notions or the reformist propaganda of Farm Security Administration (FSA) photography projects, which began once everyone had been safely conquered. Photography of this sort came to be normalizing, and an Other was thereby established, an Other always measured off the West's Normal. The "perpetual ratio" (Foucault, 1973:378) was thus maintained, as the West became the only subject, the only eye. Native Americans could not be seen looking back; they could only be seen (Portfolio I).

This coincidence itself deserves more commentary, for it derives from a social context of expansionism, a motion into the rest of the world, an imperialist acceleration. In the American Southwest, in Navajoland, this expansion was dramatic from the 1870s on, involving a series of government expeditions with explicit photographic agendas and the extension of the capitalist mandate and Manifest Destiny. I explore these themes in more detail in Chapters 2 and 3.

Early scholars denied the setting in which photography emerged (the deep and complex history of visualism) and was practiced (the shallow history of expansionist capital and imperialist conquest). As a result, two sorts of critical scholarship initially dominated the study of photography. The first type focused exclusively on aesthetics and the aesthetics of form.[14] Form aesthetics came to be relentlessly preferred above other levels of actual use and meaning. There was rarely any historical or cultural context outside the formal postures—just a transcendent aesthetic ideal. Photographs were to speak for themselves (indeed, to "say it all") only because viewers were all educated (or uneducated) to the same form assumptions—that photography was a neutral photochemical operation about which only assessments of form aesthetics were possible. This view precluded any other text, any introduced meaning, any critique at all. From this perspective, there could be, then, axiomatically fascist aesthetics, bourgeois aesthetics, where meaning was introduced *from* form, as if there were some intrinsic link between morality and aesthetics.

The second type of scholarship offered rudimentary political critique based upon a rather limited notion of representation.[15] It often argued that the photograph did not adequately represent or only represented partially, as if it were always a stereotype and that a "real" representation could be achieved photographically—"seeing is believing," "photographs never lie." The problem here is not that representations are always inadequate (of course they are inadequate) but that they never produce a truer or more accurate view. Representation is compromised because it holds a complex relation to reality—sometimes contradictory, sometimes laced with desire, fear, sometimes jeopardized, filled with resistance.[16] Indeed, the relationship of reality to representation is not something that can even be satisfactorily approached in rationalist discourse.

With the traditional, limited conceptions of representation, one obvious solution was to put cameras in the hands of the "misrepresented" subaltern. There were and are now a number of experiments in this direction. But cross-cultural photography is very problematic, for unless it can manage to *enforce* a boundary cross-culturally, it normally drags the framing practices of the dominant photographer and the technology along. As will be argued, placing the subaltern behind the camera is not a solution to the problems of representation, however much it may be vital to introducing alternative discourses; it illustrates only the photographer's specific pertinences. Photograph[er]s only present themselves—anything we think we see beyond them in the photograph is representation. I am not convinced that conventional indigenous photography gets around this problem.[17] Some less experienced or less introspective Navajo photographers acquired a reflective vision or double vision; they came to see themselves as others see them (see Chapter 8). Photography alone can never provide a truth (the real) to challenge power—that can only be an intellectual affair. It is quite as discursive as "nature," or "rights," or "law," or "poverty," or "theory," or the West's Other. But, as will be argued, for Navajo the images became the reality, and Navajo (real) emerged as imperfect or inadequate copies of their images.[18] This was a complicated issue, however, for the West's real Navajo were not exactly what they appeared. Photographs could only tell the whole story if accompanied by anthropology's text.

Navajo, Photography, and Anthropology

What, then, does it mean to be Navajo *in photographs*? This is not as sententious a question as it sounds, for photographic representations are critical in shaping responses to specific "meanings" of Navajo that have been persistently put forward. Indeed, photographs have been instrumental in bringing into being something of these "Navajo." "Reality" came to be (had to be) the representation, the photographic image. These meanings change, of course, over time, but a stubborn stability characterizes them.

Photography of Navajo by definition leans on canons of realism, the opaqueness of the subject, the transparency of the photograph. Navajo are received as real, as existing independently of the technology, of the social relations that placed them in the photograph, and of their own social relations. But they do not exist, or at least not in any necessary or nontrivial way revealed in the photograph. As noted, photographs say less about Navajo than about photographers of Navajo—indeed, in the limited ways in which Navajo appeared, photographers used amazingly few tropes, and these are remarkably consistent over time. Navajo, by definition, are set in their alterity to white men, their distance of Other accepted without so much as a whimper from viewers. They appear unproblematic as Other, and the photograph functions as document, as presentation of Navajo alterity. Non-hostile Navajo are, after all, such attractive Others (and certainly vital to a vast tourist industry in the region). To be sure, some representations were clichés, some objectionable by later historical movements, some objectionable by later Western sensitivities. But never was the alterity dissolved, even by Navajo photographers (unless the latter avoided photographs of people, a subject considered in more detail in Chapter 8). The tropes of photographs of Navajo people were always rigidly on Western terms; there has emerged as yet no setting in which instruments of gaze can present Navajo. Photography is not a medium that has a being in indigenous culture (or local presentation), though it may be used in explicit political ways by local artists.

I am not attempting to expose, reveal, or analyze a falsity about Navajo that has been perpetrated by photography. Photography is not a conspiracy; but, more important, there are no truth claims or determinant conclusions in this analysis. Of course, there are some clearly erroneous labels, claims, settings, and deliberate distortions in photography, as in Western texts, where Navajo are misunderstood, misinterpreted, or missing. But the task is to examine the nature of the entity constructed, not match it or compare it with a "real" entity it may have claimed to portray or with which it might be contrasted. Nevertheless, this register of representation is a vitally important one for the West, for it is how the West often "knows" it has knowledge of Navajo—Navajo are always framed, muted, always as the photographs show them.

To demonstrate, let us contrast the photography of another Southwestern minority group, the various Pueblo peoples, as evidence of their history and social relations with the photography of Navajo as evidence of another history and other social relations. Suffice it to say here that the West is prepared to accept in rough outline the antiquity of the Pueblo peoples to the region and thereby at least some of their claims to aboriginality and to the land on which they are found. It thus accepts Pueblo social relations in general (at least with respect to the land). Photographs confirm these claims and are considered evidential to them. This is not to say that photographers have never violated Pueblo peoples,[19] only that at least some Pueblo truths are considered in correspondence with Western truths.

Quite the contrary is true of photography of Navajo, which denies their status as aboriginals, as claimants, as indicators of their own social relations (though a naive minority popular discourse—among uninformed tourists, romantic Big Mountain supporters, etc.—regards Navajo as being in their place, as if they have always been there). Photographs are silent to any other discourse and certainly to a Navajo discourse. Anthropological orthodoxy and conventional wisdom deny them autochthonous or indigenous status, and photographs thus become evidences of their exotic and foreign origins, their hybrid and borrowed culture—Navajo as adapters.[20] In other words, Navajo exist in a space (as must all photographic subjects), but they also exist in a time (a dimension about which photography has very little to say, confined as it is to the instant past moment). Space is turned into time in the West's predatory grip on history, and thus Navajo space is denied them by the Western rewrite of their history, by the anthropological evidence of their late arrival, their adaptation, their alien and exotic character. Photography becomes a perverse asset in denying Navajo history, and they become subjects only of the West's history. The only Navajo social relations seen are those that can be placed into two visual dimensions. Metamorphic relations are not visible to photography, nor clan relations, nor healing relations, nor migrations, nor emergences from netherworlds, nor Navajo histories with European Americans. Though some of the specific Western history of Navajo is hidden to photographs by convention (for example, exploitation), so too are any and all Navajo claims to a history.

What, then, are the rhetorics of the Western photographic projects, the figures that allow us to recognize the master portrayals that forecast, that indicate something of the optical unconscious? I will argue that even though they change over time, even though one discourse penetrates and percolates into others, the projects are quite limited in number, and the same gestures appear again and again over time. There are a very limited series of frames. To extend much beyond these risks the West's "Navajo," whether or not any other "Navajo" is possible in photographic registers. Thus, there is not another history, another means of discussing photographic appropriations and inscriptions of Navajo by the West—Navajo inscriptions. Unlike ceremonial accounts involving many histories, photographs of Navajo allow for no alternative narratives. All histories are reduced to those of the West.

There is insufficient depth for much of an archaeology of Navajo photography, as the stratigraphy is mixed and jumbled, interpenetrated by other layers, or not varied enough to enable us to discriminate. We can only distinguish the tropes that were there from the beginning, and in many cases, despite the commentary of their partisans, Laura Gilpin looks like Edward Curtis, Marcia Keegan looks like Curtis, John Running looks like Curtis, Joel Grimes looks like Curtis (see Chapter 7), or Carl Moon, or Frederick Monsen. Thus, photography is even more impoverished than it might initially appear; it is not even in competition with an alternative. These limited photographic registers will be explored in some detail, but it is clear that Navajo appear only as another intention of the West, not because the "reality" of Navajo is not comprehensible but because it may well be impossible to approach in prevailing discourses of the West or in Western modes of visual representation. There certainly cannot be, in this circumstance, nonviolent representation—exposing the inability of Western humanism to adequately evince (represent) the non-West.[21] Certainly aesthetics of form dictate "success" or "interest" in many photographs from Navajoland. But Navajo, except as devices (as red rocks, trees, turquoise, silver, sheep, lichens), are irrelevant, nothing more than exotic props, colorful contrivances to Western projects.

The point is not just that Navajo social relations—Navajo texts—are ignored (though they are) but that there is no space available for them. The West cannot have its Navajo without having saturated the universe of possibilities, and the serious admission of Navajo discourse is simply impossible. Culture dictates appearance, and the West's culture has its own view of Navajo culture. A great many contemporary Western photographers accompany their photographic collections with Navajo memoirs (usually, of course, in English) or commentary. But such attempts to present Navajo "reality" presume the universalism of the predatory West. This universalism not only saturates the possible meaning of photographic referents (subjects) but also establishes "respect"—the way the West prides itself on the ostensible acceptance of its Other (a feeling of, "How good we are to 'know' them"). Of course, no direct link exists between the subject matter of the photograph and the text, revealing that this gesture is at base cynical—it constitutes an insulation, a wrap of liberal acceptance on the terms of the West (which dictates the texts worthy of inclusion). In the available examples, the relationship between the photographs and the texts are extremely problematic (cf. Chapter 7—McAuley, Keegan, Grimes, Page, Running, etc.). Unless readers and viewers suspend judgment, the relations of text to photographs are not even clear or logical. The kind of respect or dignity offered in these efforts, however sincerely motivated, is only possible on Navajo terms.[22]

In some instances, of course, Navajo have sought out or solicited photographs (Portfolio II). However, the sediments of Western narrative or Western discourse are present in all cases, evidence that Navajo behave "just like Americans." But this also says something about the very real limitations of photography. Though photography is considered innovative, in fact there is no room for innovation. Photography must lean on new subjects, new types of behavior, new things people will do in front of the camera. Its innovation depends upon how outrageous humans will be, how shameless or perverse photographers will be. As Navajo change, so, too, does the photographic subject, but because the West only has a limited series of ways in which it accepts Navajo images, photography must, in most circumstances, continually repeat itself. Navajo can only be accepted as exemplars of a tradition the West names for them (thus maintaining the tradition/modernity dichotomy so important to Western notions of progress and hierarchy), even (and especially today) if photographed in behavior considered ironic, used as pastiche, or thought humorous—herding sheep with motorized vehicles, shooting arrows with high-tech bows, participating in healing practices while wearing sneakers and t-shirts emblazoned with names of heavy-metal rock stars (see Chapter 7).

Photographs of objects of alternative social relations such as Navajo are curious. They enter Western discourse in familiar registers (what other registers might they enter under?), take on an evidential quality after so long a time, and become Western treasures, as the social relations that originally situated them are no longer very apparent, unknown, or perhaps even totally opaque. They are rather like the pyramids of Giza or the Bastille—that is, monuments of considerable beauty and character. Once the social relations that enabled their creation are no longer in place, a deliberate amnesia sets in, one that does not encourage history to be read critically. This has been called a "ruins aesthetic" in the museum world—the West neither wants to know what things might have looked like prior to the West, nor what social relations might have generated them, nor certainly which ones generated Western access. There is in this circumstance a slippery link between content and form—a link normally ironclad in the West, with its rationalist and materialist foundations. What social relations were necessary to build the Cheops pyramid or make possible the Bastille? Are Navajo as the objects and subjects of conquest (as represented photographically) themselves even necessary to their photographs? Can Navajo social relations (productive, in the Western view, of Navajo visual appearance) be photographed, be represented? Are non-Navajo photographs of Navajo nothing more than ruins, great monuments of the West's alienation, its contumaciousness? How do we account for the few very fine photographs taken by Westerners of Navajo—or is it, as Lippard (1992:37) suggested, especially in the aftermath of genocide, "simply luck?"

Navajo History

A central thesis of this volume is that photography has been very important in the situating of Western perceptions of Navajo, not simply in superficial appearances and pastoral setting but also in the establishment of a specific Navajo history and a concrete conventional wisdom of Navajo character and being in time.

Several nonphotographic Navajo histories exist. At least one of these, broadly accepted by many Navajo, suggests that in a remote past *diné* ("people of the earth's surface") came to occupy the area that today (approximately) makes up greater Navajoland. This event occurred after the *diné diyinii* ("Holy People") had freed the earth from almost all the monsters that had inhabited it, and it appeared largely as it did prior to Europeans. The *diné* had emerged from nether worlds and metamorphosed from other forms. Various adventures characterized the *diné* as they learned to live in this world, and on occasion the Holy People taught some of them how they might help other *diné* to deal with some of the remaining monsters, such as sickness. For example, one individual, *bił'áhát'íní·*, was taken by the Holy People and instructed in the healing system today known as the Nightway *(tł'éé'jí)*, which addresses maladies of the head. After the *diné* appeared on the earth's surface, the Holy People came to occupy, invisibly, the sacred places of Navajoland—the canyons,

Chapter 1

ruins, mountaintops, etc.—and remain there today. Several Navajo healing practices, such as the Nightway, include masked individuals impersonating some of the Holy People.

Although this history acknowledges that Navajo borrowed some traditions, the substance of Navajo culture came to be in this fashion, especially the orders—the proper social relations *(hózhǫ́)*—that are so essential to Navajo health and beauty. The violation of these orders brings about sickness and death and thus necessitates the great healing system, which reestablishes the essential conditions of beauty and order, the proper social relations between people and between people and "nature" (though this dichotomy does certain violence to the actual Navajo conceptions, and though nature is certainly discursive in Navajo reckoning). This history makes little claim to account for other populations and establishes no priorities for alternative histories. It sets Navajo social relations and order and provides for their maintenance and their reorder. To violate, consciously or unconsciously, such social relations—such orders—is to become sick, disordered, ugly. Navajo causality, in direct reference to innovation, creativity, the new, suggests that the world was once ordered and cannot be added to without severe consequences for the established social relations. Indeed, in this view, knowledge is limited (or cannot be added to), and there is no room for innovation, addition, adaptation, assimilation[23]—the very opposite of the Western view of Navajo character and history (that is, the notions of Navajo as borrowers, Navajo as nonauthentic, Navajo as late, intrusive, mimetic, Navajo as adaptive).

Another history assigned to the Navajo stems from conventional European-American archaeology and anthropology of the Southwest. This history, with some minor technical debate, argues that the Navajo are a people recently derived from Asia who arrived into approximately their present location (first a bit further north and further east) as late as the fifteenth century A.D.— essentially, just in time to greet the first Europeans moving north from Mexico. This history suggests that Navajo arrived with a cultural system substantially different from their current one, which in large measure has been borrowed subsequently—much of their lifeway and economy from European introductions, their great healing system from the Pueblo, weaving and silverwork and herding from elsewhere, and so forth. Navajo in this history are adaptive and assimilative. This history *does* prioritize other histories—the others, it argues, are wrong.

These two histories, at least, are in some conflict over fundamentals. It is not my purpose in this volume to debate their relative merits, nor certainly their truths and falsities. But photography becomes very important to one of these histories and is largely irrelevant to the other, and I will argue that this difference is vital to understanding some of the complexities of the photography of Navajo. To the history by which the West situates Navajo, photography is an important evidential apparatus and thus a tool of rationalist discourse. Navajo in this scheme are but information, but signs—gestures that can be captured by imaging devices. There is an established and firm hierarchy of observer, subject, representation, real, imaginary, object.

However, events that occurred long after the origins postulated in these opposing histories established the setting for photography's temporal appearance in the area. Because of claimed violations of agreements, claimed persistent raids on European-American settlers and herds—not to mention European-American expansionist needs, specifically coveted mineral deposits, nor the ambitions of redundant Civil War military men—the great majority of Navajo were rounded up in 1864 and forcibly marched ("The Long Walk"—*Hwéeldi)* from Arizona to Bosque Redondo (Fort Sumner) on the Pecos River in eastern New Mexico Territory. The first known photographs of Navajo date from and were taken at the incarceration at Fort Sumner.

The chronological history of the photography of Navajo begins with the first photographs of Navajo in captivity, taken in 1866. No known photographs of Navajo in their homeland were taken prior to that year. There was something diabolically prophetic about this, for it is a central thesis of this volume that Navajo have been essentially captive to photography ever since—to the majority discourses of photographers and to the commercial, scientific, humanist agendas of the West.

Let me close this segment by referring back to the epigram with which the chapter began.[24] This aphorism expresses something fundamental to the West's obsessions in general and is menacingly instructive to a volume on photography of non-Westerners—the "natural" privilege that should permit Westerners to be able to view, to see anything, anywhere, anytime and the consequent benefits to be gained if this vision is extended to those with the right artistic talent, character, and empathy (basically, Western Enlightenment philosophy). That this can be, and often is, a dramatically assumptive, racist, and predacious motivation never occurs to Riefenstahl, of course, nor probably to many photographers.[25] But the world of other humans is not simply available as fodder, either for photographic capture or for ethnographic predation, however compassionate the Westerner. The belief that vision must be accorded all privilege, that there exists some natural concession or fundamental freedom to extend sight everywhere, must be understood as a temporal and historical feature of expansion and power, not a biological or universally accruing human right.[26]

Portfolio II
Navajo Elected

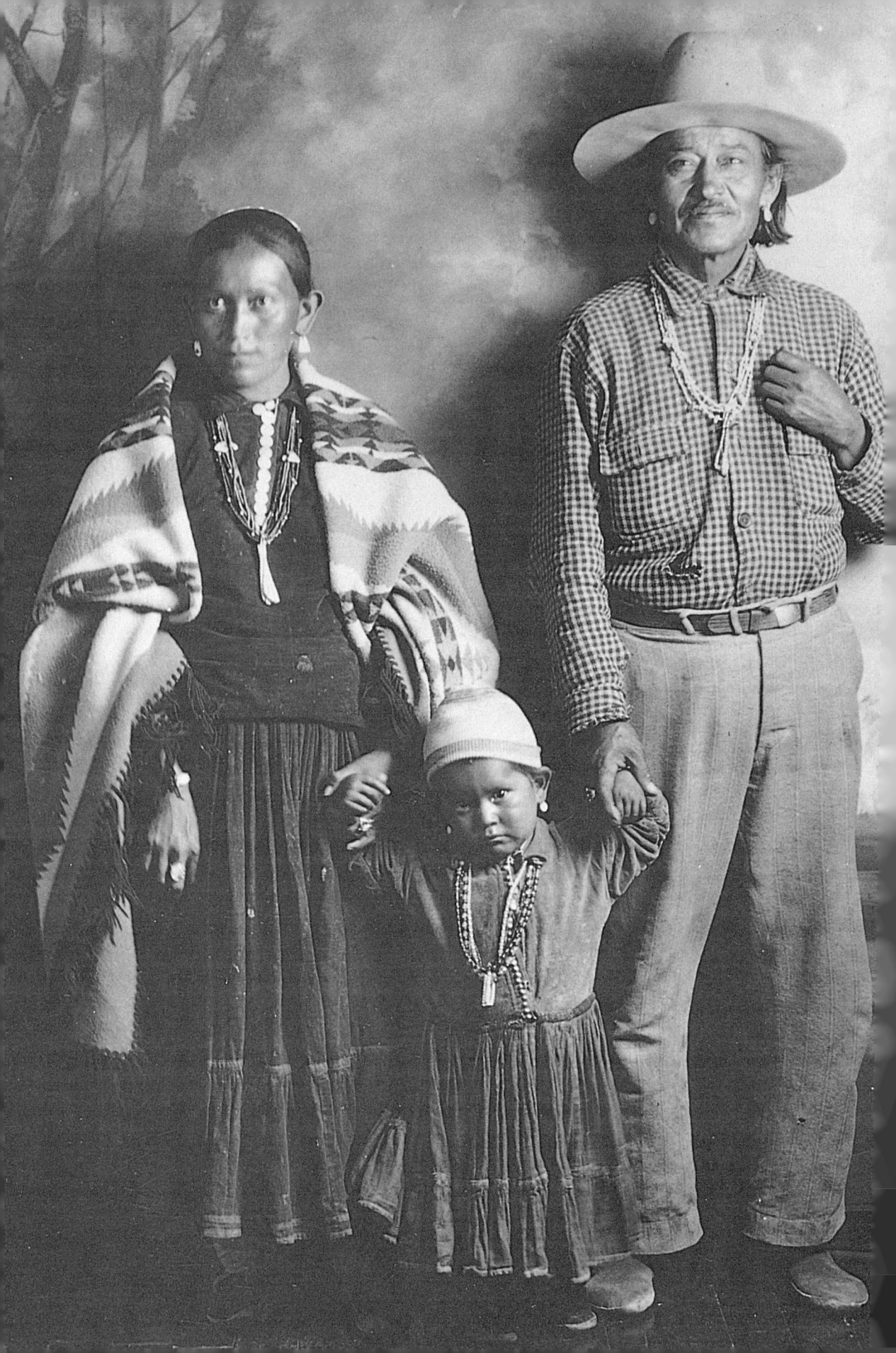

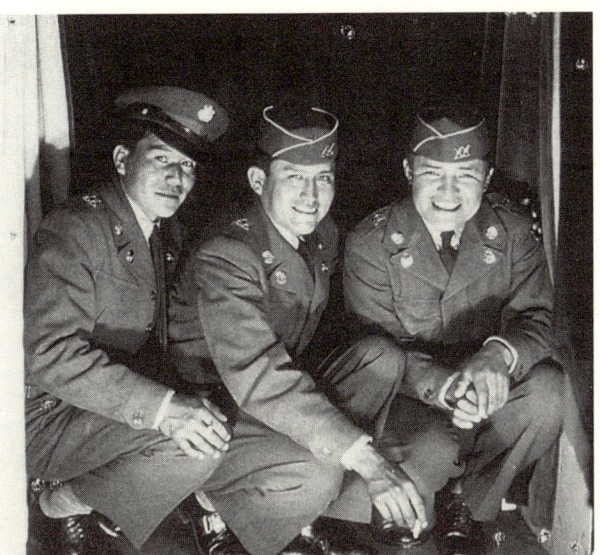

Figure 8

Figure 7. "Indian Family." Mary Ann Studio, photographer (Winslow AZ), 26 June 1931. This family appears to have solicited this photograph or at least to have willingly participated. The social relations here differ from those involved in the more common unsolicited encounters, making the Navajoland border-town photographers of special interest; they are unlike the numerous photographers who traveled to Navajoland itself to photograph. Here Navajo seem also to have escaped the posing of other studio conventions (cf. Fig. 12). Photograph courtesy National Anthropological Archives, Smithsonian Institution. NAA LOC03266400.

Figure 8. "Three Birds. Woodrow Elanger, Gilbert James, Casey F. Yazzie." Photographer unknown, n.d. (probably World War II era). Navajo dictating their own photography. This archive has many such photographs, probably most from Santa Fe Indian School alumni. Photograph courtesy Southwest Association on Indian Affairs Collection, New Mexico State Records and Archives. No. 35288.

Portfolio II

Figure 9. "Rodeo Riders at Gallup Intertribal Indian Ceremonial." *Mark Nohl, photographer, n.d. (August 1983). Navajo cowboys examine contact sheets, keenly interested in seeing themselves as through the lens of a rodeo photographer. But is the young man in the left foreground using his hat to shield himself from the current photographer? See also Fig. 17. Photograph courtesy Mark Nohl, New Mexico Magazine.*

Figure 10. "'Street Corner' or 'Fair' photography." *Milton Snow, photographer, 12-13-14 September 1952, Window Rock AZ. Note interest of children in photographer despite numerous distractions of the fair (and "Keep Smiling" note on front of camera.) See also Laura Gilpin, Neg. No. #4164[1], ACM. Fort Worth TX. Photograph courtesy Milton Snow Collection, Navajo Nation Museum, Window Rock AZ. NF 5-956.*

Navajo Elected

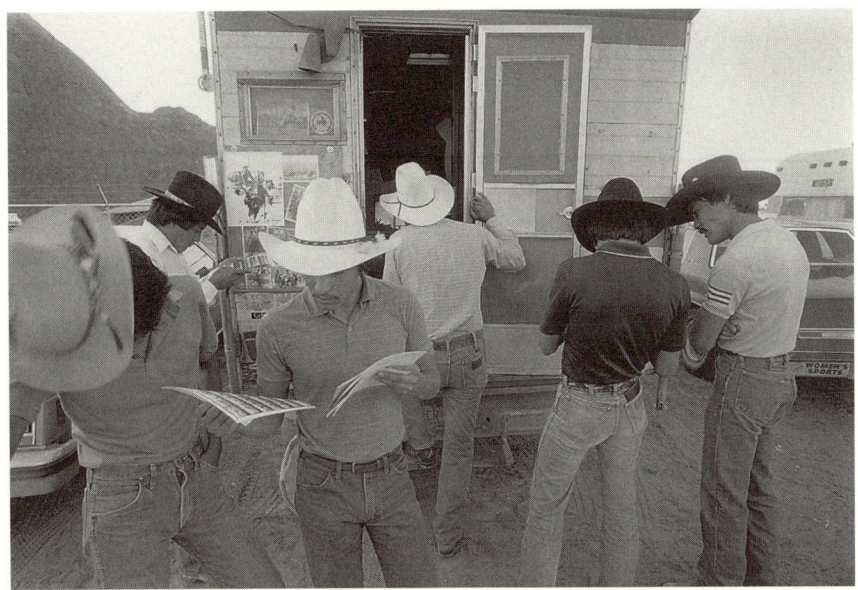

Figure 9

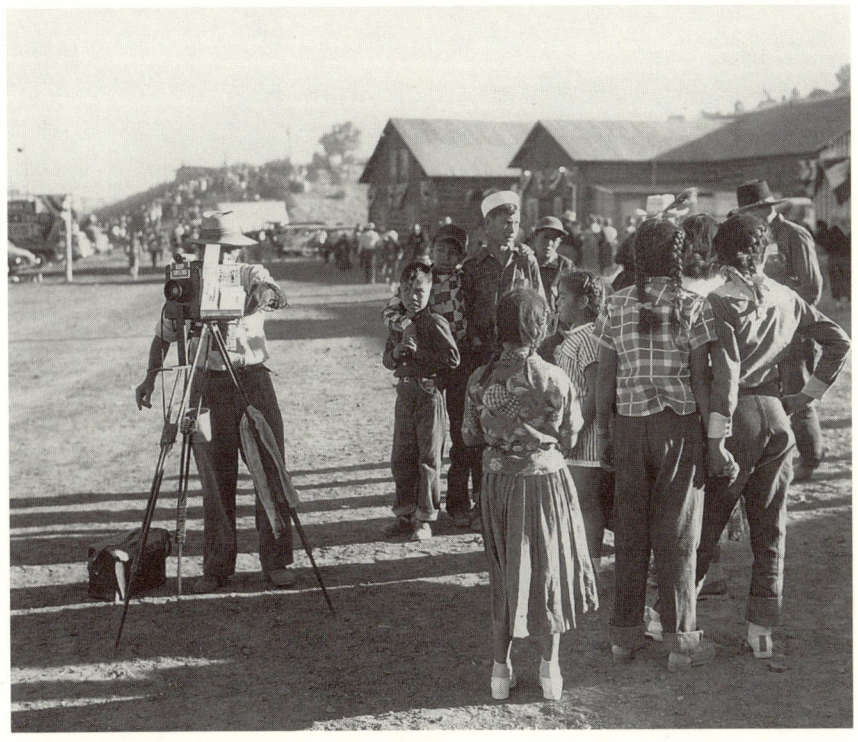

Figure 10

Chapter Two

The Registers of Photography of Navajo

Method as Political Critique

Obviously, one cannot see all photography of Navajo; well over 100,000 images are available to public and research scrutiny, scattered in dozens of archival sources and hard-to-find personal collections. But I have attempted to approach the major sources, and have at least sampled a few of the less accessible and less well-known collections and sources. Obviously, thousands remain in personal collections, and new publications with new photographers appear frequently.[1]

Having seen many tens of thousands photographs[2] of Navajo from almost a thousand known (see Appendix, Chart 1) and anonymous photographers, I can only comment in general on the most historically, theoretically, or rhetorically significant, the most dramatically different, or the most unique twentieth-century examples. Such a survey can still indicate something of the range of materials available; it can also argue the social relations of alterity that exist between photographers and Navajo and, more generally, between the West and Navajo. Even at this selectivity, I will not be able to give the appropriate attention to many photographers and collections, nor to variations and differences within and between them. By grouping some photographers I do not mean to demean one or the other, and by ignoring some photographers I do not imply their insignificance. Moreover, many photographs significant to this project are unattributed but must be noted.

Chapter 2

One of the straightforward purposes of the volume is to bring to view certain historical photographs that have not been published. I will consider a wider range than the rather rigidly fixed set of acceptable published photographs, comparing what was published with what was censored or left unpublished. Some photographs illustrate themes upon which I particularly wish to comment and are included here but might not otherwise ever have made publication. But I obviously do not mean to ignore published photographs; my central thesis is that those published played a critical role in establishing the tropes acceptable in the West and that it is necessary to look at familiar work—especially some of the classical sources and genre photographers (cf. Gilpin, Curtis, Moon, Monsen)—once again.

The study proceeded inductively. I examined collections as they came to my attention; efforts to track down one photographer, photograph, or type of photograph inevitably led me to others. Obviously, with such a methodology, I cannot claim to have located *all* publicly available photographs of Navajo, only to have found a large segment of them. The examination of unpublished (in contrast to published) photographs may seem a bit unfair, especially because so many of the photographers included here are no longer living. The unpublished photographs may include visualist gestures unrelated to the photographer's announced project. There may be experimental work—"early drafts," so to speak. Certainly this is the case with Curtis and Gilpin. Examination of the unpublished or unexhibited photographs of living photographers poses more problems; indeed, publishing *any* photographs from living photographers is difficult, for doing so often involves rights, require permissions from those photographed, and raises a host of new social relations surrounding the legalities of exposure. Such considerations confine the evidential material presented here largely to the past, but because what any photograph exposes is past after the moment of exposure, this is not as large a methodological problem as it might seem. More serious is that I cannot claim to have seen the all the work of many current photographers of Navajo. Perhaps photographers now at work will someday establish a practice that effectively critiques this volume. That would be good, as it might signify the evolution of a reflexive and self-conscious photography, with discussion and input and determination from classical subjects.

Another reason not to seek out all possible individual and personal unpublished collections is that these had less effect than published work on the situating of Navajo to the public. But some personal photos are important in indicating 1) relationships the photographer had with Navajo, and 2) differences between personal photographs and photographs with explicit other purposes—documentary, advertising, art, and so forth. Nevertheless, viewing unpublished photographs other than those contained in archives would be methodologically and logistically difficult. I will thus primarily consider the unpublished materials of Carl Moon, Frederick Monsen, G. W. James, Edward Curtis, Laura Gilpin, and others whose published materials have been important in defining the major tropes of the photography of Navajo.

A final reason for the selection of some photographs is to publish work that is uncharacteristic (J. W. Hildebrand, Milton Snow), non-normalizing, or atypical[3] or that casts new light on the classical receptions of photographs published and considered typical (Curtis, Gilpin). Still another is to indicate something of the dramatically large quantity of photography of Navajo people, as well as the dramatically narrow range of images. By *range*, I mean the variety of registers of images, the extent and boundaries of tropes established or replicated or acknowledged in archives and in print. Although I use photographs here as evidence, they are commonly used as evidential in a reflexive manner, or against themselves. Absences in the published record are here published; silences in the discourses on Navajo and photography are here given voice.

Some time ago, I submitted a grant application to secure funding for the extended visits, archival studies, and photocopying and photographic printing necessary to this project. One referee critiqued the application because I had not expressed an intent to show photographs of Navajo to Navajo for their reaction. Presumably, this individual believed that involving Navajo in judgments about photography of them by others somehow made my project more anthropological (or, perhaps, more politically correct). For a variety of reasons bearing on the structure of the current project (apart from my obvious pique that the application was rejected), I think this reaction was particularly wrongheaded.

First, there already is abundant Navajo reaction to photography, most commonly expressed in outright refusal to be photographed (which can be seen throughout this volume) and in avoidance (particularly noticeable in many of the unpublished archival photographs—see Portfolio III). One of my tasks herein is to bring to view some of these graphic "silences," for they exist in excess. These came to be photographed because the subject reacted just at the moment of the photograph or because the photographer could not eliminate them or did not notice them at the time the photograph was taken. We also have ample evidence of the specific prohibitions (e.g., of sacred settings) and inappropriate subjects (e.g., the sick or dead) or settings for photography of Navajo.[4] As will be seen (especially in Chapter 5), earlier generations of photographers had to devise all manner of ruses and deceits to get their photographs in the face of nearly universal opposition from their subjects. Almost every photographer on whom there is data mentioned Navajo resistance to photography in one way or another. Thus, many reactions already are known, but they normally are not brought to attention, for if taken seriously they make future photography of the same order problematic (at least, for ethical individuals). Liberal Western photographers can seldom tolerate such considerations; for them, usually, what is physically possible to photograph *should* be photographed.

Second, the grant referee's request presumed or implied a universalism in photographic subjecthood by which Navajo reaction would inform the photograph in some manner bearing on its form, its universality, its cross-cultural conditions of acceptance or rejection. Some of these problems have been discussed elsewhere (see Chapter 1 and Chapter 8). In this project I aim to examine the *Western character* of the photography of Navajo, and certainly Navajo have never, save through refusal, had much input into that. Third, the referee was asking once more for Navajo participation in a project inaugurated by Westerners—expecting a population that has been endlessly poked and measured and violated already to give more blood, submit to more measurements, reveal more sacred texts.

That some Navajo people were paid for having their "picture taken" (not simply photographed) or otherwise gave approval is surely not the issue. Certainly Navajo sometimes were paid to be photographed and even charged for them (Portfolio I, II), and some of these electives form an interesting corpus.[5] Determining how Navajo feel about other photographs is a curious project, however, for unless they are aware of the whole range of Navajo photography, or unless there are clear boundaries established for the types of photographs, it is difficult to see how they could offer any relevant opinions, any more than any other population unfamiliar with the conventions of photographic representation and the use of images by an alien dominant culture could do so.[6]

As set out in Chapter 1, photographs of humans often serve an othering function. This function is particularly clear in Western photographs of non-Westerners but also is commonly true across any axes of power, as in males' photographs of females. But Western photographs of cultural forms of lesser power (subalterns) most clearly demonstrate that there is something very Western about photography and about the social relations by which it is possible. Indeed, photography of subalterns became paradigmatic of such social relations. The photographer's cultural identity may mediate these issues but

The Registers of Photography of Navajo

does not solve all the problems. If there are alternatives to Western photography, the possibilities have been insufficiently explored. The assumptions that situate photography's Western, developmental, visualist intellectual hegemony are understudied and undertheorized, as is the assumption that everything and everyone is subject to photographic access and scrutiny. This rendering and constitution of alterity has aspects of both desire and denial, aversion and attraction—all stubbornly Western in expression. But difference/alterity has no axiomatic hierarchy unless constructed. The shape of the West's hierarchy and power has meant that Navajo not only act on their own beliefs and practices but also must act on and participate in those of the West.

Although the picture-taking act itself may dominate (camera over subject), photographs of Navajo were, in addition, taken by members of a dominant, colonial, and racist social form, however well intentioned the individual photographers might have been. Thus, photographs are necessarily part of the discourses normalizing the dominant social form, the dominating social relations bounding and marginalizing Navajo. Thus, in its methodological foundations, this study is a political critique of the m[t]aking of pictures of Navajo. However, it is not just an attempt to critique photography. First, I am not competent systematically to undertake such a project. Second, photography has abundant non-exploitative uses, bringing grand warmth and great pleasures to friends, relatives, families, communities—to those between whom there is love (and no additional axes of differential power).[7] Many of these sorts of photographs are illustrated here, as are the many types of photographic images displayed in Navajo homes (see Portfolio II and Fig. 11).

There are important ideological aspects to photography of landscape and photography that does not involve humans,[8] but theoretically informed and critical attention is only beginning to be paid to the photography of minority humans by non-minority humans, particularly a corpus of photography of specific humans.[9] There continue to be abundant works with little or no critical perspective, repeating the past with unapologetic and embarrassing consistency (and monotony)—see Chapter 7 for examples. The techniques and devices of marginalization for the establishment of difference, and their dramatic implications not only for theory and photography[10] but for the West in general,[11] have only begun to receive consideration.

Significantly, few sources specific to one approach to photography of Navajo exist. Practically every major photographer of Navajo—whether primarily focused on art, landscape, government and tribal policy matters, tourism, sale of the Southwest, or another theme—has also overlapped other themes. There are few radical breaks in the history of photography of

Chapter 2

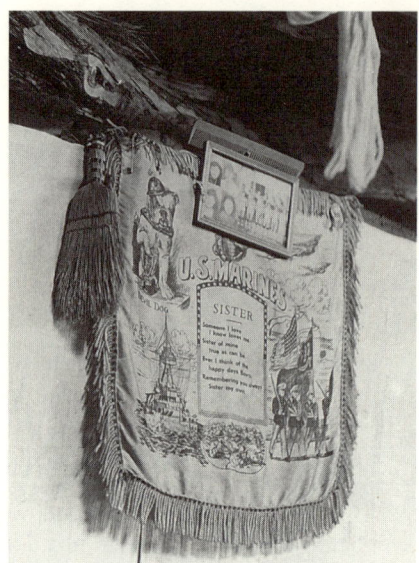

Figure 11

Figure 11. "Souvenir of Navajo War Veteran. #29." John Collier, Jr., photographer, n.d. In a small frame are school photographs and bus-station photo machine snapshots. Collier's photographs of hogan interiors frequently illustrate these sorts of decor and indicate something of Navajo choice in types of photographic imaging, as well as their patriotism. Photograph courtesy The University Museum, University of Pennsylvania. Negative No. 54-141435.

Figure 12. "Jimmie Miles and his wife." Photographer unknown, n.d., Chilocco School. Note the Western dress and the Navajo weaving on the floor. Obviously the photograph was taken before World War II, when the swastika was still a popular Native American symbol. Note the several framed snapshots, including a mounted figure (see also Fig. 88) and an adult woman and child. This photo follows a standard Western studio convention, picturing an unnamed woman with her hand on a named, seated man. Contrast this with the studio photograph in Fig. 7. Photograph courtesy Museum of Northern Arizona and Franciscan Friars at St. Michaels AZ. MS 119-32-335.

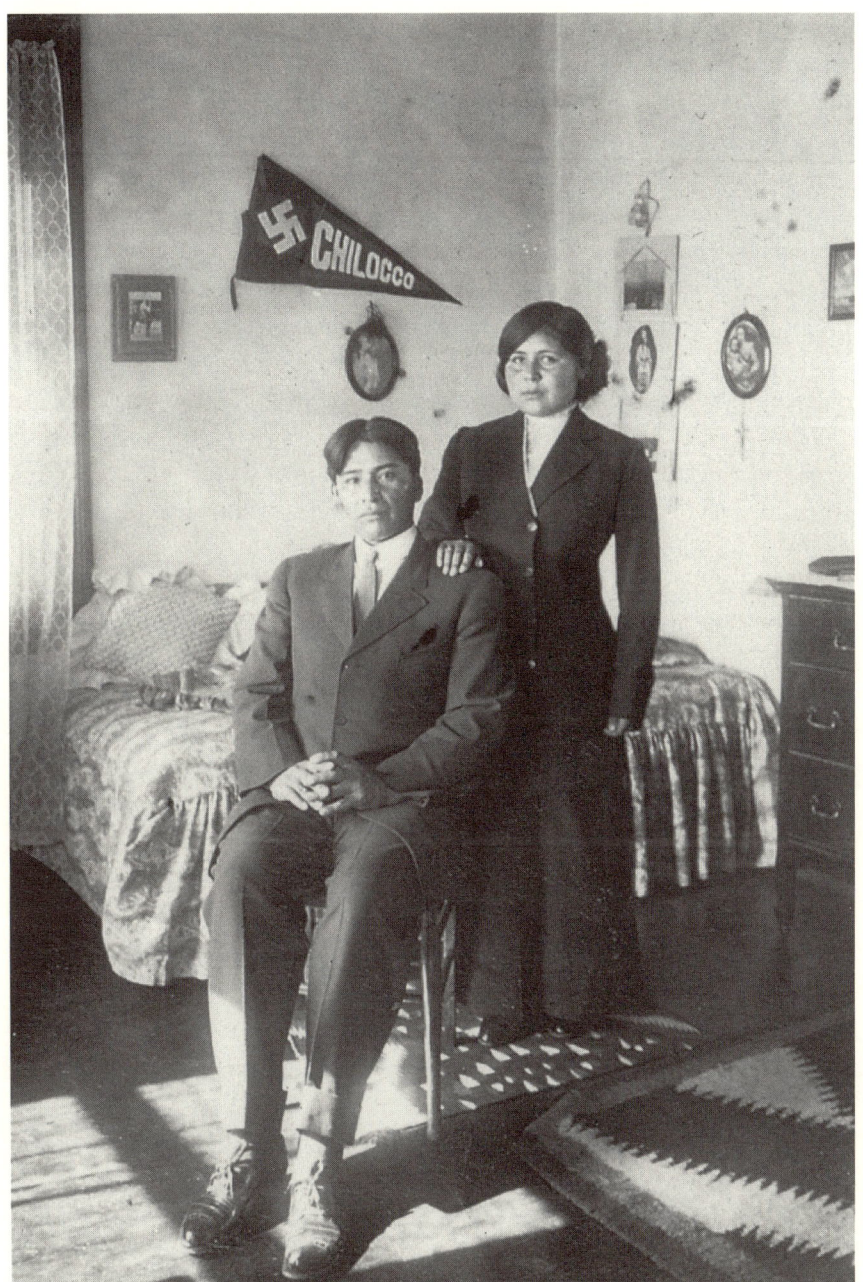

Figure 12

Chapter 2

Navajo—the early "scientific" photography often looks like the early "art" photography, and so forth. Bureau of Indian Affairs (BIA) "official" photographs also turn up in tourist sources; "art" photographs also end up as postcards and in surveillance and evidential collections—as do protest photographs and social administration photographs. And all find their way into government and tribal archives. Sediments of one photographic discourse seep into others. There is so much overlap in the ways Navajo have become acceptable to the West that there is seldom exclusivity of photographic style or discourse, perhaps (or even often) despite photographic intention. Indeed, it is principally for this reason that but a few contemporary Western photographers of Navajo have been interviewed—sooner or later, the work of most will cross genre lines, so consciousness or intentionality is not as relevant as might be suggested. I have thus only sought to interview a few major contemporary photographers of Navajo about their work, their intention, and their relationships with Navajo people.

Indigenous photography—Navajo photography of Navajo—needs more attention, but that is another study altogether, and one perhaps best undertaken by Navajo. Chapter 8 is thus quite brief. Navajo will, after all, know something more about Navajo social relations than will non-Navajo. As someone from the West, I know something more about the social relations of the West—which are, of course, the real subject matter of this book. I hope I have been sensitive to Navajo social relations with Westerners, at least insofar as they bear on photography.

But this volume does not necessarily present a consistent, coherent thesis or critique, and it has been motivated by a number of interests. Just as few Navajo asked the great numbers of photographers in Navajoland to photograph them, neither did they ask that the present study be undertaken. Indeed, except for some historical photographs and some of the more specific critiques, it may not interest very many Navajo. The same is true of most Western representations and publications. This book once again makes Navajo available to the Western gaze,[12] but perhaps it will help bring voice where there was silence. I am neither an historian of photography, photographer, photo archivist, nor photo curator. My critical postures are based on political judgments rather than a specific analytical or synthetic method. I chose the portfolios politically (how Navajo appear in the West), determined the classification of photographic registers politically (the projects guiding photographic practice), and selected images to illustrate the argument, the Navajo, and the West politically.

I assign meaning to photographs in a variety of ways, not always coherent with each other nor always consistent with some program or another. I will critique in multiple layers. Of course, the reader will do the same, but I will attempt to persuade readers to accept my view. Although I hope this is not overly coercive, it is certainly not liberal. I want to fracture, if possible, some of the existing knowledges about photographs, photographs of Navajo, Navajo, the West, and the relationship between them. This work rests on no uniform or epistemologically based foundation; appeals will be of the moment, of the event of viewing, of the specific photograph. I may lean on what can be determined about the event of the photograph, or I may ignore its specificity altogether. I seek to unsettle—even to confuse—the conventional wisdom of the photography of Navajo, if such wisdom indeed exists. I will be reading politically but not programmatically; critically, but without overall agenda. Some specific analyses are "interruptions," in the sense that a great deal of received commentary is already available about those photograph[er]s considered, which I hope to deconstruct and fracture along lines that are variable and without lattice.

By "political critique" I do not imply a totalizing notion, as in a nineteenth-century view of political project or in some Leninist sense. This exercise is not, however, anarchic—on the contrary, it is simply intended to encourage multiple views. I believe that such an approach places readers/viewers in a better position to genuinely take specificity seriously—to take Navajo discourse about Navajo on its own terms, insofar as it is possible to do so from photographs and from texts not written in Navajo. But I will also insist on specificity of reading. I will not base interpretations on some master narrative of photographic criticism or textual foundation nor on assumptions about the meanings of Navajo social relations. I am not subjecting all photos to a theoretically unified scheme of description. It (a reading, a seeing) will shift, and different questions may be asked of different photographs—not all are subjected to same objections. In attempting to avoid a consistent and coherent series of criteria (such as a machine might follow), I hope to avoid a "theory" of the photography of Navajo, a "proper" approach, or an insistence on some master reading. There is no grand theory, nor any continuum along which photography of Navajo is more or less instrumental. Representations cannot be reduced to function without loosing the "capillary" power that makes them so complexly necessary. Each reading is informed by a politics that must be argued each time—there is to be no axiomatic or assumed relationship between any content and any form, and any function will be argued, not derived from method or theory.

The critique may appear severe, but in a distinct way it contrasts severely, as do photographs; if the deconstruction and analysis appear harsh, so, too, are the photographs; if they appear too focused, so, too, do photographs. We accept the reality of photographic images in the West, even though such images simulate their subjects in only a narrow chemical or electronic sense and are dramatically and extraordinarily different from them. I attempt to unprivilege photography, much as it has been unprivileged by subalterns.

My most important task in this chapter, however, will be to call attention to the *most typical*, the *normalizing* types,[13] the photographs that constitute the Navajo visual image and establish its limits and boundaries. I will discuss the distinguishing and specific photographs that made Navajo in the eyes of Western viewers and propose a thesis for what Navajo must and have looked like to the West, why, and how photographic images situated Navajo realities. This is not to necessarily privilege photography, for the West's "view" is both determined by and determining of the photographic encounter. This "view" is a complex, "saturated field of visibility" (Butler, 1993:15) of the ways Navajo are photographed by the West and the ways in which such images have structured how Navajo can appear. I will argue that Navajo input has not affected the conventional and normalizing wisdom the West already possesses.

Valences in the Photography of Navajo

A rhetorical and subjective working classification may be established for the major Western categories of photographs of Navajo—the lenses through which Navajo are viewed, the values attached to images of this American people.[14] Rather than a scheme into which each and every photograph and every photographer of Navajo is placed, this classification is a plot of the major visual themes that are not only easily discernible but also, I will argue, important to the West's "view" of Navajo. They are not the only relevant themes, but they have a specific role, for Navajo are as visually well established as any American minority. I will argue that these are classes of major significance into which Navajo subjects have been situated and constituted. They guide both photographers and consumers and are in turn guided by established structures of conquest and racism. Historically, they established the limits and the boundaries of how Navajo would be accepted visually and how photographers would subsequently photograph Navajo. They bound and constitute Navajo culture for the West, and they situate the ways Navajo can be understood in photographs. More than one theme may be evident; a single photograph can easily convey combined and complex messages that fold, mix, fuse, and blend this scheme into itself. Thus, the common conscious and overt themes of assimilation, pastiche, and adaptation, on the one hand, and preservation, nostalgia, and pastoralism, on the other, are not separate categories but exist in practically every photograph and entries of the chart, which is presented on page 42.

The outline, like the photographs upon which it is based, is a formal representation. But I will argue these are the guiding formal visual discourses, the politically significant formal valences—literally, the "views" that have crucial importance in defining how Navajo are consumed by the West. The classes are not, in other words, arbitrary, nor are they relevant to the common form criterion often used to discriminate photographs from one another in conventional Western aesthetic judgments. Like all classifications (such as those by which the various portfolios are organized [in choice and in order of presentation]), these are regulating, but I will argue that they are informed by a political objection to or interrogation of the West's depiction of Navajo. The placement of a specific photograph or photographer in one or another category, is, of course, a matter of judgment—a political and thereby subjective judgment. These are the lenses through which the West has pictured and imagined Navajo; these are the valences that, I will argue, adhere to each photograph of Navajo. They are, to the West, some of the conditions of existence of Navajo. These categories are not flaws in an uneducated, unevolved, unenlightened West; they are the necessary features of its relationship with Navajo. They must maintain difference, a specific and shaped difference.

Motivations and intention are not so easily determined, and I will not suggest here that these were necessarily conscious (or relevant) in any case. The categories of this classification are not, then, based on perceptions of explicit photographic purposes nor announced desires, for any and all photographs are subjects of ambition and desire.[15] They are political judgments about the social relations established by/in such photographs between Westerners and Navajo, the ways in which Navajo are to "appear" to the West and the ways in which the West "views" Navajo—a specification of the "optical unconscious," as Benjamin expressed it, as well as an overt consciousness in content (such as pastiche, adaptation, assimilation, pastoralism, etc.). The categories saturate, for the West, Navajo visibility—all ways Navajo can appear. This project is possible because there are so few photographs of Navajo on Navajo terms; where Navajo appear in other terms, I will argue, they are situated by one or more of the categories noted.

For all the complex purposes and qualifications outlined, I have divided and assigned photographic fields of Navajo into the following valence classes:

Chapter 2

A)—surveillance
    1)—documentary (official, unofficial, advocacy)
    2)—anthropological (asset in communicating anthropology's view, archive, museum)
    3)—casual (early tourist, traveler, worker in area, gaze)

B)—humanist
    1)—sentimental (vanishing race, lost culture, family of man)
    2)—victims (dead, dying, non-functional or misfunctional in West's view)

C)—commercial
    1)—aestheticist (color/silver/weaving/turquoise, fashion—body parts)
    2)—landscape (extension of trees, red rocks)
    3)—studio (personal, postcard)

D)—alternative
    1)—late modernism (modernist photo gestures mocked, different voice privileged)
    2)—Navajo photographers (political, resistance, silences, effacement, defacements)

These valence classes themselves should be self-explanatory, though assigning photographs and photographers to them will be a political matter and thereby arguable. Each photographer of Chart 1 (see Appendix) about whom we have sufficient knowledge can be placed in one or more of the cells in the above plot.

Though all available photographs of Navajo may be assigned in the above classification, the composition and labeling of the portfolios involved determinations of another order. Both entailed political and critical decisions. The portfolios do not depend on quantity, nor are they meant to be exhaustive; their selection is subjective. They are meant to illustrate both positively (cf. Portfolio II) and negatively (cf. Portfolio III, Portfolio VI). Some are not necessarily critical or political but represent views not commonly seen or reflected upon (cf. Portfolio I, Portfolio V, Portfolio VIII). Others are dictated by institutional arrangements and expectations of the West that I think merit further attention (cf. Portfolio IV, Portfolio V, Portfolio VII); for example, Portfolio VII, entitled "Loom," is meant to document a stereotype of Navajo *essence*. But photography could never simply (complexly) "capture" such "reality," even if it did exist; we can see all manner of non-essential information in each photograph, as the aesthetic, social, or technical motivations guiding the photographer are exposed. As

The Registers of Photography of Navajo

a result, the structured settings deny essences far more than they communicate or reveal them.

The portfolios are these collections of both grand and painful photographs, and the thematic content (should it not be obvious) will be expanded upon in the captions. The choices and determinations are subjective and personal and thus not meant to be exhaustive nor necessarily normalizing of photographic practices or Navajo responses. They are, then, enunciations rather than representations.

*Portfolio III
Avoidance*

Portfolio III

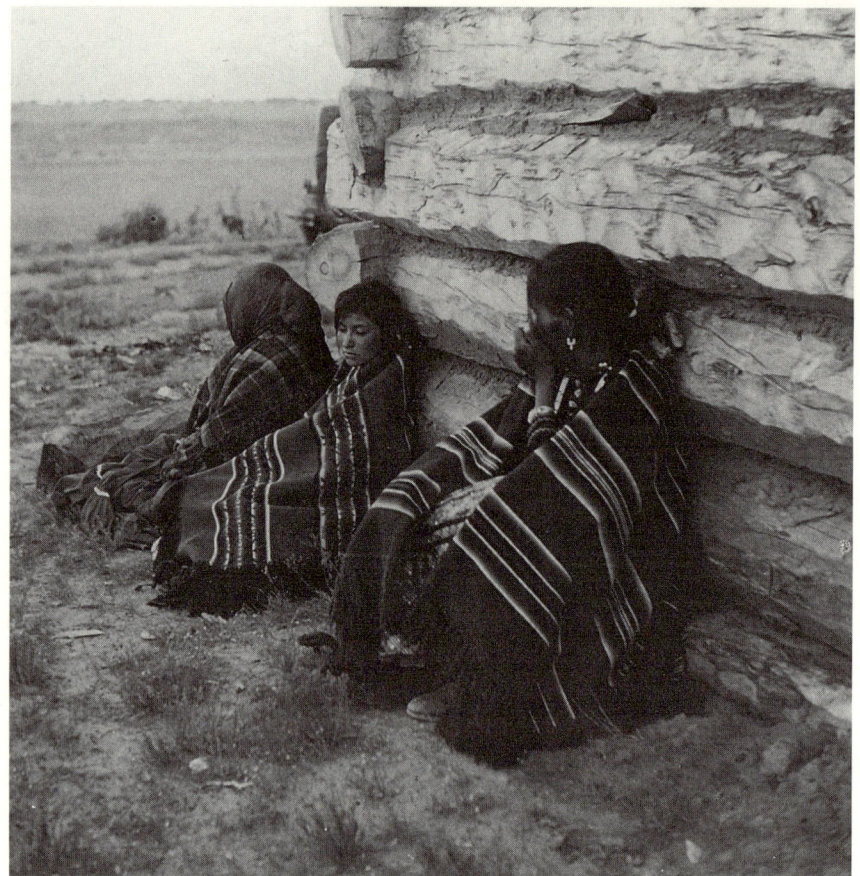

Figure 13

Avoidance

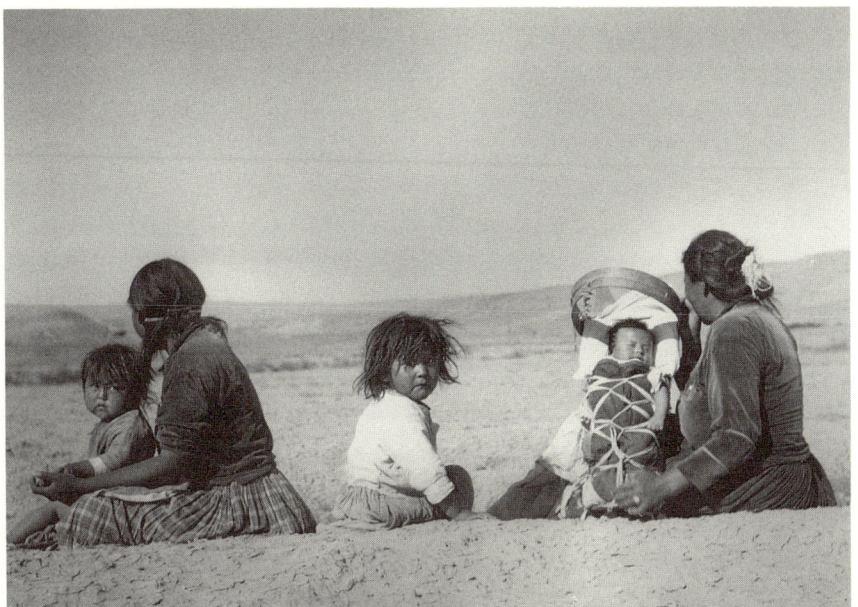

Figure 14

Figure 13. "Navajo, East Bound [sic—boundary] Association Meeting." Helen Post, photographer, ca. 1936–1941. Two women deliberately avoid the photographer, a third casts her glance downward. This reaction is seen over and over again in unpublished photographic archives; despite this refusal, note how close and intrusive the photographer is. Photograph courtesy Amon Carter Museum, Fort Worth TX, No. P1985.50.837.

Figure 14. Women with children. Photographer unknown, n.d. Though the children may still be curious and turned to the camera, all the women have deliberately turned away from the device. Such photographs are often labeled "shy women"—that is, in terms that do not condemn the photographer. Photograph courtesy Wheelwright Museum of the American Indian. #60/32.

Portfolio III

Figure 15. "Navajo hogan." Photographer unknown (possibly H. C. James), n.d. (possibly 1926). The person rushing into the hogan is probably attempting to escape the photographer. These sorts of photographs, with one individual dramatically out of focus trying to escape the photograph, are common in archives but are seldom published. Small older-style forked-stick hogan. Photograph courtesy Museum of New Mexico. Neg. No. 104650.

Figure 16. "Turquoise Bar, Waterflow NM." Photographer unknown (perhaps Billy R. Santistien), 26 August 1967, 6:40 p.m. This bar, adjacent to Navajoland on the highway between Farmington and Shiprock, exploited Navajos' lack of alternatives to alcohol consumption and was always a site of excessive drinking and accidents and a persistent source of embarrassment to state authorities along a tourist route. This photograph was gathered in an attempt to build a case for closing down the Turquoise Bar, but the patrons objected, at least to the photographer (most turn their back, and one even confronts the camera). The state, of course, eventually won, and Navajo, with ever fewer alternatives (drinking and the sale of alcohol are prohibited on the Navajo Reservation), must move to another border-town bar, equally exploitative. Photograph courtesy Cargo Collection, New Mexico State Records and Archives. No. 25780

Avoidance

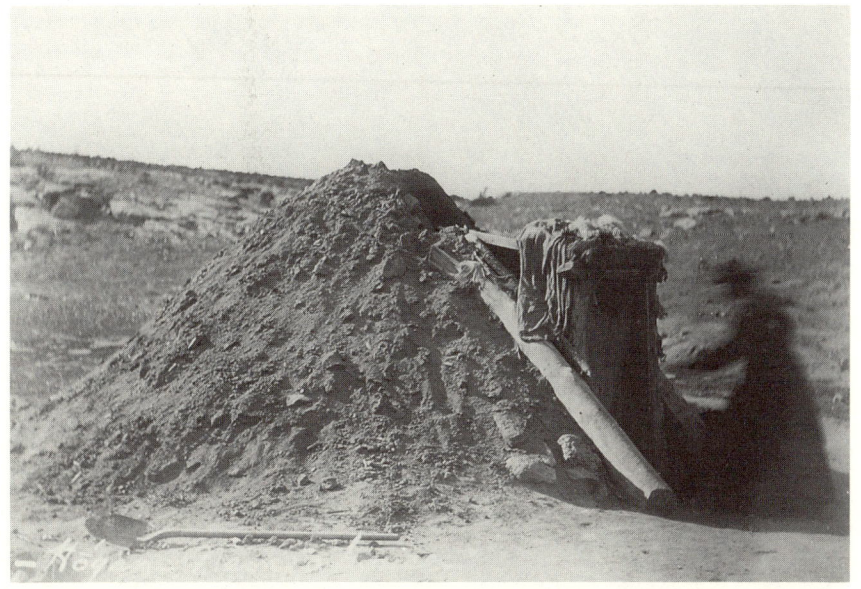

Figure 15

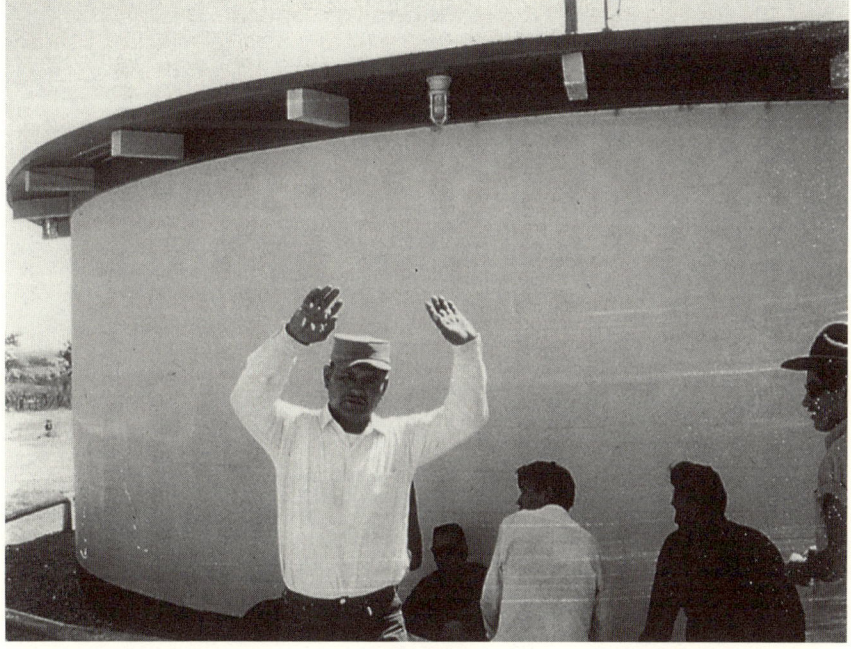

Figure 16

Portfolio III

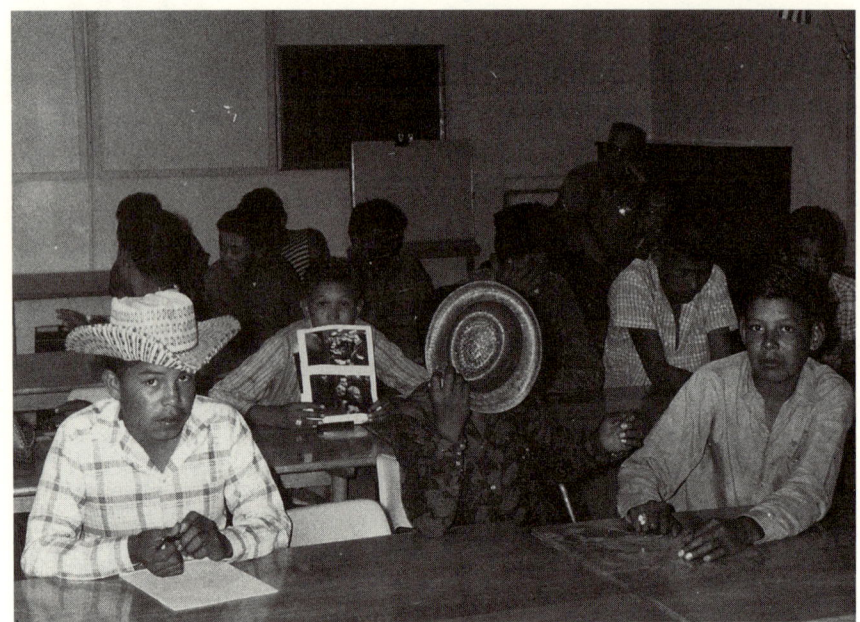

Figure 17

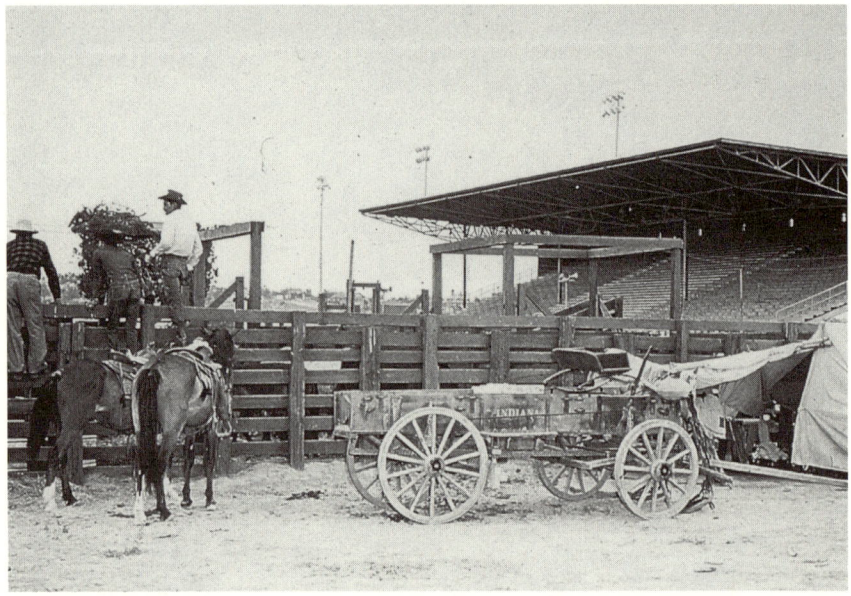

Figure 18

*Figure 17. "Classroom session at summer youth camp."
J. McKee, photographer, July 1962, Pine Springs AZ. One
lad uses his hat to shield himself from photographer (see Fig. 9),
and others use their hands to avoid the photograph. Little
seems to be going on—even the supervisor sitting in the rear
appears bored. Photograph courtesy Concho Collection, Navajo
Nation Museum, Window Rock AZ. G-8.*

*Figure 18. Behind grandstand, Gallup Ceremonial. Frank McNitt,
photographer, 1950. "By getting a special pass from the Chamber
of Commerce, Bon and I were allowed inside the ceremonial
grounds. A Navajo family had pitched this tent and were sitting
outside as we approached. When they saw my camera they
quickly went in the tent and lowered one flap. The men on the
corral turned their backs and paid no more attention." See Fig.
165. Photograph courtesy McNitt Collection, New Mexico State
Records and Archives. No. 6775.*

Chapter Three

A Historical Sketch of Nineteenth-Century Photography of Navajo

We do not go to the country of the Whites—why do they come to ours? I laugh moreover when the Whites say they wish only to observe our country! They will continue to observe and observe until nothing more remains for us.

a Somali from Brava (quoted in Norman Robert Bennett, Arab versus European, *1986:39)*

The First Photographers

I am unaware of any photographs of Navajo taken prior to their genocidal capture and incarceration at Bosque Redondo (Fort Sumner) on the Pecos River in the 1860s.[1] During this period, known as the "Long Walk" era, at least four photographers—J. G. Gaige, Nicholas Brown, Valentin Wolfenstein, and Henry Lorenzen—took photographs of Navajo at Bosque Redondo and elsewhere. At least one other photographer, William A. Smith, reportedly recorded at Fort Sumner, but none of his photographs of Navajo appear to have survived.[2] Photographs of Navajo from this period have been attributed to Cyrus Jennings, Edw. F. Weed, Charles Wimar, Alexander Shindler, Charles Gentile, and a Mr. Shepard in the various archives. These latter attributions are likely in error and may refer to the donors of the photographs; alternatively, these men may have copyrighted or printed the materials even though they were not the photographers. There is specific evidence tying each of these items to Gaige, Brown, Lorenzen, or Wolfenstein; in the case of

Gentile, there are indications that the photographs are not of Navajo. Based on the available materials, histories, and research, I have concluded that Gaige, Brown, Wolfenstein, and Lorenzen are the only Bosque Redondo–period photographers for whom we have reasonably established photographic evidence (and whose photographs have survived).[3]

J. G. Gaige was under contract with the military to photograph at U.S. Army posts, and records document his presence at Fort Sumner in the spring of 1866.[4] Gaige's photographs (or those herein attributed to him) of the Navajo at Bosque Redondo have been widely reproduced,[5] and used to date Navajo dress, weaving, and other items of Navajo manufacture and/or use. Gaige may also have taken a number of studio photographs of Navajo, probably while all were prisoners at Bosque Redondo (Navajo leaders are documented to have been in Santa Fe at least twice prior to returning to Navajoland in 1868).

We do not have details of Gaige's commission. The large outdoor photographs are documentary in an obvious sense, but there does not seem to be any central theme. Navajo appear in all the Fort Sumner outdoor photographs, but, apart from those in the husking party photos, most of the Native Americans are being counted, being held on charges, or awaiting rations or coupons;[6] rarely are they depicted doing productive work. If the photographs were supposed to decry (or support) the Long Walk, Gaige didn't succeed, although certainly they do not suggest, even in the context of the times, that the incarceration was a good idea. The studio portraits depict such exaggerated, bizarre salon postures, Navajo women and men idly and intimately draped on one another,[7] that their purpose, apart from recording details of apparel, remains unclear. We can be sure, however, that Navajo had little input and that the poses derived from other studio conventions of the time. Despite the imported posing style and pastoral studio backdrops, most individuals wear indigenous dress, with bead necklaces and rough natural color blankets with small horizontal stripes. There is little silver evident, and only an occasional man has a Western hat or jacket.

Valentin (also spelled Valentine) Wolfenstein was known to have set up portrait equipment in Fort Sumner,[8] and two important photographs of Barboncito are concretely attributed to him (Figs. 19, 20). These are dated 1867 (but probably were taken in 1868). We also have evidence that Wolfenstein photographed the treaty signing with General Sherman in 1868, though none of the latter appear to have survived.[9] Wolfenstein's diaries (Faris/R. Wolfenstein, September 1993) indicate that he actively photographed Navajo, the Bosque setting, and the military while at Fort Sumner. In an entry dated 14 March 1868, Wolfenstein notes his offer to sell his equipment to Nicholas Brown of Santa Fe. There is no indication of Brown's response, but he may have later bought some items, perhaps including some photographs.[10]

Wolfenstein uses a formal, straightforward posing style, but nothing as flamboyant as that used in the studio photographs here attributed to Gaige. He shows the Navajo with weapons, but because Wolfenstein photographed toward the end of the captivity, these may also have been appropriate individual possessions, however much the photographer deliberately used them as props. Wolfenstein took the only existing photographs of the important Navajo leader Barboncito—one, singly, sitting *en face* in a grand dignified portrait (Fig. 19), the other with Manuelito, Calletano, and a hidden fourth individual (Fig. 20). He also probably took the first family portrait of Manuelito, his wife, Juanita, and their son, Manuelito Segundo (see Fig. 21 and Roessel, 1980:209) and a portrait of Juanita standing alone (Fig. 22—noted in the archive, probably incorrectly, as Barboncito's daughter-in-law). As will be argued, several other photographs attributed to Nicholas Brown and Son may indeed be Wolfenstein's handiwork.

Nicholas Brown, a photographer who was in Santa Fe in 1866, is not specifically documented as having photographed at Fort Sumner, although I do identify some photographs of Navajo as his (see Figs. 23-27). Brown had a studio in Santa Fe, but the studio photographs here attributed to Brown may have been taken at Fort Sumner, for they are set in a room similar to that used in some of the studio photos assigned here to Wolfenstein.[11] Moreover, their subjects are not identified as important Navajo (several are children) and thus would not likely have traveled to Santa Fe. Some are labeled "captives" (see Fig. 23). In some studio photographs here attributed to Gaige (but not Wolfenstein), some Navajo also are labeled "captives," so if these ordinary Navajo had come to Brown's Santa Fe studio, the label seems peculiar.

The posing styles of the photographers differ. In Brown's photographs, the Navajo are not draped about one another, as in the portraits here attributed to Gaige. Brown's poses are also somewhat more stiff than Wolfenstein's. All three used both a figured carpet and a non-figured floor covering; a few of Gaige's photographs also include a painted backdrop missing from the studio portraits of both Brown and Wolfenstein. Brown used a slightly different chair than Wolfenstein, perhaps lending support to the theory that the Brown photographs were taken in Santa Fe. All photographs here *firmly* attributed to Wolfenstein have the same figured carpet, and some have a patterned drape on which people are sitting or leaning. Brown seems to have photographed more youth and children (unless some of these photos were indeed

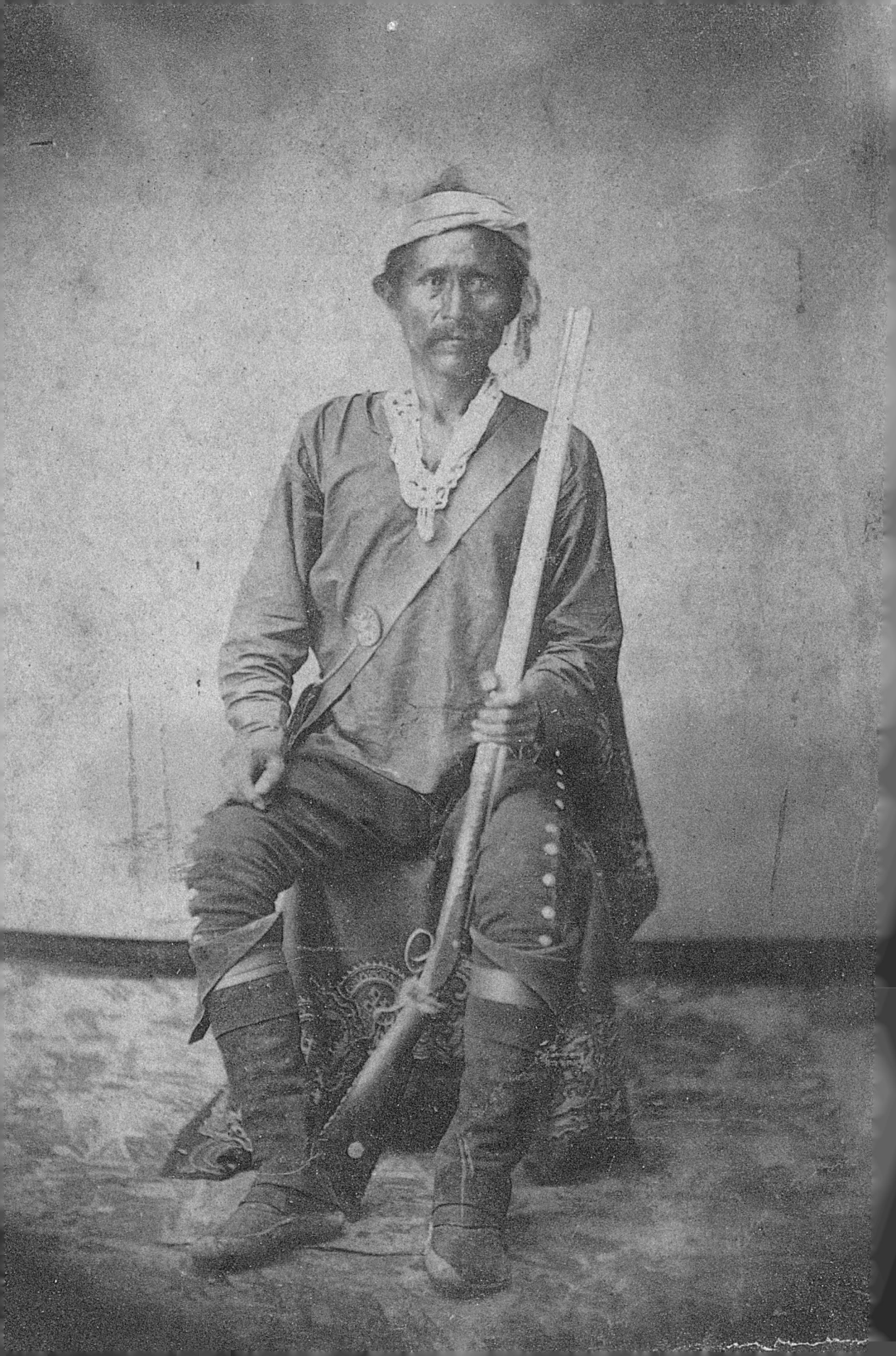

A Historical Sketch

Figure 19. "Man holding rifle. Photo by Valentin Wolfenstein. n.d. Collected by William N. Grier during Indian campaigns in the West, 1835–61. Presented by Robert Campbell in memory of grandfather, Wm. Grier." N.d. *This grand photograph of Barboncito, the great Navajo leader, was probably taken in 1868. Though published in other sources, it is reprinted here to establish an argument for the photographer (see also Figs. 20, 21). I am convinced that the attribution to Wolfenstein here is correct, though this photograph has been variously attributed to Charles Wimar, Alexander Gardner, a Mr. Shepard, and Nicholas Brown & Son. It has also appeared in the mounts of Gardner, Blackmore, and Nicholas Brown & Son (cf. National Anthropological Archives, Smithsonian Institution No. 55,766 [Neg. No. 2442]). The National Museum of the American Indian also has a copy of this photograph (see P. #7335) that is hand-tinted (perhaps by a Mr. Shepard). Photograph courtesy National Museum of the American Indian, Smithsonian Institution. P. #20816.*

Figure 19

Chapter 3

taken by Wolfenstein), Gaige and Wolfenstein more adults, groups, and important (named) Navajo.

I am aware of no direct collaboration between any of these men. However, both Gaige and Brown later worked in Chihuahua, and Wolfenstein and Brown both earlier photographed at Fort Union (Brown in September 1866, Wolfenstein sometime prior to 1868), so there could have been some sharing of facilities (the room and the figured carpet) or even photographs and negatives. None of the same Navajo appear in both Gaige and Brown photographs, but some—such as the Navajo leader Manuelito—appear in both the Wolfenstein and Brown photographs. Brown apparently photographed Navajo and sold prints and *cartes de visite* with his imprint. He also imprinted photographs taken by others (especially some here considered to be Wolfenstein's), which he bought or otherwise acquired. His frequent moves around New Mexico would suggest market demand was not great or, perhaps, that he did not know how best to market his images. They have nevertheless found their way into archives as Brown photographs, though, as noted, I suspect many of these of Navajo subjects are indeed Wolfenstein photographs later acquired by Brown. I would cautiously suggest that all the *attributed* Brown photographs illustrated here might indeed be Wolfenstein photographs.

Of the three, Wolfenstein took perhaps the most dignified photographs. The Navajo youth are generally quite glum in the photographs attributed in the archives to Brown, and peculiar posing and careful (and bizarre) arrangements characterize the studio photographs here attributed to Gaige.

The only two extant Navajo photos attributed to Henry Lorenzen reveal strikingly different and contrasting attitudes. One (Fig. 30) illustrates a Navajo woman in Western dress, confidently posed in a three-quarter portrait style; the other (Fig. 31) depicts a frightened, disheveled girl, perhaps being made to hold onto a modeling prop. The former reveals that assimilationist pressures were succeeding; the latter, that the Navajo were still clearly subject to a prying, interrogating, dominant, terrorizing West. Perhaps these earliest photographers could not transcend the desperation evident in Navajo lives with the Long Walk period, but it is not clear how much the subjects' melancholic appearance is a consequence of this genocidal event and how much represents the belligerence, hostility, fear, or confusion produced by the photographic encounter.

These earliest photographs are also interesting because the various conventions and visual rhetorics for photographing Navajo were then only beginning to be established. Some of the tropes they use seem to have been imported

A Historical Sketch

from other endeavors—especially the extravagant Gaige posing style—and (fortunately) were seldom repeated later. The bored/disgusted/despairing young boy[12] (attributed to Brown, but perhaps taken by Wolfenstein—see Roessel, 1980:202) and the frightened, disheveled girl (Fig. 31) provide somewhat unique and almost studied candid views; if such faces appeared in the work of later photographers, they never got out of the studio, for this pose did not emerge as an acceptable convention for later Navajo photographs. It is difficult to determine if all woven clothes, Navajo blankets, and other attributes were arranged by the photographers, but Navajo must have had many of these materials with them, including skin bags, hats, and weavings. The poses with weapons, especially the three-quarter views, survived as one dominant trope of Navajo photographic appearances. Numerous photographs, in varied forms, of Navajo with weapons survive down to the present (see Figs. 20, 23, 54). At least one visual register, then, was established from the beginning.

Although contemporary photography of Navajo with high-tech weapons is meant to convey modernist irony (cf. Chapter 7 herein and McAuley, 1989), it is these early Navajo-with-weapons photographs that are indeed ironic. These subjects were prisoners, stripped of offensive force, and photographs of them with such implements make perverse reference to their captivity, their conquest, and the impotence of such items. The weapons props ostensibly indicate something of Navajo ferocity, barbarism, freedom, a grotesque (and new) means of keeping Navajo savage (but captive) in the public eye after the United States had conquered and controlled them. Such photography was now to be nostalgic, primitivizing, domesticating—a mockery. Of course, because Navajo were captives well outside their homeland in these earliest photographs, there can certainly be little claim to aboriginality in dress, personal appearance, and so forth. What exists inside the frame is thus problematic and can evidence only what is outside the frame—capture and desperation.

Chapter 3

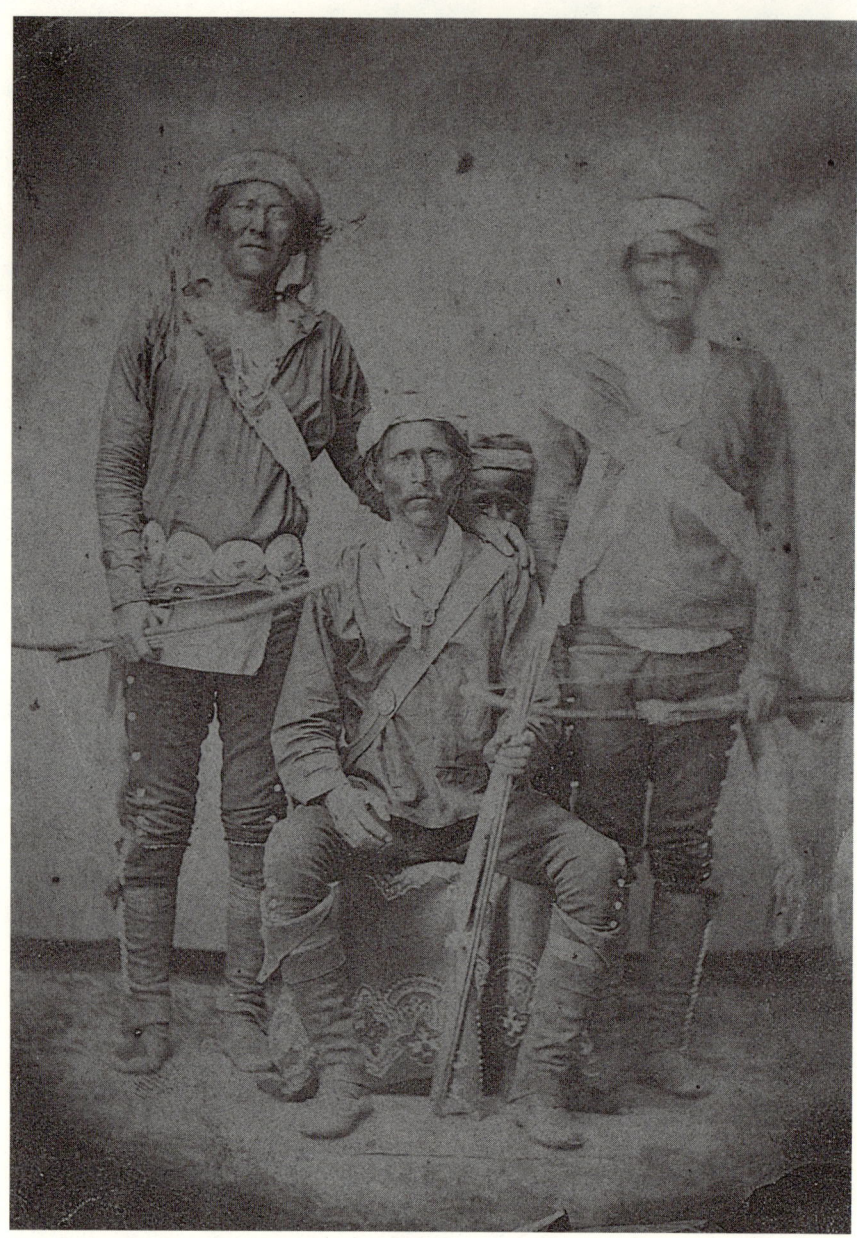

Figure 20

Figure 20. "*Three [sic-four] men holding bow and arrow. Photo by Valentin Wolfenstein. Collected by William N. Grier during his Indian campaigns in the West, 1835–61. Presented by Robert Cambell in memory of grandfather, Wm. Grier.*" *N.d. (probably 1868), probably Fort Sumner. From viewer's left, individuals are Manuelito, Barboncito, a man (or boy) barely peering over Barboncito's shoulder, and Calletano, Manuelito's brother. Clearly this photograph was taken at the same time and place as Fig. 19, 21, 22. I think the attribution to Wolfenstein is correct (see Figs. 19, 21), and here forms the basis for other Wolfenstein attributions. Photograph courtesy National Museum of the American Indian, Smithsonian Institution. P. #20815.*

Chapter 3

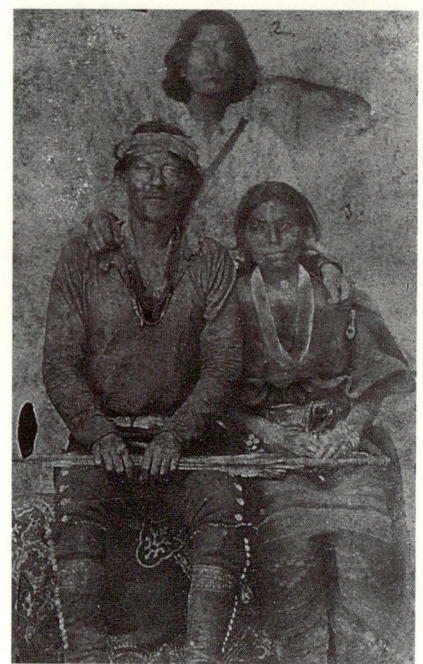 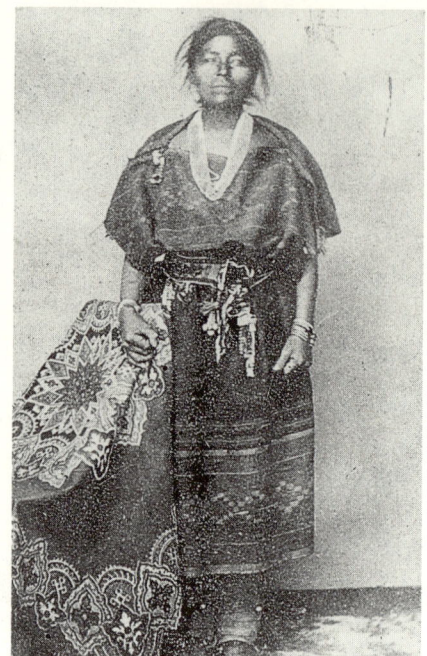

Figure 21 *Figure 22*

Figure 21. "Chief Barboncito, Chief's wife, Chief's son." Photographer unknown, probably Valentin Wolfenstein, 1868, Fort Sumner. This identification is in error in the NAA print; illustrated here are Manuelito, Juanita, and their son, Manuelito Segundo. See Figs. 19, 20, 22, for similarity to other Wolfenstein photographs. Photograph courtesy National Anthropological Archives, Smithsonian Institution. NAA Neg. No. 55,769.

Figure 22. "Mica se qui, daughter in law of Chief Barboncito." Photographer unknown, probably Valentin Wolfenstein, 1868. Drapery the same as in the Barboncito photograph (Fig. 19). This woman is Juanita, the wife of Manuelito (see Fig. 21). Photograph courtesy National Anthropological Archives, Smithsonian Institution. NAA Neg. No. 55,770.

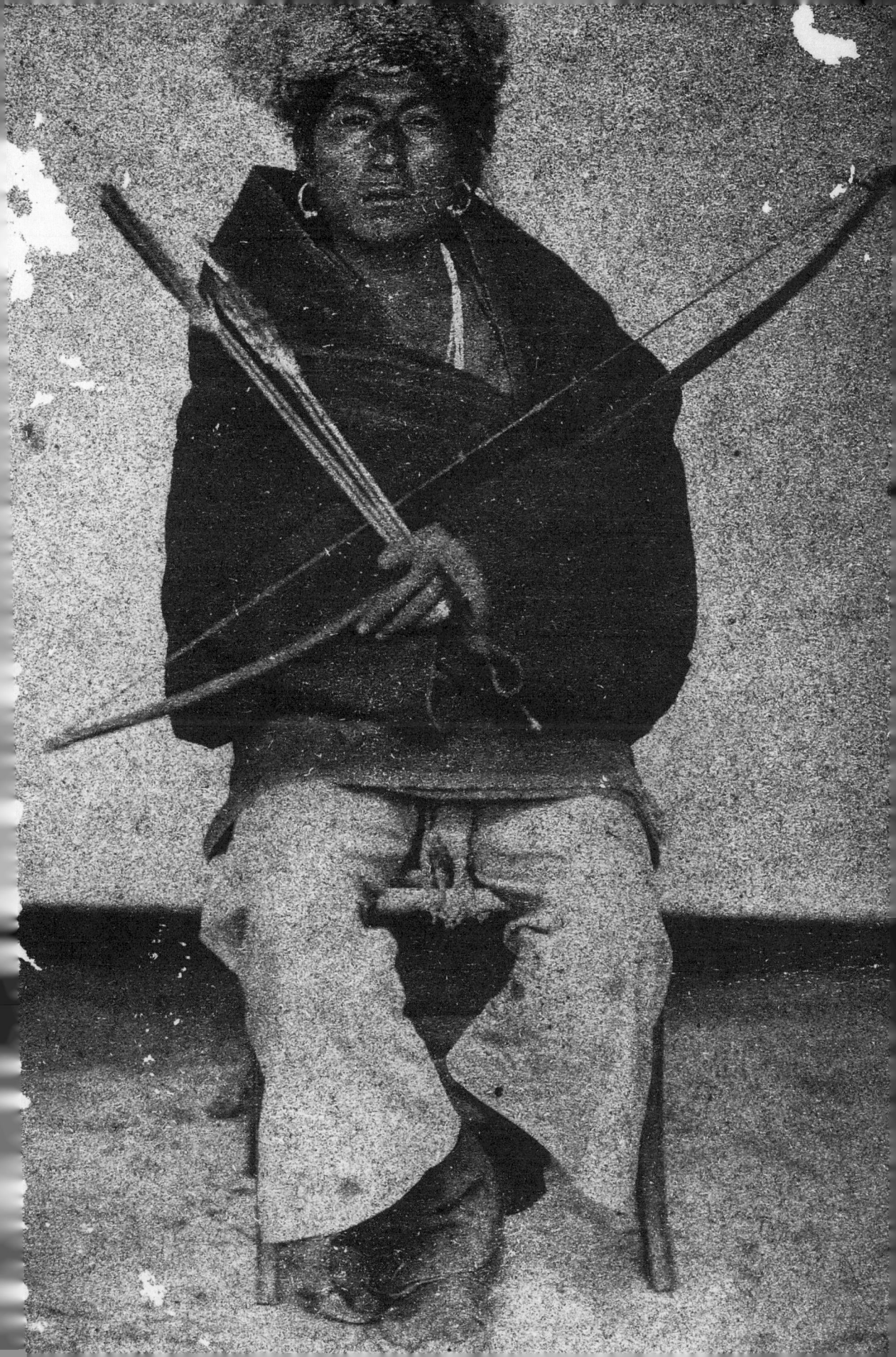

Chapter 3

Figure 23. "*Brave, captive at Bosque Redondo.*" *Photographer unknown, n.d. This photograph is on an* "*N. Brown e Hijo*" *carte de visite. If a Brown photograph, it probably dates ca. 1867–1868. This young man here has a fur cap but may indeed be the same young man illustrated in Roessel, 1980:170, with his hair down and wearing a different cap. Certainly the bow and arrows appear to be the same. This also could be, on the strength of the backdrop and chair, a Valentin Wolfenstein photograph. Photograph courtesy Arizona Historical Society Library. No. 14948.*

Figure 24. "*Boy in costume. Navaho. New Mexico. Photo taken about 1867 and presented by Ed. F. Weed.*" *This photograph was taken during the period of captivity (1864–1868), perhaps in Santa Fe, and may have been taken by Nicholas Brown or Valentin Wolfenstein. Weed undoubtedly acquired it later and presented it to the museum. The lad is dressed in cast-off clothing and has no shoes—"costume," indeed. Photograph courtesy National Museum of the American Indian, Smithsonian Institution. P. #9048.*

Figure 25. "*Two young Navaho with bows and arrows.*" *Photographer unknown (perhaps V. Wolfenstein), 1868. This photograph has also been attributed to Blackmore, Shindler, and Jackson and appears in both Blackmore and Brown mounts. If a Wolfenstein photograph, it was presumably later acquired by N. Brown. The boys seem only barely to comply with the order to strike a shooting pose, but such postures, even as impotent a threat as they present here, were popular at the time. This style is undoubtedly meant to be more humanist (nostalgic, ironic) and commercial than surveillance and documentary. Photograph courtesy National Anthropological Archives, Smithsonian Institution. NAA Neg. No. 55,087.*

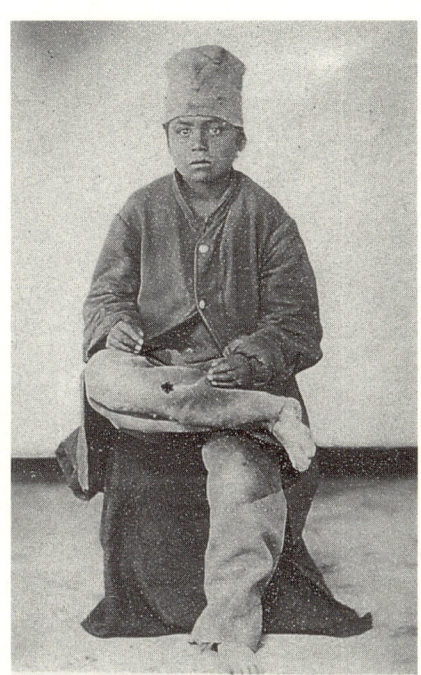

Figure 24

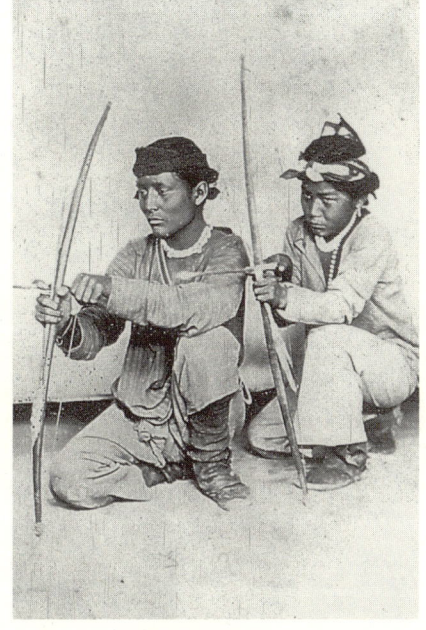

Figure 25

Chapter 3

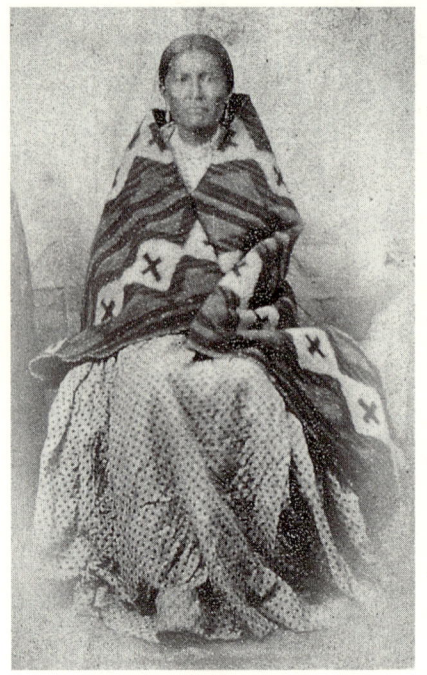

Figure 26

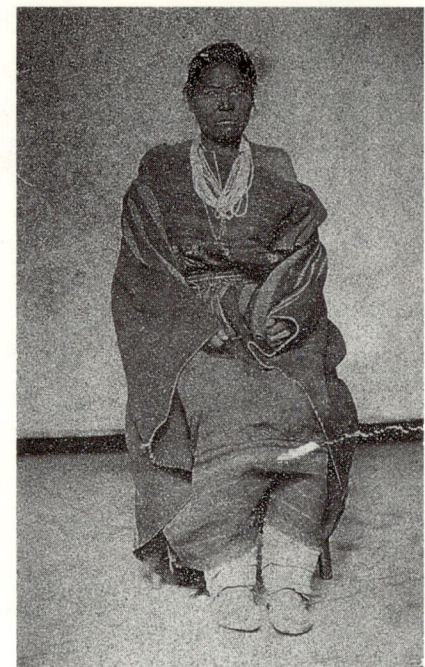

Figure 27

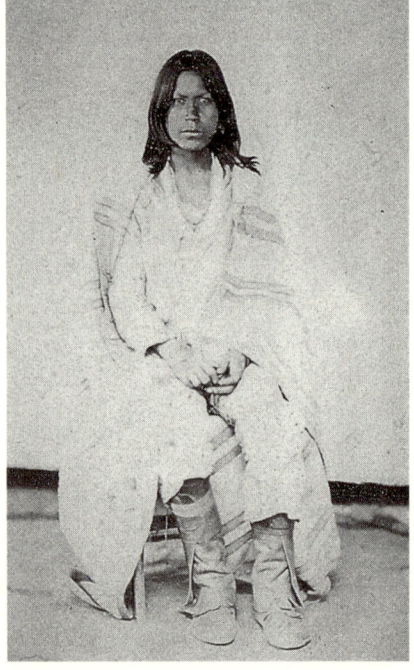

Figure 28

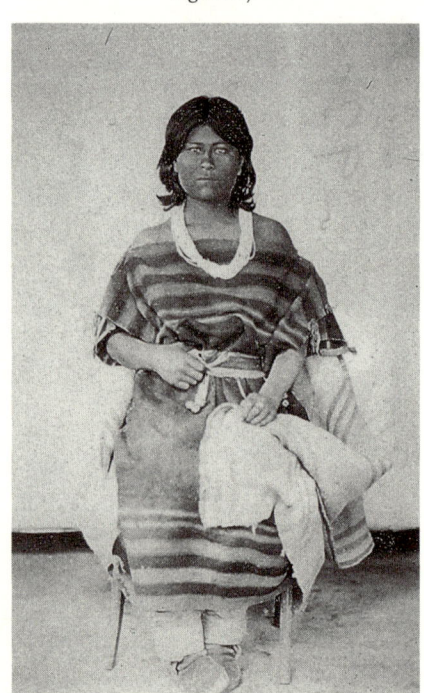

Figure 29

Figure 26. "Woman in costume." N. Brown and Sons, photographer, n.d. (probably 1867–1868), Santa Fe. This Navajo woman, with her calico skirt, cotton blouse, and Navajo weaving wrap, resembles the woman pictured in Roessel, 1980:155. This may be the way some important Navajo women dressed on visiting Santa Fe from Fort Sumner during the Bosque Redondo era. Photograph courtesy National Museum of the American Indian, Smithsonian Institution. P. #7345.

Figure 27. "Woman. Navaho. New Mexico. Photo taken about 1867 and presented by Ed. F. Weed." This is one of the studio photographs of the Bosque Redondo period that Valentin Wolfenstein may have taken. If the date (1867), however, is correct, this would probably mean it is a Nicholas Brown photograph, as Wolfenstein's diaries do not place him in Fort. Sumner until 1868. Nevertheless, the chair and studio backdrop are similar to those in attributed Wolfenstein photographs. In contrast to the woman of Fig. 26, this woman appears in traditional woven clothes. Photograph courtesy National Museum of the American Indian, Smithsonian Institution. P. #9045.

Figure 28. "Woman in costume. Navaho. Photo by Edw. F. Weed, and presented by him to museum." N.d. (perhaps 1867–1868), Bosque Redondo period. A studio photograph, possibly by Wolfenstein or Brown. There is, however, no clear evidence that this is indeed a woman, as s/he appears to have on cotton pants. Photograph courtesy National Museum of the American Indian, Smithsonian Institution. P. #7351.

Figure 29. "Woman in costume. Navaho. Photo by Edw. F. Weed, and presented by him to the Museum." N.d. (probably 1867–1868), possibly Santa Fe or Fort Sumner. Again, this is undoubtedly not a Weed photograph but may have been taken by Valentin Wolfenstein. Two other studio photographs of the period (MAI #P. 7353 and P. #7370, the former with Manuelito) are attributed to Weed, but are probably by Wolfenstein, Weed later acquiring them and presenting them to the Museum. Photograph courtesy National Museum of the American Indian, Smithsonian Institution. P. #7350.

Chapter 3

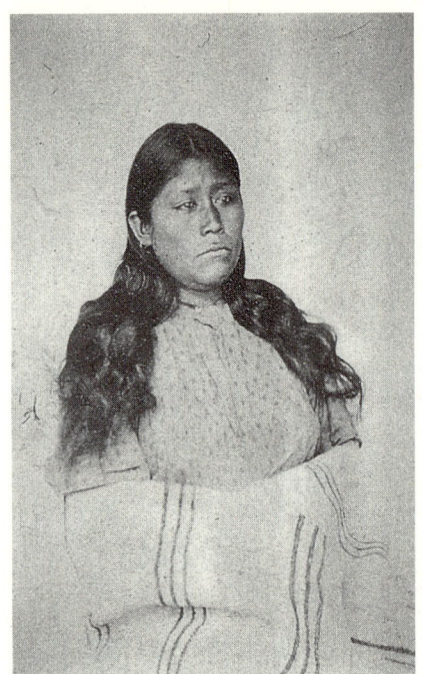

Figure 30   Figure 31

Figure 30. "Woman in costume. Navaho. Photo by Henry Lorenzen, New Mexico." N.d. (probably ca. 1868), perhaps Santa Fe. There is no reason to doubt this attribution, as there are Lorenzen photographs of this time with Santa Fe imprint (see Fig. 31). Note the formal three-quarter studio pose, calico blouse, and crude Navajo weaving wrap. Her hair, spread across her shoulders, slightly waved, is unusual. The notation "in costume," seen throughout, appears to be an archivist's convention to cover all individuals in any state of dress and contrasts with "nude." It does not designate Western versus indigenous clothing styles. Photograph courtesy National Museum of the American Indian, Smithsonian Institution. P. #7360.

Figure 31. "Woman in costume. Navaho. Photo by Henry Lorenzen, New Mexico." N.d. (probably ca. 1868), perhaps Santa Fe (see Fig. 30). This young woman, barefoot, wrapped in cotton and calico with a trade cloth overwrap, appears very disheveled and quite miserable. She is even standing with what appears to be a posing brace behind her. Certainly her captive status is evident, and there is little attempt to disguise her anguish and distress. This stands in dramatic contrast to the extravagant posed studio photographs from Fort Sumner attributed herein to Gaige. Photograph courtesy National Museum of the American Indian, Smithsonian Institution. P. #7361.

Chapter 3

Photographers, 1870–1900

After the treaty signing and return to Navajoland from Fort Sumner in 1868, there appeared an ever increasing number of photographers and photographs of Navajo. These were taken in Navajoland and elsewhere (such as Washington D.C.), many being specifically commissioned works. A Henry Hiester photograph of Manuelito and agent Theodore Dodd at Fort Defiance, dated late 1868 or early 1869 (Dodd died early that year—see Faris/Herzer, 14 April 1994, and Fig. 32), is, to my knowledge, the first photograph of individuals taken in Navajo country. Hiester was a commercial photographer brought to Santa Fe to succeed Brown, and he took several important 1870s views of Fort Defiance, Arizona, and its Navajo inhabitants.[13]

The Lt. G. M. Wheeler expedition, a broad scientific survey of the 1870s, produced Timothy O'Sullivan's Navajo photographs from 1873, and Maj. John Wesley Powell's famous geological surveys of the same decade yielded Navajo photographs by E. O. Beaman and John K. Hillers—the latter's work coming later, mostly in 1879 [Figs. 33, 34]).

These first post–Long Walk photographers illustrate the distribution of rations (Hillers), overviews of important forts (Hiester), women engaged in weaving (Hillers, O'Sullivan), landscapes of Navajo country and the White House at Canyon de Chelly (O'Sullivan), group portraits both formal and informal (O'Sullivan, Hiester), and the first series of portraits against a large background of Navajo weavings (Hillers), though Navajo weavings did appear in earlier, Bosque Redondo photographs. In the weaving photographs, Hillers gives the names of one or two people, labels others randomly ("A Navajo Wrestler," "A Navajo Pauper"—see Fig. 34), and changes the backgrounds, which sometimes end up on the subjects. Some are posed beside the weavings, in front of animal skins. Navajo men are seated in straightforward *en face* positions, two elders (the leader Ganado Mucho is one) in three-quarter *en face*. Seated facing the camera, Navajo women commonly avert their eyes (see Fig. 33). These intense, bold, open-lens Hillers portraits are qualitatively much better than the Wolfenstein, Gaige, or Brown wet plates of a decade earlier, and they illustrate not only greater variation in dress of both men and women but also a more confident presence than that evident in photographs taken when Navajo were still captives.[14]

O'Sullivan's photographs, however, demonstrate something of the disorganization following the Navajo return to the reservation. In his photographs, all taken outside, people do not appear very happy, and family scenes suggest a curious ambience of depression, despair, even fright. One portrays a

A Historical Sketch

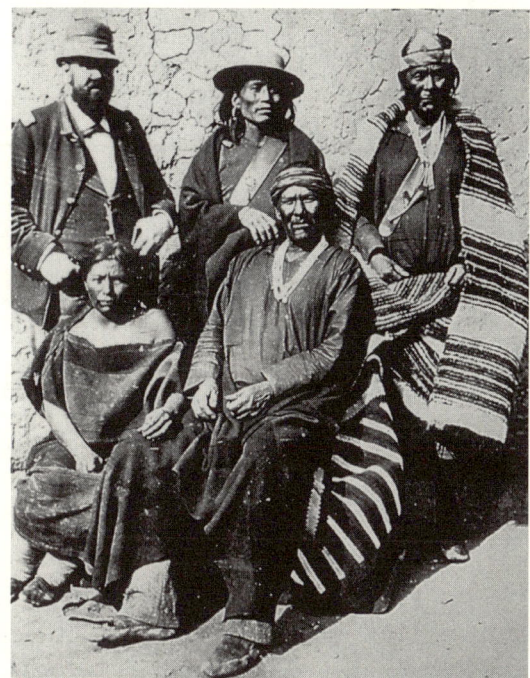

Figure 32

Figure 32. "Group including Manuelito (sitting) and wife." T. H. Hiester, photographer, ca. 1868, before 1870. Probably taken in Navajoland, just after the return from Bosque Redondo. Left to right: Col. Theodore Dodd, Navajo agent (who died before 1870—see Faris/Herzer, April 1994), Juanita (Manuelito's wife), probably Tiene su se, Manuelito, Cayetano. This represents one of the first (and few) photographs taken after the return to Navajoland from Bosque Redondo and before 1870. But there is debate about the date of the photograph and the identity of the European-American (see Chapter 3, endnote 13). Photograph courtesy McNitt Collection, New Mexico State Records and Archives. No. 5849.'

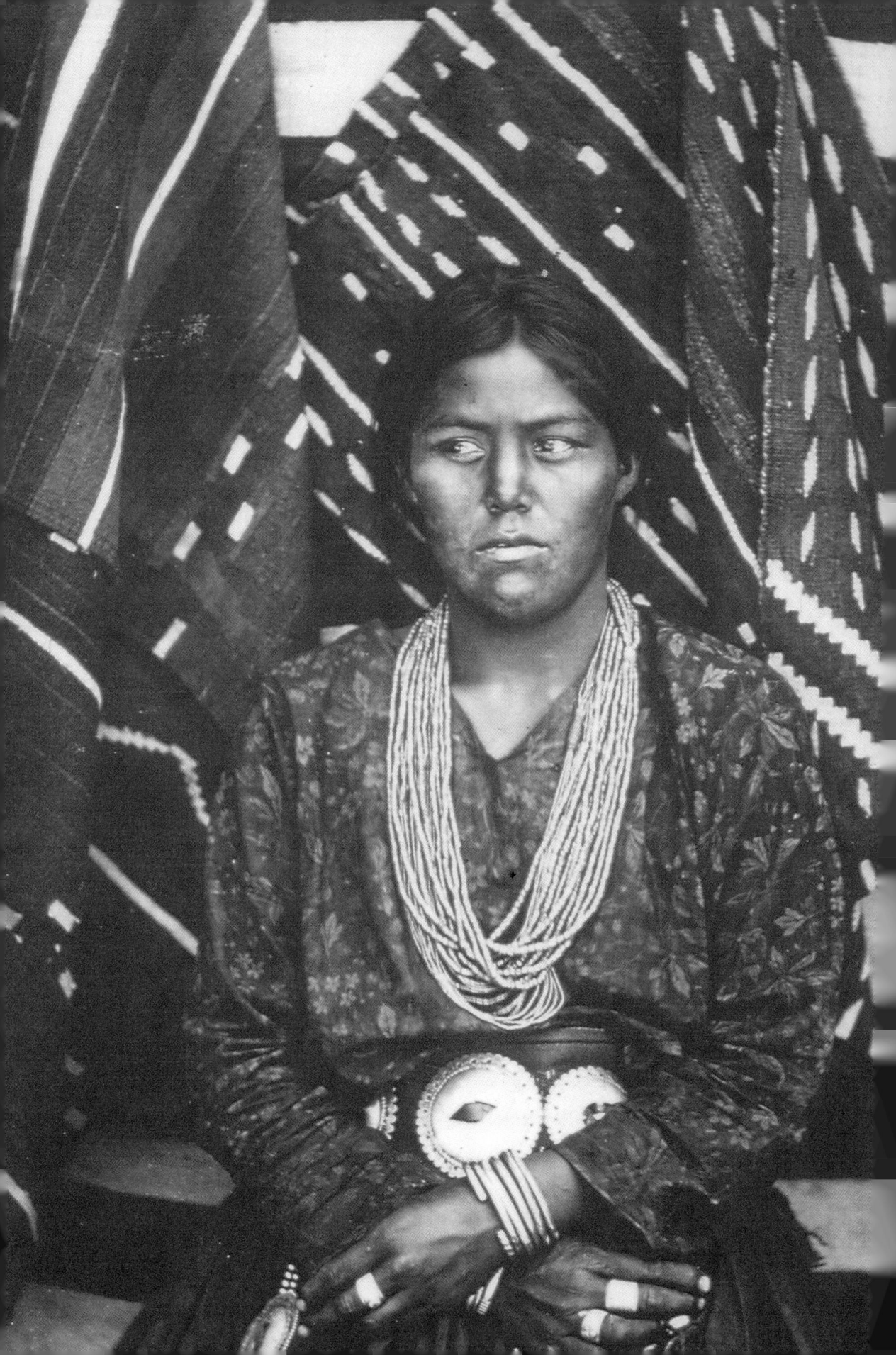

A Historical Sketch

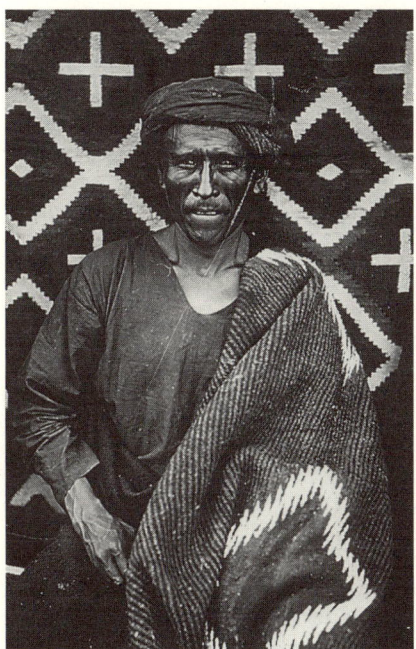

Figure 34

Figure 33. "A rich Navajo." John K. Hillers, photographer. ca. 1879. See Fig. 34. The subject's eyes are deliberately averted. Hillers posed an entire series of Navajo in front of weavings such as these and in front of animal skins. Photograph courtesy National Anthropological Archives, Smithsonian Institution. NAA BAE Neg. No. 2419.

Figure 34. "A Navajo pauper." John K. Hillers, photographer, ca. 1879. That this man is poor is evident only by his lack of jewelry (conversely, only the abundance of jewelry in Fig. 33 seems to indicate wealth). Photograph courtesy National Anthropological Archives, Smithsonian Institution. NAA BAE Neg. No. 2418.

Chapter 3

possible Apache woman with her nose cut, and many depict extremely disheveled, unkempt individuals.[15] O'Sullivan did pose individuals and families, so it is puzzling that he focused on what appear (in comparison with other photographs of the period) to be such aberrations in these more candid photographs.[16] Or, given the traumas, perhaps these photos offered a fair picture of a common state of affairs.

In 1874 a delegation of Navajo leaders, with Navajo agent H. M. Arny, visited Washington, D.C. This was the first of several delegations from Navajoland to attempt to get the United States to honor its obligations under the treaty of 1868. Studio photographer Charles M. Bell took several photographs of the visitors with props of the time.[17] These photographs duly record all ten Navajo men (named), Arny, interpreters, and one woman (Manuelito's wife, Juanita). The photo's label reads "in costume." As typically occurred in delegation photographs of the time, some of the same costume parts appear on different men, and at least one man wears a Plains shirt. Though all Navajo would have arrived in some sort of dress (usually a mix of Western and locally evolved styles), delegation photographers frequently added their own notions of what was appropriate to the circumstance.[18]

The 1880s essentially marked the end of the great surveys and much of the early official government photography of Navajo and saw the railway cross the southern edge of Navajoland.[19] Moreover, the Kodak camera and roll film became available in 1888, and the trading post networks dramatically expanded. Consequently, there was a massive increase in the number of white men who owned cameras, and their motivations were disparate. Camera clubs sprang up everywhere, and members of at least one, the camera club formed by Adam Vroman in Pasadena in 1898, visited Navajoland and photographed Navajo.[20]

Records exist from the last two decades of the nineteenth century for at least four dozen identified photographers of Navajo. Aside from those already noted, the best known, and those taking the most images of Navajo after 1880, are Christian Barthelmess, Charles Goodman, J. W. Hildebrand, George Wharton James, Sumner W. Matteson, James Mooney, Frederick I. Monsen, George Pepper, Adam Vroman, and George Ben Wittick (though several of these men photographed into the twentieth century). As noted, all negatives from William Henry Jackson's earlier photographs of Navajo failed, and though there are a few photographs attributed to Jackson dating from 1884, these are not very secure assignments.[21] And, despite attributions, I have no convincing evidence that Alexander Gardner actually photographed Navajo (though he did visit the Southwest and it would be peculiar if he did not take photos). He is documented as having photographed at El Morro, only a few miles from the Ramah Navajo location. There are occasional interesting, bizarre, outrageous, or unique late-nineteenth-century photographs from both the famous and the less-known—Dana B. Chase (Fig. 52), Elias Bonine, William Dinwiddie, George Grant, Ales Hrdlicka, John Lime, Frederic Maude, E. A. Mearns, Mickle and Jones (Fig. 35), Cosmos Mindeleff, Gustaf Nordenskiold, and Julian Scott.

As a consequence of the early technology (large view cameras), all photographs until almost the end of the century had to be carefully posed, and some photographic imposition is nearly always visible. Nevertheless, some surprisingly large collections of photographs have survived, especially from Hildebrand, James, Matteson, Monsen, Mooney (Fig. 36), Pepper, Vroman, and Wittick (see Appendix, Chart 1).

With the beginnings of easier access and easier photographic procedures (even before roll film, dry plates with prepared surfaces were available), anthropologists, traders, and government employees joined established professional photographers in taking pictures of Navajo in the final two decades of the nineteenth century. A series of distinct postures for Navajo photographs emerged as well.[22] No longer did Navajo subjects appear in the rather insecure or unsettled poses seen in earlier photos. They began to appear largely as they would to the West subsequently. During this time photographers began to produce much more candid photography (the "captured" moment) and multiple exposures of the same scene. Navajo were asked to turn a bit this way, turn a bit that way, sit, stand, and so forth (cf. G. W. James, where we have many times up to ten variations of the same photograph). Poor Juanita, the wife of Manuelito and the most photographed of all early Navajo women, had to endure James's camera through numerous poses (at least eight different photographs of this woman from the same sitting exist in the Southwest Museum's James collections). Her dignity emerges intact, however, even if her appearance is testimony to the weary task. Juanita had to sit through sessions with many photographers, everyone from Wolfenstein and Brown to Charles Bell, Hiester, Wittick, James, and undoubtedly several others. It is uncertain whether she chose to wear the traditional woven dress she is everywhere seen in or whether this was a perpetual photographers' request.

Photographic motivations during the last decade of the nineteenth century began to shift dramatically for technical, sociological, geographic, political, and economic reasons. The Kodak, the railway and the automobile, the burgeoning settlement of California and the Southwest, the clamor for statehood,

Chapter 3

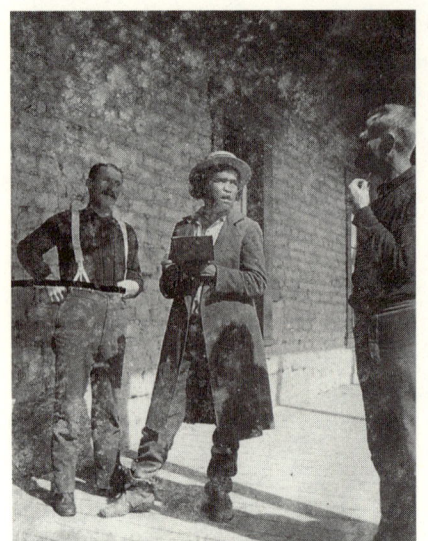
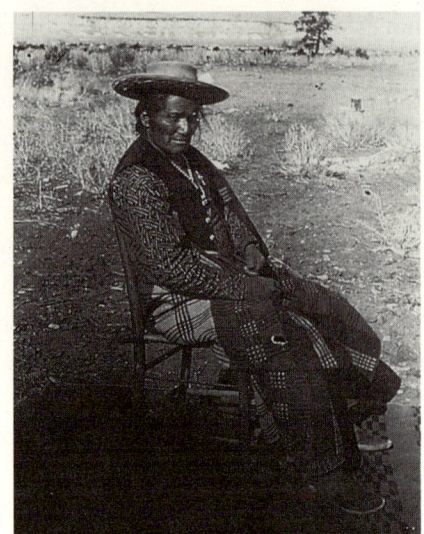

Figure 35   Figure 36

Figure 35. "Benny Green. Navajo Indian. Ft. Wingate NM 1890." This photograph is possibly by the Fort Wingate studio of Mickle and Jones. This same Navajo man is also featured in a studio setting with a Mickle and Jones imprint (1895) labeled, "Benny, an Idiotic Navajo Indian" (Museum of New Mexico, unnumbered). This individual may be Chief Mariano's nephew, Choh, photographed by Wittick in the 1880s (see Broder, 1990:128). Photograph courtesy United States Army Military History Institute. #80,495-LD.12

Figure 36. "The Navaho 'Doctor,' Fort Wingate NM." James Mooney, photographer, 1892. This comfortable photograph depicts the important Navajo medicine man, Laughing Singer. Mooney's photographs of Laughing Singer are very important in identifying him, and one is the photograph used by Washington Matthews (1897:57). They also provide a means for correcting Curtis's misidentification of Little Singer as Laughing Singer (see Fig. 75 and LOC USZ62-52674). Characteristically, Mooney's shadow is in the photograph. Photograph courtesy National Anthropological Archives, Smithsonian Institution. NAA BAE Neg. No. 2481-b-9.

and the scramble for mining, timbering, and grazing leases all meant there was money to be made. Though several photographers of this time came to argue against the prevailing assimilationist attitudes displayed toward native peoples by the U.S. government and local missionaries, their behaviors would suggest their initial motivations were otherwise.

Several of the first anthropologists took photographs before the end of the nineteenth century in Navajoland. Mooney, Pepper, Orchard, and Hrdlicka were among those who left the most images. Mooney photographed principally in the areas of Fort Wingate and Keams Canyon in the winter of 1892–1893.[23] It was his photograph of Laughing Singer that Washington Matthews used in his publications (and that helped correct Edward Curtis's erroneous identifications of this important Navajo medicine man—see Fig. 36 and Chapter 4). And Mooney produced an extended series of photographs depicting the activities (principally weaving) of "Charlie's camp." In many of these we can see Mooney's shadow, a small conceit that runs through very much of his photography (Faris/Jacknis, February 1993). He could not resist the Navajo with weapon, witness his widely published photograph of a man with shield and spear.[24] Mooney himself was photographed in Navajoland with Navajo, probably by M. C. Stevenson.[25] Here we see another emerging posture: white men with their hands on Navajo, either in jocular fashion, to get them to pose for the camera, or in a patronizing friendship (see Portfolio VI).

George Pepper, involved in archaeological efforts at Chaco Canyon on behalf of the American Museum of Natural History from 1897 until the early 1900s, left quantities of unusually well-documented photographs of Navajo working on the project and enjoying leisure and domestic activities. He also took occasional portraits and photographs of other Navajo of the region, some with the Wetherills (Chaco Canyon traders), and a series of grotesque breechcloth only, *en face* and profile physical anthropology views (Fig. 46). These were later supplemented by photographs by the Museum of the American Indian's William Orchard, who seems to have taken over some of the photographic chores of the expedition after the turn of the century. Orchard left many close-up portraits, but neither the photographs nor much other data suggest that his social relations with Navajo were anything but supervisory and perfunctory (Figs. 37, 38). Ales Hrdlicka, also at Chaco Canyon for a time, took photographs of specific relevance to his physical anthropological typologies but also a few quite candid images of children and of events that seem, in dramatic contrast to the physiognomic studies, warm and human.

George Wharton James, who left many hundreds of Navajo photographs, was widely resented (by, among others, Charles Lummis, Adam Vroman, and the physician-ethnologist Washington Matthews) for his use of the published materials of others and for the aggressive pressure he applied to local people. The resentment was probably mixed with some envy—photographers of this generation photographed anything and everything they could, and James had created opportunities that others had missed. James was a crusader, very much in the mold of the most zealous of reformers, and he was determined to get his photographs at any cost. He was convinced he knew what was best for local people and that his ends justified his means.[26] Despite his reputation, he worked with others, especially Frederic Maude, E. E. Hall, C. B. Waite, and Charles Pierce. Pierce, an established commercial Los Angeles photographer, actually did accompany James on several trips through the Southwest to photograph, processed many of James's negatives, and later bought them all.[27] The two copyrighted many Navajo photographs together. Though it is reasonably clear that most of the James and Pierce photographs of Navajo were indeed taken by James, it is impossible to sort out specifically who took each one.[28] There are also James (?) photographs credited to another Pasadena photographer, George L. Rose.[29] James was not the pictorialist Vroman was, nor was he as ashamed of less than "perfect" negatives. His method resembled that of today's photojournalists and fashion photographers, with their motor drives—get a substantial quantity of images, and perhaps a few will turn out. Given this approach, he did not worry quite as much about posing as did Monsen, Vroman, and Curtis. With his reputed aggressiveness, this may have been the only way he could work (see Figs. 39-41). Many of these men also wrote on Native Americans and did much to foster the prevailing views of the times, especially the nostalgic and sentimentalizing notions.

More interesting than these polemical individuals from elsewhere (particularly southern California and Denver) during the last decade of the century were the local photographers—the professional photographers Ben Wittick and Charles Goodman, the Army band member Christian Barthelmess, and a relatively unknown amateur, J. W. Hildebrand. Navajo individuals were frequently named in these images, some of which depicted scenes largely of Navajo making (healing practices, political gatherings, etc.). Wittick has been abundantly illustrated and discussed,[30] and it is relevant here only to note that his non-studio photographs remain quite as important and informational as others of the period, for he didn't always feel it necessary to remove items of Western manufacture from photographs. His heavily retouched studio portraits are as sociologically significant as any photographs of the time, made as they were in Gallup or Fort Wingate, where the Navajo came on one or

A Historical Sketch

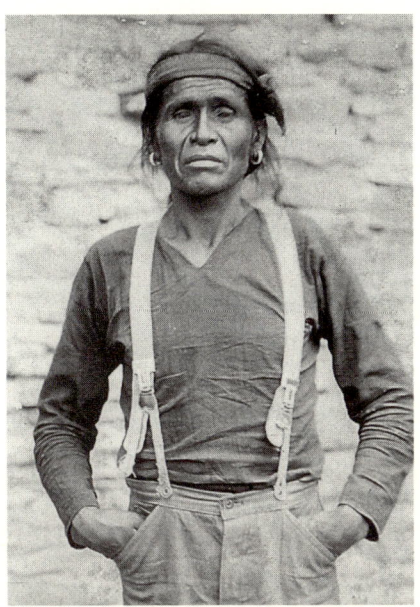
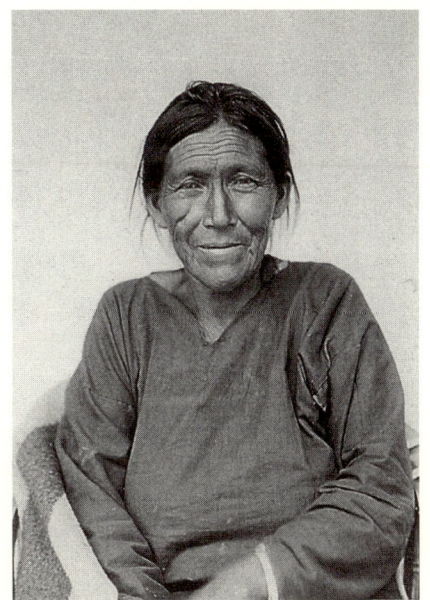

Figure 37 *Figure 38*

Figure 37. Navajo man. William C. Orchard, photographer, 1902, perhaps Chaco Canyon. Probably a workman on an archaeological excavation. Though little pleasure is indicated in this photograph, the subject has a casual posture and no fear—perhaps even a slightly bold, contemptuous, or confrontational attitude. He appears even to be looking down at the camera. Many surveillance poses (both en face and profile) photographs of this sort by William Orchard exist in the MAI archive. Photograph courtesy National Museum of the American Indian, Smithsonian Institution. P. #2781.

Figure 38. Navajo woman. William C. Orchard, photographer, 1902, perhaps Chaco Canyon. This photograph of a woman sitting, blanket in chair, suggests a somewhat shy but friendly person. She seems even to be trying to manage a smile. Her lack of jewelry suggests poverty or servitude. Nevertheless, we do not learn her name, and she is, like Orchard's other subjects, a specimen. Photograph courtesy National Museum of the American Indian, Smithsonian Institution. P. #2783.

Chapter 3

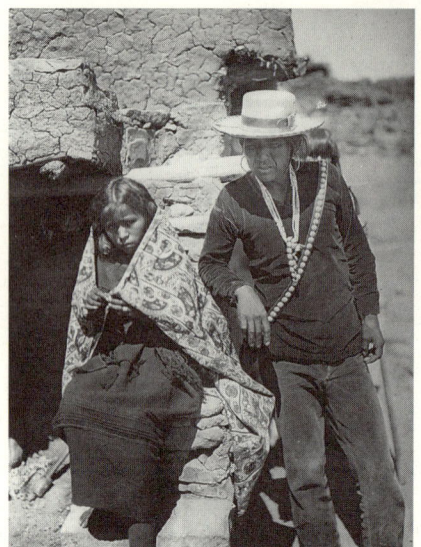

Figure 39

Figure 40

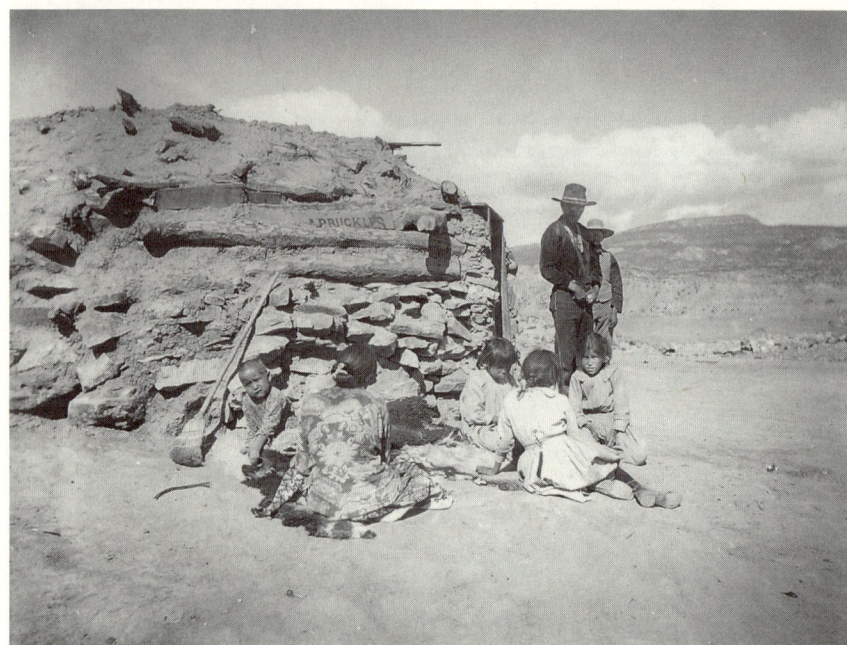

Figure 41

Figure 39. "Navajo 'Friendly' and daughter." G. Wharton James, photographer, n.d. (from 1890). James photographed this individual several times at the same sitting, adding or subtracting something from each. The young girl could even be Pueblo, judging from her dress. See Fig. 40. For "friendly" individuals, neither subject looks very pleased with the photographer. Photograph courtesy California Historical Society, Title Insurance and Trust Photo Collection, Department of Special Collections, University of Southern California Library. Negative No. 3687.

Figure 40. "Man with silver-studded bag across shoulder." G. Wharton James, photographer, n.d. (from 1890). Note that the man has lost his hat and his daughter and that adobe (complete with cracks) has been added in the darkroom above the man's head (compare with Fig. 39). Photograph courtesy California Historical Society, Title Insurance and Trust Photo Collection, Department of Special Collections, University of Southern California Library. Negative No. 3672.

Figure 41. "Peshliki's hogan and family." G. Wharton James, photographer, n.d. (from 1890). Note school uniforms on young girls, short hair on boy. Clearly Peshliki's children are in the grip of Western educational convention. Nevertheless, at least two children and an adult woman deliberately turn from the camera. "Peshliki" is an approximation of a word that translates as "silversmith." Photograph courtesy California Historical Society, Title Insurance and Trust Photo Collection, Department of Special Collections, University of Southern California Library. Negative No. 3210.

another of the missions required by their new relations with the U.S. government. Here the Navajo occupied a formal, distinctly inferior niche and were continually put in a position of supplication. Unfortunately, their business in the locations of his studios is not discussed, nor is the focus of Wittick's iconic studio photography. Wittick encouraged his subjects to hold weapons, wear jewelry and skins, and strike bold poses, well aware that no Westerners wanted to buy photographs illustrating Navajo solely as psychologically conquered peoples. Here and there we see a picturesque aged person ("Old Washie"), but more commonly young or important men and women appear. Occasionally he used a Victorian curtain, especially for more important subjects, as in a fine series of Manuelito and Juanita (see Figs. 42-44). Wittick occasionally succumbed to the lure of undress, producing series of pictures of young men with guns and breechcloths only (Fig. 45). These may have been taken in Wittick's tent studio at Fort Wingate, perhaps at the request of Dr. Washington Matthews, who actually involved himself in some physical anthropological work.[31] Photographs of certain events, such as the Council of 1891 (Fig. 47), are here attributed to Wittick.

Christian Barthelmess is the subject of a biography,[32] and most of his Navajo photographs have been published, though some are commonly attributed to others. In ethnographic work for Washington Matthews, Barthelmess was able to witness and document a portion of a nine-day Nightway healing practice,[33] but no photographs apparently exist from that research, perhaps because of resistance (Matthews himself took no photographs of Navajo healing practices as far as I can determine). While still a military bandsman, Barthelmess began studio work with Schofield in Fort Wingate in the 1880s.

Charles Goodman worked in an isolated and relatively undocumented area at Bluff, Utah, a small Mormon settlement on the San Juan River. He illustrated some of the first consequences of missionary activities (see Fig. 79 [in Portfolio V]) and the first Navajo fairs (beginning in 1899), with assemblages of people, weavings (see Fig. 196 [in Portfolio VII]), and produce. He also photographed Navajo herding and irrigated farming. Also in Utah was the Salt Lake City studio of C. R. Savage, who sometimes did printing for others.[34]

J. W. Hildebrand came west as a carpenter, building the original brick schoolhouse at Fort Defiance. He was said to have been a friend of Br. Simeon Schwemberger of St. Michaels Mission, and it has been speculated that this is where Hildebrand became interested in photography. Schwemberger and Hildebrand are said to have traded prints at times (Katharine Bartlett/Milton Snow, 17 September 1973). Hildebrand, from whom we have images dating as far back as 1895, apparently began his photography before Schwemberger,

A Historical Sketch

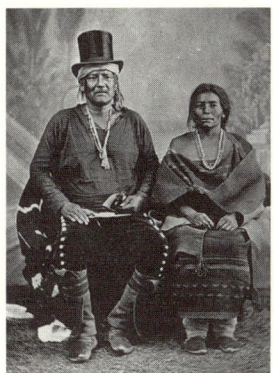
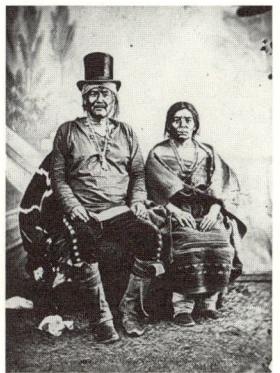
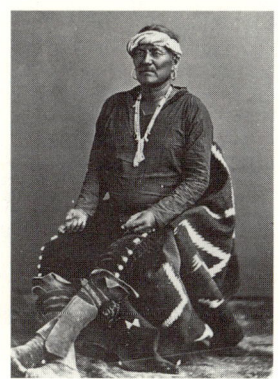

Figure 42 *Figure 43* *Figure 44*

Figure 42. "Manuelito, Navajo chief and wife. New Mexico. ca. 1881." Photographer unknown (undoubtedly Ben Wittick). This photograph is published in Roessel, 1980:216, but is included here for comparison with other photographs of Manuelito taken at the same time and place (see Figs. 43, 44). A somewhat different photograph (no pistol) is published (backwards) in Broder, 1990:43 and attributed to Wittick. Juanita is here, as always, ever dignified, having suffered through more photographic encounters than any other Navajo woman of her time. Photograph courtesy Arizona Historical Society Library. No. 30333.

Figure 43. "Manuelito, Navajo chief, and wife, Juana." Ben Wittick, photographer, June 1881, New Mexico. This photograph is also found, reversed, in Broder, 1990:43. It can be assumed that the top hat is Wittick's addition. See also Figs. 42, 44. Photograph courtesy School of American Research Collections in the Museum of New Mexico. Neg. No. 16332.

Figure 44. "Manuelito, Navajo Chief." Photographer unknown, ca. 1890. This is probably a Wittick photograph, as he photographed Manuelito with these clothes, this jewelry, and this blanket in 1881 (see Roessel, 1980:216) or 1882 (see Broder, 1990:43). The only difference is that in the attributed Wittick photograph, Manuelito has on a top hat and does not have earrings, and there is no figured backdrop (see Figs. 42, 43). Photograph courtesy Museum of New Mexico. Neg. No. 134484.

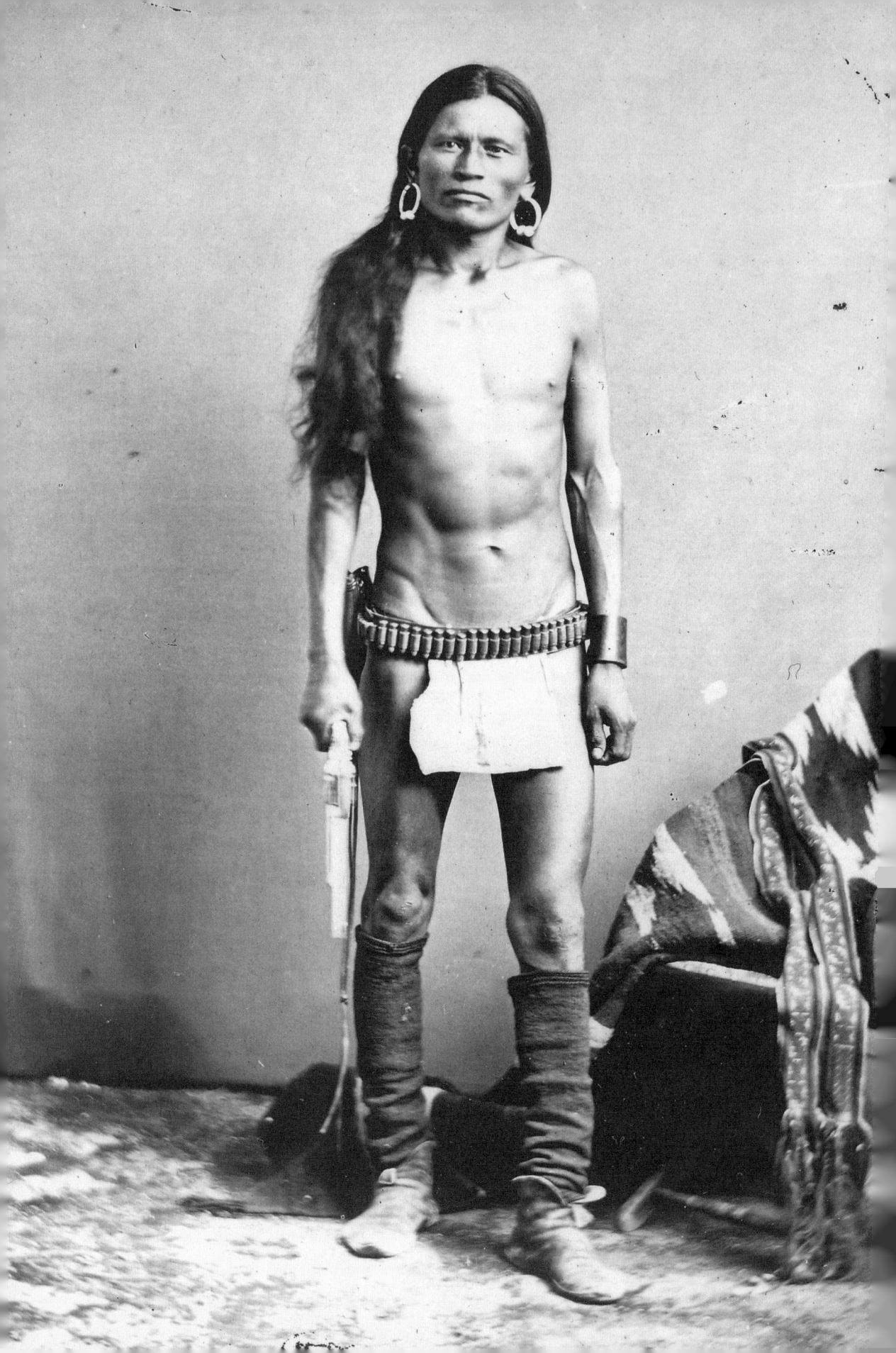

A Historical Sketch

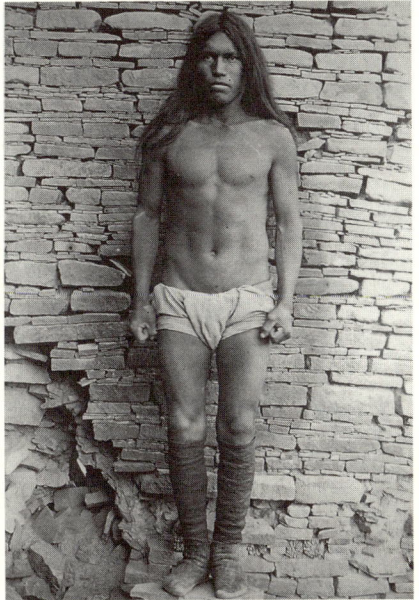

Figure 46

Figure 45. "'Charlie,' Scout under Lt. Wright." Ben Wittick, photographer, ca. 1885. It is unclear why this man is undressed, but he might have posed this way at the request of Dr. Washington Matthews, who was assigned to Fort Wingate at the time, had done research in physical anthropology, and was in possession of these specific photographs (see UMP). "Charlie" would normally have been dressed in clothing of the time, a mixture of Western and indigenous fashions of calico, denim, and so on. Photograph courtesy School of American Research Collections in the Museum of New Mexico. Neg. No. 15933.

Figure 46. "Bowlero." George H. Pepper, photographer, 1897, Chaco Canyon NM. Physical anthropology view, requiring undress (and a profile view—Neg. No. 2427), with Anasazi backdrop. The carefully folded covering and brushed hair are clearly deliberate, but were the clenched fists also instructed? This is a humiliating way to photograph anyone, but even important leaders were subjected to this sort of physiognomic portrait (cf. MAI Neg. No. P. #21222). See also Fig. 45. Photograph courtesy National Museum of the American Indian, Smithsonian Institution. Neg. No. 2426.

Chapter 3

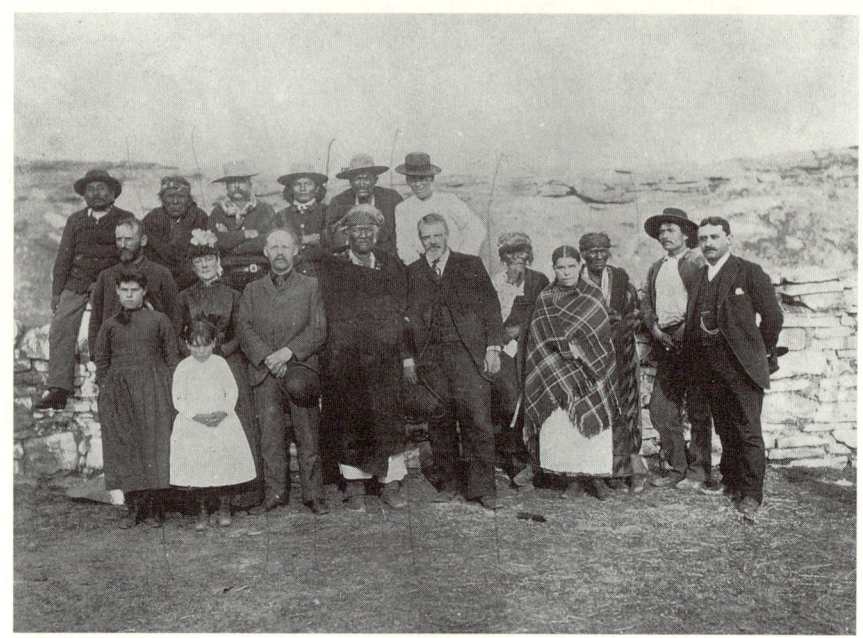

Figure 47

Figure 47. "White and Navajo Indian Council." Julian Scott, photographer (or Ben Wittick??), 20 April 1891, Fort Defiance AZ. This photograph, in the materials of the Eleventh U.S. Census, is one of the last photographs of Manuelito. From left, back row: Be-Santa-begai, Kaiga begai Soldow, Dan Dubois, Hosteen Yaga, Frank Walker (interpreter), unidentified European-American, Beochito, Juanico, Chee (interpreter). Second row: Col. W. G. Marmon (Special Agent, 11th Census), Mrs. Shipley, Agent A. D. Shipley, Manuelito, G. W. Parker (Special Agent Indian Office), Amchia, Col. John Donaldson (Special Agent, 11th Census). Front row: Vinnie Craig, Maggie Dubois. A different photograph attributed to Ben Wittick exists on this same day at this same place (see Broder, 1990:120, dated ca. 1883, from the School of American Research Collections in the Museum of New Mexico, Neg. No. 16373), with fewer individuals; the person erroneously labeled "Simon Bibo" in the MNM photograph is correctly identified as "Chee" (Dodge) in the UMP photograph. Photograph courtesy The University Museum, University of Pennsylvania. Negative No. 54-141426.

from whom we have no images until after the turn of the century.[35] He built other mission churches and continued to photograph, his images often candid, historically valuable (see Fig. 48 and Roessel, 1980:79), and certainly without agenda to eliminate signs of white men. They constitute a small, valuable, but little-known corpus. It was said that Hildebrand did not want recognition and did not want his name used (Bartlett/Snow, 17 September 1973) if his photographs were to be reproduced, though he may have collaborated with C. Kaadt (compare Fig. 199 [in Portfolio VII] with Hildebrand, Fig. 198 [in Portfolio VII]).

A number of interesting Wittick-style photographs are attributed to W. L Fetter, who once worked for D. B. Chase (see Fig. 52) in Santa Fe in the mid-1880s[36] but later worked in Gallup, where he photographed in studio (Fig. 50), and elsewhere.

Other notable late-nineteenth-century photographers, such as Elias Bonine, Frederic Hamer Maude, and Sumner W. Matteson, Jr. who photographed in Navajoland did not do so with the enthusiasm nor to the extent that they did elsewhere and are of less interest. Matteson rode a bicycle into Navajoland, making him something of a photographic subject himself. There survives a curious Matteson photograph of a Navajo man with horse belonging to a Mr. Culin (probably R. Stewart Culin, who was in the Southwest for the Wanamaker-sponsored collecting trip of the Museum of the University of Pennsylvania in 1900), with a bizarre notation about the exorbitant cost of board—$3 per day (Fig. 51). Elias A. Bonine, another Pasadena photographer, is better known for Mohave images,[37] but he persisted in the 1880s in posing Navajo males, wearing only breechcloths, against painted curtains of Grecian columns. Frederic Maude's Navajo work, far less extensive than his lantern slide photography of Western landscapes and other Native Americans, is set-piece (women weaving, families in front of hogans), undistinguished for the period, and frequently confused with Wittick or even Hillers.

Chapter 3

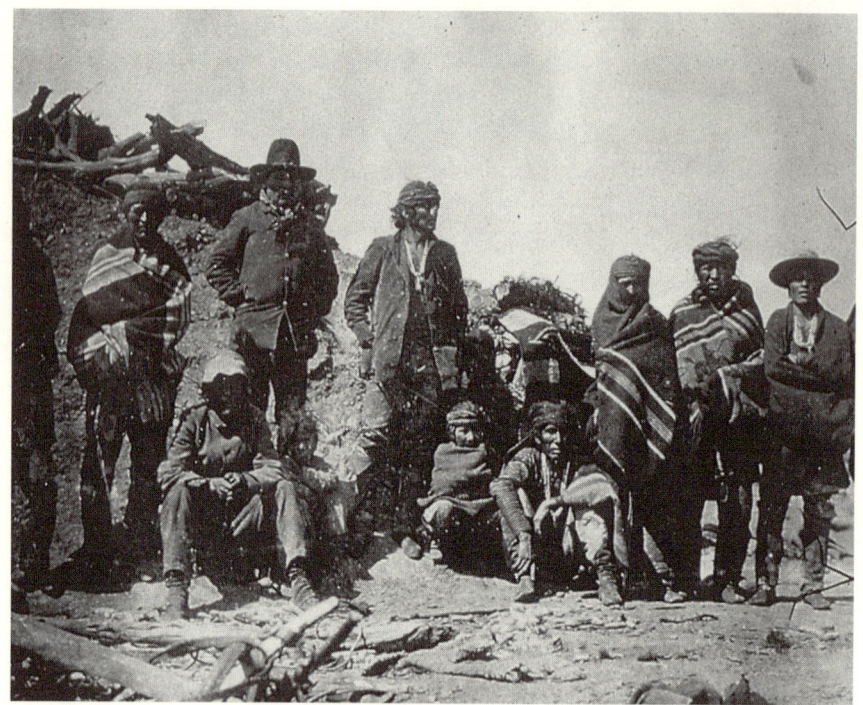

Figure 48

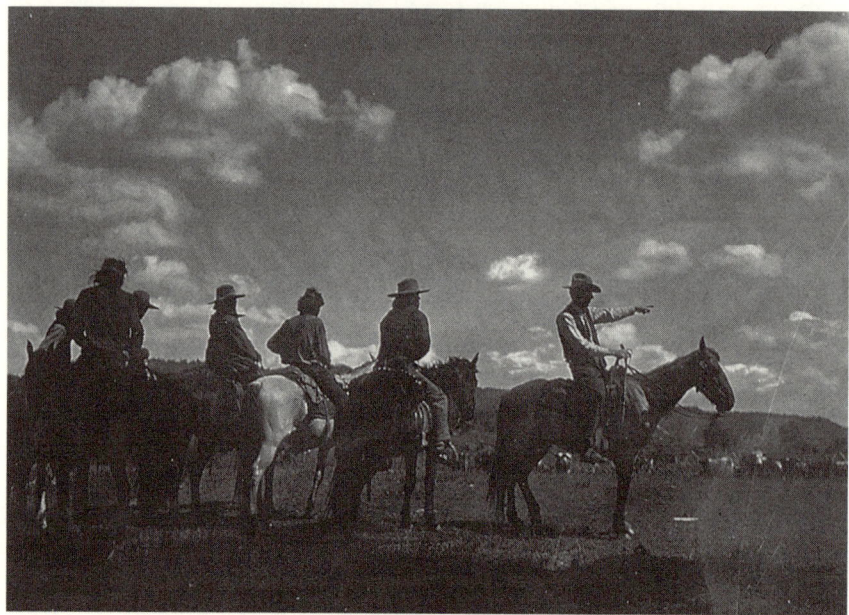

Figure 49

Figure 48. "*Navajo men in front of hogan with very long entrance way.*" *J. W. Hildebrand, photographer, n.d. (1895–1908). This photograph is one of two by Hildebrand, each with a large number of men together—clearly for some important event. The presence of the Navajo police at left also suggests the importance of the occasion. Photograph courtesy J. W. Hildebrand Collection, Museum of Northern Arizona. MS 168-E-200.4.*

Figure 49. "*Navajo men with J. B. Moore.*" *Simeon Schwemberger, photographer, n.d. (1895–1908). Moore was a trader at Crystal NM. The men are probably cowboys preparing to herd the cattle in the background. The inclusion of the cloud formations at this date reveals a deliberate exposure and compositional decision. Schwemberger and Hildebrand appear to have learned photography from one another. Photograph courtesy J. W. Hildebrand Collection, Museum of Northern Arizona. MS 168-6-22.*

Chapter 3

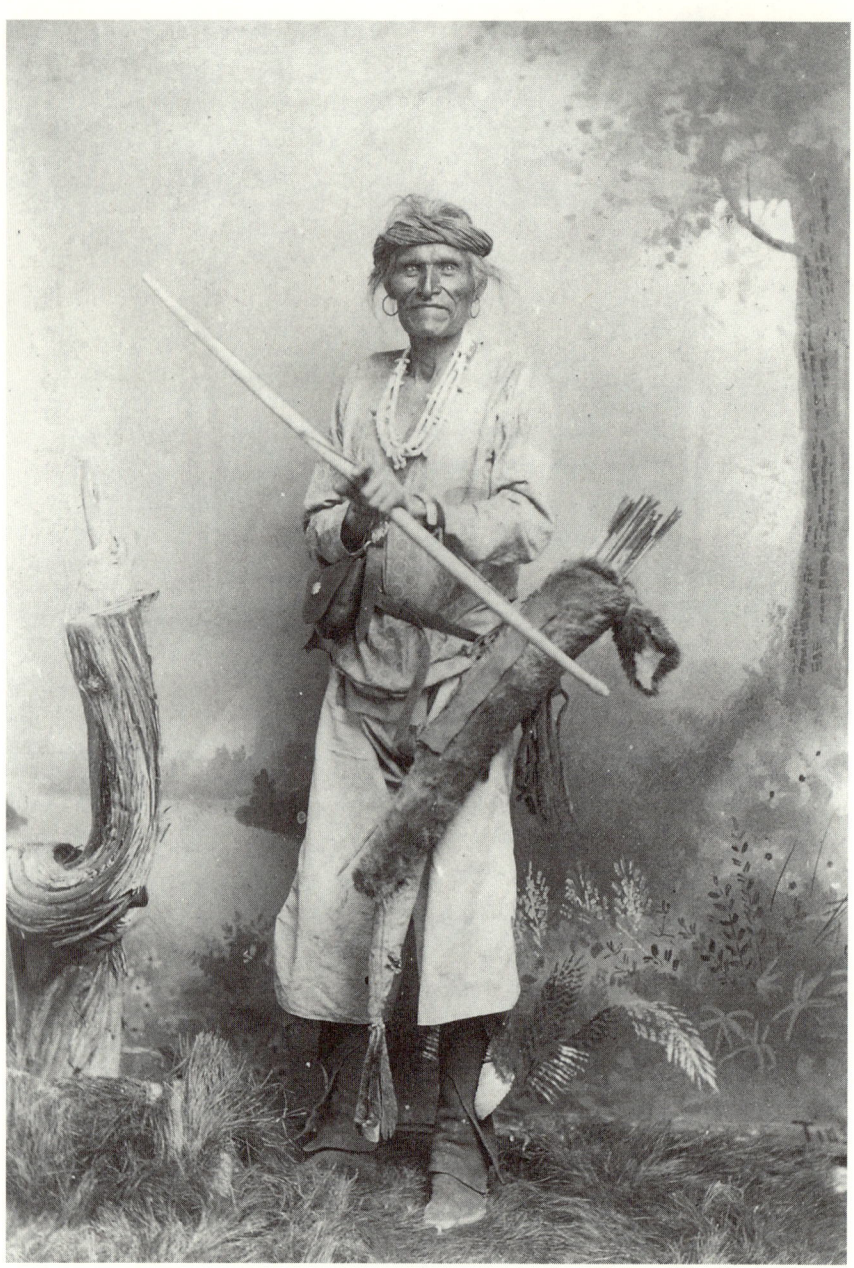

Figure 50

A Historical Sketch

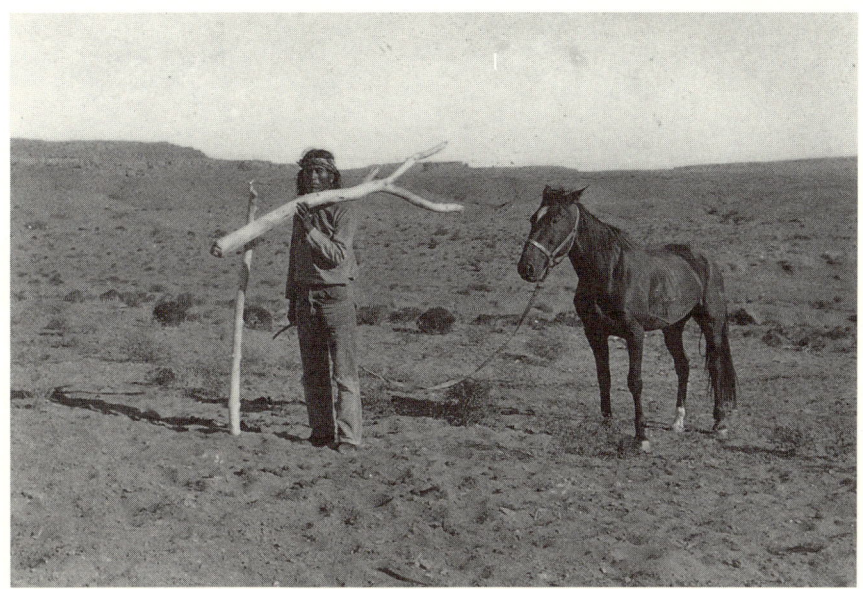

Figure 51

Figure 50. "Medicine Man." W. L. Fetter, photographer, 1890, Gallup NM. The man appears to recognize the complete absurdity of posing with bow, arrow, and quiver in the studio setting. Save possibly a small pouch tied about his waist, nothing here would identify this individual as a "medicine man." Fetter also photographed the Navajo leader Mariano in this setting (UPM Neg. No. 54-141428. Photograph courtesy The University Museum, University of Pennsylvania. Negative No. 54-141430.

Figure 51. "Mr. Culin's horse returned each morning with a full stomach and $3.00 bill." Sumner Matteson, photographer, n.d., probably 1900 or 1901. The meaning of this label is uncertain, but $3 is certainly exorbitant for a livery fee, especially as the horse does not look very well fed. Mr. Culin is undoubtedly Stewart Culin, collecting in the Southwest at the time. Photograph courtesy The University Museum, University of Pennsylvania. Negative No. 54-141432.

*Portfolio IV
Navajo in Image
1900–1950*

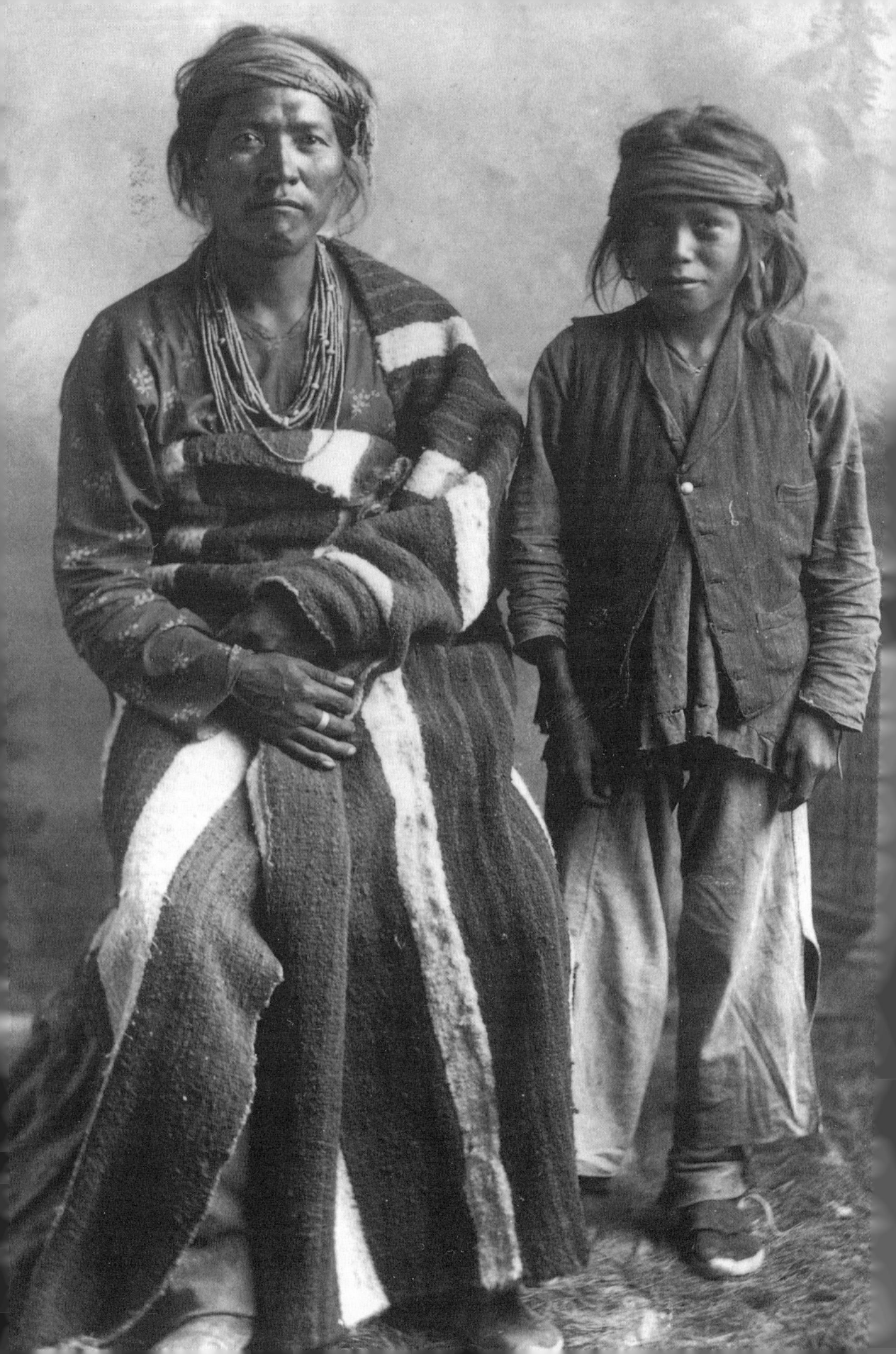

Navajo in Image

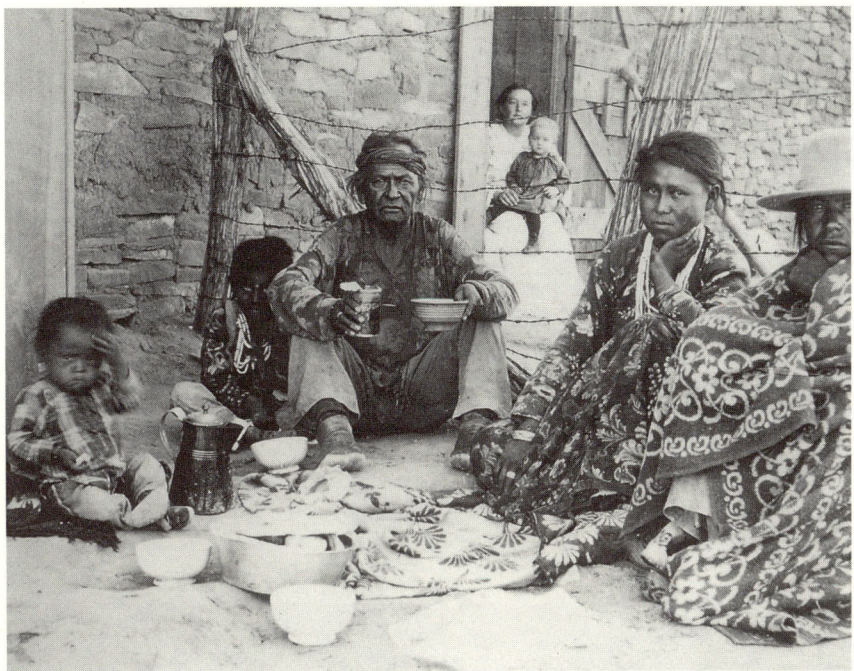

Figure 53

Figure 52. "Navajo Cheif [sic] and Son." Chase, photographer, n.d., Santa Fe NM. This Chase is probably Dana B. Chase, not A. W. Chase, as noted in the reprint by the Dry River Trading Company. These two individuals are inaccurately identified as Manuelito and son by the Dry River Trading Company. Photograph courtesy Colorado State Historical Society. No. F21,956.

Figure 53. "Old George's family." William C. Orchard, photographer, October 1900, Chaco Canyon NM. The juxtapositions of European-Americans and Navajo in this photograph (the Navajo outside the barbed-wire fence, sitting on the ground, the European-Americans, half-inside the dwelling, behind the barbed-wire fence) is probably not the deliberate subject of the photograph at this date. In any case, "Old George" does not appear pleased with the photograph, and at least one child seems to be trying to hide, another to cover his eyes. Lippard (1992:135) notes a Sumner Matteson attribution for this photograph. Photograph courtesy National Museum of the American Indian, Smithsonian Institution. Neg. No. 3758.

Figure 52

Navajo and Photography

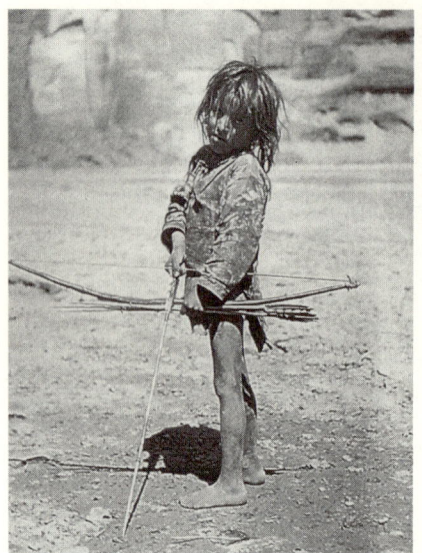

Figure 54

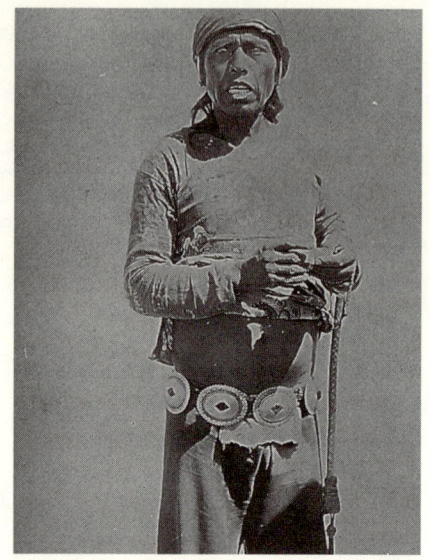

Figure 55

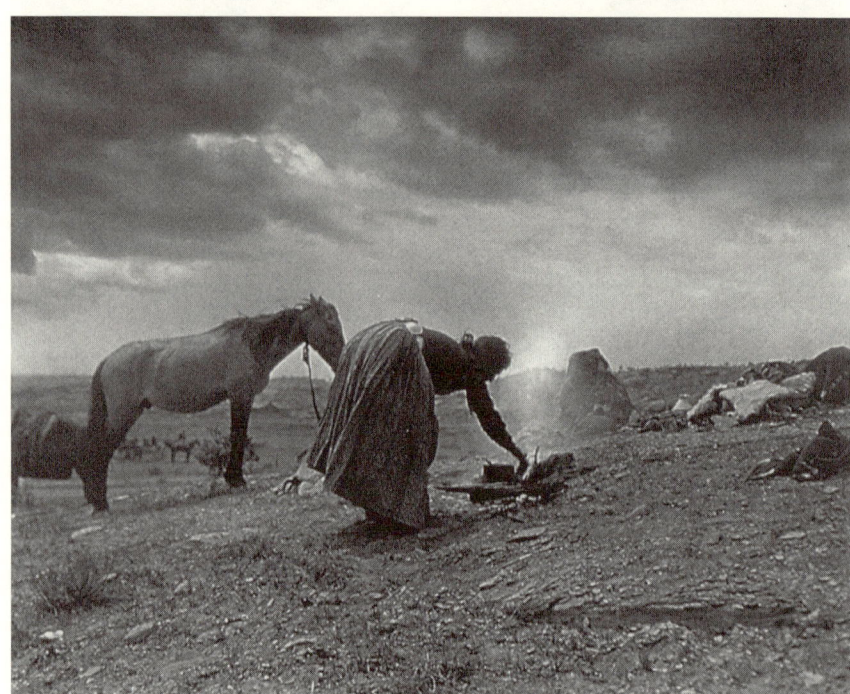

Figure 56

Figure 54. Young boy with bow and arrows. Frederick Monsen, photographer, 1896–1906. This appears to have been taken in Canyon de Chelly. This youngster either has been encouraged to look at the ready or is taking no chances with the photographer. Another photograph at the same time and place was taken with the child and his playmates, perhaps also by Monsen (see AHS No. 15794). Photograph courtesy Frederick Monsen Collections, The Huntington Library. Card No. 112.

Figure 55. Navajo man. Photographer unknown (perhaps J. F. Byrnes and Co.), 14 October 1901. Rolling a cigarette, holding a quirt, this man seems quite intently focused on something behind the photographer (see Fig. 168). Photograph courtesy National Anthropological Archives, Smithsonian Institution. NAA LOC03278600.

Figure 56. "Indian Study. Navajo woman at camp fire." Frederick Monsen, photographer, 1896–1906, Black Mesa AZ. This nice photograph could hardly have been posed. Photograph reproduced from the Frederick Monsen Collections of The Huntington Library. Card No. 100.

Portfolio IV

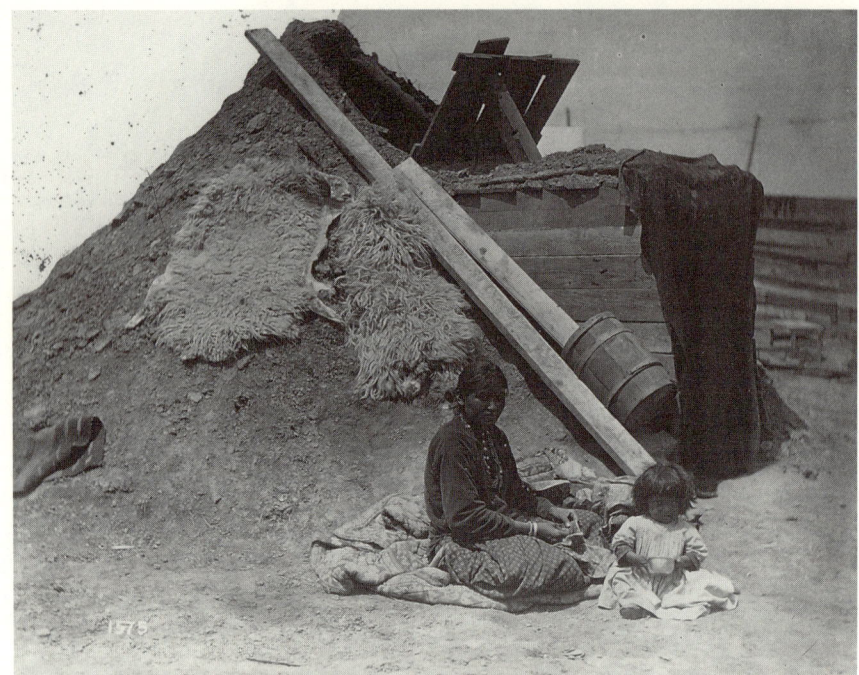

Figure 57

Figure 57. "Navajo woman and baby near hogan." Photographer may be Jesse Tarbox Beals, who photographed other Navajo at the St. Louis Exposition, 1904. This photograph would appear to be a hogan somewhere in Navajoland, but it is in fact at the Exposition itself. A nearby building can be seen near the top center, and a large brick building stands in the upper left (here masked out) in another print of this photograph. Photograph courtesy Department of Library Services, American Museum of Natural History. Negative No. 324066.

Figure 58. "She-she-nez." Delancy Gill, photographer, 1902, Washington D.C. This man is noted as being from a site on the Little Colorado River, northeast of Canyon Diablo AZ, born in 1837. The man's slightly open mouth and slightly bent-forward posture indicate some discomfort, especially with the oversized greatcoat. See Roessel, 1980:196, for en face. Photograph courtesy National Anthropological Archives, Smithsonian Institution. NAA BAE Neg. No. 2400-b.

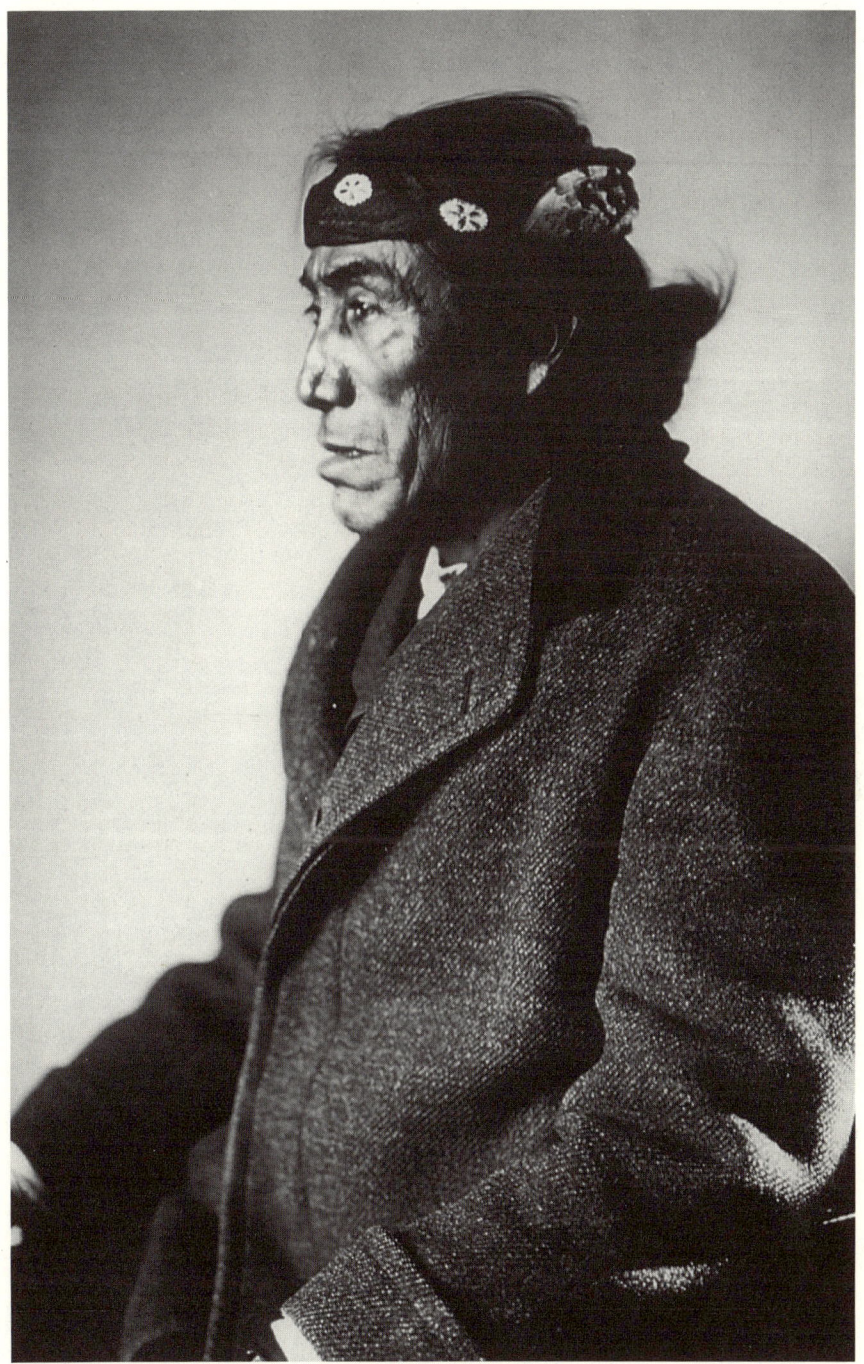

Figure 58

Portfolio IV

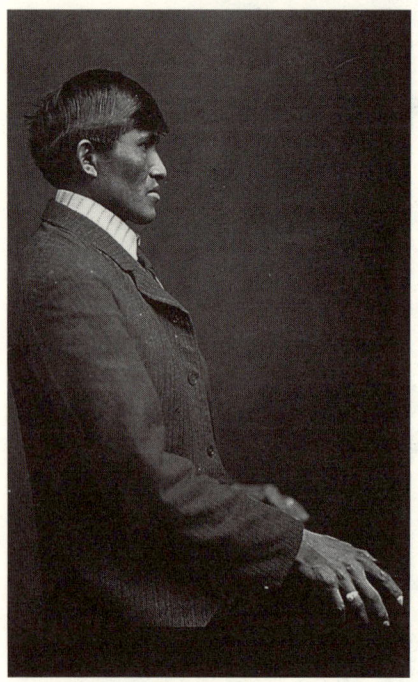 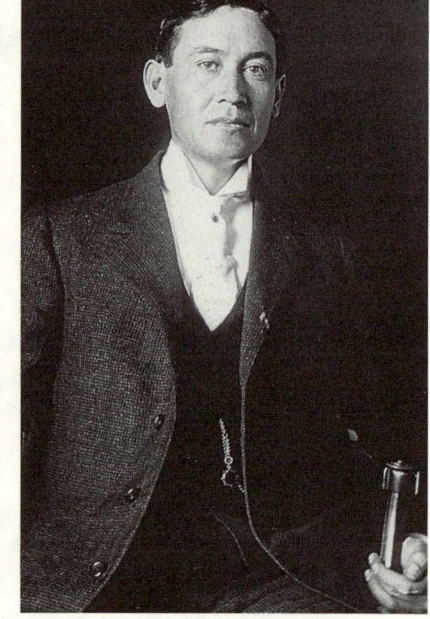

Figure 59   Figure 60

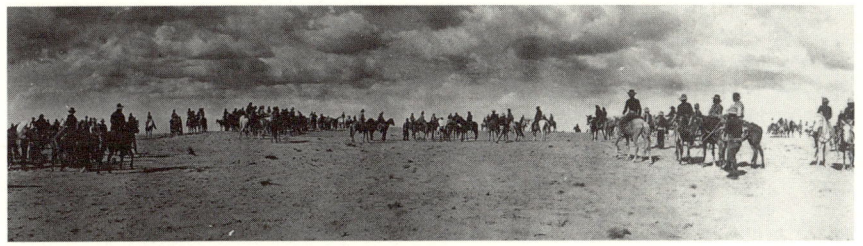

Figure 61

Figure 59. "Joseph K. Platero." Thomas W. Smillie, photographer, 25 January 1904, Washington D.C. Profile of young man. Even though he is probably a student and Christian (judging from his clothing, hair fashion, and location), he is nevertheless posed in surveillance mode (with profile and en face *[NAA BAE Neg. No. 2403-a]* views). Photograph courtesy National Anthropological Archives, Smithsonian Institution. NAA BAE Neg. No. 2403-b.

Figure 60. "John G. Walker. Mixed blood." Delancy Gill, photographer, 1909, Washington D.C. Notice the demeanor and confident stare into the camera. Walker, from Leupp AZ, born in 1880, later became Navajo agent in the Red Lake District. Only this view exists of this man. Contrast this with the required en face *and profile views of "full bloods" (even if Christian and educated, as in the case of Joseph Platero) in Fig. 59. See also Figs. 212a, b, and c. Photograph courtesy National Anthropological Archives, Smithsonian Institution. NAA BAE Neg. No. 2398.*

Figure 61. Panorama. Photographer unknown, n.d. Evidently an important gathering. For its early date, its composition, its breadth, it is a remarkable photograph. Photograph courtesy Arizona Historical Society-Pioneer Museum. NAPHS #3-32.

Portfolio IV

Figure 62. "'Tin Horn' and another Navajo, and Ida Wetherill, with Ouija [board], Kayenta, July 1920." Adelarde Law, photographer. This same "Tin Horn" is also the first clearly documented Navajo to have taken a photograph himself—see Fig. 211. Ida Wetherill is very intent on the Ouija board or perhaps just avoiding the photographer. Photograph courtesy Adelarde Law Collection, Archives of the Laboratory of Anthropology/Museum of Indian Arts and Culture, Santa Fe, Photo. #70.1/2573.

Figure 63. Miguelito at recording machine. Geoffrey O'Hara, photographer (??), February 1914 (printed). Miguelito, an important medicine man from near Ganado, here makes a sound recording at a very early date. No data accompanies the print, but it was probably sent to the Library of Congress for copyright purposes, as it appears to have been used for some sort of publication. See also Figs. 117, 169. Photograph reproduced from the Collections of the Library of Congress. LOC LC-USZ62-411054.

Navajo in Image

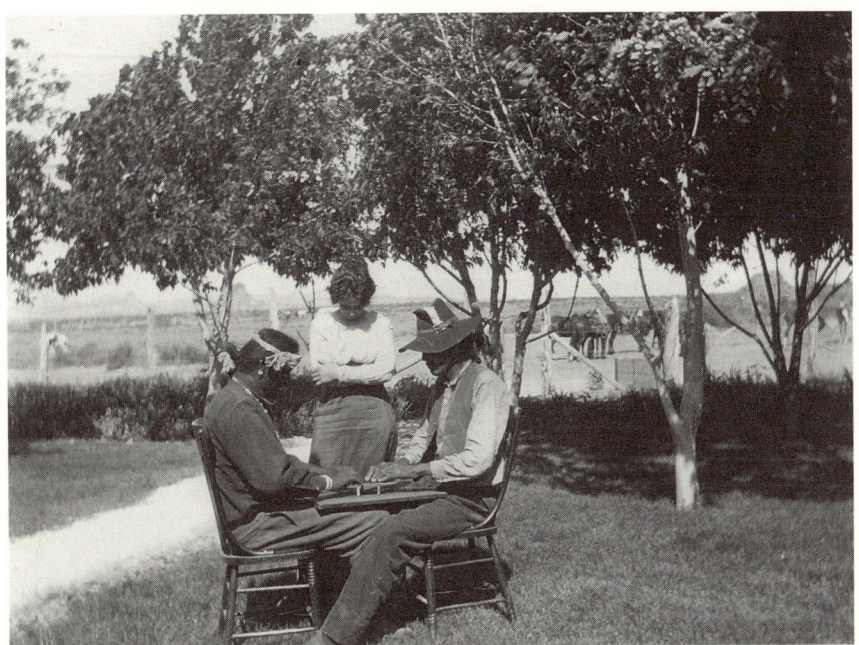

Figure 62

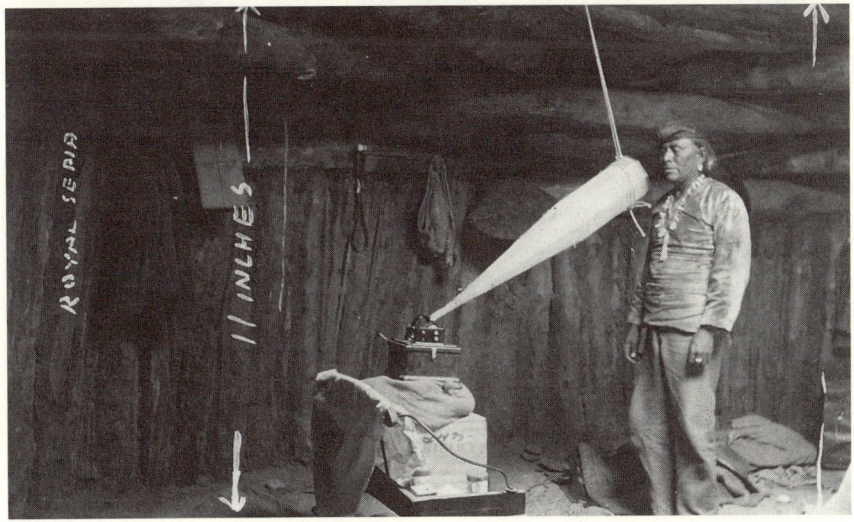

Figure 63

Portfolio IV

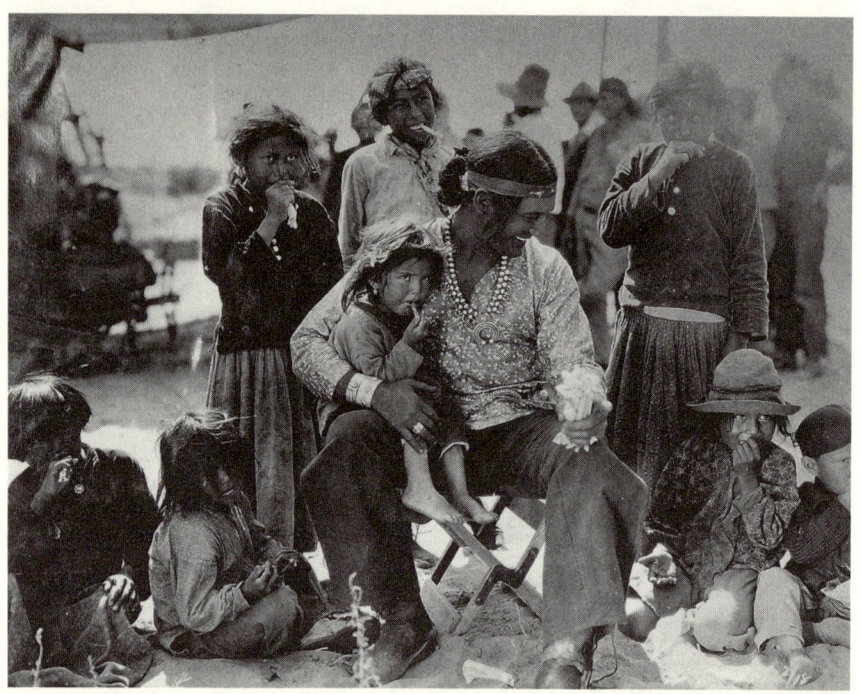

Figure 64

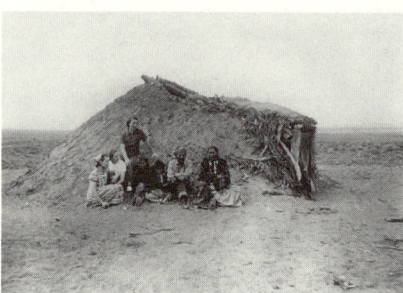

Figure 65

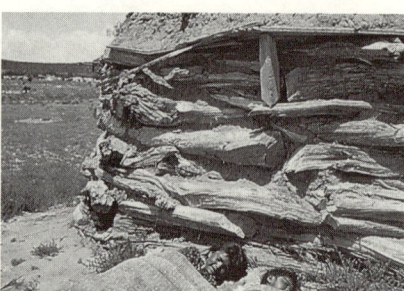

Figure 66

Navajo in Image

Figure 64. "*Each one of these bear individual names.*" Schmuckebier, photographer (??), 1930s. *Probably a title given by a weary census taker, oblivious to the delight of the man spreading candy among his children. See also Fig. 93. Census taker may have furnished the sweets. Photograph courtesy National Archives, Washington. NA/RG29 NR. Bureau of Census. Prints: Navajo Indians. 1930. Box 1. No. 29-NR-31.*

Figure 65. "*Navajo Dwelling, Hogan.*" *Photographer unknown., n.d. This isolated (at least in this view) hogan nevertheless is host to visiting European-Americans who wish their "photograph taken with Indians." We have no idea of the social relations involved nor how voluntary they might have been. In fact, the Navajo family looks trapped, even surrounded. Photograph courtesy Utah State Historical Society. Photo No. 970.44, P. 7.*

Figure 66. "*Navajo—some children taking a nap. Shows hogan construction and dirt.*" *Gretchen Swinnerton, photographer, 1936–1939. The photographer either cannot decide upon which phenomena to concentrate or was dissuaded from photographing the sleeping children by their mother and managed to include them in an ostensibly architectural photograph. Photograph courtesy G. Swinnerton Collection, Museum of Northern Arizona. MS 274-3-27.*

Chapter Four

The Vanishing Race: Edward S. Curtis

Edward Curtis hangs like a stone around the neck of the photography of Native Americans. According to Rick Hill,[1] he ranks as one of the five representational "Cs" to which every Native American must eventually react (the others being Columbus, Catlin, Christ, and Custer). He achieved this prominence not just for his monumental work *The North American Indian* (although who cannot react to it in one way or another?) but for his general thesis and its inheritances—the Vanishing Race, the Noble Red Man, the End of the Trail—and for his legacy of posing, of providing props and staging backgrounds. He championed, perhaps even inaugurated, much of the twentieth-century Western view of Navajo.

His photographs are now ubiquitous. In the past three decades Curtis, though ignored during his lifetime, has enjoyed a renaissance of substantial proportions. Shortly after his death (1952), his photographs of Native Americans emerged as popular icons; the phenomenon became so dramatic during the 1960s that today his images are somewhat clichéd.[2] "Original" prints currently sell for thousands of dollars.[3] This resurrection has also occurred among Native American specialists—indeed, after having been neglected and abused by anthropology for many years for his elaborate staging, soft focus, excessive pastoral romanticism, and sentiment, he has more recently come into vogue and now enjoys something of an anthropological "embrace."[4]

Chapter 4

The image for which Curtis most used Navajo was that of "The Vanishing Race"—the title of one of his most famous photographs and a concise description of and rationale for his entire project. Indeed, the photograph of Navajo riding single-file away from the camera into the darkness became the widespread stereotype of this theme. This turn-of-the-century media event leaned on nostalgia, as practically all indigenous Americans by this time had been conquered by European-Americans and driven into reservations. Their resistance was over, spawning a perverse public sympathy for lost savages (but two decades earlier, the same public had been clamoring for their conquest and submission). Curtis's "Vanishing Race" motivations have been examined repeatedly; it is more important here to examine in some detail his actual photography of Navajo, both published and unpublished; to establish something of his local practices while among Navajo; and to establish empirically a more adequate record, setting, and circumstance of some of the photographs.

Writings and analyses of Curtis's work by all parties have been filled with speculation, reinterpretation, and considerable outright error. At the outset, whatever else Curtis was or was not, his Navajo work was completely set up, using not only "phony" costumes, additions, and poses (*all* non-Navajo photography of Navajo has some of this) but, indeed, in some cases, actual phony Navajo. Moreover, several of the photographs of Navajo attributed to Curtis, at least two of which even appeared in *The North American Indian*, were not taken by him at all. My intention is not necessarily to condemn Curtis but rather to set the record straight; indeed, a few *unpublished* Curtis photographs of Navajo reveal not only substantial talent but also a warm and intimate relationship with at least some Navajo.

Let me begin with the imitation Navajo. In the famous photographs of Navajo Nightway masked God Impersonators—reprinted in dozens of sources—two very important God Impersonators were Charlie and Sam Day, the sons of an early non-Navajo trader at Chinle (see Figs. 67-70).[5] The Days, particularly Charlie, were absolutely vital to Curtis's work in Navajoland—he could not have done it without them. In newspaper accounts of the day[6] and in Curtis's own recorded recollections,[7] Charlie Day in fact receives abundant credit for his assistance. But Curtis does not tell us that the Days were (Navajo) subjects in the photographs[8] and certainly does not mention that Charlie Day or William Andrus or someone else might have been the photographer in several cases (Figs. 71, 72).

Curtis was only in Navajoland during the spring of 1904 and, with his family, in the summer of 1906.[9] No ceremonial photographs date from the latter period (perhaps because he was prohibited from taking such photographs—

The Vanishing Race

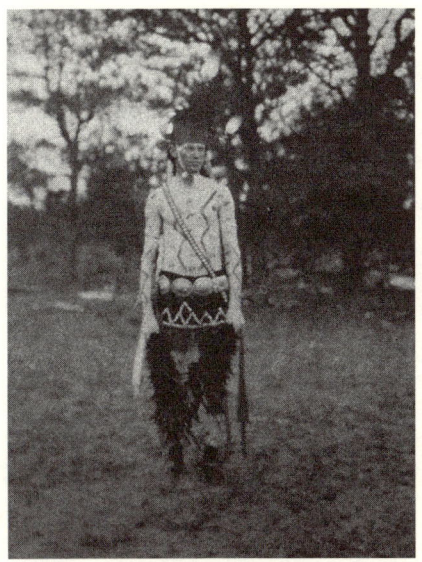
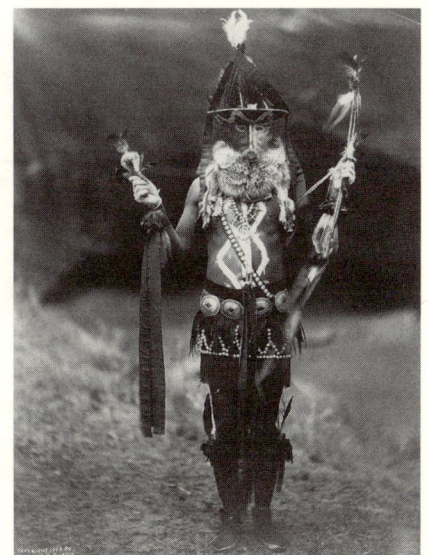

Figure 67   Figure 68

Figure 67. Charlie Day, costumed as a God Impersonator but without the mask. Photographer unknown (perhaps Sam Day II), n.d. (probably ca. 1903–1904). Note the skirt, medicine bag over the shoulder, and concha belt, all seen again and again in the photographs below. Identification by Sam Day III. Photograph courtesy Sam Day III. Enlarged and cropped by Gretchen Garner, University of Connecticut.

Figure 68. "Zahadolzha-Navaho." Edward S. Curtis, photographer, n.d. (probably summer 1904). Fringe Mouth is an important God Impersonator, especially during the last two days of the Nightway. Charlie Day is the impersonator (note skirt, bag, and belt—see Fig. 67). Curtis, 1907, Vol. 1, facing page 108. Photograph reproduced from the Collections of the Library of Congress. LOC LC-USZ62-39425.

Chapter 4

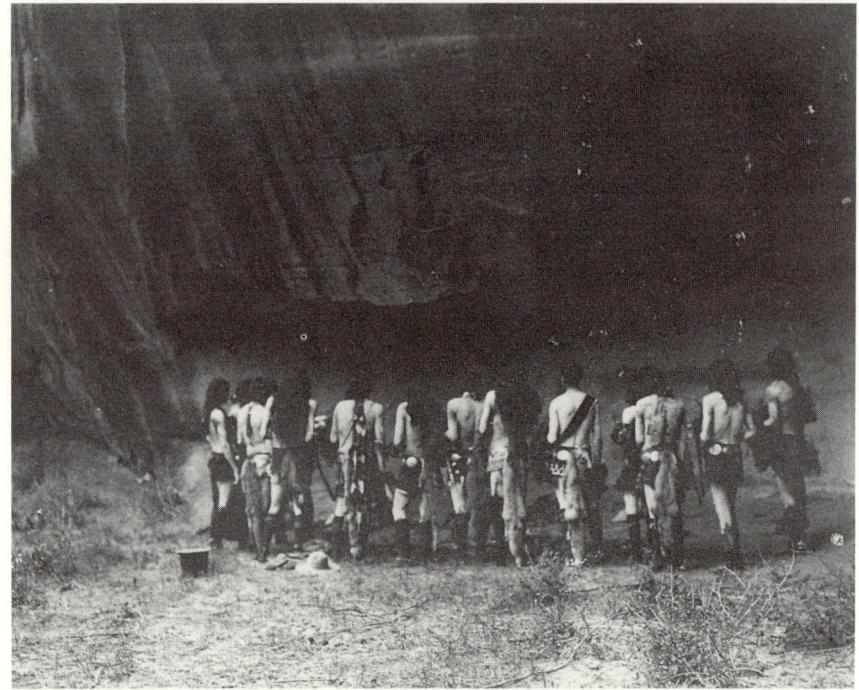

Figure 69

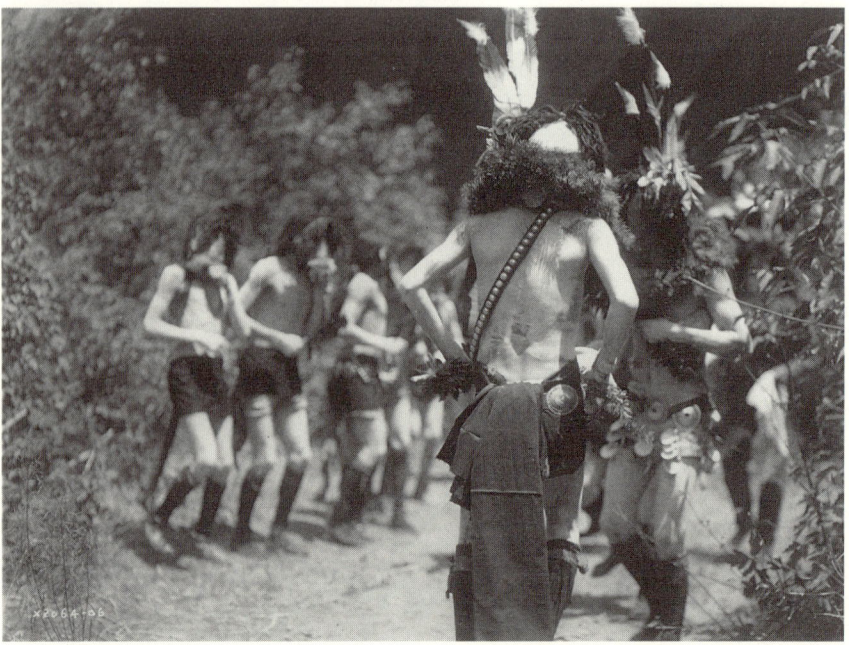

Figure 70

Figure 69. "Yeibichai Prayer." Edward S. Curtis, photographer, n.d. (probably summer 1904). Yeibichai dancers. This curious photograph may show where the dancers assembled for Curtis and costumed for the staged dance, as water, clothing, and other supplies are apparent on the ground. Most of the dancers appear unmasked, and Charlie Day is clearly recognizable (from his skirt, his lighter skin color, his height) as the fourth individual from the right, nearest the camera. To my knowledge, this is not an actual Nightway. Dancers would not gather this way for an actual Nightway; they would normally unmask only in a prepared enclosure, and it would be dark. Photograph courtesy National Anthropological Archives. NAA LOC file 03261800.

Figure 70. "Yeibichai Prayer." Edward S. Curtis, photographer, n.d. (probably summer 1904). Yeibichai dance. The dancers at right are male yé'ii; those on the left are males impersonating female yé'ii. The dancer in the foreground has substituted a cloth for a fox skin, the item attached to the back of the skirt in an actual Nightway. Curtis No 2064-06. Photograph reproduced from the Collections of the Library of Congress. LOC LC-lot 12311 (printed backwards by Curtis).

Chapter 4

Figure 71. "Emerging from Sweat." Photograph attributed to and claimed by Edward S. Curtis, n.d. (probably late 1903 or early 1904). Upon emerging from a sweat pit, the person sung over was ministered to by Talking God (?) and a female yé'ii. Photograph courtesy National Anthropological Archives. NAA LOC file 03263100.

Figure 72. "Toneneli and Haschelti." Photograph attributed to and claimed by Edward S. Curtis, n.d. (probably late 1903 or early 1904). Water Sprinkler and Talking God (?) leave in the afternoon as begging gods on the seventh or eighth day of the Nightway to solicit contributions toward payment and expenses required by the event. Curtis No. 1056-04. Photograph reproduced from the Collections of the Library of Congress. LOC LC-lot 12311.

The Vanishing Race

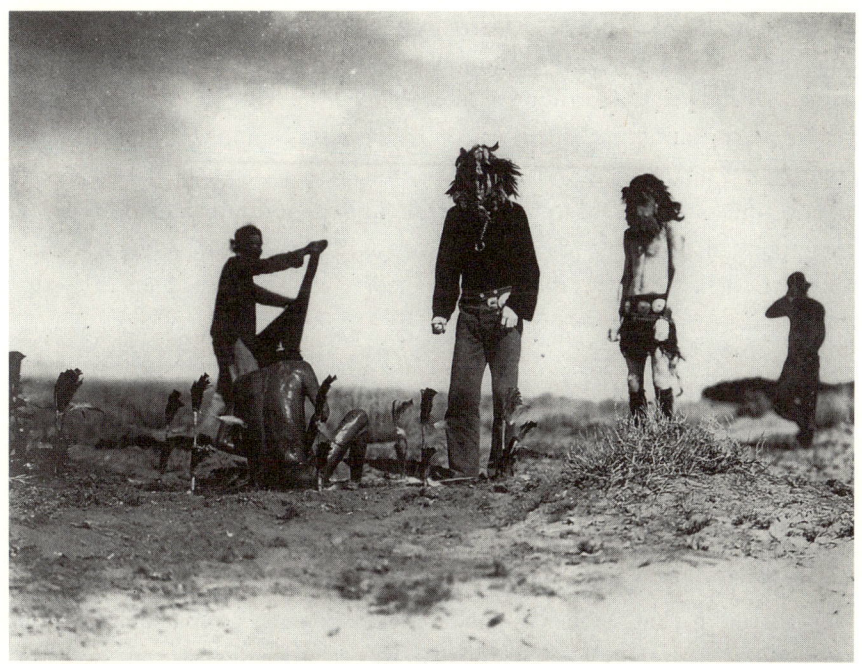

Figure 71

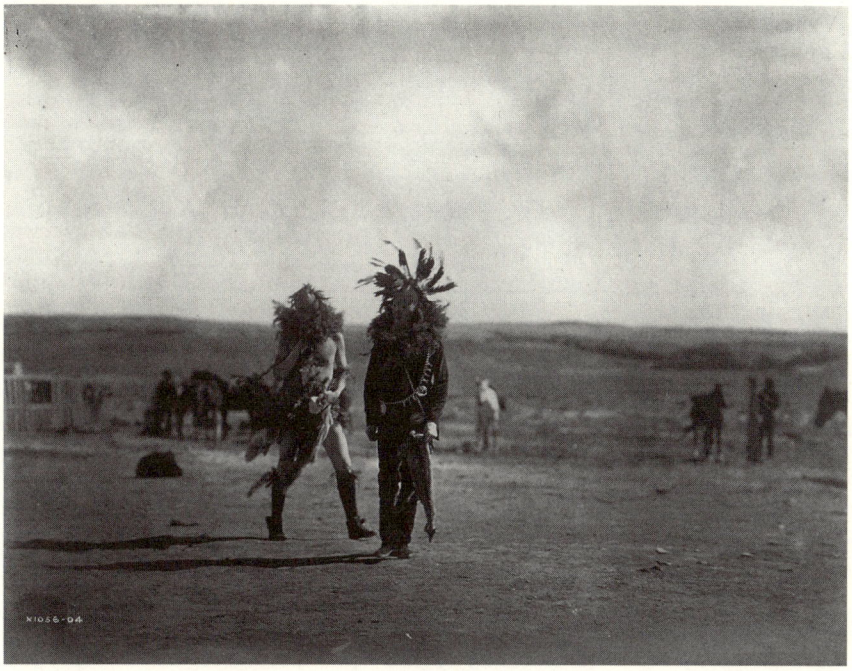

Figure 72

Chapter 4

see endnote 17). The Nightway is strictly a wintertime healing ceremony, held only after snakes and bears have hibernated, after the "male rain" (that accompanied by lightning and thunder) has stopped and the "female rain" (soft winter precipitation) has begun, after the harvest is complete and before the planting has again begun.[10] Not to be denied, Curtis arranged to stage part of a costumed dance and to pose several masked God Impersonators. In his correspondence of late 1904 and early 1905 with the Days, Curtis (in Seattle) asked Charlie Day to "strain a point and get me your Yebichai Dance description and the sand paintings, if possible" (NAU:Day Family Collection, Series 4, Box 1, Folder 30, E. Curtis to C. Day, 20 December 1904). The sandpainting sketches, made by Billy Jones, were sent Curtis a short time later, as was the Day description—all were incorporated, as if from an actual Nightway healing practice, in Volume One of *The North American Indian* in 1907. Thus, Curtis employed Navajo texts written by a non-Navajo author, Nightway sandpainting sketches drawn by a non-Nightway specialist,[11] masks and sacred material at least in part made for the photographic occasion, dances and sacred events set up for the same occasion, and even non-Navajo persons made up as Navajo! Had he been in Navajoland during the time of an actual Nightway (wintertime), none of this presumably would have been necessary.

There are other problems, however. As noted, Curtis was never in Navajoland during the appropriate season for an actual Nightway and thus had to stage all his photographs of this healing practice. Curtis straightforwardly acknowledges as much. But another series of photographs claimed and copyrighted by Curtis depict actual (unstaged) Nightway practices. Because I can find no evidence that Curtis was in Navajoland during an appropriate time, it must be concluded that these are not indeed Curtis photographs but that someone else, perhaps Charlie Day or William Andrus, took the photographs during an actual Nightway, using close relationships with local people to gain access (see Figs. 71, 72).[12]

Day, though an amateur photographer, was not unaccomplished. Stewart Culin, during his acquisition visits to the area in 1903–1904 for the Brooklyn Museum, used (and accurately credited) Charlie Day for several quite good photographs. Other sources used (or misused, since Day is not credited) Day photographs.[13]

If Day did not take these actual Nightway photographs, who did? A remote possibility exists that Schwemberger took the photographs, for he did extensively photograph a Nightway in 1905. However, Schwemberger had to pay and secure extensive permission to photograph the 1905 Nightway. He documented these steps very well,[14] but he makes no mention of having done the same in earlier years, although there is evidence that Schwemberger photographed more than one Nightway.[15] Moreover, Schwemberger, at this time a professional photographer, is perhaps less likely than Day to have given negatives to or exchanged them with Curtis.

To complicate matters more, a small photograph in the National Anthropological Archives (NAA SPC file 02279700) credited to Dr. Elizabeth Snyder illustrates the same two masked God Impersonators (probably acting as begging gods) featured in the actual Nightway Curtis claims to have photographed. W. J. Andrus has claims to a few of the others—the medicine man, some of his assistants, the person being sung over, and at least one actual Nightway sandpainting (see endnotes 12 and 16 and Figs. 75-77).

If Curtis photographed the actual Nightway sequences, he would have had no need for the Nightway text retrieved by Charlie Day, nor the sandpainting drawings from Billy Jones—he would have been able to use his own descriptions and his own photographs.[16] Moreover, the style of the actual Nightway photographs is not vintage Curtis. The images lack the formal symmetry of Curtis's work and are quite descriptive of the practices themselves. Given the flamboyance of the times and Curtis's need for publicity, we would certainly have heard much more about it had he attended an actual Nightway healing practice. After all, Curtis tells us he staged the Nightway photographs *not* because he was there at the wrong time of year but because of the resistance to his photography—a rather minor logistical matter. The type of resistance is never explained in detail, though we can probably assume it came from assimilationist bureaucrats (Navajo and non-Navajo) who resented Curtis's emphasis and manipulation to achieve some representation of "aboriginality."[17]

It is interesting that no published Navajo ceremonial photographs date from the 1906 visit, which Curtis characterizes as one of his most productive.[18] But he also relates that Charlie Day had to rescue him (and his family, which had joined him for the Navajo portion of the trip) from potential Navajo wrath over a problematic birth in Canyon de Chelly, a situation about which Curtis "years later . . . admitted he had never felt more helpless" (Davis, 1985:48).

Of course, Curtis's 1906 photography may well have been confined to nonceremonial materials as a consequence of the 1904 visit. Curtis's staging of events in 1904 certainly had repercussions for him.[19] In any case, it points up a persistent theme in the photography of Navajo—the extent to which there was resistance and, as a corollary, the extent to which photographers persisted to overcome this resistance. Navajo sensibilities clearly are not

Chapter 4

primary considerations (though Curtis does note that some Navajo were upset at his staging of the Nightway out of season).[20]

Nonetheless, the Curtis photographs are extremely interesting. Curtis apparently asked the God Impersonators to behave as they might in actual ceremonial activity (or more likely, the impersonators knew how to arrange themselves), for the postures and groupings are quite authentic.[21] He also took the familiar close-up bust portraits of each masked impersonator,[22] photographs that today are extremely useful in comparing and tracking down sets of Nightway masks out of Navajoland. Though Curtis's other Navajo photographs have had their celebrity—especially the Canyon de Chelly riders of "Vanishing Race" fame—the close-up and posed photographs of masked God Impersonators have greater comparative and historical value for contemporary students.[23]

It is clear that several of the same models used in the staged Nightway photographs posed in other photos. Curtis apparently worked with a rather narrow range of Navajo subjects, sometimes portraying them in quite different poses. The same people appear over and over again in wholly different circumstances—for example, as riders in the canyon landscapes, in portraits, in small group pictures. The same woman appears as "basket maker," as "weaver," as "Navaho woman" (see Fig. 73 and Curtis, 1907, Vol. 1, facing page 76), and as "Navaho smile" (see Fig. 74). We know the names of some of Curtis's photographic subjects, at least those who were medicine men. He identifies Laughing Singer, Tall Chanter, and Little Singer,[24] although there are some inaccuracies (see Fig. 75 and endnote 16).

Curtis photographed Navajo (or their surrogates) essentially in four dimensions—studio close-up with plain backdrop; posed "action" photograph (frequently with canyon backdrop); distant long focus of broad landscape, sometimes with humans (usually mounted), sometimes not; and silhouette. In part, these stylistic features help us distinguish the rigidly documentary Day or Andrus photographs of an actual Nightway from those Curtis set up. His published Navajo photographs use few other settings. Some of these were peculiar to Curtis, but others shared the conventions of the times. The distant landscapes, with a few Navajo crossing the field or disappearing into it, form the basis for the "Vanishing Race" trope. Although Curtis was a leading proponent of this view, the notions were part of the shallow guilt of the times (a by-product of the Progressive expansionist mentality), and they motivated many photographic poses by all sorts of photographers (cf. Monsen, Moon). Though indigenous Americans did not actually disappear or vanish, the conquest and assimilationist trends of the turn of the century had severe

The Vanishing Race

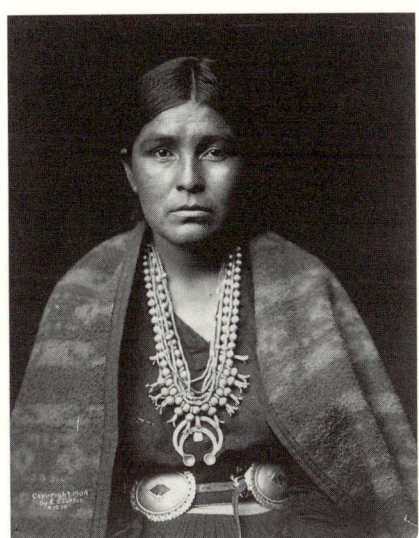

Figure 73

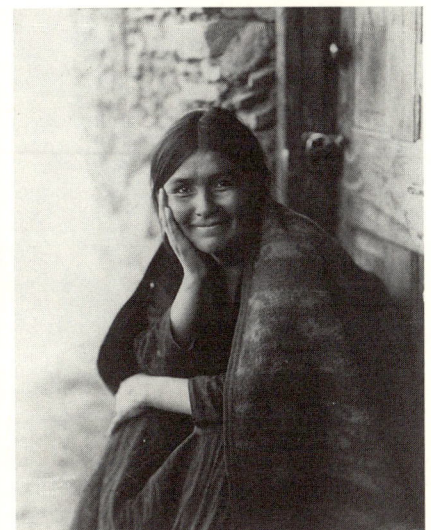

Figure 74

Figure 73. "Navaho woman." Edward S. Curtis, photographer, n.d. (probably taken summer 1903). This dour posed photograph (the same woman is similarly posed in The North American Indian *as "The Blanket Maker" [Curtis, 1907, Vol. 1, facing page 76] with skeins of wool in her hands) provides a view of Navajo common for the time (and subsequently)—bejeweled, straight-faced, sad, stoic, certainly inscrutable. The jewelry was probably added by Curtis (see Fig. 74). Curtis No. 1019. Photograph reproduced from the Collections of the Library of Congress. LOC LC-lot 12311.*

Figure 74. "A Navaho Smile." Edward S. Curtis, photographer, n.d. (probably taken summer 1903). This lovely image of the same woman as in Fig. 73 could not be of greater contrast. Indeed, her entire face changes, and years disappear. If this smile reflects Curtis's relationship with his subjects (if it is indeed Curtis's photograph), he got along very well with his local models. Here he uses no jewelry, no dark backdrop, no contrived pose. It is unfortunate that this grand photograph has not been more widely displayed (though since my initial research, it has appeared in a postcard—see "Native American Women," Pomegranate Art Books, 1993). Photograph reproduced from the Collections of the Library of Congress. LOC LC-USZ62-46943.

Chapter 4

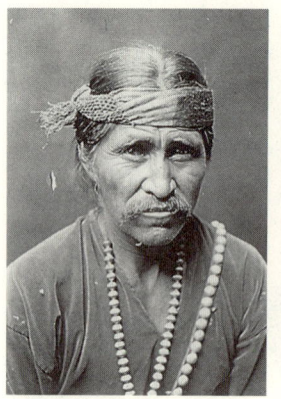 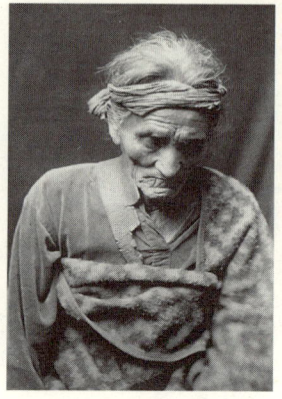 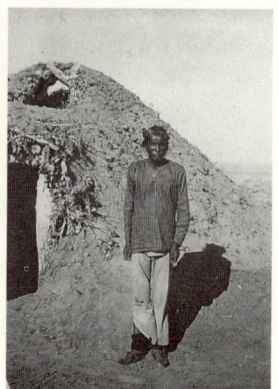

Figure 75   Figure 76   Figure 77

Figure 75. "Man who conducted singing at Yeibitchai. W. J. Andrus, September 1904." This photograph is also claimed by Edward S. Curtis and published as "The Singer." It is found in the Library of Congress's Curtis materials as LC-USZ62-52674 (Curtis No. 1061-04, labeled "The Laughing Singer"). This is not Laughing Singer but Little Singer, one of the medicine men presiding at an actual Nightway, at which Curtis was not present but the photographs of which he claims. Andrus, as noted in Fig. 76, was in the Southwest at the appropriate time of an actual Nightway and correctly labels this photograph, at least when seen in contrast with those of the actual Nightway photographs claimed by Curtis (but incorrectly labeled). Also, the MAI collections contain a photograph attributed to Andrus of an actual Whirling Logs sandpainting from an actual Nightway in 1904. Had Curtis photographed this, it undoubtedly would have been published, so it must be concluded that Andrus or Charlie Day or someone else photographed the actual Nightway. The sandpainting photograph is obviously not reproduced here. Photograph courtesy National Museum of the American Indian, Smithsonian Institution. P. #1300.

Figure 76. "Old medicine man who assisted at Yeibitchai ceremony." *Photographer listed as W. J. Andrus, 1904, Chinle AZ. Andrus, the attributed photographer for this and a slightly different pose (MAI P. #1301), was in the Southwest at this time and during the winter Nightway season. This photograph is one taken in the same studio setting as several claimed by Edward S. Curtis (but to my knowledge this specific photograph is not present in any Curtis archive). It is the same man and much like Curtis No. 1046-04 (LOC LC-USZ62-56512), a photograph very similar to one also claimed by and attributed to Curtis and widely present in Curtis archives. The label suggests that the photographer attended an actual Nightway ("Yeibitchai"), which Curtis did not. But several Navajo portraits from this studio setting have been attributed to Curtis, suggesting that he certainly could have made this photograph. However, it does not bear any numbers in the lower left, as is characteristic of Curtis prints. Old man is possibly Hatali Nez. Photograph courtesy National Museum of the American Indian, Smithsonian Institution. P. #1302. Neg. No. 37707.*

Figure 77. "Male patient in Yeibitchai ceremony." *Photographer listed as W. J. Andrus, 1904, Chinle AZ. This photograph does not appear in any Curtis archive to my knowledge (indeed, Curtis identifies another photograph of another man as "patient" [LOC Curtis No. 1059-04]). The label here is very likely correct—the medicine hogan appears newly built, as it would have been for an actual Nightway. Photograph courtesy National Museum of the American Indian, Smithsonian Institution. Neg. No. 37705.*

Chapter 4

consequences in the lives of these people. This photographic concept dictated that no one should appear happy and yielded the stoic, long-suffering, unsmiling facial expressions we know from the time. Though in many cases people were *not* happy—after all, they had no input into the types of images projected and faced incredible pressures from a variety of directions—Navajos, like most humans, are frequently happy, joking, and busy despite the immense hardships dumped upon them by European-Americans.

Curtis's studio bust close-ups are rigidly "documentary." Despite the criticism of Boas, they are frequently quite in the aseptic Boasian "scientific" style of the times and quite in accord with prevailing anthropological notions of preservation and recording (though sometimes in soft focus and with black background—see endnote 4). Curtis did, however, pioneer the "action" pose, and it is for these photographs that he has been most condemned (or, depending on the times, most heralded). The Navajo Nightway sequences feature one, two, three, or more individuals, masked and with all appropriate body paint, costume, and postures, usually posed in front of a canyon backdrop. Those posed as trios occur in the groups appropriate to actual Nightway healing activities.[25] The Days, two of the subjects in these posed photographs, were both initiated into the Nightway and certainly knew the appropriate trios and postures.

Thus, one important facet of Curtis's Navajo photography is the paradigmatic quality of his images. Non-Navajo photographers of Navajo subsequently have had either to succumb or to react to Curtis's precedent; from Laura Gilpin[26] to Leonard McCombe[27] to Keegan[28] and Running,[29] we see the ghosts of Curtis and his romantic notions of "threatened" Navajo. Indeed, more recent photographers commonly also felt compelled to photograph sacred materials and mount similar defenses in the face of Navajo objection (see Chapter 7).

Edward Curtis, then, if seen in the total universe of the photographs he took of Navajo, emerges very much as a man of the time—an exceptional pioneering photographer, a shameless faker and claimant of the work of others, but a vital source of the images so important to European-American views of indigenous Americans. It is remarkable[30] how little these images have changed. But in Curtis's total corpus we also find a few unpublished warm, sympathetic, and grand photographs (see Figs. 74, 78). Given the time he worked and the enormous numbers of photographs he took (or claimed to have taken), he could not totally escape, despite his project, the humanity of Navajo.

The Vanishing Race

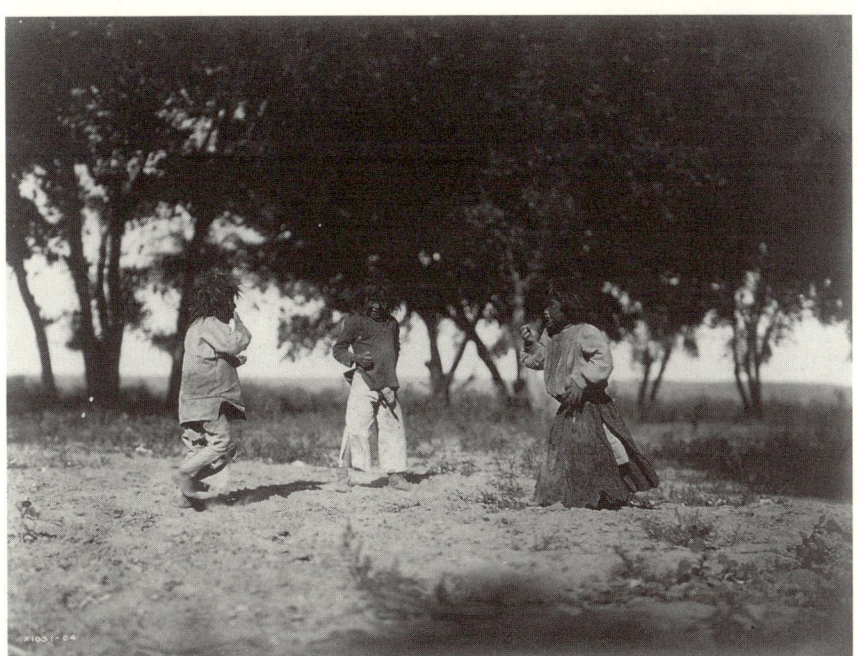

Figure 78

Figure 78. "Child Life—Cottonwoods." Edward S. Curtis, photographer, n.d. (probably taken summer 1903). Again, this delightful photograph of active, happy, dirty children at play should have been more publicly acknowledged. It, like Fig. 74, apparently did not confirm the desired image of the time. These are certainly not members of the "vanishing race." Note the low position of the camera, the center child smiling at the photographer, and the Curtis number (1031-04). Photograph reproduced from the Collections of the Library of Congress. LOC LC-lot 12311.

Portfolio V
Church and State

Portfolio V

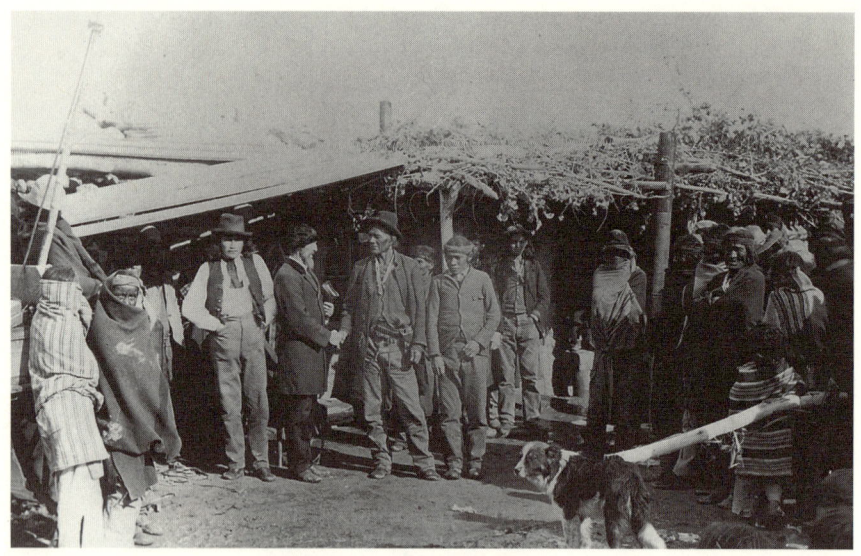

Figure 79

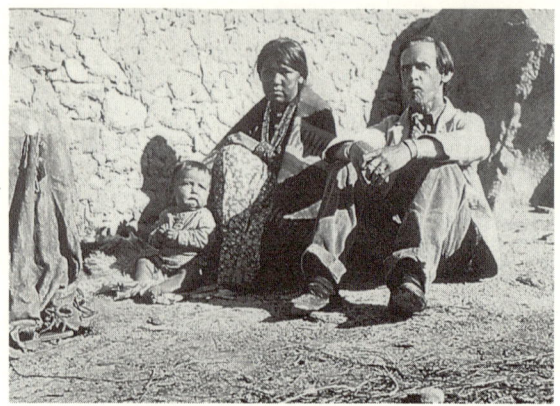

Figure 80

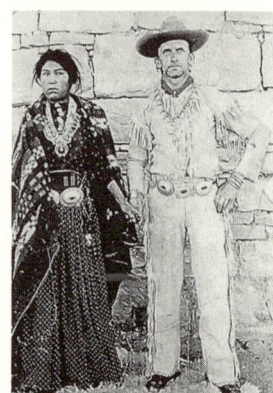

Figure 81

Figure 79. "Missionary laboring amongst the Navahos—San Juan River, Utah." Charles Goodman, photographer, n.d. (ca. 1890), near Bluff, Utah. The man shaking hands with the missionary is wearing a large pistol for the encounter. This may be Black Horse, an important leader for this region and one who distrusted Westerners. Photograph courtesy Colorado State Historical Society. No. F24,320.

Figure 80. "Squaw-man and his Navajo wife. A type of white man of early days. The picture was made in 1886." Frederick Monsen, photographer (see also Fig. 81). It is interesting that European-American men who might have taken seriously their commitments to indigenous women are the object of photographic scrutiny as well as derogation. The "squaw-man" seems also to have acquired a healthy distrust of the camera and now wears moccasins. And there is a toddler. Photograph reproduced from the Frederick Monsen Collections of The Huntington Library. Card No. 120.

Figure 81. "Woman in costume and cowboy." Photographer unknown, n.d. This photograph may depict a "squaw-man" and his wife, a European-American of uncertain class status who married a Navajo woman (see Fig. 80). His flamboyant fringed leather clothing, jewelry, and confident posture would indicate some unconventionality. The Navajo woman whose hand he holds looks far less certain about the photographic encounter. Presumably the touch between a European-American and a Navajo is more consensual in this circumstance than those photographs of Portfolio VI. Photograph courtesy National Museum of the American Indian, Smithsonian Institution. P. #11484.

Portfolio V

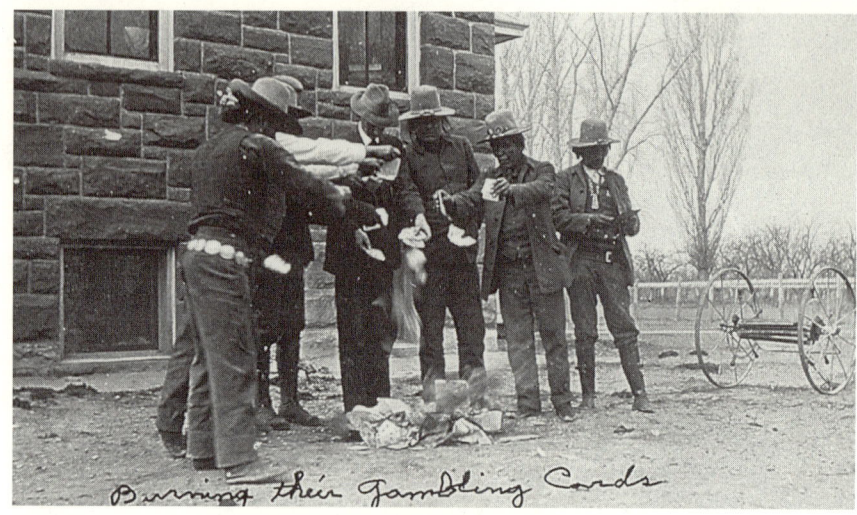

Figure 82

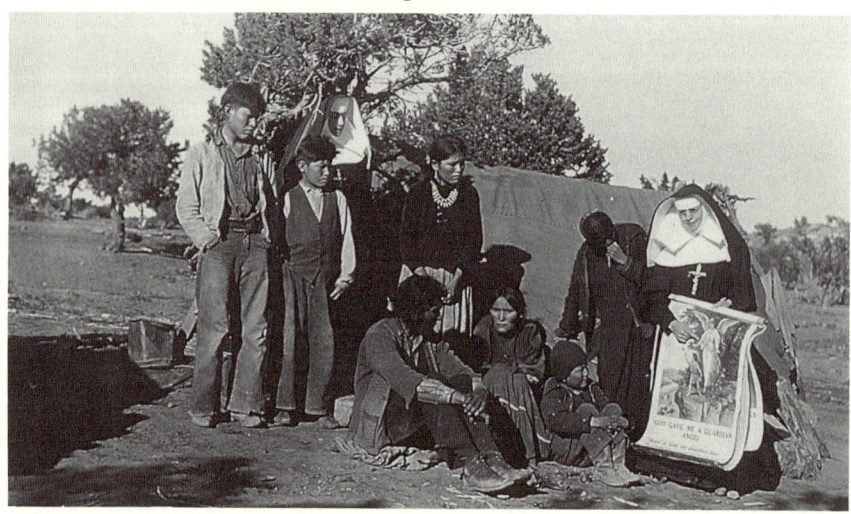

Figure 83

Figure 82. "*Burning their gambling cards.*" *Photographer unknown (perhaps Beatrice Warren), n.d. Some of the papers being dropped into the fire look like more than gambling cards. Note the European-American at the center of it all and the mission building behind. Photograph courtesy Cline Library, Special Collections and Archives, Northern Arizona University. No. NAU 412-1-49.*

Figure 83. "*Sister Antoineta—Navajo camp instruction.*" *Photographer unknown, n.d. Navajo appear utterly bored with the visit and the camera, though Sister Antoineta seems enthusiastic about both. Photograph courtesy Arizona State Museum, University of Arizona, and Franciscan Friars, St. Michaels AZ. #PIX1589-x-8.*

Portfolio V

Figure 84. "Navajo Girls at St. Michaels." *Photographer unknown, n.d. Probably a communion class. The composition of this photograph deviates somewhat from the usual straight-on style of the time (cf. Figs. 85, but also Fig. 98). Photograph courtesy Arizona State Museum, University of Arizona, and Franciscan Friars, St. Michaels AZ. #PIX1604-x-20.*

Figure 85. Navajo students performing as "Indians." Photographer unknown, n.d., St. Michaels Mission School AZ. Even more perverse costumes appear in Fig. 100. The tipi, rock forms, and trees of the backdrop curtain used here are interesting, but a Victorian curtain appears over the top, and even another appears as a Navajo weaving. Photograph courtesy Museum of Northern Arizona and Franciscan Friars at St. Michaels AZ. MS 119-52-660.

Figure 86. Navajo mothers and daughters. Photographer unknown, n.d. This juxtaposition, the traditional/modern, savage/saved dichotomy, is a popular photographic gesture in the St. Michaels archive (as well as elsewhere), as parents often visited their children at the mission school dressed in their best. Photograph courtesy Museum of Northern Arizona and Franciscan Friars at St. Michaels AZ. MS 119-145-263.

Church and State

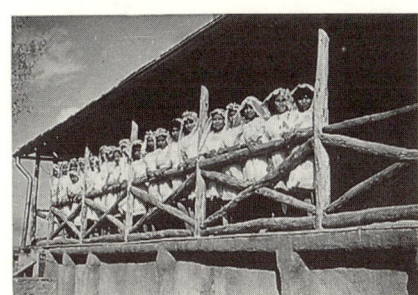

Figure 84

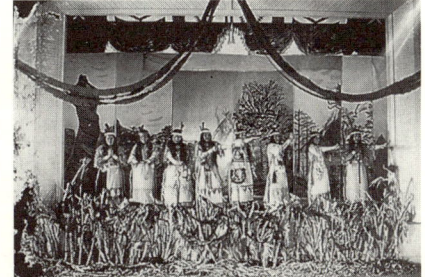

Figure 85

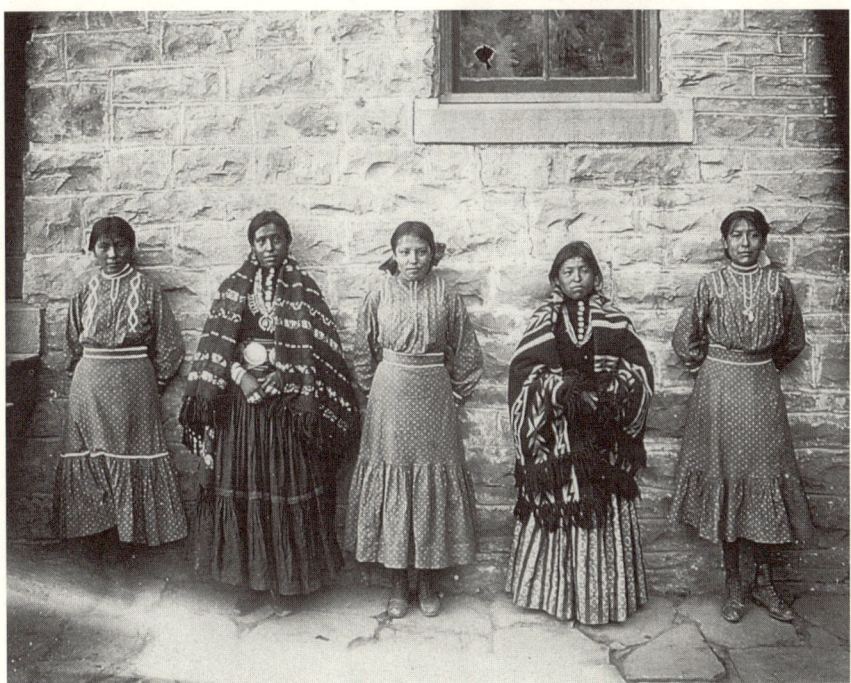

Figure 86

Portfolio V

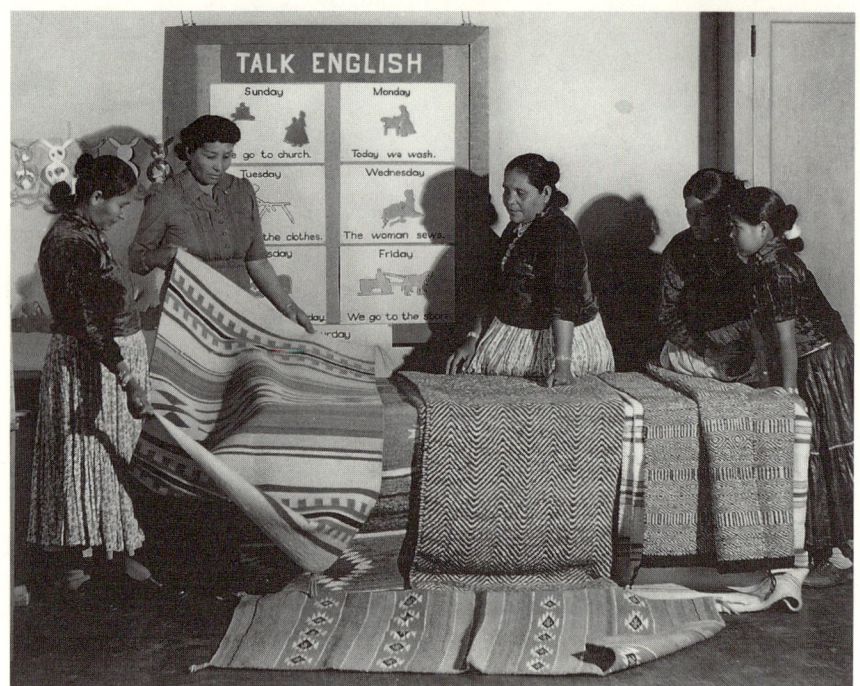

Figure 87

Figure 87. "Marie Martin instructing weavers in pattern design. One of the services rendered by the Navajo Arts and Crafts Guild." Milton Snow, photographer, 30 April 1943, Hunter's Point Day School, St. Michaels AZ. The patterns on weavings that are evident here appear to be those long well-known by Navajo weavers. Note the command on the bulletin board, with its rigorous Western weekly schedule. The grammar is also interesting—a command imperative for "Talk English," a first-person direct for most days, an indirect gendering command for Wednesday. Photograph courtesy National Archives, Washington. NA/BIA/R75 NG/Prints: Navajo Life in the Southwest, 1936–1956. Box 1. NC3-57 (A).

Figure 88. "Marine home on leave." Photographer unknown, n.d. (ca. 1944). Posing on horseback seemed to have special significance for Navajo involved in Western affairs (see Fig. 12). Photograph courtesy Arizona State Museum, University of Arizona, and Franciscan Friars, St. Michaels AZ. #PIX1606-x-3.

Church and State

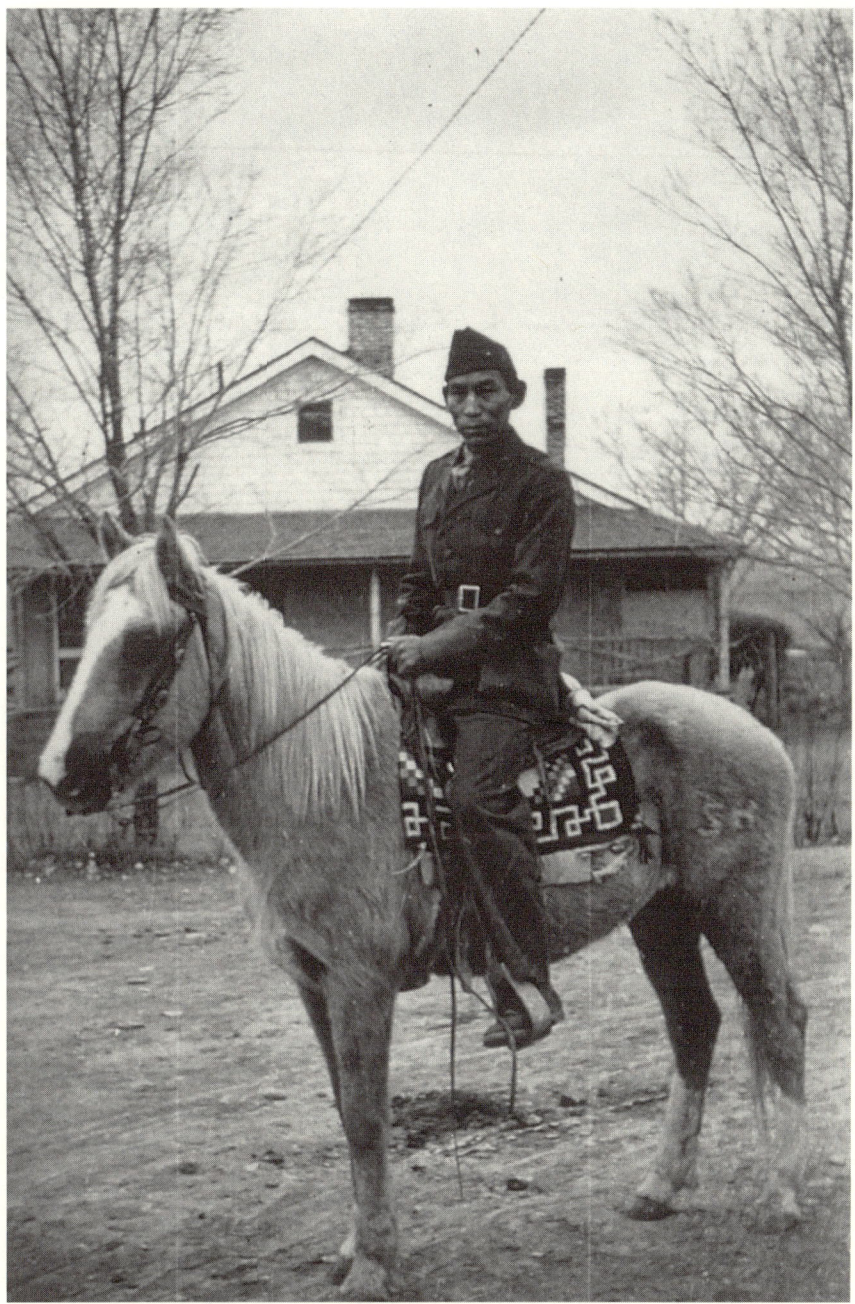

Figure 88

Portfolio V

Figure 89. "Milk and cooked cereals are good for growing children." Milton Snow, photographer, 29 October 1942, Wingate Vocational High School. Robert Henry posing. Important, if clumsy, propaganda. The institutional utensils do not help, but the choice of Robert Henry, male, in Western clothing as a model is significant in contrast to Fig. 90. Photograph courtesy Milton Snow Collection, Navajo Nation Museum, Window Rock AZ. NK 4-2.

Figure 90. "Child refusing to eat fried bread and coffee." Milton Snow, photographer, 27 October 1942, Wingate Vocational High School. Jean Henry, the model, like her brother, seems to be waiting uncomfortably for instructions. We only have Snow's word that she is indeed refusing, but she is in traditional attire. See Fig. 89. Photograph courtesy National Archives, Washington. NA/BIA/R75 NG/Prints: Navajo Life in the Southwest, 1936–1956. Box 4. NK4-61

Church and State

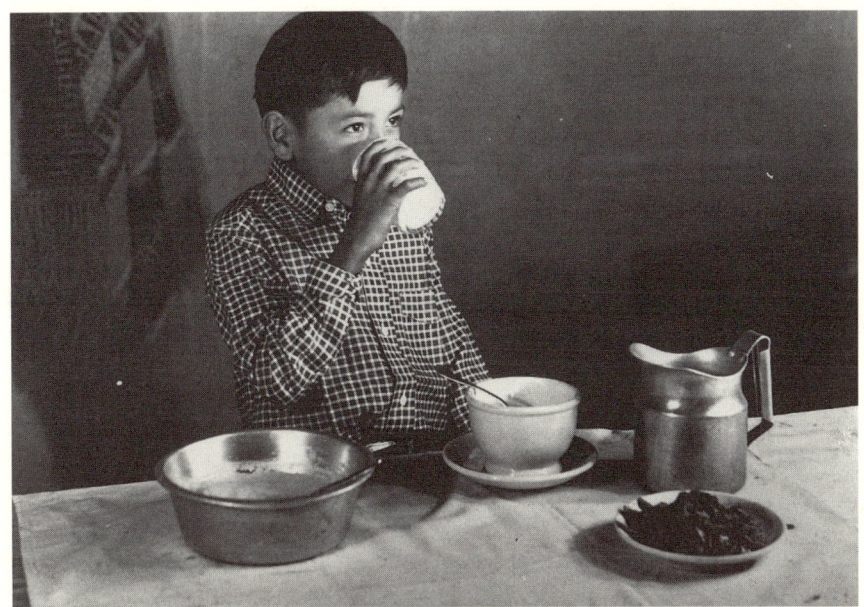

Figure 89

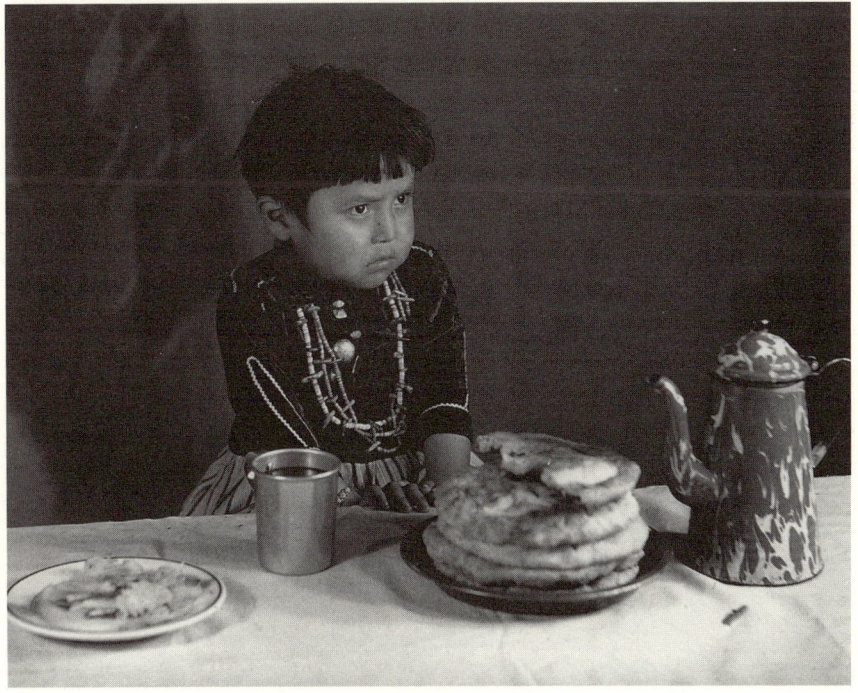

Figure 90

Portfolio V

Figure 91. "Public health field nursing." Milton Snow, photographer, November 1949. Field immunizations. Note the caution of the young boy at the rear of the hogan. We are not told what immunizations are being administered, but clearly many people have been assembled here for the occasion. The field nurse does not visit each individual hogan. Photograph courtesy Milton Snow Collection, Navajo Nation Museum, Window Rock AZ. NK 3-29.

Figure 92. "Public Health Service personnel are constantly presenting programs on personal hygiene, baby care, and improved home sanitation." Photographer unknown (probably Milton Snow), n.d. The photographic image was important to justify budgets, to prove that the BIA and other bureaucratic bodies who lived off Navajo existence were doing what they said they were doing, and to show that Navajo were being normalized to the extent assimilationists felt important and necessary. After all, these Navajo probably did not read English. There were seldom discussions (and never photographs) on conquest, racism, oppression, or exploitation. Navajo were photographed as drunks and accident victims (although, not, to my knowledge, by Milton Snow) but never were the perpetrators or Western collaborators in some of these conditions under the same surveillance as Navajo. Note the bored, captive appearance of Navajo "models" in this photograph. Photograph courtesy Navajo Nation Museum, Window Rock AZ. No number.

Church and State

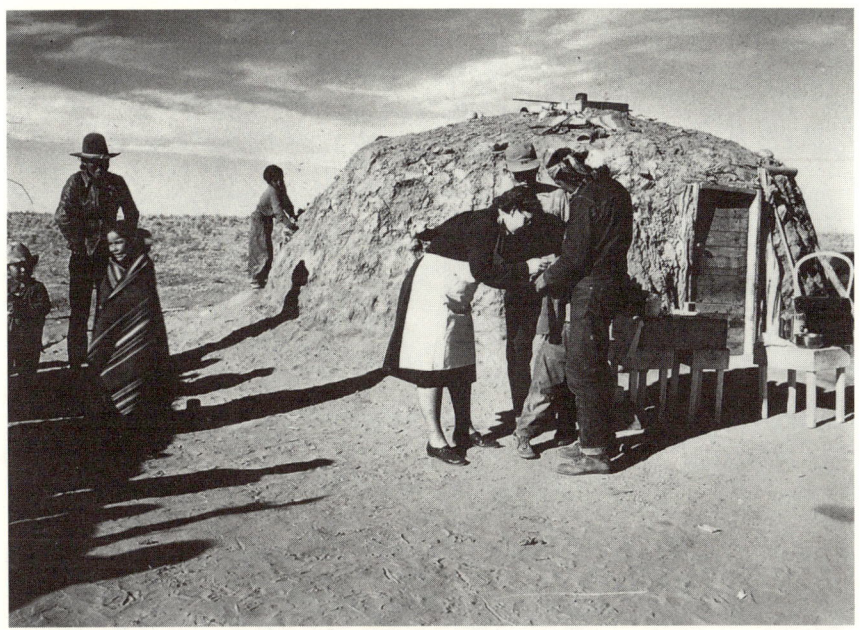

Figure 91

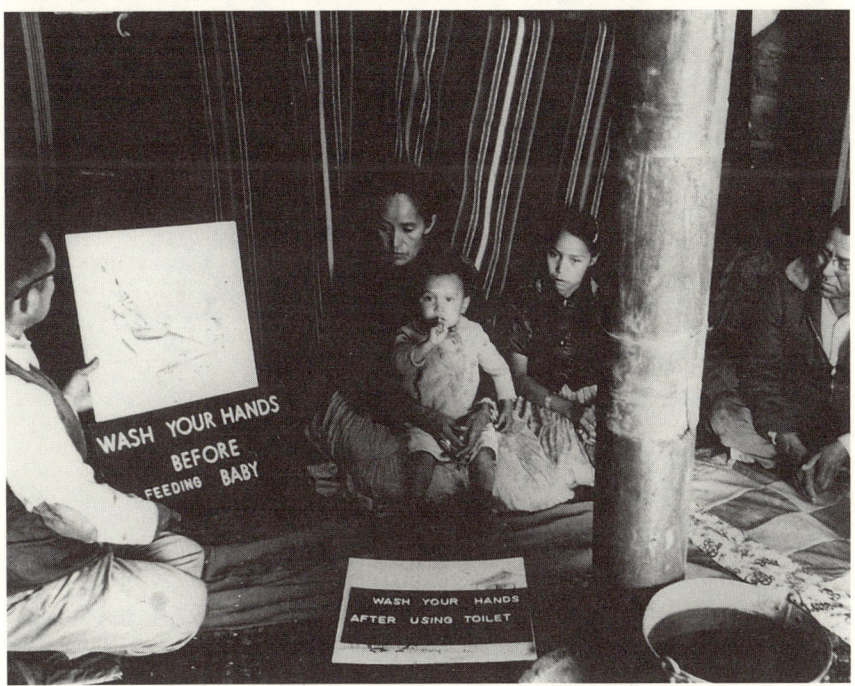

Figure 92

135

Portfolio V

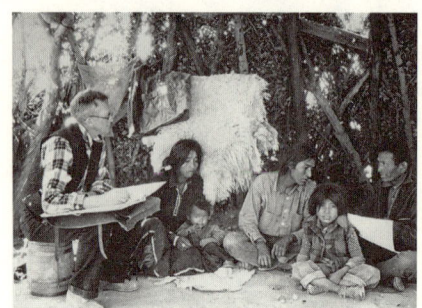

Figure 93

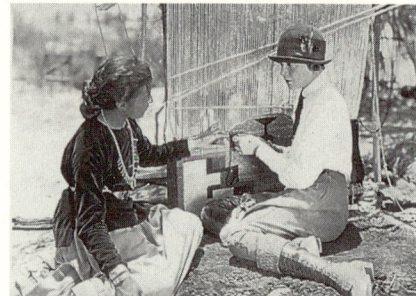

Figure 94

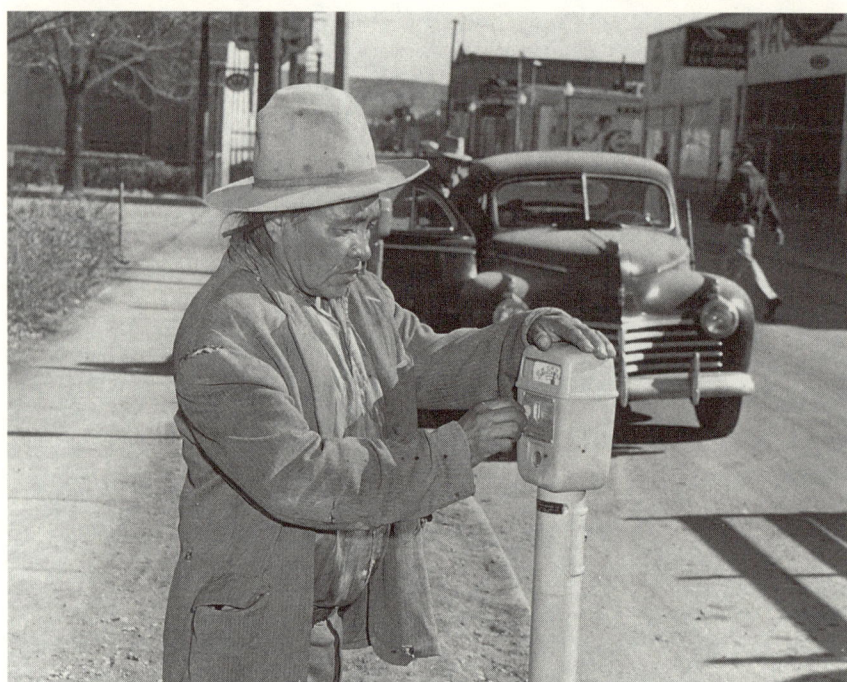

Figure 95

Church and State

Figure 93. "Rev. Smith enumerating 1930 census in Navajo Indian camp." Schmuckebier, photographer (??), 1930s. For many surveillance tasks, a bilingual Navajo was required as interpreter—in this case, clearly the man at far right. Appointing a Christian missionary as census taker may have solved government personnel problems in the task, but it could have had other implications for Navajo. See also Fig. 64. Photograph courtesy National Archives, Washington. NA/RG 29NR. Bureau of Census Prints: Navajo Indians. 1930. Box 1. No. 29-NR-25.

Figure 94. "Teaching the Paleface the art of rug weaving." Schmuckebier, photographer (??), 1930s. This photograph (taken with flash or reflector) illustrates something of the assumption of European-Americans. Though Navajo weaving is a plain weave with but a single moving heddle, its mastery requires years—not a task to be comprehended in a short time (cf. Reichard, 1936, 1939). The extent to which Navajo were contracted or simply put upon or expected to 'demonstrate' or host visitors with apparent good cheer, can be seen over and over again in the photographic archives—see Figs. 103, 104. Photograph courtesy University of Arizona Library Special Collections. No number.

Figure 95. "Gallup NM—When Parking Meters Were Installed the Local Indians Thought They Were Peanut or Gum Machines." Charlie Wunder, photographer, n.d. The use of a flash and the proximity of the subject suggest that this photograph may have been grotesquely encouraged or set up. There is also already time on the meter, as if there has been rehearsal. Aside from provisioning racist anecdotes, what is the purpose of this image? Photograph courtesy Amon Carter Museum, Fort Worth TX. Mazzulla—Navajo B.

Portfolio V

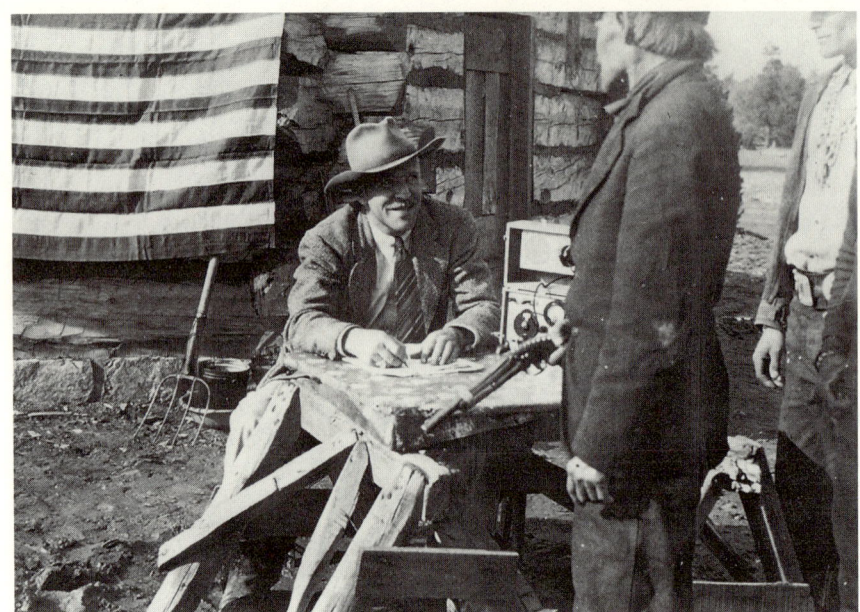

Figure 96

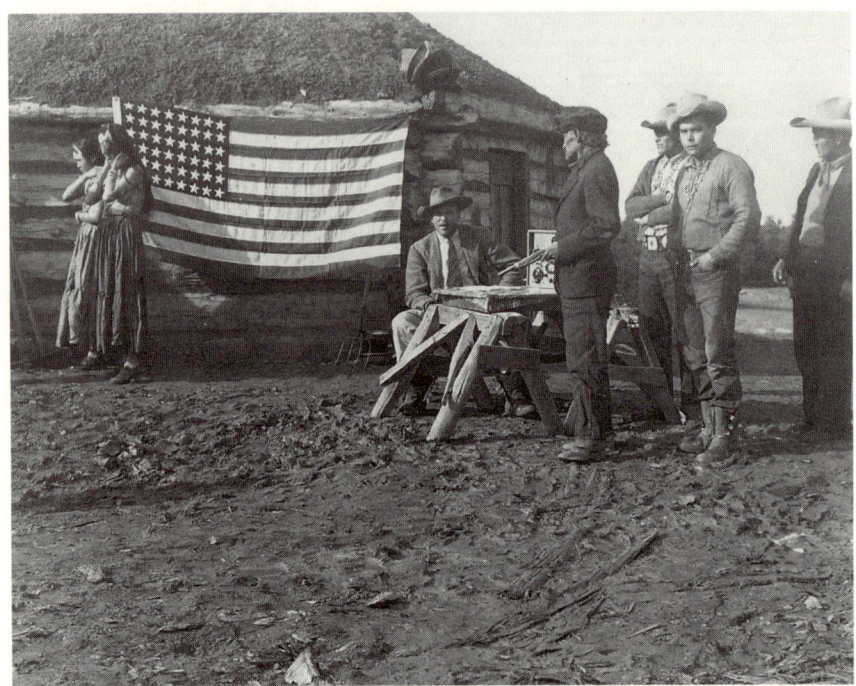

Figure 97

Figure 96. "Navajo Indians register for selective service. This old Navajo Indian came around with an Aston (1849) pistol, ready to tackle Hitler's armies." Photographer unknown (probably Milton Snow), 1941. This old man is being made to pose with his pistol while other activities take place outside the frame (see Fig. 97) of this widely published propaganda photograph. There is a third photograph of this event, published in Link, 1968:72-73, with Frank Walker, the Navajo leader, in view, as well as a man wearing an antique U.S. Cavalry blouse. Photograph courtesy National Archives, Washington. NA/BIA/RG75 N/Box 22, Navajo 229-1333. Navajo 352.

Figure 97. "John McPhee, seated, registering Navajos for Selective Service." Milton Snow, photographer (or perhaps Sumner??), 26 February 1941. This photograph is interesting for several reasons. The registrar has some sort of electronic device or receiver or transmitter on the table (with a recorded message in Navajo?), and older men pose with antique weapons. But to the left are two young girls, bare to the waist, clearly in the middle of a Navajo healing practice, perhaps an Enemyway. Government agents frequently utilized every possible gathering of Navajo for their own purposes, as it was difficult to contact or get access to great numbers of scattered Navajo except when they assembled for ceremonial occasions. Here, Selective Service registration is taking place at the occasion of a Navajo ceremonial event. Snow (Sumner??) either did not know the event was taking place or included the two female participants in the photograph deliberately. Also see Fig. 96, cropped or posed to exclude any indication of the ceremony. The significance of the hats stacked atop the hogan is unclear. Photograph courtesy Milton Snow Collection, Navajo Nation Museum, Window Rock AZ. NH 1-22.

Portfolio V

Figure 98. "Navajo Marine code talkers in formation at Camp Pendelton CA." Photographer unknown (perhaps Philip Johnston), n.d. (perhaps 1942). See Kawano, 1990 and Bixler, 1992. This photograph, though taken from above, otherwise shares something of the compositional style of Fig. 84. See also Figs. 205, 206, 207. Photograph courtesy Cline Library, Special Collections and Archives, Northern Arizona University. No. NAU 413-1176.

Figure 99. "Members of five Navajo families, who when they received $15,000 as compensation of the deaths of six of their children in a train and school bus collision in 1936, invested $5500 of the amount in Defense Bonds. Two Indian boys who were injured in the crash received $1000 apiece and purchased a $500 bond." Photographer unknown (probably Milton Snow), n.d. The buying of the bonds seems more important to the photograph than the tragedy itself, the grief or privacy of the families. Photograph courtesy National Archives, Washington. NA/BIA/RG75 N/Box 22, Navajo 229-1333. Navajo 385.

Church and State

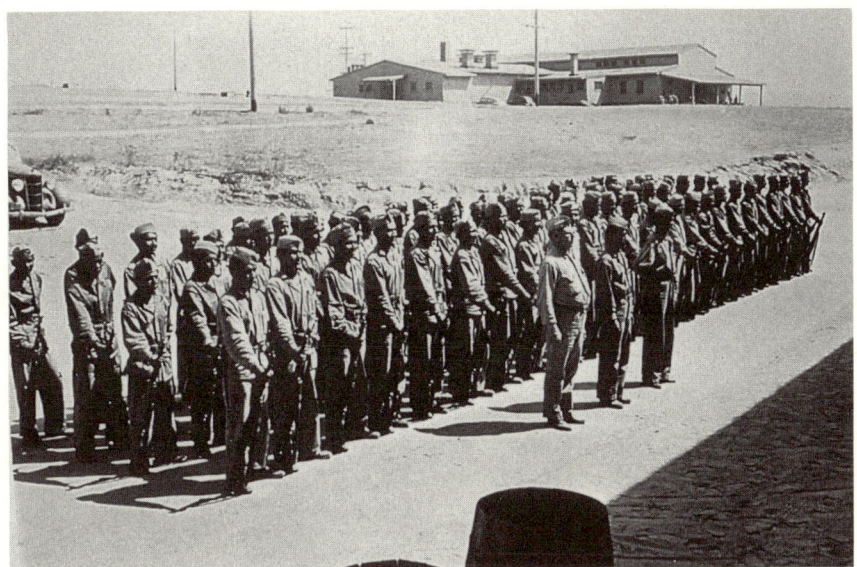

Figure 98

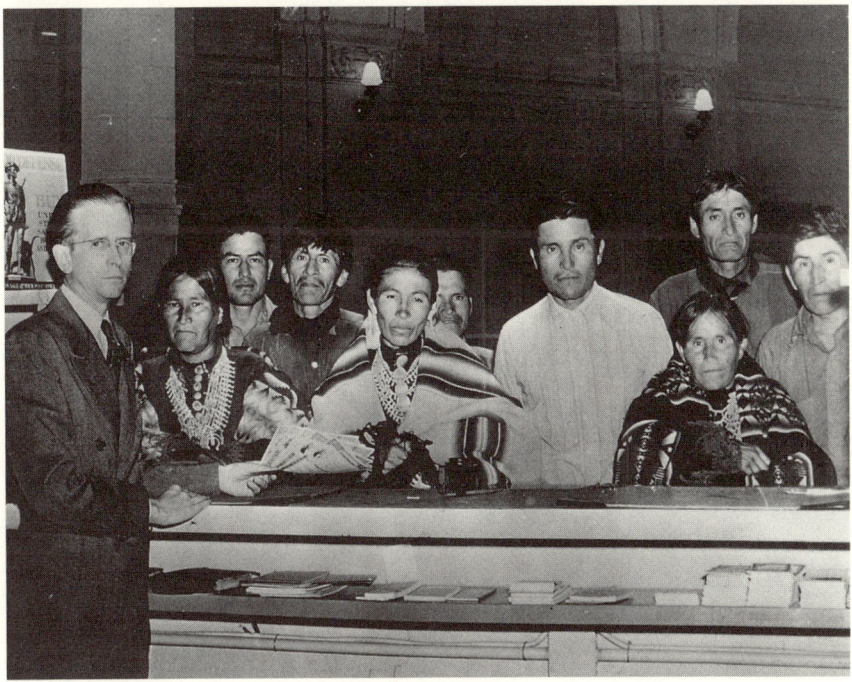

Figure 99

141

Portfolio V

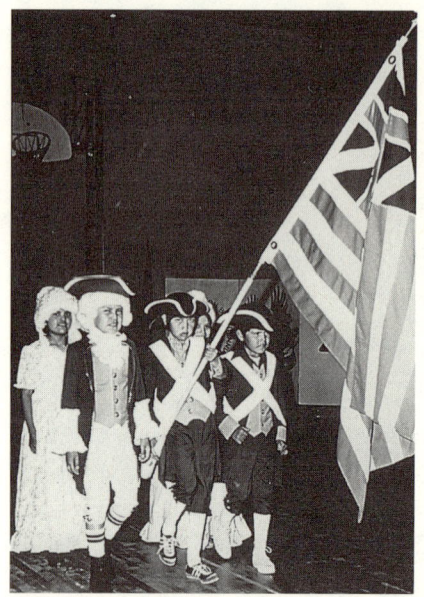

Figure 100

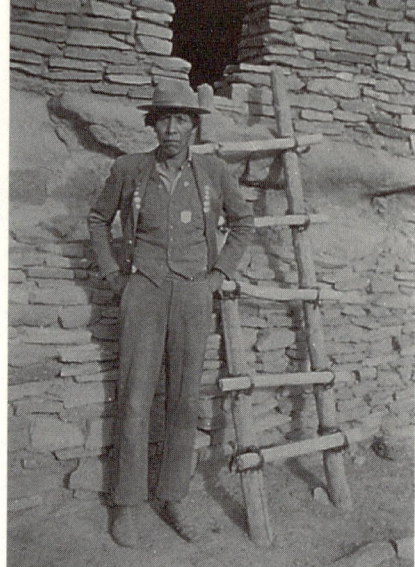

Figure 101

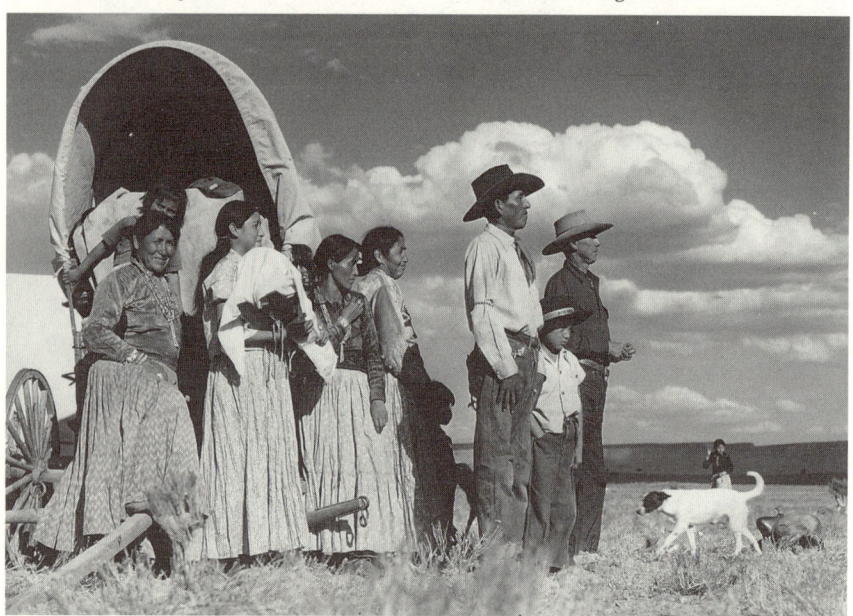

Figure 102

Figure 100. "Birth and Growth of the American Flag. Crownpoint Bicentennial Project." Photographer unknown, n.d. (ca. 1976). In perverse irony, Navajo children are costumed as colonists. See also Fig. 85. Photograph courtesy New Mexico Bicentennial File, New Mexico State Records and Archives. No. 33882.

Figure 101. "Clyde Peshlacoi with NPS hat and badge. Probably (taken) as we were leaving Wupatki and Jim, as he said in the Monthly Report, 'abdicated in favor of Clyde.' Clyde took his duties as caretaker very seriously and, in the best government tradition, went (in his wagon, with family) to visit his brother rangers at the Grand Canyon—where, we later learned with sadness, some officious NPS employee had detained him and taken the badge." Sallie (Brewer) Harris, photographer (??), 1936. Photograph courtesy Sallie Harris Collection, Museum of Northern Arizona. MS 242-2-unnumbered print a.

Figure 102. "Navajo looking into the Future to Uncle Sam." Milton Snow, photographer, 2 October 1942, near Ianbito Day School NM. Hoskie and Howard Miriam and families. This propaganda photograph was clearly very successful, being sent to World Wide Photos, Inc., as well as to Time, Inc. What they might actually be looking at is not specified. The two women at far left seem not to be interested, however, and appear amused at Snow's instructions (to look to the "future"?) or activity. Note the low position of the camera, lending a slightly "heroic" dimension to the subjects. The young boy's hat band reads "Inter-Tribal...." Photograph courtesy National Archives, Washington. NA/BIA/R75 NG/Prints: Navajo Life in the Southwest, 1936–1956. Box 4. NO6-46.

Portfolio V

Figure 103. "Royal Party from Saudi Arabia watches Indian girl weaving cloth from improved Navajo wool at SW Sheep-breeding Laboratory, Fort Wingate NM. Hamilton and Granstaff visible in background." Photographer unknown (probably Milton Snow), n.d. Note that the "girl" is dressed in Western clothing and the loom is a commercial model (quite unlike immovable Navajo upright looms), as are the heddles. Hamilton and Granstaff are politicians. See Figs. 94, 104. Photograph courtesy National Archives, Washington. NA/BIA/R75 N/Prints: Navajo A-Navajo D. Box 23. NA-24.

Figure 104. "Mr. and Mrs. Raymond Nakai (Navajo Tribal Chairman) and Harry James." Clifford E. Gedekoh, photographer, 25 November 1961, Window Rock Civic Center. James was probably booked by the Navajo Tribe or the BIA and could hardly have been the choice of the majority of Navajo people. Navajoland was a frequent site for visitors on one or another official mission, which, of course, required gracious Navajo hosts, gifts, and time and energy. Photographs are abundant in the Navajo Nation Museum photo archives with all manner of politicians (including George Wallace!), foreign potentates (see Fig. 103), and beauty queens (see Fig. 169). Photograph courtesy Navajo Nation Museum, Window Rock AZ. No number.

Church and State

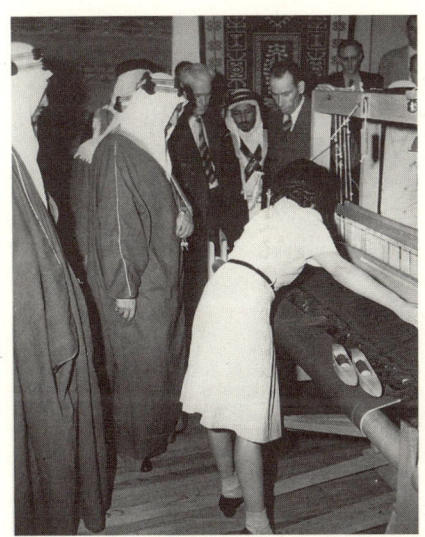

Figure 103

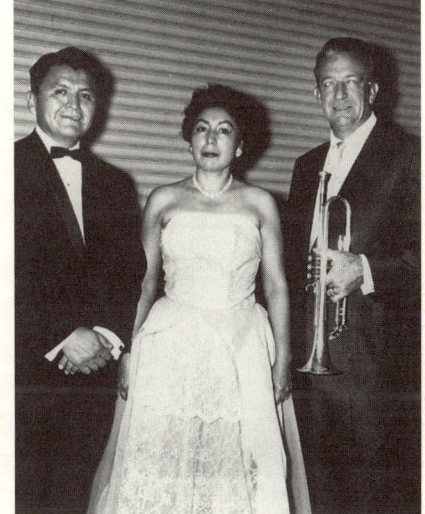

Figure 104

145

Portfolio V

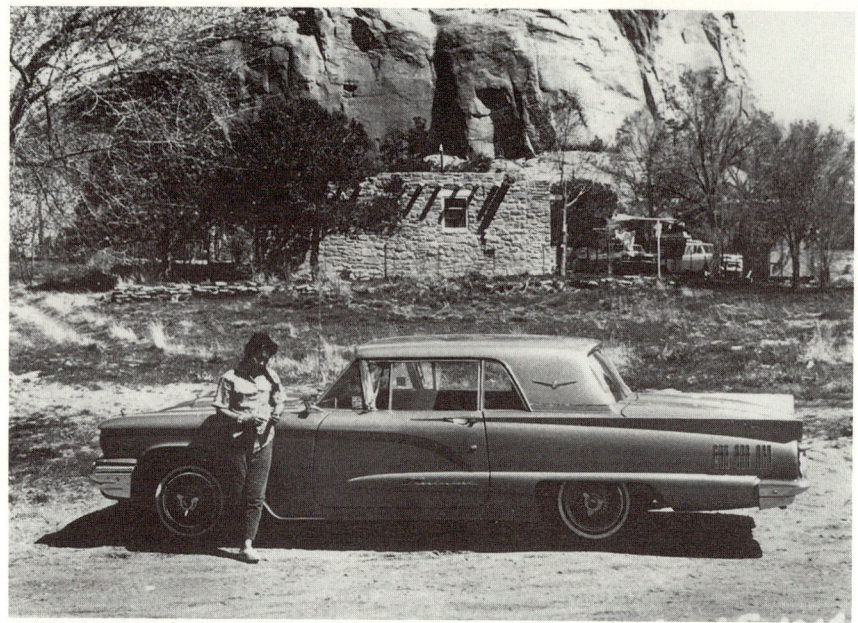

Figure 105

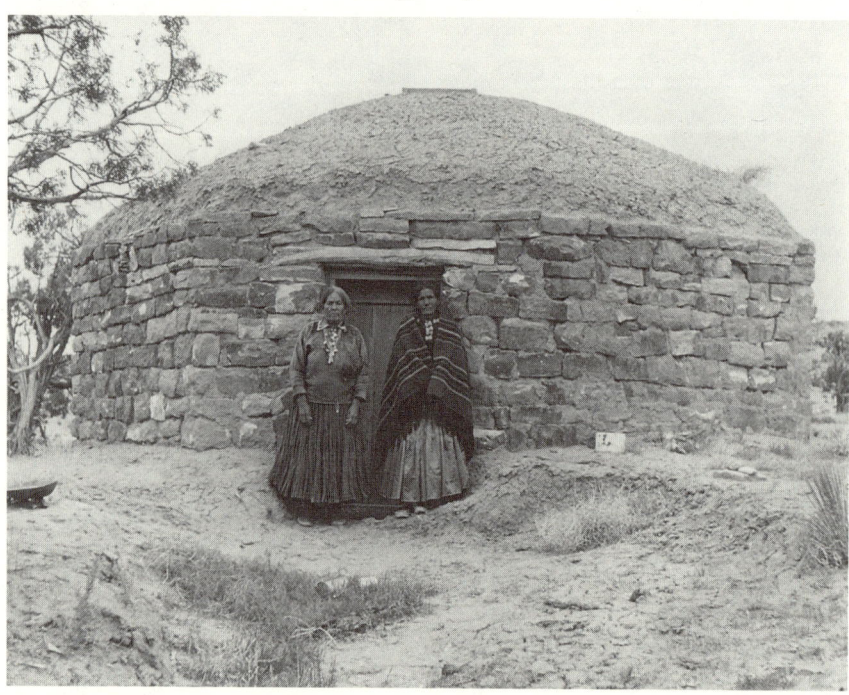

Figure 106

Church and State

Figure 105. "Domestic coming to work." Photographer unknown, n.d. (1965??), Window Rock AZ. BIA European-American personnel housing stands in the background (contrast with Navajo housing in Fig. 146). Photograph courtesy Concho Collection, Navajo Nation Museum, Window Rock AZ. X-13.

Figure 106. "Mrs. Jessy (left), and Mrs. Billy Antes standing before the substantial home place of Eddie Nakai and family which is now abandoned owing to the action of white stockmen and the Bureau of Land Management, Monticello, Utah, District 6." Clifford Gedekoh, photographer, 17 May 1955. This photograph refers to the continual problems of land and jurisdiction facing Navajo on the periphery of the original reservation area, many of whom were displaced by more legally sophisticated and well-connected ranchers. Persistent arguments that Navajo treated rangeland badly led to the devastating and vicious stock-reduction programs of Collier in the 1930s. These were later acknowledged to be excessive and ill-conceived, but the discourse was established and it still guides action. Photograph courtesy Navajo Nation Museum, Window Rock AZ. No number.

Chapter Five

Photography of Navajo to Mid-Century: Saturated Fields of Visibility

So it should hardly be a surprise that everything about being Indian has been shaped by the camera.
                        Paul Chatt Smith in Partial Recall *(1992:97)*.

The Settling of Tropes: The First Two Decades

From major archives and publications, there are over 175 known new photographers of Navajo in the first decade of the twentieth century.[1] Edward Curtis was not the only photographer of the time to visit Navajoland explicitly to impose his vision (though he was one of the more ambitious). Many of those active at the end of the nineteenth century continued their work, and several other romantic pictorialists, such as Roland Reed, Carl Moon, and James Verplanck—commonly sponsored by the railways—arrived. The studio tradition of Ben Wittick and Charles Goodman remained in place, and photographers such as William Pennington and Simeon Schwemberger, who photographed Navajo both in their studios and in Navajoland, emerged. The initial anthropological projects also began at this time in the continued work of George Pepper and William Orchard and the appearance of Alfred Tozzer and Ales Hrdlicka. And there were a few private commissions to photograph Navajo, such as Phoebe Hearst's sponsorship of Dr. Philip Mills Jones in 1902 (Fig. 107) and the Wanamaker expeditions (the first in 1909, the last in 1913— see Krouse, 1987), featuring the photography of, respectively, William C. Farabee and Joseph Dixon. Photographers such as George Wharton James,

Chapter 5

Adam Vroman, Frederic Maude, Sumner Matteson, and Frederick Monsen were still working, and administrative or semiofficial photography, such as that of Frank Churchill and, somewhat later, Leo Crane, began. Large collections of directed photography, such as the vast groupings of mission-related photographs at St. Michaels (an early Franciscan establishment near Fort Defiance), were launched or continued. Finally, increasing numbers of amateurs, both local and traveling, began taking photographs. These included the trader Charles Day (whose photographs sometimes may be attributed to more famous photographers, such as Curtis) and the interesting cowboy romantic, Earle Forrest.[2]

Photographs by amateurs—travelers and early tourists, traders, government employees—begin to appear heavily in archival and published sources of the first two decades of the twentieth century. The impression is that few people crossed northwestern New Mexico and northern Arizona without pointing a camera at Navajo. Pueblo peoples quickly began to limit photographers' access to themselves and their religious practices (the "Snake Dance" of the Hopi so important to Vroman and his colleagues was banned to photographers in the first decade of the century—see Lyon, 1988), but Navajo were dispersed and had no central political means to resist. Indeed, by the time color film appeared in the 1920s, an entire industry based on dramatic landscapes and Navajo posed in colorful dress had begun.

The Kodak, of course, also meant the end of the demand for the cabinet cards, the *carte de visite*, the studio card photograph, and the stereocard of the nineteenth century as the primary or only types of visual material on the Navajo. Anyone who might travel could now take his or her own pictures. For those who could not travel or whose skills were inadequate to the task—and as Navajo resistance to casual photography increased—cheap picture postcards became available as safe memoirs (see Appendix, Chart 2b for postcard companies). This was an important reason (as it clearly had important financial implications) to have photographs of Navajo doing what were considered Navajo activities in what were considered Navajo surroundings and behaving and looking the way it was considered Navajo should, as opposed to photographs in the earlier tradition of studio poses. These new portrayals became the sources of meaning, the images that regulated Navajo appearance. The studio poses largely dropped away except where taken at the request of Navajo for their own purposes, in postures at least in part of their choice. The latter included photographs from early studios in Southwestern towns adjacent to Navajoland (but see Portfolio IV and Figs. 58-60). These were rare in the first decades, however, for reasons of Navajo poverty, generalized

Photography of Navajo to Mid-Century

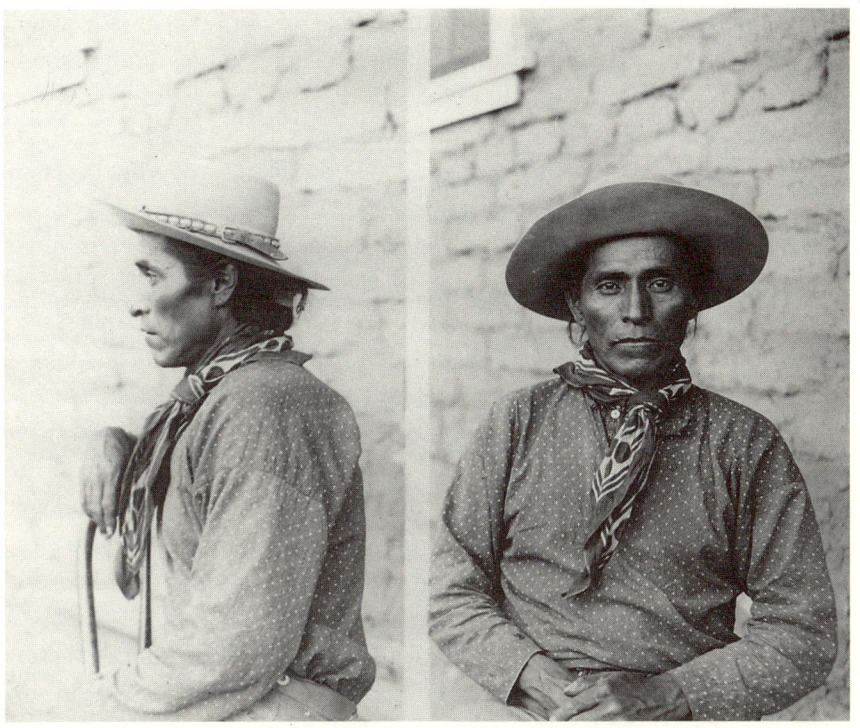

Figure 107

Figure 107a, b. "Navajo." Philip Jones, photographer, 1902, Ganado AZ. This man displays little reaction save a desire to get the encounter over with. But he regards the camera fearlessly and squarely. Dr. Jones also photographed (UCB No. 15-1598) the "Head Chief of Navajos", but we are not told his name, and he is subject to the same typical physical anthropology surveillance postures. Photograph courtesy Phoebe Hearst Museum of Anthropology, University of California, Berkeley. No. 15-1574.

Chapter 5

fear of the camera's capacity to do harm in one way or another, and simple lack of interest (and certainly a lack of interest in the representational postures required by Western photographers).

Most of the non-studio photographers of the first two decades of the century encountered resistance to their work, as Portfolio III reveals, but the familiar litany of excuses for appropriation (preservation, celebration, what the West could learn from Navajo, what Navajo could learn from the West, profit, exposure, closer friendships, etc.) continued and expanded. Indeed, the mention of resistance is ubiquitous in the writings of all early photographers, and the photographic images reveal it. McLuhan (1985:97) summarizes some of the reasons for this: "Many Indians refused to be photographed. It was their view that a portrait would bring bad luck, shorten their lives, and lead to their death. It was also believed that for the relinquishment of one's image, one's power was dissipated." McLuhan does not note simple irritation and anger at the appropriation itself, nor some of the specifically Navajo reasons for prohibiting photography of certain events, such as healing sandpainting (see Chapter 6).

Force was always a possibility, especially before the Kodak made theft of more candid photographs possible. Thus, in a revealing passage praising the merits of roll film, the Kodak, and candid photography, Monsen (1910:165) says of the older large view cameras:

> My Indian model was placed before the camera; one of my assistants
> on each side to hold him in case he should attempt to run away. The
> critical moment, however, was always when I put my head under the
> black focusing-cloth and pointed the lens straight at his heart, with my
> hand on the focusing-screw in an attitude suggesting a cannon about
> to be discharged. That was always a signal for poor Lo to move, and
> he generally did so with alacrity.

Where force didn't work, photographers employed various schemes and devices to get around resistance.[3] Monsen, trying to eliminate the "self-consciousness" (1910:166) of posed photographs, was one of the very earliest professionals to use the new Kodak candid camera and eliminate the hundreds of pounds of gear earlier photographers had to carry around. He describes his technique (1907:686–687):

> My own method of working is to carry three small camera, which fit
> in cases without covers that are slung to a belt around my waist and

are concealed under my loose coat. One turn of my hand and the camera is out and ready for use. Long practice in focusing has made it possible for me to do it almost by instinct, as a rifleman will hit the target when firing from the hip or at arm's length almost as often as when the weapon is sighted, and my subjects seldom know when they are photographed.

Indeed. By 1906 he had accumulated over 10,000 images of native peoples of the Southwest—most of which were destroyed in the San Francisco earthquake and fire of that year. His friends loaned him photographs so he could rebuild the lantern slide series with which he lectured, and thus we are left with a confused mixture of Vroman, Monsen, P. G. Gates, and Edward Kemp photographs, frequently without clear evidence of specific authorship (see Figs. 108-116). Monsen's daughter suggests that Vroman and Monsen "used each other's negatives freely and interchangeably," and during the time of the World's Fair in San Francisco, "Vroman made prints and enlargements of Monsen's negatives" (see Monsen/Kurutz, 17 June 1973).

Carl (also spelled Karl) Moon, whose romantic inclinations paralleled those of Curtis, required all his subjects to be posed ("worthy of preservation")[4] and was quite unctuous about the deceit of candid photography.[5] He nevertheless remained ever the clever white man. He relates an occasion at which a number of Navajo elders asked him to destroy a photograph (1914:12):

> One day I was visited [at his Fred Harvey El Tovar Studio at Grand Canyon] by six men of the Navajo tribe who, after much smoking and visiting, made known the real cause of their call. Directly over my desk was a framed portrait of one of the old medicine men of their tribe, who had just died. Believing that a part of his soul was imprisoned in the portrait—else how could it look so like him—they asked me if I would not destroy it, so that his spirit might be released and be at peace. I immediately took the print from the frame and tore it into bits while the men looked on with silent approval. After thanking me they each shook my hand in turn and filed quietly out of the room. They did not suspect that there might still be in existence others copies of the picture or a negative.

Moon most commonly worked in the now-established clichés and repeatedly photographed the same models, as did Curtis and many others. A weaver, Elle from Ganado, took over from Juanita, Manuelito's wife, as the most

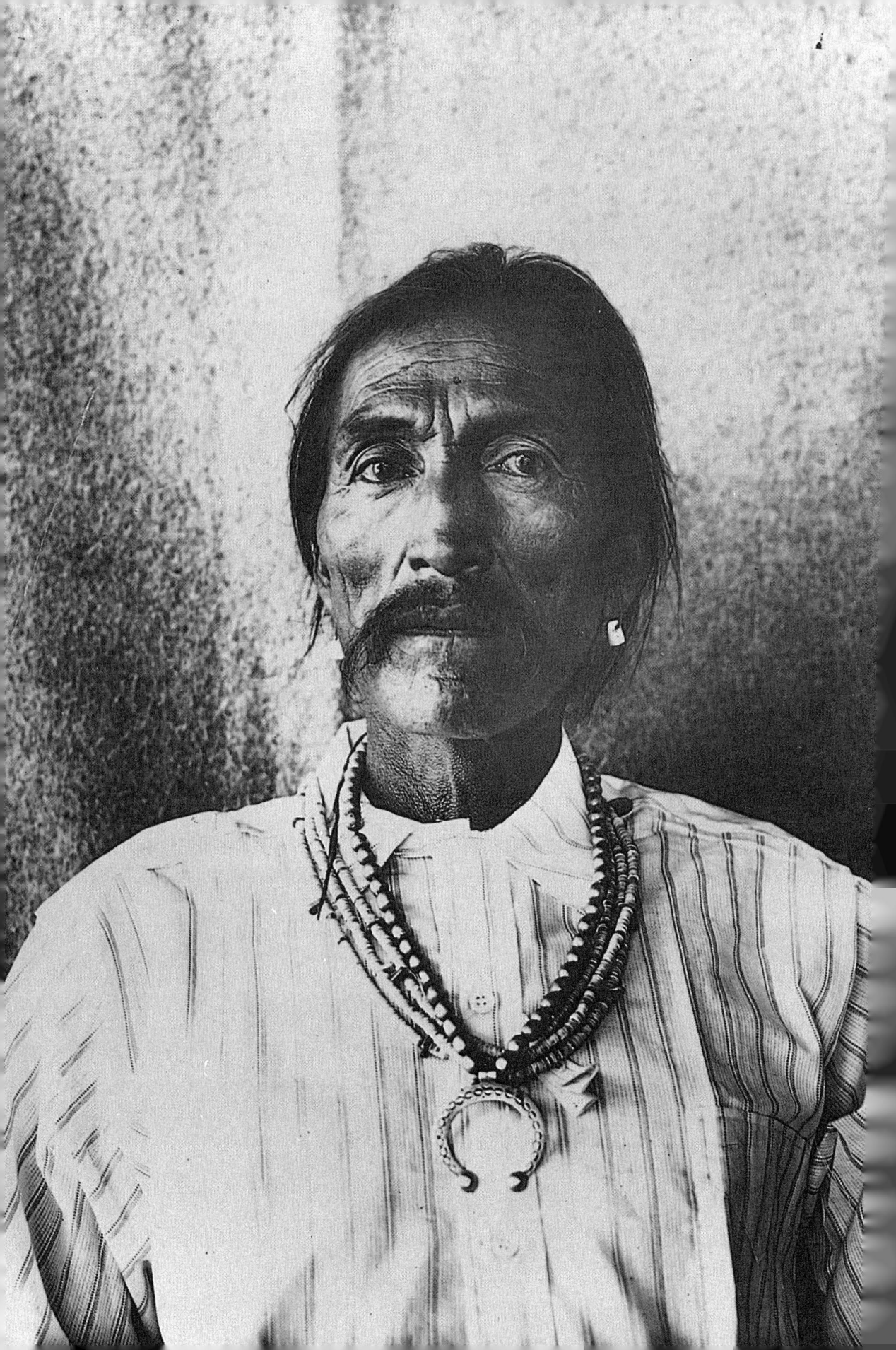

Photography of Navajo to Mid-Century

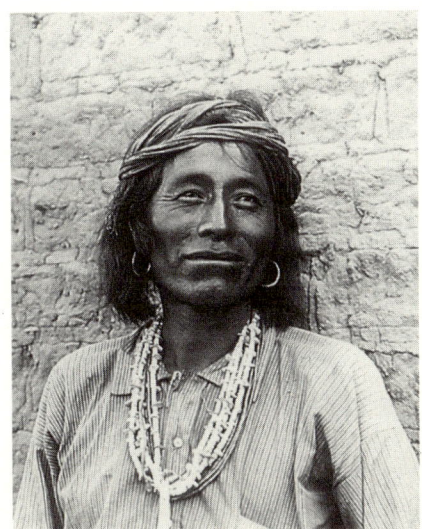

Figure 109

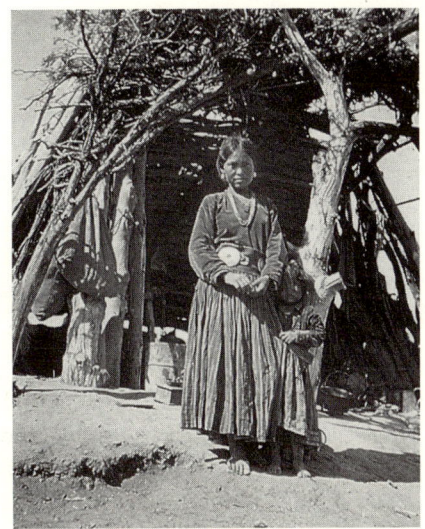

Figure 110

Figure 108. "A Navaho." P. G. Gates, photographer, n.d. This dignified (though very close) portrait appears to be of Hosteen Nez, the important leader, in younger years (see Roessel, 1980:200). Photograph courtesy National Anthropological Archives, Smithsonian Institution. NAA SPC02301100.

Figure 109. "Hostine qust-gin-ayne, the Navajo who had charge of my horses." Frederick Monsen, photographer, 1896–1906. One of the few Monsen portraits of Navajo smiling (and perhaps one of the few Navajo whom Monsen knew very well and who was getting much compensation from his encounter with European-Americans). Photograph reproduced from the Frederick Monsen Collections of The Huntington Library. Card No. 25.

Figure 110. Navajo woman and child. Frederick Monsen, photographer, 1896–1906. Despite the shy child, this is a nice photograph of a handsome and confident young mother in a summer shelter. The lower camera angle lends her some elevated deportment. Photograph reproduced from the Frederick Monsen Collections of The Huntington Library. Card No. 27.

Figure 108

photographed of all Navajo women; as she traveled to Harvey establishments elsewhere (such as the Alvarado in Albuquerque) to weave, she became the subject of undoubtedly thousands of amateur photographs. But many different poses of Elle exist from Moon alone, as well as from others (see Fig. 197). A few decades later, a particular family in Monument Valley, the Clys (cf. Fig. 161), would succeed Elle and her husband, Tom, as the favorite postcard models, as they could be endlessly photographed at a variety of "Navajo" tasks, such as sheepherding and weaving, in situ.

Despite the differences between posed and candid photographs, many of these early twentieth-century photographers were generally critical of the federal government for attempting to force assimilation and of missionaries for encouraging suppression of indigenous belief systems. Monsen even authored a text entitled *The Destruction of Our Indians: What Civilization Is Doing to Extinguish an Ancient and Highly Intelligent Race by Taking Away its Arts, Industries and Religion* (1907). Verplanck wrote a short illustrated polemical book in this same vein but was not beyond his own suppressions:

> These Indians revere the powers of nature and personify them. . . . I wonder whether any Indian songs, dances and ceremonies connected with their native religion, or any of their songs and dances at all, will survive to future ages, save as museum records (a few of them are indecent and ought, of course, to be dropped for that reason, but these are only a few) (Verplanck, 1934:10, 15).

Moon and his wife wrote children's books, James wrote several texts lauding native peoples,[6] and Curtis even got the trader Charlie Day into trouble over the recording of local healing practices (despite—or perhaps because of—the fact that the practices were set up for the camera). All railed against institutional change strategies—and how could they not? Their preservational arguments were based upon reaction to such strategies of assimilation and change. This same critique has persisted as a reason for photographic and anthropological appropriation down to the present day.

Moon's romantic posed style, often seen in dramatically lit portraits with an all-black background, is generally easy to recognize (see Figs. 117-122, 124-128, 130). But Fred Harvey, for whom he worked from 1906 to 1914, copyrighted the photographs (Harvey postcards rarely acknowledged the photographer), so it is not always easy to trace specific attributions to Moon for this period. Harvey purchased photographs from many other photographers (both professional and amateur—cf. Jesse Nusbaum) at this same time and copyrighted them under his company's name. Other photographers, such as William Simpson of the Santa Fe Railway (from 1901), became active during this period and produced early stock tourist photographs (see Figs. 131, 132).

As noted, Moon shared Curtis's nostalgic motivations and argued that photographers should record Navajo people and lifeways before they disappeared. Early twentieth-century photographers argued this point with such fervor that one might think photography itself could halt the inevitable. Somewhat later, the Fred Harvey Company published a book edited by its chief buyer, J. F. Huckel, with an incredible commentary that could only have encouraged ever more photographers: "[P]rimitive peoples unconsciously group themselves with an effect pleasing to the eye of the artist. . . .they make the picture to a degree that deliberate posing can seldom attain" (Huckel, 1926:34).

Roland Reed resembled Moon in his motivations and in making portraits against black backdrops (Fig. 130). But he was more brazen in posing young Navajo males in a state of near nudity (see Fig. 134). He seemed to have worked a great deal in the Canyon de Chelly area (Fig. 133), posing young men against rocks, on rocks, holding bow and arrow, wearing but a skin or a small loincloth about the waist. He labels at least one of these (SDM-23042) from 1913 the "Sons of Manuelito," but this seems impossible and must have been meant metaphorically. Assuming himself (like Moon) more clever than local people, Reed explains his method (Johnson, 1978:57):

> In approaching the Indian for the purposes of taking his picture, it is necessary to respect his stoicism and reticence which have so often been the despair of the amateur photographer. . . . In going into a new tribe with photographic paraphernalia, although I hire ponies and guides, I never once suggest the object of my visit.
>
> When the Indians, out of curiosity, as last inquire about my work, I reply casually, "Oh, when I'm home I'm a picture-taking man." Perhaps in a few days an Indian will ask . . . "Could you make our pictures?" My reply is non-committal . . . "I don't know . . . Perhaps." "Would you try?" "Sometime, when I feel like making pictures." Further time elapses, apparently the picture-taking man has forgotten all about making pictures until an Indian friend reminds him of his promise. Then the time for picture-taking has arrived.

Like Reed, Dr. Joseph Dixon, the principal photographer and proponent of the 1913 Wanamaker expedition (a grotesque patriotic propaganda recruitment

Chapter 5

campaign), also undressed Navajo males (see Fig. 135). Curiously, nude Navajo women never became a part of the Western image, and it is quite rare to see even a naturally (unposed) seminude Navajo woman in all the archival record (see Fig. 115).[7] (Nudity seems to have been an imagery that was reserved for the indigenous women of the Southwestern borderlands, such as the Mohave.) Dixon posed Navajo much as did Curtis, Moon, and (later) Pennington. Indeed, were the photographs not attributed, one might easily assign Dixon's photographs to one of these photographers.[8] Because many of the first- and early second-decade photographers modeled many of the same Navajo, it is sometimes especially difficult to determine the source without precise attribution detail.

Navajoland must have been very crowded during the early part of the century (ca. 1903–1913); photographers were stumbling over one another. The various fixers, arrangers, and cultural brokers, such as traders J. L. Hubbell, Charles and Sam Day, the Wetherills, and J. Moore, must have been extremely busy. Perhaps as a consequence, Charlie Day actually began to photograph and may have been published by Edward S. Curtis (see Chapter 4). Although there was some cooperation and trade in negatives and prints between photographers (Monsen, Maude, Vroman), there was also apparently theft and piracy (Wittick, Frank Randall, Edward O. Richmond) and, for some, simply unresolved confusion over who actually took the photographs (James, Rose, Pierce, Hall).

Continuing the Wittick studio tradition in Gallup[9] were a series of photographers whose postcard work—increasingly conducted at the annual Gallup Intertribal Ceremonial when it began in the 1920s—came to typify photography of Navajo at the time. Wittick's son Archie, J. R. Willis, and Tom Mullarky were among these practitioners. To this Gallup tradition came Simeon Schwemberger, who learned to photograph while a Franciscan brother at St. Michaels Mission. Schwemberger took many hundreds of photographs for St. Michaels, including an extraordinary series of a 1905 Nightway healing practice, access to which Charles Day, the trader, brokered in exchange for payment of a medicine man's fees.[10] Schwemberger left the order in 1909 and opened a studio in Gallup, but he produced his finest photography prior to that date. Like the others, Schwemberger issued postcards of his photographs. Many of these views are remarkably free of cliché (see Fig. 129 and Long, 1992). As noted previously, Schwemberger became friends with J. Hildebrand and may have taught him photography. Certainly they traded negatives; in some collections, in fact, there seems to be some confusion between the two (see Fig. 49).

Other studios existed in the border towns of Winslow, Holbrook, and Flagstaff and further afield in locales such as Albuquerque and Grand Junction, Colorado (where the Wheeler studio left some well-documented Navajo portrait photographs from 1901). Several studios handled postcards taken by their owners at the Gallup ceremonials or fairs (see Chart 2b) but only occasionally did a studio outside the Gallup establishments specialize in Navajo photographs. These commercial studios sometimes took interesting portraits, at least some of which probably were initiated by Navajo themselves.

Burton Frasher, an important postcard photographer, began his career in the 1910s. Frasher, from Pasadena, never opened a studio in Gallup but visited often and worked out of there. He left a remarkably full series of Navajo photographs—some obviously from the annual ceremonial (which by now had posing days and locations for the hundreds of photographers who wanted images) but others from travels out into Navajoland. His photographs are quite as good as those more famous (see Fig. 136) and no more aphoristic than those celebrated as art photographs of the time. The subsequent plethora of postcard companies can be seen in Chart 2. His works were often but not always labeled "Frasher Fotos"; a few came to be claimed by or attributed to other photographers.

One of the first professional photographers to secure photographs of an actual Nightway ceremony was P. Clinton Bortell, who in 1919 managed to get some pictures of a Nightway initiation and of the last evening's dance (perhaps from the same Nightway photographed by Dane Coolidge—see Coolidge, 1930:194). A postcard made from one of these Nightway photographs has today found its way into many of the archival sources of the Southwest (see Appendix, Chart 1). Another amateur of the time—Jo Mora (1904–1906), an artist from California—took a number of photographs during visits to Arizona (for hunting trips, Hopi dances). He took a series of a Nightway healing ceremony, making photos of a sweat-bath sequence, an initiation sequence, and events of the last afternoon, including a Black God visit (rare for the time).

One unique romantic cowboy, Earle Forrest, came West and began taking photographs in the Four Corners region in 1902. His many photographs nearly always specify their Navajo subjects by name (even if they are the sometimes insulting names made up by local traders), and the very well-documented collection discusses social relations, events, and Navajo resistance to photography without the unctuous defenses set forth by most professional photographers of the era (see Figs. 1, 137, 138). Forrest's book on

Chapter 5

his photographic experiences is remarkably free of the liberal sensitivities thought necessary by that time (1970).[11] The book covers his first journeys to the Southwest and a later visit in the 1920s, and though his text is filled with the caricatures of the times, Forrest sought permission to photograph Navajo and claims to have given copies to those he photographed (but see Forrest, 1970:68, for discussion of one of the many exceptions). He inaugurated small photo-dramas, playful interactions between non-Navajo and Navajo. In Forrest's example, the white man wins. Forrest himself is the non-Navajo model—it is unclear whether someone else took the photograph or whether the shutter was tripped by extended release (see Forrest, 1970:71-72). In a sequence later set up by Pennington (and copyrighted by Carpenter), the clever Navajo wins at a card game, and the white man is left without horse, saddle, or kerchief.

There is little doubt that Navajo had by now acquired a reputation as picturesque, exotic photo objects. They lived in small isolated groups and consequently were less hostile than Pueblo peoples (that is, less capable of going inside house blocks to hide, less capable of joining with numbers of other adjacent people to chase off photographers). The subjects of photographs came to include persistent themes—herding, shearing, spinning, holding lambs, combing hair, making jewelry, attending festivals[12] at the pueblos of Zuni, Zia, Jemez, Laguna, and the Hopi villages, and weaving, endless weaving (see Portfolio VII). The latter activity took place even outside cement tipis (Fig. 201), and some photos were set up to appear as if women are weaving when in fact they were not (Fig. 196). Navajo were pictured on horses, off horses, riding at chicken pulls, in cradleboards, sitting on corral fences, and in covered wagons. The pervading cliché—a Navajo family peering out from a covered wagon—came to grace the covers of the tourist magazines and maintained currency until wagons disappeared for good in the 1960s.

Amateurs participated in this photography, and the engineer H. F. Robinson contributed large numbers of intense, close-up photographs oriented about these stereotypes. (He held the record for some time, I believe, for the most *New Mexico Magazine* covers—certainly so for Navajo subjects.) Robinson and his wife, Mary, published a guide to photography of Native Americans, *Lens Studies of Indians* (1914), illustrated with photographs and commentary. His brother, Will, also published on the region; his *Under Turquoise Skies* (1928) used photographs of Navajo taken by H. F. Robinson (but this work includes a section entitled "Menace of the Nomad," reflecting a persistent form of bigotry favoring the settled over the nomadic that continues down to the present in land claims arguments between Navajo and others).[13]

Government employee Stephen Olop took substantial numbers of photographs during the 1910s in the northeastern Ute-Navajo borderland, and nurse Marie Le Tourneau Olson did likewise at the western edge of Navajoland. A decade later, Olson would return to Tuba City to photograph again. Another nurse, Florence Barker, first photographed around Immanual Mission, returning some three decades later. The latter two established friendships, sometimes labeling the photographs with the subject's names and taking detailed photographs of their families and their children. Natalie Curtis (Burlin), who came west before 1910 to record songs, left a few romantic photographs.[14]

The Hopi dances, especially the Snake Dance, attracted photographers from far and wide, as it occurred to no one that Native American objections ought to be taken seriously. (Indeed, the first ban on photography was inaugurated by a federal Indian agent, whose chief concern was that the crowding would create chaos and possibly provoke retaliation by the Hopi.) Getting to the Hopi villages required a trip through Navajoland, and this generated considerable photographic opportunities. A few photographers, such as Stuart Young, spent more time in Navajoland itself than in the Hopi settlements and came to photograph Navajo events. Young left some interesting historic photographs from the north portion of Navajoland (see Figs. 139, 140).

This period also produced the first documented photograph actually taken by Navajo (1914). The photographer, "Tin Horn," is said to have borrowed a camera and "took some very good pictures" (see Fig. 211). Tin Horn, who lived in the vicinity of Kayenta, was photographed by Adelarde Law six years later on the occasion of an Enemyway (*'Ana' í Ndáá'*), a summertime healing event that quickly became known to photographers (who sometimes used the denigrating label "Squaw Dance")—especially those on their way to the Hopi summer dances. "Tin Horn" also is shown at work on another Western obsession of the time, a Ouija board (see Fig. 62). Navajo holding cameras (usually inappropriately, and therefore clearly not taking photographs) came to be a common theme, and this racist image—first inaugurated, to my knowledge, by Frederic Maude—persists down to the present (see Portfolio I).

The cliché, however, was to reach ridiculous proportions in the hands of studio photographers such as William Pennington and Lisle Updike. The "Pen-Dike" Durango studio managed to pose, both in the studio and in Navajoland settings,[15] several individuals (Fig. 141), some of whom we know from other sources (for Pennington does not identify them), in the most absurd postures, with equally asinine labels (indeed, in at least one case, the same pose is alternately labeled "A Bad Character" and "A Strong Character" in different

Chapter 5

collections). One, a famous leader of the 1913 Beautiful Mountain rebellion named Bi-joshii,[16] is reduced to a series of mimetic action postures and silly parody (see Fig. 141). Pennington photos, with their posed themes, appeared to be popular, however (they can be found in many archives—see Chart 1)— at least, sufficiently so that William Carpenter patented a series of them under his own name in 1915. I do not know whether Carpenter purchased negatives from Pennington or simply pirated the photos, but under his name they enjoyed some publication success and appear so attributed in the introductions to Hathaway, 1990 and Goetzmann, 1991:117. The latter even seriously discusses Carpenter as if he were the actual photographer: "Carpenter, who operated out of Spokane, Washington, and Rossland, British Columbia, *traveled to Navajo country for this series*, which includes several highly unconvincing action images of ancient, frail braves on the warpath" [emphasis added]. As far as I am aware, William Carpenter produced no Navajo images, and those copyrighted by him are from Pennington.

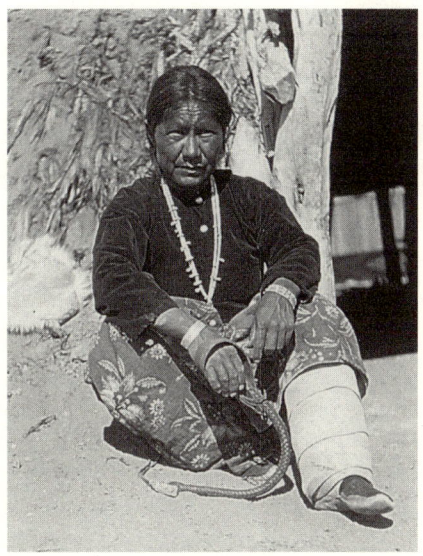

Figure 111

Figure 111. "Na da Ketche, wife of Hosteen Nez." Frederick Monsen, photographer, 1896–1906, Ganado AZ. "Good weaver, superb business woman who owns over 1000 sheep and many ponies." Wrapped in buckskin leggings and holding a quirt, this confident woman certainly looks all business. Again, the low camera placement enhances the dignity of her appearance. Monsen may have photographed another man named Hosteen Nez, or this Hosteen Nez may have had another wife also photographed by Monsen (see Figs. 108, 110, 116). Photograph reproduced from the Frederick Monsen Collections of The Huntington Library. Card No. 83.

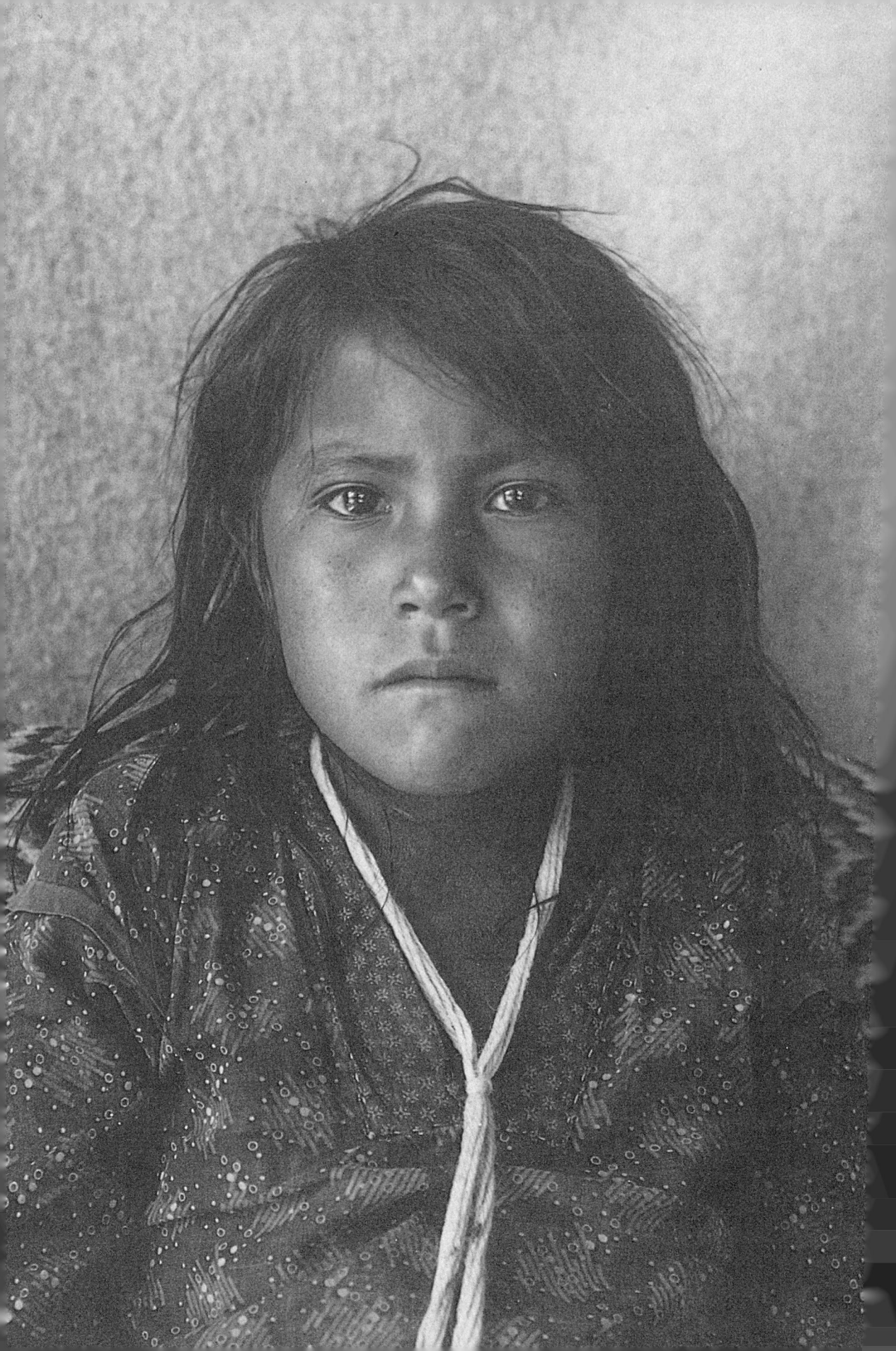

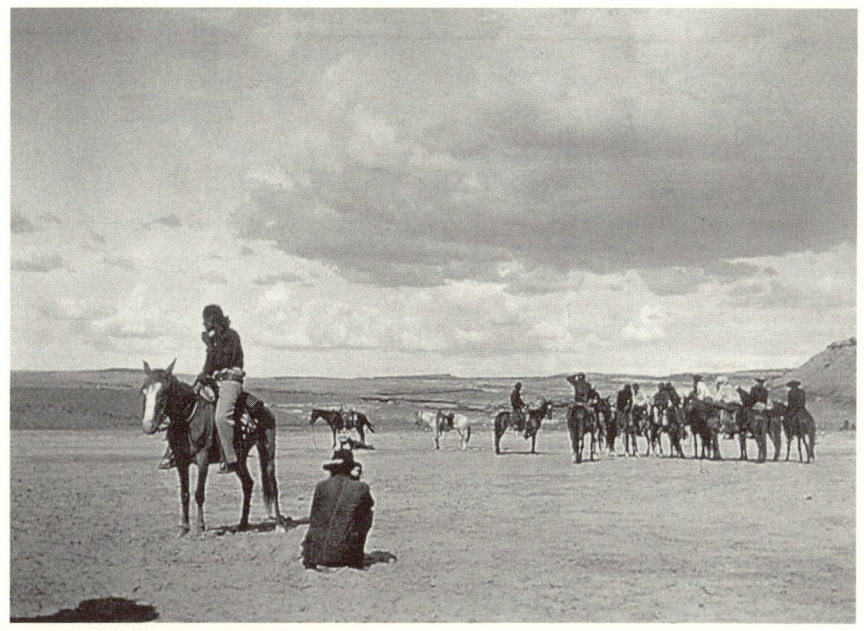

Figure 113

Figure 112. "Tsosie-bina, the Slender One." Frederick Monsen, photographer, 1896–1906, Navajo Mountain AZ. This boy, twelve years of age, is posed with a yarn necklace. Photograph reproduced from the Frederick Monsen Collections of The Huntington Library. Card No. 85.

Figure 113. "Gathering of Navajo at Chin Lee to engage in Indian sports." Frederick Monsen, photographer, 1896–1906. Monsen took a wide view of this event as well (Card 141). Photograph reproduced from the Frederick Monsen Collections of The Huntington Library. Card No. 86.

Figure 112

Chapter 5

Figure 114. "Frederick Monsen in the Navajo country." Photographer unknown, n.d. Monsen with Navajo children. These same children, of Hosteen Nez, are also photographed by Monsen (see Fig. 116). Photograph courtesy National Anthropological Archives, Smithsonian Institution. NAA (SPC02302202).

Figure 115. "Old Navajo women and their hogan or home." Frederick Monsen, photographer, 1896–1906. One woman appears to be taking care of an older woman, perhaps a sister or a mother. Photograph reproduced from the Frederick Monsen Collections of The Huntington Library. Card No. 93.

Figure 116. "Navajo Indian Children." Frederick Monsen, photographer, 1896–1906, Shiprock NM. These are the children of Hosteen Nez, a Navajo headman. Monsen's low camera placement suggests the children are at some ease with the photographer. See also Fig. 114. Photograph reproduced from the Frederick Monsen Collections of The Huntington Library. Card No. 94.

Photography of Navajo to Mid-Century

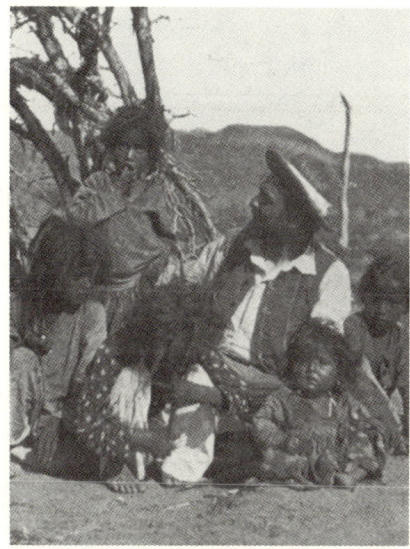

Figure 114

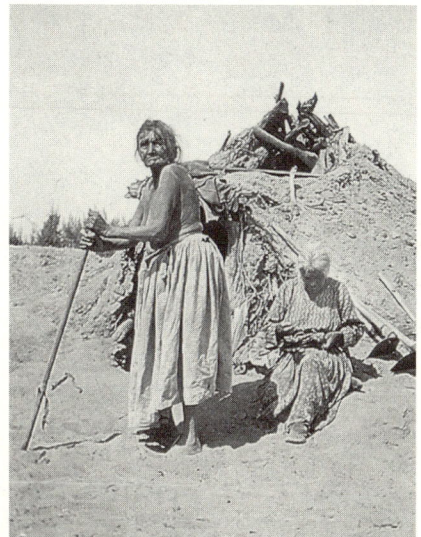

Figure 115

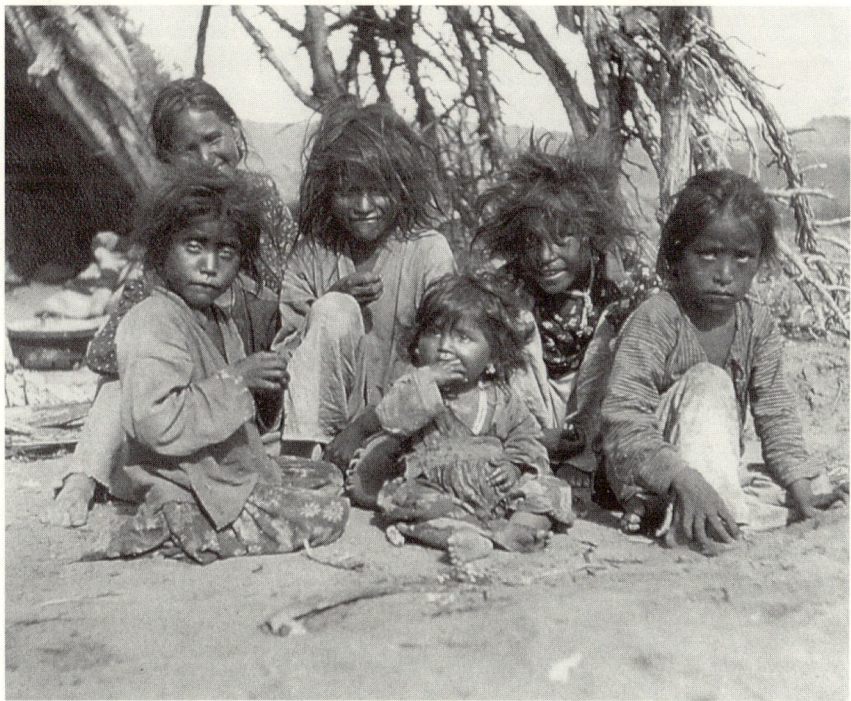

Figure 116

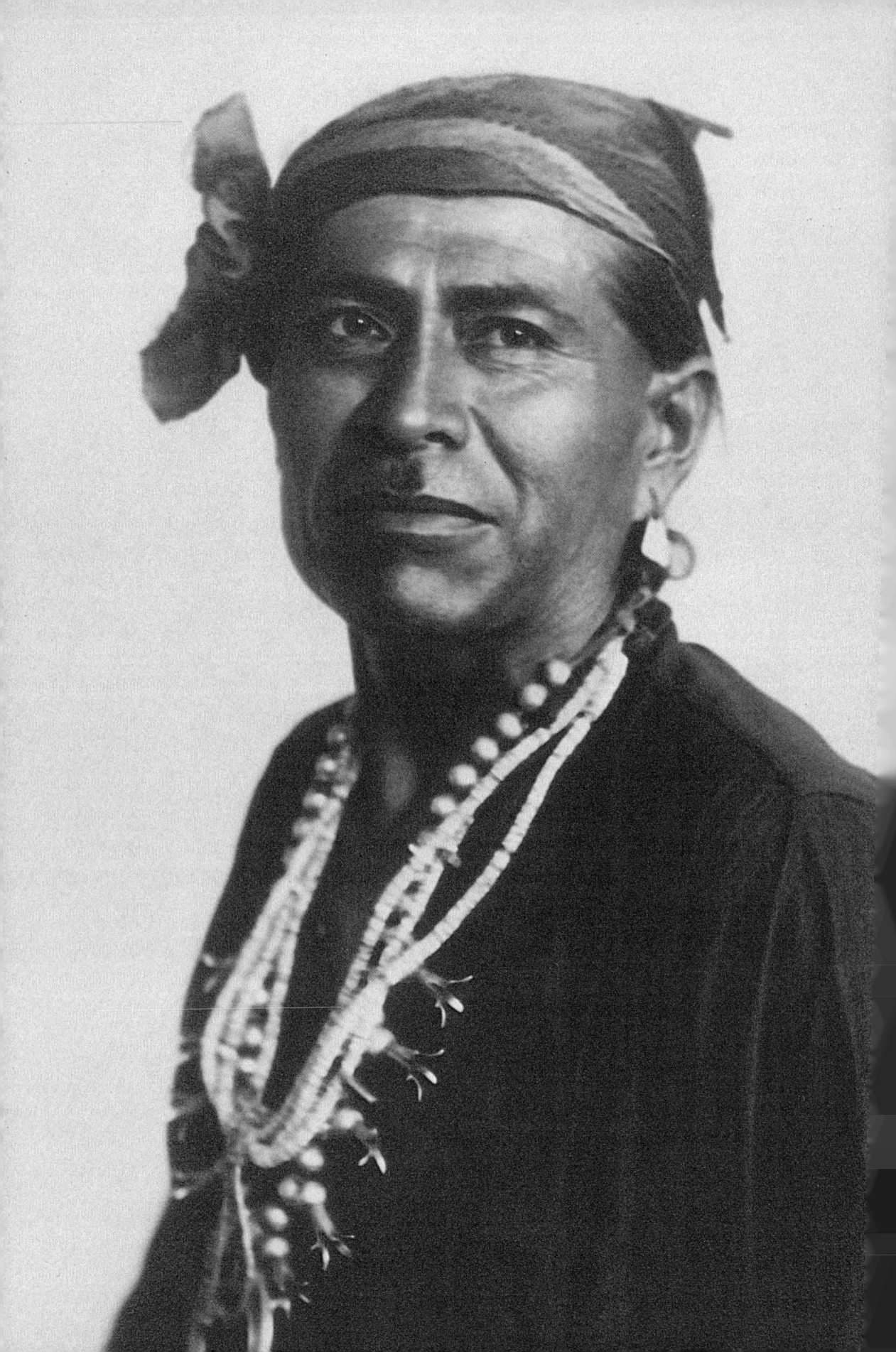

Photography of Navajo to Mid-Century

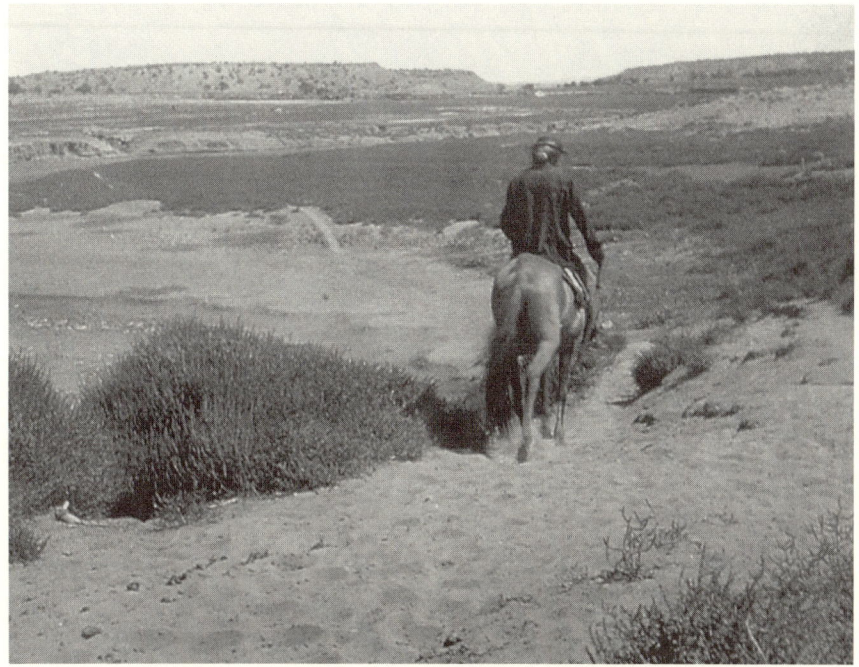

Figure 118

Figure 117. "Meguelito [sic]. Yah-otsa-begay." Carl Moon, photographer, 1903–1914. This famous, handsome medicine man was very much used to photographs of himself—see Figs. 63, 169—but seldom do we see his Navajo name. Photograph reproduced from the Carl Moon Collections of The Huntington Library. Card No. 96.

Figure 118. "Navajo land. Taken in the heart of the Navajo Reservation, Arizona." Carl Moon, photographer, 1903–1914. In this carefully composed (and posed) photograph, the rider may have had to repeat the same stretch of trail several times until Moon got the image he desired. This is an early example of the tourist cliché—Navajo riding away from the camera—seen in Curtis, Simpson (Figs. 131, 132), and many others. Of course, this type of image also had the advantage of avoiding possible hostile faces. Photograph reproduced from the Carl Moon Collections of The Huntington Library. Card No. 67.

Chapter 5

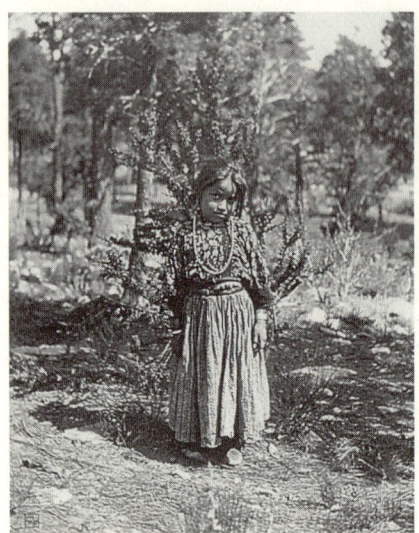 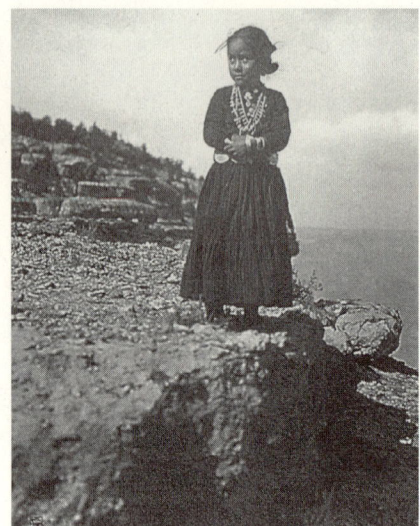

Figure 119   *Figure 120*

Figure 119. "Navajo maid." Carl Moon, photographer, 1903–1914. This coy child is also seen in other Moon photographs, and became one of his favorite child models. Photograph reproduced from the Carl Moon Collections of The Huntington Library. Card No. 85.

Figure 120. "Navajo maid. Haz pah." Carl Moon, photographer, 1903–1914, Grand Canyon. This may or may not be the same child as in Fig. 121; she looks back uncertainly, perhaps because she stands so close to the edge of the canyon. Photograph reproduced from the Carl Moon Collections of The Huntington Library. Card No. 86.

Figure 121. "Haz pah." Carl Moon, photographer, 1903–1914. Photograph reproduced from the Carl Moon Collections of The Huntington Library. Card No. 77.

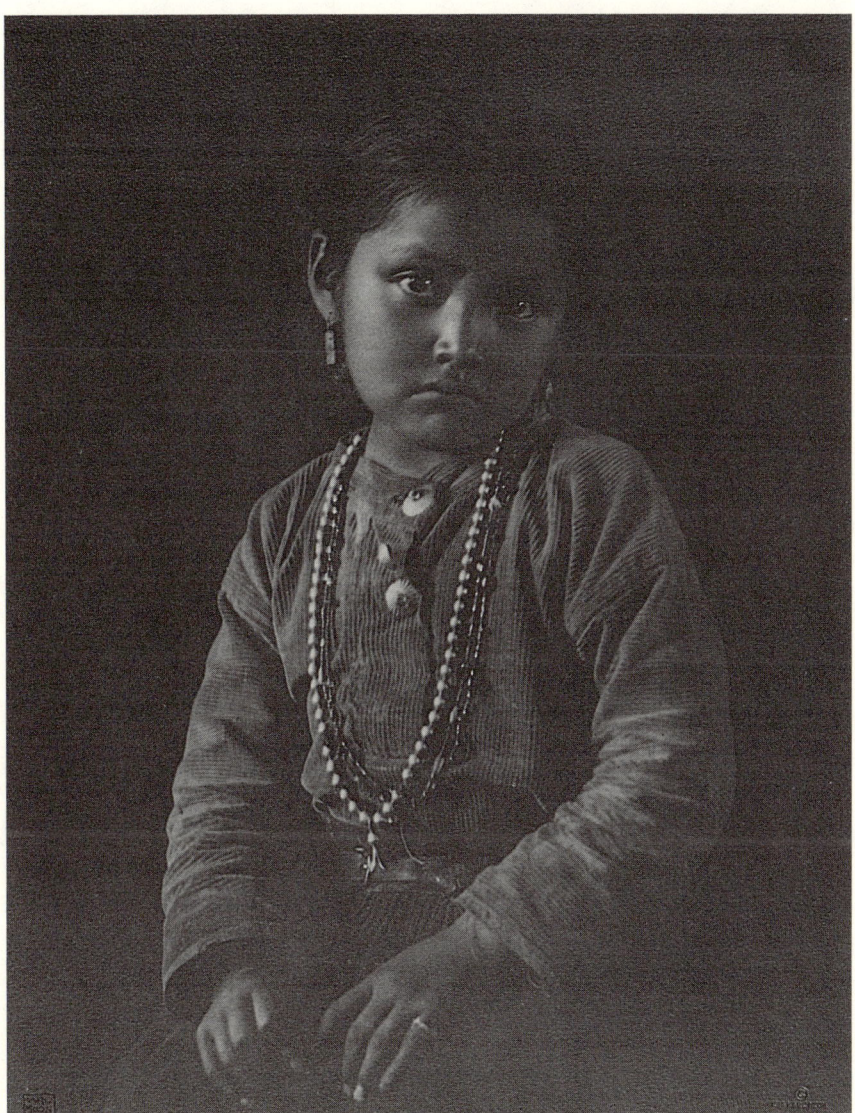

Figure 121

Chapter 5

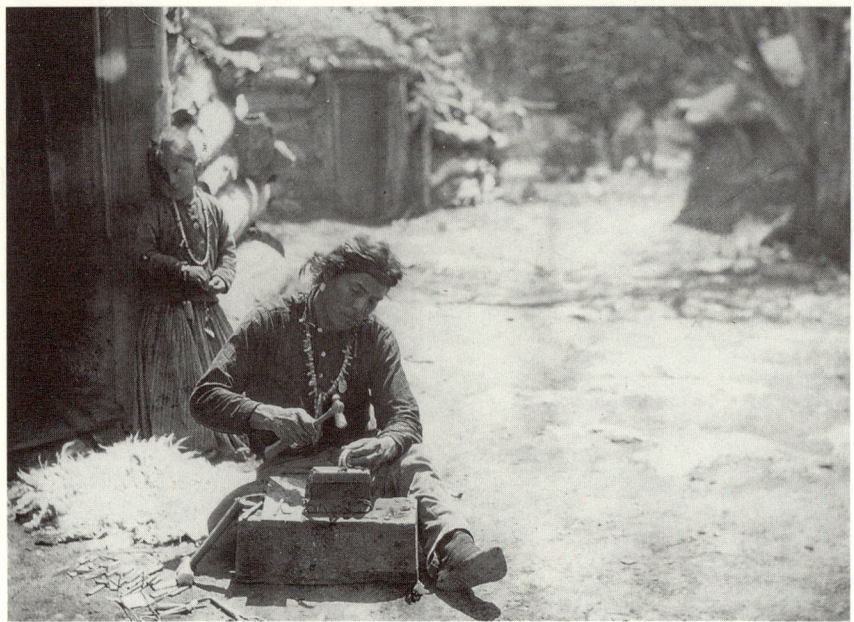

Figure 122

Figure 122. "View of silversmith at work and a young girl watching. Hogan in background." Carl Moon, photographer, n.d. Moon also used this silversmith's daughter as a model (cf. Figs. 119, 120). The silversmith may have been working at Grand Canyon; both he and his daughter were photographed extensively. From Fred Harvey Collection. Photograph courtesy National Museum of the American Indian, Smithsonian Institution. Neg. No. 31721.

Figure 123. "The Silversmith's Daughter." J. R. Willis, photographer, n.d. This photographic postcard from the Willis Gallup studios may be from a print bought from Carl Moon, who photographed this young girl extensively. Photograph courtesy Wheelwright Museum of the American Indian. #60/219.

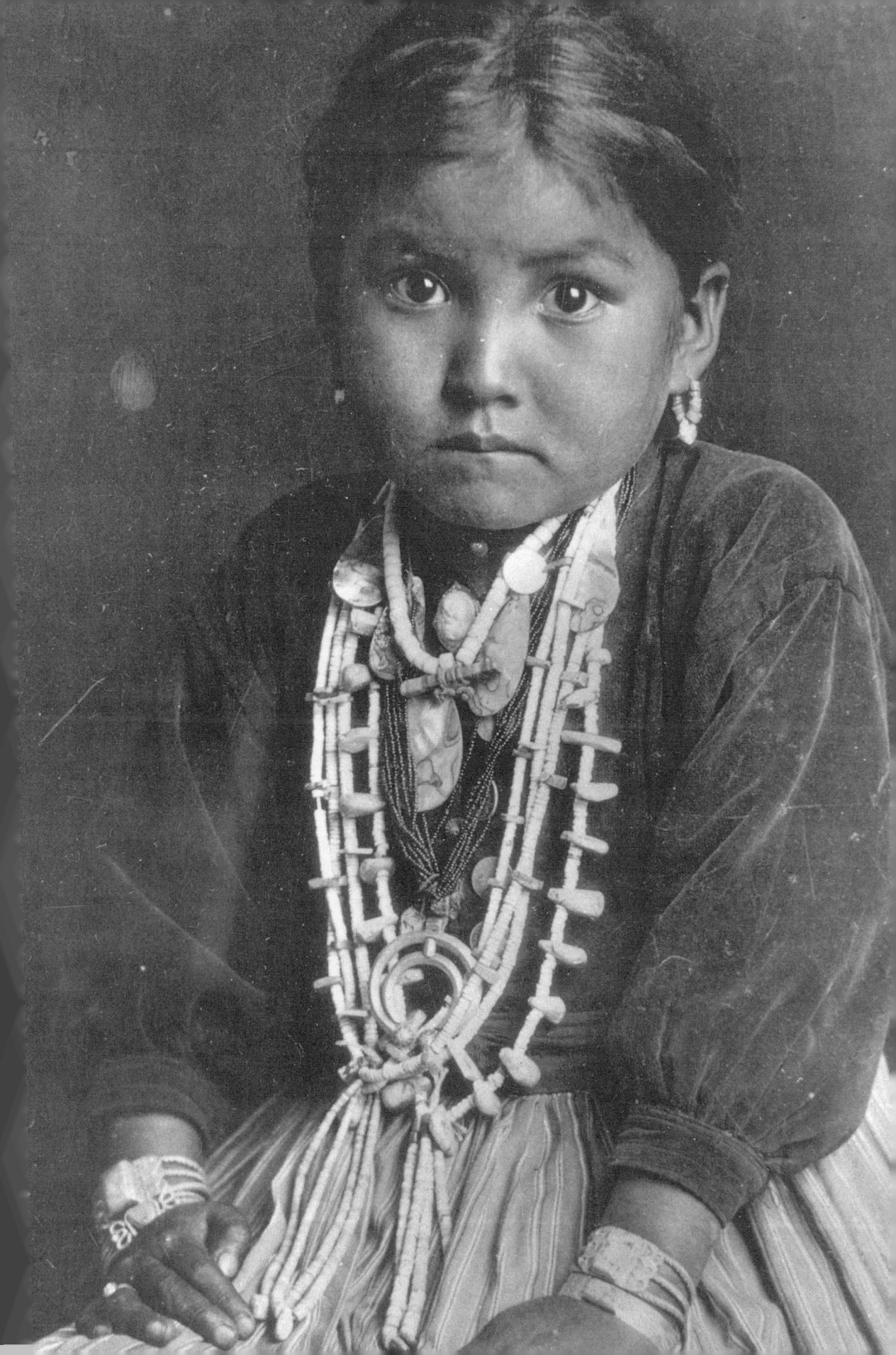

Chapter 5

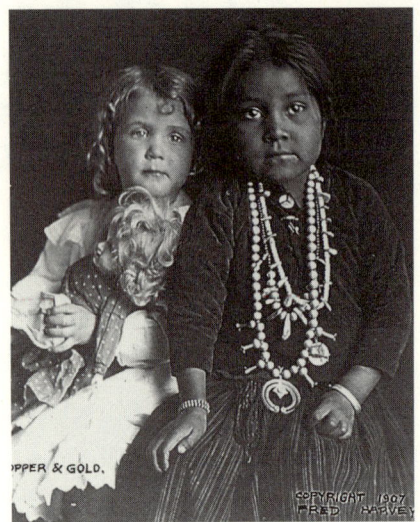

Figure 124

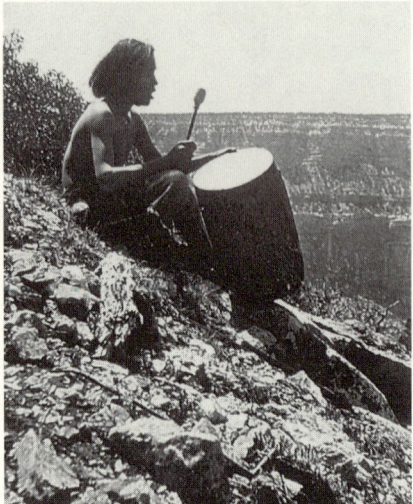

Figure 125

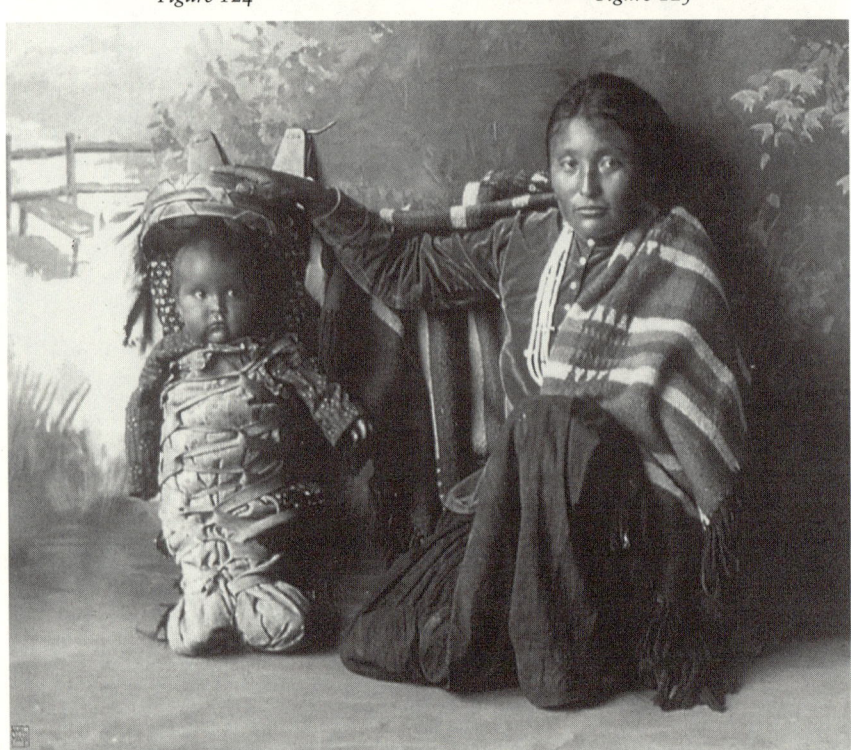

Figure 126

Figure 124. "Copper and Gold." *Photographer unknown (probably Carl Moon), 1907, possibly Grand Canyon. Navajo is copper, European-American is gold? Photograph courtesy National Anthropological Archives, Smithsonian Institution. NAA LOC 03266500.*

Figure 125. "Mountain Chant." *Carl Moon, photographer, 1903–1914. "The Navajo is fond of singing and often goes off by himself to practice his weird chants, usually in a high minor key. He knows many songs; the writer has heard him sing as many as fifty in an evening." This silly caricature, taken at Moon's Fred Harvey El Tovar studio at Grand Canyon, depicts a boy singing on the edge of the canyon (with a non-Navajo drum). But this scene has no relationship to anything that would occur naturally—Navajo today live near, but not on, Grand Canyon and do not sing to it; this certainly has nothing to do with the Navajo healing chantway, the Mountain Chant. There is indeed nothing to suggest that the model is in fact Navajo. Photograph reproduced from the Carl Moon Collections of The Huntington Library. Card No. 59.*

Figure 126. "Navajo mother and baby." *Carl Moon, photographer, 1903–1914. In his photography of Navajo, Moon rarely used this pastoral backdrop, but it does not detract from this very nice portrait of a confident and cautious mother and her child. Because the setting is so clearly a fixed studio, it is possible to speculate upon the social and economic relations between the woman and Moon. Did she request and pay for the portrait (and keep the prints), or did she receive payment to model, with all prints belonging to Moon? The painted pastoral backdrop suggests an even earlier date than the one given. Photograph reproduced from the Carl Moon Collections of The Huntington Library. Card No. 66.*

Figure 155

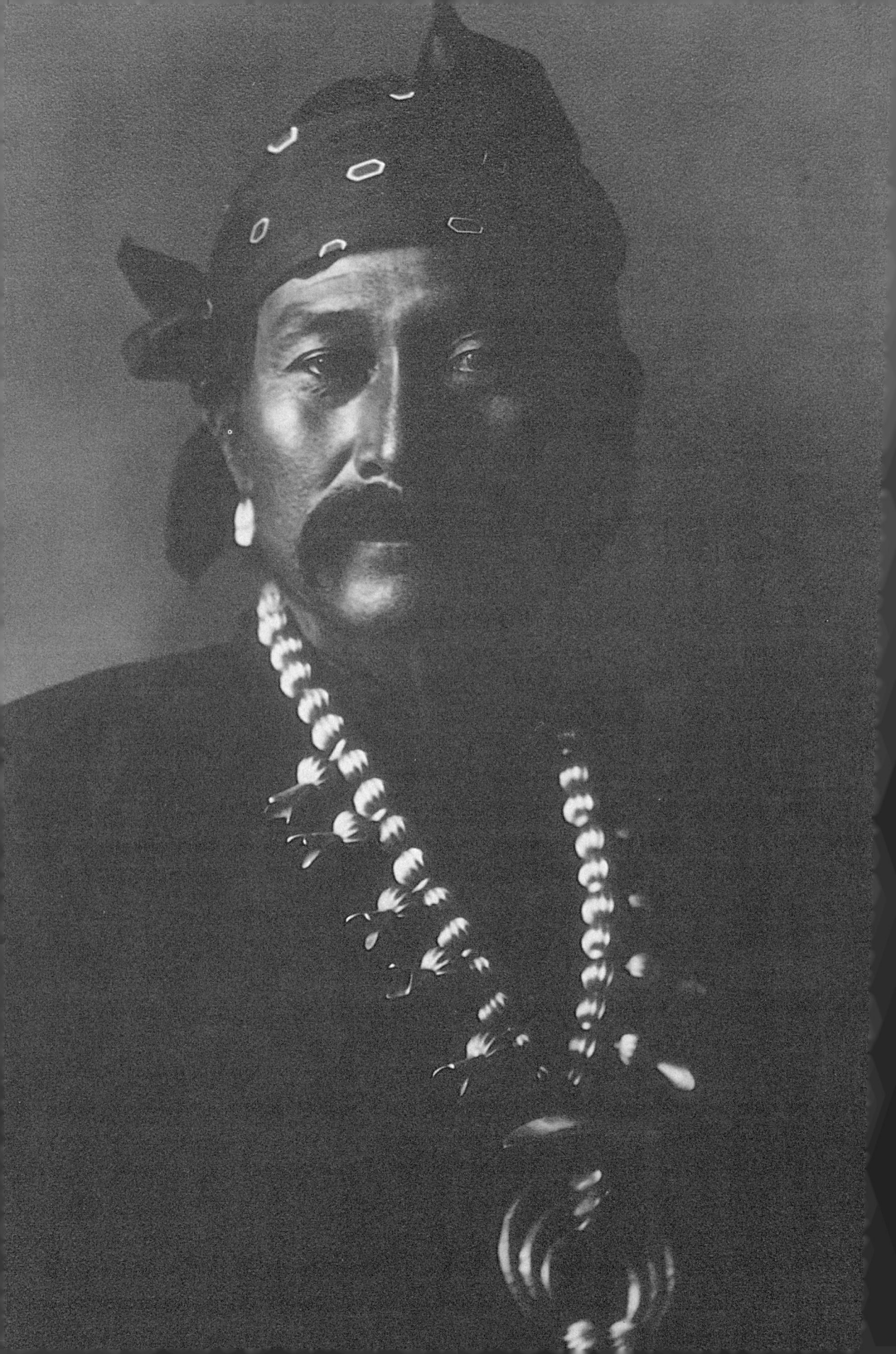

Photography of Navajo to Mid-Century

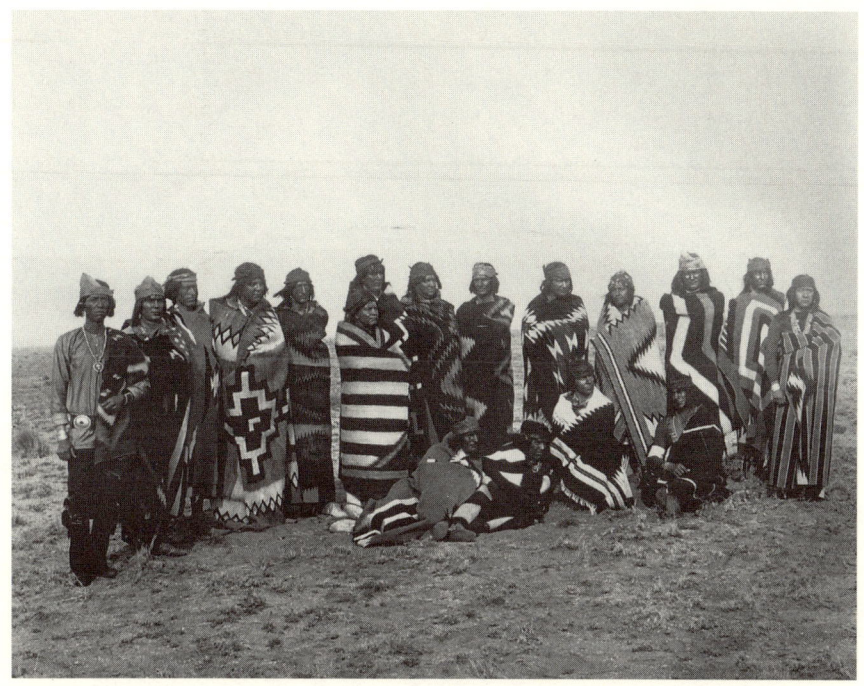
Figure 128

Figure 127. "Navajo Brigand, of the Black Mountain country." Carl Moon, photographer, 1903–1914. Moon gives no reason for assigning this label to this superb portrait of a very handsome man, but the man's downturned Mexican-style mustache and direct challenge to the lens help relay the label's message. The same necklace appears in other Moon portraits. Photograph reproduced from the Carl Moon Collections of The Huntington Library. Card No. 58.

Figure 128. "Indian Finery." Carl Moon, photographer, 1903-1914. Probably photographed when Moon had the El Tovar studio at Grand Canyon. This deliberate photograph has recently been reproduced from the photograph in a postcard, "Indians with Blankets" by Bob Wade, (oil on photo linen, 22" x 48"), with no credit to Moon. Photograph courtesy Wheelwright Museum of the American Indian. #60/23.

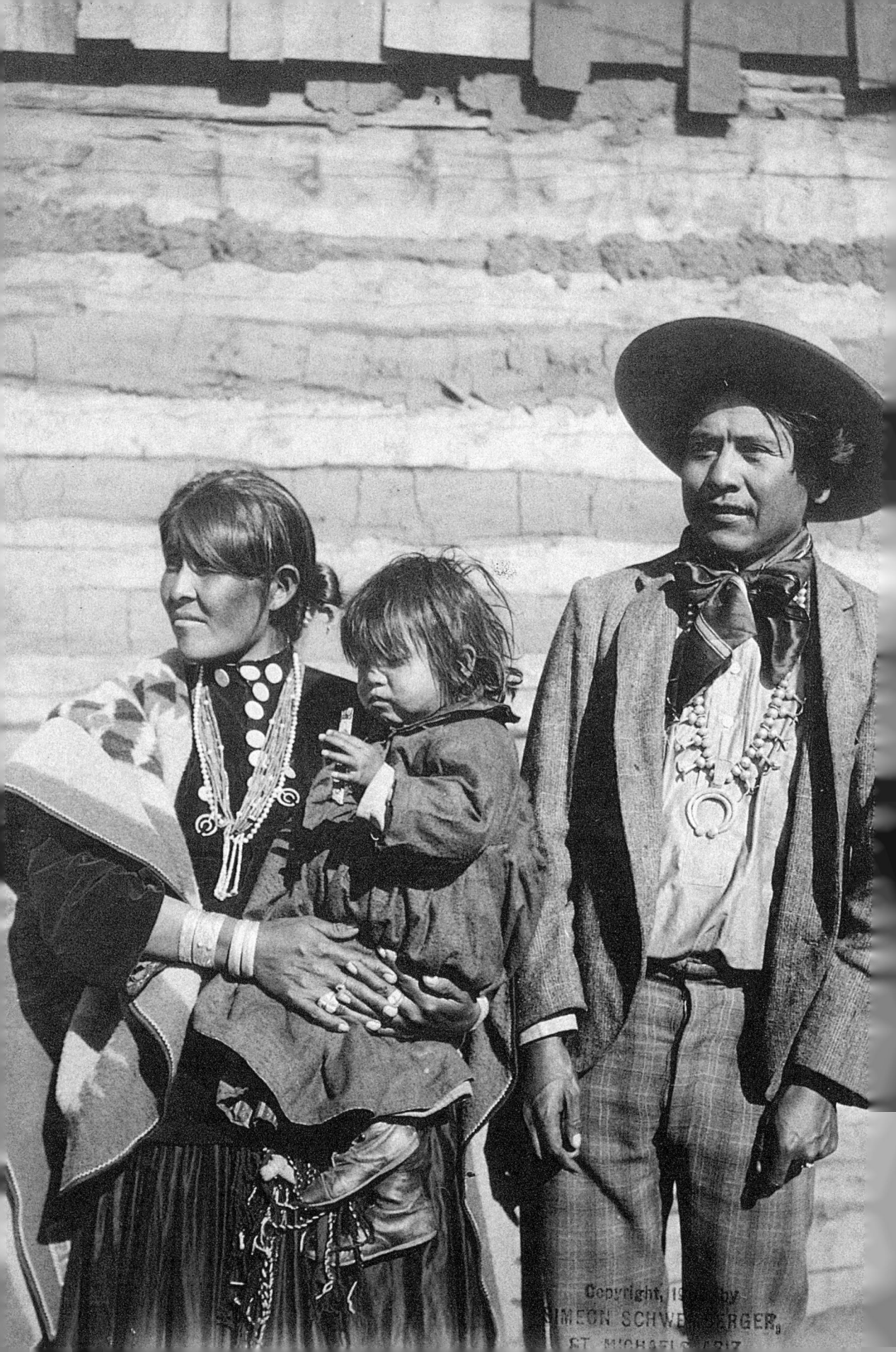

Photography of Navajo to Mid-Century

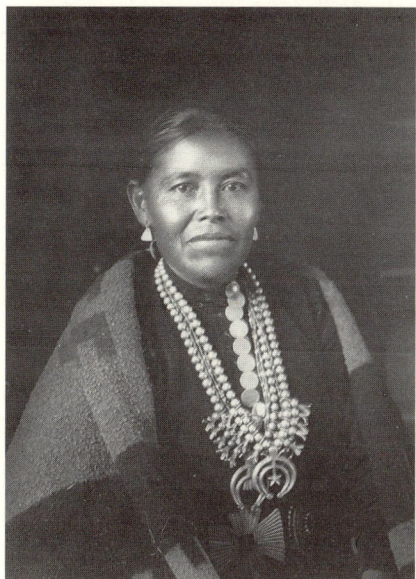

Figure 130

Figure 129. "Louis Watchman, Wife and Child. An educated Navajo, employed at Ft. Defiance, Ariz." Simeon Schwemberger, photographer, n.d. (ca. 1905). Schwemberger, a Franciscan, took many fine photographs—see Long, 1992. Photograph courtesy San Diego Museum of Man. #13909.

Figure 130. "Portrait of a Navajo woman." Photograph possibly by Carl Moon (but not attributed), n.d. This lovely portrait, very much in the Moon style, features additional jewelry and considerable darkroom retouching. It appears much later than Moon, as if it were a Parkhurst or Gilpin portrait. Fred Harvey Collection. Photograph courtesy National Museum of the American Indian, Smithsonian Institution. Neg. No. 31709.

Chapter 5

Figure 131. Navajo couple in wagon. Photographer unknown (Santa Fe Railway LA 373-22, perhaps William Simpson), n.d., near Agathla. This, and Figs. 118 and 132, both lean on the theme of Navajo disappearing into the distance—a motif first brought to prominence by Edward Curtis as the very icon of the "vanishing race." Of course, if Navajo are resistant, it is much easier to photograph them with their backs to the camera. Photograph courtesy Frank Waters Collection, Center for Southwest Research, General Library, University of New Mexico. No. 000-332-0190.

Figure 132. Navajo riders. Photographer unknown (Santa Fe Railway LA 373-29, perhaps William Simpson), n.d., Monument Valley AZ. See Fig. 131. Since at least one of these individuals may be the same as in Fig. 131, rather elaborate staging is suggested. Photograph courtesy Frank Waters Collection, Center for Southwest Research, General Library, University of New Mexico. No. 000-332-0191.

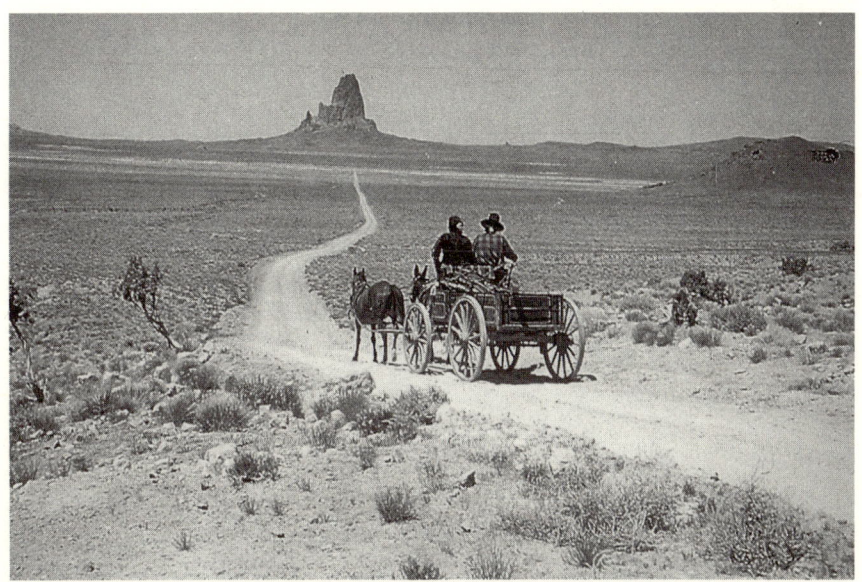

Figure 131

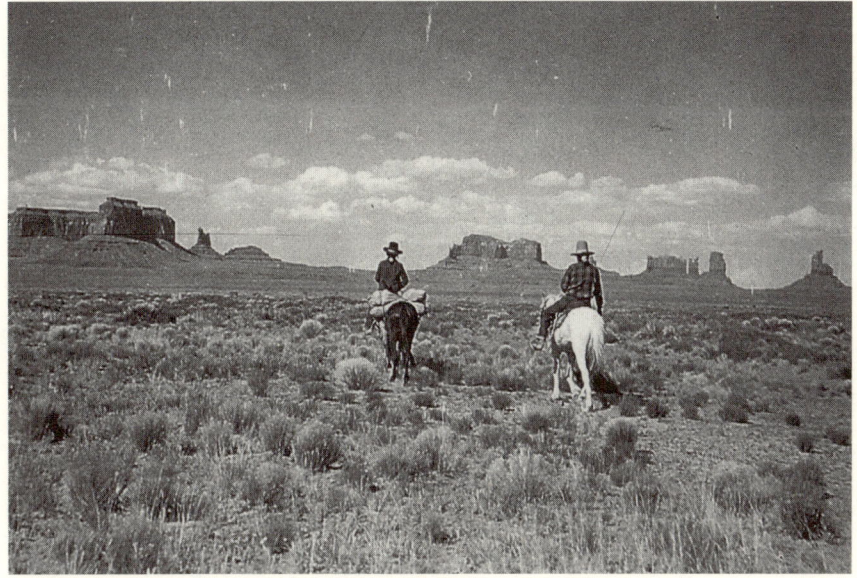

Figure 132

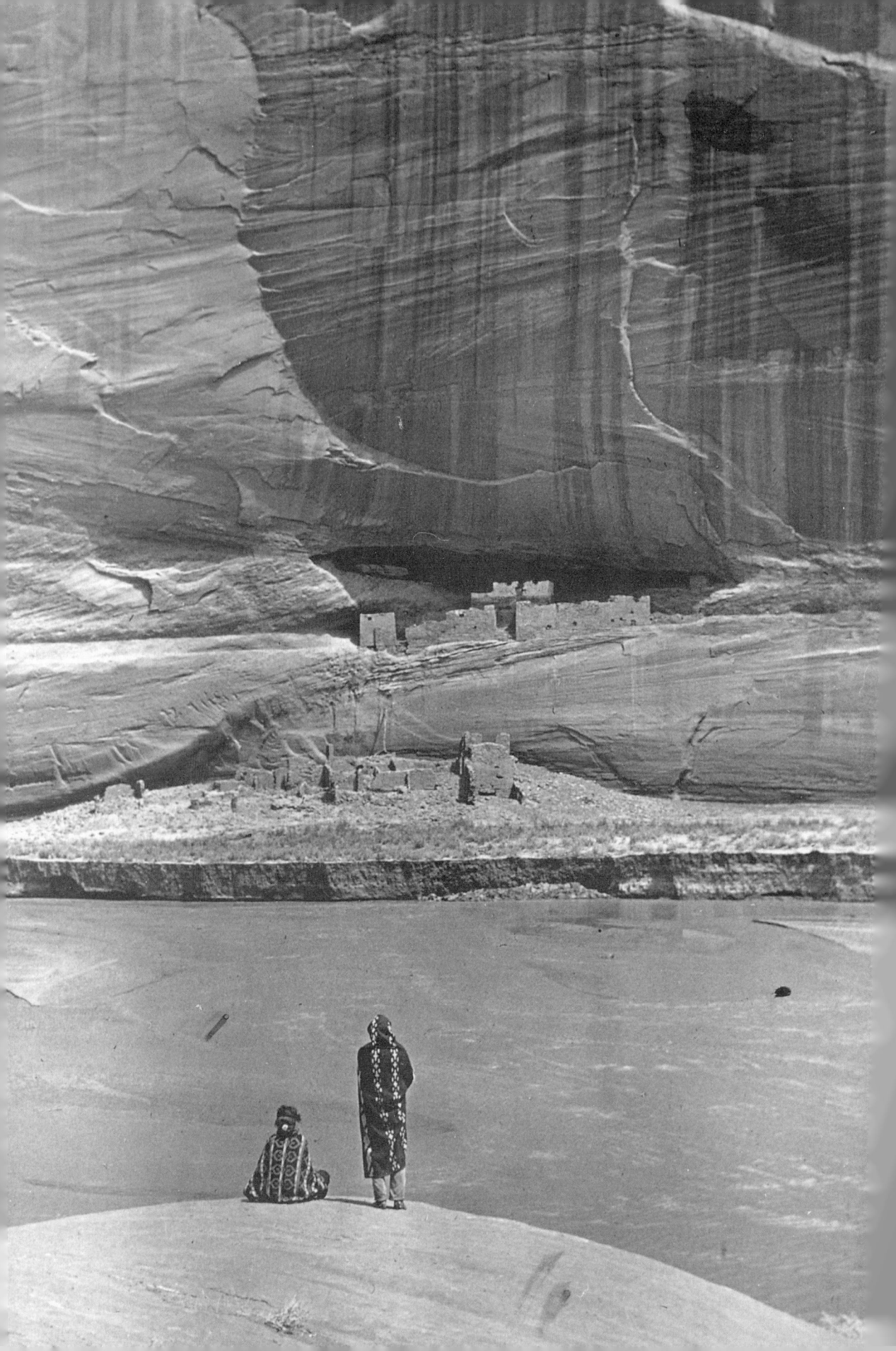

Photography of Navajo to Mid-Century

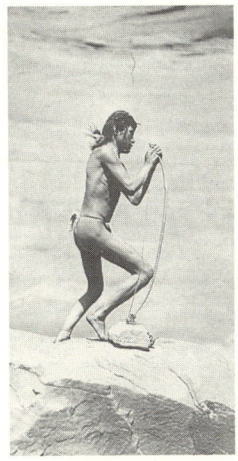

Figure 134

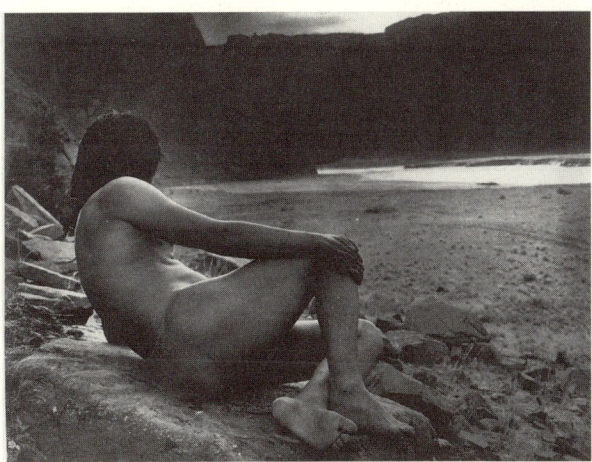

Figure 135

Figure 133. Two men (models) looking across wash at flood stage toward the White House, Canyon de Chelly. Photographer unknown (probably Roland W. Reed), n.d. (probably 1913). Photograph courtesy San Diego Museum of Man. #23041.

Figure 134. "Navajo stringing his bow." Roland W. Reed, photographer, n.d. (probably 1913). This young man posed for numerous Reed photographs. Photograph courtesy San Diego Museum of Man. #2212.

Figure 135. "The Dreamer, Canyon De Chelley. Nude, reclining, gazing at distant canyon walls through evening mist." Joseph K. Dixon, photographer, 4 July 1913. The breechcloth covering has been drawn onto the photograph. In the American Museum of Natural History Wanamaker Collection (No. 316442), a different breechcloth covering has been added to the same view. In both cases, however much these subjects were posed undressed, someone was determined to dress them, even if minimally, in the darkroom. Photograph courtesy William Hammond Mathers Museum, Indiana University. W3267.

Figure 133

Chapter 5

Figure 136. Three children with dog and sheepskin. Burton Frasher, photographer, n.d. The children seem cautious but at ease in this nice photograph. Photograph courtesy Staples Album, G. Reichard Collection, Museum of Northern Arizona. MS 22-14-p.79.

Figure 137. "Ad-de-sia, Nicholas, and Toe-hade-len, Runs Like The Water, standing on a fine Navajo saddle blanket, which I purchased. Toe-hade-len was very much afraid of the camera, and only consented to let me take his picture if Nicholas would stand with him. Even at that you can see the fear of the 'magic black box with the evil eye' on his face." Earle R. Forrest, photographer, August 1902, Meadows Trading Post, San Juan River NM. Note the attempt to get the men's Navajo names as well as those given them by Westerners (see Forrest, 1970). Photograph courtesy Earle R. Forrest Collection, Museum of Northern Arizona. MS 9-143-519.

Figure 138. "The young wife of Yellow Horse. I do not know how many wives he had, but this was a brand new one, and he was very proud of her. He wanted her picture taken, and she was not afraid of the camera. The Navajos in that section still practiced polygamy." Earle R. Forrest, photographer, August 1902, Sandoval's camp, San Juan River NM. This nice portrait is but one of many good and well-documented Forrest photographs taken in the Four Corners region of Navajoland at an early date (see Forrest, 1970). Photograph courtesy Earle R. Forrest Collection, Museum of Northern Arizona. MS 9-143-533.

Photography of Navajo to Mid-Century

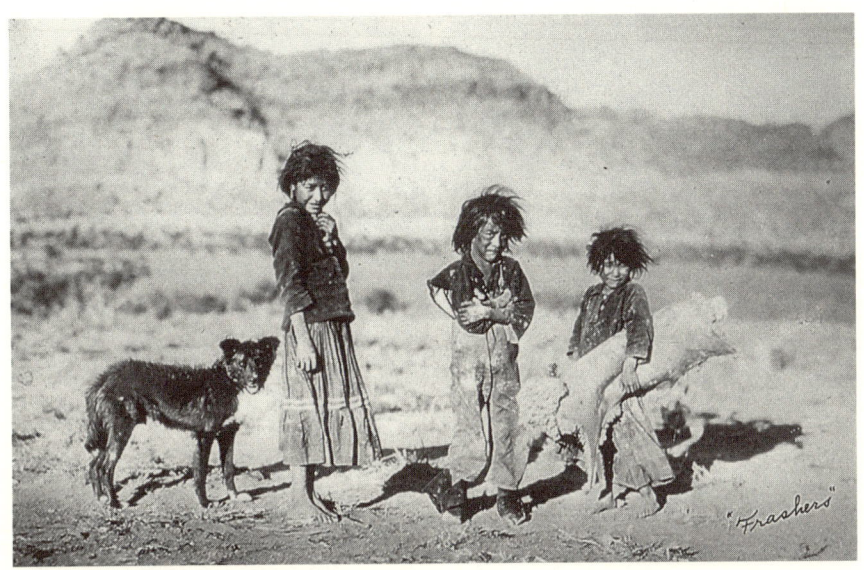

Figure 136

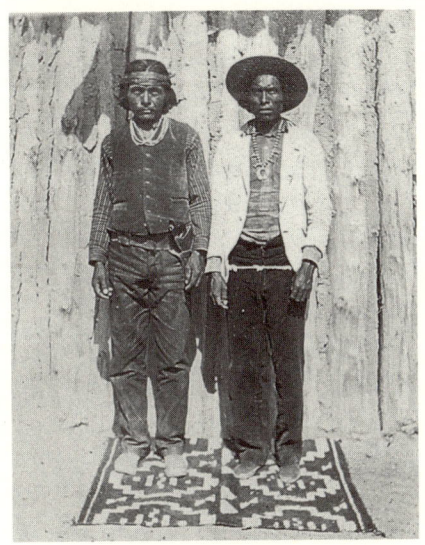

Figure 137

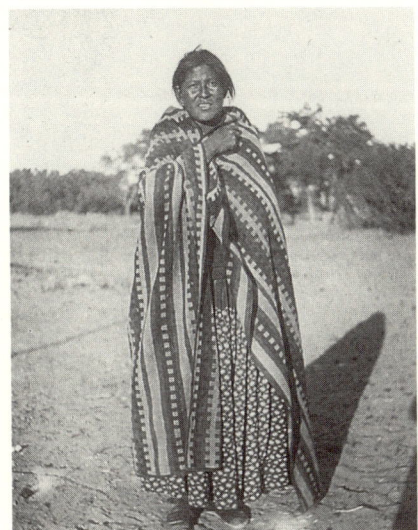

Figure 138

Chapter 5

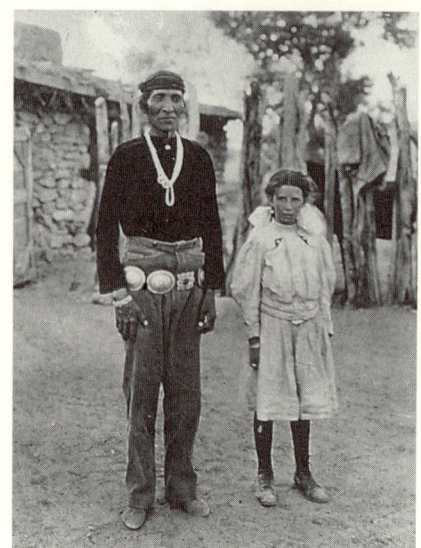

Figure 139

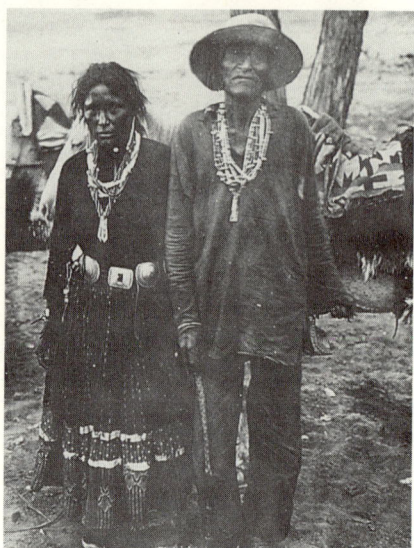

Figure 140

Figure 139. "Hoskinninni Begay and Ida Wetherill." Stuart M. Young, photographer, 1909, Oljato, UT. The son of an important leader in this region, with an important trader's daughter. Both appear to have been coaxed into the photograph. See also Figs. 62 and 140. Photograph courtesy Museum of Northern Arizona. MS 10-2-20; E-200.10.

Figure 140. "Hoskinnini and wife." Photographer unknown (perhaps Stuart Young or Neil Judd), 1908 or 1909, Oljato. This photograph is similiar to one taken by Neil Judd, who says Hoskinnini avoided any photographs of himself until 1909. Judd (1968:39) states "when Hoskininni died five weeks later, [a] photograph was blamed for his death." See Fig. 139. Photograph courtesy Arizona State Museum, University of Arizona. #PIX276.

Figure 141. "An Old Warrior." William Carpenter, photographer, copyright claimant, 1915. This is actually a Pennington studios photograph , 1914. This man, Bi-joshii, one leader of the earlier Beautiful Mountain rebellion in 1913 against BIA assimilationist attempts (see McNitt, 1962:347-358), was frequently solicited for photographs in silly caricatures. Photograph courtesy Museum of New Mexico. Neg. No. 89508. Photograph reproduced from the Collections of the Library of Congress. LOC LC-USZ62-99575.

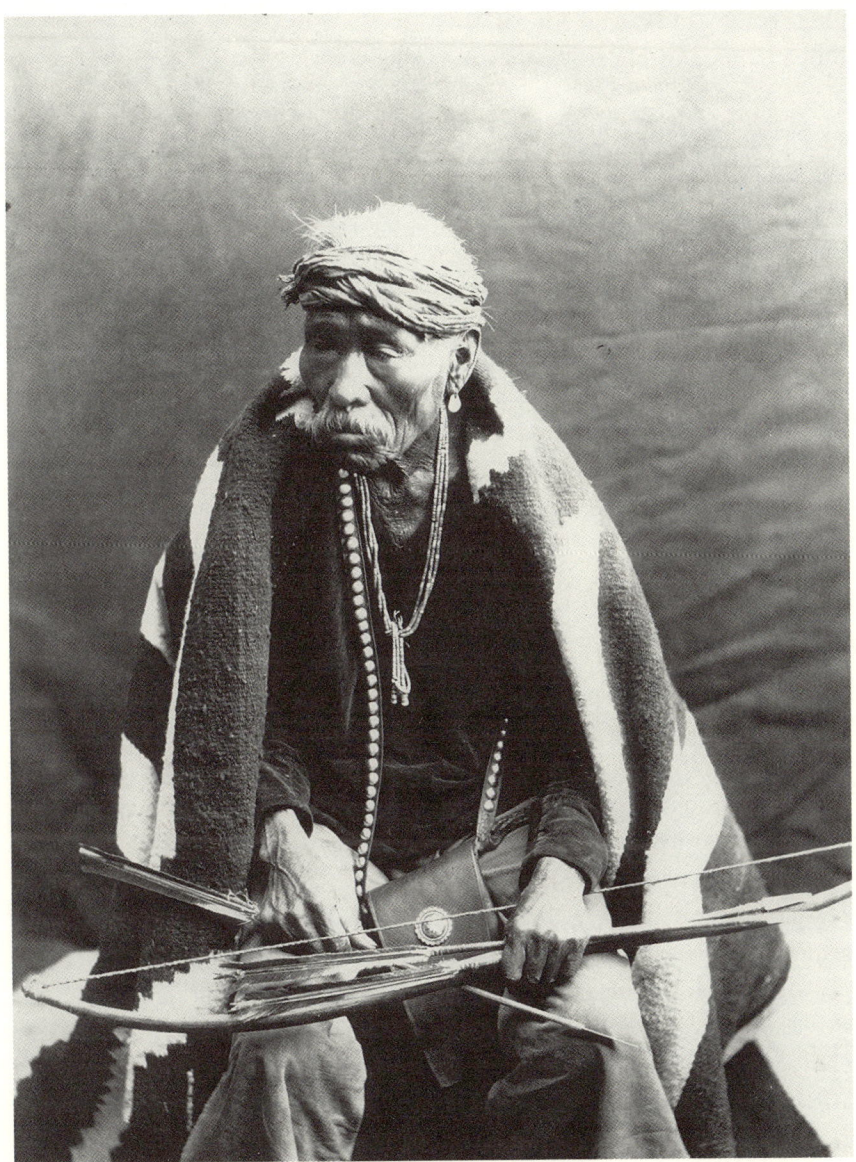

Figure 141

Chapter 5

**Photography of Navajo After 1920:
Bureaucrats, Postal cards, and Color Slides**

By the 1920s, the early enthusiasms (and some excesses) were over, and the lantern slide lecture format faded. This was replaced by the Keystone view, the commercial slide series, and the postcard with more photographic detail of Navajo life. Bureaucrats, nurses, teachers, engineers, anthropologists, and, as always, traders became more constant and consistent sources of photographs. A host of unpublished significant collections were produced by other amateurs, such as William Sassaman and Alden Stevens in 1929, L. W. Smith in 1933, and Leone Kessler in the 1930s. The first road engineer of the Navajo Service, Norman Conway, and his wife, Virginia, a nurse, left a series of labeled photographs from the period.

The traders Franc Newcomb, Gladwell Richardson, Tom Kirk, Sally Lippincott (Wagner), and Elizabeth Compton Hegemann gave us remarkable photographic series indeed—sometimes comprising several hundred images[17]—and other trader families had their own private collections (many as yet unresearched). These valuable photos usually name their Navajo subjects (frequently friends of the photographer) and have a less formal and more candid character than images taken by professionals (though in Hegemann's photographs the same necklace appears on individual after individual). Trader relations are sometimes evident, and Navajo homes often had copies of these views on display, along with those from formal studio sittings solicited by Navajo themselves in border towns.

Following statehood, both New Mexico and Arizona launched official magazines (which eventually became *New Mexico Magazine* and *Arizona Highways*) that were important and consistent sources of photographs and picture stories of native peoples. These publications catered explicitly to tourists, so photography was picturesque, commercial, and promotional, designed to attract people to the Southwest for investment, holidays, or retirement. Chart 1 indicates that dozens and dozens of photographers published with these magazines over the years.[18]

Katie Field, a rancher's daughter, married a Navajo man, John Guerro of the Alamo Navajo Reservation, in the 1930s, and took a remarkable series of candid photographs depicting Navajo ranching and other activities from a little-known and isolated area (see Fig. 142). Indeed, this material, emphasizing the well-documented extended family of her Navajo relatives, merits more research and is the subject of recent historical inquiry.[19]

In the 1920s more rich amateurs and intellectuals began traveling to the

Photography of Navajo to Mid-Century

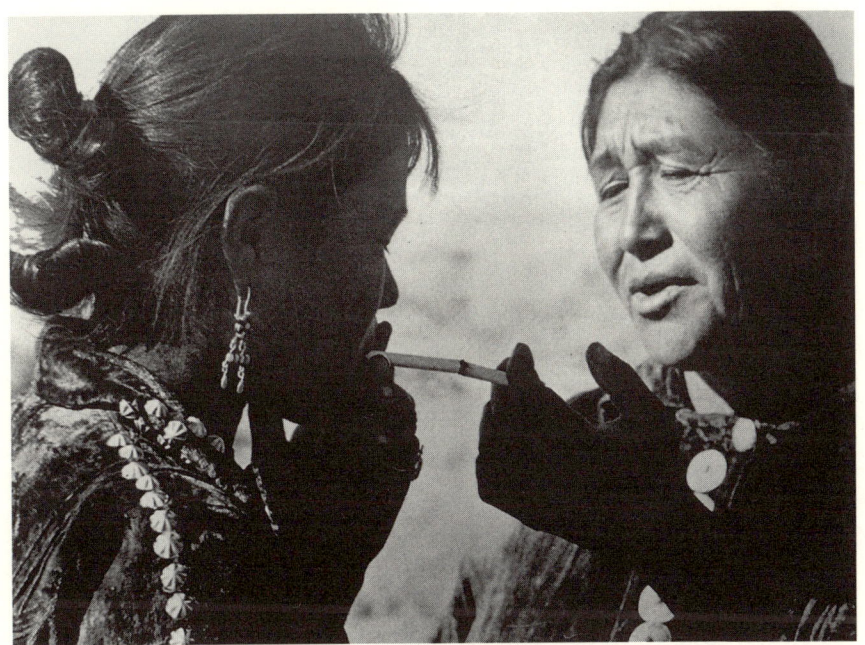

Figure 142

Figure 142. Two women lighting cigarettes from one another. Photographer unknown, n.d. Possibly Alamo Navajo community. These two women are far too involved in their lighting task to be aware of the photographer, probably because the photographer is some distance away and using a long-focus lens. Photograph courtesy Wheelwright Museum of the American Indian. #60/2372.

area for periods—such as the Californians Mary and Dane Coolidge, Laura Armer, and easterners Adelarde Law and Mary Cabot Wheelwright.[20] The Coolidges wrote of their travels and attempted some stimulating syntheses[21] with their numerous historically interesting and informative photographs. Most of these individuals photographed Navajo healing ceremonials with abandon, leaning on their ties to specific medicine men (again, commonly brokered by traders [Franc J. Newcomb in the case of Mary Wheelwright]),[22] firm local friendships, or extraordinary amounts of money (see Fig. 143). Armer even had a house built on the Hopi reservation and patronized a number of important medicine men in the western region of Navajoland. Armer, however, also an artist and successful photographer,[23] kept alive a soft-focus romanticism in some of her work, and revived external posing conventions not seen since Curtis, Moon, and Roland Reed (nude males, pastoral pictorialism). She also left abundant photographs of Navajo ceremonials[24] and made one of the earliest ciné films of a Navajo chantway, a Mountain Chant, in 1928.

Arizona photographer Forman Hanna resurrected the nude in the 1930s, though this is not, to my knowledge, illustrated in his photography of Navajo.[25] Sally Lippincott (today Sally Wagner), who with her husband owned the Wide Ruins trading post for a period, left a significant collection of photographs from the 1930s. She championed local weavers and artists, documenting a great deal of local weaving. She also photographed Navajo artists locally and on trips elsewhere (see Figs. 144, 145).

Various forms of spiritualism were in vogue at this point. Many individuals were interested in Navajo healing, and their work became a focus of dubious scholarship; Wheelwright in particular was a sponsor of research. The art colonies of Santa Fe and Taos were also becoming popular, attracting visitors (such as poet and translator Witter Bynner) who photographed Navajo as part of that ambience. Art and amateur scholarship easily mixed for these people, and their photographically illustrated publications stimulated interest in what were considered the exotic aspects of Navajo culture. As a consequence of this embrace (as if Navajo didn't have enough trouble during this period of heavy government involvement—including the devastating stock-reduction programs of BIA commissioner John Collier),[26] Navajo became a favorite focus of the Jungians.[27]

In the nineteenth century, the Franciscans at St. Michaels Mission established what is today the most substantial collection of photography of Navajo extant (outside the Snow and Concho collections of the Navajo Nation Museum). Schwemberger added hundreds of very good photographs after the turn of the century, and the collections constantly grew, with photographs of confirmation, catechism, and communion classes, of school activities, of weddings and festivals and socials, of parents visiting their children, and of nuns and priests in instructional and pastoral visits (see Portfolio V). These archives are not well known, however, and although most of the Schwemberger portions of the St. Michaels collections have been researched and attempts to catalog them all have begun,[28] they are largely inaccessible (though sizable portions of are reproduced in the photographic archives of the Museum of Northern Arizona and the Arizona State Museum). But it remains a remarkable record of Navajo/church relations over one hundred years. Unfortunately, many photographs are poorly labeled or even unlabeled, and except for some of the early Schwemberger photographs, photographer attributions and the names of individuals are often missing.[29]

The most substantial collection of photographs of Navajo of any period is located at the Navajo Nation Museum (formerly Navajo Tribal Museum) in the work of Milton (Jack) Snow and his successors and collaborators. These photographs span a period from the 1930s until the 1960s, when agencies of the Navajo and federal bureaucracies began to keep their own images (today official photographs taken at events and places in Navajoland are widely dispersed in a host of Navajo Nation and Bureau of Indian Affairs [BIA] offices). In the 1930s, the BIA established the central Navajo capital at Window Rock (previously, several semiautonomous territorially-based superintendents had shared control); inaugurated the tribal council/chapter system of Navajo government; built roads, dams, hospitals, and schools across the reservation; and realized they needed to document their accomplishments if the appropriations were going to continue. The Soil Conservation Service hired Milton Snow as its photographer to this end. Later the various different federal agencies at work in Navajoland were merged into one unit, known as the Navajo Agency (or Navajo Service), under the BIA, and Snow was retained as staff photographer. With mission expanded beyond range and soil conditions, Snow built a moving darkroom in his panel truck and, with Navajo assistants as interpreters, photographed far and wide across Navajoland on agency business. He and some of his successors, however, went much beyond the bounds of their assignments, producing tens of thousands of photographs[30] of just about every conceivable public activity. Some photographs appear to have been taken largely for aesthetic reasons or as a consequence of personal relations with individuals (Figs. 146–156).

Snow left a remarkably well-documented collection (in comparison, for example, to the poorly documented collections of many other substantial

Chapter 5

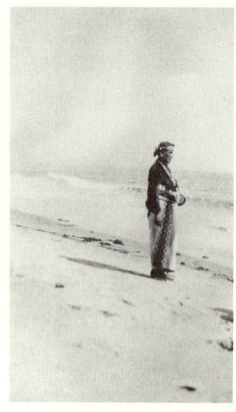
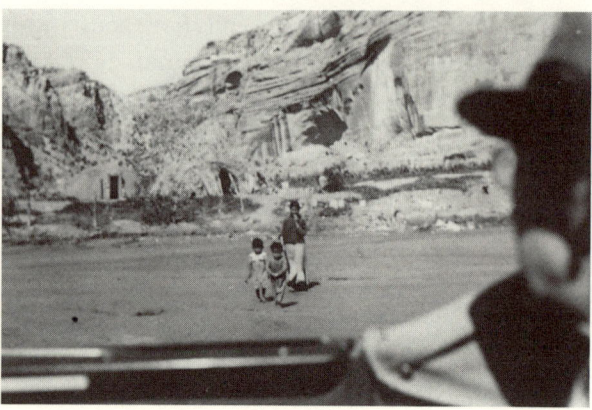

Figure 143   Figure 144

Figure 143. Hosteen Klah, at Pacific Ocean, Santa Barbara. Photographer unknown (probably Mary Wheelwright), 1927. A visit, with Wheelwright, to the western ocean, where Klah collected water from the Pacific and carried out a blessing. Photograph courtesy Wheelwright Museum of the American Indian. WM/Santa Barbara/Wheelwright Album XVI.

Figure 144. "Navajo Indians. Canyon de Chelly, Arizona." Sally Lippincott, photographer, 1938. Navajos may have been summoned to the convertible automobile so the photograph might be taken, or they may have been called over for another purpose, only to have the photograph taken opportunistically and without permission. Photograph courtesy Museum of New Mexico. No. 11251.

Figure 145. "Joe Toddy from Wide Ruins AZ at zoo in Colorado Springs CO." Photograph probably by Sally Lippincott, ca. 1939. Toddy, the father of Beatin Yazz, was probably with Lippincott in Colorado Springs to further his son's artistic career, perhaps through the Taylor Museum. This diversionary activity with an orangutan is undoubtedly innocent, but it is interesting that it is not a European-American photographed with the ape. Photograph courtesy Museum of New Mexico, Neg. No. 3153.

Photography of Navajo to Mid-Century

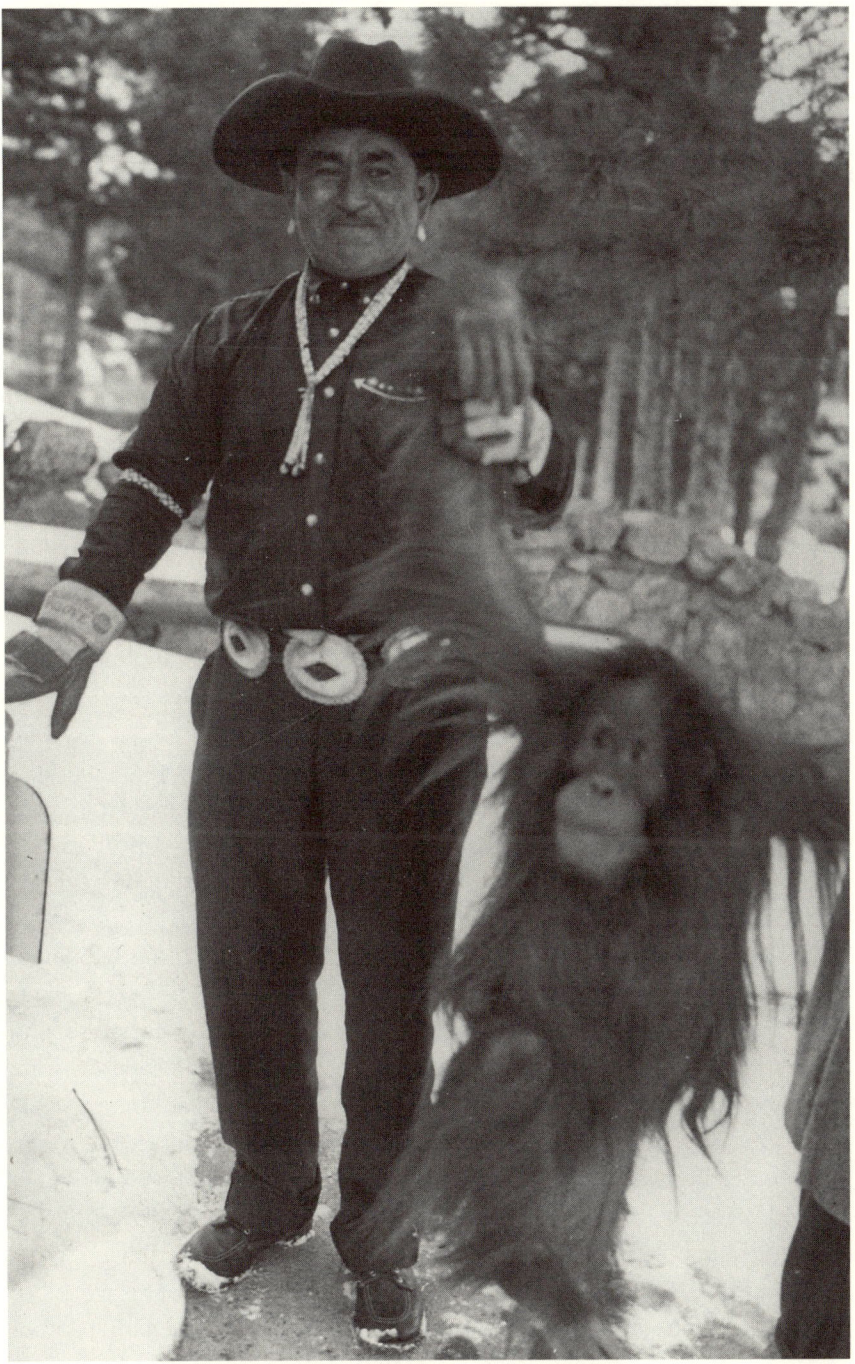

Figure 145

Chapter 5

photographers of Navajo, such as Kluckhohn or Gilpin, or the Franciscans of St. Michaels). He rarely failed to note the name of the person in the photograph, and he very commonly sent copies to his subjects, so the locations and times and circumstances are recorded. He did not attempt to photograph sacred events or practices and always asked permission to photograph. Often his work was published not only in government reports but also in nongovernment publications on Navajo. In many of these, however, the photographs are simply credited to "United States Indian Service." Snow appears not to have been overly ambitious, and only once did he publish a portfolio of his work, which he appended to a Guggenheim application to seek additional training and further pursue his craft in 1941.

Snow was afflicted with cerebral palsy, so photography was a challenge. He did not normally use a cable release, though he did occasionally balance the camera on the truck. He trained his Navajo assistants in his cataloguing scheme and taught some to photograph, print, and work in the darkroom (Faris/Gale, October 1991—see Fig. 151). Some of these aides became artists (Andy Tsinajinnie, Hoke Dennetsosi) and photographers (J. Tapaha). Snow credits others, both Navajo and non-Navajo, who helped him photograph, including Lucy Oppen, Tom Allen, Jim Thomas, H. Clay Lockett, Mike Brodi, Sombrero, and Marie Martin.

Jack Snow unquestionably was a dedicated employee. He went about documenting range conditions so others could argue for the stock-reduction program, and he photographed various forms of assimilationist propaganda encouraging Navajos to go into debt, take jobs out of Navajoland, eat differently, speak English, buy war bonds, volunteer to fight (see Portfolio V),[31] adapt, or simply to do what they normally did (weaving, farming, animal husbandry) in ways Westerners deemed more appropriate (Portfolio V, Figs. 152, 153). But he tried to avoid posing people any more than he had to, and he was said never to have photographed people without their permission, regardless of the assignment. He left no photographs that are oppressively close up, that reveal individuals in embarrassing circumstances, that compromise the dignity of people. Moreover, his interest in Navajo employment and welfare seemed to extend beyond his photographic assignment, and there are vague hints of critical commentary in some of his photographs.

The extent to which he understood the surveillance aspect of his work can be seen in his photographic classification scheme. Snow placed all his photographs into sixteen major categories, with the following internal divisions.[32]

NA Agriculture (423 total)
1. animal husbandry (32)
2. dairies (33)
3. farms (87)
4. irrigation (87)
5. gardens (53)
6. land erosion (9)
7. farming practices (45)
8. Tribal flour mills (32)
9. orchards (6)
10. poultry (6)
11. Shiprock Nursery (33)

NB Archaeology and Antiquities (25 total)

NC Arts and Crafts (588 total)
1. ceramics (0)
2. drawings, paintings (45)
3. Navajo Arts and Crafts Guild (159)
4. leatherwork (19)
7. stone carving (1)
8. silversmithing (84)
9. weaving (221)
10. woodworking (51)
11. unclassified (8)

NE Architecture, Navajo and BIA (1889 total)
1. hogan, abandoned (3)
3. hogans, ceremonial (5)
4. hogans, storage (13)
5. hogans, summer (27)
6. hogans, sweat (2)
7. hogans, tent (58)
8. hogans, winter (192)
9. hogans, interior (43)
10. hospital (84)

11. hospital projects (51)
12. missions (6)
13. Navajo Service (263)
14. boarding schools (354)
15. day schools (116)
17. warehouse, storehouse (41)
18. trading posts (233)
19. Window Rock headquarters, etc.
20. unclassified (181)

NF Education (4054 total)
1. adult education (113)
2. arts and crafts (90)
3. classrooms (371)
4. home economics (140)
5. airs, exhibits (1447)
6. first aid, childcare classes (84)
7. copies of old photos (65)
8. vocational education (173)
9. libraries (5)
10. missions (16)
11. motion pictures (121)
12. music (3)
13. pre-induction training (10)
14. physical education (191)
15. school living, waiting in lines (141)
17. youth groups and activities (585)
18. school activities (499)

NG Engineering (2036 total)
1. building construction (486)
2. draughting (20)
3. electrical (19)
4. irrigation (318)
5. land subjugation (53)
6. mining (107)
7. radio and telecommunications (35)
8. road construction (395)

Chapter 5

10. soil conservation (478)
11. water supply (125)

NH Ethnology (94 total)
1. ethnology, general (37)
2. costume (8)
3. material culture (2)
4. customs (47)

NI Forestry (803 total)
1. forests (311)
2. fire fighting (22)
3. erosion (10)
4. logging (74)
5. practices (39)
6. pre-fire suppression (29)
7. tribal sawmill (303)
9. aerial photos (11)
10. unclassified (4)

NK Health (690 total)
1. general health (91)
2. dental (14)
3. nursing (45)
4. nutrition (74)
5. various hospital interiors (64)
6. maternity (33)
7. anitation (123)
8. surgery (6)
9. trachoma (101)
10. tuberculosis (139)

NM Public Safety (309 total)
2. courts (5)
3. police (13)
4. law enforcement (117)
5. unclassified (174)

NO People (2727 total)
1. babies, most identified (36)
2. children, most identified (39)
3. students, most identified (228)
4. men, most identified (184)
5. women, most identified (92)
6. family groups (132)
7. military (151)
8. crowds (99)
9. celebrities
10. meetings, Navajo Service (97)
11. Tribal Council (1270)

NN Livestock (1102 total)
1. mules (16)
2. cattle (214)
3. Tribal cannery (33)
4. goats (8)
5. horses (204)
7. sheep (187)
8. sheep and goats, mixed (115)
9. sheep, types (69)
11. sheep, dipping and shearing (207)
12. SW Sheep Breeding Lab (17)
13. sheep butchering (32)

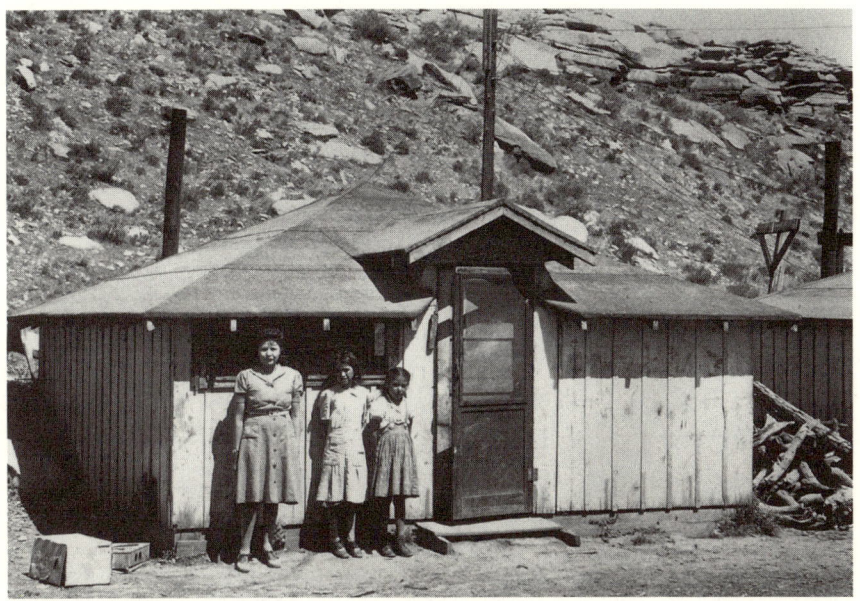

Figure 146

Figure 146. "House #79 in 'Rat Row,' Navajo employees' housing." Milton Snow, photographer, 19 June 1945, Fort Defiance AZ. BIA assimilation. See Fig. 105 to contrast with European-American employee housing of the time. Photograph courtesy Milton Snow Collection, Navajo Nation Museum, Window Rock AZ. NE 13-16.

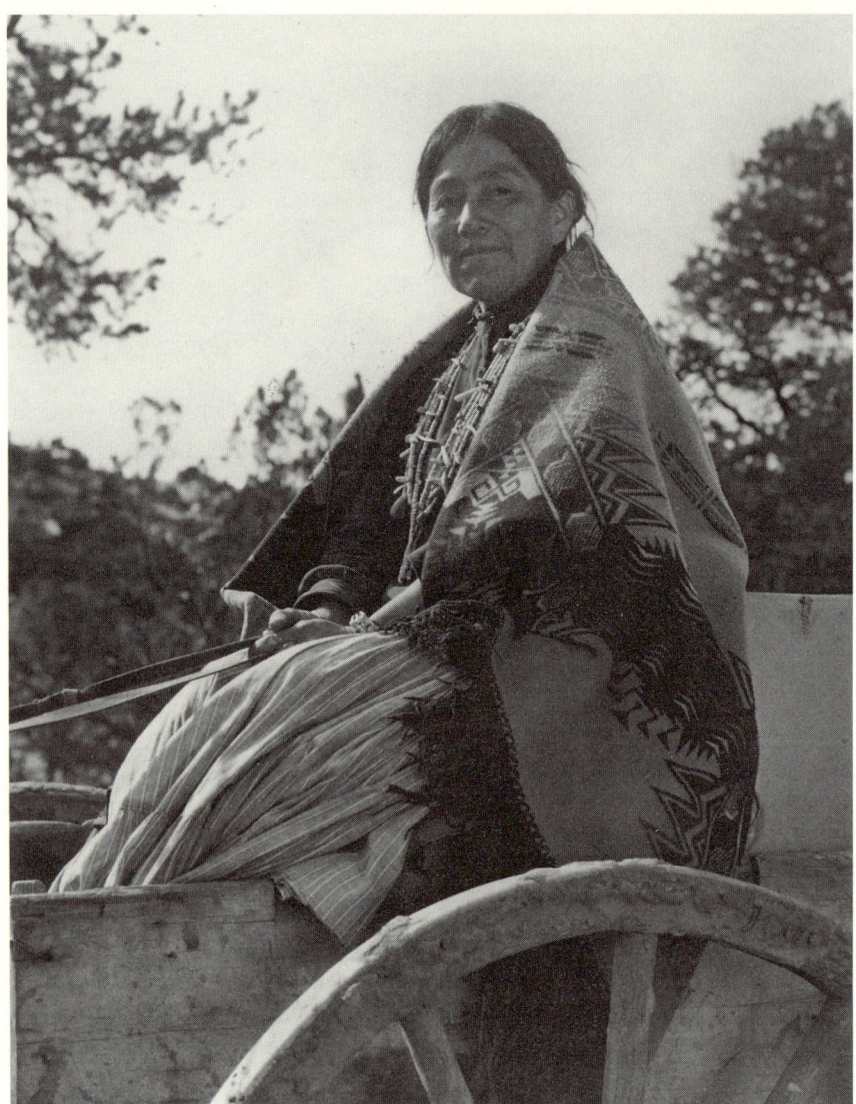

Figure 147

Figure 147. Navajo woman driving wagon. Milton Snow, photographer, n.d. A dignified grand photograph in heroic style of a confident (but unnamed) woman. Photograph courtesy Maxwell Museum of Anthropology, Selgem Number 67.128.2

Photography of Navajo to Mid-Century

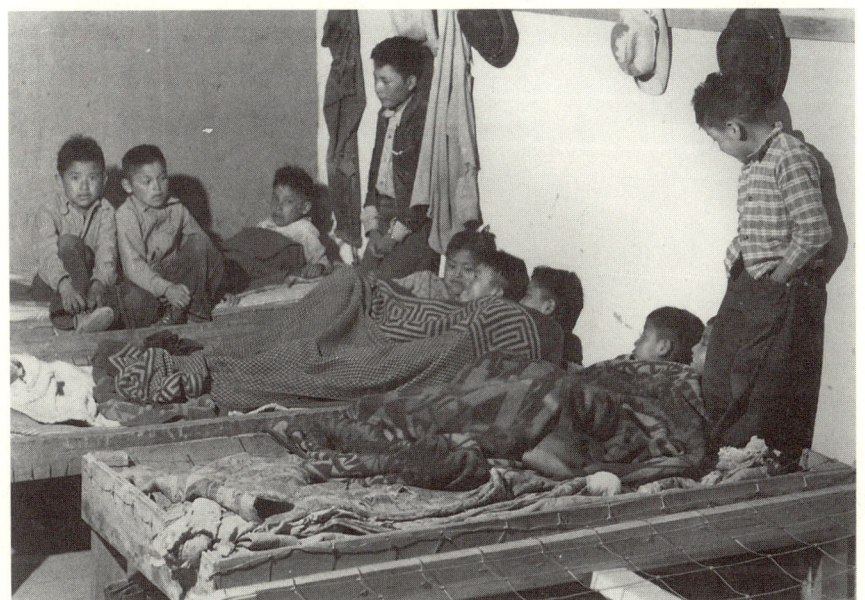

Figure 148

Figure 148. "Coyote Canyon Day School. Chapter house used as dorm as buses no longer run." Milton Snow, photographer, 29 October 1944. Snow does not say why buses no longer run. Beds made from fencing wire. Photograph courtesy Milton Snow Collection, Navajo Nation Museum, Window Rock AZ. NF 16-9.

Chapter 5

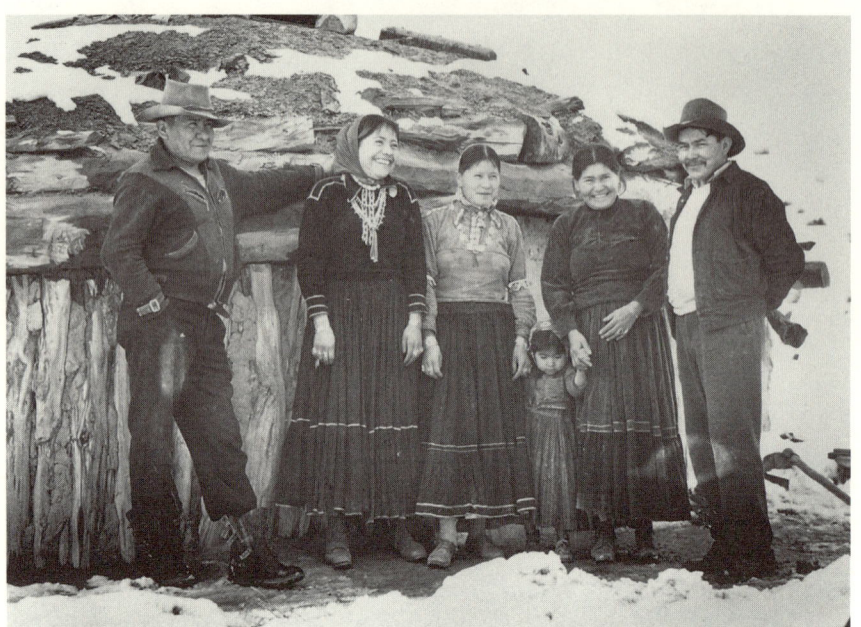

Figure 149

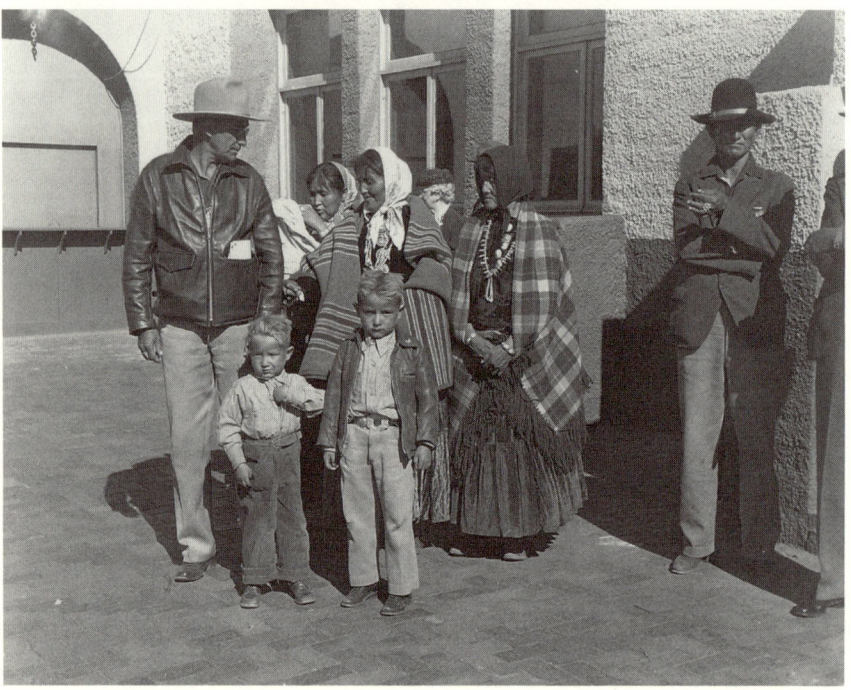

Figure 150

Figure 149. "*Frank Whitegoat's farm.*" *Milton Snow, photographer, 22 January 1945.* "*Seven miles north of Rocky Point Trading Post on Highway 66.*" *Frank Mitchell is at right. These people are clearly comfortable with the photographer, though the pose is conventional. Photograph courtesy Milton Snow Collection, Navajo Nation Museum, Window Rock AZ. NO 6-49.*

Figure 150. Billy Norton and family. Milton Snow, photographer, 10 May 1946, Gallup NM. Billy Norton, an important medicine man, was the offspring of a Fort Wingate soldier who married into an important Navajo family. Billy had two wives, illustrated here, and was one of the most photographed of Navajo medicine men, as he frequently traveled to demonstrate sandpainting to European American audiences, though when I interviewed him a year before he died (see Faris, 1990:96) he no longer spoke any English. Snow, significantly, photographed Billy without 'costume', while in the anthropological corpus, photographs of Norton and his family always required appropriate 'native dress' (cf. Wyman, in WM collections). Photograph courtesy Milton Snow Collection, Navajo Nation Museum, Window Rock AZ. NO 6-62.

Chapter 5

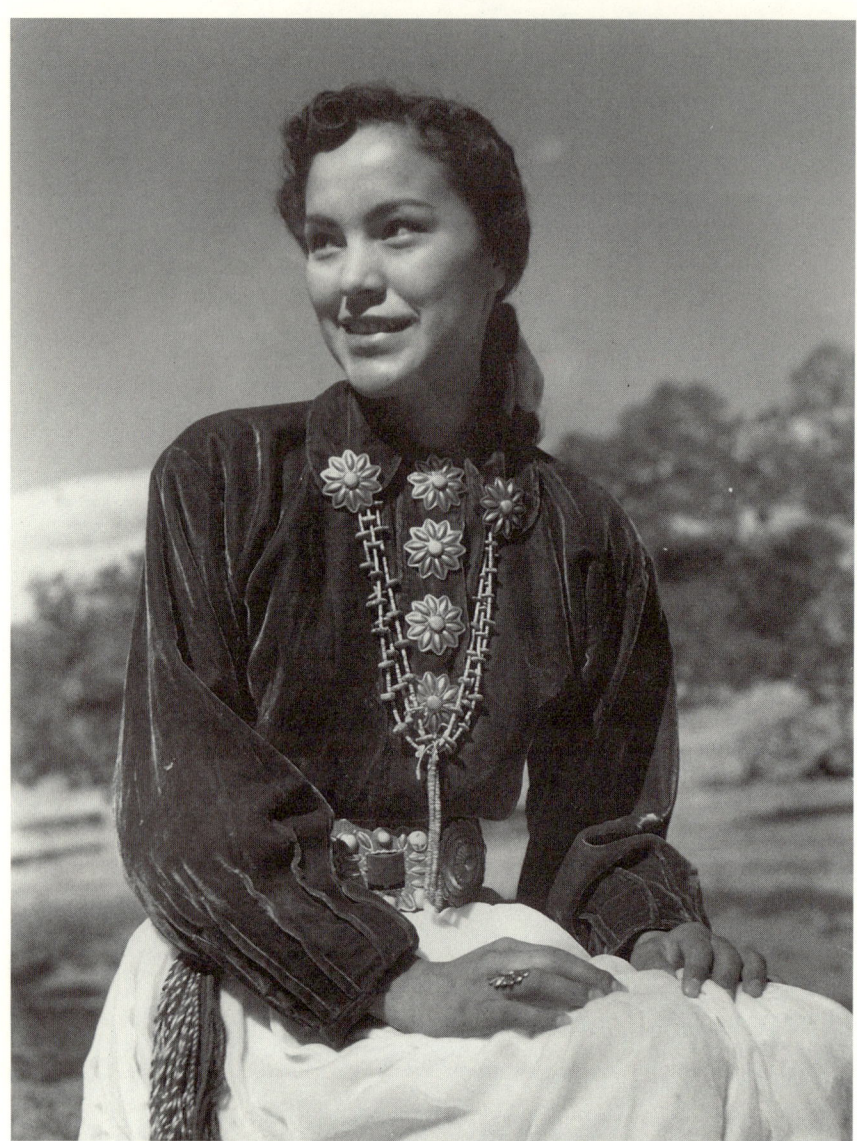

Figure 151

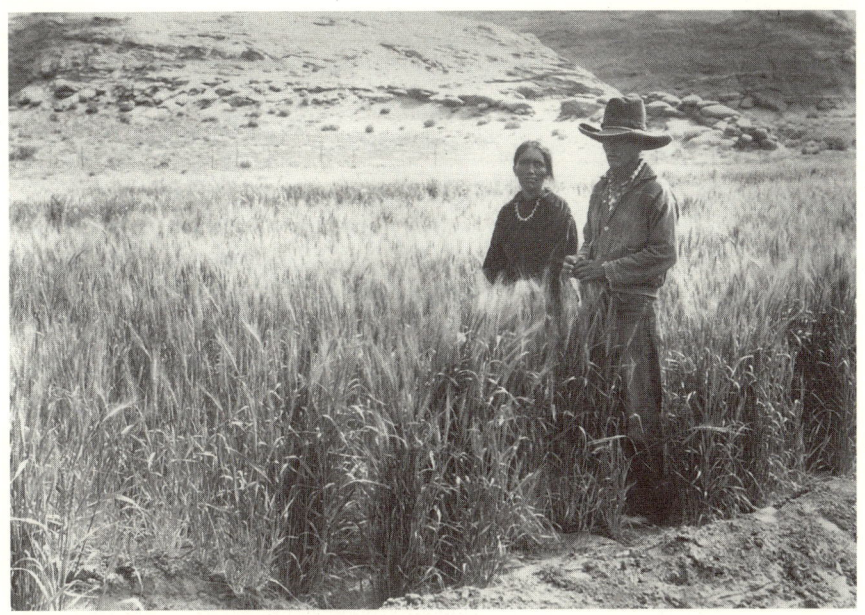

Figure 152

Figure 151. "Ida Mary Gail. 1953 Navajo Queen." Milton Snow, photographer. This young woman from Red Lake worked for Snow both in filing and in processing film. Snow taught her photography, but she confined her work primarily (and significantly) to photography of family and friends. See J. Faris/Ida Gail, October 1991. Photograph courtesy Milton Snow Collection, Navajo Nation Museum, Window Rock AZ. NF 5-1087C.

Figure 152. "Wheat crop of 1937 at Rock Point subjugation area. Growth of winter wheat. Tenants proud of their crop." Milton Snow, photographer (with D. A. Rogers), 26 June 1937. Archie Begay and wife. It is not explained why Navajo are "tenants" on their own land. This is one more U.S. government attempt to turn Navajo into farmers, a persistent pressure since the Bosque Redondo era. Photograph courtesy Milton Snow Collection, Navajo Nation Museum, Window Rock AZ. NA 4-26.

Chapter 5

Figure 153. "The Navajo Indians, although primarily sheepherders, plant their corn on dry farms along the Little Colorado River in Arizona." Tad Nichols, photographer, n.d. (1940s). Both men and women are clearly busy in the task. This appears to be a virgin site, maybe one more experiment inaugurated and encouraged by the government. Photograph courtesy University of Arizona Library Special Collections. No number.

Figure 154. "Off Reservation Employment. These are sugar beet field workers in Richfield UT. More and more Indian people are taking advantage of off-reservation employment opportunities extended through private sources, the State employment services and the Bureau of Indian Affairs." Milton Snow, photographer, n.d. From appearances here, Navajo are working under any conditions—even as migrant agricultural labor. Note also here Snow's juxtaposition of a senior and a junior woman, fixing the traditional/modern hierarchy. Photograph courtesy National Archives, Washington. NA/BIA/R75 N/Prints: Navajo A-Navajo D. Box 23. (5). NA.

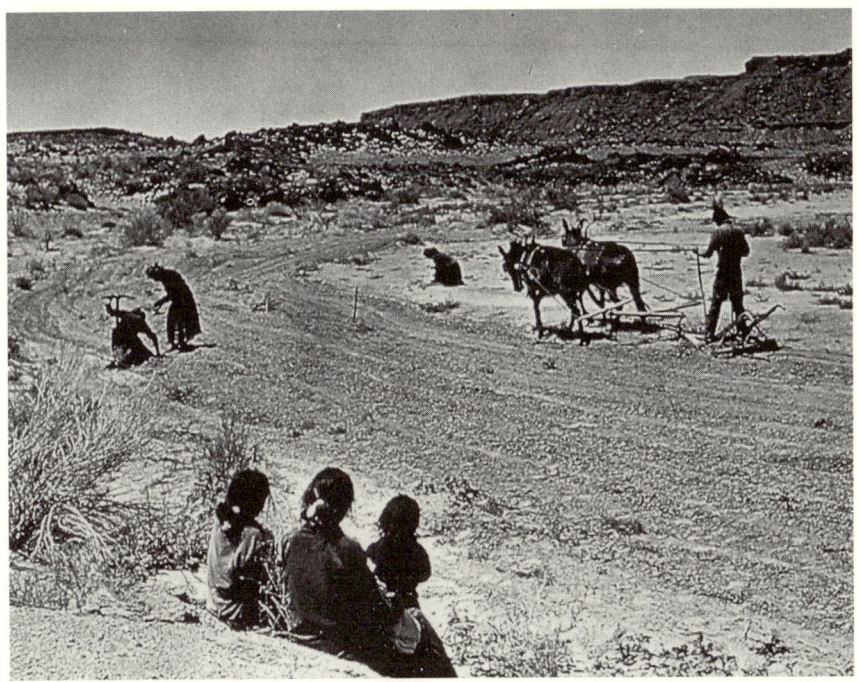

Figure 153

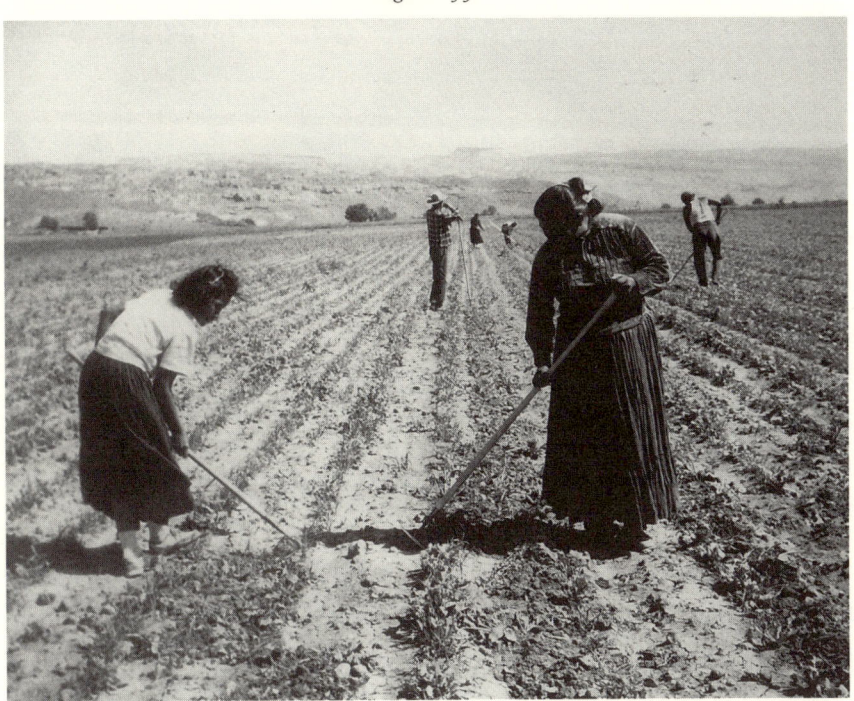

Figure 154

Chapter 5

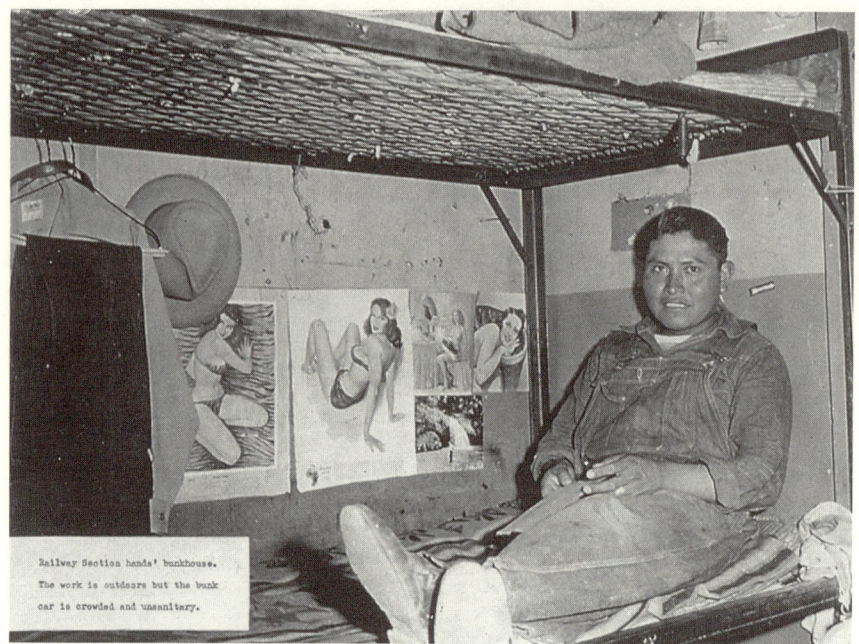

Figure 155

Figure 155. "Railway Section hands' bunkhouse. The work is outdoors, but the bunk car is crowded and unsanitary." Milton Snow, photographer, 1950s. Given the pinups, the adjective was perhaps more a moral commentary than a hygienic one, for the bunkhouse was probably no less sanitary nor more crowded than government housing (see Figs. 146, 148). The Santa Fe Railroad was an important source of wage labor in Navajoland, and workers were not always subject to the same strictures as employees of the government. Photograph courtesy Museum of Northern Arizona. E-242.3.

Photography of Navajo to Mid-Century

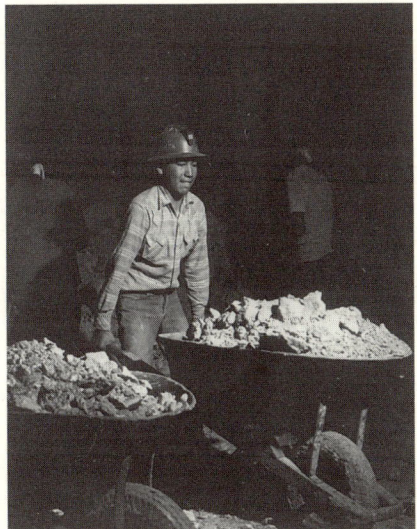

Figure 156

Figure 156. "*Navajo miner hauls uranium ore in wheelbarrow at Moonlight Mine.*" *Gene Price/James Bosch, photographers, 24 July 1957, near Monument Valley, UT. All such mines have been closed, as far as I know, but the consequences are dramatic —polluted and irradiated land, water, people. Navajoland is constantly subject to rapacious exploitation by any who promise jobs and today is being extensively strip-mined for coal (which fuels electrical plants, using Navajo groundwater, to make power for Las Vegas and California customers). Photograph courtesy Navajo Nation Museum, Window Rock AZ. Neg. No. S-322.*

Chapter 5

Several aspects of Snow's classification are interesting (as well as regulating). In addition to his care in doing his job, Snow's humanist passions emerge.[33] He obviously had little regard for some of the anthropological shibboleths (note how weak are the categories NB, Archaeology and antiquities, and NH, Ethnology), despite the fact that he worked for the Museum of Northern Arizona for a period during the mid-1930s. His greatest numbers of photographs were logically of the Navajo Tribal Council and fairs and exhibits, but these were followed in number by images of youth and their activities. Education and people are the most numerous classes. It is also interesting to note the reclassification dumped atop Snow's photographs (and his colleagues and successors) by the bureaucrats at the central BIA photographic repository, which came to be known as the Concho collection (from its location in Concho, Oklahoma).[34] Though the Concho collection at the Navajo Nation Museum contains fewer photographs than the Snow collection (despite the classification excess of the former), the majority of its photographs are by Snow and his successors and colleagues—Stan Bartos, Gene Price, James Bosch, Jack Carson, John McPhee, Cato Sells, Cliff Gedekoh, Glenn Abbeloos, C. Knell, and F. M. Hamel, among others.[35]

In sum, Jack Snow's sensitive, workmanlike photography, taken continually over some three decades of critical social change, helped flesh out the photographic record not only of Navajo peoples but also of government relations, government policies and programs, and Navajo responses (or at least acceptable responses—there is no photo documentation by anyone for responses to the government which are unacceptable). Many of his photographs are easily the equal of those from the era's far more famous arts and documentary photographers, yet he is unmentioned in the standard sources on photographers of the Southwest. Whereas Curtis, Gilpin, and other more famous professional photographers set their own agendas, situating Navajo in terms of their own personal projects, Snow's photography was largely dictated by his employers. He was, vis-à-vis the "art" photographers, considered an illustrator, an instrumentalist. But his photography in many circumstances transcended his assignment, and other things emerged, such as his warm relationship with Navajo and his respect for them on their on terms. Certainly he had better relations with Navajo people than did other photographers of the time, and most of the great corpus of his well-documented photography is now where it belongs—with the Navajo.

The anthropologists—especially the major figures Gladys Reichard, Leland Wyman, and Clyde Kluckhohn (and, at St. Michaels, the anthropological linguist Fr. Berard Haile)—appeared from the early 1920s on. Many others worked in Navajoland during this time, but few were responsible for as many photographs as Reichard, Wyman, and Kluckhohn.[36] Reichard used her talented sister, Lillian, to provide many of the photographs for her illustrated work, which also included photographs by traders (B. Staples), other amateurs, and photographers (Linda Musser, J. S. Crouse).[37] Clyde Kluckhohn was the major force in the somewhat later (post–World War II), inflated Harvard Value Studies Project, which organized around Ramah, in southeastern Navajoland (off the main reservation), generating many thousands of pages of notes and hundreds and hundreds of photographs by, among others, Kluckhohn, A. V. Kidder, Adelaide Bullen, B. Staples, Reichard, Helen Bradley, John Adair, Tom Etson, Janine Rosenzweig, R. G. Fuller, John Landgraf, David Aberle, Dorothea Leighton, Harmon Maxson, William Morgan, John Roberts, Fred Strodtbeck, Harry Tschopik, and Paul Vestal. The project not only kept photographs from the social scientists but also acquired materials from professional photographers such as Paul Woolf, Tom Mullarky, J. R. Willis, Milton Snow, and *Life* magazine photographers. It also held historic photographs from Roland Reed, Alfred Tozzer, S. J. Guernsey, C. C. Willoughby, Frank Russell, J. W. Fewkes, Washington Matthews, Bruce Barnard, and W. H. Jackson. For the entire corpus, most of the photographs are from a limited area, and a few families appear repeatedly. Dozens exist of every possible activity, including psychological projective testing, children at play, and experiments (Fig. 157). Like Reichard, Leland Wyman used his own photography and that of others, including amateurs and other anthropologists, in his publications. In each case these "anthropological" projects primarily used photography in evidential ways, but Kluckhohn and Reichard used it in part to illustrate, in part as ambience, and in part as rhetorical setting for their theoretical exegesis.[38]

The most dramatic photography/anthropology volume was (and still is) the 1951 Vogt-Kluckhohn text, *Navaho Means People,* with photography by Time-Life staffer Leonard McCombe. Though many later books focused upon Navajo with dramatic photographs, this book remains unique (some of the text was drawn from an earlier volume by Kluckhohn and Leighton, *The Navaho,* first published in 1946). It has more photographs than pages and was by the far the most heavily illustrated volume on Navajo to appear to that date. The volume is a clear social propaganda piece, and the ostensibly well-meaning title errs in at least three directions—in the spelling of *Navajo;* in the translation of that term (which is of debated meaning);[39] and in that even the term by which the Navajo call themselves *(diné)* translates not as "people" but properly as something like "visible people now occupying the surface of the world" (in contrast to *diné diyinii,* "Holy People," or those ancestors who

Chapter 5

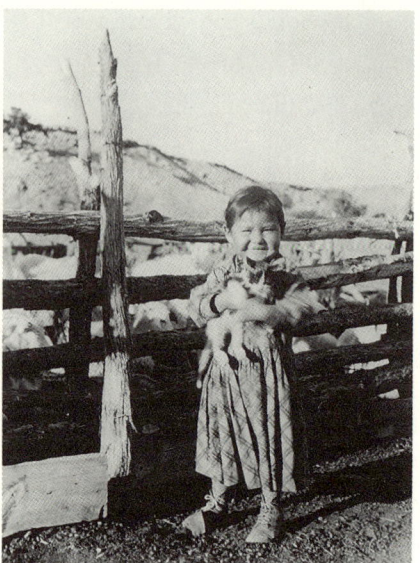

Figure 157

Figure 157. Child with kitten, Coolidge NM. Clyde Kluckhohn, photographer, n.d. See also Leighton and Kluckhohn, 1948:33 ("Animals take the place of toys and get the same rough treatment"). One of the hundreds of photographs of the Harvard Value Studies Project of the 1950s, this one appears as if it could have been taken simply in response to the charm and delight of this little girl, but it was part of an experiment, a specific surveillance. This, as many others of this archive, were not photographs of disinterested friends. Photograph courtesy Ramah Research Collection, Archives of the Laboratory of Anthropology/Museum of Indians Arts and Culture, Santa Fe, Photo #CK-26-150.

destroyed the monsters and ordered the world and who, now invisible, occupy the mountains and sacred sites of Navajoland—see Chapter 1).

McCombe only came into the project when local photographers refused to be part of it (Faris/Hight, July 1990). On learning that the authors wanted to focus on social problems in such an intrusive visual way, George Hight, a respected Gallup studio photographer (who had initially been contacted), wanted nothing to do with the project, for he had many Navajo customers and friends and wanted to continue to live and work in the community. So McCombe was contracted. He had no experience in Navajoland—he was simply hired to illustrate the text (although the text appears to have illustrated his photos in some circumstances). His spontaneous style—the photograph of the moment—yielded the capture, the intrusive and offensive action image so important to propagandists and photojournalists. There are photographs of the dead, photographs of the dying, and close-ups of those passed out from excessive alcohol consumption.[40]

Readers are familiar with the ideologies here—the passive victim, the dignified casualty, the stoic Navajo in defeat.[41] The implication is that such a condition is a Navajo problem, to be overcome by Navajo themselves. This work, with its grotesque exposure of Navajo in circumstances in which permission or payment could not have been possible, never indicts the social structure that has brought about such conditions, never offers any commentary about getting European-Americans out of the hair of indigenous Americans. Vogt and Kluckhohn (who, of course, had to direct McCombe to photograph some subjects) reserve their greatest contempt for the Native American Church and—wholly irrelevant except for Cold War rhetoric (Kluckhohn had strangely become part of the Russian Research Center at Harvard)—for the perceived dangers of communism, both of which are equated with Navajo resistance! Their conclusions are amazing (1951:159):

> [W]e may ask: after we have assisted the "backward" or "underdeveloped" area of the world to obtain what we call a "decent standard of living" by helping their people to establish improved technologies and by creating in them a desire for the manufactured products of our own industrial system, what then?. . . do we supply the material goods and improved technology and allow the communists to supply them with a new "religion" and set of values? These are certainly far from merely academic questions in the modern world. . . . One important consequence . . . if carried out too rapidly upon a "backward" people, is a period of social and political disorganization in which individuals are

Chapter 5

caught "between two worlds" and are chronically dissatisfied. But human beings will not tolerate such a state of affairs for long. If solutions are not found in the development of new coherent sets of values, they are sought by nativistic returns to the old values, or by a psychological flight from the realities of the intolerable situation by using alcohol or peyote.

Even in those photographs where Navajo are smiling at the camera and seem not to mind having their photographs taken, the text, with its dramatic assimilationist bias, conveys bizarre racist revelations. In the case of one young girl wearing jeans, a striped t-shirt, a jacket, and a bow in her hair, the caption reads: "This school girl, with a comic book in her pocket, might be taken for a white American student" (see McCombe, 1951:79).

Save the historical and museum archives, no formal state agencies in either New Mexico or Arizona systematically assembled photographs of Navajo (*New Mexico Magazine* and *Arizona Highways* simply contracted with individuals for specific stories but returned the photographs after using them).[42] Tourist photographs were taken by the hundreds (Chart 1), but apart from those that were published, most remain in private collections. Each state's tourist bureau contracted repeatedly with the same photographers, however. For New Mexico, John Candelario,[43] Johnnie Martinez, Harvey Caplin,[44] T. H. Parkhurst,[45] Wyatt Davis, Henry Miller, George Thompson, Buddy Mays, and D. W. Van Devanter, among others, left sizable bodies of photographs of Navajo; for Arizona the Manleys (Ray and Alan), Chuck Abbott, the Muenchs (Joseph, David, and Emil), Jerry Jacka, Don Dedera, and Senator Barry Goldwater are among those known for such photographs. Some of these individuals did quite as well as the celebrated art or documentary photographers and in many cases were just as close to Navajo, but they did not achieve the fame or prestige. For example, T. Harmon Parkhurst of Santa Fe, who studied under Jesse Nusbaum, photographed Navajo on many occasions (and poorly documented his photographs), producing an outstanding series of Navajo at the annual September Laguna feast day of San Jose in the 1930s (see Fig. 158) and some very fine portraits of Navajo weavers attending a conference on Navajo weaving held in at the Laboratory of Anthropology in Santa Fe in September 1933.[46]

Most of this photography is very normalizing and even rigidly stereotyped; for example, the several editions (also available in several languages) of Ray Manley's widely distributed *The Vanishing Indian* contain mislabelings, identify the same individuals differently in different editions, and include quite sloppy and racist expressions as well as outright lies (people decked in their finest jewelry and satins, with their animals on leashes—probably at fairs—are said to be just out herding, and outrageous ages are claimed for the models). Some of the tourist photographers' favorite subjects made much of their living by keeping their traditional clothing and jewelry at the ready, keeping their hogans and summer shades free of the normal detritus and accumulations, keeping their horses and sheep handy, and always having a loom erected in a photographically appropriate spot (even in summer sunshine—cf. Fig. 159). Especially for those of Monument Valley, such as Happy and Willie Cly and their family, photographers must have visited almost daily (Fig. 161); the Navajo combed their hair with grass brushes so often for photographers that it must have been difficult to keep from going bald (Fig. 160). That money was to be made can be seen in a few pitiful local advertisements (see Fig. 6) but also in the extent to which much of the collaboration became part of official Navajo policy (Fig. 2).

The National Geographic Society, of course, had a stable of staff and contract photographers it periodically loosed on Navajoland—Sam Abell, Alfred Bailey, John Breed, Bruce Dale, Terry Eiler, Charles Herbert, Steve Northup, and Susanne [Anderson] Page among them. *National Geographic* alternated between the aestheticist landscape-with-humans theme (Navajo as extensions of red rocks) and assimilationist propaganda (Navajo in two worlds and experiencing adjustment problems). And there was always the Navajo-are-just-like-us, family-of-man theme—an obliterating (of history, of place, of time, of the unique, of difference) gesture, however humanistically motivated (see Lutz and Collins, 1993:277).[47] Though *National Geographic* produced several different stories on Navajo over the years, there was never one that cogently discussed conquest, racism, exploitation, rights ceded and treaties not kept, nor even battles won by Navajo.

Many celebrated individuals also photographed Navajo, including Ansel Adams (Fig. 162), Dorothea Lange,[48] Marion Pafli,[49] and perhaps others unpublished. Eliot Porter photographed in the region, as did H. Cartier-Bresson and Edward Weston—though I am aware of no photographs of Navajo people from any of these three men. Though Roy Stryker explicitly did not consider Native Americans important to his FSA (Farm Security Administration, 1937–1942) project, FSA photographers Jack Delano and John Collier, Jr., did photograph Navajo.[50] Delano photographed them as part of the FSA project itself (taking pictures of railway work teams comprising Navajo, other Native Americans, European-Americans, and African-Americans), and Collier photographed Navajo separately, after his FSA period (see Fig. 163), with John Adair and others.[51]

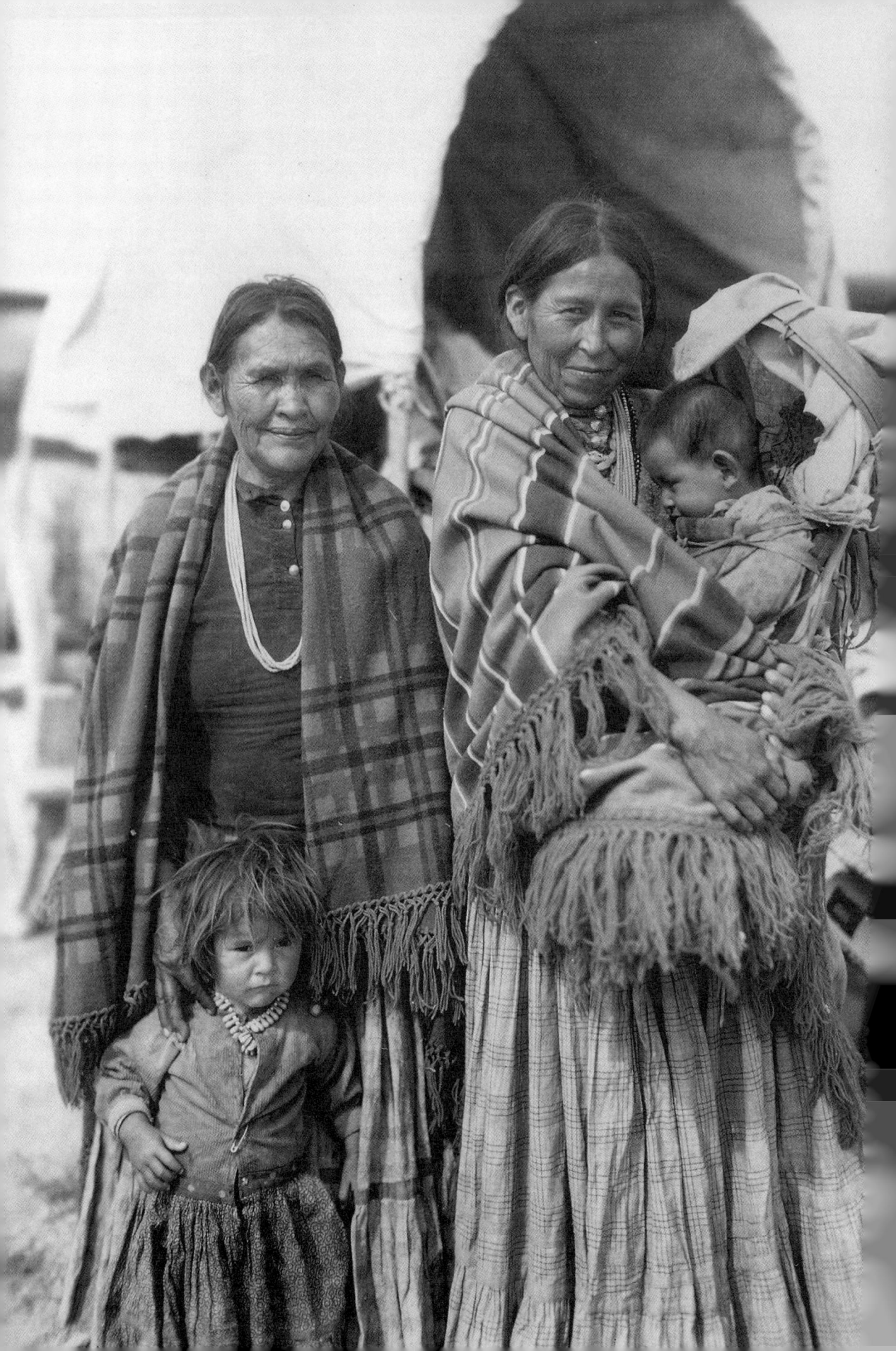

Photography of Navajo to Mid-Century

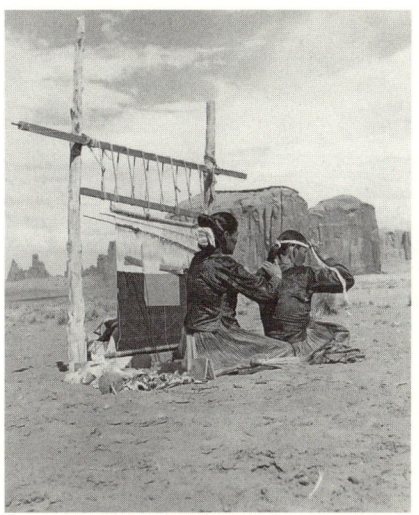
Figure 159

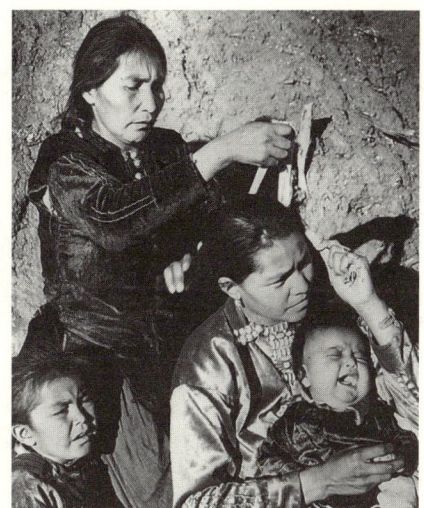
Figure 160

Figure 158. Women and children. T. Harmon Parkhurst, photographer, n.d., (1920s–1930s). This nice photograph is one of a large number Parkhurst took at the Laguna Pueblo annual fiesta, at which there were always many Navajo guests. Whereas it was sometimes difficult to photograph Pueblo peoples, Navajo were there in their finest and could not easily escape photographers at these public festivals. Photograph courtesy Wheelwright Museum of the American Indian. No number (Parkhurst prints).

Figure 159. Women, loom, hair tying. Photographer unknown, n.d. This stereotype—red rocks, weaving, velvet, hair tying—attempts to squeeze in as much "acceptable culture" as possible. It is very unlikely a woman would have set up a loom in the middle of nowhere, without shade, unless paid to do so. Photograph courtesy Wheelwright Museum of the American Indian. #60/1529.

Figure 160. "Navajo Hairdo." Willard Luce, photographer, ca. 1955. No one is posing happily (especially the children), and the subjects grow impatient with the photographer. Normally Navajo children in this distress would be instantly comforted. This photograph (with flash at close distance), another featuring the hair-fashioning cliché, portrays one of the Monument Valley families that modeled so frequently. Photograph courtesy Colorado State Historical Society. No. F36,626.

Chapter 5

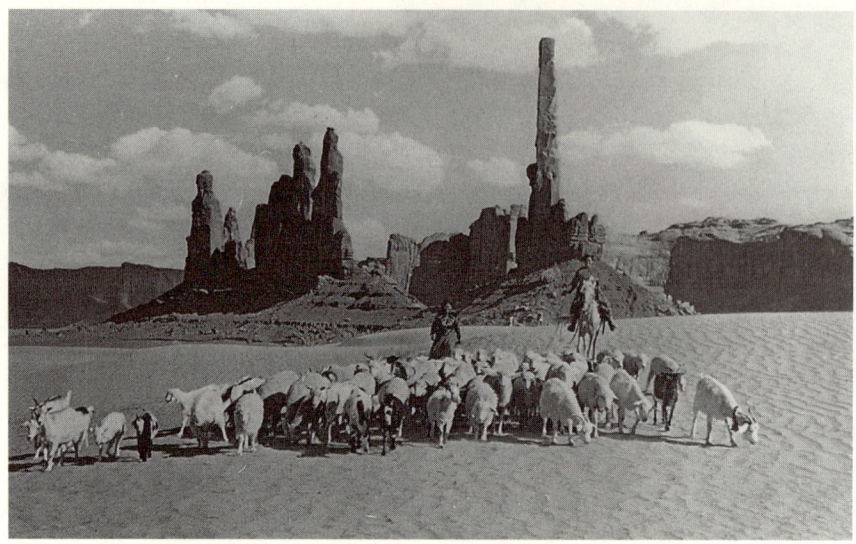

Figure 161

Figure 161. "Navajo Indians." Photographer unknown, n.d. This view typifies advertising photography—combining a dramatic physical setting with a known Navajo productive activity acceptable to the West. It would appear timeless, but goat and sheep herds and horses have been built up since the BIA's stock-reduction policies in the 1930s, and dress styles are from the late nineteenth century and later. Only a few Navajo families actually live in this section of Navajoland, but they appear hundreds of times in tourist and advertising photographs. Photograph courtesy Utah State Historical Society. Photo No. 970.4, P. 30.

Photography of Navajo to Mid-Century

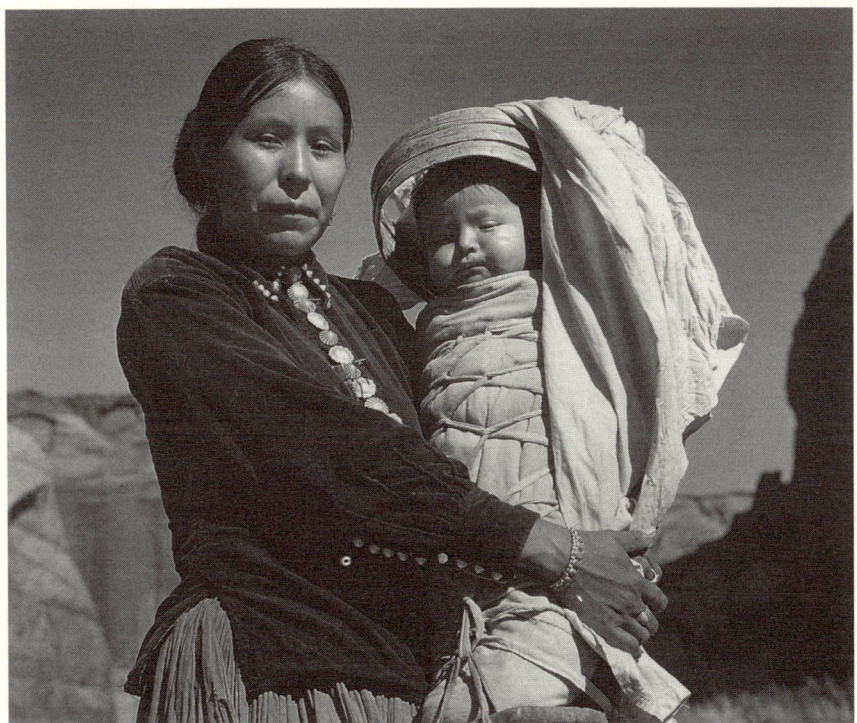

Figure 162

Figure 162. "Navaho Mother and Child, Canyon de Chelle [sic], Arizona." *Ansel Adams, photographer, ca. 1941. This is one of only a very few photographs Adams took of Navajo people and the only one not previously published to my knowledge. Perhaps expectedly, this woman and her child seem very much like trees or rocks (save that they have been prepared and are modeling for the photograph). The camera is positioned to look up from below yet still capture the cliffs behind. Any heroic or grand proportions that might emerge from this ambitious gesture (see, for example, Fig. 147) are diminished by the subjects' facial expressions and their closeness. It appears like so many other tourist cliché photos. Photograph courtesy Center for Creative Photography and Trustees of the Ansel Adams Publishing Rights Trust (Copyright © 1994, all rights reserved), #84:089:009.*

Chapter 5

Though Collier's photographs contain the normalizing themes of the time[52]—and he was not to be denied ceremonial materials—often they are more detailed and sometimes even show other photographs in the hogan interiors—for example, bus-station photomachine snapshots of servicemen (Fig. 11). These, as well as photographs by Laura Gilpin, Milton Snow and Mark Nohl (see Fig. 9 and Portfolio II), indicate that Navajo are certainly not adverse to photographs of themselves. They *are* adverse to the social relations required when others pay them to pose or take photographs in circumstances upon which they may not agree or over which they have little choice. Chapters 7 and 8 touch upon traditions of photography of agreement and nonexploitative social relations.

Alongside the BIA photographers were others commissioned by agencies and programs with private aid agendas, and these documentarians established virtually an entire photograph style of their own. To the names of Collier and Adair may be added those of Helen Post (see La Farge, 1940 and Fig. 164), Charlie Wunder, Lawrence Kafer, Peter Mygatt, and Marion Palfi.[53] These photographers often used both the humanist style (say, of Gilpin) and the harsh surveillance mode (say, of McCombe). Though usually characterized by a more sophisticated compositional style than that of mid-century anthropologists or most amateurs, they also displayed some of the subtle contempt for photographic subjects noted earlier; Helen Post, a pre–World War II photographer, is described this way (biographical manuscript on Helen Post, Amon Carter Museum, n.d.:4):

> She took most of her pictures with a 70 mm Roliflex which permitted her to glance down at her composition while maintaining unobscured eye contact with her subjects during most of a photo session. She was a past master of the old trick of using a loud shutter-cock to fool the subject into believing the picture had been taken, only to capture the true image with a barely audible click as the subject relaxed and the conversation stated again.

Charles Wunder, who worked in Navajoland after the war, even set up grotesquely racist photos (Fig. 95). But of this entire group, John Adair (see Fig. 165) stands out for having photographed in one community over generations and for involving Navajo in their own photography. With Sol Worth and Richard Chalfen, he inaugurated a program whereby Navajo made short films of subjects chosen by themselves. This pioneering effort suggested that there were cultural features determining how Navajo made motion pictures,[54]

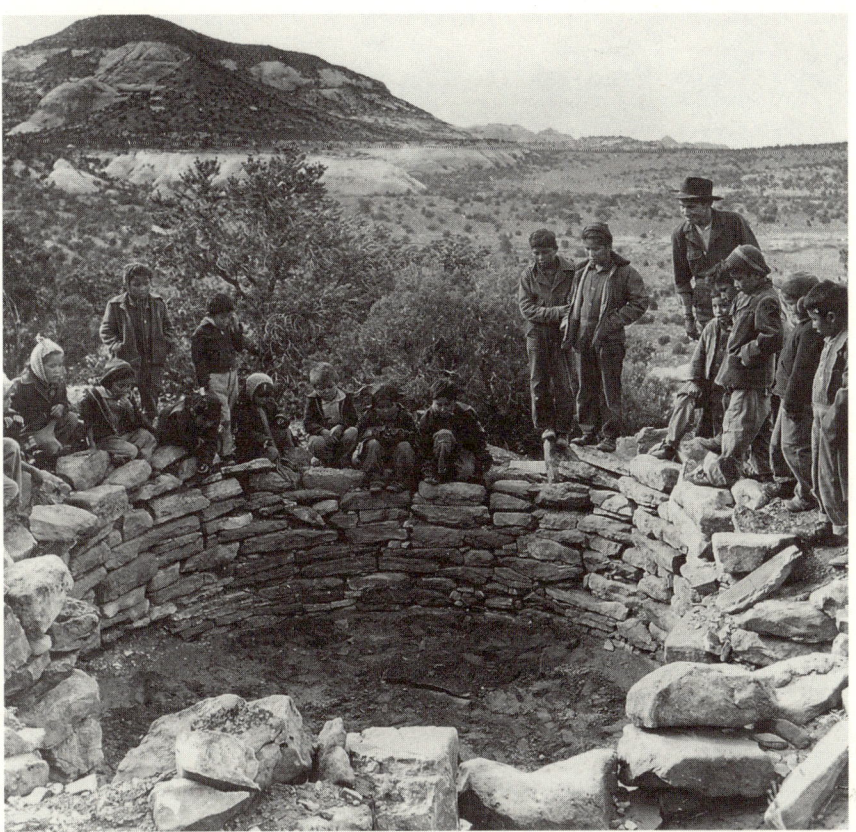

Figure 163

Figure 163. "Pupils from Navajo Mountain School on Sunday Outing. #346—Pueblo Ruins and Children." John Collier, Jr., photographer, n.d. This photograph is especially ironic, because these ruins, in the heart of Navajoland, are not considered Navajo in Western historiography, yet many of these youngsters come from round homes not unlike this kiva and regard these Anasazi ['anaasází—"enemies of the old people"—not "the ancient ones," as so commonly translated in popular discourse] ruins as contemporary with those of their own ancestors. Photograph courtesy The University Museum, University of Pennsylvania. Negative No. 54-141433.

Chapter 5

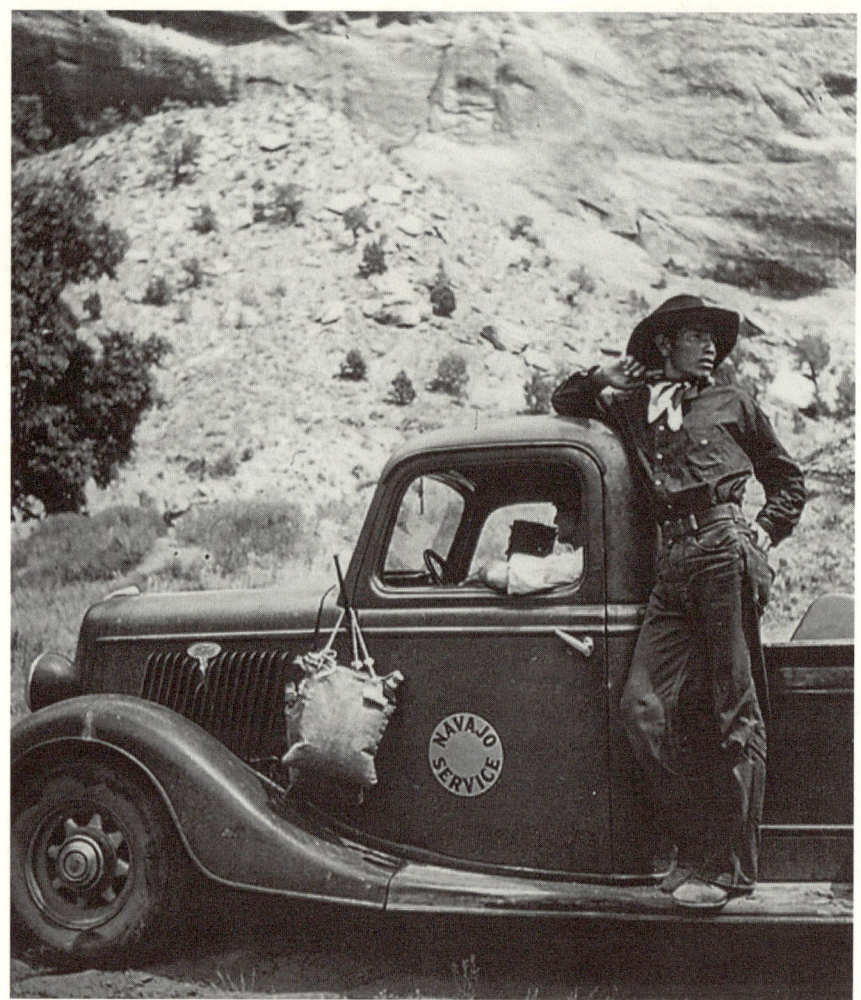

Figure 164

Figure 164. Ned Bia on pickup truck. Helen Post, photographer, n.d. (ca. 1936–1941), Canyon de Chelly. Ned was given his name from the BIA and rides outside while European-Americans ride in the cab (Navajo Service, indeed). Photograph courtesy National Anthropological Archives, Smithsonian Institution. NAA SPC02269700.

and though the project proceeded with a political naiveté and remained wedded to traditional objectivism, it yielded some insightful conclusions:

> We do it [make films] because we are anthropologists, scholars, researchers, or whatnot. We do because it never occurred to us that "they" ought to be doing it, that "they" can do it, and most importantly, that when "we" do it, we are showing a picture of our world and salvaging a culture not of others but of ourselves. Our record of them might very well be a record of us (Worth and Adair, 1972:253-254).

Adair has continued his work with the people of the Pine Springs region of Navajoland, in both ciné and still photography, and is now involved, with his photographer son, Peter, in a video-disc historical photographic project.

Of the many films, commercial and "documentary" (the differences are not always clear), one major project stands out, inasmuch as it produced many still photographs as well. This is the American Indian Film Project, which operated from the Lowie Museum (now Phoebe Hearst Museum) of the University of California, Berkeley, under the general direction of Samuel Barnett. This well-funded and well-connected enterprise filmed among several Native American groups, but the work involving the Navajo (inaugurated in 1963) was very problematic. After completing several films of healing ceremonies, the project team encountered objections from third parties (though it had secured permission both from the medicine man involved and from those for whom the healing practice was being held), and production was stopped. Weaving, silversmithing, some architecture, considerable portions of a Red Ant Way, a girl's puberty ceremony *(kinaaldá)*, a Nightway, and a Mountainway were filmed. Most of this material (at least of the healing ceremonials) has never been edited for viewing and remains in vaults at the Hearst Museum (Jacknis/Faris, 15 April 1992). Elsewhere (see Faris, 1990:22, 111, 133) I have discussed some of the more serious problems stemming from this project (at least for the Nightway portions); here it is important to note that still photographs (some of which have been published) were taken at these filmed ceremonies by William Heick, David Peri, Kenneth Foster, Max Lair, perhaps Charlotte Frisbie, and others.[55]

Few museums or universities keep photographers for extended periods— at least, not ones that journey to Navajoland at intervals. One exception is the longtime staff photographer of the Arizona State Museum, Tucson— Helga Teiwes.[56] Teiwes specializes in ethnographic photography when possible and has maintained friendships over time with local people (Fig. 166).

Chapter 5

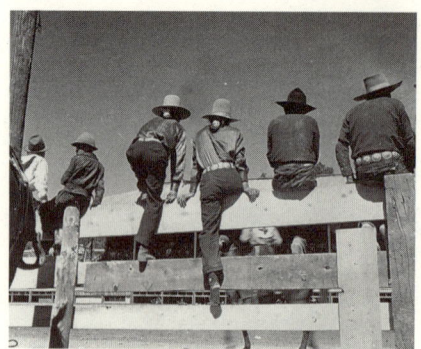 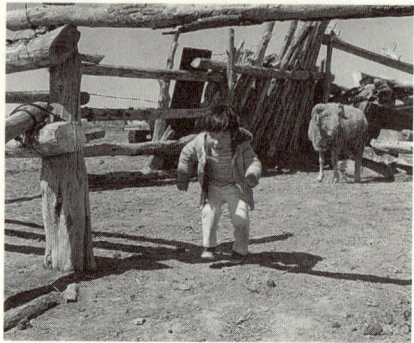

Figure 165   Figure 166

Figure 165. Men watching rodeo. John Adair, photographer, n.d. This particular type of photograph (Navajos from the back, sitting on fence) is stereotypical and can be found in the archives of many photographers of Navajo, as well as in publication (cf. Gilpin, 1968:201, 202, 205, 207). Such a pose has the local color necessary (hats, boots, hair ties, concha belts), can be carefully composed, and has no hostile faces or averted eyes (but see Gilpin, 1968:202, where a seated woman turns around to confront the camera). See also Fig. 18, where perhaps such images may be a consequence of refusal to face the photographer rather than an aesthetic choice. Photograph courtesy Wheelwright Museum of the American Indian. No number.

Figure 166. "Navajo Indian boy in pen with ram." Helga Teiwes, photographer, n.d. Photograph courtesy Arizona State Museum, University of Arizona. #38860.

Photography of Navajo to Mid-Century

This practice has served her well, and though she never pressures anyone to be photographed who does not want to, she is careful to get model releases from individuals photographed (Faris/Teiwes July 1992). Teiwes frequently photographs at fairs and has often documented contrasts in lifestyles manifest among Navajo at any given time. As a long-standing professional, Teiwes produces photographs that often easily compete with those of art photographers such as Gilpin and certainly with the legions of new "coffee table" photographers. She collaborated in one such recent volume,[57] but her photography of people is more careful, more contextual, and considerably more informed than that of the photographers discussed below (Chapter 7).

With the earlier McCombe photography volume *(Navajo Means People)*, the publication of Laura Gilpin's book *The Enduring Navajo* in 1968 (see Chapter 6), and all the other intervening projects, the photography of Navajo would seem to have exhausted the conventional directions. After World War II and into the 1960s, many photographers were sent to Navajoland on special assignments to photograph for advertising, for specific magazine stories of one sort or another, for news stories, for individual film projects (such as the American Indian Film Project), for commercial films, for special nonprofit commissions involved in development planning and training, and for various surveys, such as health-care data collection. Thus, Navajo came to enter the great American minority scrutiny network, and Navajoland matured as an ever-popular exotic domestic destination.

Portfolio VI
*Hands-on
Social Relations*

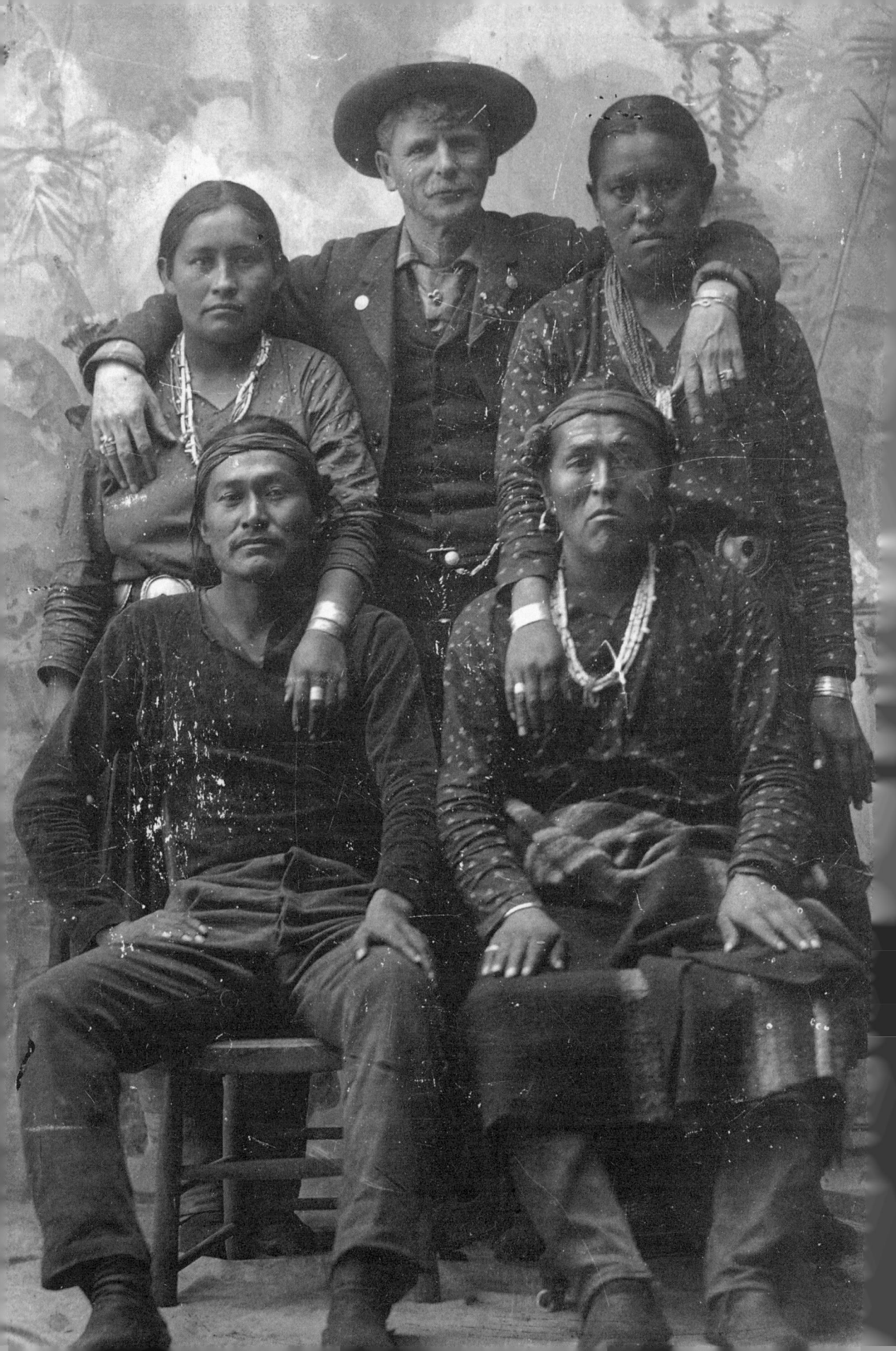

Hands-on Social Relations

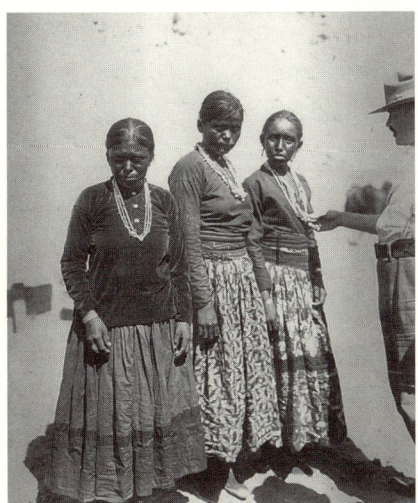

Figure 168

Figure 167. Four Navajo with European-American. Photographer unknown, n.d. The draping of the women's hands over the seated men (perhaps their husbands) is probably instructed. The standing man, however, seems simply to be taking liberty. Photograph courtesy Colorado Historical Society. No. F36,850.

Figure 168. "Unidentified Navajo women." Photographer unknown (perhaps J. F. Byrnes and Co.), n.d. (perhaps 1901). See Fig. 55 for another possible J. F. Byrnes photograph. See also Fig. 169, with European-Americans examining jewelry being worn by Navajo. There seems to be more puzzlement or hostility directed toward the photographer than toward the very presumptive European-American man at viewer's right. Photograph courtesy Museum of New Mexico. Neg. No. 39598.

Figure 167

Portfolio VI

Figure 169. "*Texas Frontier Centennial, 1836–1936. To Dorothy Hubbell from the Woodards.*" *Photographer unknown (perhaps Woodard), 1936. This is the medicine man Miguelito not long before his death. Note the Navajo in the background, probably camped at the site during an exhibition at the Centennial. One of the beauty queens is holding Miguelito's necklace, and thus this photograph resembles Fig. 168—both depict Westerners placing their hands on Navajo and examining jewelry being worn by Navajo Photograph courtesy University of Arizona Library Special Collections. N-11,469.*

Figure 170. "*Fannie (seated) and John Wetherill.*" *C.M.W., photographer (probably C. M. Wood), n.d. (ca. 1925). Though the familiarity might suggest otherwise, John Wetherill is probably not the father nor husband of the Navajo woman in this photograph. Photograph courtesy Arizona State Museum, University of Arizona. #1089.*

Hands-on Social Relations

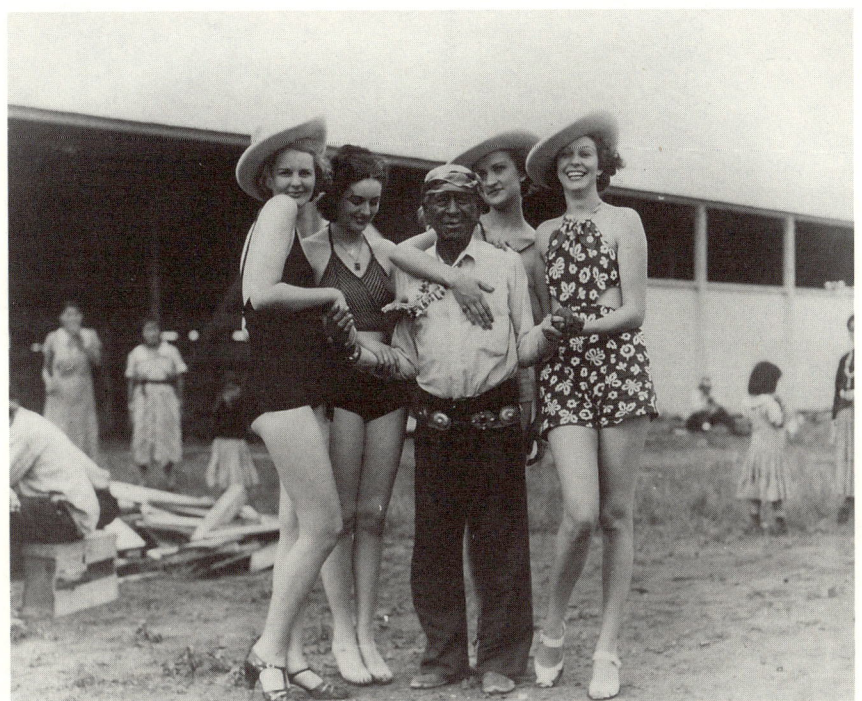

Figure 169

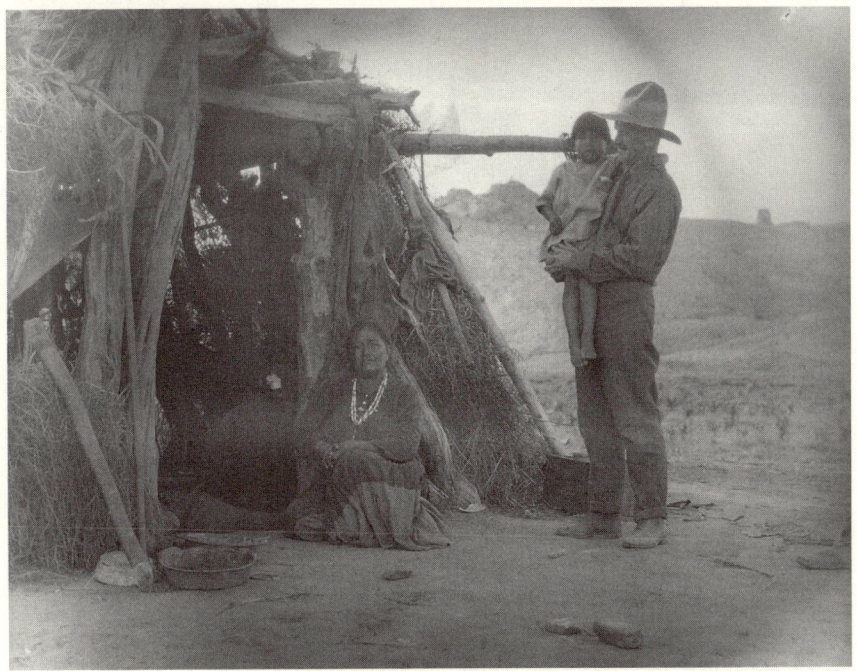

Figure 170

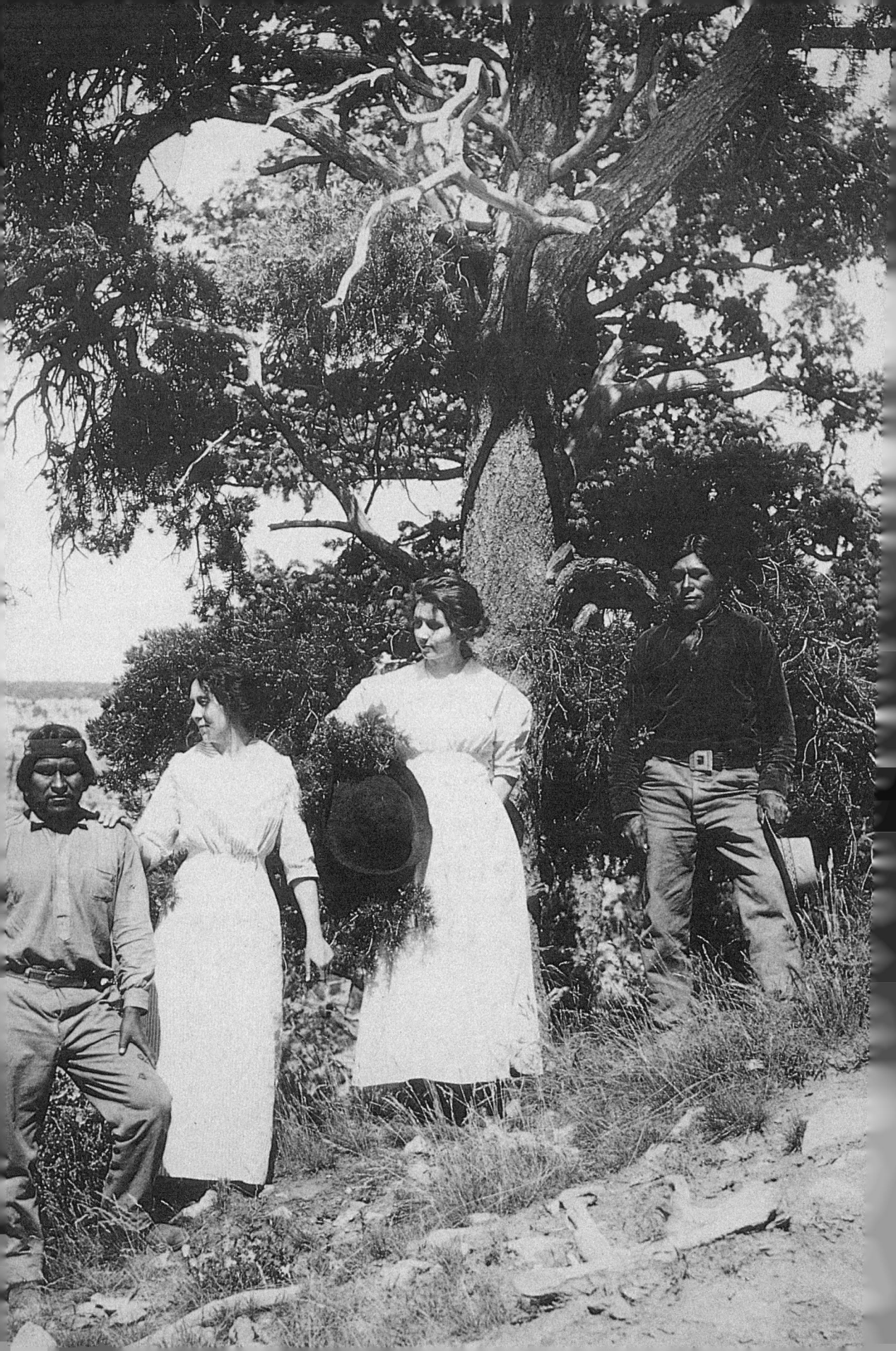

Hands-on Social Relations

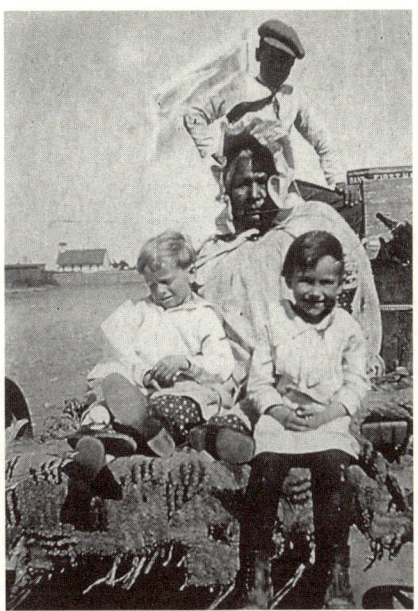

Figure 172

Figure 171. "Navajo Indian Men and Anglo Women: Grand Canyon." Emory Kolb, photographer, n.d. Kolb maintained a studio at Grand Canyon and presumably had Navajo employees (or access to other Navajo employees at Grand Canyon) as props for photographs. Notice the hand on the shoulder—as if with this gesture some sort of legitimate contact is established. Photograph courtesy Emory Kolb Collection, Cline Library, Special Collections and Archives, Northern Arizona University. No. 568.6193.

Figure 172. "Delivina Maxwell." Photographer unknown (perhaps John Grassham or A. B. Harris), ca. 1924. Delivina Maxwell was a Navajo servant of Lucien Maxwell of Fort Sumner, New Mexico. Only the child at right, Ida Harris (the daughter of A. B. and Lenida Harris), is identified. Delivinia is said to have gone in the room to see if Pat Garrett had killed Billy the Kid at the Maxwell house in Fort Sumner. Was Delivinia a Navajo child who never went home from the Bosque Redondo captivity? Note the children's excessively familiar behavior—Westerners of all ages handling Navajo of advanced age. Photograph courtesy John Grassham Collection, New Mexico State Records and Archives. No. 29570.

Figure 171

Portfolio VI

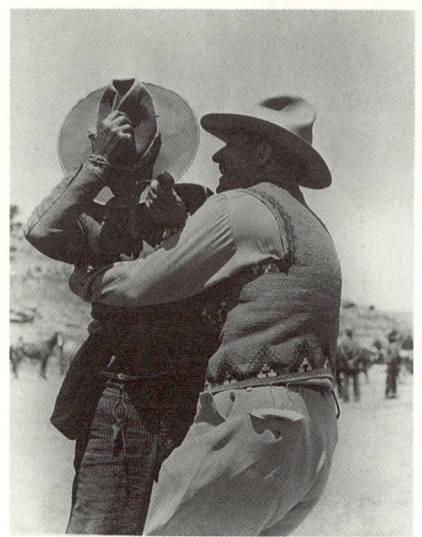

Figure 173

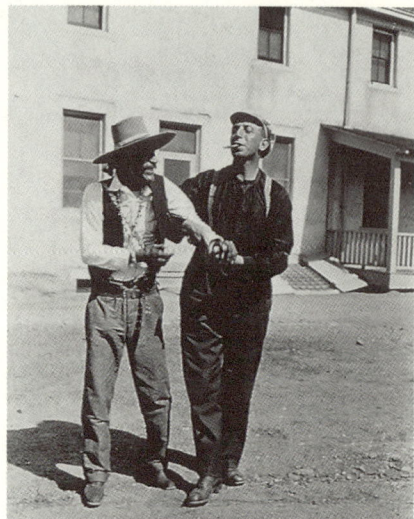

Figure 174

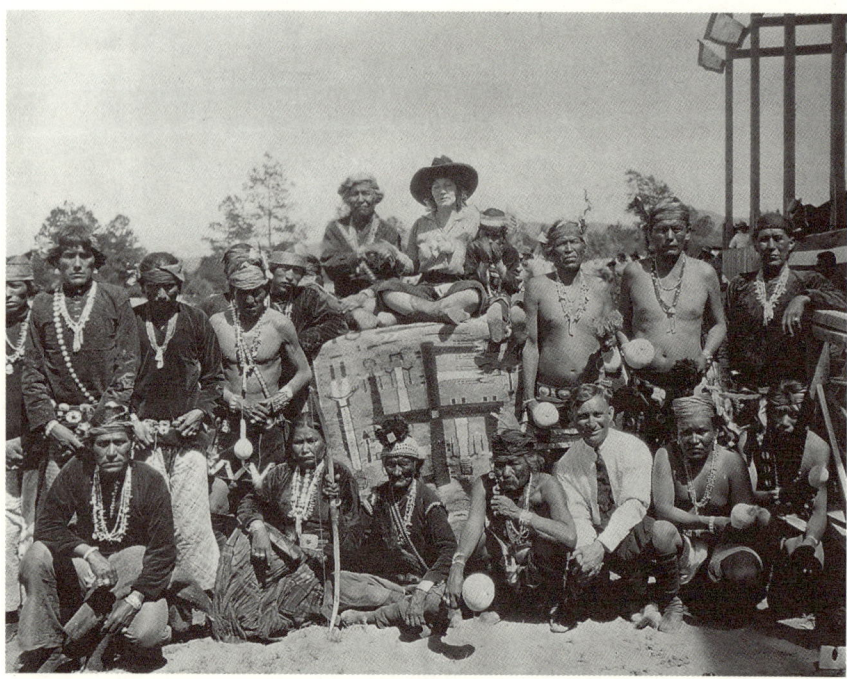

Figure 175

Figure 173. "Born and raised on the Navajo Indian Reservation, in western New Mexico, Roman Hubbell, a popular Indian Trader, is shown here clowning with a conservative old Navajo Indian, trying to convince him to pose for the photographer." Wyatt Davis, photographer, n.d. (ca. 1945??). Although this is undoubtedly in good-natured jest, archival collections contain very few photographs of Navajo putting their hands on European-Americans. Photograph courtesy Museum of New Mexico. Neg. No. 7299.

Figure 174. "Gishin Biye and Fr. Celestine." Photographer unknown, n.d. European-Americans clowning with Native Americans. Photograph courtesy Arizona State Museum, University of Arizona, and Franciscan Friars, St. Michaels AZ. #PIX1577c-7.

Figure 175. "Mike Kirk with a dance team in 1925." Photographer unknown (perhaps Tom Kirk). Probably at Gallup Intertribal Ceremonial. Haske Yazzi in front row with bow; note European-American woman in rear, as well as rare sandpainting-design weaving. Photograph courtesy San Diego Museum of Man. No. 5357e.

Chapter Six

The Endearing Navajo: Laura Gilpin

A number of hagiographic articles in the past decade, a well-received major biography, and several recent retrospective exhibitions of her work have made possible a more detailed critical examination of Laura Gilpin's photography of Navajo. Certainly there have been sufficient uncritical examinations of this work.[1] Gilpin's extensive Navajo photography also bears on a number of other issues, as a lawsuit was brought in 1985 against her estate (Gilpin's photographs were bequeathed to the Amon Carter Museum, Fort Worth, Texas) charging invasion of privacy (specifically relying on the subtorts of unlawful public disclosure and misappropriation of likeness).

Laura Gilpin grew up in the American West and was formally trained in arts and photography. Her first contact with Navajo came when she accompanied a friend, Elizabeth Forster, to Navajoland in 1930.[2] Forster, a field nurse, accepted an appointment at Red Rock on the New Mexico portion of the Navajo reservation and thus came to know local people in the region very well. As a consequence, Gilpin's first photographs of Navajo were of people from this section of the reservation, especially those who worked for Forster or had close contact with her. Gilpin's principal photographs of Navajo people date from 1930 to 1933 (when Forster left the reservation) and from 1950 until the publication of *The Enduring Navaho* in 1968. She produced some sporadic photography of Navajo after that and had started work on a grand volume about Canyon de Chelly at the time of her death in 1979.

After her first visits, Gilpin gave many illustrated public lectures, exhibited,

Chapter 6

and published postcards of her Navajo images (see Appendix, Chart 2b). She was not alone, of course; during the forty-year period between 1930 and 1970 hundreds of photographers pursued "documentary" and "cultural/landscape" themes in the photography of Navajo. This period coincided with the BIA's most substantial impacts on Navajo: the introduction of the representative council and the chapter political system, the initiation of the devastating stock-reduction program (see endnote 26, Chapter 5, and endnote 7, this chapter), the expansion of compulsory schooling, and the extension of voting franchise. In her 1968 volume, Gilpin attempted to document something of the changes that had taken place since her earliest visits, taking photographs of some of the same subjects she had depicted twenty-five to thirty-five years earlier. She paid attention to successful acculturation and "The Coming Way," presenting change as unproblematic if handled by the right people and carried off without resistance. But her purpose was to photograph a people in their landscape, in harmony with the setting (or her view of that harmony—which always implied a very traditional and very clean Navajo or Navajo settlement), successfully adapted, structured by the gaze of Western humanism.[3]

Gilpin is abundantly championed for many reasons. She endured in an environment that was not easy, particularly for women, and she was apparently overburdened with heavy responsibilities by relatives, companions, and friends for most of her life.[4] Like Edward Curtis, she made very little money during her lifetime. But, like a number of other professional women of her time in the Southwest, especially in Santa Fe and Taos,[5] she possessed a form of class confidence,[6] a comfort with hierarchy, and an acceptance of at least some of the prevailing orders that enabled her to secure—to take for granted—access to Navajo. She could insert herself in a more or less confident fashion into the affairs of cultural brokers (Navajo leaders), BIA officials, and the white patrons of Santa Fe. A number of New Deal politicians endorsed her Navajo endeavors, though she was more politically conservative than many of them, and she endorsed their analyses of and solutions to Navajo problems.[7] She resurrected an old notion dormant since the time of Monsen and Moon—the "romantic enlightened," the dignified, stoic Navajo (without the victimization, for Gilpin distanced herself from the "realist" photography of Navajo assimilationist problems—as in the work of McCombe [1951]). Gilpin didn't want photographs of Navajo succumbing to conquest;[8] she wanted photographs of Navajo successfully adapted (that is, silently persisting, not giving BIA bureaucrats or other officialdom any trouble). Indeed, she seemed to share the view of Kluckhohn and Vogt (in McCombe, 1951:142) that those who found "relief in becoming followers of Navaho demagogues" presented a problem on a par with alcoholism and other deprivations. Presumably she was referring to the radical critics of BIA policies and programs and to the Native American Church, with its peyote ceremonies. Gilpin liked her Navajo in their place, long-suffering, adaptive, self-sufficient—neither resisting nor succumbing.[9] She possessed these characteristics herself, and so (she thought) should they—Navajo as sort of colorful Yankees.[10] Gilpin was not against change, as long as it was the change New Deal planners envisioned and wasn't messy. But she did not like resistance or refusal; she liked adaptation and cooperation and cleanliness—and, above all, landscape. Gilpin says of McCombe (1951), "The Navaho are a characteristically happy people, and a people to whom the land is everything! In that book not one landscape" (Sandweiss, 1986:88).[11] Such photography was also offensive, one could argue, but Gilpin called no attention to the dramatic injustices, the bleak poverty, the appalling conditions it illustrated, nor to the intrusive and assuming photographic style. After all, they had their landscape.

Gilpin's generation had a John Collier–inspired attitude toward Navajo.[12] In the words of her biographer, Gilpin "represents a new humanistic strain in landscape photography that regards people and the landscape as an integrated whole" (Sandweiss, 1986:101). But this is hardly how Navajo view harmony—it's a white man's view of integration, the "harmony" that generated things such as the devastating stock-reduction programs or the Jungian embrace of Navajo as the perfect exemplar of universal order and primitive archetype. This view embodied the social administration philosophy of the BIA, the patronizing humanism, the pastoral romance—and Gilpin did a great deal to ensure a specific and appealing prototype of dignity. Her work included lots of white man's Mother Earth. *The Enduring Navaho* became, in the words of one reviewer, "The Endearing Navaho" (quoted in Sandweiss, 1986:104). But she had disdain for Navajo who might emerge as anything else, for those who resisted BIA policies and who adopted peyote and the Native American Church. Indeed, the endpapers of Gilpin's very successful book (first published in 1968 but now in its seventh hardbound printing and its second paperback printing) contain small photographs of Navajo body parts doing acceptable things—doing things Gilpin thought Navajo ought to do, some "traditional," some Western. This hierarchical view was very popular with the BIA and had a strong historical component as well. There are no fingers wrapped around liquor bottles, no defiant fists in the air, no hands holding guns pointed at the photographer. Gilpin represented the romantic edge of that Collier generation; she wanted Navajo pure, washed, and clean. As an example, she argued (cf. Sandweiss, 1986:316) against the current spelling

Chapter 6

of *Navajo*, claiming a Spanish "corrupting influence" (as, of course, did Vogt and Kluckhohn, as well as Collier), and apparently always arrogantly felt that she was representing a Navajo view.[13]

Much is often made of Gilpin's regard for Navajo and Navajo custom. She is quoted as saying that "this time [in *The Enduring Navaho*] the people would be the theme, and the landscape the background" (Sandweiss, 1986:86). Yet we read later that Gilpin in fact delayed the Navajo book because of "a severe drought, which meant there wasn't a cloud in the sky in a land where normally the skies are superb and on which I count much" (Sandweiss, 1986:87). Nor did Gilpin's respect and regard for Navajo custom extend so far that she was to be denied photographs of healing practices (known in popular nomenclature as "ceremonials"). She acknowledged the Navajo resistance to photography of sacred materials used in such healing; but whereas Curtis got his pictures by staging them, Gilpin simply persisted, stating that she relied on the "building up of human relations to the point where I have such permission given [to photograph]. No one knows how long it takes to build this all up . . . two, three or even more trips and visits to finally win through" (Sandweiss, 1986:89). Gilpin did not understand that resistance had nothing to do with the degree of friendship but simply reflected the fact that Navajo believed a photograph of a sandpainting, for example, preserved something of a creation that is properly to be consumed wholly in the healing practice; failure to so consume it leaves it open to potential ill use and does not most effectively use the creation. Gilpin's view that it was simply a matter of "building up of human relations" or rapport or trust reveals how little she really understood Navajo culture. She wrote (1968:3), "To understand the Navaho people, even in small measure, it is essential to know at least some part of their symbolic ritual"—the last two words using the denigrating vocabulary of Western cynicism and disbelief.

Gilpin's extensive series of a Nightway healing practice at Pine Springs in October 1952 includes about a dozen photographs of the outside dancing on the ceremony's last night.[14] Though most lighting comes from an overhead electric or a lantern, in one photograph Gilpin actually used a flash (Fig. 176)! She did not try it again. All Gilpin's photographs of Nightway sandpaintings were from a different Nightway healing ceremony, taken extremely early in the year (28 September 1951—the Nightway is normally not held until after the first frosts) near Shiprock. She photographed a seventh- or eighth-day sandpainting, known as a radial Fringed Mouth sandpainting.[15] The point is, resistance was sufficiently strong that she only got access to bits and pieces of various healing practices, at different times, and so far as her

The Endearing Navajo

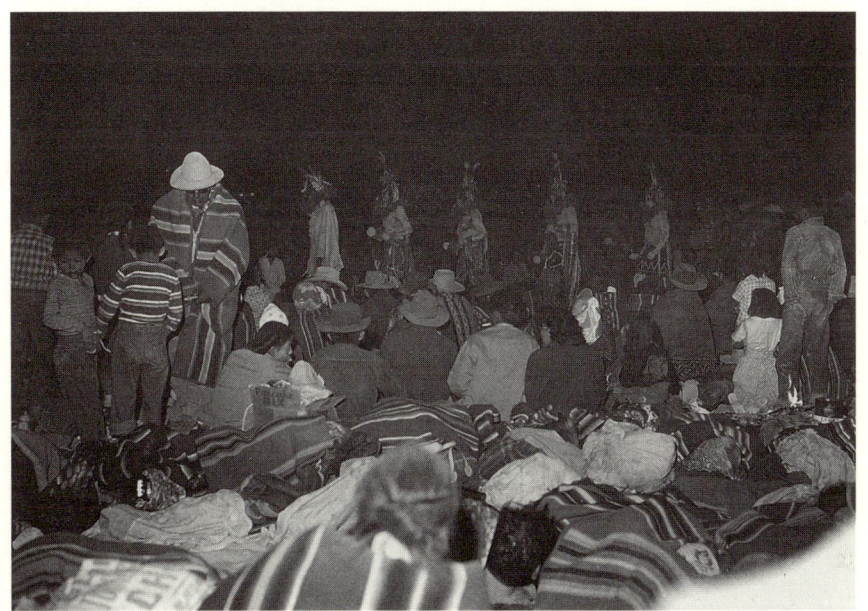

Figure 176

Figure 176. "Night of Yeibichai." Laura Gilpin, photographer, n.d. (probably 15 October 1952). Nightway, ninth evening, Slim First Dancers. flash. Many Gilpin photographs of this Nightway last night exist, including some published (see Gilpin, 1968:244), but she never again used the flash. This photograph was never published. Photograph courtesy Laura Gilpin Collection, Amon Carter Museum, Fort Worth, Texas. P1979.228.690. Copyright 1981.

Chapter 6

photographs indicate was never allowed to photograph a single Nightway healing ceremony in its totality.

Her genuine concern for Navajo did not override her concern for recording certain images—for example, of the Nakai family posing in front of the American flag that draped their son's coffin. He was killed in France during World War II, and the flag was presumably given the Nakai family after his burial. It is certainly a poignant photograph,[16] and the sorrow and despair are apparent. But how many exposures did Gilpin take for this particular photograph, and how many different poses did she try to achieve the desired end?[17] Do we know something of Mrs. Nakai's feelings in the circumstance, save the obvious distress? Was she asked if this were an acceptable trade—their son for the nation (it must be remembered that this death may have taken place before Navajo had the right to vote)? To Gilpin, the great patriot, the image illustrates one of the necessary heavy sacrifices Americans must make—but we know less of the Nakais' reaction. In this circumstance, is Gilpin not skating the edge of exploitation or banality to have set it all up so deliberately, to provoke a setting that would maximize the visual image (the stoic Navajo in grief) in the white public's mind? To Gilpin the Nakai boy's death was undoubtedly an acceptable sacrifice, but to the family? The conspicuous pain evident in their faces generates in both viewer and in subject a discomfort; we feel as if we should not be witness to this.

Inflated claims are made for Gilpin (and, though normally a modest person, Gilpin did steadfastly insist she represented "*their* view" [Sandweiss, 1986:110—italics in original]). Her biographer, Sandweiss, states that Gilpin's work remains vital as a unique document of New Deal Navajo history overlooked by other photographic surveys of the time.[18] Certainly it is important, but other archives contain thousands of photographs (cf. the Milton Snow and Concho collections of the Navajo Nation Museum) of this same period by individuals having better access, better understanding, and, in many cases, just as much technical skill.[19] These photographers did not spend so much time on lighting and posing—they were not "fine art" photographers, did not exhibit, and were not well-connected in Santa Fe. These attributes (usually referred to collectively as "sensitivity") are too often used to distinguish Gilpin from her contemporaries. But however well-intentioned, Gilpin was just one more non-Navajo representing Navajo. Some claims for her are simply not true. For example, Sandweiss states that Gilpin "never lent props to her subjects as Edward Curtis did, or took snapshots without consent" (1986:54). Yet we see Gilpin's favorite Navajo blanket time and time again, arranged on people who look every bit as posed as Curtis's Navajo, and we see backgrounds arranged to accord more with *her* aesthetic vision of what Navajo should look like (Fig. 177). Indeed, her Navajo blanket, her Pendleton blanket, and her arrangement of setting can be seen many, many times in her unpublished archive.[20] And in many of her candid photographs it appears that consent was not secured (see Fig. 176).

Though her partisans decry comparison with Edward Curtis, we know that a Curtis photograph of Canyon de Chelly hung in her family home and was an early and continual inspiration to her.[21] Gilpin lived at a different time; rather than documenting dying cultural entities, she was persuaded by her progressive Protestant outlook to regard Navajo as enduring and assimilating with dignity and grace. In fact, at times Gilpin shared exactly the same motivations as Curtis, remarking of one of her works: "I consider this one of my best photographs because I believe it portrays truly the individual character and the patient resignation of a member of this vanishing race" (Sandweiss, 1986:55).[22] Though we are told she moved away from this perspective, the romance and nostalgia, the posing and props, and the shallow understanding of the indigenous culture are still there.

Feminists[23] have called attention to Gilpin's humanizing of the landscape—her putting people, particularly women, back into it. They argue that the famous mother and child at the edge of the Shiprock photograph actually create the Shiprock in the distance by their gaze (Fig. 179). But this conclusion fails to acknowledge that Gilpin also published the same photograph without the mother and child—who were, on this evidence, simply framing devices, props, exotic compositional contrivances (Fig. 178).[24] Clearly her photographs were set up—that is not something necessarily to be critical of, but it also cannot be ignored in light of Gilpin's reputation as a chronicler of Navajo. "Mrs. Francis with Corn" (Fig. 180), "Navahos by Firelight" (Fig. 181), and "The Little Medicine Man" (Fig. 182) are not just people in ordinary postures doing ordinary things; "Navahos by Firelight" is, in fact, Navajo by flashbulb.

Sandweiss says the famous photograph "Hardbelly's Hogan"[25] demonstrates that Navajo "accepted Laura" and indicates "calm implacability"; Hardbelly's wives were "sitting peacefully" for the photograph, "no one acknowledged Laura's presence," and the picture was lit by "sunlight filtering through the overhead smoke hole" (1986:54). However, everyone looks very stiff and uncomfortable, and the very postures of people do not suggest self-arrangement. And if the only light available was that coming through a smoke hole, Gilpin would have had to instruct her subjects not to move while she took the long exposure necessary (she used a large view camera for all

Chapter 6

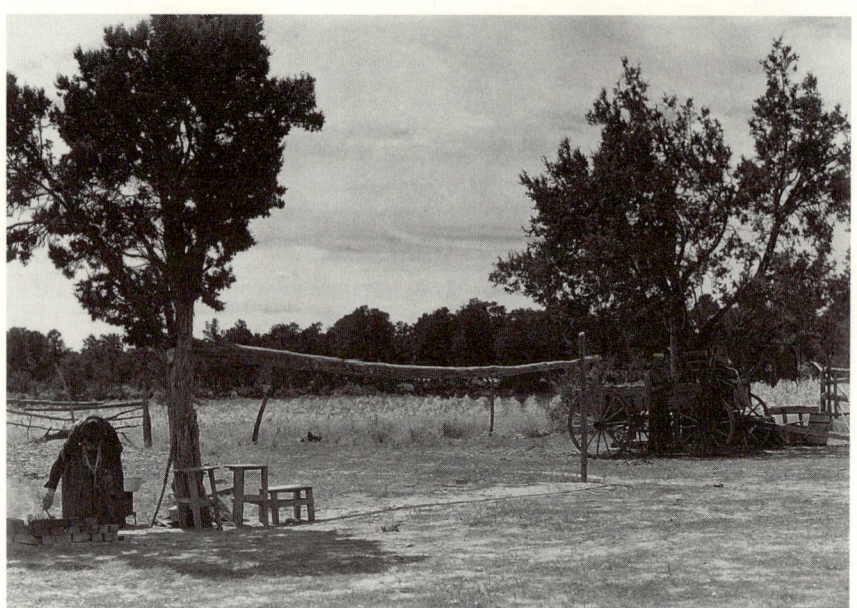

Figure 177

Figure 177. "Scene on Yazzie Farm, Pine Springs." Laura Gilpin, photographer, 17 October 1952. One of a series of a homesite, each cleared of unacceptably conspicuous Western debris. A homesite with this bare appearance would be regarded by Navajo as abandoned or inhabited by poverty-stricken individuals. In others of the series of this homesite, Gilpin draped Navajo weavings along the horizontal pole (something else that would not normally be seen in any Navajo homesite). Photograph courtesy Laura Gilpin Collection, Amon Carter Museum, Fort Worth, Texas. Gilpin negative # 3729 [6]. Copyright 1981.

The Endearing Navajo

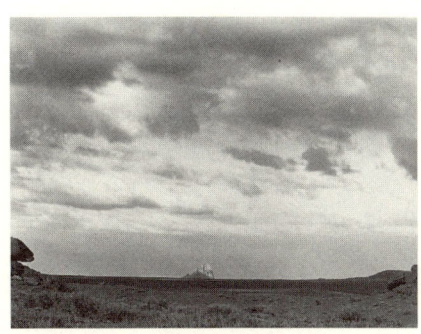
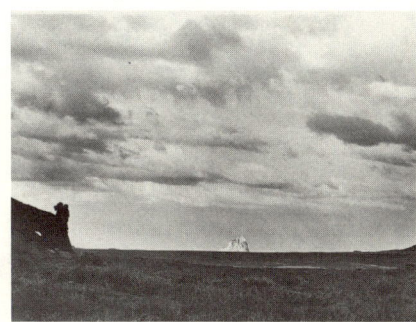

Figure 178 *Figure 179*

Figure 178. "Shiprock from the West, Evening." Laura Gilpin, photographer, 1932. See Fig. 179. Photograph courtesy Laura Gilpin Collection, Amon Carter Museum, Fort Worth, Texas. Gilpin negative # 2857.1. Copyright 1981.

Figure 179. "Shiprock, New Mexico." Laura Gilpin, photographer, 1932. See Fig. 178. Photograph courtesy Laura Gilpin Collection, Amon Carter Museum, Fort Worth, Texas. P1979.128.392. Copyright 1981.

Chapter 6

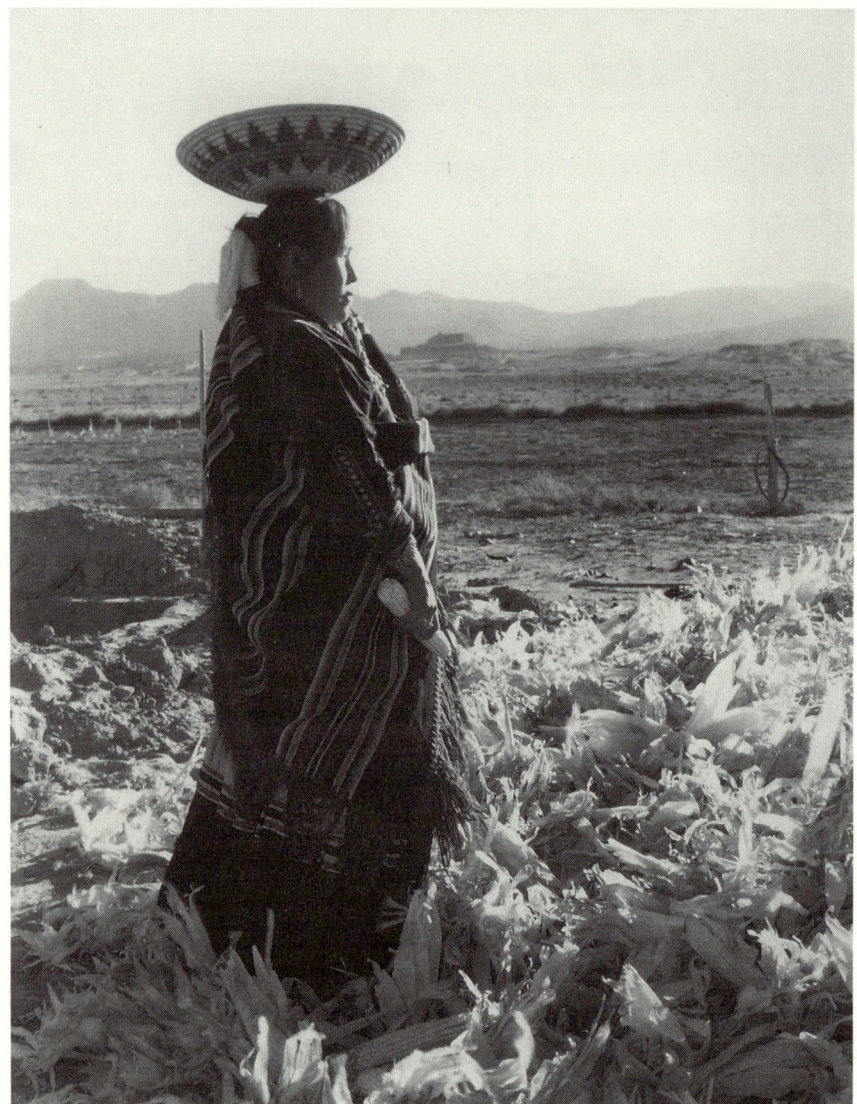

Figure 180

The Endearing Navajo

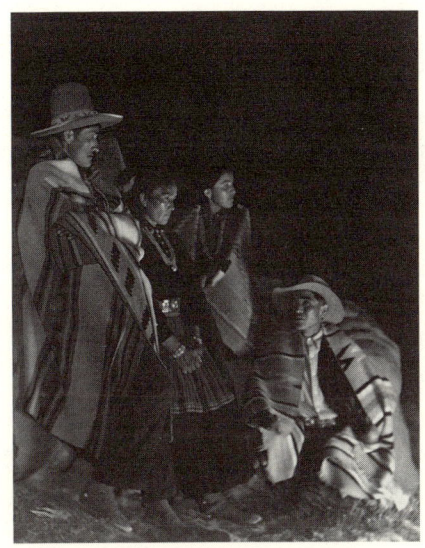
Figure 181

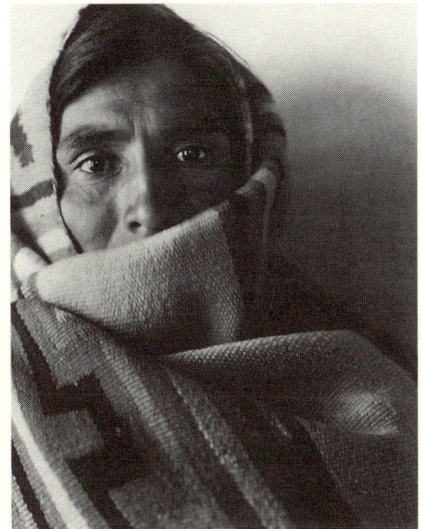
Figure 182

Figure 180. "Mrs. Francis with Corn." Laura Gilpin, photographer, 1933. Photograph courtesy Laura Gilpin Collection, Amon Carter Museum, Fort Worth, Texas. Gilpin Negative No. 2897.2. Copyright 1981.

Figure 181. "Navahos by Firelight." Laura Gilpin, photographer, 1933. Gilpin's blankets. See also Fig. 190. Photograph courtesy Laura Gilpin Collection, Amon Carter Museum, Fort Worth, Texas. Gilpin negative #2904.4. Copyright 1981.

Figure 182. "The Little Medicine Man." Laura Gilpin, photographer, 1932. Gilpin's blanket. Photograph courtesy Laura Gilpin Collection, Amon Carter Museum, Fort Worth, Texas. P1979.128.704. Copyright 1981.

245

Chapter 6

of her Navajo photographs). Indeed, the shadows and lighting suggest possibly a reflector, if not a bounced flash. Though persons who worked with her said Gilpin was said to have been embarrassed by some of her earlier excessively romantic and posed Navajo photographs (such as "Navahos by Firelight"),[26] "Hardbelly's Hogan" apparently was not judged such a photograph, and it appeared in her 1968 book. Gilpin speaks of the conditions of the making of the photograph, taken during Elizabeth Forster's visit to the senior man.[27] Forster is seen in the photo administering medicine (she has moved to the far side of the patient, presumably so Gilpin would not photograph her from the back, as all her medicines are still on the near side), and Hardbelly's wives and a son also appear. Gilpin says, "I wondered if I dared ask to make a picture. To my surprise they seemed pleased I wanted to" (1968:31). In the circumstances, they also had little choice.[28]

Sandweiss tells us that the task was to "document a particular people and their way of life" and that the "empathetic feelings that existed between her and her subjects add to the emotional impact and import of her work and in no way distract from its value as an extraordinary document of Navajo life" (1986:56). But, as with Curtis, the motivating tropes for Gilpin are a type of preservational documentary and her own view of what was worthy of preservation. Her partisans insist that she made photos of Navajo only after asking and paid for them by providing prints to the subjects. In many situations, however, consent was clearly not (or could not have been) obtained. Gilpin did complain, however, about how the excessive modeling fees paid by wealthy amateur photographers made it difficult for her (presumably with little or no money to offer) to get permission to photograph.

Comparing materials from the unpublished archive with published photographs indicates that there was hardly an unproblematic Navajo photograph. One of the surprising features of the archive is the number of photos taken for each usable one. This may not be unusual for photographers in general, but it is surprising for a documentarian or chronicler. There are over thirty unpublished photographs, for example, of the "Old Lady Long Salt Hogan" image (only a few photos of this image were published).[29] It is not without significance, perhaps, then, that Gilpin is quoted as saying of this sequence: "[W]e have found when visiting families such as this, that a time comes when their courtesy to us has been fulfilled, their curiosity is satisfied, and their normal work must be resumed. It is well to be sensitive to this approaching moment and to take one's leave before wearing out a welcome" (Sandweiss, 1986:91). Like so many other photographers, Gilpin leaned on Navajo courtesy and the dramatic power differential between them

The Endearing Navajo

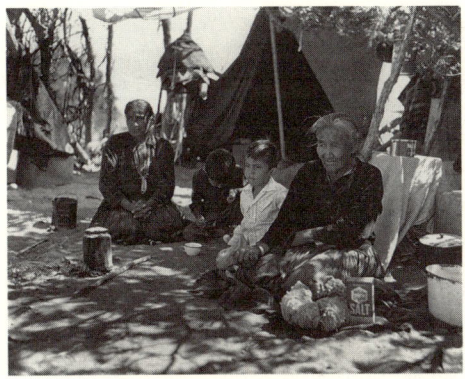
Figure 183

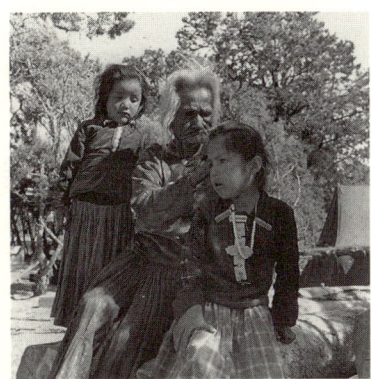
Figure 184

Figure 183. "Navajo Family." Lee Boltin, photographer. August 1954. This family also appears in the Gilpin photographs (cf. Gilpin, 1968:70-71) of "the summer hogan of Old Lady Long Salt," made about one year earlier. Boltin must have had the same interpreter as did Gilpin, for these people are not in an easily accessible location (Navajo Mountain). Photograph courtesy Department of Library Services, American Museum of Natural History. Negative No. 2A 3695

Figure 184. "Navajo Family." Lee Boltin, photographer, 1954. This family (as well as "Old Lady Gray Salt") also appears in the Gilpin collections (cf. Gilpin, 1968:44), photographed at the head of Navajo Canyon within a year of Boltin's photograph. Photograph courtesy Department of Library Services, American Museum of Natural History. Negative No. 6965 #175.

Chapter 6

and herself to secure the images. Even she could recognize when they tired of the exercise, of having cameras pointed at them. (The same family group was descended upon within a year by two major photographers—see Figs. 183, 184—probably because they were not too resistant and because a cultural broker and/or interpreter had some access to the family.)

In a sequence surrounding the image "Group in Hogan Door, Red Rock" (see Figs. 185-188), Gilpin suggested that she took the photograph because the hogan shape replicated the rounded hill in the landscape background.[30] She published it despite a blurred feature—the movement of one individual. But there are several more unpublished photographs of the hogan and its family *without* the background rounded hill (suggesting perhaps the round form features were darkroom discoveries). However, the most interesting thing about the entire sequence is the small boy second from right, who consistently refuses to look at the camera or deliberately moves during each exposure. It would appear that throughout these multiple exposures of the same family, Gilpin may have been attempting to get the young boy to look at the camera or stay still. Other unpublished images contain occasional instances of resistance or of dramatic photographic manipulation (see Figs. 189-190).[31]

As with the FSA photographers Walker Evans and Dorothea Lange, suit was eventually leveled at Gilpin's estate, in this case by her Navajo Madonna (Lilly Benally and her son Norman). When asked what Gilpin's reaction would have been to the suit, Sandweiss proposed that she would not have been upset, that "she probably would have talked to the woman and that would have been the end of it" (Eauclaire, 1989:46). The details of the lawsuit's argument, however, would suggest otherwise. This suit highlights some of the disadvantages Native Americans face in European-American-based legal matters and the extent to which rulings protect photographers, who can argue their photographs were of public facts and views, however much the Native American subjects of the photographs may feel differently. Little redress is possible given existing statutes and torts concerning privacy, especially the segments considering what are specified as "persons of reasonable and ordinary sensitivity."

Because the final settlement (23 May 1989) was reached out of court, the details were kept from public knowledge, and attorneys for both sides were asked not to comment. The attorney for Lilly and Norman Benally honored this request, but the Amon Carter attorney talked with the press and revealed that the agreement "didn't call for an absolute prohibition" on use of the "Navaho Madonna" but merely limited its uses—it could be used for "educational purposes" that were not publicly specified.[32] The Amon Carter attorney also revealed that the terms and restrictions of the settlement expired with the death of the subjects.[33]

The original suit, based on invasion of privacy, stemmed from Navajo belief that public exposure of photographs can possibly have bad effects for those depicted.[34] The plaintiffs argued that they had not given permission for the publication of the photo, nor indeed had it been sought by Laura Gilpin (contradicting claims that she always sought releases for her photographs of people), who had published it and exhibited it extensively, nor by the Amon Carter Museum, nor by three magazines that had recently used the photograph, two with the explicit permission of the Amon Carter Museum. The museum initially argued, rather callously, that New Mexico jurisdiction did not apply (as it was a Texas entity). This position was denied on appeal. But the invasion-of-privacy tort eventually came to plague the plaintiffs, as it was found that they were not, in expressing their fear of such exposure of their image or in simply objecting to such exposure, "reasonably sensible." The district court, in initially granting summary judgment for the defendants, indicated the Benallys had made no claim that the publication was offensive to an ordinarily sensible person, only that it was offensive to traditional Navajos.[35] The case was successfully appealed and eventually settled out of court, as noted.

Several other points about the lawsuit are worth noting. First is the fact that it concerned but a single photograph, the "Navaho Madonna." The Gilpin collections of the Amon Carter Museum include at least eleven other photographs of Lilly Benally, but the out-of-court settlement applies only to the single image. Presumably, then, the other photographs are not subject to the announced restrictions on publication that apply to "Navaho Madonna," though this has not been tested as far as I know. (Interestingly, in the unpublished photographs of Lilly Benally in the archive, she is depicted more often in nontraditional dress than in the silver and velvet traditional attire of the Madonna portrait.) The attorney for the plaintiffs told me[36] that he did not know these other photographs existed. The defense attorneys presumably were aware of their existence but did not reveal this information.

That Navajo are adjudicated not to be persons of ordinary sensibility has many implications. The plaintiff's attorney mentioned (October 1991) that the presiding district judge in the case (Juan Burciaga) lamented this conclusion and urged a change in the statutes to address it. But Moreland (1991:277) convincingly argued that the concluding finding is absurd:

Chapter 6

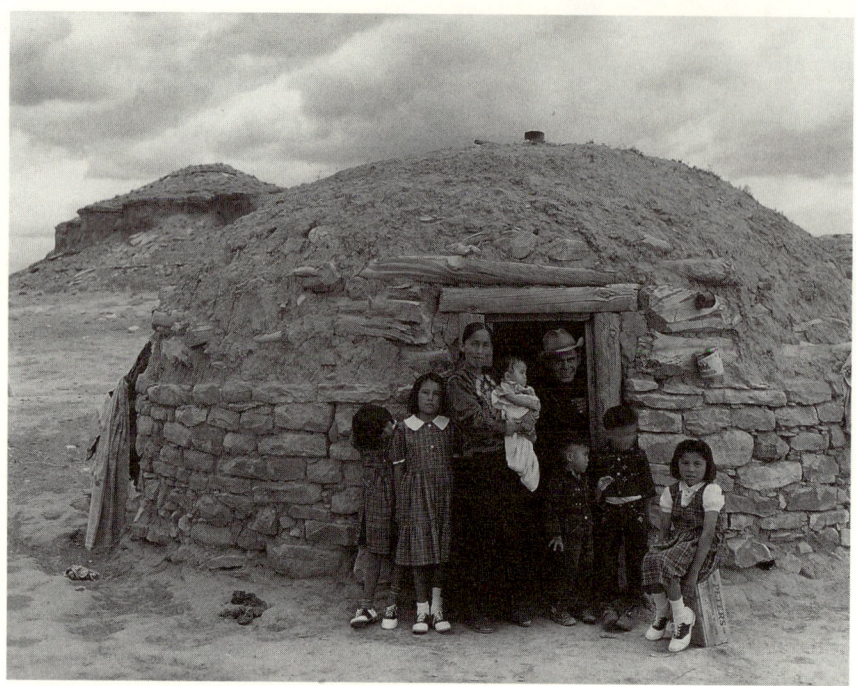

Figure 185

Figure 185. "Group in Hogan Door, Red Rock." Laura Gilpin, photographer, 17 September 1950. Published in Sandweiss, 1986. Girls in school uniforms (but note young boy at right). Photograph courtesy Laura Gilpin Collection, Amon Carter Museum, Fort Worth, Texas. Gilpin negative # 2924.1. Copyright 1981.

The Endearing Navajo

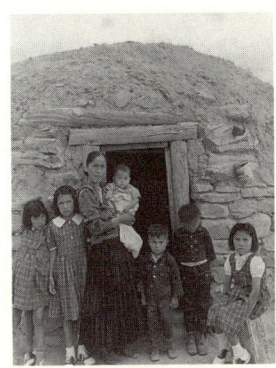
Figure 186

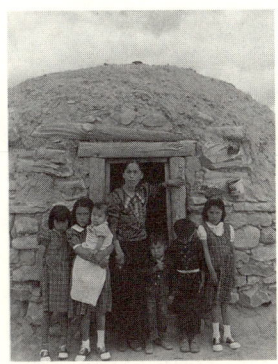
Figure 187

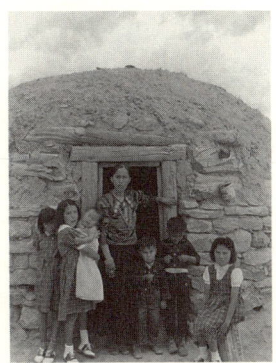
Figure 188

Figure 186. "Group in Hogan Door, Red Rock." Laura Gilpin, photographer, 17 September 1950. Unpublished. Same setting as Fig. 185. Photograph courtesy Laura Gilpin Collection, Amon Carter Museum, Fort Worth, Texas. Gilpin negative # 2924 [2]. Copyright 1981.

Figure 187. "Group in Hogan Door, Red Rock." Laura Gilpin, photographer, 17 September 1950. Unpublished. Same setting as Fig. 185. Photograph courtesy Laura Gilpin Collection, Amon Carter Museum, Fort Worth, Texas. Gilpin negative # 2924 [3]. Copyright 1981.

Figure 188. "Group in Hogan Door, Red Rock." Laura Gilpin, photographer, 17 September 1950. Unpublished. Same setting as Fig. 185. By the time of this pose, others besides the young boy are tiring of the photographic experience. Photograph courtesy Laura Gilpin Collection, Amon Carter Museum, Fort Worth, Texas. Gilpin negative # 2924 [4]. Copyright 1981.

Chapter 6

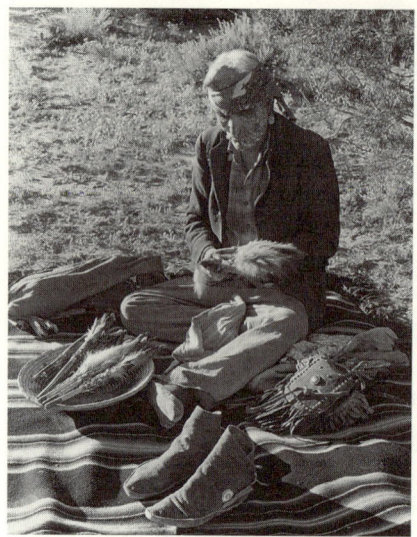
Figure 189

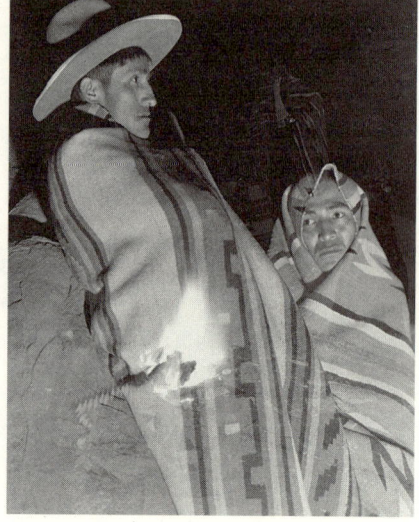
Figure 190

Figure 189. "Medicine Man, Pine Springs." Laura Gilpin, photographer, 1952. This man suffered a skin disease or a pigment loss, but in other prints I have seen of this photograph, Gilpin touched up his face in the darkroom. The published version (in Gilpin, 1968:214) of this print is printed more darkly. Photograph courtesy Laura Gilpin Collection, Amon Carter Museum, Fort Worth, Texas. Gilpin negative # 3722 [3]. Copyright 1981.

Figure 190. "Navahos by Firelight." Laura Gilpin, photographer, 1933. Unpublished. Campfire imposed (possibly dual exposure). Blankets are Gilpin's (see Fig. 181). Photograph courtesy Laura Gilpin Collection, Amon Carter Museum, Fort Worth, Texas. Gilpin negative # 2904 [5]. Copyright 1981.

Even if the findings in the Indian privacy cases weren't irrelevant and absurd, beautiful neurotics nonetheless have their rights. The plaintiffs were not beautiful neurotics, however, and they were not being unreasonable. They were merely attempting to protect their basic human needs, and thus their basic human rights to privacy.

He went on to argue (1991:277) that because conventional European-American law seems inadequate to these rights and needs, tribal courts and judiciaries must take up the task to ensure that privacy is respected.

Portfolio VII
Loom

Portfolio VII

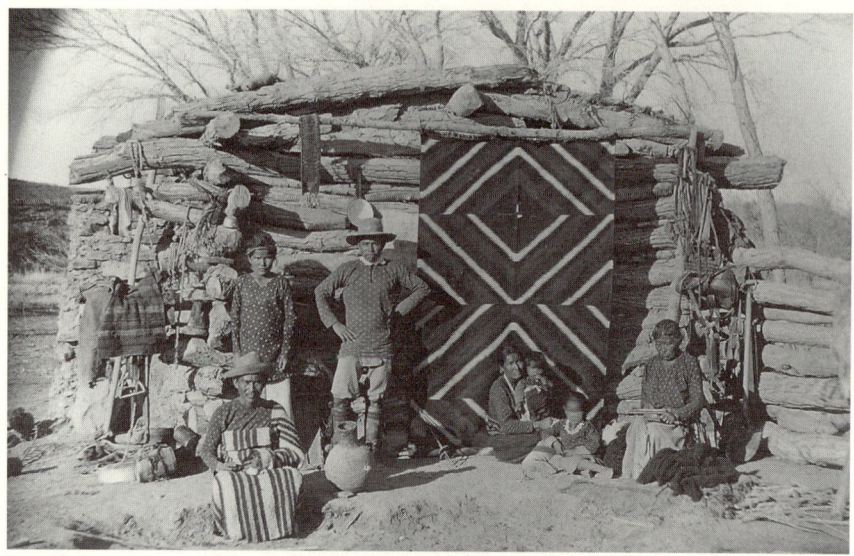

Figure 191

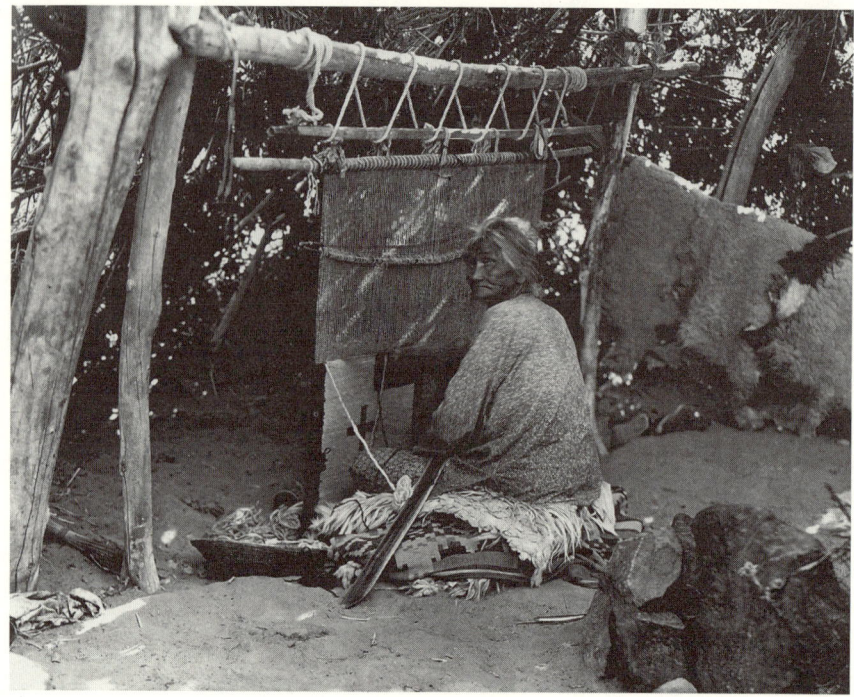

Figure 192

Loom

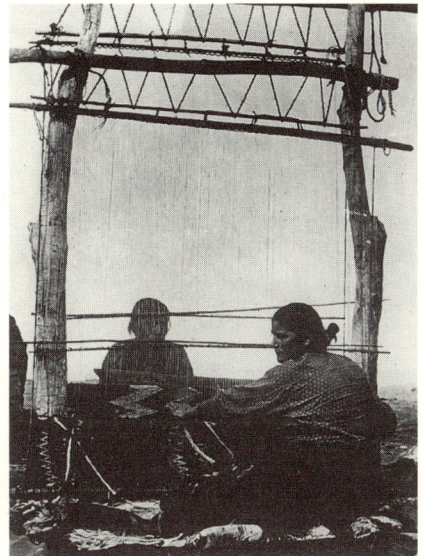
Figure 193

Figure 191. "House built by Manito, Navaho Indian. A family of blanket weavers." Charles Goodman, photographer, n.d. Probably before 1900 (1884–1902). Note unusual weaving and large pot or pitched basket. Photograph courtesy Colorado State Historical Society. No. F20,543.

Figure 192. "Navajo woman weaving rug, seated, 3/4 view of face, before primitive loom in summer hogan." Joseph K. Dixon, photographer, 4 July 1913. A very similar photograph of this same setting has been erroneously assigned a date of "around 1850" in the recent Time-Life book, People of the Desert (see Woodhead, 1993:167). Photograph courtesy William Hammond Mathers Museum, Indiana University. W3263.

Figure 193. "Navajo weaver." J. Hildebrand, photographer, ca. 1895. This is not, as might appear initially, simply another woman sitting idly on the other side of the warp; it is an interesting illustration of two rugs strung from the same structure, and both women are weaving. In such an arrangement, weaving is a social affair. Photograph courtesy Museum of New Mexico. Neg. No. 808.

257

Portfolio VII

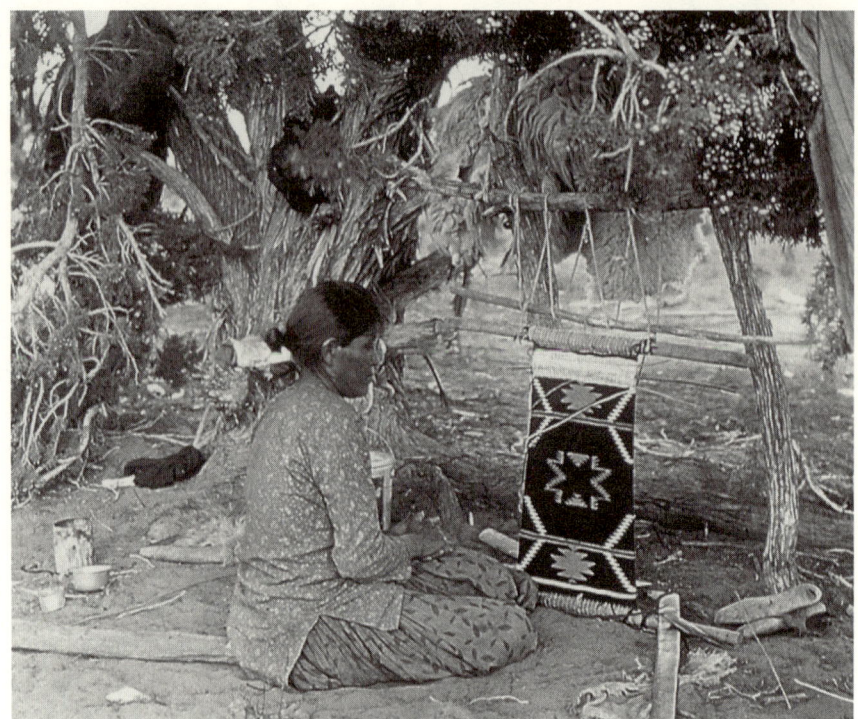

Figure 194

Figure 194. "Navajo woman weaving blanket." Frederick Monsen, photographer, 1896–1906, Jeddito Springs AZ. This woman has stopped weaving for the photograph or has been placed in front of the loom while not weaving. Interestingly, the weaving is not a blanket (not even a saddle blanket) but probably a special order placed by a trader or rich patron for a set of weavings for a specific use and design. See, for example, the slightly larger but otherwise identical weaving in Fig. 195, indicating that these were weavings to a specific special order. A Navajo weaver would not normally make weavings of exactly the same design in different and abnormal sizes. Photograph reproduced from the Frederick Monsen Collections of The Huntington Library. Card No. 91.

Loom

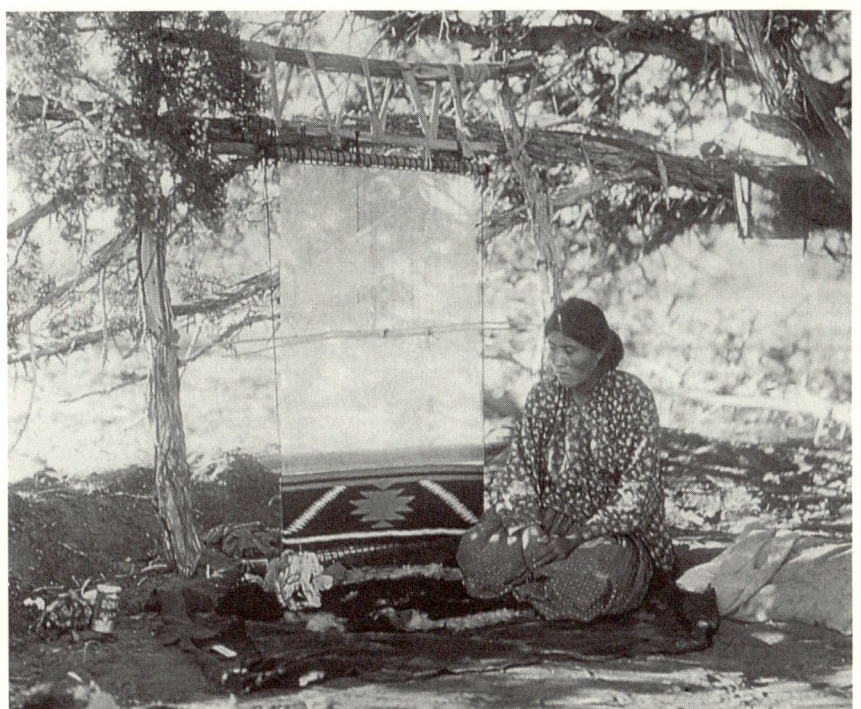

Figure 195

Figure 195 "Navajo blanket weaver." Frederick Monsen, photographer, 1896–1906, Jeddito Springs AZ. See the smaller but otherwise identical weaving in Fig. 194, indicating these were weavings to a specific special order. Light from behind the warp threads became a successful and favorite photographic element (see Fig. 193). Photograph reproduced from the Frederick Monsen Collections of The Huntington Library. Card No. 92.

Portfolio VII

Figure 196. "*Navajo Blanket maker.*" *Charles Goodman, photographer, n.d. (1884–1902). Perhaps Bluff, Utah. Clearly this arrangement has been set up for the photograph, for the weaving illustrated does not appear fastened at the bottom of the loom. Moreover, the branches in the background seem to have been simply propped up. Perhaps the photograph was taken at a fair, where a weaving demonstration or loom was rapidly mounted and not intended to be used. Goodman photographed extensively at fairs. Photograph courtesy Colorado State Historical Society. No. F36,627.*

Figure 197. "*Elle at loom, with daughter.*" *G. Wharton James, photographer, n.d. Elle, from Ganado, who, with her husband Tom, was probably the most-photographed Navajo woman of the first quarter of the twentieth century. She was a fine weaver and set up with a loom at the Fred Harvey Alvarado Hotel and Santa Fe Railway station in Albuquerque, where thousands of tourists took her photograph. Photograph courtesy California Historical Society, Title Insurance and Trust Photo Collection, Department of Special Collections, University of Southern California Library. Negative No. 5888.*

Loom

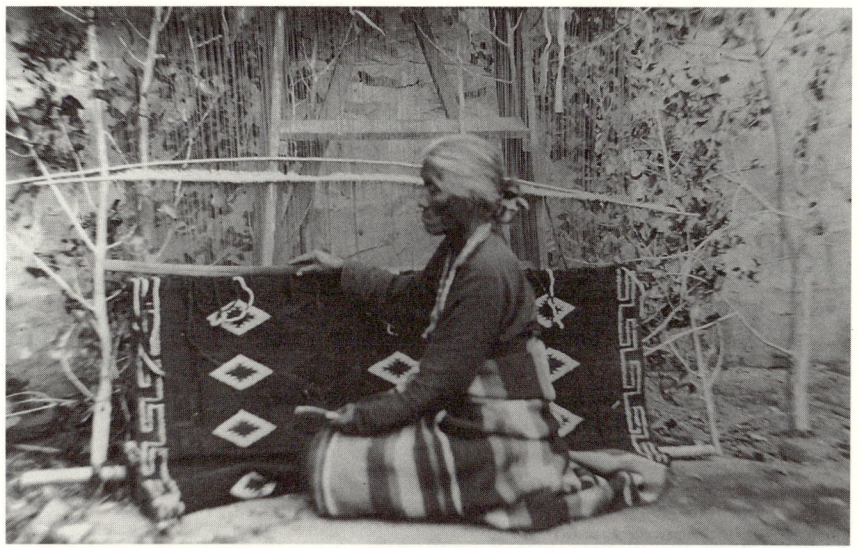

Figure 196

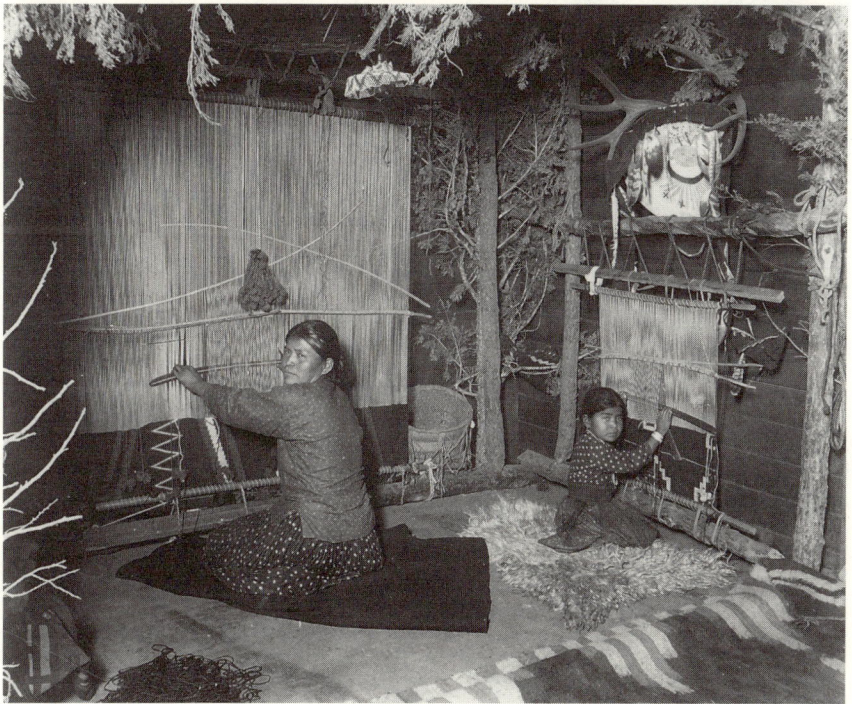

Figure 197

261

Portfolio VII

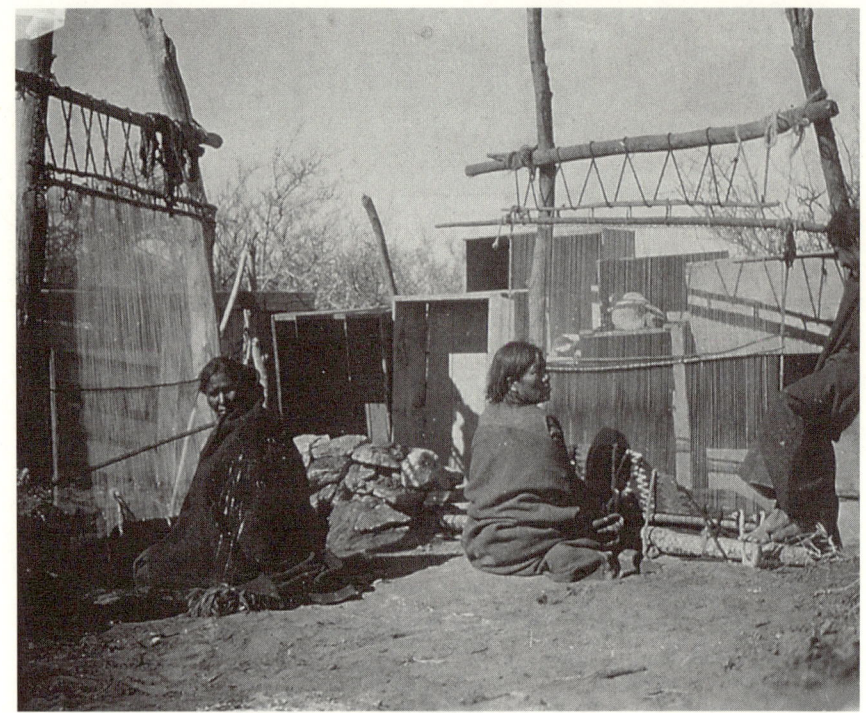

Figure 198

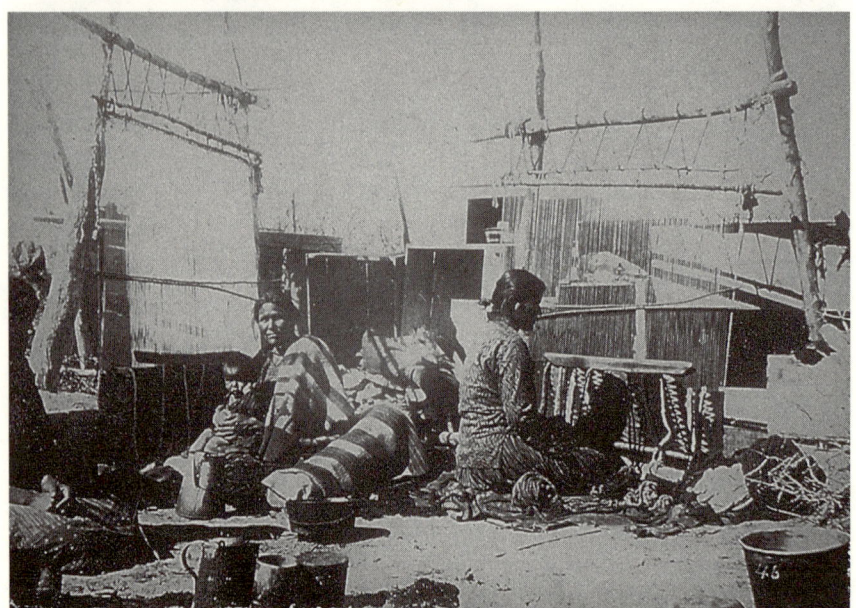

Figure 199

Figure 198. Navajo women at looms. J. W. Hildebrand, photographer, n.d. (1895–1908). An unusual number of large wooden crates stand in background (perhaps for shipping of Navajo weavings??). J. L. Hubbell was said to have had some 300 Navajo weavers "working for him" at one point (see M'Closkey, 1993:384), and weavings in this period (and in some areas until much more recently) were frequently bought by the pound and shipped all over the nation. For a view of the same weavers at a slightly different time, with children and unremoved items of Western manufacture, see Fig. 199. Photograph courtesy J. W. Hildebrand Collection, Museum of Northern Arizona. MS 168-E-200.5.

Figure 199. Women weaving, perhaps cooking, child minding. Christian Kaadt, photographer, 1899–1905. Note here the numbers of crates and boxes, perhaps used to ship Navajo weavings in bulk. See Fig. 198 for the same scene photographed at a slightly different time by a different photographer—perhaps Kaadt and Hildebrand collaborated. The items of Western manufacture here in the foreground (pots, pans, buckets) are missing in Fig. 198. Photograph courtesy Southwest Museum, Los Angeles. P39528.

Portfolio VII

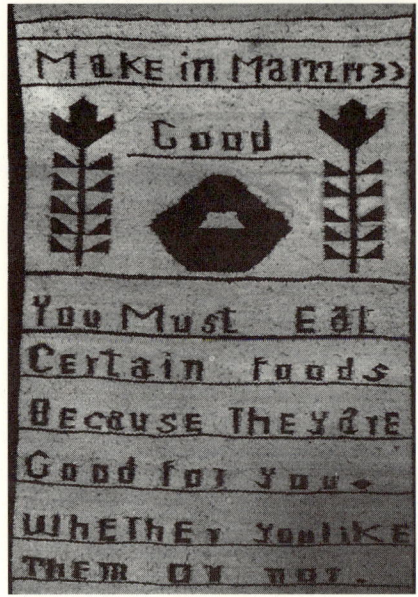

Figure 200

Figure 200. "Typical modern rug—showing what should be discouraged by traders." Milton Snow, photographer, 1 June 1936. The weaving seems to express the desired BIA and Protestant virtue, including the weaver's resigned, humorous admonition and her own judgment of the piece as "Good," including the month and year of weaving. She has clearly and delightfully violated the conventional market view that weavings are timeless, hold sacred meanings, and must always be anonymous. Photograph courtesy National Archives, Washington. NA/RG 114/Soil Conservation Service, 1933–1937 NM.

Figure 201. "Navajo weaver." T. Harmon Parkhurst, photographer, ca. 1935. Navajo at tourist site (concrete tipi, commercial loom, man wearing Navajo blanket), probably Holbrook AZ. The weaving, as a "properly" assigned Navajo custom, carries most of the load for Navajo-ness in this caricature, as does the Navajo weaving draped about the man (Navajo did not at this time normally wear their own weavings, preferring to don commercial blankets, as does the woman at the loom). Photograph courtesy Museum of New Mexico. Neg. No. 3141.

Figure 201

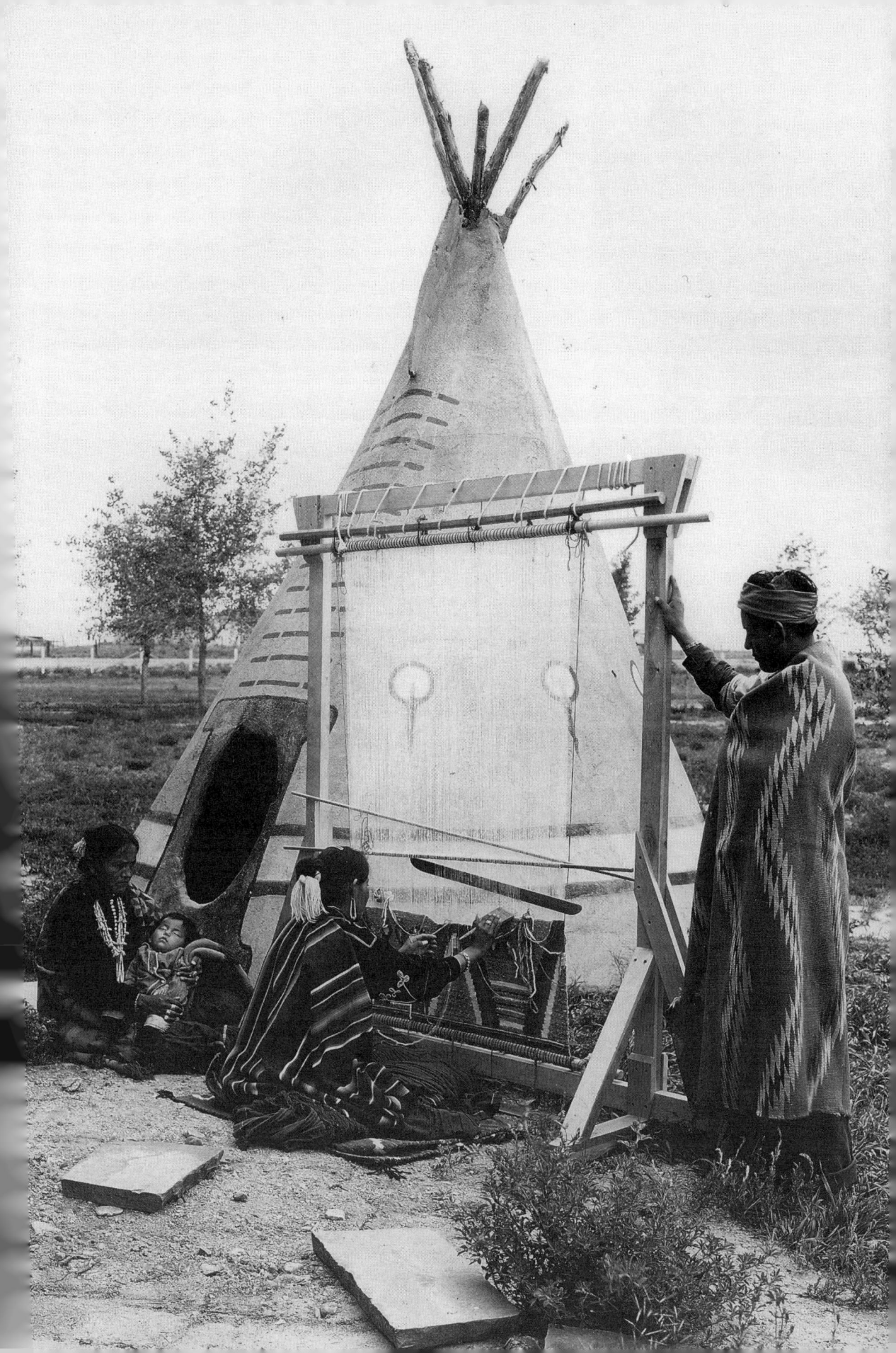

Chapter Seven

Selling Navajo Images: Contemporary Picture Books and Photographic Modernism

One of the consequences of the early establishment of most possible Western registers in Navajo photography was competition between photographers, especially between a photographer and his or her predecessor. Different practitioners did not deviate greatly from each other in thematic content or photographic essentials; rather, discriminations primarily took place discursively. Each photographer claimed to have some new perspective, more authentic perception, increased understanding, greater familiarity, better relationships, special insight, or heightened sensitivity vis-à-vis Navajo. This is particularly true of the biographers of such photographers, who made such arguments to justify publication and discriminate their subject from the undifferentiated others. There seems to me about this analysis a sort of defense, a need to rationalize, to absolve, to exonerate, almost as if without it the personal motives would be too stark, the similarities with earlier (and other) photographers and their motives too apparent.

Over time, with increased liberal sensitivities, shifts in reasoning and styles of appropriation occurred. The clever white men from the era of Monsen (outsmarting Indians unfamiliar with the technology) and Post (concealing the exact time of exposure) gave way to the litany of those today who are supposed to be more respecting of Navajo (Susanne [Anderson] Page, Marcia Keegan, John Running, Joel Grimes, Skeet McAuley), more aware of their plight (Mark Gaede, Roswell Angier), or ever aiding them—photographically—

Chapter 7

in their struggles (Running, Abigail Adler, Dan Budnick, Lisa Law, Karen Marshall, Janet Bingham). Not even the radical allies of Navajo bother to significantly critique the camera, or photography, or the nature of the encounter, and there is usually only implied criticism of other photographers.[1]

Intellectually, modernism had triumphed, pulling along some of the newer photographers. These latter were of several types. One might be called anti-aestheticists—those who revolted from the formalist aesthetic dictates of their predecessors. For photographers in this category, including Robert Frank (Figs. 202, 203) and Fedor (Fig. 204), Navajo were simply more Americans under casual anti-studio surveillance.[2] As such, this was at once an incorporating and an obliterating movement. Nothing distinctively Navajo emerged, only an underbelly of America useful to Frank's project, sort of a reciprocal to Steichen's "family of man"—high modernist reality surveillance leveling as opposed to universalist romantic leveling.

There also came to be in this tradition a more specific photojournalistic emphasis and frequently a focus on victims. Following McCombe (1951), there appeared the quite unpleasant book by Gaede (1988), a former Museum of Northern Arizona staff photographer. Gaede principally photographed victims—the dead, the dying, the broken—in stark black and white. But he showed us little about why these conditions pertained—he simply hoped his photographs would have some redeeming value by presenting the situation as a real problem, at least for the victims illustrated: "All of the portraits reproduced in this book were taken with the permission of the subjects, most of whom were paid. The portraits were never forced or exposed clandestinely. All of the newsworthy images were taken spontaneously without permission as permitted by law" (Gaede, 1988:no pagination).

The definition of "newsworthy," of course, rests with the European-American photographer, as does the law. To appeal to the law in this case seems particularly unfortunate—indeed, Gaede describes how he was threatened after photographing accident victims and had to be rescued by the police.[3] In some portraits, it is clear money was the only reason the subject gave permission:

> For years she has walked the streets of Gallup. A small man usually accompanies her and they sort trash bins together for a living. Her face is a mask, but in the one good eye something of the woman can be seen. Perhaps she isn't as old as the first impression portrays. When the photographer previously requested photographs, she would always respond "no pictures, no pictures!" But this time she gave in, probably for the little money offered (Gaede, 1988:photograph 73).

He seems challenged and determined to overcome her clear resistance. His raw presentation never discusses murder, rape, or exploitation. Rick Hill (1993:11), in a review of Gaede, makes the point clearly:

> The point here is that maybe, if Gaede really wants to change the condition of the street people, he should look at the real problem. It is not cultural suicide committed by Indians, it is usually murder or at least a form of genocide. He should point his camera at the craftshop owners, the bootleggers, the rapists, and the cowboys in their pickup trucks.

This victim realism had a currency, however, such that half the Navajo represented in a photographic volume, *New Mexico, USA*, published by the Santa Fe Center for Photography, appear in photographs of this offensive sort.[4] Here again, the reader/spectator/guard is provided with no information on context—just an inscrutable warts-on-view of New Mexico. (It is significant that Navajo are the only New Mexico population portrayed so harshly in the book.) Given the prevailing Western discourses about Native Americans, it seems irresponsible not to discuss the circumstances of Navajo incarceration, the threat to the photographer, or the power enabling him to take such photographs. What was Angier doing in the Gallup jail's drunk tank? Is there anything "newsworthy" (and thus enabled by law) about this? Was there any model release, any payment? Was there any choice given the subjects?

More recently (and much more overwhelmingly), an unending series of picture books have appeared on the region and its indigenous inhabitants. With the emergence of the Southwest as a desired retirement and vacation location, photography (especially color photographs) became the text and came to speak more and more for itself. It no longer seemed quite so necessary to have a narrative that the photographs illustrated or that explained the photographs; pictures of Navajo stood by themselves, as if in a gallery. This approach commonly resulted in blatant tourist caricatures or more pictorially dramatic and extreme photographs—all well within the hackneyed canon of types known since the early decades of the twentieth century. The very sparse narrative texts accompanying these albums are generally insulating rather than explanatory—introductions and commentary by the rich and famous (Robert Redford, Tony Hillerman, N. Scott Momaday, Stewart Udall)—and humanist organizations (Sierra Club, Friends of the Earth), camera and film manufacturers (Kodak), or mining companies (Union Carbide) often sponsor such photographic projects. The last few lines of a common Blessingway song (often that sung before dawn on the last morning of a

Chapter 7

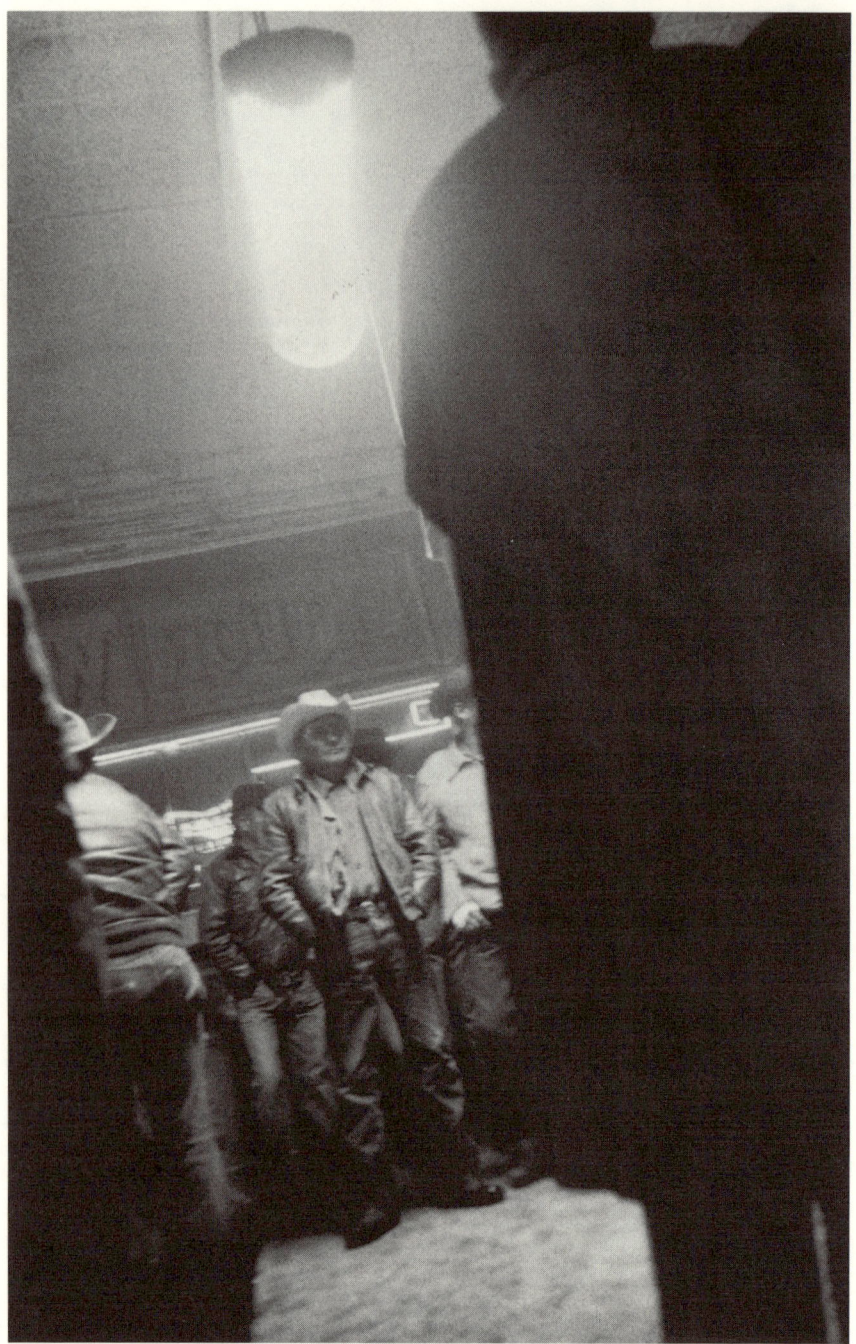

Figure 202

Selling Navajo Images

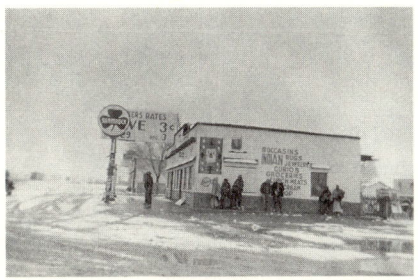

Figure 203

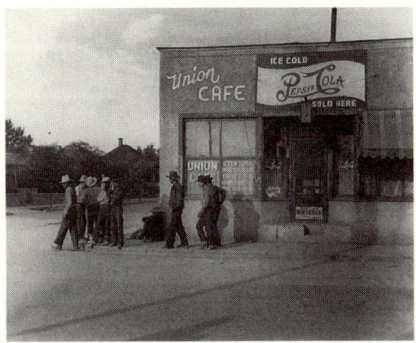

Figure 204

Figure 202. "Bar—Gallup, New Mexico, 1955." Robert Frank, photographer. See Frank, 1978; Coke, 1979. Photograph courtesy University of New Mexico Art Museum, Museum purchase. #78.176.

Figure 203. "Indians Leaning on Shamrock Station, 1956." Robert Frank, photographer. See also Fig. 202. Photograph courtesy University of New Mexico Art Museum, Museum purchase. #89.27.2.

Figure 204. "Navajo Indians in front of Union Cafe." Ferenz Fedor, photographer, ca. 1940, Gallup NM. Compare with the Robert Frank photograph, Fig. 203, *made more than a decade later. This photo anticipates the rise of casual modernist surveillance.* Photograph courtesy Museum of New Mexico. Neg. No. 101699.

Nightway healing ceremony)[5] are repeated—in varied forms—over and over again. There is lots of walking in beauty and lots of Mother Earth—white man's Mother Earth.

Four such photographers will be discussed here—Susanne [Anderson] Page, Marcia Keegan, John Running, and Joel Grimes—but there are many others. What one sees as exploitation (posing), another sees as giving the subject some command over the conditions of the photograph. What one extols as evidence of their acceptance (allowing the camera at random), another sees as evidence of aggressive behavior. One sees payment for photographs as just, another as polluting and mercenary. One eschews the long focus lens as voyeurism; another adopts such lenses to highlight or to produce a more intense or poignant photograph, often with all background out of focus and obliterated. One sees the photographs as a means of preserving disappearing customs, another as evidence of vitality. All claim (or their commentators claim for them) to have greater insight into Navajo than their predecessors or colleagues. Though there can be little doubt about the sincerity of these individuals and their naive quests, there is also no doubt that their projects are obstinately Western—essentialist and/or patronizing—and stress just what photography stresses best—a timelessness, an obliteration of the exploitative history that makes it possible to photograph Navajo. They ignore a Navajo history itself that is so dramatically at odds with conventional wisdom[6] and the persistent vision and imaging on Western terms. It must be remembered that a continual focus on the "beautiful" and the "traditional" (even if it is expressed in pickup trucks and sneakers) still erects hierarchies ("ugly" and "modern") and thus totalizes Navajo experience. It also reiterates that knowledge of Navajo existence is a privilege of the enlightened West. As noted, this is not a Navajo existence on Navajo terms; "traditional" is limited to a period of less than 100 years, and Navajo claims to aboriginality are not considered legitimate.

Most of the Navajo photographs in Page's *A Celebration of Being* (1989) appeared earlier in *Song of the Earth Spirit* (n.d. [1973]). The latter text did not use real names, but the former did.[7] In the first volume, photographs have to speak for themselves; there are no labels, and the accompanying text is only occasionally relevant to the photographs. The second volume is similarly organized but has a list of photographic labels at the end. Both volumes offer much discussion of the subtleties of Navajo culture, but the understandings are very superficial—much like the telephoto photographs that isolate people from any surroundings.[8] In her descriptions, Navajo order [*hózhǫ́*] becomes "harmony," another indication of the West's shallow assimilation of Navajo concepts. In accordance with the dictates of the Friends of the Earth,[9] there are only clean, isolated Navajo and bare landscapes (where we occasionally do see a photograph with a wide angle of view), never littered with Pampers, beer cans, old refrigerators, junk automobiles, tires, and other debris of previous consumption.[10] Sometimes the latter, in the Navajo view, are indications of desired wealth and status, whereas a homestead devoid of any evidence of prior purchases is a homestead of poverty or even a *ch'į́įndii* (ghost hogan).[11] But Page's extreme close-up portrait photographs and common use of a long focus lens mean that backgrounds are not often in focus, so not much evidence of Western detritus is visible in any case.

When she does not "capture the moment" with a close-up using a long focus lens (which makes it difficult to discriminate Navajo from Hopi or to see any specificity at all),[12] she sometimes takes her models out to a "photogenic" site—red rocks, or backlit vista. Though it is commendable that Page attempts to stress the commonalties between Hopi and Navajo (but thus deliberately avoids the issues of land disputes), she does so by extirpating significant differences and eliding massive injustices perpetrated upon Navajo by the federal government in the Joint-Use Area.[13] She apparently has plans for a large photo volume on Navajo,[14] but this had not appeared by the time of the current research. She did participate in the very problematic *Millennium* television series, and her still photographs appear in the book derived from the series.[15] Here she photographed a short, set-up healing involving sandpainting and took pictures of *jish* (the ingredients of sacred bundles used in healing) and training sessions for healers. Though she undoubtedly had permission from those involved, she did not seem to realize that such photography and discussion are nevertheless very problematic (and even offensive) to a large majority of Navajo, especially among the more serious *hataalii* (medicine people). And she discusses witchcraft, normally a restricted topic, in *Song of the Earth Spirit*. But her close-ups with long focus lenses and her insipid and sentimental approach have made her very important friends in high places—in the Navajo Nation, in the federal government, and with rich liberals.

Page notes, "I have tried to photograph people the way I feel they see themselves, rather than the way an outsider might want to see them" (1989, rear jacket). Although this sounds commendable, how do we know how they "see themselves"? Did she ask photographic subjects how they wanted to be "seen"? Do Navajo "see themselves" (their distinctiveness, their difference, their specific culture) in terms that are accessible to photographic imaging? Page's work, firmly in the Steichen mold, largely obliterates specificity for generalization on Western terms—children, family, land, animals. Navajo once again appear like colorful Westerners in dramatic landscape. Page was once was photo editor for the United States Information Agency's *American Illustrated*, so she is well equipped for diluting propaganda. The jacket cover of *A Celebration of Being* (1989) says of her: "Throughout her career, Susanne Page has been drawn to *private people* in out-of-the-way communities, and her sensitivity to them and their ways of life has resulted in *thousands* of moving photographic images" (emphasis added).

Marcia Keegan published her first extensive volume of Navajo photographs, *Mother Earth, Father Sky* (1974), for preservational reasons, to capture dying traditions, "eager to record . . . for posterity" (Keegan and Frontier Photographers, 1990:9). One might assume that if she were wrong—that if traditions did not die—there would be less need for any more photography. But in her last volume, *Enduring Culture* (1990), where she admits that she was indeed wrong, she now photographs to celebrate that the traditions did not die! With every contingency thus covered, it would appear the Navajo have no escape from ever more photography. Keegan tells us she did not know the older photographs (the "Frontier Photographers") that are juxtaposed with her own in the 1990 volume. This is very difficult to believe if she spent any time at all in the Southwest, where the photographs of Curtis, Frasher, Hillers, Lummis, Parkhurst, Willis, Moon, and Vroman are iconic and ubiquitous. It is also peculiar inasmuch as she deliberately poses her subjects, "giving them the opportunity to willingly, consciously participate in the making of documents about themselves" (Keegan and Frontier Photographers, 1990:11). Given the similarities between Keegan's photos and those of the "Frontier Photographers," it is hard to believe the Native Americans posed themselves. Of course she had seen many of the earlier photographs. Sadly, however, she celebrates the similarity rather than her inability to make different photographs after almost a century. Keegan jams together all Southwestern Native Americans into one belief system, renders her own rationalist understanding, and then appropriates it: "[B]y studying these peoples' attunement to the spirit forces of the Earth, the rest of us may learn how to hold in check the dangers than threaten to annihilate our planet" (Keegan and Frontier Photographers, 1990:13). In the first volume (1974), the texts are all translations of healing chantways. For Navajo, these are specific ordering or instructing procedures handed down from the Holy People. Her lack of understanding of indigenous belief systems is dramatic: "I have tried to recreate [through the photographs] the sense of wonder and harmony with nature which is the integral part of Indian life. The chants that are included are expressions of the Indian spirit evoked by the natural beauty that surrounds them" (Keegan, 1974:7).

The only Navajoland photographs of "Frontier Photographers" are a landscape by Curtis and a landscape by Wittick. Keegan's own photographs of Navajo are curiously juxtaposed with "Frontier" Hopi photographs (one of basketmakers, another of hair brushing with a grass brush).[16] Where Page concentrates on universalist themes—Navajo as sympathetic people just like anyone else—Keegan focuses upon customary activities and, everywhere she can, ceremonial practices. With shocking evolutionism, she contrasts Native Americans with "modern man" (Keegan and Frontier Photographers, 1990:12). She unctuously claims (Keegan and Frontier Photographers, 1990:11–12):

> I would no more dream of photographing private rites than I would think of stealing a church crucifix—and I would be the first to break the camera of anyone else who tried. What moves me to such a state of reverence is not simply a conservative or old-fashioned turn of mind—it is a firsthand appreciation for the power of the living esoteric reality that informs the lives of the Southwestern Indians.

I was once a guest at a private museum setting at which a Navajo sandpainting (having previously been done for an exhibition) was going to be consumed (that is, used and thereby obliterated). Keegan had apparently made arrangements (despite resistance from other Navajo present) with the medicine man involved to photograph it (and was in attendance for this purpose only). However, at one point in this particular practice, all women in the room are asked to leave. Keegan at first balked, then left only after making arrangements for a male companion to photograph the sandpainting consumption! Unquestionably, Keegan is the most naive and crudely assuming of the four picture-book photographers noted here. In a review, Gill (1991:31) gently sums it up: "She shows that what is most enduring among us is the unconscious act of dominating Native Americans even when we intend to praise them."

John Running is often assumed, from his name, to be Native American, and this assumption has undoubtedly served him well. He is one of the most sought-after commercial photographers for Native American themes, particularly in the Southwest, and his photographs illustrate all manner of publications—from beer-company commercial calendars to activist productions. He has furnished photographs to stock companies (the source of difficulty in at least one case), and his work is widely available. His photographic *métier*

Chapter 7

runs from hackneyed photographs of the aged[17] and powwow dancers to Penn/Avedon-like fashion studio photographs of Navajo pictured on all-white backgrounds, as if suspended. Like the other picture-book photographers discussed here, he does not do innovative work, either photographically or ethically; his photography fails to reveal any unique social relations with Navajo. He is in high demand because his range of photographic styles gives him much latitude. He is also an instructor in contemporary Native American photography at the Santa Fe Photographic Workshops, where all students are photographers.[18] Running takes photographs for the annual Adolph Coors brewery calendar, commonly of powwow dancers, sometimes in extreme close-up,[19] and he will photograph objects or extensive technical sequences (say, of weaving) if the commission so demands. His insufficient attention to the use of his photographs, however, has resulted in a lawsuit in at least one case, in which he sold to a photo agency a photograph that later was used in a rock album cover. (The album cover was subsequently photographed and destroyed by fire in the video production of the featured rock group.) This suit, as with others involving Native Americans (see Chapter 6), stemmed from the unanticipated use of the photograph beyond the permissions thought to have been given.[20] In interview, Running has stated:

> I don't like a lot of what goes on when some professional photographers decide they're going to photograph Native Americans. . . . I discourage the tendency to invade a person's privacy, and I tell people that to do this endeavor properly [invade privacy??], you have to spend time with people. . . . Twenty-three years ago, when I first started photographing Native Americans, I though that the reason many Indians didn't like me taking their picture was because of some belief they had about my camera capturing their spirit. . . . It took me a while to understand that my rationale was way off target . . . that the reason I was having difficulty with Native American subjects was because I wasn't treating them respectfully as individuals. . . . I started not only asking for permission and working toward better understanding these people, but I also gave photographs back to them, and showed them that my work wasn't exploiting their religious objects and wasn't portraying them in a glamorized way (Villani, 1993).

This, of course, is the litany of them all, beginning in the modern era with Laura Gilpin (see Chapter 6). Somehow, once a photograph has been given them and they have been "respected," the obligations are over, and the machinations of capital or personal ambition take over. Running should have returned to his original rationale, for it was closer to the truth in most cases. He just didn't want to believe it, and instead justified his appropriation on the tired and worn saw of greater friendships and more respect. In an earlier volume, Running actually specified this more precisely—"Polaroids for them, regular film for me" (Running, 1985:98)—and continued, "leaving my picture with the people I photograph is not as important as leaving my spirit with them" (1985:153), almost as if they had been waiting for this. Running, like most other photographers, assumes his "genuine concern for his subjects, their lives, and a culture" (*Ibid.*:xiv-xv) should obligate local people to pose for his photographs, bring them to accept his camera, impel them to admire his concern.

Of course close friendships and respect are factors—as they are in photographs of family and friends (where no one would even consider sale to agencies who might use the photographs in unanticipated ways). But the consistent assumption of access is never questioned—the assumption that respect, familiarity, promises, and a Polaroid grant the photographer title to Navajo subjects. (It should perhaps be mentioned here that I have never, despite having been in dozens and dozens of Navajo homes, seen one of these Polaroids.)

One of the newest picture books, involving perhaps the most saccharin photographs of the four, had sanction from the top. Joel Grimes apparently sought (and received) Navajo Tribal Council support, got cooperation from the Navajo Office of Broadcast Services, and was assigned several guides to help him during the tenure of his project (at least he didn't simply wander about Navajoland without permission, trading polaroids for photographic access). He says his task ("to portray the Navajo people in a sensitive manner, allowing all of us to see who they really are—a proud and beautiful people" [Grimes 1992:191]) was made more difficult by the fact that "for more than a century there have been those who have carried a camera of disrespect" (1992:190). His photographs of people are nearly all carefully constructed, interspersed with song and prayer texts (in Navajo and English), narrative in English, and landscape photographs. Indeed, there is no discrimination between landscape photographs (which constitute about a third of the total) and photographs of people—Navajo and red rocks. The book is insulated by a foreword by Stewart Udall, an historical (or Western historical) introduction by Garrick Bailey and Roberta Glenn Bailey, both songs and prayer texts, and an intelligent cultural narrative by Navajo journalist Betty Reid. Grimes himself supplies a revealing two-page note and acknowledgment. His brief, straightforward and honest comment is refreshing,

Chapter 7

especially in comparison to the usual unctuous and/or breathless remarks of the other picture-volume photographers. He notes the compensations furnished for photographs (money, potatoes, flour) and identifies most subjects by their name, occupation, and location. This is important, for the non-landscape photographs in the volume are nearly all portraits, not images of people actually working at their occupations or engaged in other activity. Grimes notes that his project took three times as long as scheduled, cost four times as much as anticipated, and suffered from the "endless numbers of rejections from people I approached for portraits." He also laments that "despite my vigorous campaign to seek permission to photograph these events [Navajo religious ceremonies] . . . in every case I was asked to leave before any pictures were taken" (Grimes, 1992:190–191). Grimes explains:

> It took more than a dozen rejections before I realized there was a good reason for my lack of success. The Navajo people have lost much to the invasion of Anglo-American society. To pursue photography of their religious ceremonies would be just one more injustice heaped upon them. If one goal of this book is to assist in the preservation of the Navajo culture, surely exposure of their sacred rites could only negate such an aim (1992:191).

At least he accepted these rejections and did not attempt to secure the photographs of sacred materials in other ways. But Grimes does not seem to see a problem in the photography of Navajo people in non-sacred settings. His photographs are carefully posed and lighted, perhaps making possible some control by subjects. Consequently, some of the photographs are interesting, such as the two images of one of Grimes's collaborators, Dewayne Johnson of the Navajo Office of Broadcast Services, who carefully never allows his face to be fully photographed. Of the photographs of people in the book, about a third find their subjects averting their eyes or hiding their faces. Navajo still treat the camera as a possible tool of "disrespect" and attempt to protect their own subjecthood through avoidance. Though Grimes tells us (1992:191) he is not going to illustrate "social and political problems," nevertheless later (1992:193) we are told the Navajo "foe" is, amazingly, "popular culture." There is no mention of racism, oppression, sickness, disease, unemployment, capitalist penetration, consumerism, access, choice, or the federal government's newest genocidal relocation scheme; nor does he cite his own work as a prime exemplar of Western "popular culture"—the naive consumption of Navajo images. If one of his goals is preservation, the photographs of Navajo as bearers or consumers of "popular culture" must be regarded as a type of pastiche or collage. It is certainly not popular culture in a bad light (indeed, one portrait is of a Navajo rap singer). But because the clear aim is no bad light (pun intended), this volume, like the others, is ultimately an advertisement for tourism and more photographers. Come capture these views yourself; come gaze at such beautiful and proud people. Be pleased with yourself for admiring them.[21]

Navajo (and other native peoples) do not exist to provide boundaries to the West, to furnish perimeters of Western self—the frontiers of the West's desire—nor to guard Western conscience, to assuage guilt, render ablution, constitute moral lesson. Photography of Navajo is the securing of difference on Western terms, when difference may exist on cultural terms and subjective terms not available to visual media (however much the West may see [understand] it or want to see [visualize] it). Navajo photographic subjecthood is not existential, their alterity spectacle, their being forever instructive. Will the West ever accept difference without appropriation? When will "respect" mean leaving them alone, leaving the cameras at home?

"Respect," appreciation of the "power" and "dignity" of the images, people's faces (and other body parts), the "beauty" of their existence in their homeland, are the expressions heard over and over again. But there is never sufficient respect to not bring cameras; power is never discussed as the variable that gives Westerners image access; and dignity and beauty are never mentioned as things that cannot be appropriated by imaging but can only be secured on local terms and in local social relations. Navajo subjecthood is always defined by outsiders. It is revealing that these books are often sponsored by regional museums or prominently featured in their gift shops—which are simply adjuncts to the Southwest's vital tourism industry,[22] itself an enterprise shot through with saccharin assumption at best and racism at worst. Museum staffs sometimes privately bemoan this tourism but depend vitally on it for their survival. Hence they cater to such imagery in their exhibition strategy. Didactic or critical exhibits are usually only mounted by Native American–dominated institutions (such as the Institute for American Indian Arts in Santa Fe) and occasionally by fine arts galleries whose funding is institutionally or privately secure.

Kenji Kawano has produced a sensitively photographed volume, entitled *Warriors* (1990), devoted to the Navajo code talkers. Code talkers were used in the Pacific theater in World War II to communicate in Navajo—a "code" the Japanese could not break (Navajo code talkers actually further "coded" their own language with local usages, substitutions, etc.). Navajo code talk

Chapter 7

was very instrumental in U.S. marine victories in the Pacific from 1942 to 1945—see Figs. 205-207.

Kawano, a Japanese newspaper photographer *(Navajo Times)*, illustrates some 75 of the approximately 250 code talkers still living. He was strongly supported by all associated with the project, and the depth of field of his photographs allows the very informational settings to speak. These careful portrait photographs illustrate more about contemporary Navajo than all the photographic art books and coffee-table "beautiful" books noted in this chapter. The subjects are photographed for their history (and they comment, variously, on that history), not because their image conforms to some Western aesthetic caricature.

One further volume—Skeet McAuley's *Sign Language* (1989)—sits in the space of this chapter rather uncomfortably but has received great critical acclaim.[23] McAuley is concerned with irony, especially the irony of juxtaposition, of curious mix, so important in global modernism.[24] McAuley's irony, however, is more humorous, more wry, and somewhat forced. Unlike the casual (but prying) appearance of Frank's 35mm photography (see Figs. 202, 203), McAuley's photographs are nearly all very carefully composed and/or posed. So that this is not seen as disrespectful, however, the volume is cushioned with an introduction from N. Scott Momaday; commentary on some of the Navajo photographs by medicine man Mike Mitchell; a very successful insulating essay by Navajo poet Lucy Tapahonso; and, should all this not be enough, an historically and aesthetically situating essay by photographic historian Martha Sandweiss. That the volume appears in the *Aperture* series ensures its photographic acceptance and seal. McAuley takes no chances.

Certainly the book avoids the banal sentimentalizing and aestheticizing of the coffee-table volumes noted above, as well as the invading scrutiny of the victim photographers (McCombe, Gaede, Angier). One of its goals is irony, pastiche.[25] Another is to call attention to the environmental (and cultural) precariousness of the region by juxtaposition, and not necessarily by exposure of ecological devastation—indeed, it is not very clear McAuley is objecting at all. There is, however, an incoherence in the volume, a schism between text and image. Its attempts to make environmental statements, to image irony, for example, are conspicuously ignored by Mike Mitchell's Navajo commentary on many of the photographs (curiously, there is almost no commentary whatsoever on the photographs of Apache, the other Native American group illustrated). Sandweiss (McAuley, 1989:77), in an essay that generally praises McAuley for his irony, calls attention to Mitchell's comments:

280

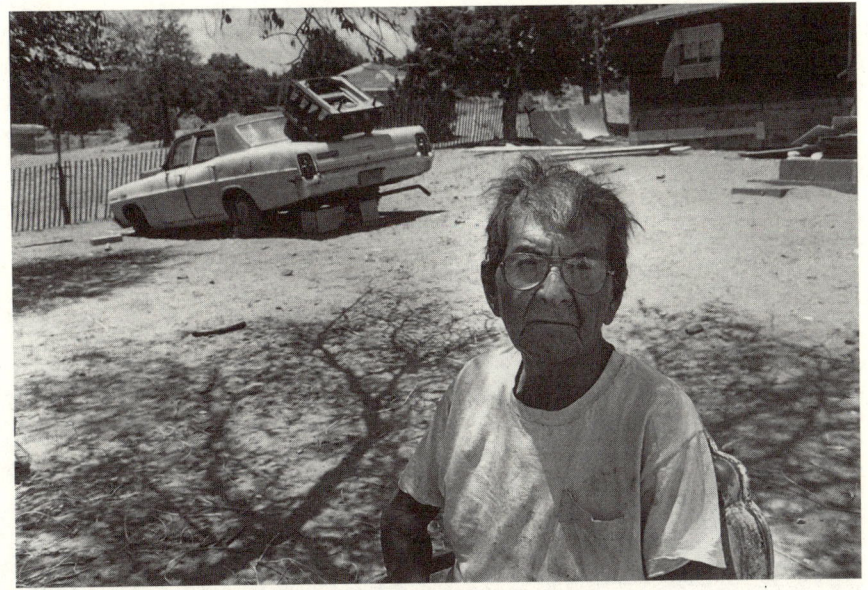

Figure 205

Figure 205. "Lee H. Begay." Kenji Kawano, photographer, 1987. "I was in combat training on Okinawa . . . rough days, rough nights. I was eighteen years old." This man, and the men of Figs. 205-207, were photographed for a particular historical episode Navajo were celebrating (or at least commemorating), not because their images conformed to some Western notion of how Navajo were to appear. These photographs have all been previously published. See Kawano, 1990:27. Photograph by permission of L. H. Begay and Kenji Kawano.

Chapter 7

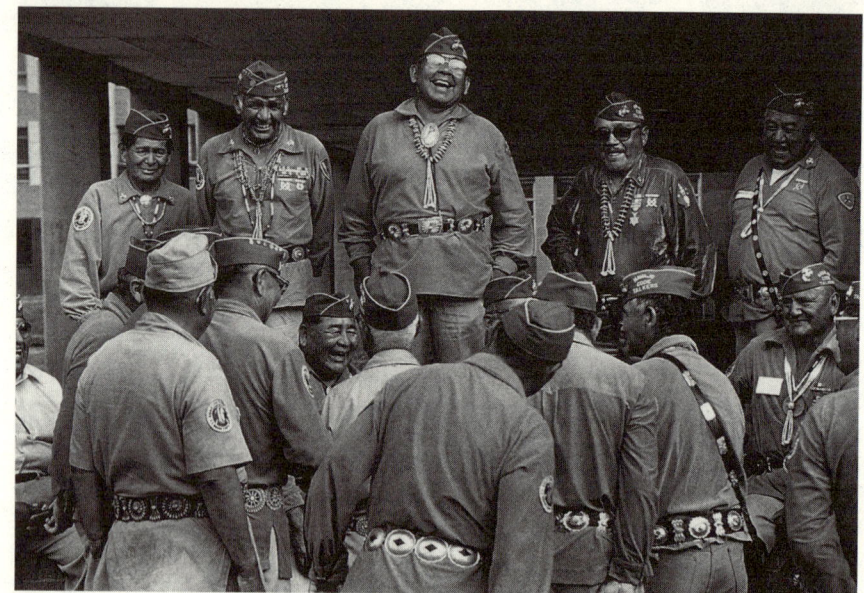

Figure 206

Figure 206. "Navajo Code Talkers in Washington DC." Kenji Kawano, photographer, 1983. These distinguished World War II veterans, comfortable with one another and the photographer, enjoy a laugh. See Kawano, 1990:xiv. Photograph by permission of Kenji Kawano.

> I look at McAuley's pictures in one way; Mitchell looks at them in another. Where I see evidence of material change, Mitchell sees evidence of spiritual continuity. While I seize on the incongruity of the new, he focuses on the continuing force of the ancient. It is humbling for me to be reminded that what I see as funny or ironic or beautiful in these pictures is not necessarily funny or ironic or beautiful to any of the people who come out of the culture that the photographer depicts.

This is a revealing (and refreshing) statement from a photographic commentator whose biographical work on Gilpin is characterized by a silence to such matters.

Perhaps a more generous interpretation might position Mitchell's commentary as a ground and McAuley's photographs as an expansion, an indication of precariousness, of change, or potential loss, or just ironic adjunctions. If so, then the photos cease to be ironic and become illustrative. That is why the volume seems unsettled and confused. And in this circumstance, McAuley's wit, his cleverness, becomes rather irrelevant, a conceit, or even mistake. There is one photograph (McAuley 1989:33) of two Navajo medicine men, Alfred Yazzie and Andy Natonabah (neither named by McAuley), said to be discussing the Navajo "lease-purchase of Sacred Mountain land, Rough Rock, Arizona, 1986" (this is land adjacent to the San Francisco Peaks near Flagstaff, Arizona—considered one of the most important Western Navajo sacred sites). Given McAuley's project, we are supposed to respond to the irony of two traditional medicine men (both specialists in several healing practices but sharing at least the Nightway in their repertoire) dressed in typical Western clothing, both with short hair, seated in the Navajo Resource Center of Rough Rock Community School, surrounded by modern furniture, maps, globes, papers, fans, paintings, photographs, and a large sign reading "Strategies of Teaching in Bilingual and Bicultural Courses." I would venture to say, however, that there is nothing at all ironic in this to the two medicine men nor to any other Navajo viewers. They are perfectly comfortable here, discussing the lease-purchase of the land adjacent to the San Francisco Peaks as naturally as if they were talking about the sacred esoteric details of a healing practice in a remote region of Navajoland in the depths of a winter night. There is no novelty for them in McAuley's juxtaposition. The irony depends on an outmoded Western view of the limited ways in which Navajo are expected to appear; if that view is jettisoned, the irony disappears, and the photographs cease to be remarkable at all.

Chapter 7

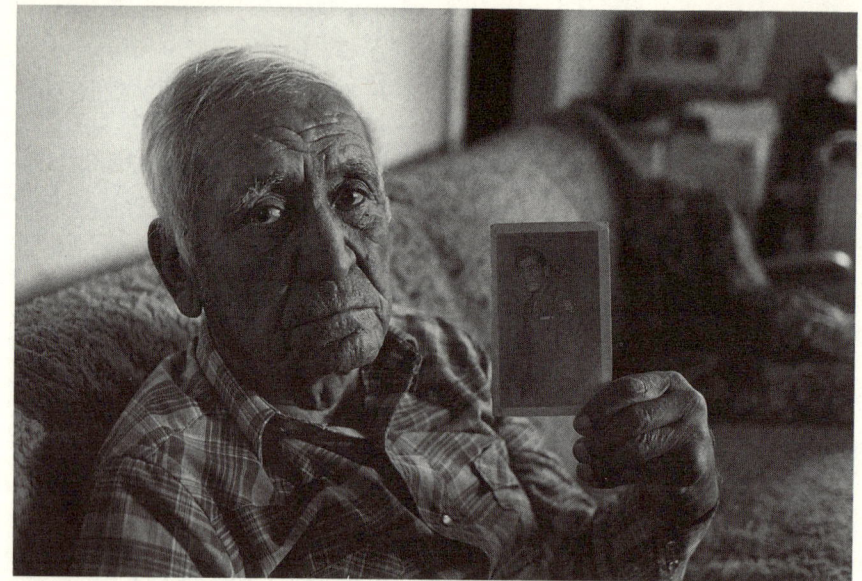

Figure 207

Figure 207. "Wilson Keedah, Sr." Kenji Kawano, photographer, 1987. "I went to war because there were no jobs on the reservation." See Kawano, 1990:56. He holds a saved studio photograph of himself at the time. Photograph by permission of W. Keedah, Sr. and Kenji Kawano.

A more detailed examination of the modernist irony in McAuley's photographs suggests a casualness, a retreat from the strictured dictates of studio formality, despite the careful use of a view camera. But these are not snapshots—they are not Robert Frank's casual 35mm photographs. The juxtapositions are careful, not casual, the photographs formal, the irony studied (even strained). That humor underlies many of the constructions (rather than just an underbelly of photography of Navajo in its classical content and form) is, of course, a somewhat different matter. In several cases it works, formally (as in a photo of a red gas pump in the foreground with red rock monoliths in the distance [p. 67]; in the careful formal juxtaposition of the road cuts and bulldozer tracks [p. 61]; the horizontal pipeline and parallel rock tables [p. 54]; the green football field and black track so scrupulously contiguous to red sand and Monument Valley [p. 47]; and the witty political statement of the photograph "Entering Hopi land from Navajo land, Arizona, 1985" [p. 71]). These are all landscapes. But other photographs, especially those accompanied by a commentary from Mitchell, seem to mock the seriousness of Mitchell's words. Mitchell censors or erases the young European-American boys that appear in "Pictograph and tourist, Betatakin ruin, Navajo National Monument, Arizona, 1983" (p. 23) and in "Interior of Navajo weaver's hogan, Monument Valley Tribal Park, Arizona, 1985" (p. 65) but comments carefully on all other details in each photograph. He certainly validates the Navajo content in the photograph (and thus constitutes one justification for the photographs) but ignores the other material so vital to McAuley's irony. Perhaps it is not funny to Mitchell, or not ironic, or not of sufficient interest to deserve comment. Certainly Navajo have a rich sense of humor—but this is not what is being subtly revealed here. Something of this rich cultural humor comes out in Tapahonso's accompanying essay—Navajo humor simply fails to make it in the photographs. The humor and the wit is distinctly non-Navajo—subjects are juxtaposed to challenge cliché, but there is no theoretical appeal, and McAuley relies on visual interruption for his point. Navajo could, indeed, be anyone else; they are contrivances for Western humor. The boundaries and limits challenged here are Western, with Western visualist imagery. McAuley cannot have it both ways, all ways. The attempt to do so is unfortunate and results in a somewhat incipient and theoretically confused work, one whose ambition outpaces its organization and design. In one respect, that is sign language, indeed.[26]

Portfolio VIII
Mimesis

Portfolio VIII

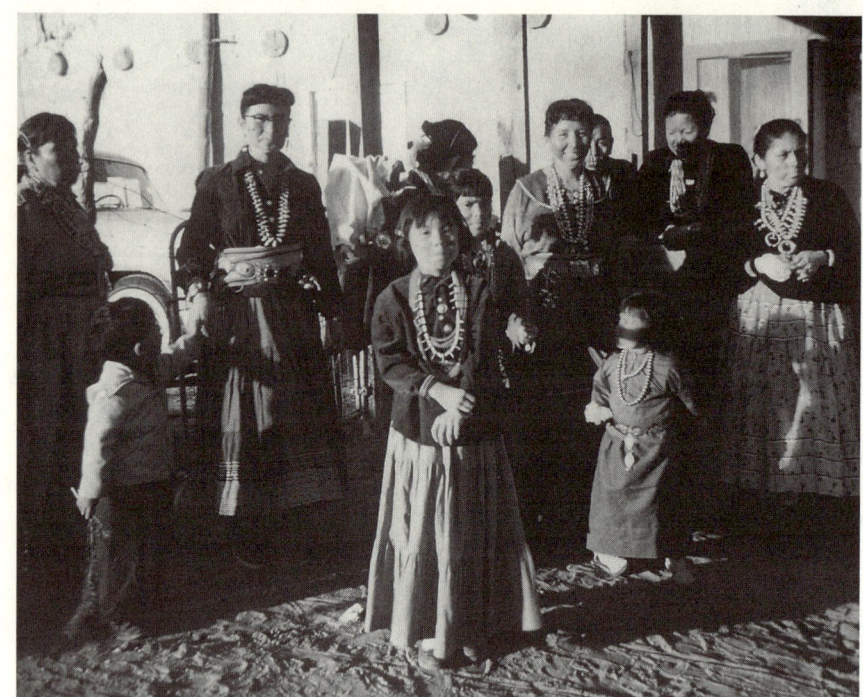

Figure 208

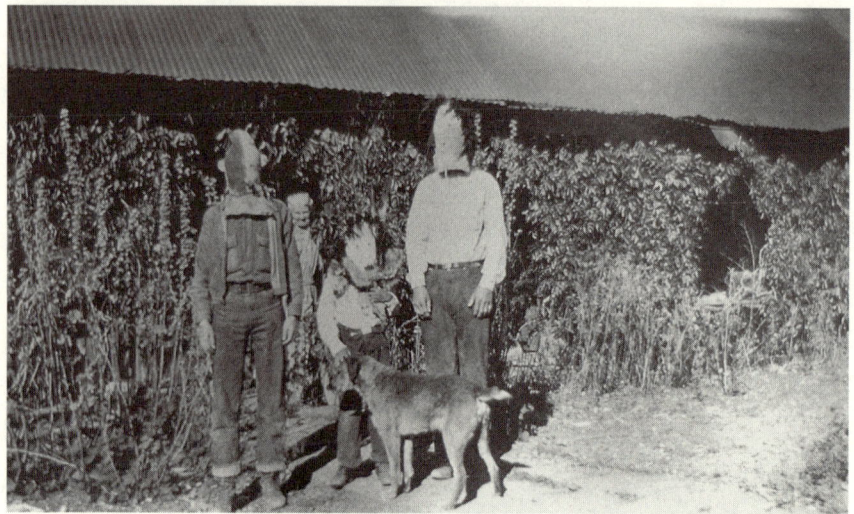

Figure 209

Figure 208. "*Navajo impersonators at Cochiti Christmastime dance spoofing Navajo.*" *Sally Wagner, photographer, ca. 1958. Though this sort of spoofing is taken in good nature by most Navajo, it is significant that there is no acceptable Navajo spoofing of Pueblo peoples. Sally Wagner Collection #8458, Box 187:3. Photograph courtesy New Mexico State Records and Archives, Santa Fe.*

Figure 209. "*Mrs. Day, Sr., wife of the pioneer trader Samuel E. Day, in front of her screened porch at St. Michaels, Arizona with her son Sam Day and his young son, Sammie. Mike Harrison also in group. They are all wearing Navajo buckskin dance masks.*" *Elizabeth Hegemann, photographer, 1926. Sammie (whose mother is Navajo) appears to be wearing a Talking God mask, Sam Day II is wearing the mask of an ordinary male yé'ii, and Mike Harrison wears the mask of a Fringed Mouth, none with any of the necessary attributes. Even though Sam Day II had been initiated into the Nightway and had a Navajo wife, his basic cynicism is revealed here, as such a display outside a proper Nightway healing ceremony would be considered sacrilege by most Navajo medicine men. Hegeman Collection #F10. Photograph courtesy Arizona State Museum, University of Arizona. ASM Neg. No. 7215.*

Portfolio VIII

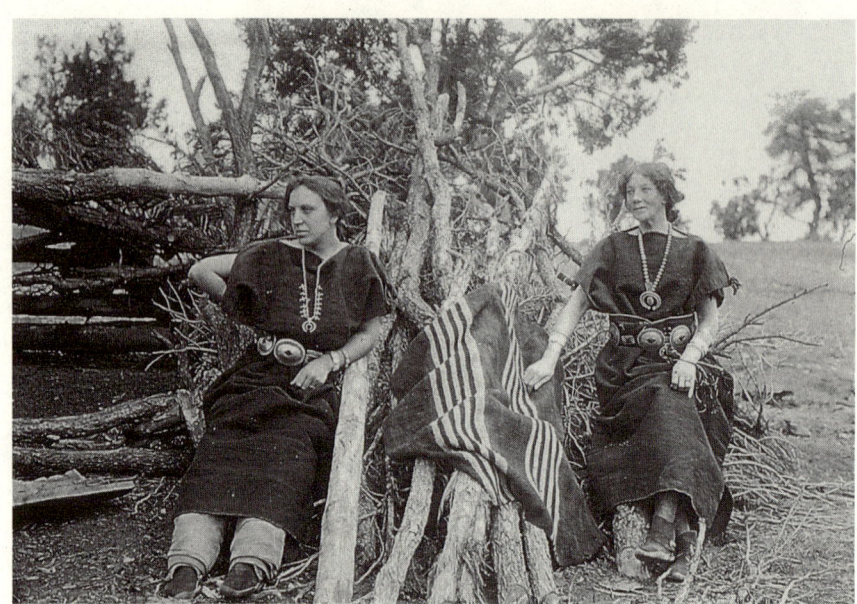

Figure 210

Figure 210. European-American women wearing Navajo woven dresses. Photographer unknown, n.d. Though dressed as early Navajo women, complete with moccasins, deerskin leggings, woven belts, and jewelry, the subjects are safely protected from any of the rigors of the life of Navajo women. Photograph courtesy Museum of Northern Arizona and Franciscan Friars at St. Michaels AZ. MS 119-15-147.

Chapter Eight

Navajo Photographers

And the liberation of representation into a domain of signification always opens onto a pattern or structure of absences—that which it is the task of the representation to bring forward as a 'making present.'
   S. Stewart, Crimes of Writing *(1991:6)*

The Navajo photographers that came to my attention during the course of this research are listed in Chart 3 (see Appendix). There are undoubtedly many others (especially with the spread of camcorders into schools and offices in Navajoland and with the number of students in the photography curricula at various colleges in the Southwest).[1] This chapter will be short, both because production as well as critical commentary of indigenous photography is beginning to move, as it should, into Navajo hands and because the total number of Navajo photographers listed in Chart 3 equals less than 15 percent of the total of Chart 1 (Appendix). A few of these individuals have done historic and unique work, the vast majority are not employed in photography, and only a minority have published or exhibited or are quoted in the various sources I have consulted. There exist, to my knowledge, two vaguely systematic lists of Navajo photographers. One comes from the Heard Museum, Phoenix, where Navajo are incorporated into a roster of selected contemporary Native American photographers compiled by Gloria Lomahaftewa (updated April 1991). The other is a register of Native American photographers compiled in June 1990 by the University of New Mexico Native American Studies Department's Southwest Native Photographer's Directory Project (sponsored by the Society for the Preservation of American Indian Culture). Chart 3 has been derived from and comprises the photographers on these lists, plus others that have come to my attention during my research.

Chapter 8

Figure 211. "*Camp scene taken by 'Tin Horn.'*" Tin Horn, photographer, 6 July 1914. See Fig. 62. Tin Horn, the first Navajo photographer on record, made this photo on the occasion of an Enemyway at Kayenta AZ. His ostensible subject, the European-American, has been moved left of center so that Tin Horn might include a Navajo child, a woman (probably the child's mother), horses, donkeys, and tack. Photograph courtesy Arizona State Museum, University of Arizona. #PIX278-x-8.

Navajo Photographers

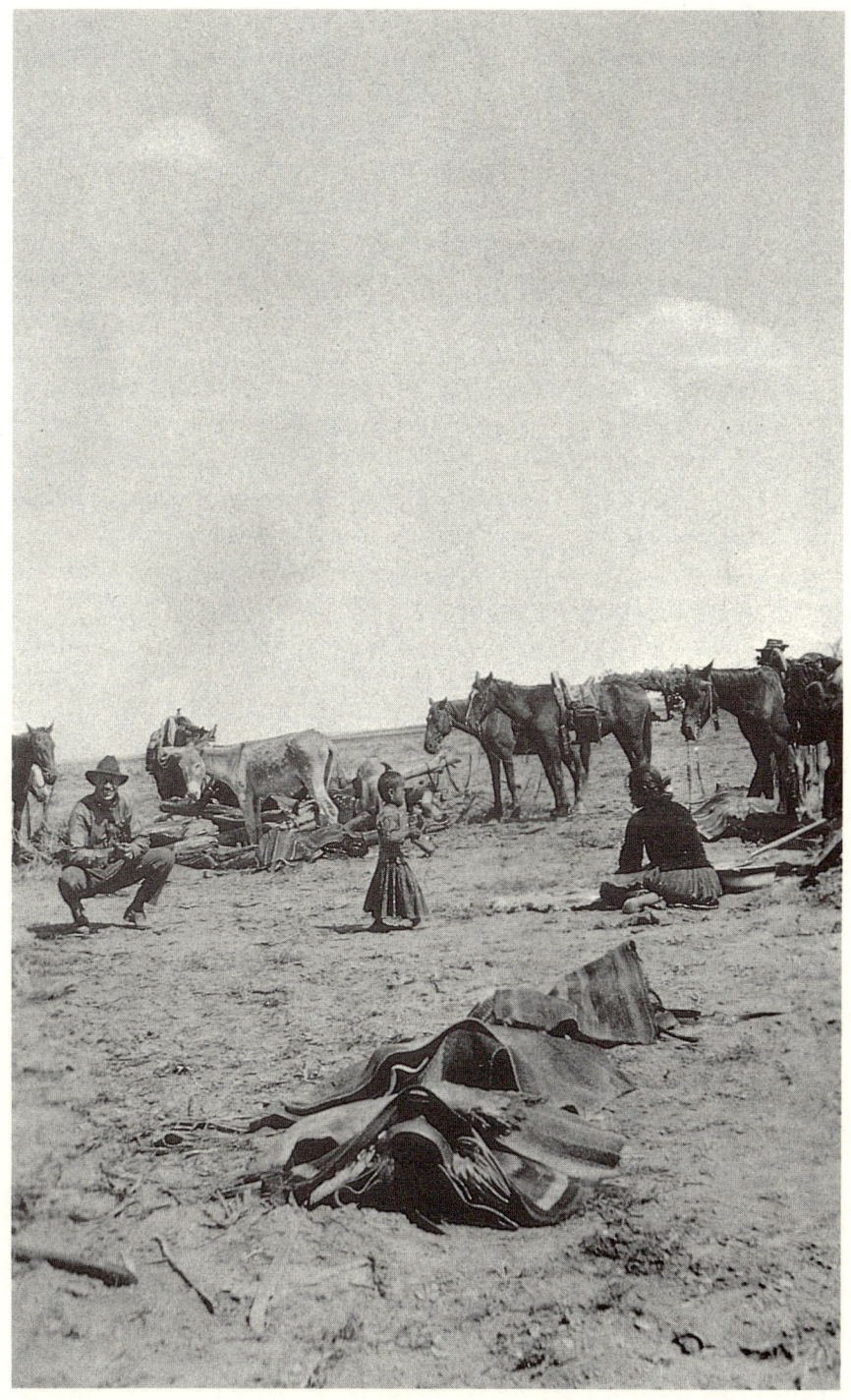

Figure 211

Chapter 8

Most of the individuals of Chart 3 who have exhibited have done so in rather minimal ways—for example, at senior exhibitions for their photography curricula. Though there are some interesting projects now underway (such as Arlene Bowman's, Anna Boyd Whitesinger's, and undoubtedly others of which I am unaware), only four or five Navajo photographers are widely recognized.[2] Of these, Monty Roessel and Hulleah Tsinhnahjinnie (a photojournalist and an artist, respectively) are best known.

Roessel began photography by printing and sorting his father's photographs.[3] He studied journalism, with a minor in photography, and photojournalism was thus logical. As a photojournalist Roessel often worked on assignment, but as he gained greater and greater experience his desire to work on his own projects increased, and he began to do freelance photography. Today,[4] though he still takes commissions (both for picture stories and individual commercial assignments), he tries to work out his own picture stories as much as possible. He has worked for various newspapers in Navajoland and was the editor of one, and he regularly publishes in regional magazines of the Southwest. He is on retainer to the Blackstar agency.

Roessel does not feel that being Navajo gives him any necessary advantage in securing photographs—on the contrary, he thinks it is thus sometimes easier for people to say no to him. His method is to schedule all his photography as much ahead of time as possible to give people the opportunity to say no (which, he reports, about half of them do). In about half the cases, he secures model releases from those he photographs. He is not particularly interested in landscape photography and tries to do illustrated narratives, particularly of naturally occurring social events. At this he has been quite successful, publishing repeatedly in *Native Peoples*, *New Mexico Magazine*, and many other periodicals. He also has received assignments for specific photographs. Nevertheless, Roessel tries not to pose individuals in his illustrated narratives and photographs events that are already scheduled to take place. He does not like to have to "represent Navajo" himself and claims it makes him feel guilty to do so. Some of his work has been criticized by some Navajo for "telling too much" (for example, he "got some heat" for a recent article on an Enemyway in *Native Peoples*), but Roessel maintains that he generally knows what not to include in a photograph or a photo story. His photographic style is not exceptional, but his articles are visually noteworthy for their graphic silences (what is *not* photographed) and dignified portrayals. Roessel's photographs do not contain the uncomfortable faces so frequently seen in Western photography of Navajo people, and he likes photographing people who trust him. He thinks it makes a difference to photograph "from the inside." In an interesting and revealing statement, Roessel says, "Off reservation, I'm not a person, I'm a photographer, behind the camera, and capable of all the callousness sometimes necessary to photograph people you don't know. But here [on the reservation], I'm a Navajo, not a photographer." Roessel's photography seems to exemplify what Benjamin has called "double vision"—that is, he sees Navajo as they see themselves as well as how non-Navajo see them.

At a recent symposium on Native American photography,[5] Roessel read the results of a project he had inaugurated (see also Chapter 2): He took some of the classic photographic sources (including Gilpin, *The Enduring Navaho*, and Kluckhohn/Vogt/McCombe, *Navaho Means People*) to his local chapter house to show people the books and ask their opinion of them. Roessel freely admitted he liked many of the photographs in both of these books— at least, *as* photographs—but many people, especially older ones, were very upset at the photography of ceremonials and of the sick,[6] the drunk, the dying, and the dead.[7] They especially wanted to know who had given permission to take such photographs. These Navajo offered little commentary (save recognition) on the vast majority of the other photographs in the volumes.[8]

Hulleah Tsinhnahjinnie (her father is the Navajo painter, Andrew Tsinajinnie),[9] was formally trained at the California Academy of Arts and Crafts and is today a freelance artist and sometime teacher in San Francisco.[10] Tsinhnahjinnie sees herself as a continuation in a long line of native peoples who have made images to communicate.[11] Her exciting work is explicitly political, not only altering the boundaries of photography itself but also linking native peoples' issues with wider global struggles against oppression and for control of their own representations. She is very much aware of the power of photography and, as a committed activist, sees her work as a locus of struggle to represent and "compensate" for what she calls "imbalances"—including not only the genocidal history of the West vis-à-vis Native Americans but also racism and sexism in general.[12] For Tsinhnahjinnie the use of the term *imbalance* is complexly interesting, for it refers both to the Navajo notion of imbalance (a condition of being out of order and thus potentially dangerous and ugly) and to the imbalance of relative power between the classic subjects of photography and photographers (and between Native Americans and the West). The two are merged in the photographic relationship between Native Americans and the West, where the traditional subjects—those photographed—are placed in a position/posture/pose of potential danger and ugliness.

Tsinhnahjinnie regards Native Americans as her primary audience and public and is not very sanguine at this point about non-Native audiences

Chapter 8

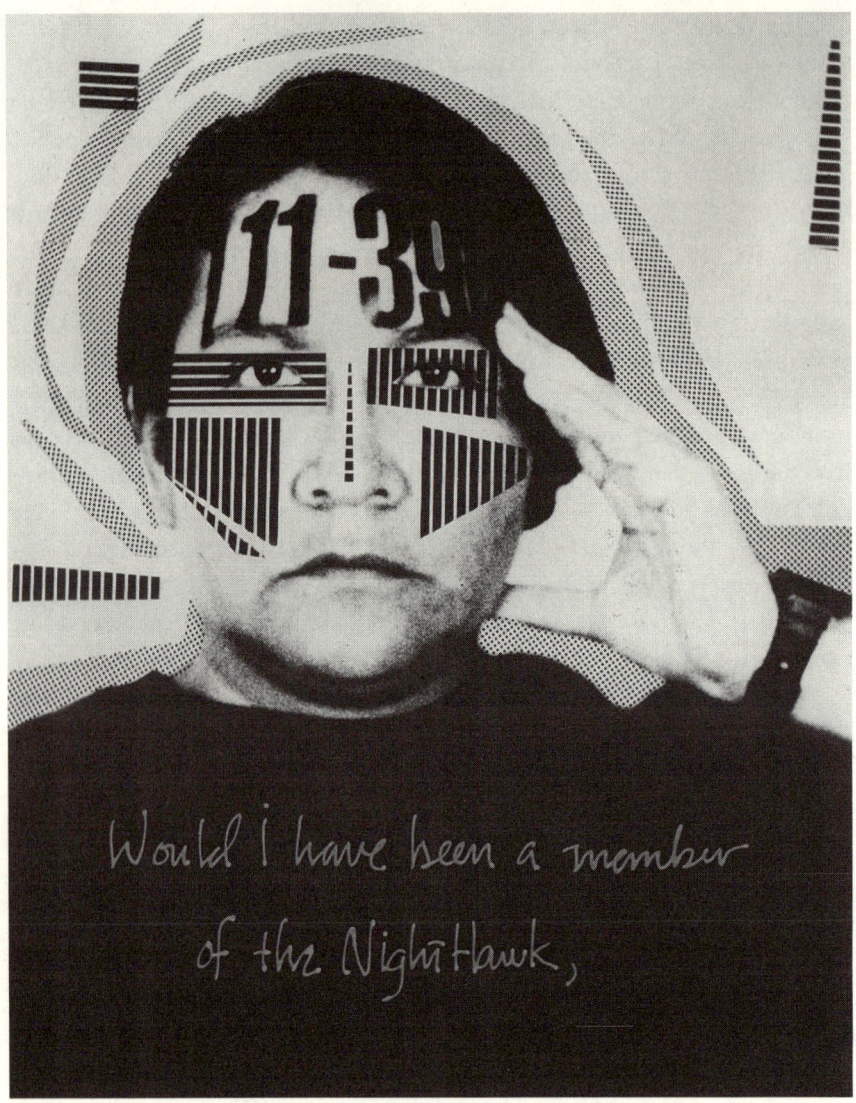

Figure 212a

Navajo Photographers

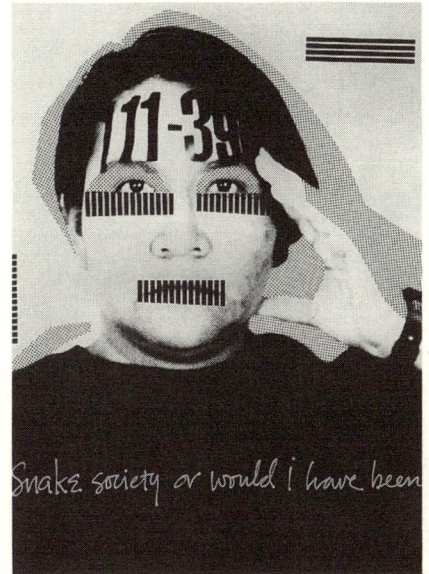
Figure 212b

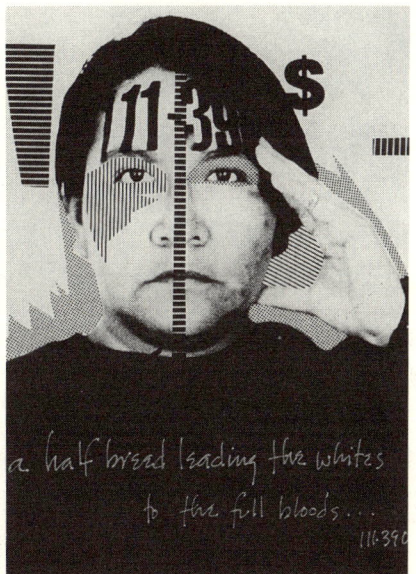
Figure 212c

Figure 212a, b, c. "Census makes a Native Artist," from the "Creative Native" series. Hulleah Tsinhnahjinnie, photographer (and model), 1991. Originally from a series, these three photos form a collage 40" x 30." They were stimulated by the "good intentions" of Public Law 101-644, signed into law in 1990, which required Native artists to prove their Native heritage. As Tsinhnahjinnie is Seminole/Creek/Navajo, her "exact identity" in "full-blood" terms is questioned by the West, and she is defined by her census number, tattooed across her forehead. The text raises the problematic issue of the West's setting identities (especially in terms of "blood" quotas), defining who is and who isn't a native artist, and imposing exterior identification criteria upon Native Americans, as if it were a "gift" to local people to protect them from non-Native American creations posing as Native American. Tsinhnahjinnie likens such "gifts" to the blankets given Native Americans in the last century—items sometimes laced with smallpox (see Tsinhnahjinne, 1993a). Photographs courtesy Hulleah Tsinhnahjinnie.

understanding her work. Indeed, she seems almost suspect of her recent successes and embrace by Western curators. She does not subscribe to universalistic criteria for photographic judgment and is highly critical of Western standards of critique and opinion judgment of Native American production.[13] She sees her work as part of Native Americans' fight for survival on their own terms and explains the late appearance of Native American photographers on these very grounds—the earlier, more direct struggle for physical survival made it impossible to consistently make artistic statements. But she honors the early Native American photographs—including the boarding school snapshots, the bus-station machine photographs—and notes the early importance of the native-held camera to friendships and family.[14]

Tsinhnahjinnie has been widely exhibited in recent years (San Francisco, Santa Fe, Boston, Philadelphia, New York, Phoenix) and has curated several exhibitions on her own. She was selected as one of the inaugural Native American photographers for the opening of the Smithsonian Institution's National Museum of the American Indian in New York City in 1994. Her style is informed by several photographic and artistic combinations—whatever is necessary to make her points in a way she feels is accessible to local communities. The elements she employs include collage, mixes of photography and painting, framing experiments, and careful posing of subjects. Her works are often didactic, and she uses herself as a model in some series. Her political points are directed not only at wider Western audiences but also toward Native communities on issues of local concern. For example, in the recent controversy of what constitutes "Indian" in the production of art, Tsinhnahjinnie mocked the requirements of census numbers (assigned by the Bureau of Indian Affairs) to define "native" by presenting a portrait of herself as native with her census number tattooed across her forehead. She likens census numbers to other such assignments made by outsiders with power, such as the blankets (infected with small pox) given to Native American communities by the same Western agencies (see Fig. 212a, b, c). She defends the productions of local artists struggling in any epoch against the cynical critiques of later Westerners[15] and to this extent involves herself in criticism of the genre of Western critical attention to "Indian art"—indeed, of the entire Western enterprise of patronage.

Thus, while making politically explicit art and affirming and drawing inspiration from earlier, less politically overt Native American art traditions, Tsinhnahjinnie maintains a distinct posture of producing photography for the consumption of Native American communities rather than political art to convert Westerners. She has achieved a position of importance, however, in wider politically engaged photographic circles as a consequence of her didactic style, clear commitments, and creative work. Tsinhnahjinnie's photography is far more presentational than representational, which makes it rather unique, exciting, and, thus, vastly more innovative than all the Western photography of Navajo put together.

There is no necessary feature of their work that identifies these two photographers as Navajo, save perhaps the subject matter and their careful awareness of cultural boundaries, limitations, and propriety. This dictation of what does *not* appear is an assumption of power, for it has always been the prerogative of those with power to dictate silences, absences. They choose not to expose some images. What does not appear, what does not have to be labeled, listened to, is in this case reserved for the deliberation and contemplation of an indigenous community of shared understanding. It is denied to the West for exhibit. It may be that what does not appear is thus inalienable and perhaps incommensurate with the West. To that extent, these two photographers produce "anti-photographs," or photographic refusals.

Nor is there is here a "ghettoization" of Navajo photography. It is neither so personalistic that is ceases to have anything but local relevance—indeed, in the case of Tsinhnahjinnie, the appeal is global (but not in some essentialist or diluting sense to a greater universal)—nor so arcane that it has no meaning to a wider audience. But in that it is politically critical of Western social relations with Native Americans, Navajo photography forces the West to look, if it will, at these relations and to examine its own categories, obsessions, and drives.

Chapter Nine

Conclusions

Reality is not an imperfect copy of its images
　　　　　　Rey Chow, Writing Diaspora

Navajo exist to the West largely in photographs. Indeed, photographs far outnumber any other portrayals of Navajo, most of which lean on photographic conventions, if not on specific photographic themes, styles, or postures.[1] This *photographic* nexus is somewhat exceptional for a non-Western people. But photography's particular predatory success in depicting such populations has been noted throughout,[2] requiring a more critical look at the practice itself. I have argued against photography's neutrality as a technology, with its assumed transparency to reality, and called attention to the projects inherent in the camera's inscriptive gaze, the fix of its focus. By calling attention to the erasures constituted by photography's boundaries/frames, I have specified the absences, the graphic silences, the social relations not illustrated.

This study has been organized to call attention to photography's Western essence (its dependence) and hence the limitations of the photographic enterprise in communicating cross-cultural experiences and social relations. Photographs, I have argued, are signs without meanings—they are non-iconic, have no axiomatic syntax—despite the West's most fervent wishes that they mirror some transcendent reality. There has always been confusion over photography's simulation and social reality; as representations they are in a peculiar relationship to the real as part of a discourse—involving a field of viewers, those for whom they are intended, those who consume. They are only agreed upon and structured for conception *by other discourses*. For Navajo, these

Chapter 9

are largely discourses premised on the hierarchies of civilized/savage, sedentary/nomadic, anthropological knowledge/local ideology, West/Other. Thus, there appear to have been finite ways the West could *view* Navajo, and I have drawn attention to the persistence of certain stubborn themes in photography of them.

I also have discussed the power inherent in being able to and being allowed to photograph—as seen in the various discourses that made photography of Navajo so important (to control, to preservation, to essentialist projects) and the laws that facilitated it. Photography conferred the power to censor what was seen and what was not seen, to establish a field for the West's relations with Navajo in photographs, to select some Western social relations with Navajo and to ignore others. It thereby enabled the West to objectify and dominate—Navajo are not photographing the West.

Though some of these arguments are not specific to Navajo, they have particular pernicious significance for photography of Navajo. Power in representation, however, is not simply instrumental, and the relation between power and knowledge is not always straightforward.[3] Non-photographic discourses are relevant. Moreover, Navajo, like most humans in increasing contact with the West, are sometimes attracted to photographs (witness the longtime presence of photographs in Navajo homes); there is now a small but growing body of photographs *by* Navajo.

Navajo have been photographed with a series of discursive lenses, through which they came to exist to the West. First they were hostiles, savages (and unphotographed—their resistance would have precluded use of the slow, large format view cameras of the time), then captives—they were models of conquest, taught a lesson. The lesson was that they were not to interfere with the West's aggressive expansion into their homeland. The earliest photographs of Navajo fix them as conquered, as prisoners. This representation erased Western genocide or any Navajo reality previous to their existence as incarcerated objects. In these, the Bosque Redondo photographs, Navajo posed as instructed by their captors.

After the failure of the Fort Sumner experiment (which was never judged wrong or immoral and was terminated only because it was too expensive), photography was unsettled for a few years, as if the West didn't quite know how to depict Navajo outside captivity. Then came the initial surveillance photographs, followed by the beginnings of a slight nostalgia for unconquered Navajo—and commercial display. Quickly, during the chaotic invasion of traders, railways, and the Kodak, the dominant photographic tropes were established. Transportation and tourism made Navajo as accessible as most other Southwestern Native Americans, if not more so. With this development, there came to be a relentless focus on aesthetics (as opposed to registers of meaning and use). By the turn of the century, or shortly thereafter, practically all photographic types to be seen subsequently had come into focus.

With the first major photographers in Navajoland at this time, romantic, pastoral, and sentimental photographic themes emerged—Navajo now domesticated, well on their way to vanishing (at least, vanishing as a challenge to Westerners), as if their potential extinction satisfied Western consumers in some perverse or cathartic way, a type of ruins aesthetic. Navajo were best consumed in photographs of what was assumed to be Navajo culture made in what was assumed to have been aboriginal Navajoland. Shortly after 1900, however, a non-visualist discourse came into being—anthropology,[4] which set the Navajo outside their claimed homeland, without much culture, until just before the arrival of the Europeans. This scenario had Navajo coming south as Europeans came north, borrowing all subsequent culture from their neighbors. This discourse became an unyielding barrier through which the photographic interpretation of Navajo was to subsequently labor.

But photography's rigid presentism made the establishment of such non-visual discourse difficult. All the photographic evidence of the time portrayed Navajo after—in this view—having borrowed all their new culture. The casual consumer of photographs, the tourist, only saw the Navajo in velvet, silver, turquoise, red rocks, sheep, and weaving, as if that were their atemporal, autochronous way of life. How very necessary, then, became the experts; for ocular vision is deceiving, seeing cannot be believing—all that people saw in photographs of Navajo was new, borrowed, adapted, and the beings bearing it were not the origin of any of it. The borrowings—silver, weaving, sheep, Navajoland—looked good on them and around them. Despite the photographic appearance, since they were not from here, their rights to claims in the area were debatable.

The anthropologist endeavored to tell novices and naïfs what lurked beneath the surface, what was behind appearance, to spawn his cynical text—to privilege reason over "reality." But how was the expert to fix appearance and still privilege the message that all you see is adapted, borrowed? How, if all is borrowed and adapted, was he or she to posit an ethnic identity based at least in part on appearance? Here entered *Navaho Material Culture* (1971), a decidedly unfashionable anthropological subject for the time, especially among theoretically ambitious authors. The book was filled with photographs as evidence, creating a sort of baseline—for despite the fact that none of what characterized Navajo visually was their own, it could now be

Chapter 9

fixed on them, and with any shifts they were no longer real Navajo. It was an exercise in what might be called the arbitrariness of identity in the hands of the West.

Subversively, however, as late modernism identified adaptation and change as essential to the Navajo character (when practically all change had been precipitated by the West!), so too did newer (Western) additions to Native Americans (pickup trucks, sneakers) become the photographic rage. Generally it would not be until after mid-century that Navajo as adapters could be part of photographic portrayal itself—the pastiche, with the unremoved evidences of more recent non-Navajo additions appearing in the photograph as an acceptable new part of Navajo life. Here, of course, there was obvious irony—Navajo and helicopters, Navajo and pickups, Navajo and cameras, Navajo and parking meters, Navajo with high-tech bows and arrows (cf. Portfolio I, Figs. 54, 92, 95, 98, and Chapter 7). But more often the juxtapositioning was used in humor, often a type of racist humor—not so funny to Navajo.

What of Navajo claims to their own homeland and a culture on their own terms? Navajo "views" of themselves have never seemed to bother European-Americans. Indeed, they have a convenient way of disposing of Navajo views—such views are "myth" (or sometimes, more politely, "oral tradition"), as opposed to Western "history." The photograph then illustrates or reveals myth, not history. Appearances are not realities, so the need for science was secured—for science can "see" beneath appearances, ferret out truths, realities, laws. Only Western reason made veracity possible.

It is possible to deconstruct the early twentieth-century nostalgia for a Navajo in the region prior to Europeans (leaving aside, for the moment, that such sentiment was indeed for the Indian fighter, for the white conqueror). There is, in Western wisdom, very little time that this was possible. It is a patronizing and phony nostalgia for a Navajo that never existed in the West's mind. This is a small matter for most photographers of Navajo, however, for photographically the West's Navajo always have had to exist in some continuum along the lines of traditional/modern, non-Western/Western—otherwise there would be little reason to take photographs of them at all. This historical view fixes or controls Navajo alterity, establishes hierarchies—there are "no Frenchmen without wogs, no masters without slaves, no class without exploitation, no property without exclusion" (Cixous and Clément, 1986:70–71). Navajo enter this structural hierarchy in a photographic form that requires as well the eremitic anthropological caveat—all you see in the photo is borrowed, and you're recent to the area. With photographic and anthropological capture, all space in which Navajo might exist was saturated.

Conclusions

With perverse mockery and pernicious irony, Navajo came to be mimicked, in caricatures that would be denounced as racist should such mimesis pertain to any other contemporary minority (Portfolio VIII). Strange indeed that a culture denied integrity of its own is so much the focus of mimicry.

One of the few and most persistent Navajo photographic images is that of stubborn refusal (Portfolio III). Such photographs are not often published, because they reveal a Navajo input not usually sought.[5] However, they exist in abundance in archives. In a subversive alliance with such subjects, and to extend this notion of objection, I have insisted on writing a history that includes such imagery as part of the corpus of the West's photography of Navajo. As such, it is a political critique. Of course, such studies are distinctly unpopular, and it is considered unfashionable and excessively strident to continue to raise such issues. But I insist upon doing so here because, however rhetorical it may sound, there is still a lack of careful histories of exploitation and detailed deconstructions of histories written by conquerors. Political critique is not old, not tired, but anthropologists and scholars from allied disciplines who might be examining photography have simply not done complete, thorough work and have ignored important bodies of data and important critical positions. Nor have they examined the mechanisms of their own rhetorics. The restless Western academic drives should not move beyond detailed and careful histories so fast and far that exploitation cannot be recognized and oppression cannot be pointed out, that framing is not examined, that censoring is not investigated, that deconstruction of hallowed hierarchies is not possible and does not take place. Photographic gestures have never been without agenda, without intention, without desire.

There is, nevertheless, not a coherent unitary theoretical nor political position in this work. I set forth no totalizing critique, for doing so would reduce the specific critiques to but an expression of some master scheme. The "reality" of Navajo representation too complex for such an overarching analysis, and appropriating all photographic practices in a single theory would be impossible. Moreover, a theoretical unity would subvert the alterity Navajo reality should preserve. Power/knowledge relations are never simple—if they were, a solution to abuse would be equally simple. These photographic discourses conceal within them conflicts and contradictions of the West, as well as Navajo resistance to the West. The great photographic caricatures of Navajo so widespread in Southwestern tourist sources and literature (promoted as well by the Navajo Nation leadership—see Fig. 2) have in them desire, delight, and fear, or they would not be so successful. Representation is intention, but not straightforwardly. This slippage, this eliding between representation and intention, is the space in which much of photography's power rests. It is one locus of photography's appetite.

The complete absences in representation, the graphic silences, encompass Navajo views of their own history and Navajo social relations unknown to the West, as well as much of Western social relations with Others. To the casual Western photographic consumer—the viewer, the spectator—photographs do not reveal this absence, and Navajo culture is not something unrepresented. It could be as it appeared—aboriginal, genuine, indigenous. But for Western science Navajo are not as they appear; they are something else—borrowers, late arrivals, adapters, people without aboriginal culture who simply mimic others. They are, then, in this latest discursive movement, essentially nothing but reflection. Photography, itself rigidly confined to mimesis, was not particularly good at revealing this anthropological concept.

It was better at portraying Navajo outside the rigid images established from the turn of the century. As pickup trucks and sneakers replaced wagons, horses, and moccasins, and as modernism triumphed over earlier studio and formalist motivations, photographs revealed that Navajo are indeed adapters, borrowers, with no culture of their own save pastiche, but now in obvious, trivial ways.[6] That Curtis (and sometimes Gilpin) removed items of the West from many of their photographs is no more significant than that McAuley and Grimes included them. The ranges of possible Navajo social relations are limited, as are relations between Navajo and non-Navajo. Hysterical Navajo, sexy Navajo, contradictory Navajo, inconsistent Navajo, for example, are outside the boundaries of normalizing photographic discourse.[7] Any social relations that authorize Navajo outside Western terms are simply unphotographed or unphotographable. Thus, many of the photographs of Chapters 3, 4, and 5 are similar in appearance to those of Chapter 7—the first case suggesting potential disappearance, the latter, persistence. Marcia Keegan might speak for most photographic motivations of the twentieth century—the camera had to be used to preserve Navajo because Navajo might disappear or celebrate Navajo because they didn't. In no case can Navajo escape the Western photograph. Both the output and meaning are thereby regulated.[8]

I am not attempting to deny a livelihood to contemporary Western photographers. Indeed, were they to rely on commissions from Navajo and serve actual Navajo interests (rather than their own, Western view of such interests), they would be welcome. (I have abundantly indicated Navajo interest in being photographed.) Photographers are not likely to abuse people they regard as clients rather than subaltern Others, nor photograph in circumstances their clients do not dictate.[9] To stand on some absolute right to make photographs is to resort to the most Western and capitalist of foundations—individual rights, the extension of rights to those with property (the camera), the absolute right to be able to see anyone, anywhere. It is to stand on power. Navajo people ought to be able to prohibit non-Navajo from making photographs of them (at least within Navajoland) without permission. And they ought to be able to specify any further use of or access to existing photographs of Navajo in very exact terms. If Navajo culture is so vital to photographers of it, then Navajo culture should be taken seriously in its concerns about photographic exposure, as noted the in lawsuits discussed in Chapter 6.

It does not seem unreasonable in the circumstance to consider the camera somewhat like a firearm—something not to be pointed at people with whom there is not a social relation of hostility. Such a conception would challenge the West's notion of press freedoms. If nothing else, however, perhaps this study has indicated something of how very assuming such notions indeed are. There must be what Foster (1988:ix) has called a "thickening" of experience, which involves not only locally driven cultural "exposure" but, more important, *different* moral and ethical considerations.[10] As Jay (1984:9) has suggested, "photography rarely involves an aesthetic decision, but usually a moral or ethical one."

A popular notion today, especially among photographers and anthropologists,[11] is that the anthropological and photographic encounter is actually mediational and really best understood as one of negotiation—that oppressed and oppressor influence one another and at least to some extent mutually structure their relationship, that there be collaboration in the representation. This may, to a limited extent, be more true today than it once was. But the history of photographic exploitation (in tandem with other Western discourses guiding the enterprise) has yet to be fully understood and cannot be dismissed as partisan in favor of some contemporary normative view (exactly what "mediation" implies). Moreover, to marginalize exploitative history is to deny some new information and continue some suppressions. Of course, Navajo history and the history of the photography of Navajo are not monolithic; they are filled with contradictions and complexities. Depicting any reality is a complicated process. Novelists and poets are probably better at it than historians and documentarians (notwithstanding some of the conceits of contemporary modernist anthropologists *en vogue*) because they are commonly more experienced with the subversions entailed in such indeterminacy. Certainly there are important anthropologists and contemporary theorists at work in these directions.[12] I am less sanguine about the involvement of photographers in inaugurating such projects. And it is not excessively cynical to

Chapter 9

suggest that these new collaborations and mediations may well be another method for securing maintaining Western access, one more expression of a sinister Western parasitism, an elision that disguises who really and ultimately has power. In this sense, theory can be seen as the method, the form of knowledge and understanding of the *spectator*, as suggested by the epigram to the previous chapter. In the Navajo case, money, class, and academic patronage have not restored their history nor generated an alternative photographic practice.

There is little innovative in the suggestion that photographs of Navajo are photographs with non-Navajo agendas and not worth the effort of an entire book. But non-Navajo photographs are, in tandem with other powerful Western obsessions, commonly argued to be evidential of something Navajo because photographs do not lie, because seeing is believing, because methods of proof are often so dependent on images. A concomitant Western intellectual concept at work here is that social relations can be made visible. Still another Western truth at risk in this study is that images can expose human essentials, communicate something significant and non-trivial about us all. I have argued that these are all unfortunate notions.

On examination of the total archive, and with a more explicit critical orientation, the celebrated makers of Navajo images can be examined more thoroughly. Laura Gilpin emerges as something less than a saint, Edward Curtis as something less than a villain. The appearance of exciting new Navajo photographers and the persistent use of photographs by Navajo in their homes indicates the complexity of visual imagery both within and across cultural boundaries. But also "coming to light" (pun intended) in such an endeavor is the continuing resistance to Western photography—where Navajo people do not dictate the terms and conditions of the photograph, alternative discourses or representation—and the notion that there can be *another* cultural attitude toward the camera. There are very limited ways in which photography reveals much of Navajo cultural significance and very extensive ways in which it suggests power relations between those making the images and those being imaged.

Years of photography and newer photographic motions have not enriched Navajo representation; they have only revealed the poverty of its possibilities and the leveling of alternatives and actualities. There is no longer anything oppositional about regarding Navajo as special victims, nothing new in considering them special human beings.

This volume has a political orientation. But the politics have only partially been struggles over representation—partially, but not specifically nor pro-

Conclusions

grammatically. I have argued a politics of opening possibility—but possibility limited to Navajo on their contested fields. Navajo are not the West's Other. Whatever this volume yields, it at least reveals—and hopefully bridges—the gap between signified and signifier, between representation and represented. Navajo, then, are no longer the West's Other (ultimately, in leveling, the civilized barbarians to the West's barbarous civilized), and photography, heretofore the instrumental solution to the humanist sovereign panoptic, might emerge free to new potentiality.

Notes

Chapter One

1. Cf. Fabian, 1983:106; Faris, 1992b; Tyler, 1984. Some would argue this is a Western motion of even longer standing—all the way back to Plato and shadows on cave walls (cf. Rorty, 1980)—or even a product of the projective activity of speech itself (cf. Derrida, 1976; 1993). Tyler (in Clifford and Marcus, 1986:130) discusses well the implications of visualist ideology for referential discourse, its "presumption of representational signification," and the failure of the entire enterprise in ethnographic matters.
2. Cf. Crary, 1990; Levin, 1993. Photography was hardly a unique, singular invention. At the time of its emergence there were actually several different technical processes in experimentation simultaneously—that is, lots of photographies were competing for acceptance. Some (for example, Fox-Talbot) even had to be persuaded to pursue their experiments.
3. Cf. Pinney, 1992a.
4. This should be read not as an essentialist statement but as a critique of the view that a photograph speaks its subject by its reference—that it conveys a neutral image of what was in front of the lens. It is a critique of the view that photographs are opaque (or alternatively, transparent to reality), that photographers and photographic culture are not in every way the makers.
5. Postmodern photographers, somewhat like surrealists, attempt to obliterate those boundaries, whereas modernists toyed with them, flirted with the edges, deliberately called attention to them, or suggested them slightly differently—but never effectively transcended such boundaries nor established alternative power relations that might challenge the existence of such boundaries. Indeed, photography, as commonly practiced, cannot do so. In a new study, Krauss (1993) discusses this idea.
6. The medium of photography has been argued to be inherently pornographic, as—incapable of being an erotic art—it "presents us with the object of lust rather than a symbol of it"; it "gratifies fantasy of desire long before...expressing the fact of it" (Scruton, 1981:602–603). Some feminists argue that because photography was normally a process of the symbolic order (rather than the real or the imaginary and rather than the signifying order), it could thus not escape the domination of the father.
7. See Sontag, in Goldberg, 1981:516.
8. Cf. Walton, 1984.
9. See here especially Worth and Adair, 1972, but also Faris, 1992a, 1993b.
10. Cf. Banta and Hinsley, 1986:127; Collier, 1967:passim.
11. Cf. Pinney, 1992a.
12. Cf. Edwards, 1992.
13. See also in this regard Albers and James, 1988, and Coombes, 1994.
14. There is considerable debate about photographic aesthetics—especially in the genre of "art" photographs. Soloman-Godeau (1985), for example, persuasively argues that if photography is going to lean on the world, on reality (to distinguish itself from, say, painting), it effectively jettisons the possibility of a genuinely photographic aesthetic.
15. Cf. Berger, 1972, 1980, 1982.
16. Cf. Young, 1990.
17. Cf. Faris, 1992a, 1992b, 1993b; Moore, 1992; but see also Turner, 1992, Ginsburg, 1994.
18. See the epigram to Chapter 9.
19. They certainly have—see Lyon, 1988.
20. A typical example is K. Brower, 1967, a photographic book with abundant images of Anasazi ruins (considered by Western authorities to have been built hundreds of years before Navajo arrival in the area) but filled with quotations from Navajo healing texts and commentary from Navajo philosophy. This is all the more remarkable in that the text itself was organized by a leading academic authority on Navajo, Stephen C. Jett.
21. Indeed, as Todorov has put it (1984:71):

Notes to pp. 19–31

it is impossible...to desire both cultural diversity and familiarity with culture other than our own; for familiarity is the final step toward the disappearance of that diversity. [This, in effect, requires us face the prospect of being] anti-humanist, to oppose the intermixing of cultures.

22. Navajo have commonly been represented as bearers of a beautiful and meaningful culture. But once they are represented, there is no attempt (nor need, as it has been superficially established within a humanist discourse of acceptance on Western terms) to seriously consider that culture. In other words, the exercise is basically to establish them as human beings—the issue isn't that their cultural values or notions might be superior to the West's or preferable to the West's or even *different* from the West's. To do so, indeed, would be implicitly to criticize the West. How do Navajo critique the West? Rarely, for they are all too aware of the very significant power differentials. If they actually act, they are labeled terrorists and killed or jailed. Their only real way of criticizing the West that doesn't immediately bring down something on their head is to simply be themselves, to *do* their own culture. What if they banned cameras on the reservation? What if they declared everything save the main highways private property and prosecuted anyone found there or found taking photographs?

23. When once asked about the sources of his creativity and the inspiration for his painting, the surrealist Magritte remarked, "I do not feel I am 'adding' something to the world: where would I get what I am adding if not from the world?" [20 June 1957] (Alexandrian and Waldberg, 1980:74–75). Magritte, in this sense, would have been quite comfortable with Navajo thinking. Perhaps, indeed, this is one of the reasons Magritte gave up painting, as he realized its limitations in "saying" anything—the inability of painting (visual imaging) as a means by which to "discuss" these matters. This ever-changing/never-changing, creative/conservative axis is argued in more detail in Faris, 1990. But it also points up here—in dramatic difference—photographic imaging and the "new" in Navajo cosmology and in Western cultural practice.

24. Riefensthal's plea, stemming from her long photographic experience, is described mostly in terms that feature her as innocent victim in her recent memoirs (Riefenstahl, 1987; 1992—but see also Faris, 1988a, 1993a). Despite her grotesque propaganda heritage during the Third Reich, her outlook (pun intended) here reveals the rigidly Western motivations in her "quest for Great Art" and how very Western was the Nazi movement in its fundamentals, especially in many of its cultural expressions.

25. Cf. Ammann, 1993 for a recent example.

26. There are today, of course, abundant experimental works in vision and film that attempt to call attention to the peculiarly Western "view" of sight and to discuss it further and/or transcend it (cf. Tyler, 1984; L. Taylor, 1993; Krauss, 1993; Trinh, 1989). For theoretical discussion, see Krauss, 1988.

Some historians of ethnographic photography actually argue that the problem is that photography and visual inscriptions have been ignored for the written word and that the balance should be redressed (cf. Scherer, 1988, 1990). Though not attempting to privilege the written, on the strength of the experience with the photography of Navajo, this study would clearly argue to the contrary, *against* photography's ascendancy or any further authority.

Chapter Two

1. Except for a very few cases, all photographic materials I have examined have been available as publication or as archive. I have not tried to examine personal collections that have come to my attention if they are not archived (and thus accessible) or available in publication. There are some rather substantial collections not (yet) available, such as those of trader families, studio photographers from towns surrounding Navajoland, and non-Navajo personnel serving in government or missionary capacities. The extant Navajo bibliography of published photographs alone would require years to examine thoroughly.

2. As examples, there are over 15,000 photographs in the collections of the Navajo Nation Museum, Window Rock, Arizona, and over 10,000 photographs in the St. Michaels Franciscan Mission collections, St. Michaels, Arizona.

3. These are not always the same, of course, as archives are filled with images of Navajo resisting photography, but such images are seldom published. See also Portfolio III and endnote 13 below.

4. Cf. Lyon, 1988.

5. Gilpin notes the extent to which "modeling fees" were being paid and expresses regret at the effects of this practice on her own photographic projects (driving up her costs, perhaps compromising her because she, too, might be required to pay or pay more); see also Dennis (1993) and Chapter 7 herein. As the Benally lawsuit involving Gilpin's photograph makes clear, however, payment is not the singular issue at stake for Navajo (see Chapter 6).

6. Moreover, it is being done—but by Navajo of Navajo. Monty Roessel inaugurated just such a project in showing Gilpin (1968) and McCombe (1951) to people of his local chapter house. This is recorded in Roessel (1995) and discussed in Chapter 8 herein.

7. This is not to endorse the oppressive social relations that sometimes exist between kin nor the stifling hegemony of certain family structures—structures photography has frequently recorded so poignantly and, in doing so without the addition of critical commentary, helped to constitute and reinforce (see Fig. 12). Of course, the abundant extensions into art and the aesthetic alterations of images are well known.

8. Cf. Krauss, 1985a.

9. Cf. Graham-Brown, 1988; Hill, 1989; P. Taylor, 1988; Lippard, 1991, 1992; Powers and Hill, 1995. There were objections to the intrusive nature of photography from its very beginning, especially after the widespread availability of the candid camera. The rights of subjects and alternatives have certainly been discussed—see Garner, 1977; Edelman, 1979. Milgram, in Garner (1977:6), discusses the power implied in the photograph itself, the power to censor and control one's image, and the power of those who are able to control their imaging:

> President Carter was willing to meet with representatives of the PLO but was unwilling to have his photograph taken. Extremely interesting the way he feared the effect of the photography, but not the fact [of the meeting] itself.
>
> When Henry Kissinger visited Ian Smith in Rhodesia he refused to allow a photograph showing the two of them together—in other words, the photograph creates a kind of bond. Things happen in the photograph, and neither Carter nor Kissinger wanted this particular reality to be disseminated. The lengths to which people will go to avoid certain photographs evidence the power of photography.

Milgram also notes that there is no technical reason that cameras could not have developed that would have shown the photographer as well as the subject simultaneously.

Henderson carefully discusses some of the implications of current laws of photographic access. She notes a common photographic attitude—"you can decide what not to publish, but you can never publish what you didn't take" (1988:104)—and correctly notes that photographic releases protect the rights of photographers, not those of subjects. Perhaps most discouraging of all in Henderson's research (1988:105) is the finding that "among fellow professionals, it is a sign of competence and reliability to be able to get pictures regardless of the circumstances, an ability seasoned photographers are assumed to possess and novices are rewarded for acquiring." See also Ammann, 1993, and Dennis, 1993.

10. Cf. Law, 1989. McGrane, 1989:116. Travel (with photography as its record) became in the twentieth century a mode of seeing and important to the establishment and maintenance of difference.

11. Cf. Goetzmann and Goetzmann, 1986, and Truettner, 1991—the latter a book based on an exhibition at the National Portrait Gallery in Washington, D.C. that provoked a storm from conservative congressmen for suggesting there could be any interpretation of—or attitude toward—the conquest of the American West other than Manifest Destiny.

12. It is important again point to out that I try not to include many photographs that have already appeared in print. Thus, many important historic photographs are not here included (see Chapter

4). For some comparative purposes, and to illustrate a point, however, there will be a few photographs that have already appeared in publication. Moreover, as noted, to avoid including many living people (from whom permission must be secured to publish), most photographs will thus be of historical individuals and by historical photographers. Certainly many contemporary photographers, especially given my critical scrutiny and polemic, would hardly be anxious to have me examine their unpublished work.

13. *Most typical* and *normalizing*, of course, are not necessarily the same. There may well be normalizing gestures that are not very typical.

14. Obviously there are leakages and sediments of one category into others, and another analysis might assign some photographers differently, even using the same classification. However, the issue of different classifications is, I would argue, a political debate. As a regulating and ordering procedure, as a methodology of power or the will to truth, classifications situate, establish differences, fix alterity. In giving expression to the possible ways any corpus can be divided, classifications also give it meaning and strata of significance. Inasmuch as I argue against other classifications on political grounds, it is important to see this one in explicit politically instrumental terms, and I will so argue it. I will try to argue for a posture of articulation or enunciation rather than representation, if articulation is possible in photographic terms (in this regard, see Haraway, 1992:311).

15. Intention, of course, is distinctly social and cultural. For example, in the West there are many more photographs of marriages and birthdays and vacations than of divorces, funerals, or sickness, so actual numerical counts of photographs may be one (but only one) indication of intention.

Chapter Three

1. Robert Roessel, Jr.'s account (1980) prints many of the vital early materials and a selection of other early Navajo photographs to 1910. It is an essential reference for viewing the earliest images. As we know more today, it is possible to assign some of the photographs unattributed and correct mistaken attributions (pp. 35–62, 171, all possibly J. G. Gaige; p. 209, probably Valentin Wolfenstein; pp. 85–86, 152, 172–179, 214, Charles M. Bell; pp. 170, 202, 203, Nicholas Brown; and possibly pp. 155 and 162, either Nicholas Brown or Valentin Wolfenstein; pp. 163 [left], 185, Christian Barthelmess; p. 189, E. A. Mearns; pp. 157, 158, 187, 216, 217, 218, 222, 228 [left], and possibly 215, Ben Wittick; p. 225, J. R. Riddle; pp. 107. 194, 198, 199, 201, and possibly 169, Carl Moon; pp. 79, 191, and probably 233, J. W. Hildebrand; p. 195, Charles Day; p. 232, attributed to W. Ray Swartz, also attributed to G. Wharton James; p. 236 [bottom], Stuart M. Young, 1909; p. 234 [top], William H. Simpson; p. 226, F. Monsen; pp. 167, 168, 208 [top], possibly Jesse Beals; and p. 94, attributed to F. H. Maude, is also attributed to J. Hillers and copied by Ben Wittick). The caption and attribution number of p. 229 (top) actually belongs to the bottom photograph on the same page. I have reproduced very few of the photographs that appear in Roessel, 1980, or elsewhere (cf. La Farge, 1956; Frink, 1968; Link, 1968; Trafzer, 1982; Bighorse, 1990).

A brief but useful summary of the chronological history of photographic resources of Navajo is found in Brugge, 1983. Also very essential are Rudisill, 1973, and Fleming and Luskey, 1986, and references therein. For general commentary with some biographical detail, see Coke, 1979; Keegan, 1990; and Bush and Mitchell, 1994. Caution is urged, however, with these latter three, as there are mistakes (cf. Chapter 7, endnote 22).

There are occasional claims for photographs predating Bosque Redondo. In a recent Time-Life book, *People of the Desert* (Woodhead, 1993:167), a photograph of a Navajo woman weaving is captioned "taken around 1850." The photograph, from the University Museum of the University of Pennsylvania (Neg. No. 134541, copied from Lantern Slide 1512), has the notation "1851," probably left over from an earlier numbering system. How this date got inaccurately reported to the Time-Life photography editors is unknown (Pezzati/Faris, 9 March 1993). But in the Wanamaker archives of the Indiana University William Hammond Mathers Museum, this photograph is attributed to Dr. Joseph K. Dixon, taken at Ganado, Arizona, 4 July 1913 (see Fig. 192). There is also noted an "Old No. 1856, 15, #25" on this image, presumably an older numbering system. This may indeed be the source of the error. Dixon, as noted in Chapter

5, photographed for the Wanamaker expeditions, and many Wanamaker-sponsored photographs also rest in the University Museum of the University of Pennsylvania. Rodman Wanamaker (and well as his father, who also sponsored expeditions) was a Philadelphia department store magnate. However, concluding that Dr. Dixon indeed was (always) the actual photographer is problematic, as there were other photographers along on the 1913 expedition.

2. See Rudisill, 1973:55.

3. Copies of several of these earliest photographs are in the National Anthropological Archives attributed to A. Zeno Shindler (a Washington studio photographer—see Fleming and Luskey, 1986:231), and many appear in his catalog (1869), as well as the later Jackson catalogs (1874, 1877). Much of this misidentification results from the fact that Shindler made copies of several of these earliest photographs in 1868, and they appear in his exhibition catalog of 1869. As far as I am aware, there are no existing photographs of Navajo originally by Shindler. Jackson's two catalogs (1874, 1877) note ten Charles Bell photographs of the 1874 delegation to Washington, and his 1877 catalog adds a Wolfenstein photograph of Barboncito (who died in 1870 and so was not part of the 1874 delegation) and another Bell 1874 photograph of Nabona Primero to the original ten.

Several other early prints in the National Anthropological Archives, Smithsonian Institution, Washington, D.C. (Neg. No. 55,767; 56768) from the Wimar collections originating from the City Art Museum, St. Louis, MO, are attributed to Charles Wimar. Other than the note "photo by Wimar" penciled on the back of these photographs, however, there is no evidence that Wimar was indeed the photographer (on Wimar, see Stewart, *et al.,* 1991). They are undoubtedly photographs taken by Valentin Wolfenstein or Nicholas Brown and purchased, collected, or given to Wimar.

Edw. F. Weed is noted as having been the photographer (and having presented copies to the Museum) for several photographs of Navajo in the National Museum of the American Indian, Smithsonian Institution, New York, that are here attributed to Nicholas Brown or assigned to Valentine Wolfenstein. I have no information on Weed, and he is not listed in the standard sources on early Western photographers (cf. Rudisill, 1973; Fleming and Luskey, 1986; Mautz, 1986). It will be assumed here that Weed was only a donor. "Henry Lorenzen, N. M." is noted as the photographer on two National Museum of the American Indian images of Navajo that look not unlike Nicholas Brown or Valentin Wolfenstein images. Lorenzen was known to have been in New Mexico, but I have no information that would further corroborate these attributions. Nevertheless, they are here attributed to Lorenzen, based on the MAI designations. They are not photographs I have seen previously published.

The label "photo by Charles Gentile & Co." is noted on a print identified as Navajo (MAI print #7344). This individual does not look Navajo, and I have no other information on Charles Gentile nor from elsewhere that would merit identifying this photograph as Navajo. In 1914, several photographs from the Bosque Redondo era here attributed to Gaige were copyrighted by Cyrus Jennings—but again, Jennings is undoubtedly not the photographer. And it has been noted that Bosque Redondo photographs are suggested for William A. Smith (see Fleming and Luskey, 1986:70-72, 243; Rudisill, 1973:55), but none of these have survived or been located. Finally, there is a "Mr. Shepard" designation on one Wolfenstein photograph of Barboncito from the National Anthropological Archives. I have no data on Shepard, who was possibly but an artist who tinted the print.

4. See Rudisill, 1973:28. The *Santa Fe Weekly Gazette* of 26 August, 1865 (Vol VII, page 2, column 5), reveals:

> Mr. Gage [sic] who is now in the city, is engaged, under contract with the Quartermaster, in taking photographs of the different Military Posts in this Department. Mr. Gage [sic] is a competent artist and will no doubt, take first rate views of the various localities.

After his work at Fort Sumner in the spring of 1866, Gaige later moved to Chihuahua and eventually to Arizona, where he died in 1869 (*Weekly New Mexican,* 27 July, 1869). The identification of J. G. Gaige as the photographer of the Bosque Redondo outdoor group photographs was first tentatively made by Richard Rudisill (1973:28). I am very much indebted to him for further discussion of these materials with me (but it must be clear the extension of assignment of Gaige as the photographer of the lavish studio photographs is my own). The tentative attributions of the Wolfenstein photographs, except for Fig. 19 and Fig. 20 (which are attributed to Wolfenstein in the National Museum of the American Indian, Smithsonian Institution, New York City [MAI]), are my own, based upon differential posing styles, dress of subjects, items of furniture, background, floor covering, and the other apparent distinctions between Gaige, Brown, and Wolfenstein photographs.

5. Cf. Frink, 1968, La Farge, 1956; Link, 1968; Brugge, 1983; Roessel, 1980.

6. For these photographs, see Frink, 1968:65–77; Link, 1968:1–9; and Roessel, 1980:35–55.

7. See Roessel, 1980:57, 58, 59, 61, 62; Frink, 1968, La Farge, 1956.

8. Rudisill, 1973:63.

9. Rudisill, 1973:63.

10. Indeed, the famous photograph of Barboncito, here attributed to Wolfenstein (based on that attribution in the MAI), is also found on a Nicholas Brown *carte de visite*, as are some others here attributed to Wolfenstein (based on similarities of style, dress, props, etc.). Those with Nicholas Brown imprints could mean either that Brown is indeed the photographer or that he bought the photographs from Wolfenstein. I think there are persuasive reasons to trust the MAI Wolfenstein attributions and then to expand from them to make some other Wolfenstein attributions of photographs with Brown imprints. First, these Wolfenstein photographs from MAI are to my knowledge, the *only photographs of Navajo* attributed to Wolfenstein. Second, we have specific diary information that places Wolfenstein at Fort Sumner in 1868. And third, Wolfenstein may have sold equipment and photographs to Nicholas Brown. From Wolfenstein's diaries of the time, we know he contemplated selling his photographs and photographic equipment to Brown. The entry of 14 March 1868 (written while at Fort Union) reveals: "Today I try to work. Nothing succeeds. I feel terribly discouraged. Therefore I write Brown in Santa Fe and to Booth in Las Vegas and offer my equipment for sale for four hundred and fifty dollars." There is no indication in the diaries of the outcome of this offer. Clearly it was not taken up immediately, and in about three weeks Wolfenstein reached Fort Sumner, where he stayed until July, taking pictures of Navajo, of the Fort, of the treaty signing. It may well be that Wolfenstein shortly later made some arrangement with Brown, perhaps including outright sale of the photographs to Brown. It seems more likely that Wolfenstein sold photographs to Brown (who later issued them as his own *carte de visite*) than that Brown took photographs attributed in the MAI sources to Wolfenstein and that Wolfenstein bought them from him. Certainly Brown did issue photographs taken by others for his *carte de visite*. And if indeed these Barboncito photographs were taken by Brown, how did the Wolfenstein attribution come to be? Wolfenstein went on to California in 1868, and it seems unlikely that Wolfenstein might have acquired Brown photographs that later were to be attributed to himself. Herein, until further information is forthcoming, I will assume that Valentin Wolfenstein produced the photographs of Barboncito and thereby others taken at the same time and place (cf. Fig. 21, 22).

11. Brown is documented as having traveled to Chihuahua in 1867 (Rudisill, 1973:16) and may have photographed at Fort Sumner at this time.

12. Roessel, 1980:202.

13. See Fleming and Luskey, 1986:238 and Rudisill, 1973:33. According to Rudisill (Faris/Rudisill, August 1990), Hiester may have also worked with O'Sullivan at Zuni. Though Rudisill (1973:33) suggests Hiester came to Santa Fe first in 1871 (and may not have worked in Navajoland until 1877), if the date of Dodd's death before 1870 is correct, then the Hiester photograph of Dodd with Manuelito (Fig. 32) must have been taken prior to the attributed 1871 (indeed, in late, 1968 just after the return from New Mexico); or perhaps the European-American in the photograph is someone other than Dodd. He has been identified as Capt. Frank Bennett (a later agent to the Navajo) in Berlant and Kahlenberg, 1991:105, which makes possible the 1871 (or later) date of the photograph. At this writing, the precise identification of the European-American in the photograph is still uncertain, and the identification given in Berlant

and Kahlenberg, 1991, is not corroborated. Indeed, until this is resolved, the attribution of the photograph to Hiester is in doubt—or, at least, the date of Hiester's photography of Navajo is in doubt (Herzer/Faris, 12 December 1994).

14. There is one photograph of Navajo with which I am familiar from E. O. Beaman, the original photographer with the Powell expedition (see Fleming and Luskey, 1986:131 and SWM P9733). Beaman quarreled with Powell and was dismissed, which eventually gave Hillers the opportunity to become the expedition's photographer (see Fleming and Luskey, 1986:109).

15. See Horan, 1966: 292–296.

16. See Horan, 1966; Newhall and Newhall, 1966; Roessel, 1980; Snyder, 1981, for O'Sullivan's Navajo photographs. Though some noted in catalogs were not indeed found in the standard O'Sullivan sources, I am familiar with nine different photographs of Navajo attributed to O'Sullivan. As far as I am aware, all O'Sullivan Navajo materials have been published in the noted references. Of all the great surveys, no photographs of Navajo survive from the Hayden survey on which William Henry Jackson was a photographer. All those Navajo photographs that are noted in his two catalogs (1874, 1877) are by other photographers. Jackson is on record as having photographed in Navajoland in 1877, but these negatives all failed (Fleming and Luskey, 1986:108). Despite this, misidentifications abound. In the Southwest Museum are three photographs attributed to "W. H. Jackson, 1884" on the back in pencil. All are dated 1884, and though they certainly could have been produced by Jackson, they are a curious size for the date (3 ¾ by 2 ¾ inches) and must be considered doubtful attributions.

In a new publication, Dippie (1992:133) cites a photograph of Carnero Mucho (a famous Charles Bell 1874 portrait of the leader lying against a rock, holding bow and arrow) as that of W. H. Jackson (presumably because it is from Jackson catalog[s] No. 1034—where the identification as Navajo is correct, though the photograph is not attributed to Bell), misidentifying the man as "Mariamie" (RAI 1164).

17. See Roessel, 1980, for publication of many of these; and see Fleming and Luskey, 1986, for commentary on delegation photography. At least three photographs (of the Navajo leader Manuelito, his wife, Juanita, and their son, Manuelito Segundo) of the 1874 Washington delegation photographed by Charles Bell have been occasionally attributed to James Thurlow (see Rudisill, 1973:57; Frink, 1968:81). The three are posed in Bell style, with Bell props, and the Thurlow attribution, on the strength of the information thus far available, must be considered in error.

18. In a couple of later delegation portraits attributed to Bureau of American Ethnology engraver Delancy Gill (1902 and 1909), Navajo are posed in total Western dress, as are most other notable visitors. Though these are more distinguished portraits, even here, however, we get both *en face* and profile images of these individuals—a common pattern in criminal recording and *de rigueur* for anthropological surveillance photography of the time (but compare Figs. 58 and 59 to 60).

19. The Santa Fe Railroad, as well as the Fred Harvey Company, its entrepreneurial concessionaire, employed many photographers to sell the indigenous landscape and local people. Among the earliest were William H. Jackson, Adam C. Vroman, William E. Kopplin, Carl Moon, William H. Simpson, Edward H. Kemp, Frederic H. Maude, and Fred Harvey himself. Photography and the railways have been the subject of several studies (cf. McLuhan, 1985), and Harvey and the Santa Fe Railway itself generated an entire aesthetic (and a host of more recent nostalgic museum exhibitions). Many others, of course, sold photographs to both Harvey and the Santa Fe Railway, and there is little doubt that these two sources, plus other tourist companies and hotels, were important outlets and sponsors for photographers of the times. Indeed, patronage by the Santa Fe Railway or the Fred Harvey organization was the chief source of income for several photographers for specific periods (cf. Jackson, Moon, Simpson). Publication of photographs to accompany book texts was more limited until the turn of the century, but photographic postcards proliferated, as did illustrated camera magazines. A popular form of traveling entertainment was the hand-tinted lantern slide show and illustrated lecture, and many postal cards and lantern slides were from the same photographs. A good overview of some of these photographers, particularly those from Southern California (Vroman, James, Monsen, Maude, Lummis) is Jutzi, n.d.

20. See Fleming and Luskey, 1986:244. Though Vroman made several trips, the club members who also photographed Navajo included Crandell, Hoopes, and Rose. Vroman has been the subject of specific study (cf. Mahood, 1961; Webb and Weinstein, 1973 [there are dating and attribution errors in the Navajo portion of the latter reference]), though dozens and dozens of his Navajo photographs have never been published. Today most original Vroman materials are at the Southwest Museum and the Natural History Museum of Los Angeles County. Copies of some of these materials, however, are widespread. In the view here (and referring only to the photographs of Navajo), inflated claims have been made for the innovative character of Vroman's images, and his unpublished materials are unremarkable and typical. They focus on archaeological activities or Navajo leading the rich and famous to the Hopi "Snake Dances" (in fact, once the "Snake Dances" were closed to photographers, Vroman abruptly gave up Southwestern photography). Indeed, many of Vroman's photographs of Navajo are labeled "On the Way to the Snake Dance." To these activities Navajo are often simply adjunctive as laborers or spectators, and Vroman's collecting ambitions and touring arrangements to Hopi seemed to dictate many of his Navajo photographs. He apparently preferred photographing Pueblo peoples.

Many others photographed Navajo while on the way to the Hopi villages. A particularly good set of ordinary Navajo activities was so photographed by the Yale paleontologist Charles Emerson Beecher in 1900 (ASM archive).

21. In the Southwest Museum is an attribution on the back of a photographic print, "William Henry Jackson," probably by Mrs. Hector Alliot, wife of the Museum Director [1909-1919] and is undoubtedly in error. This print (P. 37326) looks very much like (and probably is) a G.W. James photograph.

22. I would not suggest these "postures" were specific to Navajo, nor even peculiar to native peoples. Many were from studio poses and conventions of the day. Herein, however, the task is to document and discuss all possible visual registers and the implications of their application to Navajo.

23. See Kavanagh, 1993.
24. See Fleming and Luskey, 1986:170.
25. See Roessel, 1980:231.
26. See also Fleming and Luskey, 1993:36-39.
27. See Kurutz, 1978.
28. See also Jutzi, n.d.
29. See Hathaway, 1990:78.
30. See Broder, 1990; and Olivas, 1970. As elsewhere for photographers of this period, there is persistent confusion over attribution. Wittick certainly printed the photographs of others (Hillers, for example). Photographs here attributed to Wittick have also been elsewhere attributed to A. F. Randall, E. O. Richmond, and Julian Scott (see also Fleming and Luskey, 1986:242, and especially Rudisill, 1973:48-49). As elsewhere, there was probably loaning/borrowing/purchasing/piracy of one by another in these days. Herein Wittick will be noted as the photographer if his name appears on the photograph and there is no convincing information to the contrary.
31. See Halpern and McGreevy, 1996. It is of some significance that whereas today studio photographs (and negatives) normally belong to the sitter/purchaser, in these early sittings of Native Americans all photographs and negatives belonged to the photographer. Obviously Native American sitters could seldom pay for them.
32. Frink, 1965.
33. See Faris, 1990:20.
34. Fleming and Luskey, 1986:243; Roessel, 1980:87.
35. See Long, 1992.
36. Rudisill, 1973:20.
37. See Berezin, 1982.

Chapter Four
1. In Hammond, 1993:27.
2. See, for example, Deloria, 1982:11.

3. Considerable confusion exists over the Curtis "originals." It appears likely that many, if not most, of the original glass plate negatives used in *The North American Indian* were deposited in and eventually discarded by the Morgan Library in New York. I am aware of only a few that survived. The relevant photographs reprinted herein are from existing contact photoprints at the Library of Congress and the National Anthropological Archives, sent to the former for copyright registration purposes, or original contact prints made from copy negatives that Curtis made available elsewhere. The numbers were inscribed by Curtis on many of the original negatives. Those "original" Curtis prints widely for sale may be printed from the copper photogravure plates used to print the photographs in *The North American Indian*, or from one or another more intermediate or derived process, and in the worst cases, actual pages from the twenty-volume set. Because only 3,000 copies of *The North American Indian* were printed (a minority of these were accompanied by a large additional portfolio of photographs), this supply is clearly diminishing. And there are also circulating other Curtis prints from negatives or copy negatives from his independent studio work—many of which appeared as well in *The North American Indian*, some of which did not. Curtis's Navajo materials seem to have all been on dry glass plates.

The Library of Congress possesses both published and unpublished Curtis photographs of Navajo—thirty-six of the former and ninety-one of the latter (in *The North American Indian*, 1907, Volume 1 [and its photographic folio supplement], there are a total of fifty-five photographs of Navajo published, including the sandpainting sketches). The National Anthropological Archive Curtis Navajo photographs are from 1) private donations of Curtis prints from several sources and 2) prints from the Library of Congress, some of which are duplicates of those now existing at the Library of Congress, others of which appear not to be. Those Library of Congress prints sent to the National Anthropological Archives (or Bureau of American Ethnology, as it was known at the time) were transferred at a period in the early decades of this century when the Library of Congress felt it had too many "Indian photographs" and was trying to dispose of many of them (Faris/J. Kearns, 12 March 1991).

4. Boas, the instigator of a "scientific" anthropology (and historical particularism as cultural relativity) dismissed Curtis—even going so far as to write to President Theodore Roosevelt (who had written an introduction to *The North American Indian*). Of course, Boas himself set up and staged photographs in the most dramatic way (cf. Holm in Davis, 1985:ix). But Curtis was (probably as a consequence of Boas's criticism) championed by Boas's enemies in anthropology at Harvard, the Bureau of American Ethnology, and the American Museum of Natural History (see Graybill and Boesen, 1976:28). See also, for example, the recent general hostility of anthropology (cf. Holm, 1983; Scherer, 1990) to Lyman (1982—with an introduction by Vine Deloria, Jr.) for what was considered to be an attack on Curtis (see also Holm's defense of Curtis in his forward to Davis, 1985—incidentally also a book with an appreciation by the photographer and historian Beaumont Newhall). Lee, 1980:312, summarizes the new defense:

> [I]f Curtis . . . [remained] true to his own intentions, then it becomes futile to accuse him of "dishonesty." If Curtis' goals in making these films were achieved as the contextual analysis suggested, then perhaps Curtis should be commended for creating a truly "ethical" work of art.

This represents a new resurrection after more than half a century of neglect and abuse. Interestingly, however, for all the new anthropological embrace, Curtis is not represented in any illustrative Navajo material in the volumes thus far produced of the new *Handbook of North American Indian*—a series where the rationalist tropes of accuracy and authority reign and where photographic materials must not bear any taint of inauthenticity. It is perhaps worthy of note that such care seems to fall away in some caption detail—for example, on page 554 of Volume 10 (*Southwest*—the volume which includes Navajo) of the *Handbook of North American Indians*, Figure 15, a Mountain Way sandpainting is mislabeled as a Nightway in an important article on the Navajo Ceremonial System (Wyman, 1983). The very publication of actual sandpainting photographs is, of course in Navajo view, to be avoided at all costs. This perhaps reveals something about anthropology's subtle but continuing contempt for indigenous practices, even at such exalted levels as the Smithsonian Handbook series. Curtis photographs have been used, however, in non-Navajo photographic materials in the Handbook series (Scherer/Faris, 13 July 1994). Faris, 1993c and 1993d, are in error in suggesting otherwise.

Moreover, the deceit of the more recent anthropological embrace fails to address the earlier condemnations—certainly Curtis's work is no less staged, the props no more authentic, the subjects no less posed than work by his predecessors. Perhaps more than anything else, the anthropological community's insecurity was exposed as it scrambled to get aboard the Curtis resurrection. This is a commentary on anthropology, not Curtis, for the recent defenses of Curtis outside anthropology may be considered persuasive (or not) on their own terms. Strangely, anthropology has not bothered to research the copious Curtis photographs of Navajo.

Certainly another common fashionable attitude toward Curtis is to compare him to others of his generation, such as Vroman (cf. Misrach, 1992), and to thereby demean him. There is little question that many of Vroman's photographs, particularly of Pueblo peoples, are very fine—however, on the strength of just the photographs of Navajo, Curtis's work is quite as impressive, or more so. Curtis, probably as a consequence of the immensity of his project, is also compared with his successors and predecessors, both favorably and unfavorably.

5. I located this photograph in a personal collection of family photographs belonging to Sam Day III in the course of other research—but also after developing suspicions for sometime about the muscular and very tall Navajo appearing in some of Curtis's photographs. It should also be noted that both Charlie and Sam Day II had grown up in the area and were fluent in Navajo. And according to Sam Day III, whose mother is Navajo, both his father and his uncle had been previously initiated at Nightway (and thus could participate legitimately in subsequent Nightway) prior to participating in Curtis's staged Nightway dance. The issue does not, then, center on the appropriateness of the Days' participation in the ceremonial nor on some criterion of "authenticity"—it is Curtis's duplicity (see also Portfolio VIII below, for more Navajo mimesis).

6. See *Seattle Sunday Times*, 22 May 1904

7. Davis, 1985:47.

8. This might have been suspected, however, from what Curtis does tell us. In the flamboyant *Seattle Sunday Times* (22 May 1904) account:

> As everything was in readiness for the dance Curtis did not delay another moment. As soon as the crowd had drifted away, Curtis put off for the mountains. When he started, he could not see one of the "faithful fourteen," and as a matter of fact, he did not know whether he would ever see them again or not.
>
> Charlie was with him, and by and by they came to a little wooded grass covered ravine in the heart of the foothills. "Put your camera up there," said Charlie, and when that had been done they seated themselves and waited.
>
> It wasn't very long before Curtis saw that he was not to be disappointed. Down the ravine came fourteen of the queerest, most fantastically dressed figures Curtis ever saw in his life. It would be impossible to describe the dance. The camera alone has the power to do that, but Edward S. Curtis of Seattle saw what no other white man had seen before.

One could reasonably ask how Charlie Day knew exactly where the *yé'ii* dancers were to appear—but indeed, Charlie *participated* as a dancer (see especially Fig. 69) and led the dance team to the precise location of Curtis's ciné camera. In fact, the lead dancer (cf. Lyman, 1982:69, Fig. 43) of the *yé'ii* dance team was probably Charlie Day. If so, then Charlie was not one of those who "seated themselves and waited." Because this dance was photographed both in ciné and stills (and from careful comparison, it does not appear the stills are taken from the ciné), Curtis clearly had assistants. Fleming and Luskey (1993:112) note that Adolph F. Muhr became Curtis's darkroom assistant in 1904, but it is not clear if he was on this trip, nor which members of Curtis's family were along in the first trip. His family did spend time with him on the second visit to Navajoland.

9. See Davis, 1985:47.
10. See Faris, 1990.
11. Faris, 1990:123.
12. Curtis negative numbers appear on most of those prints of *actual* Nightway in the Library of Congress collections. They were copyrighted (most claimed copyrighted in 1904—judging by Curtis's negative numbering system), but many were actually copyrighted somewhat later—judging by the technical date of copyright by the Library of Congress), and two of these *actual* Nightway photographs, probably by Charlie Day or W. J. Andrus, were copyrighted by Curtis (both actually in 1905, though Curtis claims 1904) and published in *The North American Indian* (see Curtis, 1907, Vol. 1, facing pages 116, 124). There is one photograph—LOC LC-USZ62-96725 (also found, with a different label, "Ceremony with Yeibichai," also attributed to Curtis, in the NAA [Copy Neg. 74-7221])—in the LOC collections of an initiation, "Initiation, Outdoors, 1905 [*sic*]," attributed to and claimed by Edward S. Curtis, but undoubtedly by Andrus or Charlie Day, taken probably late 1903 or early 1904. It is one of the initiation of boys (no girls are visible, though they may also be initiated at this time) to the secrets of the masks—which occurs during one of the later days of the Nightway. The same Talking God (?) and Female *yé'ii* that have been seen in Figs. 71 and 72 are administering in the initiation (the Female *yé'ii* gently whips the boys with the two yucca stalks he is carrying). In this photograph, the medcine man, probably Little Singer, is seated at right.
13. See Mitchell, 1910.
14. Long, 1992:passim.
15. Faris, 1990:119.
16. There is an actual Navajo sandpainting photograph in the Curtis materials in the Library of Congress ("Sand Painting—Wind Doctor," LOC LC-USZ62-59799, Curtis No. X1043-04), probably by Speech Man. It depicts a Navajo Windway sandpainting, known as "Cactus People, Many Heads, Ascending Branches," very similar to the same sandpainting reproduction found today in the Huckel Collection of the Taylor Museum of Colorado Springs, CO. The Navajo Windway is also a healing practice normally confined to the fall and winter. Had Curtis actually taken this photograph, we certainly would have heard about it. This photograph is very likely by Charles Day or perhaps by W. J. Andrus, who photographed an actual Nightway sandpainting in 1904 (at least, it is attributed to him in MAI archives) and may indeed be responsible for other Curtis Nightway photographs. There are several photographs in the National Museum of the American Indian in New York attributed to "W. J. Andrus, Chinle, 1904," two of which are clearly also claimed by Curtis (Negative No. 37706—"Man who conducted singing at Yeibitchai"—see Fig. 75; and Negatives No. 37707 and No. 37708—"Old man who assisted at Yeibitchai"—see Fig. 76), at least as known from LOC collections and elsewhere. (It should be noted that Curtis misidentifies the "man who conducted singing" as Laughing Singer, when it is in fact Little Singer. Laughing Singer is clearly and correctly identified by Mooney [Fig. 36]). Two other photographs, however, *look* like Curtis's and are of the same general subjects as the other photographs, but they do not exist in any other Curtis collections I have examined (Negative No. 33705—"Male Patient at Yeibitchai, Chin Lee, 1904"—see Fig. 77; and Negative No. 33708—"Old man who assisted at Yeibitchai"—see Fig. 76). Andrus, who was in New Mexico in 1904, was involved in the acquisition of pottery, which found its way into the MAI collections—and, significantly, Andrus was present during the winter months of 1903–1904, when a Nightway ceremony could properly be held. Andrus could have been the photographer for all the *actual* Nightway photographs and sold or given the negatives to Curtis, or perhaps *vice versa*, with the photographs entered the MAI collections attributed to the donor. Four of these photographs, portraits, are in the Curtis style (which lends credence to the theory that Curtis is the actual photographer), but the labels on the photographs claimed by Andrus suggest someone more familiar with the Nightway than Curtis might have been, unless he were told these details by someone close to the Nightway and close to the men of these photographs. Another photograph is, as noted, of an actual Whirling Logs Nightway sandpainting, and if Curtis had actually photographed a Nightway sandpainting, he would not have had to get the sketches from Billy Jones, which were eventually published. As noted above, he would have

certainly published the photograph, for he described the Nightway healing practice in some detail in Volume One of *The North American Indian*.

17. Curtis (1904) does acknowledge the hostility of Navajo themselves to his photography. The correspondence, however, refers to something other than the resistance of Navajo.

18. See Davis, 1985:47ff.

19. See Faris, 1990:54–55, and Faris, 1993:386. Curtis photographed, both in still and ciné, portions of a staged Nightway healing ceremonial, and in Volume One of *The North American Indian* (1907) he gives a day-by-day account of the nine-day reordering practice (also popularly called the Yeibichai). He claims to have photographed dancers and dances, pit sweatbaths, initiations, and masked God Impersonators, and there are Nightway sandpainting sketches reprinted in his 1907 account. But from Curtis's correspondence to the Day family, it is clear Curtis, as noted, set it all up. He got his Nightway account from Charlie Day through the mails sometime after 20 December 1904 (see NAU:Day Family Collection, Series 4, Box 1, Folder 30, E. Curtis to C. Day) and his sandpaintings from a local Navajo, Billy Jones (who was not a Nightway medicine man but who may have helped at the large sandpaintings in actual ceremonials [indeed, there are some significant errors in these Billy Jones sandpainting reproductions—see Curtis, 1907:118, 120, 122; Faris, 1990:123, 138]), who sent sketches to him sometime after January, 1905 (see NAU:Day Family Collection, Series 4, Box 1, Folder 23, E. Curtis to C. Day). And he had local Navajo set up a few rounds of the dance for the last night of the Nightway so that he might film it (with, again, the vital assistance of Charlie Day, the non-Navajo trader's son, and Billy Jones, who made for Curtis a basket of sacrificial cigarettes [NAU:Day Family Collection, Series 4, Box 1, Folder 30, Curtis to C. Day, 20 December 1904] as well as the Nightway sandpainting reproductions noted). Indeed, the actual Nightway sandpainting photographed by W. J. Andrus in 1904 is quite different from the sketch sent Curtis by Billy Jones (compare Curtis, 1907:facing page 120, to MAI #P. 1297). For controversy over Curtis's ciné footage of Navajo, see Faris, 1993d.

20. See Lyman, 1982:67.

21. See Curtis, 1907, Vol. 1, facing pages 112, 114.

22. See Curtis, 1907, Vol. 1, facing pages 136, 140.

23. Those masks featured in the close-up studio busts are of one set, those photographed with the canyon background are of the other set. Some masks of the canyon background and some of the bust series together appear to be the mask set today in the Field Museum in Chicago. Navajo, as noted, regard the public display of such masks in such a way as sacrilege. See also Faris, 1993d:384–385, and Faris, 1990 (Chapter 5 and associated Chart 12 notes), for more detail of the "Curtis" masks.

24. See Faris, 1990:Chart 7.

25. See Curtis, 1907, Vol. 1, facing page 114—Monster Slayer with Born for Water, and with Water Sprinkler. The former two never appear without one another.

26. See Gilpin, 1968. "One photographer who must surely be excepted from this evaluation [lacking a sympathetic sense of purpose] is Laura Gilpin, whose deeply committed studies of contemporary life are truly a continuation of Curtis" (Coleman and McLuhan, 1974:VI). This assessment contrasts, of course, with that of Gilpin's biographers, who saw her as something qualitatively different from Curtis and in much firmer touch with her subjects (cf. Sandweiss, 1986). As will be seen, I am not convinced her differences, given the differences in time, technology, and outlook, were that great. See Chapter 6.

27. See McCombe, 1951.

28. Keegan, 1974, 1990. In a rather amazing exercise, Keegan unapologetically likens the work in her 1990 volume to that of the earlier pioneer photographers, including Curtis. See Chapter 7.

29. Cf. Running, 1985.

30. And at times very depressing—cf. Keegan, 1990.

Chapter Five

I paraphrase the term "Saturated Fields of Visibility" from an excellent essay by Judith Butler (1993:15).

1. By "new," I mean photographers not previously identified as late nineteenth-century photographers. Obviously, some late nineteenth-century photographers of Navajo produced into the twentieth century as well. And this number of twentieth-century photographers includes many amateurs and individuals whose few photographs found their way into print or into archives.
2. Forrest, 1970.
3. An interesting, well-researched, and informed novel, Charles Fergus's *Shadow Catcher* (1991), relates the story of the Wanamaker expedition of 1913 and the photographic role of Joseph Dixon. Dixon's bombastic posed propaganda photos are contrasted with candid photography, and a persistent tension in the novel is based about the ethics of using secreted candid images from a concealed button-hole camera rather than posed large view camera photographs.
4. Indeed, Moon claims to have destroyed as many as half of his negatives because they were not up to this standard. Moon has been shamelessly copied, not only because Fred Harvey often used his photographs without attribution but also because less careful contemporary artists apparently have done so. A popular postcard of an oil on photo linen by Bob Ward, "Indians with Blankets" (22" x 48"), is from a known Carl Moon photograph of Native Americans wrapped in Navajo blankets (Fig. 128). Ward does not bother to acknowledge or attribute Moon. Interestingly, this photograph may have been taken in California, even, perhaps, at the Southwest Museum building site, where Charles Lummis assembled native peoples, draped them with Navajo blankets, and had them photographed (see NAA Neg. No. 54,630).
5. Nevertheless, Moon was not above its use:

> To break down the prejudice and superstition of the Indian's attitude toward the camera, in those early days [1909], I found it necessary to hide all photographic apparatus until I had gained a friendly footing with the chief men of the village or tribe I was visiting. Then later, I would produce my camera as if it were an afterthought or second consideration, rather than the thing that stood for my business among them. To photograph ceremonies and dances, the camera often had to be hidden in a paper bag or wrapped in something that looked innocent and yet would leave an aperture for the lens and shutter-trigger (Moon, 1923b).

In fact, Moon is noted for having done so, as has his ingenuity in arranging it. He once attended a harvest dance at Santo Domingo but was firmly told to leave his camera at home. Instead, he disguised it in a sack of crackers and snapped pictures as he watched (Kirk/Mack, n.d. [1988]).
6. James, 1908.
7. There has been photography with nude female models, both European-American and Navajo (cf. Hanna for an early example), in Navajoland, with its red rocks, blue sky, clouds, and Anasazi ruins. These have not, to my knowledge, been published, especially those using Navajo models.
8. It should be emphasized that many photographs in the Wanamaker collections (University Museum, University of Pennsylvania; William Hammond Mathers Museum, Indiana University) are neither by William Farabee (of the earlier expedition) nor by Joseph Dixon (of the 1913 expedition). Many, particularly in the 1913 expedition, were made by other photographers or assistants. Wanamaker (and later his son) was a Philadelphia department store magnate who claimed to be sponsoring a gigantic monument to the American Indian in New York Harbor to rival (or complement) the Statue of Liberty. The 1913 Expedition of Citizenship traveled all over the nation's Indian reservations, and at each stop (where the Bureau of Indian Affairs had been instructed to lay on all facility), the assembled had to listen to Edison recordings of speeches by the President (Wilson), Wanamaker, the secretary of the interior, the acting commissioner of Indian affairs, and the expedition's leader, as well as live speeches by Joseph Dixon (also commonly the expedition's photographer) and BIA inspector James McLaughlin. The "Declaration of Allegiance," which each Native American group was required to sign, read:

> We greatly appreciate the honor and privilege extended by our white brothers, who have recognized us by inviting us to participate in the ceremonies on this historical occasion.
>
> The Indian is fast losing his identity in the face of the great waves of Caucasian civilization, which are extending to the four winds of this country, and we want fuller knowledge, in order that we make take our places in the civilization which surrounds us.
>
> Though a conquered race, with our right hands extended in brotherly love, and our left hands holding the Pipe of Peace, we hereby bury all past ill feeling and proclaim abroad, to all the nations of the world, our firm allegiance to this nation and to the Stars and Stripes, and declare that henceforth and forever, in all walks of life and every field of endeavor, we shall be as brothers, striving hand in hand, and will return to our people and tell them the story of this Memorial, and urge upon them their continued allegiance to our common country (Anon., 1913:15).

For their pledge, each reservation ("tribe") got an American flag from Wanamaker. Ground had been broken for the monument at Fort Wadsworth in New York Harbor in February 1913. This initial ceremony involved a demeaning admission by the assembled Native American leaders of their past sins in resisting the white man:

> I lament the ignorance of my forefathers. We would not now be driven into the small places of the earth had our grandfathers dealt with wisdom with reference to our lands and our homes, and I can now see that the open road for happiness and prosperity among my people is to join hands with the white brother, and receive into our own lives the civilization and education that he offers, and join with our white brother in supporting the flag (ibid.:7).

At the groundbreaking, the red, white, and blue of the flag was endowed with symbolic significance wholly at odds with the conventional symbolism for such colors. White became the trail of purity, red was the blood necessary to shed to keep the flag out of the dust and to put "a steel plowshare into the virgin prairies" (Ibid.:13), and blue was what held the field of stars, stars of war and peace and love, now to be dedicated "toward his brothers and toward the white man" (ibid.:13).

The monument was never built, of course, but the expedition proceeded, taking the time, energy, and allegiances of those at each place it stopped (but see Fergus, 1991 for some subtle resistances). Nor did Native Americans get citizenship out of it; this was not forthcoming until at least a decade later, and in portions of Navajoland not until 1948.

9. A few other studios did work in the region of Navajoland during this period. These included the Fort Wingate studio of Mickle and Jones (see Fig. 35) and the Gallup studios of Mishler and Walker, William Fetter, (see Fig. 50), and J. Riddle. For some territorial-period photographers of Gallup and environs listed in Rudisill, 1973, I have no evidence of photography of Navajo.
10. Many of these, plus some other of Schwemberger's remarkable photographs, are the subject of a recent book (Long, 1992)—a book that, unfortunately, seems never to have been proofread.
11. Forrest, 1970.
12. The photography of Navajo at Pueblo festivals and feast days became commonplace, as the Navajo were considered more colorful in dress and accouterments than their Pueblo hosts. Parkhurst, for example, took dozens of photographs of Navajo at Laguna feast days, as did amateurs. Navajo could be photographed with impunity at Pueblo feasts, guests as they were. One such photograph—of two Navajo women and a child against a Pueblo ladder—appears in Scherer, 1973:91. The caption says the women "are standing in front of what is probably a Government building on the reservation, because most Navajos lived in sod-covered huts called hogans," but it is clearly a Pueblo dwelling, possibly at Laguna or Jemez or Zuni, on one of the

local feast days. Curiously, this volume makes other ethnographic mistakes about Navajo—for example, a hand-rotated spindle illustrated in a Mooney photograph (p. 45) is described as a "foot rotated spindle," and the colors of black and white wool (p. 15) come not from clay and charcoal, as suggested, but from the natural colors of sheep themselves.

13. Cf. Whiteley, 1987—but see also Faris, 1990:24.

14. See Babcock and Parezo, 1988:95. Indeed, the Southwest began to attract independent women, sometimes of wealth, in anthropology, the arts, letters, and Indian rights and education. Many of these women also photographed Navajo.

15. The Pen-Dike studio lasted from 1910 until 1912, when the two went their separate ways. Apparently Pennington continued in the studio, with Updike traveling and taking photographs, which the two sold. Pennington also teamed with Rowland in 1914 in a number of Navajo portraits of the same sort. Sets of numbered limited editions of the Navajo photographs came to be offered by Durango trading companies in 1974.

16. Bailey and Bailey, 1986:110.

17. See Newcomb, 1964; Richardson, 1986; Hegemann, 1963.

18. Unfortunately, no central photographic archive exists for these magazines' photographs, as most were (and are) commissioned on a contract basis and retained by the photographer. Both magazines keep indexes, however, on subject.

19. See Plett, 1986, and Faris/Walt, May, 1994.

20. See Babcock and Parezo, 1988:175, 209.

21. See Coolidge and Coolidge, 1930; and Faris, 1990:56.

22. Babcock and Parezo, 1988:53.

23. Palmquist, 1991:9.

24. See Armer, 1962; Berry, 1929.

25. See Sawyer, 1985.

26. The controversial stock-reduction program, inaugurated by Commissioner John Collier in the 1930s, required Navajo drastically to reduce herds, ostensibly to reduce soil erosion. A majority of people lost most of their assets and were not even able to eat the animals killed. More recent scholarship suggests the reduction program was excessive, did not serve to reduce erosion so much as anticipated, and was thus largely unnecessary. See Parman, 1976; Roessel and Johnson, 1974. See also Chapter 6, endnote 7.

27. Cf. Sandner, 1979.

28. Long, 1992; Butler/Faris, 19 November 1990.

29. Copies of some (but by no means all) of the St. Michaels photographs exist at the Special Collections Library of the Cline Library of Northern Arizona University, Flagstaff, and at the Photography Archives of the Arizona State Museum, Tucson. Some (but not all) of these external copies duplicate each other.

30. The Navajo Nation finally acquired the BIA/Milton Snow Collection (as it is known) in 1985 from the Bureau of Indian Affairs after years of unkept promises to return it, repeated attempts to secure it, etc. (cf. *Navajo Times Today*, 17 July, 1985:1; 14 November 1985:1). It should also be noted that although the vast majority are there, some Snow photographs are not in the Navajo Nation Museum collections, as they apparently earlier made their way elsewhere while under the care of the BIA. Many are in the National Archives, Washington; the Maxwell Museum of the University of New Mexico; and elsewhere (including some from commercial stock companies). Though a few of these external Snow photographs are copies, many are unique. Some attempt should be made to assemble copies of all of them for the Navajo Nation Museum.

31. It is interesting to note the extent to which, in the dominant assimilationist motions, Navajo are shown buying bonds and volunteering to fight in World War II and subsequent conflicts. In 1993, for example, there were still signs all over the reservation welcoming home soldiers from Desert Storm (1991) and expressing support for the operation. The images of assimilation have become the realities. See Portfolio VIII.

Prior to the outset of the Persian Gulf war, a petition against it was circulated among faculty of Navajo Community College. The petition had been initiated by non-Navajo faculty, and although a few Navajo signed it, most signatures were from non-Navajo. The lack of Navajo support was explained by the fact that Navajo were basically very "patriotic." That Navajo faculty did not behave as anticipated by non-Navajo faculty is a clear example not only of Navajo patriotism (Navajo were, as usual, disproportionally represented in the Persian Gulf theatre as troops, and many had relatives or knew of individuals in the war) but also of the persistent failure of Navajo to conform to one or another Western stereotype of how they should behave.

32. The categories N [Maps], NJ [Geology], NP [Rangeland], and NQ [unclassified] are unrepresented in the internal divisions. Numbers in parentheses are the negatives available for each. Gaps in lettering and numbering sequences are Snow's.

33. However, on the strength of his classification, Snow seemed to have known men by name more often than women.

34. All museums and archives have classification systems—sometimes inductively derived from collections, sometimes imposed upon the collections. All are Western and announce what is important to Westerners, for classification is a great rationalist normalizing and commanding device—it situates and orders and imposes organization in the terms of those who are classifying. The quite incredible Concho photographic classification scheme is:

A. Agriculture
Aa1. field preparation, planting, cultivation
2. growing crops
3. harvesting
4. harvested crops
5. insect control
6. fertilizing and application
7. noxious weed control
8. farming misc.
9. farm demonstrations
10. historical agriculture
Ab Orchards
1. planting
2. pruning
3. insect control
4. diseases
5. harvest and produce
6. orchards
7. Tribal Nursery
Ac Irrigation
1. diversions, canals, ditches
2. water applications
3. irrigated fields and misc.
Ad Farm Training
1. training farm
2. farm trainees and activities
3. results of training
B. Lakes, Rivers, Dams
1. Morgan Lake
2. White Cone Lake
3. Tsailee Lake
4. Wheatfields Lakes
5. Round Rock Lake
6. Ganado Lake
7. Mariano Lake
8. Red Lake
9. Lake Powell and Glen Canyon Dam
10. Navajo Lake and Dam

11. Whiskey Lake
12. misc. lakes
13. misc. streams
14. misc. rivers
C. Fish
1. fish stocking
2. fish die off
3. fish management
4. fish eradication
D. Wildlife
a1. predator control—poison
a2. predator control—trapping, shooting
a3. rodent and pest control
b1. mammals
b2. birds
b3. reptiles, mollusks
b4. insects, arachnids
b5. fish
b6. flora
b7. trees
c1. game birds stocking
c2. deer stocking
c3. beaver stocking
c4. bear control
c5. zoo and animal exhibit
E. Navajo Culture
1. housing
2. native foods
3. home slaughtering
5. cooking and food preparation
6. misc. arts and crafts
7. ceremonials, seat baths
8. dress
9. transportation
10. misc.
11. Navajo people
F. Navajo Government
1. Window Rock/capital

2. Tribal Council
3. council house
4. chairman
5. councilmen
6. inauguration
7. chapter houses
8. voting
G. Navajo Social Activities
1. Navajo Fair
2. rodeo
3. civic center
4. dances
5. athletics
6. youth camps
7. youth activities
8. civic and social groups
10. border town shows
11. Gallup Ceremonial
12. Indians—non-Navajo
H. Tribal Activities and Enterprises
1. Navajo Forest Products Industries
2. Navajo Tribal Sawmill
3. Navajo Tribal Utilities Authority
4. design and construction
5. Tribal Motor Pool
6. tribal heavy equipment
7. tribal water development
8. First Navajo National Bank
9. arts and crafts
10. cull livestock buying
11. horse buying
12. emergency feed grain
13. tribal work relief
14. Navajo Police
15. tribal misc.
J. Scenery
1. Grand Falls
2. Monument Valley
3. Canyon de Chelly
4. Canyon de Muerto
5. Coal Mine Canyon
6. Mystery Valley
7. White Mesa
8. Black Mesa
9. Shiprock Mt. and Rt. 1
10. Navajo Mt. area
11. Window Rock area
12. Todilto Park
13. Kayenta
14. high country
15. Dilcon area
16. Indian Wells
17. Nazlini
18. Boundary Buttes
19. Leupp earth cracks
20. Mexican Hat area
21. Comb Ridge
22. nearby Utah
23. nearby Colorado
24. nearby Arizona
25. nearby New Mexico
26. clouds, sunsets
27. windows and bridges
28. Painted Desert
K. Antiquities
L.a. Cattle
1. parasite control
2. injury, defects, deformity
3. diseases
4. castrating, branding, dehorning
5. disease prevention and control
6. poisoning, bloat
7. supplemental feeding
8. desirable bulls and cows
9. reservation cattle
10. off-reservation cattle
11. beef breeds
12. dairy breeds
13. cattle feeding
14. marketing
15. cattle, misc.
L.b. Sheep
1. parasite control
2. injury defects
3. blue tongue
4. sore mouth
5. scabies
6. misc. diseases
7. castrating, docking, vaccinating
8. poisoning, bloat
9. supplemental feeding
10. improved rams
11. reservation sheep
12. off-reservation sheep
13. sheep breeds
14. sheep, misc.
L.c. Wool
1. shearing and handling
2. wool grading
3. wool schools
4. marketing
5. wool crop
6. wool, misc.
L.d. Goats
1. mohair types
2. mongrel types
3. castrating, shearing
4. disease, deformity, injury

Notes to p. 208

5. goats, misc.
L.e. Horses
1. general
2. diseases, parasites, injury
3. castrating, branding, shoeing
4. breaking
5. horses, misc.
L.f. Mules, Burros
L.g. Hogs
L.h. Poultry, Rabbits
L.i. Livestock, misc.
1. home slaughter
2. commercial slaughter
3. corrals, handling, equipment
4. cull buying
5. horse buying
M. Agricultural Extension
1. 4-H
2. home economics
3. tours
4. schools
5. home safety
N. Soil Moisture Conservation
1. soils
2. wind erosion
3. water erosion
4. formation of soils
5. detentions, spreader
6. stream protection
7. Colo. River Story series
8. wind breaks, tree planting
9. SMC education
10. man's contribution to erosion
O. Range
1. sites and conditions
2. plants
3. poisonous
4. general scenes
5. brush control
6. re-seeding
7. pitting and ripping
8. fencing
9. stock water
10. Chinle-brushed reseeded
11. range studies and transit
12. winter range
13. range tours
P. Forestry
1. forests, general
2. insect control, aerial
3. red rot
4. logging
5. tree species
6. fires

7. clean up
8. schools and training
9. timber loss through injury
10. insects, diseases, parasites
11. misc.
12. unauthorized cutting
13. forest regeneration
Q. Roads
1. unimproved roads and trails
2. surfaced roads
3. bridges
4. road deterioration
5. road hazards
6. construction
R. Realty
1. oil wells
2. oil refineries
3. gas and oil lines
4. gas pumping stations
5. helium plants and lines
6. uranium and rare metal plants
7. uranium, general
8. coal—hand mining
9. coal—Utah mining and construction
10. coal—strip mining
11. coal—exposures
12. coal, misc.
13. building stones, clays
14. copper
15. misc.
S. Recreation and Tourism
1. Rt. 1 series
2. Rt. 12 series
3. Rt. 3 series
4. Rt. 89 series
5. littering
6. camping
7. fishing
8. accommodations
9. road signs
10. horse back riding
11. winter sports
12. water sports
13. misc.
14. national parks
15. tourists
16. Page—1st Navajo Council
T. Schools and Education
1. reservation schools
2. dormitory and boarding facilities
3. advanced education
4. a day in a boarding school
5. results of education

U. Credit
1. housing
2. livestock
3. private enterprise
4. education
V. Visual
1. posters
2. displays
3. brochures and pamphlets
4. misc. illustrations
W. Electrical Power
1. Arizona Public Service
2. Glen Canyon Power
3. Navajo Tribal Utility Authority
4. changes in Navajo living through electricity
5. misc. power lines, etc.
X. Misc.
1. trading posts
2. Indians, non-Navajo
3. VIPs
4. government officers
5. public health officers
6. personnel training officers
7. safety officers
8. misc.
9. four corners
10. communities
11. poverty
12. war
17. law and order

35. The Concho collection photographs are all but useless to most researchers, as they are devoid of descriptive information, rarely dated, and missing important attributional data. They are 5" x 7" glossy black-and-white photographs stoutly glued to a stiff backing, with no information at all on the open side of the backing. In some cases there appears to be information on the back of the photographs, but it is impossible to get this information without destroying the photograph. The information appears to have been placed on the photographs by the local agency photographers before they sent it to the depository, then ignored and obliterated by Concho bureaucrats.

36. Some archaeologists, following the work of Pepper at Chaco Canyon, assembled interesting ethnographic photographs of Navajo, some of whom worked on their crews, others whom they encountered during their expeditions. Grace Nicholson photographed with Tozzer in 1912, and one particularly good and intimate series from D. S. Byers, a member of the 1933 Harvard-Peabody Utah Floating House Expedition, incorporates images of Navajo in ordinary activities and jocular interaction with the non-Navajo archaeologists.

37. Especially see Reichard, 1936, 1939.

38. The numbers of anthropologists now working in Navajoland gave rise to jokes that the typical Navajo family consisted of a man, a woman, two children, and an anthropologist. There are probably a great many private collections of photographs from students and researchers of this period that have never been published and have not yet found their way into archives. Unexamined photographic collections, for example, were said to exist in the estate of John Roberts (see Roberts, 1951).

39. Probably a place-name—see Bailey and Bailey, 1986:12.

40. The photographer actually followed people around—from downtown Gallup to the hills outside town—to grab the most photographically "appropriate" moment. McCombe secured a photograph of a mother nursing her infant while drinking and photographed the same miserable individuals all over the local landscape. McCombe clearly had the cooperation of authorities, for he photographed in courtrooms and in police stations, where Navajo were subject to sanctioning procedures. It is very unlikely he sought the same from most of his Navajo subjects.

41. There is an entire tradition of photographing beautiful victims (from the FSA photographers to Salgado—see Curtis, 1989, and Edwards, 1991) and/or poignant gore (Meiselas, 1987, 1988). Proponents argue that such images make for effective political statements—needless to say, they do not share the perspectives guiding the arguments here.

42. Mark Nohl became *New Mexico Magazine*'s first official staff photographer in 1973, but the magazine still largely contracts with individuals for stories and photographs. Though much of Nohl's work is done on assignment, he also works independently and teaches New Mexican

landscape at the Santa Fe Photographic Workshops. Nohl has by now probably photographed more of New Mexico than anyone else.
43. Coke, 1979:33.
44. Ibid., 35.
45. Ibid., 21.
46. Several other photographic series of some interest exist. One, a collection of photographs from the 1950s of the remaining widows of the Navajo Scouts (very old women still receiving U.S. government military pensions from their husbands' service in the Apache campaigns), was sent to the Concho archive. In the limited amount of time I was allowed to spend with these photographs, I was unable to determine the photographer. In another, an extended series of Navajo preparing to make the trip to Fort Sumner at the 100th anniversary of the 1868 treaty signing, individuals are named and have given their locations and clan affiliations. These photographs are archived at the Wheelwright Museum in Santa Fe; though unattributed, they were probably taken by Betsy Frith.
47. See Lutz and Collins, 1993:277. There is an abundant literature critiquing this sort of exhibition style in content and form. Here the most relevant problems are its universalizing authority, its assumption to speak for everyone—the omnipotent eye that sees but is never seen. The burden and the arrogance of a transcendent aesthetic ideal are consequences of such style.
48. Faris/Thau Heyman, March, 1992.
49. Coleman, 1993; Lindquist-Cock, 1983.
50. See Collier, 1993:15.
51. Cf. Tremblay, Collier, Jr. and Sasaki, 1954.
52. Collier, 1967.
53. See Lindquist-Cock, 1983; Sorgenfrei and Peters, 1985; Coleman, 1993.
54. Many of the claimed culturally specific features of these ciné experiments also apply to still photographs, but some are particular to ciné. For example, Navajo filmmakers put together scenes in sequential patterns that differ from non-Navajo (see Worth and Adair, 1972).
55. Cf. Wyman, 1983; Gill, 1979.
56. See Babcock and Parezo, 1988:195.
57. Lindig, 1991—with photographs by Teiwes.

Chapter Six
1. Cf. Sandweiss, 1986 (especially extensive bibliographical entries, page 302), 1987, 1988; Coke, 1979; Hust, 1989; Halpern, 1972.
2. Forster and Gilpin, 1988.
3. Sandweiss (1986:47), in a commentary on a self-published Gilpin booklet entitled *Mesa Verde National Park*, states: "It introduces the idea of an ancient and genuinely romantic *American* past rooted in the American landscape [emphasis in original]." Such unreflective assimilationist sentiment characterized Gilpin. This gesture also appropriates Native Americans prior to European invasion as part of the past of European-Americans (cf. Trachtenberg, 1994).
4. Though Gilpin was close to Eliot Porter and Ansel Adams and always decried any suggestion that her gender had anything to do with her successes and failures (she was refused employment in the photography program of the Farm Security Administration; indeed, Stryker deliberately avoided Native Americans—cf. Collier, 1993:15), men tended to command landscape photography in the Southwest at that time. It is not excessively cynical to suspect that she was encouraged to concentrate on photography of Navajo and other indigenous people, avoiding the crowded male-dominated landscape field. Notwithstanding such speculation, her landscape photography is quite as good as the very finest of the time (cf. Garner, 1987:16–17).
5. Cf. Babcock and Parezo, 1988; Norwood and Monk, 1987.
6. McGreevy, 1993.
7. The extent to which Gilpin was blind to (or ignorant of) the bitter history and social relations Navajo have had with the West and the extent to which she seemed to basically accept the BIA view can be seen in her preface (Gilpin 1968:vii):

> Their traditional mode of living—simple, carefree, undisturbed by the great
> pressures of our complex civilization—is being changed through their
> adaptation to an utterly alien existence.
>
> In past years nature provided sufficient pasture for the Navaho flocks and
> sufficient arable land for their simple farming, while the trading posts offered a
> market for their products. Today the Navaho find themselves with a
> population more than three times greater than their land can support.

This BIA judgment was the basis of the stock reduction program that impoverished many Navajo, making them easily available for cheap wage labor. There is now evidence that this analysis was far too severe, and much of the program unnecessary (cf. Roessel and Johnson, 1974; Parman, 1976). Certainly the way it was implemented was very unfortunate.

8. Sandweiss, 1986:88.

9. Nevertheless, in the Gilpin archives are several of her photographs of drunks, including some in nighttime flash photography. They are not all in the close-up invasive style of McCombe, however, nor to my knowledge have any of them been published. Indeed, they seem hesitant, tentative, and Gilpin never gets very close. It seems as if Gilpin does not like the encounter and is uncomfortable with it.

10. Sandweiss, 1986:102, calls attention to this: "In her text, Laura ascribes to the Navajo the personal qualities she valued herself."

11. Indeed, Sandweiss argues (1986:88) that for Gilpin, "McCombe's grim depiction of their way of life seemed almost a personal affront."

12. John Collier was Franklin D. Roosevelt's New Deal Commissioner of Indian Affairs. The Navajo were a particular "favorite" of Collier's, although some of his devastating policies would suggest otherwise, and he was personally very unpopular in much of Navajoland.

13. As noted above, the word *Navajo* is not an indigenous term for *diné* ("earth surface people," or "people of the earth's surface"—as opposed to "Holy People" [not "people of the earth," as Gilpin translates it, 1968:20]), as Navajo call themselves. The precise origin of the term *Navajo* [*Navaho*] is speculative, but it is a foreign word. This debate over spelling indicates how little Gilpin bothered to learn very much about Navajo. Indeed, Gilpin's curious insistence here borders on the aesthetics of purity/corruption so characteristic of photographers such as Leni Riefenstahl. Contrary to Gilpin's notions of purity, the Navajo adopted the spelling *Navajo*.

This notion of cleanliness and purity also infected Gilpin's photography to a large extent. Her aestheticizing impulses included sometimes removing trash and items of European manufacture that are often discarded outside hogans. It is frequently assumed that a hogan with nothing outside it (no cast-off items, no evidences of money spent in the past) is either a *ch'įįdii* hogan [hogan in which someone has died, therefore abandoned], or the home of someone too poor to have cast off items of wealth. Compare, for example, the unarranged hogan in the background of Fig. 205, with Gilpin's clean studies (Fig. 177).

14. See Gilpin, 1968:237–246.

15. There appears to be some confusion, as Gilpin also photographed begging gods on 27 September 1953 (mislabeled in the archive as a "Squaw Dance"). This photograph is not of a "Squaw Dance" (Enemyway) because these particular masked God Impersonators are not involved in that particular healing ceremony, because they are characteristic of the final days of a Nightway, and because this date is almost too late for an Enemyway, normally a summer healing practice (but, as noted, it is also almost too early for a Nightway). It is hard to know if the date is wrong on this photograph as well as the information. Gilpin's Navajo photographs are in general poorly documented and labeled largely in instrumental terms.

16. See Gilpin, 1968:249.

17. Curiously, in a review of Native American photography, McRae says of this photograph (1989:337) that "such images could probably not have been taken in the days of slower shutter speeds and large format cameras," when all indications are that this was exactly what was used. Indeed, the unpublished archives include several of this pose, and some were rejected because one of the children moved at the time the shutter was opened (obviously at a slow speed).

Moreover, in the unpublished alternative poses for this published image, furniture is moved around, Mrs. Francis is standing, then sitting, children are moved around, and Francis has his hat alternately on and off.

18. Sandweiss, 1986:57.

19. It is strange that nowhere in Gilpin (1968) nor in Sandweiss (1986) is there any mention of Milton (Jack) Snow, whom Gilpin must have known. She must also have been familiar with his extensive work in Navajoland and his reputation among Navajo. Yet we get the impression Gilpin was the first serious photographer to have "gained people's confidences," to attempt to "sensitively and carefully document aspects of their daily existence."

20. It should be noted that in this period Navajo seldom wore Navajo weavings. Navajo wore Pendleton or other commercial blankets available from traders.

21. Sandweiss, 1986:19.

22. Given the difference in time, technology, and mission, Curtis and Gilpin are indeed comparable. If the total corpus of Curtis Navajo photographs is considered, a much better photographer and human being emerges than suggested by his critics (cf. Lyman, 1982). In my view, the same cannot be said of Gilpin's Navajo photography—her very best work is published, and though any unpublished archive obviously contains photographs that are not so good technically, the Gilpin archive also contains, as noted, many photographs of people who do not look at all happy with the photographer's presence.

23. Cf. Hust, 1989.

24. The Navajo woman and her child ("Ethel and Albert," from Red Rock) were not casual passersby; they had to be brought to this location.

25. Gilpin, 1968:31.

26. Cf. Brush/Faris, December 1991.

27. Gilpin, 1968:31-32.

28. Navajo photographer Monty Roessel asked many of his relatives and others of his chapter house (Lukachukai) to comment on the photographs in *The Enduring Navajo*. He reported [1995] that many were disturbed by photographs such as "Hardbelly's Hogan" and wondered just how it was that Gilpin had been allowed to take photographs of someone who was that ill. They were also disturbed by the photographs of sacred items and of healing practices. They argued they were not "enduring Navajo," just "real Navajo."

29. Gilpin, 1968:70

30. Sandweiss, 1986:89.

31. A medicine man, with his sacred paraphernalia spread out before him, is suffering from a skin disease or a pigment loss in his face (see Fig. 189). Gilpin painted out his condition before publication or exhibition (Gilpin, 1968:214). In the archive as well is some interesting experimental work, including a photo montage and a deliberate double exposure in which a campfire is superimposed over/under the widely published romantic image "Navahos by Firelight." As far as I am aware, she never exhibited nor published this photograph (Fig. 190), but Gilpin was said to have chastised Meridel Rubenstein for her own experiments in this direction (Faris/Rubenstein, November 1991). It should be pointed out, however, that Gilpin graciously championed a number of young women photographers, several of whom worked as her assistants. At least two among these are the talented contemporary photographers Meridel Rubenstein and Mary Peck. Indeed, in my experience, all of Gilpin's acquaintances and assistants speak of her with great fondness (Faris/Brush, December 1991; Faris/Rubenstein, November 1991; Faris/Rudisill, 1990).

32. Sandweiss, 1986, Plate 62. This photograph, in the Laura Gilpin Collection of the Amon Carter Museum, was, as a consequence of the suit, unavailable to me for publication here (and in Faris, 1993c); as noted, no information is officially forthcoming on the exact nature and settlement of the legal claims. Even though the attorney for the Amon Carter Museum stated that the settlement meant that the photograph ("Navaho Madonna") could be selectively used for educational purposes (*Santa Fe New Mexican*, 10 June 1989), my own attempts to secure its use for a scholarly paper were denied (Stewart/Faris, 21 January 1991), and every attempt to determine the exact reason for the denial was met with obfuscation. In a later personal con-

versation with the curator of photography (Faris/Southall, October 1991), he stated that despite his repeated attempts to secure it, the museum, now hypersensitive, had not yet gotten a statement from its attorneys on just what to tell persons requesting its use. This is unfortunate, for it would tell us something more about Navajo views of their photographic images, as well as the hegemony of European-American views/outlooks/obsessions in the legal codes, if the details of the suit were made public.

33. Sandlin, 1989.

34. A host of reasons for this have been articulated at various times and places (see Chapter 2 above). It is argued that such wide exposure of an image in the hands of strangers can be used by those of evil intentions. It has been argued that such exposure is in itself dangerous—that the gaze of so many people is undesirable. And it has been argued that a photograph, inasmuch as it freezes the subject, is potentially dangerous, for the same might happen to the subject, particularly if the photograph is not in the hands of loved ones, and that appearance in the photograph could mean a type of disappearance in reality. Each of these reasons has an articulated logic behind it, and none is irrational, save under existing privacy torts.

35. Moreland, 1991:244. Moreland goes on to argue that the court was incorrect, that indeed this was not the basis of the Benally affidavits (1991:244). But, he explains, "the court concluded that Navajos do not have the ordinary sensibilities of reasonable people, and that American Indians are not reasonably sensible people...and are therefore not protected" (1991:245).

36. Faris/LeCuyer, October 1991.

Chapter Seven

1. Practically all of the photographers noted in this chapter have taken (made) some extraordinarily and even generous photographs of Navajo people. Without doubt, each established friendships, and certainly all feel their work honors and is respectful. However, this chapter is concerned with how the genre of this photography is hackneyed, its humanist intellectual foundations old, very assuming, and very Western. I do not provide illustrations from these photographers, as books in which these photographers have published are easily available. And as most of the Navajo individuals photographed are still living, permission to publish here would be difficult to obtain. For many of these same reasons, I have also not researched the unpublished photographs of these photographers. As a consequence, this chapter is not illustrated, and there are references to work published. This means this entire volume has a largely forensic appearance, and photographs illustrated are mostly of Navajo individuals and photographers who are now history.

2. Some commentators seemed to take this quite literally. For example, in a book on the photography of New Mexico, Coke (who, teaching at the University of New Mexico, certainly should have known these subjects were Navajo and thus that picture-taking had risks that would not have pertained with non-Navajo), comments on one of Frank's Navajo photographs (1979:34):

> Reproduced in *The Americans*, Frank's major book, was a picture neither poignant nor depressing taken in New Mexico of a group of ranch hands standing around a fluorescent-lighted bar in Gallup. This offhand shot with a 35mm camera conveys the macho character of the men at leisure in their clubhouse. It is as if the photographer was fascinated by what he saw and wanted to get on film a glimpse of the tough cowboys but was afraid to show himself, or at least show his camera, and so shot the picture from a seated position across from the bar, which created a canted, keyhole view surround by black.

Whatever Frank's motivations, that this photograph of Navajo was so analyzed reveals an extraordinarily *blasé* and uninformed attitude on the part of photographic commentators toward ethical and cultural issues at a surprisingly late date.

3. See Gaede, 1988:Photograph 59.

4. See Erdman, 1985. In one case (page 43), an unnamed Navajo jail inmate threatens the photographer (Roswell Angier).

Notes to pp. 272–276

5. See Faris, 1990:73–74.
6. See Chapter 1, Chapter 9, and Faris, 1993e.
7. The issue of anonymity has a particular history in anthropology, but its use in photography seems quite peculiar, especially if individuals' faces appear. Gilpin largely ignored Navajo names, as does Keegan; Running does so partially, as does McAuley. It is a sinister fiction (another of the deceits of anthropology, like "participant observation") of using pseudonyms in ethnography as devices to protect "informants." If revelation of the names would get people in trouble locally, then why write the ethnography at all? If it were to get people into trouble with oppressive authorities, then why not attack such authorities? If it were to protect the ethnographer, then s/he may as well write fiction, because for all purposes that is what it becomes. If revelation of "informants" were to create some potential embarrassment for them or others, why undertake the project initially? If the object were *exposé*, then presumably the naming of names would be important and relevant. If not, do not one's obligations to acknowledge require naming? Not naming in photographic acknowledgment is simply bogus, for persons may be presumably recognized or identified by their photograph.
8. Isolation from background with long focus lenses also removes other local practices, some perhaps with important features of history and specificity. It is certainly an explicit *photographic* gesture imported to the project. Contrast with Kawano (see Figs. 205-207).
9. Friends of the Earth sponsored the Anderson, n.d. [1973] publication.
10. Contrast Page, 1989, with Kawano, 1990.
11. See also, in this regard, comments on Gilpin, Chapter 6.
12. This is very much like Leni Riefenstahl's photography of the Southeast Nuha—see Riefenstahl, 1976; Faris, 1988a; 1993a.
13. The Joint-Use Area was a portion of the Navajo and Hopi reservations previously jointly used. From the 1970s on the Navajo were denied access by a legal judgment. See Redhouse, 1985; Kammer, 1980; Benedek, 1992.
14. See Page, 1989:114.
15. Maybury-Lewis, 1992.
16. Keegan (Keegan and Frontier Photographers, 1990:116) specifies the brush as yucca, but though it may be tied with a yucca strip, the traditional Navajo brush [*bé'ézó*] is of grass.
17. And body parts of the aged, such as weathered hands—see also the endpapers of Gilpin, 1968, for an earlier expression of this gesture, and Foxx and Karasik, 1993, for a more recent example.
18. The Santa Fe Photographic Workshops are a vital asset to the region's view of itself as tourist destination, advertising location, and inspirational center. Mark Nohl, something of the state's official photographer since 1973 (when he became the first full-time staff photographer at *New Mexico Magazine*), also teaches—New Mexico Landscape—at the Santa Fe Photographic Workshops. Also on its staff is Lisl Dennis, who in addition runs her own photography workshops (Travel Photography Workshop in Santa Fe). Dennis, in a recent latently racist column entitled "The Ethics of Tipping" (1993), argues for denying subjects the last right to their own self—the right to demand some return for photographs taken of them. "Subjects," in Dennis's view, are best rewarded by the nature of the relationship they have with the Western photographer (echoing here John Running's "spirit," which he wishes to leave with local people). In an amazing turnaround, subalterns, the victims of the West, appear best when they are being nice to photographers and not demanding of compensation. The question with which she headlines the column (Dennis, 1993:74) is: "When you put money in the hands of a subject, what are you doing to photographers who follow?"
19. Zig Jackson, a Native American photography instructor at the Institute for American Indian Arts in Santa Fe (see Villani, 1992), has followed Running on numerous occasions and has photographed "Running photographing Indians." He relates that after one such close-up of a pow-wow dancer, the dancer took a swing at Running (Faris/Jackson, November 1991). Running's persistence, however, suggests he seems not to learn from these rejections. My own efforts to interview Running and secure a syllabus for his Santa Fe Photographic Workshops course were unsuccessful.

20. This suit was not settled as of this writing, and Running has in interviews refused to comment on the case (cf. Villani, 1993). In its complaint, however, it bears much similarity to the lawsuit leveled against the Amon Carter Museum and the estate of Laura Gilpin (see Chapter 6).
21. Cf. in this regard, Goldin, 1973.
22. There are, of course, many, many other picture books (cf. Trimble, 1986, published by the Heard Museum)—some even more trivial (cf. Parker, 1991)—and the extraordinarily confused and vulgar volume, with photographs by Foxx (Foxx and Karasik, 1993), published by Harry Abrams. And the Museum of New Mexico recently published the smaller volume *Time Among the Navajo* (Hooker, 1991—photographs by Helen Lau Running), which describes and photographically illustrates several traditional practices (non-ceremonial) in which Hooker became interested as a consequence of her teaching in Navajoland. The text is meant to be instructive, but because it contains no regional variations nor method for including practices (such as jewelry making, sale or barter of handmade items, or transportation—all certainly traditional practices), it is descriptive only of the persons, situations, and practices encountered inductively and/or for which interviews could be secured. As it is only available in English in an expensive edition, its use in Navajoland is problematic.

There are also, perhaps predictably, photographic (or heavily illustrated) children's books, taking photographs from a number of stock agencies, as well as individual photographers. Osinski, 1987, for example, uses, among others, John Running photographs.

There are newer generalized books on photography of Native Americans (cf. Fleming and Luskey, 1993; and Bush and Mitchell, 1994) that include photographs of Navajo. Some are focused on historic photographic materials, whereas others involve contemporary photographers as well. Bush and Mitchell, 1994, which wisely involves both classic and contemporary photography, is nevertheless particularly problematic. It filled with typographical, editing (cf. pp. 50, 239, where *some* changes in spelling between the photograph label and the information on the photograph occur but others do not) and research errors (bibliographical references to Coke, 1979, listing some "Indian photographs" but not others) and carelessness (p. xvii, where reference is made to Navajo, but the cited photographs do not illustrate Navajo; p. xviii, where the famous Curtis photograph of riders in Canyon de Chelly is labeled [mistakenly] "The Vanishing Race" in the text but labeled [correctly] on the photograph itself on p. 211 as "Navajos in Canyon de Chelley, 1904"). Moreover, there are misattributions (which more detailed and careful research could have revealed—cf. pp. 128, 129, where two Charles Bell photographs are mislabeled as William Henry Jackson photographs) and very questionable nomenclatures (p. viii—"American Indian" to refer to Inuit and Alaskan Natives), as well as the publication of photographs of events and objects considered sacred and therefore no longer (at least in 1994) to be published (pp. 185ff—Hopi "Snake Dances").

23. McAuley's Navajo photographs hang in Santa Fe photographic galleries along with the Navajo photographs of Curtis and the Navajo photographs of Gilpin. One wonders if those who appear in the photographs ever knew their image would be displayed, in several cases almost life-size, in the elite photographic shops on the plaza in Santa Fe, selling for thousands of dollars?
24. Cf. Clifford, 1988:146.
25. Irony, a high modernist gesture, may juxtapose the powerful and the powerless, but there is a basic cynicism about human agency in such affiliation. The very nature of irony's reliance on difference, on exposure or mixing of boundaries, hinges on humor, or perhaps corruption, never on explicit critique or objection to the power relations. In such a gesture, the determination of difference is always the prerogative of the photographer, never the subjects.
26. There were new projects, different projects, in progress at the time of this research. John Craig, a photographer whose previous work was in "geoscapes" (landscape/human building erosion), spent various periods during the past ten years with the Hunter family of Black Rock Canyon. His photographs are distinctly different from any thus far seen—they are specific, candid, and familiar, yet in every case they maintain a cultural integrity and context. This work is still in preparation, as it is a joint project of Craig and the Hunters. See Chapter 8 for brief commentary on the emergence of Navajo photographers.

Chapter Eight

1. For example, each annual student exhibition at the Institute of American Indian Art in Santa Fe usually includes work from two or more Navajo photographers. The same is probably also true of most photography curricula at the region's colleges and universities. It should be pointed out, however, that there has been no systematic attempt to assemble a list of all Navajo photographers from IAIA nor any other specific source. A systematic study of Navajo photographers is another research project altogether, one most appropriately done by Navajo photographers.
2. Very few Navajo individuals make a living through their photography. Jonas John, a commercial and landscape photographer with a studio in the northwest corner of New Mexico is one of the more successful (see Brenner, 1993a, 1993b). Others have been successful photojournalists (e.g., Paul Natonabah).
3. Robert Roessel, Jr.—the author of *A Pictorial History of the Navajo from 1860 to 1910*.
4. Faris/Roessel September 1991.
5. *Images Across Boundaries: History, Use, and Ethics of Photographs of American Indians*, sponsored by the Museum of New Mexico's Museum of Indian Arts and Culture and the Institute of American Indian Arts, Santa Fe, New Mexico, 2–3 April 1993.
6. As in Gilpin, 1968.
7. As in McCombe's photography, 1951.
8. Echoing, perhaps, Mike Mitchell's commentaries on Skeet McAuley's photographs—that is, a silence to much of Western notions of significance in content—see Chapter 7 above.
9. Father and daughter spell the name differently.
10. She had a visiting appointment on the photography faculty of the Institute of American Indian Arts in Santa Fe in 1993.
11. Images ranging from petroglyphs and ledger drawings to contemporary artists—see Tsinhnahjinnie, 1993c:30.
12. Tsinhnahjinnie, 1993b:28.
13. Tsinhnahjinnie, 1993b:27–28.
14. See also in this regard Lippard, 1992.
15. Such as the critique that the style of some of the early Santa Fe Indian School "studio school" painters suffered from "Bambi influence" (cf. Brody, 1971:145).

Conclusion

1. In summer 1992 I noted a painting on leather at the Museum of Northern Arizona's (Flagstaff) annual Navajo Art and Crafts Exhibition show. The image was a careful copy of a famous Gilpin Navajo photograph! I do not think the graphic was meant to be ironic.
2. Cf. Edwards, 1992. Of course there is an entire television channel devoted in part to photography of non-Western peoples—the Discovery Channel. Though it is considered more educational or highbrow than the mainstream networks, with their fictional presentations in sitcoms and soap operas, the appeal of programs with "anthropological" content ("Terra X," "Magical Journeys," "Strange Planet") is distinctly prurient, as their advertising makes clear.
3. Cf. Foucault, 1973; Young, 1990.
4. After all, without theory, without an anthropological "explanation," then Navajo might exist as truly other. Anthropological understanding is, in this sense, appropriative, an act of reduction. Theoretical understanding is also, as noted, a knowledge form of the spectator (cf. Young, 1990:141).
5. But cf. Angier, in Erdman, 1985:43, and Chapter 7 above.
6. The subversion of alterity to a normative pastiche is one prime motivation of contemporary anthropological theory and celebration (cf. Marcus and Fischer, 1986). This motivation can be seen especially seen in anthropology's foundational position of relativism—a type of Western project that basically preserves contempt for existence outside the equivalence of culture—the universal leveling—that anthropological relativism espouses. Readers are directed to McGrane, 1989:129; and Faris and Wutu, 1986:7, for an argument that relativism is essentially a patronizing notion and a position firmly within epistemological reasoning, inasmuch as it indicates by its equivalence how little such culture really means to such analysts.

7. This is not to imply that things would be fine if Navajo were photographed in all postures in which Westerners are photographed. All Navajo postures and social relations and individual expressions are not assumed to be within the visual imaging boundaries of the West, nor capable of nor relevant to photographic scrutiny. The "family of man" gestures of patronizing incorporation are completely Western in their definition and range and in their domesticating implications. For example, families are photographically constituted in Western terms, and there are few photographs of Navajo families as constituted by Navajo (for instance, pictures of a husband and his two wives—one being the daughter of the other by another man—or images of avoidance between a woman and her son-in-law).

8. In this regard, see Alloula, 1986:4.

9. This is not to imply that the Navajo hierarchical or bureaucratic apparatus (Navajo Office of Broadcast Services, Navajo Office of Tourism, Navajo Nation) always has the best interests of its citizens in mind. These institutional mechanisms are quite as involved in "selling" certain Navajo images as are the tourist bureaus of Arizona and New Mexico. But at least any mistakes are Navajo mistakes. Navajo may be (or should be) more aware of the limits of various visual endeavors, the social relations not subject to photographic scrutiny, etc. This is why contemporary Navajo photographers are often more interesting for what they leave out than for what they photograph (see Chapter 8).

10. This means *a conscious and enunciated politics*, for, as argued, most photographers of people make moral or ethical decisions prior to making aesthetic ones. The problem lies with the political foundations of such decisions.

11. And most especially anthropologists who photograph or encourage Others to photograph— see Turner, 1992; Ginsburg, 1994.

12. Cf. Marcus and Fischer, 1986; Marcus, 1990; Fischer, 1992.

Appendix

AC	Amon Carter Museum, Fort Worth
AHS	Arizona Historical Society, Tucson
AHSF	Arizona Historical Society, Northern Arizona Division, Flagstaff
AMNH	American Museum of Natural History, New York
ASL	State of Arizona, Department of Library, Archives, and Public Records, Phoenix
ASM	Arizona State Museum, Tucson
AZHi	*Arizona Highways*
AZS	Arizona State University Library, Carl Hayden Collection, Tempe
BAE	Bureau of American Ethnology (all materials now NAA)
BAN	Bancroft Library, University of California, Berkeley
BM	Brooklyn Museum, New York
CCP	Center for Creative Photography, University of Arizona, Tucson
CHS	Colorado State Historical Society Library, Denver
CON	Concho Collection, Navajo Nation Museum, Window Rock
DAM	Denver Art Museum
DART	Hood Museum, Dartmouth College
DMNH	Denver Museum of Natural History
HM	Heard Museum, Phoenix
HMCNAP	Heard Museum Contemporary Native American Photographers List
HNAI	*Handbook of North American Indians*, Volume 10, Smithsonian Institution, Washington
HUN	Huntington Library, San Marino, California
IAIA	Institute of American Indian Art, Santa Fe
LAB	Laboratory of Anthropology, Museum of New Mexico, Santa Fe
LAC	Los Angeles County Museum of Natural History
LCM	Lake County Museum, Curt Teich Postcard Archives, Wauconda, IL
LOC	Library of Congress, Washington D.C.
MAI	National Museum of the American Indian, Smithsonian Institution, New York
MNA	Museum of Northern Arizona, Flagstaff
MNM	Museum of New Mexico, Photography Archives, Palace of the Governors, Santa Fe
MPM	Milwaukee Public Museum
NA	Still Pictures Branch, National Archives, Washington D.C.
NAA	National Anthropological Archives, Smithsonian Institution, Washington D.C.
NAPHS	Arizona Pioneers Historical Society, Flagstaff
NAU	Cline Library, Northern Arizona University, Flagstaff
NCC	Ned Hatathli Cultural Center Museum, Navajo Community College, Tsaile, AZ
NMM	*New Mexico Magazine*
NMSRA	New Mexico State Records and Archives, Santa Fe
NNM	Navajo Nation Museum, Window Rock
NPM	*Native Peoples Magazine*
NPSWACC	National Park Service Western Archaeological and Conservation Center, Tucson
OM	Oakland Museum, Oakland, CA
PMH	Peabody Museum, Harvard University, Cambridge
PRM	Pitt Rivers Museum, Oxford University, Oxford
RAI	Royal Anthropological Institute, London
SDM	San Diego Museum of Man
SHM	Sharlot Hall Museum, Prescott
SWM	Southwest Museum, Los Angeles
USAMI	United States Army Military History Institute, Carlisle, PA
UCB	University of California, Berkeley, Phoebe Hearst Museum

Appendix

UMP   University Museum, University of Pennsylvania, Philadelphia
UCR   Keystone-Mast Collection, University of California, Riverside
UNM   Special Collections, University of New Mexico Library, Albuquerque
UNMAM   Museum of Art, University of New Mexico, Albuquerque
UNMM   Maxwell Museum, University of New Mexico, Albuquerque
UNMNSS   University of New Mexico Native American Studies Survey of Navajo photographers in New Mexico and Arizona, University of New Mexico, Albuquerque
USC   California Historical Society Collections, University of Southern California, Los Angeles
USHS   Utah State Historical Society, Salt Lake City
UUAZ   Special Collections Library, University of Arizona, Tucson
VSP   Value Studies Project, Laboratory of Anthropology, Museum of New Mexico, Santa Fe
WHM   William Hammond Mathers Museum, Indiana University, Bloomington
WM   Wheelwright Museum, Santa Fe

< >   documented period of photography of Navajo, if specifically known
[ ]   specific information and/or comments on photographer or cited photographs
F   additional materials in author's files
[N]   Navajo photographer
—##   number of prints of Navajo in source, if specifically known

Chart 1. List of photographers or others with published photographs of Navajo, or significant publicly accessible collections of photographs of Navajo, or attributed photographs of Navajo, or publicly noted as photographers of Navajo.

Abbeloos, Glenn. MNA. [Staff photographer, spring 1970 and summer 1969 issues; sheep shearing at Wupatki.]

Abbott, Chuck. HNAI:525; AZHi, June 1943. [See Cummings, 1952; d. 1973.]

Abell, Sam. Contemporary. [National Geographic Society contract photographer.]

Aberle, David. VSP. F.

Adair, John. MNM—5; WM; MAI—1. [See Worth and Adair, 1972.] F.

Adair, Peter. [Son of John Adair.] F.

Adams, Ansel. CCP-4. <1941; 1948>. [Many landscapes without people in Navajoland.]

Adams, Ron and Brownie. AZHi, June 1940. F.

Adler, Abigail. WM. [See Kammer, 1980.]

Ahrens, Gene. AZHi, June 1975.

Alexander, Ruth Laughlin. [Southwest author, private photographs.] F.

Allen, Angie. [Perhaps photographer, formerly head of records, Navajo Tribal Administration.] [N].

Allen, Grace E. MAI. [Several presented by her, Albuquerque Fair scenery, 1901.]

Allen, Norton. AZHi, August 1950..

Allen, Tom. NNM. [Helped Milton Snow in 1941—perhaps not a photographer.] [N]?

Allison, David. Contemporary. NCC. [Much donated material on exhibit, 1993; was told in each case college insisted on having model releases, and specific permission of individuals portrayed.]

Alrire, Frank T. UUAZ. [1940].

Anderson, Dale W. Contemporary. NMM, December 1992, February 1993 [NPM, Spring 1994; and advertisement—San Juan Medical Center, Farmington].

Anderson, Mike. [See Worth and Adair, 1972.] [N]

Anderson, Ralph Hopewell. MNM—31; AZHi, August 1946. [Worked in late 1920s.]

Anderson, Susanne. [See Anderson, 1973; Page, 1989; see Susanne Page below.]

Anderson, William M. AZHi, August 1979.

Andrews, Dr. Enos. [See Fleming and Luskey, 1986:232; Rudisill, 1973:10. Operated N.

Brown's late-1860s studio in Santa Fe during Brown's absence; no specific evidence he photographed Navajo.]
Andrus, W. J. MAI—4. [1904. Two photos similar to or exactly like Curtis's; may be Curtis photos, or Andrus may have furnished Curtis with photos; d. 1922. Aragon NM.] F.
Angier, Roswell. Contemporary. [See Erdman, 1985:43.]
Apoian, Jeff. [See Osinski, 1987; Nawrocki Stock Photography.]
Applegate, Meidel. [See Christenson, 1987:13.]
Arentz, Dick. [See Bingham, 1982.]
Armer, Laura. WM—many; SWM—5. [See Palmquist, 1991.] F.
Armstrong, Don. Contemporary. NMM, May 1994. [Navajo rodeo.]
Arnold, Oren. ASM. [1900–1980; editor and freelance writer, 1940s.]
Arviso, Tom, Jr. Contemporary. [*Navajo Times* editor; mostly sports photography.] [N]
Ashton, Charles. Contemporary. [Portraiture.]
Atkeson, Ray. AZHi, August 1950.
Avery, Jennie. MNM—2. [Collector only; probably not a photographer.]
Babbitt, Herb. NAPHS. <1920s–1950s>.
Bagshaw, Cradoc. Contemporary. WM.
Bailey, Alfred. DMNH. [Director of Denver Museum of Natural History for thirty-three years; 1947 trip to Monument Valley. See Bailey, 1947.]
Bailey, Vernon. NAA. [1908; mostly architecture.] F.
Baird, Lucy H. NAA. [Sarony studio imprint—perhaps not photographer?]
Baker, A. J. UUAZ; SDM. [1926 postcard for Fred Harvey, Detroit Publishers, and same photo for Herz Postcards, San Diego.]
Baker and Johnston. NAA ["Indian Pictures," Evanston, Wyoming.]
Balster F. S. CHS; UMP. ["Rocky Mountain Views"; 1910s; cabinet cards; optician and jeweler, Durango CO. See Mautz, 1986:25, noted as 1893.]
Bancroft, Dick. Contemporary. NCC. [Photograph for American Indian College Fund brochure of Navajo students, Courtney Gorman, Norman Kee.]
Barker, Florence. NAU. [Photographed Immanuel Mission ca. 1920s. Worked as nurse??. Also made return visit.]
Barnes, ??. UUAZ. [Collector only?? Also a Willis-Barnes Gallup postcard firm.]
Barrett, Samuel A. MPM—18. [Expeditions from MPM in 1910–1911, 1925 with Navajo photographs; headed American Indian Film Project for Lowie Museum, University of California, Berkeley, in 1960s.]
Barthelmess, Christian. MNM—6 with Schofield, 1 without; NAA—12 'Barthlmess and Schofield, Ft. Wingate'; SWM—1. [1854–1906; worked with Washington Matthews in 1880s. See Frink, 1965; Fleming and Luskey, 1986:233; Rudisill, 1973:12.]
Bartos, Stan. NNM. <1960s-1975>. [Succeeded Milton Snow at Navajo Agency of BIA.]
Bass, Bill. UUAZ. [Arizona Color Card Co. Postcard no. 76.]
Bate, G. H. HNAI:598; NAA. <1920s>.
Beals, Jessie Tarbox. UMP—3; AMNH. [1904 St. Louis Exposition photos.]
Beam, George. CHS. [Denver photographer, probably photographed for Denver & Rio Grande Railway; photographs of Navajo taken at Mesa Verde.]
Beaman, E. O. SWM. <ca. 1874>. [Photographer who left Powell expedition; replaced by John Hillers.]
Bedinger, Margery. NMM, July 1932. [Gallup ceremonial.]
Beecher, Charles Emerson. ASM. [Yale paleontologist, took photographs en route to Hopi, 1900; also collected Robinson, Detroit Publishers, Peabody Company, etc.]
Begay, Alberta. [See Hubbard, 1994:34, 53.] [N]
Begay, Charlene. [See Page, 1989:116: "Perhaps one the best photographs she (Susanne Page) ever produced (a black-and-white of a Navajo grandmother) was taken by five-year-old Charlene Begay."] [N]
Begay, Rudy. Contemporary. [Three photos in IAIA 1993 student exhibition.] [N]
Beissigger, ??. PRM–4 [St. Michaels, 1925?]

Appendix

Bell, Charles M.(?) W. NAA; MNM; SWM; PMH; MAI. <1874>. [1848–1893; Washington studio photographer; all photographs copies of 1874 delegation photographs. See Fleming and Luskey, 1986:106-109; 230; Bush and Mitchell, 1994:50, 127, 128, 129, 295.]
Benally, Susie. [See Worth and Adair, 1972.] [N]
Benally, Suzanne. Contemporary. [See Lippard, 1992. Boulder CO educator, poet, essayist.] [N]
Bennett, Kay. HNAI:613. <1970s>. [Gallup singer Kaibah; record album cover photograph?] [N]
Bennett, George. MNM-1. [See Rudisill, 1973:13; see also Brown entry in Rudisill, 1973.]
Bennett, Ruby. Contemporary. UNMNSS; HMCNAP. F. [N]
Berendzen, Harry. [See Berendzen, n.d. (1990?). Photographer of oral storytellers in Lake Valley School project.]
Bergere Family Collection. NMSRA. <1920s>. [Family and neighbor photographs around St. Michaels and Ganado.]
Bernard, Bruce M. LAB. [1926.]
Berneimer, Charles L. AMNH; USHS [1864–1944; self-funded expeditions; many photographs in expeditions by J. Wetherill].
Bernstein, ??. NMM, July 1950. [Tourist photo, article on Gallup Ceremonial.]
Berrett, Pat. Contemporary. [Albuquerque commercial photographer, contracted to take up-to-date photographs of Navajo for Cameron Trading Post, AZ.]
Bia, Fred. UNMNSS, HMCNAP. [Trained with Weston and Adams. See Bia 1983.] [N]
Bindell, Stan. NPM, July/August 1993. [Editor, *Navajo-Hopi* Observer.]
Bingaman, Jesse. NMM, July 1939. [Teacher at NM Western.]
Bingham, Janet. [See Bingham, 1982.]
Bingham, Sam. [See Bingham, 1982.]
Biren, Joan E. [Postcard by Helaine Victoria Press, Inc., Martinsville IN; Navajo at end of Longest Walk in 1978, Washington, D.C.]
Blackford, John L. AZHi, June 1943.
Blackwood, Beatrice M. PRM–22. <1820s>. [1889–1975; Oxford lecturer.] F.
Blanchard, Kendall A. [See Blanchard, 1977.]
Bledsoe, William.
Bliss, William P. [See Fleming and Luskey, 1986:233; Rudisill, 1973:14. Partnership with Wittick, no specific evidence of photography of Navajo.]
Bloomer, Peter. Contemporary. WM; AZHi, September 1976. [Flagstaff photographer.]
Boardman, ??. UCR. [Stereo image, 1905; perhaps exposition, perhaps not even Navajo subject.]
Boltin, Lee. AMNH—6. [Staff photographer; photographs of ceremony; also segments for CBS Adventure series "Way of Navajo."] F.
Bond, D. Clifford. AZHi, June 1941. [See Christenson, 1987:10ff.]
Bonine, Elias A. SWM—4. <1880s>. [1843–1916; see Fleming and Luskey, 1986:233; Berezin, 1982. Studio in Pasadena, CA.] F.
Bonnell, John. WM; HNAI:598. <1950s>. [Scottsdale AZ.]
Borden, John. Contemporary. [Producer and principal camera—"Seasons of the Navajo" (1984 video).]
Bortell, P. Clinton. NAA; LOC; MNM; SWM; NAW; SDM; AZS; UNMM; WM. <1910s–1920s>. [Postcards, early photographs of Klah Nightway on last day.]
Bosch, James. NNM; NAW; HNAI:632. <1950s>. [Worked with Gene Price; successor to Milton Snow and Stan Bartos.]
Bowen, Dennis. Contemporary. [Videocamera operator, Heard Museum.] [N]?
Bowman, ??. SWM—1.
Bowman, Arlene. Contemporary. ["Navajo Talking Picture," film shown at the Native American Film and Media Celebration, 1992. Film of grandmother and "a journey of discovery for an acculturated young Navajo woman."] [N]
Boyd, Harry. [Trader, had two families, the second by a Navajo wife, Jesse Long Boyd. Both photographed extensively, and now their daughter, Anna Boyd Whitesinger, also a photographer, is documenting both families.]

Boyd, Jesse Long. [See Harry Boyd.] [N]
Bradfield, Wesley. MNM—4. [See K. Chapman below; see M. Keegan, 1990.]
Bradley, Helen. LAB (VSP).
Bradley, Zorro. NPSWACC.
Bradshaw, Bob. AZHi, September 1978. [Produced slides (Bradshaw's Photo Shop, Sedona AZ); also Smith-Southwestern postcard, Tempe.]
Branham, Mary. NMM, October 1959. [With Hiddon.]
Branstead, Robert. [See Christenson, 1987:8ff, 24.]
Bratley [Brantley??], Jesse Hastings. HNAI:500; DMNH; NAA. <1900s>. [See Fleming and Luskey, 1986:74; early teacher at Hopi.]
Breed, Jack. AZHi, August 1946.
Breed, John B. HNAI. <before 1939>. [National Geographic Society photo of child being treated with Chiricahua Windway sandpainting.]
Brenner, Malcolm. Contemporary. [*Farmington Daily Times* staff photographer; photo of Jonas John at Shiprock, *Santa Fe New Mexican*, 20 September 1993.]
Brewer, Jimmie. NPSWACC. <1938>. [Wupatki, Sarah Peshlakai.]
Broderick, T. R. <1960s>. [Navajo Agricultural Projects photographs.]
Broeske, Fritz. MNM—1. [1937.]
Brook, Baylor. SDM—many. [Geology professor, San Diego State.]
Brown, Annette T. [Director of Public Television, Salish Kootenai College. Degree from NYU in film and television production. See Tribal College: *Journal of American Indian Higher Education* 6(1):24–25, 1994.] [N]
Brown, Dean. <1936–1973>. [May have photographed Navajo, but no specific evidence exists.]
Brown, Edsel. Contemporary. [Artist at NCC, works in museum in video production; brother of Norman P. Brown.] [N]
Brown, Nicholas. NAA; MNM; MAI; AHS; HNAI. [See also son, William Henry; 1860s–1880s Santa Fe studio photographers; early in partnership with George Bennett. See Rudisill, 1973:16; Fleming and Luskey, 1986:233. May have photographed at Fort Sumner and may have bought outfit of Valentin Wolfenstein. *Carte de visite* with N. Brown & Sons imprint found widely in archives.]
Brown, Norman Patrick. Contemporary. [Video and photography; teaches drama and art at Gray Hills School, Tuba City.] [N]
Brown, William Henry. MNM—1. [Son of Nicholas Brown.]
Brown, W. Cal. NAA. [See Rudisill, 1973:16; landscape and portrait photography. Also served as federal marshal.]
Brucker, Reinhard. [See Osinski, 1987; photographs in children's book.]
Brumm, Elsa. MNM—2. [Trip up Canyon de Chelley, 1920.]
Brugge, David. HNAI. [National Park Service historian; photography involved in land claims documentation.]
Buckwalter, ??. CHS. [A collector, probably not a photographer. Most may be of an exposition, perhaps in California.]
Budnik, Dan. CCP; NPM, 4(3), 1991 (cover). [Kammer, 1980; Big Mountain, 1981].
Buehman, Al. [See Cummings, 1952; Navajo loom and weaver; Hosteen Luca.]
Bullen, Adelaide. LAB.
Bullock, Dale. NMSRA. [Several photos in collection, perhaps some by Bullock.]
Burdeau, George. IAIA. [Filmmaker, communication arts program; taught Navajo students.]
Bureau of Reclamation. NMM, September 1959. [Uncredited Milton Snow photograph?]
Burckhalter, David. [See Osinski, 1987; Tom Stack Associates agency.]
Burge, J.C. MNM—1. [See Rudisill, 1973:18; ca. 1839–1897.]
Burke, Bill. [Perhaps trader near Houck in 1920s.]
Burns, J. Robert. AHS.
Burns, Robert. UUAZ. [*AZ Daily Star*, Tucson.]
Burnett, David. Contemporary. [Contact Press Images; *New York Times*, 21 February 1993:15; *London Sunday Times Magazine*, 17 January 1993; *Life*, July 1993.]

Appendix

Bussolini, Karen. Contemporary. [*New York Times*, 28 November 1993:33; Bruce Museum, Greenwich CT, exhibition of Navajo weaving.] F.
Butler, Eva L. MNM—1. [1941.]
Butman, W. C. LOC. [See Rudisill, 1973:18; Albuquerque studio, 1904.]
Buvens, Anna Edna. MNM—ca. 10. [Whipple AZ, 1939.]
Byers, D.S. PMH. [Photos taken during Peabody Utah Floating House expedition.]
Bynner, Witter. MNM. [Santa Fe poet, author; Chaco Canyon, Santa Fe Fiesta.]
Byrnes, J. F. (and Co). SWM; UUAZ. [1901 photos credited to Santa Fe Railway Passenger Dept, Chicago. Byrnes may have taken photos, or may only be the studio that duplicated them.]
Cablemant, ??. SDM. [1926.]
Cabral, Al. Contemporary. [See Eichstaedt, 1994:7.]
Cadzow, Donald A. [Member of Hodge expedition to Hawikah. See Bush and Mitchell, 1994:238, 297.]
Camp, Woodfin. [See Kammer, 1980. Perhaps only advertising agent.]
Campbell, Myrtle and Gilbert. ASM; AZS—20. <1940s>.
Cameramann International, Ltd. [See Osinski, 1987.]
Candelario, John. NMM, February, March 1941, November 1945 (covers and articles).
Cannon, Lee. Contemporary. [See Scudder, 1982. Navajo relocation, also Navajo protests in Phoenix.]
Caples, Ron L. AZHi ???
Caplin, Harvey. MNM; UNMM; WM. [See Kluckhohn, Hill, Kluckhohn, 1971:151. Smith-Southwestern postcard, Tempe; with Barnes in Southwest Post Card Co., Albuquerque.]
Carlson, Gus. NAPHS.
Carr, Lena. Contemporary. NMM, November 1988. [Filmmaker, K-Karr Productions.] [N]
Carpenter, D. W. <1890–1915>. [La Junta CO.]
Carpenter, William J. LOC; SDM. [Probably did not photograph Navajo, but is credited with (and copyrighted) several Pennington photographs, 1914–1915. See Goetzmann, 1991.]
Carson, Jack. NNM; CON. [1958.]
Carson, ?? SWM—1.
Cerba, Charles. MNM—1.
Chambers, Robert and Mary (Riordan). NAPHS. <ca. 1910-1930>.
Chamberlain, ?? SDM—18. [album, ca. 1911, at SDM. Collector? Photographer?]
Chapman, Kenneth. MNM—ca. 86. [Collected as well as photographed—many photos collected are those of H. F. Robinson and W. Bradfield.]
Chase, A. W. CHS. [Photo "Navajo Chief Manuelito and Son, No. 95., A. W. Chase Photo, Santa Fe NM," published by Dry River Trading Co., Tucson 50-2; see Fleming and Luskey, 1986:235. A. W. Chase noted as working on Coastal Survey, California, pre-1876; perhaps just a collector. Probably not the same person as Dana B. Chase. The Dry River Trading Co. attribution to A. W. Chase is wrong (as is the identification of subjects as Manuelito and son). This Navajo photograph is indeed probably by Dana B. Chase. CHS gives credit to "Chase" (no first initials specified) and identifies subjects as "Navajo Cheif [*sic*] and Son" (not as Manuelito). See also Bush and Mitchell, 1994:126.]
Chase, Dana B. [See Rudisill, 1973:19. Noted as having studio in 1884 in Santa Fe, also in 1888. One of operators was L. Fetter (see below). Probably took the Navajo photograph attributed in previous entry to A. W. Chase.]
Choate, J. N. NAA; MNM; HNAI. [1842—1902. Widely published photographs (1882–1895) taken at Carlisle School, PA, of Navajo students just arriving, and again after some time at school. Cf. Bush and Mitchell, 1994:90, 91, 297.]
Chowder, Jack. [Photographer for children's book, *Tonibah and the Rainbow*.]
Chulow, Dennis. UNMM—2. [Photographs in Sinclair College.]
Churchill, Col. Frank C. MAI—ca. 22 (1903-1907), DART—ca. 30 (1903-1909). [U.S. Indian inspector, 1899–1909 (d. 1912). Photographed mostly at Tuba City and western reservation.]
Clah, Al. [See Worth and Adair, 1972.] [N]

Appendix

Clark, F. C. NA. [BIA archives, NA; one photo, Navajo education.]
Clark, Mica.
Clarkson, Mrs. James. MNM—5. [Ran Indian Detours coaches for Fred Harvey; probably principally a collector; many by Kemp (see below).]
Clayton, Robert Alan. [Photographer/designer; author, with J. B. Hathaway, of *Quiet Pride*, book on elders of the West. See also Camera and Darkroom 15(12):46–47, 1993.]
Cobb, William Henry. MNM. <1880–1890>. [1860–1909; Albuquerque photographer. See Fleming and Luskey, 1986:235; Rudisill, 1973:21.]
Collester, Doris. NAA. [Perhaps collector only, with Carlos Motezuma.]
Collier, Charles. LOC. [1951 photo of outdoor sandpainting.]
Collier, John, Jr. UMP—ca. 60. [1913–1993. Farm Security Administration photographer, *Farm Quarterly* photographer. See also Collier, 1986; Bunker and Adair, 1959; Tremblay, Collier, and Sasaki, 1954.]
Collier, Michael. AZHi, August 1979.
Collins, Glenn C. SHM [ca.1911].
Colton, Harold. MNA. [Director of Museum, occasional photographs.]
Condie, Le Roy. NA. [Language consultant to BIA education and mission schools. BIA archive.]
Condyles, Kirk. Contemporary. [Impact Visuals; Photo Graphics. Navajo/Hopi conflict, Navajo resettlement, and Big Mountain activism.]
Conklin, Paul. Contemporary. HNAI. [Contract schools photographer. See also Woodhead, 1993:144–145; Doherty and Doherty, 1989:61.]
Content, Majorie. <Early 1930s>. [Photographed women of Shonto and Red Lake.]
Conway, Norman. MNM—ca. 28. [1887–1977. First road engineer on Navajo reservation. Wife, Virginia, was registered nurse and also photographed Navajo people. Most photographs printed by Mullarky Studios, Gallup.]
Conway, Virginia. [See Norman Conway, above.]
Coolidge, Dane. BAN—113; AZS—10; MNM; WM. <1913-1920s>. [See Coolidge and Coolidge, 1930. Many photos of Alamo Navajo area.]
Coolidge, Mary Roberts. [See Dane Coolidge, above; see Coolidge and Coolidge, 1930, and Coolidge, 1929.]
Cooper, Ed. UUAZ. [Exxon travel club *Vista*, Spring 1983.]
Cooper, Valda. NMM, October 1955. [Farmington NM reporter.]
Cooper, ??. SWM—1. [1929, with Frasher.]
Copeland, Alan. [See Gordon, 1973. Activist, news photographer??]
Cordis, Isabelle Dye. [Seventh-Day Adventist missionary, Holbrook AZ, 1940s. See Stirling, 1961.]
Cosgrove, Harriet. MNM—3.
Cowan, John L. MAI.
Coze, Paul. AZHi, July 1950.
Craig, John. Contemporary. [Hunter family, Black Rock Canyon; book pending.]
Crandall, ??. SWM-1. [Contemporary with Vroman, Camera Club; participated in Navajo photos of Navajo in 1897 trip.]
Crane, Leo. MNA. [Superintendent at Keam's Canyon. Government reports frequently illustrated with his photographs.]
Crank, Dan L. UNMNSS. Contemporary. [Poet and photographer, Dennihotso AZ; see Crank, 1988. Published for Navajo Fair, Maisels Traders, Navajo tribe.] [N]
Crass, F.C. MNA. [See Cummings, 1952. Photo of Sam Chief and son, 1919.]
Crews, Cari. HM. [Photos of sandpainting for museum.]
Cronyn, T. [Canyon de Chelly, 1939–1940.]
Cross, Guy C. MNM—1. [See Woodhead, 1993. Close-up portrait of "Hoshkay Yazhie, Navajo Medicine Man."]
Cross Studios. [See Guy Cross.]
Cross, A. E. SWM. [Copied Hillers.]
Crouse, J. S(?) MNA. [Studio photographer. See Reichard album, photograph of Charlie Turquoise, Ayanbito NM.]

Appendix

Crowder, Jack. <1950s>. [Author/photographer, *Albuquerque Tribune*.] F.
Cruz, Anna. [UNM photographer, taught Navajo, hosted Cartier-Bresson and wife to Navajoland.] [N]
Cummings, Byron. LAB—2. [Trip to Rainbow Bridge.]
Cunningham, Helen Zeta. MNM—1; NMM, November 1947. [Teacher.]
Curtis, Edward S. LOC; NAA. <1903–1906>. [See abundant entries in bibliography, especially Rudisill, 1973:21. 1868-1952. Assisted by Adolph Muhr from 1904, also Cunningham, McBride; other assistants were probably family members. See Faris, 1993d.] F.
Curtis, Natalie [Burlin]. PMH; NAA. <Before 1907>. [1875-1921. See Babcock and Parezo, 1988:95.]
Dailey, A. A. HM. [Atchison, Topeka &Santa Fe, Fred Harvey photographer.]
Dale, Bruce. [See *National Geographic Magazine*, December 1972. See also Eiler, Northup.]
Damon-Sandoval, Christi. [1994 IAIA student exhibition.] [N]
Daniels, Elton. UNMNSS; HMCNAP. [Exhibited at Millicent Rogers Museum.] [N]
Daniels, Nancy. SDM—62. [1981, see also Dodson, Walter.]
Day, Charles. NAA; BM; NMM, October 1952. [See Daniel Holmes Mitchell, Edward S. Curtis, and Dr. Elizabeth Snyder; see also Culin Journals, 1903, Woodhead, 1993; Faris, 1993d.]
Davis, Wayne. NMSRA; AZHi, August 1979. [St. John's, AZ photographer.]
Davis, Wyatt. MNM; NMSRA; WM. [New Mexico Department of Development photographer, 1930s. Brother of Stuart Davis. See Keegan, 1990. Many photographs apparently lost.]
Dawson, Roger H. NMM, January 1936. [WPA photographer.]
Dedera, Don. ASM; AZS.
Degginger, E. R. UUAZ. [Spring 1983 issue of Exxon travel club *Vista*, "In the Land of the Navajo" (18:4, p. 8).]
De Huff, Elizabeth Willis. UNM. [Photographer (??); perhaps related to J. Willis.]
Delano, Jack. MNM. [See Rabinowitz, 1993. FSA photographer, photos of railway workers in Gallup, Winslow, etc.]
Dellenbaugh, F. S. MAI. [Did apparently photograph, though no clear evidence he photographed Navajo. Probably collector only; some are C. M. Bell. See Jackson catalog, 1877.]
de Muth, Don.
Den Dooren, K. C. [See Bahti, 1971:35.]
Dennetsosi, Hoke. NNM. [Helped Snow, 1942. Probably not a photographer; artist and illustrator, Rough Rock Press.] [N]
Dennis, Lisl contemporary. ["Travel Photography Workshop in Santa Fe"; see Dennis, 1993. Advertises "feel comfortable photographing people."]
Deschinnie, Jonny. [Rock Point councilman, *Navajo Times*]. F. [N]
Deschiny, Janet. [See Hubbard, 1994:65.]
DeWald, Howard. HM. [Photos of Gallup Ceremonial parade.]
Dickerson, Warren C. SWM; HNAI. [1901 photos of Los Angeles Indian Arts and Crafts Exhibition. Most active 1910–1915, although photographed up into 1930s.]
Diers, Don. [See Frink, 1968:107. Studio in Sheridan WY, with Rockford. Miss Indian America contestants.]
Dietrich, Dick. Contemporary. UUAZ; AZHi, September 1978 [Thunderbird Cards, Beautyway postcards, Williams AZ. Photo USA agency.]
Dietrich, Margaretta. MNM—ca. 2.
Dimock, Julian. NAA.
Dinwiddie, William. NAA. [1894.]
Dixon, Dr. Joseph Kosuth. AMNH; WHM; UMP. [One of the photographers on Wanamaker expeditions, 1908–1913 (see Fergus, 1991; Rudisill, 1973:24; Krouse, 1987; Fleming and Luskey, 1993:103). Rollin Lester Dixon, his son, led the motion-picture unit. By time of 1913 expedition "of Citizenship," the group had added John Scott (NYC) and W. B. Cline (Rochester), on loan from Eastman.]
Dodge, Natt. NPSWACC. [Photographer (??) of Navajo with bear, 1944.]

Appendix

Dodson, Jim. SDM—52. [1981 Canyon de Chelly. See also Daniels, Walter.]
Donator (??). MNM. [1901, in Carlos Hall collection.]
Donaldson, John. UMP. [Special Agent for 1890 Census in Navajoland; took photographs, purchased photos (from Wittick), etc., for reports; see also Scott.]
Dorsey, G. A. NAA. [May have photographed at 1904 World's Fair at St. Louis.]
Doucette, Forrest. AZS—2 [1927.]
Douglas, F. PMH. [1951.]
Dunbar, La Vera and Felix. AZHi, August 1967.
Dunlop, Joan. Contemporary. [See Osinski, 1987.]
Durham, Bart. Contemporary. WM. [Also printed for others.]
Eames, E. Leslie. UUAZ—2; SWM. [Dentist, pre-1948.]
Ebron, ??. NMM, July 1953. [Photography of Navajo beauty contestants in Gallup.]
Edwards, David. [See Christenson, 1987:2.]
Edwards, E. K. CHS. [Edwards and Sons, Denver, 1920–1930s; see also Frink, 1968:93, 95.]
Edwards, Page. 1940s. [See Eichstaedt, 1994:25.]
Eichman, Mary. NMM, May 1943. [Gallup resident.]
Eichstaedt, Peter H. Contemporary. [See Eichstaedt, 1994.]
Eiler, Terry. *National Geographic Magazine*, December 1972. [Secondary photographer; Mugwump Studio, Athens, Ohio.]
Elkort, Martin. NMM, March 1960. [Advertising, commercial, Farmington.]
Ellinger, Ed. UUAZ. [Petley studio, Albuquerque.]
Elliot, Hugh, and Ruth. NAA. [1909, Rochester IN.]
Elliot, Bryce. MNM—4.
Elmer, Carlos. Contemporary. UUAZ.
Emerson, Gloria. Contemporary. IAIA. [N]
English, ??. NNM; CON. [Navajo Fair photographs, 1960s.]
Erb, Don. [See Kluckhohn, Hill, and Kluckhohn, 1971. Atchison, Topeka, & Santa Fe photographer.]
Erdoes, Richard. HNAI. [See Erdman, 1985. Santa Fe photographer and writer, 1970s.]
Etcitty, Al. Contemporary. NCC. [Video technician, also photography and ciné.] [N]
Etson, Tom. LAB (VSP).
Euler, Robert. [See Dobyns and Euler, 1972, 1977.]
Evans, K. E. NMM, April 1969.
Evans, Floyd B. SWM—11. ["Associate of Photographic Society of America." See *Masterkey*, 1947.]
Ewing and Hilton. UNM. <1908>. [See Rudisill, 1973:26.]
Fanshel, Susan. Contemporary cinéphotographer. ["A Weave of Time" (1986 video).]
Far West Photography. NNM. [Albuquerque studio, Navajo Fair, 1960–1970s.]
Farabee, William Curtis. UMP; PMH. [Curator at University Museum, University of Pennsylvania, at least through 1920. First photographs in 1904; on early Wanamaker expeditions. Extensive glass slide collection at UMP; Chicago Slide Co, Geo. Bond Slide Co, Santa Fe Railway.]
Farber, Joseph C. HNAI. [1970s. Commercial.]
Farber, Roy. [See Jett and Spencer, 1981 (perhaps only assistant to Jett).]
Faris, Chester E. HUN. [Superintendent, Navajo Agency, 1930s.]
Farlow Collection. PMH. [Photographer??]
Fedor, Ferenz. MNM—ca. 16; NMM, July 1947.
Fellin, Olivia. NMM, June 1958. [Gallup librarian.]
Fergusson, Erna. UNMM. [Albuquerque, Southwestern writer, popularizer.]
Fetter, W. L. UMP. [Established a studio opposite Plummer and Wickham Building (corner of 2nd and Coal) in Gallup, September 1889–February 1890. Purchased outfit of Ben Wittick, of Fort Wingate, and had studio both there and in Gallup. Probably same as L. Fetter, who operated Dana B. Chase studio in Santa Fe in 1884–1885. See Rudisill, 1973:20, 26, and Lyon/Rudisill, 29 August 1975.]

Appendix

Fewkes, J. W. PMH. [1850–1930. See Rudisill, 1973:26-27.]

Field, Katie WM; UNM; NMM, November 1986. [European-American rancher's daughter; married Alamo Navajo man, John Guerro. Extensive ranch photography and events in area, 1920s-1930s.] F.

Fisher, Egbert Fr. [St. Michaels priest who took photos with Schwemberger. See Long, 1992:3.]

Flaherty Collection. MNA. [Photographer??]

Fleming, Rex. <1930s–1940s.> [Arizona, National Park Service.]

Follett, Orno. [First Seventh-Day Adventist missionary to Navajo. See Stirling, 1961.]

Forbes, A. A. SWM.

Forlow, Doreen E. Contemporary. [NMM Vacation Guide 1995; Navajo rodeo.]

Foster, Kenneth. WM. [Former director, Wheelwright Museum. Participated in 1963 American Indian Film Project.]

Forrest, Earle, R. MNA. <1902–1907 and 1926–1929>. [See Forrest, 1970; Rudisill, 1973:27.]

Foxx, Jeffrey Jay. Contemporary. [See Foxx and Karasik, 1993.]

Francis, Perry. HMCNAP. [N]

Francisco, Janelle. [See Hubbard, 1994:65, 66.] [N]

Francisco, Nia. Contemporary. [See Beck *et al.*, 1977.] [N]

Frank, Lois Ellen. NMM, December 1990.

Franklin, Dwight. UUAZ. [1913.]

Frasher, Burton. [1888–1955. California postcard photographer ("Frasher Fotos"), in most Southwestern photographic archival collections. See Keegan, 1990; see Pasadena City Museum.]

Freeman, John. WM. [SVE color cards, Publix Agency (see Chart 2c below).]

Frink, Maurice, Jr. <1960s>. [Author/historian. See Frink, 1968. Elkhart, IN.]

Frisbie, Charlotte. HNAI:544. [Red Ant Way photos, 1963.]

Frith, Betsy. WM. [Photographed, individually, each Navajo participant in 1968 commemoration of Long Walk prior to leaving for Fort Sumner from Navajoland.]

Fritz, Mary A. NMSRA. [Photo of Roman Hubbell.]

Fronske, R. W. SDM; AZHi, August 1946. [Local studio photographer, Flagstaff. Dexter Press, Pearl River, NY postcard.]

Fuller, R. G. PMH. [1913. Photographed with C. C. Willoughby. See also Fleming and Luskey, 1986:237.]

Fuller, Tim. Contemporary.

Funk, Elizabeth. [Cook at St. Michaels during Schwemberger's period; may have taken photos, especially those with Schwemberger in them. See Long, 1992.]

Fusco, Paul. Contemporary. [Magnum Agency photographer.]

Fuss, Eduardo. NMM, March 1984.

G., F. D. NAA. [1901. Possibly Soule photograph. See Fleming and Luskey, 1986:243.]

Gaede, Mark. HNAI. [1970s. See Gaede, 1988. Staff photographer, MNA, 1968, 1970 (summer).]

Gaige, J. G. MNM. [Said to have photographed at Bosque Redondo and had a contract to photograph military posts with U.S. Signal Corps. See Fleming and Luskey, 1986:70, 237; Rudisill, 1973:28.]

Gail, Ida. [Worked for Snow, who taught her photography.] [N]

Garcia, ??. AC. [Platinium print, for Fred Harvey.]

Garner, Virginia. AZHi, January 1945.

Gardner, Alexander. NAA. [1821–1882. Delegation photographer; see Fleming and Luskey, 1986:231; Rudisill, 1973:29. Did visit Southwest, but no evidence that he took photographs of Navajo *in situ*. Photographed for General Palmer; see Missouri Historical Society, St. Louis.]

Garrett, Norman Rhoads. AZHi, August 1946.

Gates, P. G. SWM; NAA; HNAI. [See Fleming and Luskey, 1986:196, 237. Also noted in correspondence of F. Monsen's daughter with Huntington Library.]

Gedekoh, Cliff. MNM; NNM; CON. [Employed by Navajo Tribe, and SMC Cartographic Section, Concho OK series. Also worked for R. Van Valkenburgh in land claims.]
Gentile, Charles (& Co). MAI. [Claimed and attributed to Gentile, but probably taken by N. Brown and Sons or V. Wolfenstein.]
Giddings, Kirk. NMM, April 1990.
Gilbert, Hope. MAI. [Photograph of F. W. Hodge, E. Vogt.]
Gill, Delancy. NAA. [Delegation photographer, early 1900s. Also Bureau of American Ethnology engraver.]
Gilles, Cate. Contemporary. [Activist. See *Cultural Survival* 17(4):passim (Winter 1994).]
Gillingham, ??. MNM—1.
Gilpin, Laura. AC—thousands. [1891–1979. Prints and postcards available in most Southwestern archives. See Sandweiss, 1986, 1987; Faris, 1993c.]
Glaha, B. D. NAA. [1941. Bureau of Reclamation near Kayenta.]
Gleason, Herbert W. NAA. [1913.]
Goddard, Pliny. AMNH. <1909–1910>. [Photos, mostly in taking apart forked-stick hogan to transport back to museum. Some weaving carding, silverworking.]
Gonzalez, Don. Contemporary. [Lawrence Livermore National Laboratory, Livermore, CA, perhaps staff photographer. See "Educational Revolution on the Reservation" in *Winds of Change*, Winter 1993:12ff (American Indian Science and Engineering Society).]
Goodman, Charles. NAA; MNM; SWM; CHS; MAI; NPSWACC. In Prudden Collection. <1884–1902>. [Bluff, Utah; first Navajo Fair. San Juan Studio (??). See Rudisill, 1973:30.]
Goodman, Jack. USHS. [See *New York Times*, 28 December 1969.]
Goodwin, Victor. NA. [BIA archive. Navajo ITE Circuit Breaker Co.]
Goldwater, Barry. AZHi, August 1946; HM; MNM; NA. [BIA archive. See also Rosebrook, 1993.]
Gonners F. CHS. [Durango studio. Photos of Buckskin Charlie with Navajos?]
Gordon, Suzanne. [Activist. See Gordon, 1973.]
Graber, Julie. Contemporary. [See Plevin, 1995.]
Graham, Lord. LAB. [1929.]
Grant, George A. NPSWACC. [1891–1964. National Park Service photographer.]
Grassham, John. NMSRA. <1920s>. [Photographer??]
Gregory, Herbert. [United States Geological Survey geologist; <1900–1920>]. F.
Griffin, John. [See Dobyns and Euler, 1972, 1977.]
Grimes, Joel. Contemporary. [See Grimes, 1992.]
Guadagnoli, Nello. [Gallup studio photographer. Owns the studio once held by Mullarky and approximately fifty Schwemberger glass plates (perhaps also studio location of Schwemberger's Gallup studio).]
Guernsey, S. J. PMH; LAB. <1914–1917>. [Probably while on archaeological expedition.]
Gus, Larry. Contemporary. [Los Angeles freelance photojournalist. Sygma/Photo News Agencies. Listed in some guides as Larry Guf.] [N]
Haas, Ernst. [Magnum photographer. Likely to have taken photographs of Navajo during visit.]
Haesler, J. A. NNM. [Filmmaker. Staged dance in November 1938 for film "Navajo People."] F.
Hall, Carlos. MNM. [Artist. Probably collector only.]
Hall, Douglas Kent. NMM, August 1989. [Santa Fe; Navajo rodeo.]
Hall, E. E. SWM. [See Fleming and Luskey, 1986:237. Confusion with 1897 photographs attributed to James and Maude.]
Hall, Edward T. [Anthropologist. See Hall, 1994.]
Hall, Gary. DMNH. [Staff photographer, 1980s.]
Hall, Sharlot. SHM [ca. 1910].
Halseth, Odd. WM; ASM; AZS. [See Keegan, 1990. Phoenix archaeologist and architectual historian. Some photographs for H. H. Tammen, 1930.]
Hamel, F. M. NNM; CON. [1954; sheep disease, vaccination.]
Hamilton, Parker. NPSWACC; MNA. [1955– ; MNA staff photographer, 1960–1962. Possibly NPS publicity photographer. Trading posts.]

Appendix

Hanna and Hanna. MNM; NMSRA. [1938; see B. Scott.]

Hanna, Forman. AHS; ASM; NPSWACC. <1930s>. [1882–1950. See Sawyer, 1985.]

Hanna and Mau [Maupin]? ["Travelling Photographers"—probably 1910s, around Fort Defiance.]

Harrill, Bruce G. MNA. [1971; sheep and goats.]

Harrington, J. NAA.

Harrington, M. R. SWM—3. [Also known as MRH.]

Harris, A.B. NMSRA. <1920s>. [Photographer??]

Harris (Brewer, Pierce, Van Valkenburgh), Sallie. MNA. [Wupatki (as Brewer); land claims in field (as Van Valkenburgh).]

Harrison, Carter H. MNM. [Mayor of Chicago. Several times brought son west for health.]

Harter, H. H. NNM; CON. [Sheep shearing, "old way."]

Harvey, Bob. [See Kluckhohn and Wyman, 1940.]

Harvey, Fred. MAI. [Photographs in all archives. British immigrant. Atchison, Topeka, & Santa Fe concessions from 1876. Actually did some photography, but his own are usually mixed with those who photographed for him. Detroit Publishing Company.]

Harvey, Katherine MAI. [1931.]

Haskett, Bert. ASM.

Haussamen, Walter. NMM, August 1961.

Havens, C. C. NA. [1940s; BIA archives.]

Hayden, Carl T. AZS. [1877–1972. Arizona politician. Many Civilian Conservation Corps photographs (Dedera, Mullarky). Probably collector only.]

Haynes, Murrae. Contemporary. [See Eichstaedt, 1994.]

Heald, Weldon F.

Hedlund, Ann. [See Two Bears, 1995.]

Hegemann, Elizabeth Compton. NAA; HUN; ASM: MNA. <1924–1934>. [Trader's wife; see Hegemann, 1963 (containing over 320 captioned illustrations).]

Heick, William R. WM; HNAI. [1963; American Indian Film Project.]

Heid, Graham. [See Christenson, 1987:22.]

Heisey, Adriel. Contemporary. [Aerial views of Navajoland.]

Henderson, Esther. AZHi, June 1943. [NY Institute of Photography, 1940s. Married Chuck Abbott. See Henderson, 1987; Cummings, 1952.]

Herbert, Charles. WM; HNAI; AZHi, August 1967. [1950s; see Dobyns and Euler, 1972. National Geographic Society. SVE Color Cards. Western Ways Features.]

Herdeg, Walter. MNM. [*Scribner's Magazine*, 1939.]

Heron, Michael. [Studio photographer, New York. See Rosnek and Stacey, 1976; Doherty and Doherty, 1989:passim; Woodfin Camp and Associates.]

Herz, Harry.

Hiester, Henry T. MNM; NMSRA. <1869?–1878>. [Principally around Fort Defiance; see Fleming and Luskey, 1986:238; Rudisill, 1973:33. Operated out of Nicholas Brown studio, Santa Fe in 1870s. L. M. Melander and Brothers stereographic card sets.] F.

Hight, George. MAI; SDM; NMM, September 1953. [Gallup studio photographer. Some posed ceremonial photographs.]

Hildebrand, J. W. MNA; MAI. [1908 or earlier.] F.

Hill, Ted.

Hill, Willard W. NAA. [See Kluckhohn, Hill and Kluckhohn, 1971:64, 65.]

Hillers, John K. NAA; MNM; NA; PMH; AC; BAN—10. <1870s>. [1843–1925. Represented in most archives. See Rudisill, 1973:34–35; Keegan, 1990; Frink, 1968. Widely copied.]

Hinchman, Fred K. SWM—34. [Southwest Museum photographer, education outreach coordinator, 1930–1945].

Hirschmann, Fred. [NPM 4(3) (1991), on Churro sheep.]

Hodge, Marie. SWM. [Wife of F. W. Hodge.]

Hoeffer, Paul. DMNH. [Early professional photographer. Also ciné.]

Appendix

Hoffman, Martin. [See Yazzie, 1971.]
Holien, Sigred. NMM, June 1956. [Albuquerque journalism student.]
Hooper, King. [See Stirling, 1961. Seventh-Day Adventist missionary.]
Hoopes, Homer E. NAA. [1902. Part of Vroman Camera Club. See Fleming and Luskey, 1986:196, 238.]
Hoover, Grace. [See Christenson, 1987:6, 25.]
Howard, Judith. MNA. [1920; Montrose CA. In Eberle Collection, MNA.]
Hoyt, Herman S. MNM—ca. 15.
Hrdlicka, Ales. NAA, PMH. <1898–1905>. [Chaco region.]
Hubbard, Elmer. UUAZ. [Fronske Studio, Flagstaff.]
Huber, ??. MNA. [1980; photography of loom.]
Hucko, Bruce. Contemporary. WM. [Formerly Education Curator, WM.]
Huff, J. Wesley. NMM, June 1945. [Gallup newsman.]
Hunt, George W. P. AZS. [1923 Federal Air Project photographs.]
Huston, Fred. CHS. [Oklahoma City.]
Hutchison, Sonny. Contemporary. [Cinéphotographer—"How the West was Lost" (Discovery Channel and 9R USA-TV, 1993. See C. Wheeler below.]
Hyde, B.T.B. MNM. [1920; Utah. Perhaps collector of photography of Lewis Cartier?]
Hyde, Philip. [See Brower, 1967.]
Imhof, Joseph. UNMM. [Artist and painter.]
Indian Rights Association. NAA.
Indian Service Photograph. NMM, December 1953. [Probably Milton Snow.]
Inter-Tribal Indian Ceremonial Association. NMM, July 1981.
Jacka, Jerry D. Contemporary. AZHi, September 1978. [Commercial. See NPM passim; Doherty and Doherty, 1989:57. Petley postcard, Albuquerque; Smith-Southwestern postcard, Tempe.]
Jackson, H. SWM—1; CHS—4. [1941.]
Jackson, W. H. PMH; SWM—4. [1843-1942. See Fleming and Luskey, 1986:239; Rudisill, 1973:36–37. Despite claims (cf. Bush and Mitchell, 1994:128, 129), it is questionable that any actual Jackson photographs of Navajo survived.]
James, G. Wharton. SWM; USC; HUN; HNAI. <From 1890s>. [Represented in most archives; see Rudisill, 1973:37; Fleming and Luskey, 1986:36ff; James, 1908; partnerships with Hall, Pierce, Maude.] F.
James, H. C. MNA. [1926.]
James, H. L. NMM, January 1974. [Geologist, New Mexico Highway Department.]
James, Nathaniel. Contemporary. ["Seasons of the Navajo" (1984 video).]
Jay, Nelson D. MNM. [1938.]
Jennings, Cyrus. LOC. [Copyrighted (1914) photographs of Navajo in captivity during Bosque Redondo period undoubtedly taken by others.]
Jenson, Frank. USHS; AZHi, August 1967. [See *New York Times*, 28 December 1969.]
Jett, Stephen. HNAI. [See Jett and Spencer, 1981.]
Jim, Rex Lee. [See Bingham, 1982.] [N]
John, Cindy. [See Four Winds 1(4):1820 (1980).] [N]?
John, Jonas. Contemporary. HMCNAP. [Studio photographer; see Brenner, 1993.] [N]
Johnson, ?? Contemporary. [Southwest Indian leaders; Impact Visuals.]
Johnson, Pyro D. <1950s>. [Tourist postal cards.]
Johnston, Bernice. AHS.
Johnston, Philip. NAU; SDM. [1892– . Old missionary family; helped set up World War II Navajo code-talkers.]
Jones, Dr. Philip Mills. UCB—75. [1902; Hearst photographer sent to Navajoland to secure images.] F.
Jordan, Jean. NMM, August 1983.
Judd, Neil. MNA; NAA. <1909–1929>. [See Cummings, 1952.]
Kaadt, Christian. SWM. <1893–1905>. [See Fleming and Luskey, 1986:240.]

Appendix

Kafer, Lawrence. LOC. [1952; see Mygatt below; New Mexico Department of Welfare.]
Kahn, Alta. [See Worth and Adair, 1972.] [N]
Kalman, Béla. [See Kalman, 1987.]
Kammer, Jerry. Contemporary. [See Kammer, 1980.]
Kawano, Kenji. [See Kawano, 1990; *Navajo Times*.]
Kay, Virginia.
Kay, Louis.
Keams, Geraldine (Geri). Contemporary. [Filmmaker, actor, storyteller; Hozhoni Films.] [N]
Keatly, Vivien B. AZHi, August 1950.
Keaton, Lud. AZHi, August 1979.
Kegley, Max. AZHi, June 1943; August 1946.
Keegan, Marcia. Contemporary. [1942– . See Keegan, 1974, 1990; Doherty and Doherty, 1989:passim; Bush and Mitchell, 1994:303.]
Kellogg, Harold. MNM—ca. 9; NMM, May 1944. [1940s; children's books.]
Kelly, Charles. MNM; UUAZ—1.
Kelley, Klara Bonsack. [See Kelley and Francis, 1994.]
Kemp, Edward. MNM. [Perhaps most of those in Clarkson and Kopplin collections. See McLuhan, 1985. Lost originals in 1906 San Francisco earthquake.]
Kennedy, George, Jr. NMSRA. [Collector, photographer?]
Kennedy, Joe. Contemporary. NMM, September 1989. [Staff photographer for *Farmington Daily Times*; series on the Long Walk (weekly feature from about early October 1991 to early 1992).]
Kent, Dick. Photography. NMM, February 1989. [Studio, Gallup Ceremonial.]
Kershaw, Kathleen. [See Gordon, 1973.]
Kessler, Leone. MNM—21. [Lived in Navajoland.]
Keur, Dorothy. UNMM.
Keystone. UCR, MNM. [Keystone Mast collection at UCR (California Center of Photography). Many are Underwood and Underwood.] F
Khanlian, Richard. NMM, August 1986.
Kida, Jeff.
Kidder, A. V. PMH; MNM; ASM. [1914; mostly noted as having donated photographs.]
King, Cletus. [MNA staff photographer, Winter 1969.]
King, George R. SWM—3.
King, Monica. Contemporary. [Videocam, Heard Museum, Phoenix.] [N]
Kirk, Ruth, MNM—2; NMM, August 1934, July 1938.
Kirk, Tom. SDM—21. [Trading family (Mike Kirk, brother, also photographed), Chinle, from 1910.]
Kite, Alan [see *El Palacio* 75(3):8, 9, 13. 1968].
Kitsman, Barbara Emerson. Contemporary. HMCNAP. [N]
Kluckhohn, Clyde. LAB; VSP. [250 photos before and during Value Studies Project; see Kluckhohn, 1923; Kluckhohn, Hill, and Kluckhohn, 1971.]
Knapp, William. LOC. [1905 copyrighted Ganado stereo prints.]
Knee, Ernest. MNM.
Knell, ??. UMP. [1943. USDA, Southwest Range and Sheep Breeding Laboratory, Fort Wingate, NM.]
Koch, Barbaraellen. NMM, March 1980.
Koenig, Seymour. [see Koenig and Koenig, 1986].
Kolb, Emory. NAU. [1913; Grand Canyon studio.]
Koonce, H. N?? [Postcards, Petley Studios, Phoenix.]
Kopplin, William Ernest. <1907–1912>. [1882– . See McLuhan, 1985. Advertising department of the Santa Fe Railway; tinted lantern slides and collected (and made lantern slides from) photographs from other early photographers.]
Kopta, Emory. MNA; MAI. [1953. Photographer and sculptor. Some Bradfield attributed to Kopta; studio at Grand Canyon.]

Korth, Fred G. WM. [Chicago, Harriet Williams Collection.]
Krause, Warren. AZS. [1950s–1960s; perhaps collector only.]
Kukens, Glen. SWM—1. [1939.]
Laatsch, Marilyn. [See Collier, 1986. Filmed, with Collier in 1975, Rough Rock Community School, resulting in privately published manuscripts.]
Laboratory of Anthropology. NMM, May 1933.
La Fonda (Hotel). MNM—15. [Collection donated, mostly of exhibitions. No photographer indicated.]
Lair, Max. WM. [Perhaps Max Lere. Photographed 1963 American Indian Film Project with Kenneth Foster.]
Lamar, Newton. NNM. <1950s–1960s>. [Navajo Fair photos.]
Lambert, Marge. NMSRA.
Lamphere, Louise. [See Kluckhohn, Hill, Kluckhohn, 1971:131–132.]
Lancaster, Joseph. [See *Outdoor Photography*, April 1993. Instructor, De Chelly Galleries, Inc. Advertises tours: "Dinehtah, Land of the People"; "Photographic Adventure with the Dine People."]
Landgraf, John. LAB, VSP.
Lang, C. B. MAI [1903, Chinle.]
Lange, Dorothea. OM. [Farm Security Administration photographer. Navajo primarily photographed from considerable distance; probably took photos while married to Maynard Dixon.]
Latham, Kit. [See Chowning, 1994.]
La Voy, Merl. UCR [1932.]
Law, Adelarde. LAB—18. [July 1920, Kayenta.]
Law, Lisa. Contemporary. [Activist, artist, Santa Fe. *Crosswinds* newspaper story on relocation, weaving project. See Erdman, 1985.] F.
Leighton, Alexander H. [See Leighton and Leighton, 1944.]
Leighton, Dorothea C. NAA; LAB; VSP. [See Leighton and Leighton, 1944; Leighton and Kluckhohn, 1948.]
Lennihan, Mark. Contemporary. HNAI. [Activist, uranium mining, power plants. See *Cultural Survival* 17(4):passim, Winter 1994; *Gallup Independent*; Bingham, 1982.]
Leupp, C. R. [See Coolidge and Coolidge, 1930.]
Levy, Jerrold E. HNAI. [1960s; University of California Navajo Health Education Project.]
Lime, John. NAA. <1894–1904>.
Lincoln, Everett. [1993. IAIA student exhibition.] F. [N]
Lindsay, William. SWM.
Link, Martin. NNM. [Former director, NNM. See Link, 1968.]
List, Cleo. NNM—ca. 75. <1913–1915>. [Teacher, Shiprock. Family album.]
Little Turtle, Carm. Contemporary. [1952– . Apache-Tarahumara photographer, widely exhibited. Hand-colored modernist prints.]
Lockett, Clay. NNM; UNMM. [Assisted M. Snow, late 1930s; later trader in Arizona.]
Loeffler, Jack. [see *El Palacio* 75(3):10. 1968.]
Long, Paul. MNA. <1960s>. [MNA staff photographer, 1962–1966. See Long, 1992.]
Lord, C. E. MNM; SWM. [Santa Fe, Taos.]
Lorenzen, Henry. MAI—3. ["Photo by Henry Lorenzen, N. M."; very early, Bosque Redondo–period photographs. See Rudisill/Faris, 15 Feb 1992; noted in 1867 in Central City, CO in Mautz, 1986; *carte de visite* with Santa Fe imprint.]
Lothrop, S. K. PMH.
Love, Marian F. MNM—1. [Santa Fe.]
Love, Randy. MNA. [Cinéphotographer for "The Navajo: An Ancient Gift," MNA video, Tellens Group, Inc., 1982.]
Lowe, J. MNM. [Collector only?]
Lowman, Herbert A. AZHi, June 1943.
Lown, Lynn. Contemporary. [See Rosenak and Rosenak, 1994.]

Appendix

Lloyd, Harvey. [See Trimble, 1986.]
Luce, Willard. CHS. [1955.]
Luke Air Force Base. AZS—10. [Operation Haylift, 1967, during winter storm.]
Luckert, Karl. HNAI. [See Luckert, 1979.]
Lummis, Charles F. SWM—25; MNM. [See Keegan, 1990; Traugott, 1994.]
Mang, Fred, Jr. HNAI. <1970s>. [Ganado; National Park Service photographer.]
MacLaren, Maggie. [Seaich Corp postcard, Salt Lake.]
Manley, Alan. AZHi, September 1978.
Manley, Ray. WM; AZHi, August 1946. [*Arizona Highways* slides (Wyman Collection); SVE color cards; also Shostal Association.]
Manley, Roger. Contemporary. [1952– . Student of Gilpin; Roswell Museum of Art exhibition, 1986. See Bush and Mitchell 1994:266, 305.]
Marshall, Karen. Contemporary. ["Caretakers of the Earth" exhibition, OK Harris Gallery, New York City, January 1993.] F.
Marshall, Louise I. HM. [1930s; see Beatrice Warren.]
Masters, Paul W. MNM—20. [Schools.]
Martin, Marie. NNM. [Worked with M. Snow, perhaps not a photographer?] [N]
Martin, Robert H. MNM—1. [Santa Fe. Woman weaving at Gallup.]
Martin, Jon Dorsey. Contemporary. HM. [Winslow.]
Martinez, Johnnie S. NMM, February 1976 and subsequent. [Bureau chief, *Santa Fe New Mexican*.]
Maryboy, Nancy. NCC. [NCC, Diné Studies. Mostly landscape photography for museum, 1992.] [N]
Mathews, Truman. MNM—2. [Santa Fe architect.]
Matteson, Sumner W. NAA; MPM—5; SWM—3; UMP—1. [1867–1920. Denver, from 1890s. One of two photographers on Charles Dorsey's Field Museum McCormick Hopi Expedition, 1900–1901. *Field and Stream*. See Casagrande and Bourns, 1983; Fleming and Luskey, 1986:240; Rudisill, 1973:41; Fleming and Luskey, 1993:39ff; Bush and Mitchell, 1994:306.]
Matthews, Washington. AMNH; NAA; PMH; UMP. [From 1880s; see also Goddard.]
Matthiessen, Peter. Contemporary [Activist; see Matthiessen, 1980.]
Maude, Frederic H. SWM-hundreds; HM; MAI. [1858–1960; "Frederic Maude & Co., Landscape Photographers, Los Angeles"; 1890s, Smithsonian, with Scherman?; also with James. Sometimes printed as Wittick. See Fleming and Luskey, 1986:240; Bush and Mitchell, 1994:306.]
Maupin, ??. SWM. [See Hanna, above.]
Maxson, Harmon. LAB; VSP??
Mayer, C. AMNH. [See McLuhan, 1985:14. Early tourists with Navajo.]
Mayhew, Carl. LOC. [1922, Flagstaff; perhaps only copyright.]
Mays, Buddy. MNM; NMSRA; NMM, August 1990. [Widely published commercial tourist photographer.]
McAllester, Susan. [See Shaffer, 1987.]
McAllester, David. SDM; WM. [Photographed and recorded Jim Smith.]
McAuley, Skeet. CCP. [1951– . See McAuley, 1989; Bush and Mitchell, 1994:306.]
McChom, George L. [1949 photograph of sweat lodge (printed in an article discussing the return of the Snow collection to the Navajo in *Arizona Republic*, 19 January 1985.) Perhaps BIA or Navajo agency employee??]
McCombe, Leonard. WM. [See Kluckhohn and Vogt, 1951; Time/Life staff photographer.]
McCombs, Edward. NCC. [Photographer for NCC activities (cf. *Navajo Times*, 16 July 92; NCC general catalog; public relations; McCombs, 1987).]
McDermott, Michael. Contemporary. NMM August 1995.
McDonough, Timothy M. [*Winds of Change*, Winter 1993:82ff. Photographed 1992 American Indian Science and Engineering Conference in Washington D.C., several Navajo participants and student winners.]

Appendix

McCulloch Bros. ASM; AZS. [1930; also Dorothy and Herb McCulloch.]
McFarlane, Lawrence. Contemporary.
McGee, W. J. NAA.
McGibbeny, J. W. NMM, July 1957; AZHi, August 1946. [*Arizona Highways* slides.]
McGinnies, W. G. NNM. [1940s, photographed Senator Marerich in Navajoland.]
McIntosh, Donald. ASM. [In Francis Uplegger Collection.]
McKee, ??. NNM; CON. [1962; Pine Springs classroom.]
McKinney, Durwood. NAPHS. <ca. 1920–1940>.
McKittrick, Margaret. MNM—5; NMSRA. [Also known as Mrs. Norris Burge, field investigator for Eastern Association on Indian Affairs, later to became National Association.]
McLaughlin and Co. [See Marshall, 1948. Agency contracted to *Collier's*.]
McLaughlin, Herb and Dorothy. AZS; AZHi, August 1968.
McNitt, Frank. MNM; NMSRA; NMM. [See McNitt, 1962.]
McPhee, John C. NNM; NA. <1930s–1960s>. [Publicity, sheep dipping, propaganda, draft and conscription photographs in BIA archive.]
Meagher, Joseph. AZHi, August 1967.
Mearns, [Means??] E. A. NAA. [1890s.]
Measelle, Bill. SDM—291. <1940s–1950s>. [Schoolteacher, vacationer; Navajo Mountain.]
Melander, L. M. and Bro. [1880–1886; Chicago company that issued several Southwest Indian stereo sets, including photography of Hiester and of Brown.]
Merkel, William. [See Stirling, 1961; Seventh-Day Adventist missionary.]
Merriam, Douglas. Contemporary. [See Zolbrod, 1995.]
Mickle and Jones. USAMI. [1895, Fort Wingate studio.]
Middleton, Mark. MNA. [MNA staff photographer, 1975–1984.]
Milo ??. NMSRA. [Santa Fe photographer; public events.]
Miller, Henry A. NMSRA. [Perhaps New Mexico Department of Development photographer.]
Miller A. HNAI; NAA. [1890s; pirated many Wittick and Randall photos. See Fleming and Luskey, 1986:241.]
Miller, Joseph. NPSWACC; AZHi, January 1943. [See Miller, 1941.]
Milner, ??. NMM, January 1933.
Mindeleff, Cosmos. HNAI; NAA. [1890s.]
Minkler, Sam. UNMNSS. [Some video.] [N]
Mishler, Calvin, and Horace H. Walker. NAA; MNM. [1908, Gallup studio. See Rudisill, 1973:42.]
Mitchell, Percy. WM. [ca. 1981.] [N]?
Mollhausen, H. H. ASM.
Monsen, Frederick. HNAI; LOC; NAA; SDM; SWM—12; HUN—ca. 54. [1865–1929. See Fleming and Luskey, 1986:241; Bush and Mitchell, 1994:307.]
Monserratt, Pat. [See Osinski, 1987; Root Resources.]
Montezuma, Carlos/Doris Collester. NAA [Artists, probably collectors only.]
Moon, Carl E. (also spelled by him "Karl"). HUN—ca. 47. [1878–1948. Represented in most archives. El Tovar Studio at Grand Canyon (many noted with Fred Harvey copyright), 1904–1910; AMNH purchased a portion of his collection from an exhibition there, 1910; commissioned to Huntington Library for photographs and paintings (sold to illustrate color in photographs), 1914–1915. Postcards listed as K. Moon & Co. See Rudisill, 1973:43; Bush and Mitchell, 1994:217, 308.]
Mooney, James. HNAI; NAA; AC; SDM. <1890s>. [1861–1921. See Rudisill, 1973:43; Jacknis, 1990; Kavanagh, 1993.]
Moore, Terrance. [See Gordon, 1973.]
Mora, Jo. NAU; HM. <1904-06>. [1876–1950s?; California artist. Photos of Gallup Fair; several daytime photos of Nightway.]
Morgan, Barbara. <1920s–1930s>. [Photographed in Navajoland; *In American Grain*].
Morgan, Margaret. [1926– ; Princeton, NJ photographer. See Bush and Mitchell, 1994:284, 308.]
Morgan, Rose. [Journalist, photographer, filmmaker, on staff of TV station in Farmington

Appendix

NM. Hosts program on Navajo.] [N]
Morgan, William. LAB; VSP.
Morris, Earl CCP [1924, workmen at Canyon del Muerto, ceremony at Newcomb].
Morrow, Don. NA. <1940s–1966>. [BIA archive (education); see Thompson, 1975. Worked on ciné material in 1944 with Tad Nichols and Fred C. Clark on Indian health; see *Rocky Mountain Empire Magazine*, 13 August 1950.]
Muench, Joseph. UAZ; AZHi, September 1939. [*Arizona Highways* slides; Petley postcard, Phoenix; Exxon travel club magazine, *Vista*, Spring 1983. Some Muench images claimed by Mike Roberts.]
Muench, David. UAZ; AZHi, August 1976. [Exxon travel club magazine, *Vista*, Spring 1983.]
Muench, Emil. [Smith-Southwestern postcard, Tempe.]
Muir, Gertrude Hill. AZS. [1909–1981. Librarian, MNM, perhaps only collector.]
Mullan R. (Reed?) HM. [Contemporary crafts photographer.]
Mullarky, W. Tom. MNM; WM; NTM; UNMM; SWM; AZS. [Gallup studio, in most Southwestern archives. Many postcards of Navajo subjects. See Frink, 1968.]
Munk, Joseph Amasa. SWM—46. [1912. See SWM Leaflet #16, "Southwest Sketches."]
Munson, L. [See Osinski, 1987; Root Resources.]
Murkett, Delaine. [1994 IAIA student exhibition.] [N]
Musser, Linda. MNA. [1930s. Took, along with Lillian Reichard, many of the photographs in the MNA Reichard and Staples albums.]
Muth, Vesta. [See Stirling, 1961; Seventh-Day Adventist.]
Mygatt, Peter. LOC. [Santa Fe; with Kafer, 1952, photographed for New Mexico Department of Welfare.]
Nagelman, Tony. Contemporary. [American Indian College Fund brochure.]
Naswood, Evangelita. [See Hubbard, 1994:60.] [N]
Natonabah, Paul. HNAI; NMM, August 1993. [1944– ; *Navajo Times* staff photographer. See Bush and Mitchell, 1994:271, 308.] [N]
Nawrocki Stock Photo. [Osinski, 1987.]
Needham, C. E. (and Mrs.). SWM—2. ["Navajo who stood trial."]
Neel, David. [See Neel, 1994.]
Nelson, Johnny. [See Worth and Adair, 1972.] [N]
Nelson, Otto. DAM?? [ca. 1914.]
Newcomb, Franc. WM; MNM. [See Newcomb, 1964.]
Newcomer, E. D. HM. [*Arizona Republic* photographer.]
Nez, Bethany. [See Hubbard, 1994:67, 71.] [N]
Nichols, Tad. AHS; UUAZ: AZHi, August 1946. [Tucson, 1940s. Navajo education, health. Cameraman for Fred C. Clark on Navajo ciné production. See Morrow, above.]
Nicholson, Grace. PMH; MNM. [Pasadena, 1912. Perhaps Peabody employee. Photographed and collected for Tozzer.]
Niehuis, Charles. ASM. [Perhaps collector only.]
Noel, H. B. NMSRA. [Early trader.]
Nohl, Mark. [1950– . NMM staff photographer since 1973.]
Nordenskiold, Gustaf. NMSRA; NPSWACC. [1891.]
North, Charles. NAA. [Chicago, 1952. Atchison, Topeka, & Santa Fe Railway; local fairs.]
Northrop, Jack J. MNM; AZHi, June 1940. [Whipple, AZ.]
Northup, Steve. [Secondary photographer, *National Geographic Magazine*, December 1972.]
Notah, James. NA. [BIA archive.]
Nusbaum, Jesse. MNM; MAI; NAA. [1887–1975. See Rudisill, 1973:44–45. 1915 photographs for La Fonda. Taught T. Parkhurst.]
Odyssey Productions. [Chicago. See Osinski, 1987.]
O'Hara, Geoffrey. LOC. [New York; 1914.]
Olop, Stephen. DMNH. [ca. 1913; federal employee.]
Olson, Marie (Le Tourneau). NAU. [Initially nurse at Tuba City (1919); some photographs of return trip many years later.]

Oppen, Lucy. NNM. [Helped Milton Snow (probably not a photographer).] [N]?
Orchard, William C. MAI. <from 1900–??>. [??–1948. Supported Department of Anthropology, MAI. Collaborated with G. Pepper.]
O'Sullivan, Timothy H. [1840–1882. Copies in most major collections. Photographer on 1873 Wheeler expedition (west of 100th meridian). See Rudisill, 1973:45; Frink, 1968; Snyder, 1981; Horan, 1966; Newhall, 1966.]
Otizen, Dick (Fred??). MAI.
Pack, John. SDM. [ca. 1975; see Pack, n.d.]
Page, Susanne. [See Page, 1989. Susanne "Paige" in Mayberry-Lewis, 1992; Woodhead, 1993:129; see Susan Anderson above.]
Palfi, Marion. CCP. <1967–1969>. [1907–1978. See Linquist-Cock, 1983; Sorgenfrei and Peters, 1984; Coleman, 1993.] F.
Pancoast, Chalmers Lowell. NMM, June, September 1950.
Parker, ?? UMP. [San Diego studio.]
Parker, Brian. [See Osinski, 1987; Tom Stack Associates.]
Parker, Kathryn. [See Parker, 1991:52.]
Parkhurst, T. Harmon. MNM; HNAI; WM; SWM. [1930s–1952. See Keegan, 1990.] F.
Parks, Betty. NAPHS.
Parrin, Edwin O. [Listed in Anthony catalog, "chief of Navajo," 1862 (date undoubtedly too early)—perhaps commissioner of Ute?]
Pattison, S. F. ASM. [1914, Kayenta. Professor, University of Minnesota.]
Pennington, William. WM; MNA; NPSWACC. [1875—ca. 1939; Worked for Army at Fort Wingate. Studio in Durango; partner with Rowland, also Updike. See Rudisill, 1973:46; Frink, 1968; Dobyns and Euler, 1972, 1977. Claimed by Carpenter, 1915.] F.
Pepper, George. HNAI; MAI; UNMM; PMH. <1890s-1904>. [1873–1924. Chaco. See Keegan, 1990. Some Richard Wetherill attributed to Pepper.]
Peri, David. [See Gill, 1979; American Indian Film Project, 1963.]
Peterson, Jim. <late 1960s>. [See Sandner, 1979.]
Petley, Robert. [See Petley postcards.]
Photo Source International. [See Osinski, 1987.]
Photri. [See Osinski, 1987.]
Pierce, C. C. SWM; HUN; LOC. [1853–1946; Los Angeles studio. In most Western archives. See Fleming and Luskey, 1986:242. Most attributed Pierce are probably G. W. James (purchased in 1901), but Pierce did also photograph. See Kurutz, 1978.]
Pillsbury, Dorothy. MNM. [New Mexico author, probably collector (of Snow).]
Pinkerton, Charlotte. LAB. [1910s, studio in Chicago. Slide work for the Cincinnati Museum—probably not photographer of Navajo slides.]
Poley, H. S. NAA. [ca. 1864-1949; Colorado Springs (1912-1913). See Rudisill, 1973:47; Denver Public Library.]
Poling, Lesley. NMM, January 1980.
Porter, Milton. NAA. [Albuquerque studio 1908; sometimes with H. Neff. See Rudisill, 1973:47–48.]
Post, Helen M. NA; AC; NAA. [1906–1979; New York City. See Leighton and Leighton,1944; La Farge, 1940. BIA archive, Indian Service, schools. See Parezo and Babcock, 1988:120.] F.
Post, Louis. CHS. [Dispatch expedition, 1902.]
Powell, Maj. John Wesley. [1870s. "Major Powell's Stereo Views."]
Preston, Sheldon. [College student intern, *Navajo Nation Today.*] F. [N]
Price, Gene. HNAI; NNM; NA; MNM. <1950s>. [BIA archive. Successor to Snow. See Bosch above.] F. [N]?
Price, Robert C. NAA; LOC. [1906; New Mexico State professor. See Rudisill, 1973:48.]
Proper, ??. UNMM. F.
Putnam, ??. AC. [Putnam & Valentine, photographers, Los Angeles. Worked for Fred Harvey, Grand Canyon.]

Appendix

Purviance, C. E. MNA; SWM. [1940s; MNA staff photographer.]
Raffins ??. UCR. [Perhaps Raven?? 1905; Grand Canyon; Keystone.]
Rainer, Howard. Contemporary. [Taos Pueblo photographer.]
Randall, A. Frank. NAA. [1880s. Frequently confused with Wittick. See Fleming and Luskey, 1986:242; Rudisill, 1973:48–49.] F.
Rau, William. HM. [Philadelphia; confused with Wittick.]
Raymenton, ??. SDM.
Redman, C. E. NMSRA. [Albuquerque; commercial photographer.]
Reed, Allen C. AZHi, August 1950.
Reed, Roland W. NAA; LOC; SDM; SWM. [See Fleming and Luskey, 1986:242; 1993:99ff.]
Reichard, Gladys. NMM, March 1939, August 1954; MNA; UNMM. [See Parezo and Babcock, 1988:51; Reichard, 1936, 1939.] F.
Reichard, Lillian. MNA. [Photographer; took most photographs for Dezba series for sister, Gladys. See Reichard, 1939.]
Reiter, Winifred. NMM, April 1939.
Richardson, Gladwell. NAU; NAPHS; AZHi, August 1968. [Trader; see Richardson, 1986.]
Richmond, Edward O. MAI; SWM; CHS. [1897; some claimed may be Wittick. See Rudisill/Faris, 15 Feb 1992.] F.
Riddle, J. R. MNM. [1880s; see Rudisill, 1973:49–50. Itinerant, following railway.]
Ridgeway, Ryder. AZS. [1900.]
Rinehart, Robert H. [Phoenix, early 1900s. "Views of Arizona and Salt River Valley."]
Rittenhouse, Jack D. SWM. [ca. 1947.]
Roan, Toni. [See Hubbard, 1994:72.] [N]
Robert, ??. NMM, July 1949; NMM, March 1967.
Roberts, H. Armstrong. NA; AMNH; MNM; NMM, January 1939. [See Osinski, 1987; BIA archives.]
Roberts, John. LAB; VSP; HNAI:500. [See also Roberts, 1951.] F.
Roberts, Mike. UAZ. [Postcard image claimed by Joseph Mueuch.]
Robinson, B. H. ASM; AZS. [1920s.]
Robinson, Dorothy Fulwiler. AZS. [1895– . Librarian, AZS; wrote several books that remained unpublished. Wife or relative of B. H. Robinson.]
Robinson, H. F. MNM—16. [c. 1865–1956; see Rudisill, 1973:50. Also photographed Dixon on 1913 Wanamaker expedition; see Bush and Mitchell, 1994:310.]
Rodgers, J. William. NMM, March 1931. [Accompanied B. I. Staples and Navajo on trip east.]
Roessel, Monty. Contemporary, NPM passim; NMM passim; HMCNAP. [Photojournalist; see Roessel, 1995.] F. [N]
Roessel, Robert A., Jr. HNAI. [See Roessel, 1980.]
Rogers, D. A. NTM. [Helped Snow, probably not a photographer.]
Rogers, L. W. NA. [1950; BIA archive, agricultural methods.]
Root Resources. [See Osinski, 1987; J. Blank; P. Monsarratt; L. Munson.]
Root, Lindsay F. NMM, February 1953.
Rose, G. L. SWM—2. [California; Camera Club. Contemporary with James, Maude, Vroman. See Hathaway, 1990:78.]
Rosen, P. B. HNAI. [1980s; Uranium poisoning.]
Rosenthal, S. H., Jr. AZHi, August 1967.
Rosenzweig, Janine. LAB; VSP.
Rosenak, Chuck. NMM, August 1987. [Santa Fe collector; Rosenak and Rosenak, 1994.]
Rottloff, Blanche Miller. MNM. [–1993; 1920s, amateur photographer who lived with Navajo for periods.]
Rowland, ??. [1914; studio in Durango, CO. See Pennington, above.]
Rubenstein, Meridel. Contemporary. [See Rubenstein, 1977. Instructor in photography IAIA.]
Rumel, Hal. USHS. [See *New York Times*, 28 Dec 1969.]
Running, John. Contemporary. AZHi, September 1978. [Flagstaff; photographed for United

States Department of Agriculture, 1970s. See Osinski, 1987; Running, 1985; Bennett, 1987. Navajo relocation photographs. Instructor, Santa Fe Photography Workshops.]
Running, Helen Lau. [See Hooker, 1991.]
Ruohomaa, Kosti. NMM, August 1942. [Photograph repeatedly used in advertising for Gallup Intertribal Ceremonial.]
Russell, Frank. PMH. [1900; mostly Keams Canyon and Hopi country.]
Russell, Gail. NMM, August 1989.
Russell, R. W. [Partner of Wittick. See Fleming and Luskey, 1986:243; Rudisill, 1973:51.]
Rymes, Marguerite. NMM, September 1984. [Missionary among Jicarilla in 1930s; Navajo appear in article about Jicarilla Apache by Joanne Rijmes.]
Salvador, Jim. NMM, April 1981.
Samuelson, Jon [see *El Palacio* 75(3):26. 1968].
Sanborn, ??. UNMM. F.
Sandlin, Scott. NMM, December 1984. [1980s; Albuquerque journalist, covered Gilpin lawsuit. See Bailey and Bailey, 1986:215.]
San Juan Studio. NAA. [1900s; perhaps run by Goodman?]
Santistien, Billy. <ca. 1967>. [Journalist?]
Santa Fe Railway. MNM; NMSRA; WM; NTM. [Many photographers; probably many photos by Simpson.]
Sarbo, ??. [Commercial photographer. See Bixler, 1992; slide series widely published.]
Sassaman, William H. MNM; NAA. [1929; see Stevens, below.]
Saunders, Charles F. SWM; HUN. [Also known as CFS.]
Savage, C. R. [1832–1909; Salt Lake City studio used by W.H. Jackson to produce prints in 1870. See Fleming and Luskey, 1986:107, 234; Rudisill, 1973:52; Bush and Mitchell, 1994:311. May have been copied by C. W. Carter.]
Savony. NAA. [Studio photographer unspecified—Lucy H. Baird?]
Saylor, Galen H. SDM. [1978 Gallup Ceremonial.]
Sayles, E. B. ASM. ca. <1939–1945>.
Seib, Al. Contemporary. [*Los Angeles Times* photographer.]
Sekaer, ??. NA. [BIA archives; 1940.]
Scherman, ??. NAA. [With E. H. Maude?]
Scheinbaum, David. Contemporary. [Santa Fe gallery owner; see Scheinbaum, 1987.]
Schneider, Jack. HNAI. [1970s; photographed for United States Department of Agriculture.]
Schmuckebier, ??. UAZ. [1930s; photos of Reverend Smith and 1930 census. Photographer or collector?]
Scholder, Veda. [See Stirling, 1961; Seventh-Day Adventist missionary.]
Schroeder, Al. NMSRA. [NPS historian; also collector.]
Schwemberger, Simeon. MNA—81; MNM; LOC; SDM; SWM. <1904-1910>. [1867–1931; Gallup studio (1908–1911). See Long, 1992; Rudisill, 1973:52; Keegan, 1990. Produced 73 postcard views in 1909; St. Michaels has 400 glass plates, and ca. 50 glass plates and similar number of negatives are in Guadagnoli shop in Gallup.]
Scott, B. L. [1924; Albuquerque photographer? See Hanna and Hanna.] F.
Scott, Julian. UMP. [1890; with John Donaldson, special agent of the 1890 census. Said to have taken several photos, but may have bought most of them from Wittick and others.]
Seib, Al. Contemporary [*Los Angeles Times* photographer].
Sells, Cato Jr. NNM. [1971; Navajo Service.]
Seltzer, Carl. PMH. [1934; physical anthropology.]
Shaffer, Douglas L. HM. [Stills from video, "Seasons of the Navajo," with Chancey and Dorothy Neboyia.]
Shaffer, Elizabeth. NMM, February 1942.
Shepard, ??. [Cited as artist or photographer on early Barboncito photograph in Blackmore collection (here attributed to Wolfenstein); see NAA 55,766; probably only tinted print.]
Shepardson, Mary. [See Shepardson, 1986.]
Shindler, A. Zeno. NAA. [1823–1899; Washington studio photographer. See Fleming and

Appendix

Luskey, 1986:231. Attribution of photographs of Navajo to Shindler in error, despite appearance in his 1869 catalog.]
Shufeldt, R. W. HNAI:500; NAA. [1880s; photographed with Wittick. See Rudisill, 1973:53.]
Simpson, William H. HNAI; NAA; MNM; LAB. [1901; publicity director, Atchison, Topeka & Santa Fe. See Rudisill, 1973:53.]
Sipes, Paul, W. NA. [BIA archive; 1952.]
Sisson, ??. MNA. [T. C. Flaherty Collection.]
Skrondahl, ??. NMM, July 1954; UNMM. [Albuquerque photographer.]
Slinky, Leann. [See Hubbard, 1994:62.] [N]
Smillie, Thomas. W. NAA; MNM; AC. [1904; Smithsonian; probably Washington studio photographer. See Fleming and Luskey, 1986.]
Smith, Albert G. MNA. [Staff photographer 1966–1968.]
Smith, Lillian, W. MNA—37. [Prior to 1933.]
Smith, William A. [See Rudisill, 1973:55; Fleming and Luskey, 1986:70, 243. One of official photographers at Bosque Redondo treaty signing, 1868; no surviving photographs.]
Smith, W.M.L. NPSWACC. [1936.]
Snow, Milton (Jack). NNM—13,000; CON; UNMM; SDM; NA; MNM; WM; NMSRA; MNA; AZS; UMP; AZHi, June 1943. <1937-1958>; [BIA/Soil Conservation photographer; Wide World Photos, Inc.; MNA staff photographer, October 1934–1935. See Thompson. 1975; Parman, 1976. Among those listed as assistants are Lucy Oppen, Tom Allen, Jim Thomas, H. C. Lockett, Marie Martin, Mike Brodi, Sombrero, D. A. Rogers.]
Snyder, Elizabeth, Dr. NAA; MNA. <1903-1905>. [Photographs of Begging Gods, Nightway. Same photographs claimed by Daniel H. Mitchell (Mitchell, 1910) to be from Charles Day.] F.
Southern Navajo Reservation (Snow??). NMM, October 1933.
Southern Pacific Railway Co. NA. [BIA archive.]
Spencer, Virginia. [See Jett and Spencer, 1981.]
Spencer, Katherine (Halpern). [See Parezo and Babcock, 1988:60.]
Spillane, Marilyn. NMM, April 1981.
Sparks, Gene. AZHi, August 1943.
Stack, Tom & Associates. [Photo agency; see Burckhalter, Parker.]
Standard Oil Co. NA. [BIA archive.]
Staples, B. MNA. [Trader; many photographs in family albums actually taken by Linda Musser.]
Steege, Dorothy. NAPHS. [ca. 1900.]
Steen, Charles. NPSWACC. [National Park Service employee; 1950 Navajo laborers in Canyon de Chelly.]
Stevens, Alden. MNM—ca. 13. [1929; see Sassaman, above.]
Stevenson, M. C. NAA; MNM. [1850–1915; see Rudisill, 1973:55.]
Stewart, Dorothy. MNM—ca. 5.
Stirling, Betty. [See Stirling, 1961.]
Stockman, J. [See Cummings, 1952.]
Stoffel, Fred. NA. [ca. 1969; BIA archive, education.]
Stone, Les. [Sygma/Photo News, photographed Veteran's Day, November 1992.]
Stone, R. H. MAI. [1920s.]
Stowell, H. W. MNM. [Albuquerque commercial photographer; postcards.]
Stravis, ??. MNA—2. [1955, Shonto AZ.]
Strodtbeck, Fred. LAB; VSP.
Sumner, ??. NNM. [1941; Selective Service in Navajoland.]
Supplee, Charles. ASM. [See Supplee, 1971.]
Swartz, W. Ray. SWM. [1898.]
Swinnerton, Gretchen Parshall. MNA. [Pre- and post–World War II.] F.
Switzer, W. H. NAPHS. [ca. 1910–1950; Willow Springs Trading Post.]
Tapaha, Carmelita. UNMNSS; HMCNAP. [Exhibited at Millicent Rogers Museum.] [N]
Tapaha, J. NNM. [1986; Bureau of Roads; photographed Jack Snow.] [N]
Tapahe, Loren. [1993; publicist, journalist, editor of *Window Rock Scene*.] [N]

Taylor, Arthur. MNM—7.
Taylor, James Earl. NAA. F.
Teiwes, Helga. ASM; SDM. [ASM staff photographer; see Parezo and Babcock, 1988:194; Weaver, 1974; Lindig, 1991.] F.
Tepfer, Gary. NCC. [1993 exhibition at Ned Hatathli Museum; from Utah.]
Thayer, Frank S. UNMM; SDM; MNM. [Denver photo publisher, postcards. Perhaps not a photographer.]
Thompson, Ernest. UNMNSS. F. [N]
Thompson, George W. NMSRA; UNMM; UNM; NMM, July 1949 and many subsequent. [Perhaps New Mexico Department of Development photographer; postcards.]
Thompson, Hernandez. SWM. [Maybe George W. Thompson?] F.
Thurlow, James. [1874–1879; Manitou Springs, CO photographer. Hayden Survey. See Frink, 1968; Rudisill, 1973:57.] F.
Tietgens, Rolf. NMM, October 1943 (cover).
"Tin Horn." ASM. [1914; earliest Navajo photographer, probably near Kayenta. Also photographed by Law in 1920.] F. [N]
Tisinger, Richard. NNM. [ca. 1930.] F.
Tomkins, Kent.
Toadlena, Brent. IAIA. [IAIA student exhibition.] [N]
Townshend, Richard Baxter. RAI. <1903>. [British photographer, mostly at Jemez and Hopi (photographed Navajo there); collector.] F.
Tozzer, Alfred. PMH. [1901; see Tozzer, 1902, 1909.]
Trimble, Stephen. NPM, Fall 1992. [1950– ; see Trimble, 1986, 1993; Shaffer, 1987; Bush and Mitchell, 1994:313.]
Trockur, Fr. Emanuel. [See Long, 1992:3; St. Michaels priest, took photographs along with Schwemberger.]
Trueblood, ??. SWM—13.
Tschopik, Harry. HNAI; LAB; VSP; PMH. [See Kluckhohn, Hill, Kluckhohn, 1971.]
Tsinajinnie, Andy. NNM. [1937; artist. Helped Snow. Uncertain if he photographed or not.] [N]
Tsinhnahjinnie, Hulleah (Helen). HMCNAP. [1954– . Vallejo, CA; artist; widely exhibited. See Bush and Mitchell, 1994:277, 313.] F. [N]
Tsosie, Derek. [See Hubbard, 1994:41.] [N]
Tsosie, Keith. [See Hubbard, 1994:42.] [N]
Tsostie, Betty. [1993 IAIA student exhibition.] F. [N]
Tsotsie, Maxine. [See Worth and Adair, 1972. Sister of Mary Jane] [N]
Tsotsie, Mary Jane. [See Worth and Adair, 1972. Sister of Maxine]. [N]
Tsotsie, Will. UNMNSS. [N]
Turner, A. E. NAA. [1960s; Bureau of Reclamation—Glen Canyon.]
Tucker, Mrs. John (Helen Hendry Tucker, Dee Dee Tucker). MNM. [1946.]
Tucker, ??. NNM. [Photographed Wingate schools (perhaps a teacher).]
Turner, Christy. MNA. [MNA staff photographer.]
TransWorld Airlines. NMM, July 1950; MNM.
Twitchell, Ralph. MNM. [Probably collector only.]
Two Bears, Davina R. [See Two Bears, 1995.] [N]
Twomey, Arthur.
Underhill, Ruth. [See Underhill, 1953.]
Underwood and Underwood. UCR; MNM; MAI. [Underwoods actually took Navajo photographs between 1903–1905. See Keystone, above.] F.
Undritz, Lt. F. R. MNM. [United States Army, Nogales AZ (stationed at Fort Wachuka).]
United States Army Signal Corps. NMM, June 1943. [Probably Snow photograph.]
Uplegger, Francis. AZS. [1939; collection only?]
Valdez, Leroy. UNMNSS; HMCNAP. [N]
Van Doren, Wilma. NMM, August 1958; MNM.
Vanderbilt, Paul. NAA. [1920s; photographer?]

Appendix

Van Devanter, D. W. MNM—2. [Gallup?]
Van Luchene, Bob. UUAZ. [Commercial photographer; Petley Studio, Phoenix.]
Van Ness Seymour, Tryntje. [See Shaffer, 1987.]
Van Oosting, R. L. WM. [1927.]
Vassilopoulos, S. G. Contemporary. [Commercial—Southwest Indian Foundation (Gallup) 1995 calendar.]
Vento, Joseph. NMM, March 1987.
Vernon, David C. MAI. [Large collections, presented to MAI by Laurence S. Rockefeller. All photographs taken by others. Probably collector only.]
Verplanck, James D. [See Verplanck, 1934.]
Vestal, Paul. LAB; VSP (?).
Vicenti, Dan. HNAI. [1960s; community health specialist.] [N]
Victor, Manuel. ASM.
Vogt, Evon, Jr. LAB; VSP.
Vogt, Evon, Sr. MNM. [Family photos, Ramah, etc.]
Voth, Henry. SWM. [Missionary, anthropologist.]
Vroman, Adam C. LAC—33; SWM—115; SDM—6. <1895–1904>. [1856–1916; see Fleming and Luskey, 1986: 244; Mahood, 1961; Webb and Weinstein, 1973; Keegan 1990; Bush and Mitchell, 1994:209, 314.]
Vroman, Harry.
Wagner, Sallie (Lippincott). MNM—ca. 75; NMSRA; HM. [Mostly Wide Ruins area; many arts and crafts.]
Waite, C. B. SWM. [1893; Los Angeles photographer. Traded photos with Maude.]
Walian, W. W. ASM.
Walker, John. UUAZ. [1970.]
Wallace, John D. HNAI. [1960s; chapter house dedications.] [N]
Wallace, Norman G. AZHi, June 1940.
Walpole, Alton. AZHi, August 1976.
Walt, Henry. NMM, November 1986. [Archaeologist; Alamo Navajo.]
Walter, Barbara. SDM—23. [1981; Canyon de Chelly. See Daniels and Dodson.]
Walters, Anna. NCC. [1992; Canyon del Muerto.]
Walton, W. W. AZS. [1930s; Halseth Collection.]
Wanamaker, Rodman. AMNH; WHM; HM; MAI. [1910s; financed the Dixon photographs of the Wanamaker expeditions. Most attributions to Wanamaker are by Dixon or others.]
Wapaha, Kendra. [See Hubbard, 1994:64.] [N]
Warner, Paul. MAI. F.
Warren, H. W., and Beatrice Warren. HM. [1930s; traders; Kayenta and Cameron. Beatrice also traveled with Louise I. Marshall.] F.
Warrens, Mr. and Mrs. Keith. NAU. [1900s; traders; Cedar Ridge, Red Lake, Tuba City AZ.]
Wasley, W. W. ASM. [1950s; see Bailey and Bailey, 1986.]
Watchman, Louise. [See Berlant and Kahlenberg, 1991.] [N]?
Waters, Frank. UNM. [Southwest author; collector, primarily.]
Watkins, Robert. NMM, July 1949. [Gallup Intertribal Ceremonial.]
Weber, David. HNAI. [1950s; photographed for Santa Fe *New Mexican*.]
Watson, John. NNM. [BIA photographer.]
Weed, Edw. F. MAI—ca. 6. [Some photographs dated 1867; attributed to him and presented by him. Some look like Gaige photographs or other earliest photographers—some identical, some unique.]
Weidner, Tesbah??. [Heard Museum; possibly photographer or filmmaker.] [N]
Weightman, George A. LAB. [1887; Albuquerque; one photo of weaver.]
Weston, Edward. [Many landscapes in Navajoland.]
Wetherill Bros. MNM—1.
Wetherill, John. MNA; ASM [Kayenta area; many photographs still in family].
Wetherill, Richard. UNM [Chaco Canyon area].

Werntz, Carl. MNM. [Artist; partner with Simpson.]
Wexler, Ira. [See Wexler, 1993.]
Wharton, James George. SWM—thousands. [G. Wharton James—see above.]
Wheeler, Chris. [1993; cinéphotographer, "How the West was Lost" (Discovey Channel and KUSA-TV). See Hutchison above.]
Wheeler, D. N. NAU. [1901; studio, Grand Junction CO.] F.
Wheelwright, Mary Cabot. WM. [1930s principally.]
Whitesinger, Anna Boyd. IAIA. [1946– ; see Boyd; Bush and Mitchell, 1994:9, 258, 315.] F. [N]
Wilbur, Richard. NMM, October 1953.
Williams, Lee. NMM, May 1984. [Journalist.]
Williams, Shane. [See Hubbard, 1994:89.] [N]
Williams, Wende. [1994 IAIA student exhibition.] [N]
Williamson, ??. UNMM. F.
Willoughby, C. C. PMH. [1913; photographed with R. Fuller.]
Willis, J. R. NAA; LOC; MNM; ASM. [Gallup studio, widespread postcard photographs; also postcards as Willis-Barnes. See Rudisill, 1973:62; Keegan, 1990.]
Wilson, Elita. WM; NMM, July 1950. [Collection at WM.]
Wilson, Fred. AZS—2. [1940.]
Wilson, H. K. NAA. [1916; albums, photographer?]
Wilson, Paul A. MNM.
Wilson, Tom. NA. [BIA archive, education.]
Wimar, Charles (Carl). MNM. [1828–1862; claims are that Wimar took famous 1868 Barboncito series of photographs, but he undoubtedly did not. Originals at St. Louis Museum of Art.] F.
Winsor, Romana Hill. UAZ. [1961.]
Winters, Charles. [With Jean Simonelli, currently working on photographic book.]
Winters, Wayne. NMM, March 1951.
Wittick, Ben. MNM. <1880s–1890s>. [1845–1903; see Rudisill, 1973:62–63; Fleming and Luskey, 1986:245; Olivas, 1970; Broder, 1990; Bush and Mitchell, 1994:119, 123, 125, 316. Partnerships with R. W. Russell and A. F. Randall (?). Copied Hillers and others. Studios in Fort Wingate and Gallup.] F.
Wittick, Archie. MNM. [Son of Ben; see Rudisill, 1973: 62.]
Wolcott, Marion. NMM, May 1960. [Navajos at Jemez.]
Wolf, Joy. CCP—4. [1985; Big Mountain, Tuba City.]
Wolfenstein, Valentin. MAI. [1868; Bosque Redondo. See Rudisill, 1973:63; Fleming and Luskey, 1986:70, 245.] F.
Wood, C. M. MAI; ASM. <1916–1925>.
Woods, Betty. NMM, July, September 1939, 1950, 1951. [Probably took own photographs to illustrate articles. Husband (Clee) may have taken some.]
Woolf, Paul J. WM; MAI; AMNH—ca.100; LAB—ca. 185. [New York City commercial photographer. See Kluckhohn, Hill, Kluckhohn, 1971:180.] F.
Worth, Sol. [See Worth and Adair, 1972.]
Wright, Don. AZHi, July 1970.
Wright, Ralph. DMNH. [1980s; see also Gary Hall above.]
Wunder, Charlie. HNAI; SWM; AC. [1940s, Denver photographer; see Frink, 1968.]
Wurmfeld, Hope. [1939– ; New York City photographer and artist. See Bush and Mitchell, 1994, 269, 316.]
Wyaco, Virgil. [Navajo consultant on film "Navajo Moon"; perhaps not a photographer.] [N]
Wyckoff, Jerome. [See Osinski, 1987.]
Wyman, Leland. HNAI; WM. [See Kluckhohn, Hill, Kluckhohn, 1971:245, 259. Large personal collections.]
Yazzie, Alfred. [Videocam recording for Navajo Studies Program, Rough Rock Community School.] F. [N]
Yazzie, Herbert. [1965– ; while BYU student published photographs in student magazine. See

Appendix

Bush and Mitchell, 1994:281, 317.] [N]
Yazzie, Jerry. [Sports photography for *Navajo Times* (cf. 16 July 1992).] [N]
Yazzie, Shanna. [See Hubbard, 1994:88.] [N]
Yazzie, Venaya Jaye. [1994 IAIA student exhibition.] [N]
Young, Alan K. NPM, March 1991.
Young, Robert. NA. [1960s; BIA archive, education.]
Young, Stuart M. MNA; NAU. [1908- .] F.
Zehrt, Jack. AZHi, August 1950.

Chart 2a. Color slide companies with photographs of Navajo people
1. *Arizona Highways* "Color Classics." *Arizona Highways* made available slides of most of its color photographs. Navajo indexed under IN designation. [cf. Chuck Abbott, Laura Gilpin, George Hight, J. H. McGibbeny, Ray Manley, Joseph Muench, Allen C. Reed.]
2. Atkins Travel Slides, Inc.
3. Bradshaw Color Studio (Sedona AZ).
4. Jack Breed.
5. Keystone View Co. (Westwood NJ?) [Underwood and Underwood.]
6. Pacific Steropticon Co. (Los Angeles CA). [Many of F. Maude's lantern slides.]
7. Pana Vue. [All Wheelwright sandpainting slides, plus Monument Valley scenes.]
8. Roben Co. (Sedona AZ). [Set at SDM.]
9. Sarbo. "Sarbo-Seens" (Albuquerque NM).

Chart 2b. Postcard companies with cards imaging Navajo people
1. American Indian Contemporary Arts, San Francisco, CA (Tsinhnahjinnie).
2. Amon Carter Museum, Ft. Worth, TX (Curtis).
3. Arizona Color Card Co., Phoenix, AZ (Bill Bass) (UUAZ).
4. Aztec Curio Co., Albuquerque, NM (AC, Mazzulla Collection).
5. Azusa, Denver, CO (Vroman).
6. Babbitt Brothers Trading Co., Flagstaff, AZ.
7. Balke R. L. Indian Trading Co., Phoenix, AZ (SDM).
8. Beautyway, Flagstaff, AZ (Wittick, H. Caplin, Curtis, Monsen).
9. Geo. Bond & Co., Chicago, IL. Large numbers by several photographers, many ending up in Wanamaker lantern slide collection (UMP).
10. C. T. American Art, Phoenix AZ (?), 1930s.
11. Candelaria Colorgraphics, Albuquerque, NM. Contemporary.
12. Chicago Transparency Co., Chicago, IL. Large numbers by several photographers, many ending up in Wanamaker lantern slide collection (UMP).
13. L. L. Cook, Milwaukee, WI.
14. Detroit Publishing Co., Detroit, MI. Set up and run by W. H. Jackson (some Fred Harvey Co., A. J. Baker, C. Bortell).
15. Detroit Photographic Co., Detroit, MI (1901). (SDM).
16. Dexter Press, Inc., West Nyack, NY (Gilpin).
17. Dexter Press, Pearl River, NY (Fronske) (SDM).
18. Dry River Trading Co., Tucson, AZ (A. W. Chase, W. Pennington) (CHS).
19. Frasher, Pomona, CA (Frasher).
20. Fotofolio, New York, NY (O'Sullivan).
21. Fronske Studio, Flagstaff (Hubbard) (UUAZ).
22. Gilpin Publishing Co., Colorado Springs, CO. Mostly Meriden Gravure (Gilpin).
23. Fred Harvey Co., Kansas City, MO. Some are Detroit Publishing Co. (Karl Moon, Jesse Nusbaum).
24. Williamson-Haffner Co. Denver, CO.
25. Herz Post Cards, San Diego, CA.
26. Harry Herz, Phoenix, AZ.
27. J & O Curio, Santa Fe, NM (HUN, Mary Austin Collection).

Appendix

28 Lollesgard Speciality, Tucson, AZ, 1947 (some Frasher).
29 D. T. Malonee (Phoenix AZ). Produced for Curt Teich Postcards. (LCM).
30 Alfred McGarr Advertising Service, Albuquerque, NM (H Armstrong Roberts).
31 Karl Moon & Co.
32 Mullarky, Gallup, NM (Mullarky).
33 Museum Graphics, Redwood City, CA (Gilpin) (AC).
34 Natural Color Post Card, Milwaukee, WI (E.C. Kroop Co.).
35 Navajo Nation Historical Preservation Department, Window Rock, AZ. Commemorations of Navajo Historical Preservation Week, 1991 (Snow) (NNM).
36 Navajo Tribal Nation Museum, Window Rock, AZ. Co-produced with Beautyway, Flagstaff, AZ (Hillers, Wittick).
37 Newman Post Card Co., Los Angeles and San Francisco, CA (SDM).
38 W. E. Noble, Monument Valley, AZ, ca. 1955 (perhaps Manley).
39 Old Trail News Agency, Santa Fe, NM (New Mexico State Tourist Bureau).
40 Old West Collectors Series, Kustom Quality, El Paso, TX (Wittick, among others) (CHS).
41 Pen-Dike, Durango, CO (W. Pennington).
42 Petley Southwest, Inc., Albuquerque, NM. Contemporary (Jacka, Ellinger).
43 Petley Studios, Phoenix, AZ (Koonce, Josef Muench, Van Luchene) (UUAZ).
44 Bob Petley, Phoenix, AZ.
45 Petley Greetings, Inc., Albuquerque, NM. Postcard with eight Navajo views—each one also subject of distinct individual postal card.
46 C. T. Photochrom. An imprint of Curt Teich Postcards. (LCM).
47 C. T. Photo Colorit. An imprint of Curt Teich Postcards. (LCM).
48 Photo USA Thunderbird Postcards, Williams, AZ. Contemporary (D. Dietrich, J. Muench).
49 Pomegranate Artbooks, San Francisco, CA (Curtis) (LOC).
50 M. Rieder Publishing, Los Angeles, CA. Published in Germany (SDM).
51 Roben Co., Sedona, AZ (UUAZ).
52 Seaich Corp., Salt Lake City, UT. Contemporary.
53 Adolph Selige Co., St. Louis, MO.
54 Smith-Southwestern, Tempe, AZ. Contemporary.
55 Southwest Arts and Crafts, Santa Fe, NM. Some C. T. American Art (Fred Harvey, Jesse Nusbaum).
56 Southwest Post Card Co., Albuquerque, NM (Mullarky, Geo. Thompson, Barnes and Caplin).
57 Simeon Schwemberger, St. Michaels, AZ. Some seventy-three different views.
58 SVE Color Cards, Phoenix AZ (R. Manley, C. Herbert, J. Freeman).
59 H.H. Tammen Co. (also spelled Tanmen). Postcards (Halseth—1930s) (UNMM, CHS, SDM).
60 Curt Teich Postcards (Chicago IL). [C. Abbott, H. Caplin, B. Frasher, E. Henderson, D. Kent, K. Moon, T. Mullarky, G. Thompson, J.R. Willis]. See also C.T. Art Colortone; C. T. Photochrom; C. T. American Art; C. T. Photo Colorit; Curteichcolor.] (LCM).
61 Frank Thayer, Denver, CO, 1906.
62 Thunderbird Postcards, Williams, AZ (D. Dietrich, J. Muench).
63 Utah Parks Co. (WM).
64 Helaine Victoria Press, Martinsville, IN. Contemporary (Biren).
65 Williamson-Haffner, Co., Denver, CO. (WM).
65 J. R. Willis, Inc., Gallup, NM. Babbitt Bros, J. R. Willis, and Southwest Arts and Crafts all had a postcard with the exact same weaving image. Willis-Barnes in some postcards (Willis).

Chart 2c. Commercial stock photograph companies containing photographs of Navajo people
1 Arizona Photographic Associates, Inc., Phoenix, AZ. Indian Tribal Series—cf. Dobyns and Euler, 1972, 1977.
2 Blackstar, New York, NY (M. Roessel).

Appendix

3 Cameramann International, Ltd., New York, NY.
4 Contact Press Images, New York, NY (D. Burnett).
5 Mugwump Studio, Athens, OH (Terry Eiler).
6 Fotowest Picture Agency, Santa Fe, NM.
7 Michal Heron, New York, NY (Michal Heron).
8 Willard Luce, Provo, UT.
9 Nawrocki Stock Photo (J. Apoian).
10 Odyessy Productions (R. Frerck).
11 Photri, New York, NY.
12 Photo Bank, Scottsdale, AZ.
13 Photo Source International, New York, NY.
14 Photo USA (D. Dietrich, J. Mueuch).
15 Publix (J. Freeman).
16 Root Resources (P. Monsarratt, L. Munson, J. Blank).
17 Shostal Associates (R. Manley).
18 Southwest Pictures.
19 Stock Images, Denver, CO.
20 Sygma/Photo News, New York, NY (Les Stone, Larry Gus).
21 Tom Stack Associates (B. Parker, D. Burckhalter).
22 TWYC, Williams, AZ (Thunderbird Postcards).
23 Western Ways Features (C. Herbert).
24 Wide World Photos, Inc. New York, NY (M. Snow).
25 AP/Wide World Photos, New York, NY.

Chart 3. Navajo photographers.
1 Allen, Angie. Formerly head of Navajo Tribal Administration Records—photographer?? F.
2 Anderson, Mike. See Worth and Adair, 1972. F.
3 Arviso, Tom, Jr. *Navajo Times* editor (mostly sports photos). F.
4 Begay, Alberta. See Hubbard, 1994:34, 53. Tse Ho Tso Middle School, Window Rock (1992).
5 Begay, Charlene. See Page, 1989:16. F.
6 Begay, Rudy. IAIA 1993 student exhibition. F.
7 Benally, Susie. See Worth and Adair, 1972. F.
8 Benally, Susanne. Educator, poet, essayist; see Lippard, 1992; IAIA. F.
9 Bennett, Ruby. HMCNAP; UNMNSS; F.
10 Bia, Fred. Studied with Ansel Adams and Cole Weston. See Bia 1983. HMCNAP; F.
11 Bowen, Dennis. Videocam operator, Heard Museum. F.
12 Bowman, Arlene. Filmed "Navajo Talking Picture." F.
13 Boyd, Jesse Long. Married Harry Boyd, trader, mother of Anna Whitesinger. F.
14 Brown, Annette T. Director of Public Television, Salish Kootenai College. Degree from NYU in film and television production. See Tribal College: *Journal of American Indian Higher Education* 6(1), 1994 [24–25].
15 Brown, Norman. Education Department, Chinle. F.
16 Brown, Norman Patrick. Video and photography. Teaches drama and art at Gray Hills school, Tuba City (same as No 15?). F.
17 Carr, Lena. Contemporary Navajo filmmaker. See NMM, November 1988. F.
18 Clah, Al. See Worth and Adair, 1972. F.
19 Crank, Dan L. Contemporary. Poet and photographer, Dennihotso AZ; see Crank, 1988. Photographed at Navajo Nation Fair, Maisels. UNMNSS. F.
20 Cruz, Anna. UNM photographer, may have taught Navajo students (perhaps not Navajo?). F.
21 Damon-Sandoval, Chiristi. 1994 IAIA student exhibition.
22 Daniels, Elton. Exhibited at Millicent Rogers Museum. HMCNAP; UNMNSS; F.
23 Dennetsosi, Hoke. Illustrator, helped Snow (1942); perhaps not a photograher. F.

Appendix

24 Deschinnie, Johnny. Rock Point councilman, *Navajo Times*. F.
25 Deschinny, Janet. See Hubbard,1994:65. Window Rock, AZ (1992).
25 Emerson, Gloria. Educator, IAIA. F.
26 Etcitty, Al. NCC video technician; also photography and ciné. F.
27 Francis, Perry. HMCNAP; F.
28 Francisco, Janelle. See Hubbard, 1994:65, 66. Tse Ho Tso Middle School, Window Rock (1992).
29 Francisco, Nia. See Beck, 1977. Navajo NM. F.
30 Gail, Ida Mary. Worked for Jack Snow, who taught her photography, 1950s. F.
31 Gus, Larry. Los Angeles, freelance photojournalist. Also sometimes spelled Guf. F.
32 Jim, Rex Lee. See Bingham, 1982. F.
33 John, Cindy. See *Four Winds* 1(4), 1980:18–20. (Navajo?)
34 John, Jonas. Contemporary Four Corners commercial. See Brenner, 1993a, 1993b. HMCNAP. F.
35 Keams, Geraldine (Geri). Contemporary filmmaker, actor, storyteller; Hozhoni Films. F.
36 King, Monica. Videocam operator, Heard Museum. F.
37 Kitsman, Barbara Emerson. HMCNAP; F.
38 Kahn, Alta. See Worth and Adair; 1972. F.
39 Lincoln, Everett. 1993 IAIA student exhibition. F.
40 Martin, Marie. NNM. Worked with M. Snow; perhaps not a photographer?
41 Maryboy, Nancy. NCC. Diné studies, 1992. F.
42 Minkler, Sam. Educator, NAU. See Bingham, 1982. UNMNSS. F.
43 Mitchell, Percy. WM. 1981. Perhaps not Navajo? F.
44 Morgan, Rose. Journalist, photographer, filmmaker, on staff of TV station in Farmington NM. Hosts program in/on Navajo. F.
45 Murkett, Delaine. 1994 IAIA student exhibition.
46 Naswood, Evangelita. See Hubbard, 1994:60. Tse Ho Tso Middle School, Window Rock (1992).
47 Natonabah, Paul. Photojournalist, AP stringer, *Navajo Times*, *Arizona Republic*, NMM 71(8):1993 [30–35]. See Bush and Mitchell, 1994:290, 308. F.
48 Nelson, Johnny. See Worth and Adair, 1972. F.
49 Nez, Bethany. See Hubbard, 1994:67, 71. Tse Ho Tso Middle School, Window Rock (1992).
50 Preston, Sheldon. *Navajo Nation Today*, college student intern. F.
51 Price, Gene. Public health employee, old Navajo Tribal Museum, 1950s. F.
52 Roan, Toni. See Hubbard, 1994:72. Tse Ho Tso Middle School, Window Rock (1992).
53 Roessel, Monty. Photojournalist, now freelance, Blackstar Agency. F.
54 Slinky, Leann. See Hubbard, 1994:62. Tse Ho Tso Middle School, Window Rock (1992).
55 Tapaha, Carmelita. Exhibited at Millicent Rogers. HMCNAP; UNMNSS. F.
56 Tapaha, J. NNM. Bureau of Roads, 1986. F.
57 Tapahe, Loren. Publicist, journalist, editor, *Window Rock Scene*, 1993. F.
58 Thompson, Ernest. UNMNSS; F.
59 "Tin-Horn." ASM. 1914. Earliest known Navajo photographer, near Kayenta. F.
60 Toadlena, Brent. 1993 IAIA student exhibition. F.
61 Tsinajinnie, Andy. Helped Snow, 1937. Not a photographer?? F.
62 Tsinhnahjinnie, Hulleah (Helen). Contemporary artist, photographer; widely exhibited. Daughter of Andy Tsinajinnie. See Bush and Mitchell, 1994:277, 313. HMCNAP. F.
63 Tsosie, Derek. See Hubbard, 1994:41. Larry C. Kennedy School, Phoenix (1993).
64 Tsosie, Keith. See Hubbard, 1994:42. Larry C. Kennedy School, Phoenix (1993).
65 Tsostie, Betty. 1993, 1994 IAIA student exhibitions. F.
66 Tsotsie, Will. Society for Photographic Education Conference, Santa Fe, 1990. F.
67 Tsotsie, Maxine. See Worth and Adair, 1972. Sister of Mary Jane. F.
68 Tsotsie, Mary Jane. See Worth and Adair, 1972. Sister of Maxine. F.
69 Two Bears, Davina R. See Two Bears, 1995.

Appendix

70 Valdez, Leroy. HMCNAP; UNMNSS. F.
71 Vicenti, Dan. See HNAI. Community health specialist, 1960s. F.
72 Wallace, John D. See HNAI. Councilman, 1960s. F.
73 Watchman, Louise. F.
74 Weidner, Tesbah?? Heard Museum. F.
75 Whitesinger, Anna Boyd. IAIA, UNM. See Bush and Mitchell, 1994:9, 258, 315. F.
76 Williams, Shane. See Hubbard, 1994:89. Window Rock High School (1992).
77 Williams, Wende. 1994 IAIA student exhibition.
78 Wyaco, Virgil. Navajo consultant on film "Navajo Moon"; not a photographer? F.
79 Yazzie, Alfred. Nightway singer, did videotaping for Navajo Studies Program at Rough Rock Demonstration School. F.
80 Yazzie, Herbert. BYU, published in student magazine. See Bush and Mitchell, 1994:281, 317.
81 Yazzie, Jerry. Sports photographer for *Navajo Times*. F.
82 Yazzie, Shanna. See Hubbard, 1994:88. Tse Ho Tso Middle School, Window Rock (1992).
83 Yazzie, Venaya Jaye. 1994 IAIA student exhibition.

Bibliography

Interviews, Personal Conversations
(J. Faris) Sina Brush, December 1991
(J. Faris) Ida Gail, October 1991
(J. Faris) Helen Herzer, April 1994
(J. Faris) Therese Thau Heyman, March 1992
(J. Faris) George Hight, July 1990
(J. Faris) Ira Jacknis, February 1992
(J. Faris) Zig Jackson, November 1991
(J. Faris) Jerry L. Kearns, March 1991
(J. Faris) Stephen LeCuyer, October 1991
(J. Faris) Jonathan Morse, August 1991
(J. Faris) Kathy M'Closkey, April 1994
(J. Faris) Monty Roessel, September 1991
(J. Faris) Meridel Rubenstein, November 1991
(J. Faris) Richard Rudisill, August 1990
(K. Bartlett) Milton Snow, September 1973
(J. Faris) Tom Southall, October 1991
(J. Faris) Helga Teiwes, July 1992
(J. Faris) Henry Walt, May 1994
(J. Faris) Robert Wolfenstein, September 1993

Correspondence

19 November 1990.	Kris Butler to James Faris
20 December 1904.	E. S. Curtis to Charles Day
22 February 1905.	E. S. Curtis to Charles Day
12 December 1994.	Helen Herzer to James Faris
15 April 1992.	Ira Jacknis to James Faris
[n.d.] 1988.	Dorothy Kirk to Brita Mack
29 August 1975.	Luke Lyon to Richard Rudisill
17 June 1973.	Courtenay Monsen to Gary F. Kurutz
9 March 1993.	Alessandro Pezzati to James Faris
15 February 1992.	Richard Rudisill to James Faris
13 July 1994.	Joanna Scherer to James Faris
21 January 1991.	Paula Stewart to James Faris

Books, Articles, Manuscripts

Adams, Monni. 1987. Looking Beyond the Photographic Image. *Visual Resources* 4:273–281.

Akin, Louis. 1907. Frederick Monsen of the Desert—The Man Who Began Eighteen Years Ago to Live and Record the Life of Hopiland. *The Craftsman* 11(6):678–682.

Albers, Patricia C., and William R. James. 1983. Tourism and the Changing Photographic Image of the Great Lake Indians. *Annals of Tourism Research* 10:123–148.

Albers, Patricia C., and William R. James. 1988. Travel Photography. A Methodological Approach. *Annals of Tourism Research* 15:134–158.

Alexandrian, Sarane, and Patrick Waldberg. 1980. *Rene Magritte*. New York: Filipacchi Books.

Alloula, Malek. 1986. *The Colonial Harem*. Minneapolis: University of Minnesota Press.

Ammann, Karl. 1993. Hostile Places and Sensitive Subjects. *Outdoor Photography* 9(3):48–71.

Anderson, Susanne. n.d. [1973]. *Song of the Earth Spirit*. Edited with foreword by David R.

Bibliography

Brower. Celebrating the Earth series. San Francisco and New York: Friends of the Earth, McGraw Hill.
Andrews, Ralph W. 1962. *Curtis' Western Indians.* New York: Bonanza Books.
———. 1965. *Photographers of the Frontier West.* New York: Bonanza Books.
Anonymous. 1913. The Rodman Wanamaker Expedition of Citizenship to the North American Indian. Under the leadership of Dr. Joseph Kossuth Dixon. Privately printed.
Arizona Highways. 1967. *A Treasury of Arizona's Colorful Indians.* Phoenix: Arizona Highways.
Armer, Laura Adams. 1962. *In Navajo Land.* New York: David McKay.
Arreola, Paul R. 1986. George Wharton James and the Indians. *Masterkey* 60(1):11-18.
Babcock, Barbara A., and Nancy J. Parezo. 1988. *Daughters of the Desert: Women Anthropologists and the Native American Southwest 1880–1980.* Albuquerque: University of New Mexico Press.
Bahti, Tom. 1971. *Southwestern Indian Tribes.* Las Vegas, NV: K. C. Publications.
Bailey, Alfred. 1947. Desert River Through Navajo Land. *National Geographic Magazine* 92(2):149-172.
Bailey, Garrick, and Roberta Glenn Bailey. 1986. *A History of the Navajos.* Santa Fe: School of American Research Press.
Baker, Will. 1983. *Backward: An Essay on Indians, Time, and Photography.* Berkeley: North Atlantic Books.
Bal, Mieke. 1992. Showing, Telling, Showing Off. *Critical Inquiry* 18(3):568–579.
Baldinger, Jo Ann. 1992. Navajo Poet. *New Mexico Magazine* 70(8):30–35.
Banta, Martha, and Curtis Hinsley. 1986. *From Site to Sight: Anthropology, Photography, and the Power of Imagery.* Cambridge: Peabody Museum of Harvard University, Harvard University Press.
Barrett, Terry. 1990. *Criticizing Photographs: An Introduction to Understanding Images.* Mountain View, CA: Mayfield Publishing Company.
Barthes, Roland. 1981. *Camera Lucida.* Translated by Richard Howard. New York: Hill and Wang.
Beck, Peggy V., Anna Lee Walters, and Nia Francisco. 1977. *The Sacred: Ways of Knowledge, Sources of Life.* Tsaile, AZ: Navajo Community College Press.
Becker, Howard S., ed. 1981. *Exploring Society Photographically.* Chicago: University of Chicago Press.
Benedek, Emily. 1992. *The Wind Won't Know Me: A History of the Navajo-Hopi Land Dispute.* New York: Alfred A. Knopf.
Benjamin, Walter. 1969. *Illuminations.* New York: Schocken Books.
———. 1972. A Short History of Photography. *Screen* 13(1):5–26.
Bennett, Noel. 1987. *Halo of the Sun: Stories Told and Retold.* Photographs by John Running. Flagstaff: Northland Press.
Bennett, Norman Robert. 1986. *Arab Versus European: Diplomacy and War in Nineteeth-Century East Central Africa.* New York: Africana Publishing Company.
Berendzen, Margaret, ed. n.d. [1990?]. *Oral History Stories of the Long Walk:* Hwéeldi Baa Hané. By the Diné of the Eastern Region of the Navajo Reservation. Crownpoint, NM: Lake Valley Navajo School.
Berezin, Ronna H. 1982. Unknown Photographer of the West: Elias A. Bonine. In *Pasadena Photographs and Photographers 1880–1915*, Mary Melissa Patton and Ronna H. Berezin, eds. Pasadena: Pasadena Historical Society.
Berger, John. 1972. *Ways of Seeing.* Harmondsworth: Penguin Books.
———. 1980. *About Looking.* New York: Pantheon.
———. 1982. *Another Way of Telling.* New York: Pantheon.
Berkhofer, Robert F., Jr. 1978. *The White Man's Indian.* New York: Alfred A. Knopf.
———. 1988. White Conceptions of Indians. *Handbook of North American Indians.* History of Indian-White Relations volume, William Sturtevant, ed. Volume 4:522–547. Washington: Smithsonian Institution Press.

Berlant, Anthony, and Mary Hunt Kahlenberg. 1991. *Walk in Beauty. The Navajo and Their Blankets.* Salt Lake City UT: Peregrine Smith Books.
Berry, Rose S. 1929. The Navajo Shaman and His Sacred Sand-Painting. *Art and Archaeology* 27(1):3-16.
Bia, Fred. 1983. *Of Mother Earth and Father Sky.* Rough Rock AZ: Rough Rock Press.
Bighorse, Tiana. 1990. *Bighorse: The Warrior.* Noel Bennett, ed. Tucson: University of Arizona Press.
Bingham, Janet, and Sam Bingham, scribes. 1982. *Between Sacred Mountains: Navajo Stories and Lessons from the Land.* Tucson: Sun Tracks and University of Arizona Press.
Bixler, Margaret T. 1992. *Winds of Freedom.* Darien CT: Two Bytes Publishing.
Biesele, Megan. 1980. Reclaiming a Cultural Legacy: The Ju/'hoansi of Namibia. *Aperture* 119:50-57.
Blanchard, Kendall A. 1977. *The Economics of Sainthood: Religious Change Among the Rimrock Navajos.* Rutherford NJ: Fairleigh Dickinson University Press.
Bolton, Richard, ed. 1989. *The Contest of Meaning.* Cambridge: Massachusetts Institute of Technology Press.
Brenner, Malcolm. 1993a. An eye for *Tse' Bit A'i. The Daily Times* (Farmington, NM), 29 August 1993.
———. 1993b. He knows "the rock" like no other. *Santa Fe New Mexican*, 20 September:A7.
Brierly, Dean. 1993. The Frontier Photography of Charles F. Lummis. *Camera and Darkroom* 15(12):48-53.
Broder, Janis. 1990. *Shadows on Glass: The Indian World of Ben Wittick.* Savage MD: Rowman and Littlefield, Inc.
Brody, J. J. 1971. *Indian Painters and White Patrons.* Albuquerque: University of New Mexico Press.
Brower, David. n.d. [1973]. Foreword. In Susanne Anderson, *Song of the Earth Spirit.* San Francisco and New York: McGraw Hill.
Brower, Kenneth, ed. 1967. *Navajo Wildlands.* Text by Stephen C. Jett. Photographs by Philip Hyde. San Francisco and New York: Sierra Club and Ballantine Books.
Brugge, David M. 1983. Navajo Prehistory and History to 1850. In *Handbook of North American Indians.* Alfonso Ortiz, ed. Volume 10:489-501. Washington: Smithsonian Institution Press.
Buck-Morss, Susan. 1989. *The Dialectics of Seeing: Walter Benjamin and the Arcades Project.* Cambridge: Massachusetts Institute of Technology Press.
Bunker, Robert, and John Adair. 1959. *The First Look at Strangers.* New Brunswick NJ: Rutgers University Press.
Bush, Alfred L., and Lee Clark Mitchell. 1994. *The Photograph and the American Indian.* Princeton: Princeton University Press.
Butler, Judith. 1993. Endangered/Endangering: Schematic Racism and White Paranoia. In *Reading Rodney King/Reading Urban Uprising*, Robert Gooding-Williams, ed. New York: Routledge.
Burgin, Victor, ed. 1982. *Thinking Photography.* London: Macmillan.
Burnett, Ron, ed. 1991. *Explorations in Film Theory: Selected Essays from Ciné-Tracts.* Bloomington: Indiana University Press.
Casagrande, Louis B., and Phillips Bourns. 1983. *Side Trips: The Photography of Sumner W. Matteson, 1898-1908.* Milwaukee: Milwaukee Public Museum and the Science Museum of Minnesota.
Chapman, Arthur. 1921. The Sand Painters of the American Desert. *Travel* 15-17 (January).
Chow, Rey. 1993. *Writing Diaspora: Tactics of Intervention in Contemporary Cultural Studies.* Bloomington: Indiana University Press.
Chowning, Emily Blair. 1994. Weaving a Legacy. *Arts and Antiques* 17(6):92-98.
Christenson, Andrew. 1987. The Last of the Great Expeditions: The Rainbow Bridge/Monument Valley Expedition, 1933-1938. *Plateau* 58(4).

Bibliography

Cixous, Hélène, and Catherine Clèment. 1986. *The Newly Born Woman*. Translated by Betsy Wing. Manchester: Manchester University Press.
Clayton, Robert Alan (with J. Bourge Hathaway). 1992. *Quiet Pride*. Hillsboro OR: Beyond Words, Inc.
Clifford, James. 1988. *The Predicament of Culture: Twentieth-Century Ethnography, Literature, and Art*. Cambridge: Harvard University Press.
Clifford, James, and George E. Marcus, eds. 1986. *Writing Culture. The Poetics and Politics of Ethnography*. Berkeley: University of California Press.
Coke, Van Deren. 1979. *Photography in New Mexico: From Daguerotype to the Present*. Foreword by Beaumont Newhall. Albuquerque: University of New Mexico Press.
Collier, John. 1962. *On the Gleaming Way*. Chicago: Sage Books.
Collier, John C., Jr. 1967. *Visual Anthropology: Photography as a Research Method*. New York: Holt, Rinehart and Winston. Revised and expanded edition, Albuquerque: University of New Mexico Press, 1986, with foreword by Edward T. Hall, and Malcolm Collier as additional author.
Collier, Malcolm. 1993. John Collier, Jr.: Cultural Diversity and the Camera. In *Threads of Culture: Photography in New Mexico, 1939–1943*. The Pinewood Collection of FSA Photography. Santa Fe: Museum of New Mexico.
Coleman, A. D. 1993. Marion Palfi. *Camera and Darkroom* 15(10):42–51.
Coleman, A. D., and T. L. McLuhan. 1974. *Portraits from North American Indian Life: Edward S. Curtis*. New York: A & W Visual Library [Outerbridge and Lazard, Inc.].
Conkelton, Sheryl, comp. n.d. [1985]. Directory of Photographic Collections, California Museum of Photography, University of California, Riverside.
Coolidge, Mary Roberts. 1929. *The Rain-Makers: Indians of Arizona and New Mexico*. Boston: Houghton Mifflin.
Coolidge, Dane, and Mary Roberts Coolidge. 1930. *The Navajo Indians*. Boston: Houghton Mifflin.
Coombes, Annie E. 1994. *Reinventing Africa: Museums, Material Culture and Popular Imagination*. New Haven: Yale University Press.
Crank, Dan. 1988. Poetry. *Diné Be'iina'* 1(2):119–124.
Crary, Jonathan. 1990. *Techniques of the Observer: On Vision and Modernity in the Nineteenth Century*. Cambridge: Massachusetts Institute of Technology Press.
Crimp, Douglas. 1980. The Photographic Activity of Postmodernism. *October* 15:91–100.
Cross, Guy, and Judith Wolf, eds. 1993. Re-Thinking Representation. *THE* 2(7):15–20 (August 1993).
Cummings, Byron. 1952. *Indians I Have Known*. Tucson: Arizona Silhouettes.
Curtis, Edward S. 1904. Sacred Rites of the Mokis and Navajoes. *Seattle Sunday Times*, 27 November, Part V.
———. 1906. Vanishing Indian Types. The Tribes of the Southwest. *Scribner's Magazine* 39(5):52–61.
———. 1907. *The North American Indian*. Volume One. Cambridge: The University Press.
———. 1972a. *Portraits from North American Indian Life*. Introductions by A. C. Coleman and T. C. McLuhan. New York: A & W Visual Library [Outerbridge and Lazard, Inc.].
———. 1972b. The North American Indian: A Selection of Photographs by Edward S. Curtis. Introduction and text compiled by Joseph Epes Brown. *Aperture* 16 (4).
———. 1976. *Visions of a Vanishing Race*. Text by Florence Curtis Graybill and Victor Boesen. New York: Thomas T. Crowell.
Curtis, James. 1989. *Mind's Eye, Mind's Truth: FSA Photography Reconsidered*. Philadelphia: Temple University Press.
D'Emilio, Sandra, and Suzan Campbell. 1991. *Visions and Visionaries: The Art and Artists of the Santa Fe Railway*. Layton UT: Peregrine Smith Books.
Davis, Barbara A. 1985. *Edward S. Curtis: The Life and Times of a Shadow Catcher*. Appreciation by Beaumont Newhall. Foreword by Bill Holm. San Francisco: Chronicle Books.

Deloria, Vine, Jr. 1982. Introduction. In Christopher M. Lyman, *The Vanishing Race. Photographs of Indians by Edward S. Curtis*. Washington: Smithsonian Institution Press.

Deleuze, Gilles. 1986. *Cinema 1: The Movement-Image*. Minneapolis: University of Minnesota Press.

———. 1989. *Cinema 2: The Time-Image*. Minneapolis: University of Minnesota Press.

Dennis, Lisl. 1993. The Ethics of Tipping. *Outdoor Photography* 9(3):74–75.

Derrida, Jacques. 1976. *Of Grammatology*. Translated by G. Chakravorty Spivak. Baltimore: Johns Hopkins University Press.

———. 1993. *Memoirs of the Blind*. Translated by Pascale-Anne Brault and Michael Naas. Chicago: University of Chicago Press.

Diné of the Eastern Region of the Navajo Reservation. n.d. [1990?]. *Oral History Stories of the Long Walk*: Hwéeldi Baa Hané. Crownpoint, NM: Lake Valley Navajo School.

Dippie, Brian W. 1992. Representing the Other: The North American Indian. In *Anthropology and Photography 1860–1920*. Elizabeth Edwards, ed. New Haven and London: Yale University Press and the Royal Anthropological Institute.

Dixon, Joseph R. 1987. Images of Indians—Controlling the Camera. *Northeast Indian Quarterly* Spring/Summer 1987:23–26.

Dobyns, Henry F., and Robert C. Euler. 1972. *The Navajo People*. Phoenix: Indian Tribal Series.

Dobyns, Henry F., and Robert C. Euler. 1977. *The Navajo Indians*. Phoenix: Indian Tribal Series (Albuquerque: Center for Anthropological Studies).

Doherty, Craig, and Katherine M. Doherty. 1989. *The Apaches and Navajos*. New York: Franklin Watts.

Eauclaire, Sally. 1989. Proof of Who We Are: An Interview with Writer and Photocurator Martha Sandweiss. *Southwest Profile* 12(7):44–51.

Edelman, Bernard. 1979. *Ownership of the Image*. Translated by E. Kingdom. London: Routledge and Kegan Paul.

Edwards, Elizabeth. 1990. The Image as Anthropological Document. Photographic "Types": The Pursuit of Method. *Visual Anthropology* 3:235–258.

Edwards, Elizabeth, ed. 1992. *Anthropology and Photography 1860–1920*. New Haven and London: Yale University Press and the Royal Anthropological Institute.

Edwards, Susan E. 1991. Photography and the Representation of the Other: A Discussion Inspired by the Work of Sebastiao Salgado. *Third Text* 16/17:157–172.

Editors of El Palacio, comps. 1981. *Navajo Weaving Handbook*. Introduction by Nancy Fox. Santa Fe: Museum of New Mexico Press.

Eichstaedt, Peter. 1994. *If You Poison Us*. Santa Fe: Red Crane Books.

El Palacio. 1968 75(3), Autumn 1968.

Erdman, Barbara, ed. 1985. *New Mexico USA: A Photographic Essay of New Mexico*. Santa Fe: Santa Fe Center for Photography.

Fabian, Johannes. 1983. *Time and the Other: How Anthropology Makes its Object*. Chapter Four: The Other and the Eye. New York: Columbia University Press.

Faris, James C., and Keo Wutu. 1986. Review Article: Beginning Anthropology. *Critique of Anthropology* 6(2):5–23.

Faris, James C. 1972. *Nuba Personal Art*. London: Duckworths.

Faris, James C. 1988a. "Southeast Nuba": A Biographical Statement. In *Anthropological Filmmaking*, Jack Rollwagen, ed. New York: Harwood Academic Publishers.

———. 1988b. ART/artifact: A Review Essay on Museum and Anthropology. *Current Anthropology* 29(5):775–779. Reprinted in *ART/artifact: African Art in Museum Collections*. New York: Center for African Art, 1989.

———. 1990. *The Nightway: A History and A History of the Documentation of a Navajo Ceremonial*. Albuquerque: University of New Mexico Press.

———. 1992a. Anthropological Transparency: Film, Representation and Politics. In *Film as Ethnography*, Peter Ian Crawford and David Turton, eds. Manchester: Manchester University Press.

———. 1992b. A Political Primer on Anthropology/Photography. In *Anthropology and Photography 1860–1920*, Elizabeth Edwards, ed. New Haven and London: Yale University Press and the Royal Anthropological Institute.

———. 1993a. Leni Riefenstahl and the Nuba Peoples of Kordofan Province, Sudan. *Historical Journal of Film, Radio and Television* 13(1): 95–97.

———. 1993b. A Response to Terence Turner. *Anthropology Today* 9(1):12–13.

———. 1993c. Photography and the Navajo: Some Preliminary Comments on Classical Inscriptions. *exposure* 29(1):31–40.

———. 1993d. The Navajo Photography of Edward S. Curtis. *History of Photography* 17(4):377–387.

———. 1993e. Taking Navajo Truths Seriously: Consequences of the Accretion of Disbelief. In *Papers from the Third, Fourth, and Sixth Navajo Studies Conferences.* Window Rock: Navajo Nation Historic Preservation Department.

———. 1995. Photographing the Navajo: Scanning Abuse. In *Images Across Boundaries*, W. R. Powers and Richard Hill, eds. Albuquerque: University of New Mexico Press.

Fergus, Charles. 1991. *Shadow Catcher.* New York: Soho Press.

Fischer, Michael M.J. 1992. Orientalizing America: Beginnings and Middle Passages. *Middle East Report* 22(5):32–37.

Fleming, Paula Richardson, and Judith Luskey. 1986 [1988]. *The North American Indians in Early Photographs.* New York: Dorset Press.

———. 1993. *Grand Endeavors of American Indian Photography.* Washington: Smithsonian Institution Press.

Forrest, Earle, R. 1970. *With a Camera in Old Navaholand.* Foreword by Katherine Barlett. Norman: University of Oklahoma Press.

Forster, Elizabeth, and Laura Gilpin. 1988. *Denizens of the Desert: A Tale in Words and Pictures.* Edited with an introduction by Martha A. Sandweiss. Albuquerque: University of New Mexico Press.

Foster, Hal, ed. 1988. *Vision and Visuality.* Dia Art Foundation Discussions in Contemporary Culture No. 2. Seattle: Bay Press.

Foucault, Michel. 1973. *The Order of Things. An Archaeology of the Human Sciences.* New York: Vintage Books.

Fowler, Don D. 1972. *In a Sacred Manner We Live: Photographs of the North American Indian by Edward S. Curtis.* Barre MA: Barre Publishers.

Fowler, Don D. 1989. *The Western Photographs of John K. Hillers: Myself in the Water.* Washington: Smithsonian Institution Press.

Foxx, Jeffrey Jay, and Carol Karasik. 1993. *The Turquoise Trail.* New York: H. Abrams.

Frank, Robert. 1978. *The Americans.* Millerton, NY: Aperture.

Frankenberg, Ruth. 1993. *white women, race matters: The Social Construction of Whiteness.* Minneapolis: University of Minnesota Press.

Frink, Maurice (with Casey Barthelmess). 1965. *Photographer on an Army Mule.* Norman: University of Oklahoma Press.

Frink, Maurice. 1968. *Fort Defiance and the Navajos.* Boulder, CO: Pruett Publishing Company.

Frisbie, Charlotte J. 1987. *Navajo Medicine Bundles or* Jish: *Acquisition, and Disposition in the Past and Present.* Albuquerque: University of New Mexico Press.

Gaede, Marc. 1988. *Bordertowns.* Marnie Walker Gaede, ed. La Canada CA: Chaco Press.

Garner, Gretchen. 1977. A Psychologist Looks at Photography (interview with Stanley Milgram). *The New Art Examiner*, May 1977:6–7, 23.

Garner, Gretchen. 1987. *Reclaiming Paradise. American Women Photograph the Land.* Duluth: University of Minnesota, Tweed Museum of Art.

Georgakas, Dan, and Lenny Rubenstein. 1983. *The Cineaste Interviews: On the Art and Politics of the Cinema.* Chicago: Lake View Press.

Gibbs, Michael. 1990. Critical Realism. *Perspektief* 39:38–58.

Gidley, Mick. 1977. *The Vanishing Race: Selections from Edward S. Curtis'* The North American Indian. New York: Taplinger Publishing Company.

Gill, Sam. 1979. *Songs of Life: An Introduction to Navajo Religious Culture.* Leiden: E. J. Brill.

———. 1991. Tribal Poses (review of Broder, 1990 and Keegan and Frontier Photographers, 1990). *New York Times,* 2 June, p. 31.

Gilpin, Laura. 1968. *The Enduring Navaho.* Austin: Univerity of Texas Press.

Ginsburg, Faye. 1991. Indigenous Media: Faustian Contract or Global Village. *Cultural Anthropology* 6(1):92–112.

———. 1994. Culture/Media: A (*mild*) polemic (1993 Forman Lecture). *Anthropology Today* 10(2):5–15.

Goetzmann, William H. 1991. *The First Americans.* Washington D.C.: Starwood Publishers.

Goetzmann, William H., and William N. Goetzmann. 1986. *The West of the Imagination.* New York: W. W. Norton.

Goldberg, Vicki, ed. 1981. *Photography in Print.* New York: Simon and Schuster.

———. 1991. Fiddling with History in a Cause that Seemed Just. *New York Times,* 17 November, Section 2:35, 42.

———. 1992. Photography and the Sin of Voyeurism. *New York Times,* 8 March, Section 2:1, 37.

Goldin, Amy. 1973. Diane Arbus: Playing with Conventions. *Art in America* March/April 1973:73.

Gordon, Linda. 1988. Writing Culture, Writing Feminism: The Poetics and Politics of Experimental Ethnography. *Inscriptions* 3/4:7–26.

Gordon, Susan. 1973. *Black Mesa, The Angel of Death.* New York: John Day Company.

Graham-Brown, Sarah. 1988. *Images of Women: The Portrayal of Women in Photography of the Middle East 1860–1950.* New York: Columbia University Press.

Graybill, Florence Curtis, and Victor Boesen. 1976. *Edward Sheriff Curtis: Visions of a Vanishing Race.* New York: Thomas Y. Crowell.

Greenblatt, Stephen. 1993. Kindly Visions (review of Lutz and Collins, 1993). *The New Yorker,* October 1993:112–120.

Gross, Larry, John Katz, and Jay Ruby, eds. 1988. *Image Ethics: The Moral Rights of Subjects in Photographs, Film and Television.* New York: Oxford University Press.

Grimes, Joel. 1992. *Navajo: Portrait of a Nation.* Foreword by Stewart L. Udall. Englewood, CO: Westcliffe Publishers, Inc.

Guterson, Ben. 1993. Peyote Prayers. *New Mexico Magazine* 71(8):30–36. Photographs by Paul Natonabah.

Gupta, Sunil. 1986. Northern Media, Southern Lives. In *Photography/Politics Two,* Patricia Holland, Jo Spence, and Simon Watney, eds. London: Comedia/Photography Workshop, Methuen & Co.

Hall, Edward T. 1994. *West of the Thirties: Discovery Among the Navajo and Hopi.* New York: Doubleday.

Halpern, Katherine Spencer. 1972. Review: The Enduring Navajo (Laura Gilpin). *American Anthropologist* 72(3):993.

Halpern, Katherine Spencer, and Susan Brown McGreevy, eds. 1996. *Washington Matthews and the Beginning of Navajo Studies.* Albuquerque: University of New Mexico Press.

Hammond, Harmony. 1993. Resistances: Cultural Tourism and Native Resistance Through Self-Representation. *THE* 2(5):27–29 (June 1993).

Haraway, Donna. 1992. The Promises of Monsters: A Regenerative Politics for Inappropriate/d Others. In *Cultural Studies.* Lawrence Grossberg, Cary Nelson, and Paula Treichler, eds. New York: Routledge.

Hathaway, Nancy. 1990. *American Indian Portraits.* San Francisco: Chronicle Books.

Hegemann, Elizabeth Compton. 1963. *Navaho Trading Days.* Albuquerque: University of New Mexico Press.

Heider, Karl. 1980. *Ethnographic Film.* Austin: University of Texas Press.

Henderson, Lisa. 1988. Access and Consent in Public Photography. In *Image Ethics: The Moral Rights of Subjects in Photographs, Film, and Television,* Larry Gross, John Stuart Katz, and Jay Ruby, eds. New York: Oxford University Press.

Bibliography

Henderson, Esther. 1987. Looking Backward. *Journal of Arizona History* 28(4):409–430.
Hill, Rick. 1989. In Our Own Image: Sterotyped Images of Indians Lead to New Native Art Form. *Muse*, Winter 1989:32–37. (Reprinted in 1993—*exposure* 29[1]:6–11).
Hockings, Paul, ed. 1975. *Principles of Visual Anthropology*. Mouton: The Hague.
Holland, Patricia, Jo Spence, and Simon Watney, eds. 1986. *Photography/Politics:Two*. London: Comedia/Photography Workshop, Meuthen & Co.
Holm, Bill. 1983. Review: The Vanishing Race and Other Illusions (Christopher Lyman). *American Indian Art*. Summer 1983:68–73.
Hopson, Rex C., ed. 1989. *New Mexico Magazine Cumulative Index, 1923–1988*. Santa Fe: New Mexico Magazine.
Horan, James D. 1966. *Timothy O'Sullivan: America's Forgotten Photographer*. New York: Bonanza Books.
Hooker, Kathy Eckles. 1991. *Time Among the Navajo. Traditional Lifeways on the Reservation*. Foreword by Danny K. Blackgoat. Photographs by Helen Lau Running. Santa Fe: Museum of New Mexico Press.
Houk, Rose. 1995. *Navajo of Canyon de Chelly. In Home God's Fields*. Tuscon: Southwest Parks and Monuments Association.
Hubbard, Jim (selector). 1994. *Shooting Back from the Reservation. A Photographic View of Life by Native American Youth*. Foreword by Dennis Banks. New York: The New Press.
Huckel, J. F., ed. 1926. *American Indians: First Families of the Southwest*. Kansas City: Fred Harvey Company.
Hust, Karen. 1989. the landscape (chosen by desire): Laura Gilpin Renegotiates Mother Nature. *Genders* 6:20–48.
Jacknis, Ira. 1984. Franz Boas and Photography. *Studies in Visual Communication* 10:2–60.
———. 1990. James Mooney as Ethnographic Photographer. *Visual Anthropology* 3(2–3). (Special issue: Picturing Cultures: Historical Photographs in Anthropological Inquiry. Joanna Scherer, ed.)
Jackson, W. H. 1874. *Descriptive Catalogue of the Photographs of the United States Geological Survey of the Territories for the Years of 1869 to 1873, inclusive*. United States Department of Interior, Miscellaneous Publications No. 5. Washington: Government Printing Office.
———. 1877. *Descriptive Catalogue of Photographs of North American Indians*. United States Department of Interior, Miscellaneous Publications No. 9. Washington: Government Printing Office.
James, George Wharton. 1908. *What the White Race May Learn from the Indian*. Chicago: Forbes and Company.
Jay, Bill. 1984. The Photographer as Aggressor. In *Observations: Essays on Documentary Photography*, D. Featherstone, ed. Carmel, CA: Friends of Photography.
Jett, Stephen C., and Virginia E. Spencer. 1981. *Navajo Architecture. Forms, History, Distributions*. Tucson: University of Arizona Press.
Johnson, Patricia London. 1978. The Indian Photographs of Roland Reed. *The American West* 15(2):44–57.
Jutzi, Alan H. n.d. Southern California Photographers and the Indians of the Southwest 1888–1910. Unpublished manuscript, Huntington Library, San Marino, CA.
Kalman, Béla. 1987. *Indian Country: America's Sacred Land*. Text by Tony Hillerman. Flagstaff: Northland Press.
Kammer, Jerry. 1980. *The Second Long Walk: The Navajo-Hopi Land Dispute*. Albuquerque: University of New Mexico Press.
Kavanagh, Thomas W. 1993. A Catalog of the James Mooney Photograph Collection in the National Anthropological Archives. Manuscript, William Hammond Mathers Museum, Bloomington, IN.
Kawano, Kenji. 1990. *Warriors: Navajo Code Talkers*. Flagstaff: Northland Publishing Company.
Keegan, Marcia. 1974. *Mother Earth, Father Sky: Navajo and Pueblo Indians of the*

Southwest. New York: Grossman Publishers. (Second Edition, 1988.)
Keegan, Marcia, and Frontier Photographers. 1990. *Enduring Culture: A Century of Photography of the Southwest Indians.* Santa Fe: Clear Light Publishers.
Kelley, Klara Bonsack, and Harris Francis. 1994. *Navajo Sacred Places.* Bloomington: Indiana University Press.
Kluckhohm[n], Clyde. 1923. The Dance of Hasjelti. *El Palacio* 15(12):187–192.
Kluckhohn, Clyde, W. W. Hill, and Lucy Wales Kluckhohn. 1971. *Navaho Material Culture.* Cambridge: Harvard University Press.
Kluckhohn, Clyde, and Dorothea Leighton. 1946 [1958]. *The Navaho.* Cambridge: Harvard University Press.
Kluckhohn, Clyde, and Evon Vogt. 1951. *Navaho Means People.* Photography by Leonard McCombe. Cambridge: Harvard University Press.
Kluckhohn, Clyde and Leland Wyman. 1940. An Introduction to Navaho Chant Practice. *American Anthropological Association Memoir* 53.
Kobbe, Gustav. 1911. Photographing the Indian from Life. *New York Herald*, magazine section, 19 February 1911:12.
Koenig, Harriet, and Seymour Koenig. 1986. *Navajo Weaving/Navajo Ways.* Katonah NY: The Katonah Gallery.
Krauss, Rosalind. 1985a. Photography's Discursive Spaces. In *The Originality of the Avant-Garde and Other Modernist Myths*, Rosalind Krauss, ed. Cambridge: Massachusetts Institute of Technology Press.
———. 1985b. Photographic Conditions of Surrealism. In *The Originality of the Avant-Garde and Other Modernist Myths*, Rosalind Krauss ed. Cambridge: Massachusetts Institute of Technology Press.
———. 1988. The Im/Pulse to See. In *Vision and Visuality*, Hal Foster, ed. Dia Art Foundation Discussions in Contemporary Culture, Number 2. Seattle: Bay Press.
———. 1993. *The Optical Unconscious.* Cambridge: Massachusetts Institute of Technology Press.
Krouse, Susan Applegate. 1987. Filming the Vanishing Race. In *Visual Explorations of the World.* Jay Ruby and Martin Taureg, eds. Aachen: Edition Herodot, Rader Verlag.
Kurutz, Gary F. 1978. "Courtesy of Title Insurance and Trust Company..." The Historical Collection at the California Historical Society's Los Angeles History Center. *California History* 57(2):186–194.
La Farge, Oliver. 1956. *A Pictorial History of the American Indian.* London: Spring Books.
———. 1940. *As Long As the Grass Shall Grow.* The Face of America series, Edwin Rosskam, ed. New York: Longmans, Green and Company.
Laxalt, Robert, and John Steffer. 1983. In the Land of the Navajo. *Vista* 18(4):6–9.
Law, Mary E. 1989. *Confronting the Uncomfortable: Questioning Truth and Power.* New Haven: Yale University Art Gallery.
Leahy, James. 1977. Notes on the Navajo Films. *Film Form* 1(2):76–100.
Lee, William Beachum. 1980. *The Nature of Reality in Ethnographic Film: A Study Based on the Work of Edward Sheriff Curtis.* Ph.D. Thesis, University of California, Los Angeles.
Leighton, Alexander H., and Dorothea C. Leighton. 1944. *The Navaho Door: An Introduction to Navaho Life.* Cambridge: Harvard University Press.
Leighton, Dorothea, and Clyde Kluckhohn. 1948: *Children of the People.* Cambridge: Harvard University Press.
Lesy, Michael. 1973. *Wisconsin Death Trip.* New York: Pantheon Books.
Levi-Strauss, David. 1991. Photography and Belief. *SF Camerawork Quarterly*, Spring 1991:5–7.
Levin, David Michael, ed. 1993. *Modernity and the Hegemony of Vision.* Berkeley: University of California Press.
Lew, Julie. 1990. Hollywood's War on Indians Draws to a Close. *New York Times*, 7 October 1990, Section H:15.
Linden, Eugene. 1991. Lost Tribes, Lost Knowledges. *Time* 138(12):46-56.

Bibliography

Lindig, Wolfgang. 1991. *Navajo: Tradition and Change in the Southwest.* Photographs by Helga Teiwes. Zurich: U. Bär Verlag.
Linquist-Cock, Elizabeth. 1983. Marion Palfi: An Appreciation. *The Archive* 19:4–11.
Link, Martin A., ed. 1968. *Navajo: A Century of Progress, 1868–1968.* Window Rock, AZ: Navajo Tribe. [K. C. Publications].
Lippard, Lucy. 1983. *Overlay: Contemporary Art and the Art of Prehistory.* New York: Pantheon Books.
———. 1990. *Mixed Blessings: New Art in Multicultural America.* New York: Pantheon Books.
———. 1991. Doubletake: The Diary of a Relationship with an Image. *Third Text* 16/17:135–144.
———, ed. 1992. *Partial Recall.* New York: The New Press.
Lloyd, Jill. 1984. Old Photographs, Vanished Peoples, and Stolen Potatoes: The Relationship Between Anthropology and Photography as Modernist Phenomena. *Arts Monthly* 8(3):13–16.
Loizos, Peter. 1993. *Innovation in Ethnographic Film: From Innocence to Self-consciousness, 1955–1985.* Chicago: University of Chicago Press.
Long, Paul V. 1992. *Big Eyes: The Southwestern Photography of Simeon Schwemberger, 1902–1908.* Albuquerque: University of New Mexico Press.
Looney, Ralph. 1972. The Navajos. *National Geographic Magazine.* December 1972:740–780.
Loy, Dana. 1980. Artist Profile: Clifford Beck. *Four Winds* 1(4):18–20.
Luckert, Karl W. 1979. *Coyoteway: A Navajo Ceremony.* Tucson: University of Arizona Press; and Flagstaff: Museum of Northern Arizona Press.
Lutkehaus, Nancy. 1989. "Excuse Me, Everything is Not All Right." On Ethnography, Film, and Representation: An Interview with Filmmaker Dennis O'Rourke. *Cultural Anthropology* 4(4):422–437.
Lutz, Catherine A., and Jane Collins. 1993. *Reading National Geographic.* Chicago: University of Chicago Press.
Lyman, Christopher M. 1982. *The Vanishing Race and Other Illusions: Photography of Indians by Edward S. Curtis.* Washington: Smithsonian Institution Press.
Lyon, Luke. 1988. A History of the Prohibition of Photography of Southwest Indians Ceremonials. In *Reflections: Papers on Southwest Culture History in Honor of Charles H. Lange.* Anne V. Parry, ed. Archaeological Society of New Mexico Papers, No. 14.
Lyons, Nathan, ed. 1966. *Photographers on Photography.* Englewood Cliffs: Prentice Hall.
McAuley, Skeet. 1989. *Sign Language: Contemporary Southwest Native America.* New York: Aperture Foundation.
M'Closkey, Kathy. 1993. Some Ruminations on the Textile Production by the Navajo and the Inuit. In *Papers from the Third, Fourth, and Sixth Navajo Studies Conferences.* Window Rock, AZ: Navajo Nation Historic Preservation Department, pp. 379–389.
McCombe, Leonard. 1951. *Navaho Means People.* Text by Evon Z. Vogt and Clyde Kluckhohn. Cambridge: Harvard University Press.
McCombs, Edward. 1987. Navajo Images: A Portfolio. *Diné Be'iina'* 1(1):25–31.
McDowell, Steve. 1994. Images Across Boundaries. *El Palacio* 99(1&2):38–45.
McGrane, Bernard. 1989. *Beyond Anthropology.* New York: Columbia University Press.
McGreevy, Susan Brown. 1993. Daughters of Affluence: Wealth, Collecting, and Southwestern Institutions. In *Hidden Scholars. Women Anthropologists and the Native American Southwest,* N. Parezo, ed. Albuquerque: University of New Mexico Press.
McKelvey, Nat. 1950. Movies Remake the Redman. *Rocky Mountain Empire Magazine.* 13 August 1950:4.
McLuhan, T. C. 1971. *Touch the Earth: A Self-Portrait of Indian Existence.* New York: E. P. Dutton [Outerbridge and Dienstfrey].
———. 1985. *Dream Tracks: The Railroad and the American Indian 1890–1930.* With photographs from the William E. Kopplin Collection. New York: Harry N. Abrams, Inc.
McNitt, Frank. 1962. *The Indian Trader.* Norman: University of Oklahoma Press.

McRae, William. 1989. Images of Native Americans in Still Photography. *History of Photography* 13(4):321–342.

Mack, Brita. 1985. Preface. Shadow Catchers: Photographs of Native Americans in the Huntington Library. Exhibition, The Virgina Steele Scott Gallery. Huntington Library, San Marino, CA.

Maddox, John Lee. 1923. *The Medicine Man*. New York: Macmillan.

Mahood, Ruth I. 1961. *Photographer of the Southwest: Adam Clark Vroman 1856–1916*. New York: Bonanza Books.

Malcolm, Janet. 1980. *Diana and Nikon: Essays on the Aesthetic of Photography*. Boston: Godine.

Manley, Ray. 1983. *The Vanishing Indian: A Portfolio*. Text by Clara Lee Tanner. Tucson: Shandling Lithographic Company, Inc.

Marcus, George. 1985. A Timely Rereading of *Naven*: Gregory Bateson as Oracular Essayist. *Representations* 12:66–82.

———. 1990. Imagining the Whole. *Critique of Anthropology* 9(3):7–30.

Marcus, George, and Michael Fischer. 1986. *Anthropology as Cultural Critique*. Chicago: University of Chicago Press.

Marshall, Jim. 1948. Twilight on the Navajo Trail. *Collier's*, 7 February 1948:20–48.

Matthews, Washington. 1897. *Navaho Legends*. Boston: Houghton Mifflin and Co.

Matthiessen, Peter. 1980. Battle for Big Mountain. *GEO* 2:12–30.

Mautz, Carl. 1986. *Checklist of Western Photographers*. Brownsville, CA: Folk Image Publishing.

Maybury-Lewis, David. 1992. *Millennium: Tribal Wisdom and the Modern World*. New York: Viking Press.

Meiselas, Susan. 1987. Susan Meiselas: The Frailty of the Frame, Work in Progress. A Conversation with Fred Ritchin. *Aperture* 108:39–41.

———. 1988. Some Thoughts on Appropriation and the Use of Documentary Photographs. *exposure* 27(1):11–15.

Mercer, Kobena. 1993. Reading Racial Fetishism: The Photographs of Robert Mappethorpe. In *Fetishism as Cultural Discourse*, Emily Apter and William Pietz, eds. Ithaca: Cornell University Press.

Metz, Christian. 1985. Photography and Fetish, *October* 34:81–90.

Michaels, Eric. 1989. *For a Cultural Future: Francis Jupurrurla Makes TV at Yuendumu*. Art and Criticism Monograph Series, Volume 3. Sidney: Art and Text Publications.

Miller, Joseph. 1941. *Arizona Indians: The People of the Sun*. New York: Hastings House.

Misrach, Myriam Weisang. 1992. Developing History. *Antiques and Fine Art* 9(2):77–83.

Mitchell, Daniel Holmes. 1910. *God's Country*. Cincinnati: Ebbert and Richardson Company.

Mitchell, W.J.T. 1986. *Iconology: Image, Text, Ideology*. Chicago: University of Chicago Press.

Monsen, Frederick Immam. 1907. The Destruction of Our Indians: What Civilization Is Doing to Extinguish an Ancient and Highly Intelligent Race by Taking Away its Arts, Industries and Religion. *The Craftsman* 11(6):683–691.

———. 1907. Life and Customs of Indians of the Pueblos Shown in Exhibit of Monson [sic] Pictures. *The Brooklyn Daily Eagle*, 7 January 1907 (photographs).

———. 1910. Picturing Indians with the Camera. *Photo-Era* [American Journal of Photography] 25(4):165.

Moon, Carl. 1914. Photographing the Vanishing Red Man. *Leslie's Illustrated*, 10 March 1910.

———. 1923a. Navajo's Plea for His Dances. *New York Times Magazine*, 18 November 1923:7, 13.

———. 1923b. Idyls of the Vanishing Indian Preserved for a Wondering Future. *Christian Science Monitor*, 6 April 1923.

———. 1982. *Photographs and Illustrations of the American Southwest. Catalogue 83: A Selection of Vintage Photographs, Original Art and Related Materials*. San Francisco: Argonaut Book Shop.

Bibliography

Moore, Rachel. 1992. Marketing Alterity. *Visual Anthropology Review* 8(2):16–26.

Morden, Terry. 1986. Documentary. Past. Future? In *Photography/Politics Two*, Patricia Holland, Jo Spence, and Simon Watney, eds. London: Comedia/Photography Workshop, Methuen & Co.

Moreland, J. William. 1991. American Indians and the Right to Privacy: A Psycholegal Investigation of the Unauthorized Publication of Portraits of American Indians. *American Indian Law Review* 15(2):237–277.

Mulvey, Laura. 1989. *Visual and Other Pleasures.* Bloomington: University of Indiana Press.

Nadel-Klein, Jane. 1991. Picturing Aborigines: A Review Essay on After Two Hundred Years: Photographic Essays on Aboriginal and Islander Australia Today. *Cultural Anthropology* 6(3):414–423.

Navajo Times Today. 1985. 17 July, 14 November.

Neel, David. 1994. NMAI Update. *Smithsonian Runner* 94(3):3 (photographs).

Newcomb, Franc J. 1964. *Hosteen Klah: Navaho Medicine Man and Sand Painter.* Norman, OK: University of Oklahoma Press.

Newhall, Beaumont, and Nancy Newhall. 1966. *T. H. O'Sullivan, Photographer.* Rochester: George Eastman House, Inc.

Nichols, Bill. 1981. *Ideology and the Image: Social Representation in the Cinema and Other Media.* Bloomington: Indiana University Press.

Nicholson, Adam, and David Burnett. 1993. Shooting the Neutron Breeze. *The Sunday Times* (London), 17 January 1993:30–31.

Nixon, Bruce. 1991. The Editorial Eye; Shadowy Evidence and Our Chiefs and Elders at San Francisco Camerawork. *Artweek* (Los Angeles) 22(3):11.

Norrell, Brenda. 1991. Navajo Family Farms. *Native Peoples* 4(3):38–40.

Norwood, Vera, and Janice Monk, eds. 1987. *The Desert is No Lady: Southwestern Landscapes in Women's Writing and Art.* New Haven: Yale University Press.

Northern, Tamara. 1993. *To Image and To See.* Hanover NH: Hood Museum of Art, Dartmouth College.

Olivas, Authur. 1970. *The Wittick Collection, Volume 1.* Santa Fe: Museum of New Mexico Press.

Osinski, Alice. 1987. *The Navajo: A New True Book.* Chicago: Children's Press.

Overstreet, William. 1992. The Navajo Nightway and the Western Gaze. *boundary 2* 19(3):57–76.

Owens, Craig. 1993. Improper Names. In *Unsettled Objects.* Published in conjunction with the exhibition AMERICA *Invention* by Lothar Baumgarten. New York: Solomon R. Guggenheim Museum, pp. 101–110.

Pack, John. n.d. [ca. 1975]. *The Ganado Portfolio.* Privately printed.

Page, Susanne. 1989. *A Celebration of Being.* Foreword by Robert Redford. Afterword by Jake Page. Flagstaff: Northland Publishing.

Palmquist, Peter. 1991. *A Directory of Women in California Photography 1900–1920.* Eureka CA: Eureka Printing Company.

Parezo, Nancy, and Barbara Babcock. 1988. *Daughters of the Desert.* Albuquerque: University of New Mexico Press.

Parezo, Nancy, ed. 1993. *Hidden Scholars: Women Anthropologists and the Native American Southwest.* Albuquerque: University of New Mexico Press.

Parker, Kathleene. 1991. *The Only True People: A History of the Native Americans of the Colorado Plateau.* Denver: Thunder Mesa Publishing.

Parman, Donald L. 1976. *The Navajos and the New Deal.* New Haven: Yale University Press.

Patton, Mary Melissa, and Ronna H. Berezin. 1982. *Pasadena Photographs and Photographers 1880–1915.* Pasadena, CA: Pasadena Historical Society and Ronna H. Berezin.

Peterson, Nicolas. 1985. The Popular Image. In *Seeing the First Australians*, I. and T. Donaldson, eds. Sidney: Allen and Unwin.

———. 1989. A colonial image: penetrating the reality of the message. *Australian Aboriginal Studies* 2:59–62.

———. 1993. Constructions of Aboriginal Feminity and the Family in Early Twentieth Century Photography. Unpublished joint seminar paper, Department of Prehistory and Anthropology, Australian National University.
Pinney, Christopher. 1989a. Appearing Worlds. *Anthropology Today* 5(3):26–28.
———. 1989b. Representations of India: Normalization and the "Other." *Pacific Viewpoint* 29(2):144–162.
———. 1990a. The Quick and the Dead: Images, Time, and Truth. *Society for Visual Anthropology Review* 6(2):42–54.
———. 1990b. Explanations of Itself. *Society for Visual Anthropology Review* 6(2):62–65.
———. 1992a. The Parallel Histories of Anthropology and Photography: Or the Impossibility of a Photo-Graphy. In *Anthropology and Photography 1860–1920*, Elizabeth Edwards, ed. New Haven and London: Yale University Press and Royal Anthropological Institute.
———. 1992b. Future Travel. *Visual Anthropology Review* 8(1):38–55.
Plett, Nicole. 1986. Alamo Navajo Rediscover Their Heritage. *New Mexico Magazine* 64(1):25–28.
Plevin, Nancy. 1995. Time Looms Heavy. Santa Fe *New Mexican*, 9 July:A1–6. Photographs by Julie Graber.
Pollock, Floyd Allen. 1984. *A Navajo Confrontation and Crisis*. Tsaile, AZ: Navajo Community College Press.
Powers, Willow Roberts, and Richard Hill, eds. 1995. *Images Across Boundaries*. Albuquerque: University of New Mexico Press.
Pratt, Mary Louise. 1992. *Imperial Eyes: Travel Writing and Transculturation*. London and New York: Routledge.
Rabinowitz, Jay. 1993. Jack Delano and the Railroad Photography Project in New Mexico. In *Threads of Culture: Photography in New Mexico, 1939–1943*. The Pinewood Collection of FSA Photography. Santa Fe: Museum of New Mexico.
Redhouse, John. 1985. *Geopolitics of the Navajo-Hopi Land Dispute*. Albuquerque: Redhouse/Wright Publications.
Reichard, Gladys. 1936. *Navajo Shepherd and Weaver*. New York: J. J. Augustin.
———. 1939. *Dezba, Woman of the Desert*. New York: J. J. Augusin.
Richardson, Gladwell. 1986. *Navajo Trader*. Tucson: University of Arizona Press.
Riefenstahl, Leni. 1976. *The People of Kau*. New York: Harper.
———. 1987. *Memoiren*. Munich: Albrecht Knaus Verlag GmbH.
———. 1992. *The Sieve of Time: The Memoirs of Leni Riefenstahl*. London: Quartet Books.
Rijmes, Joanne. 1984. Jicarilla Apaches: Stone Lake in the 1930s. *New Mexico Magazine* 62(9):40–43.
Roberts, John. 1951. *Three Navaho Households: A Comparative Study in Small Group Cultury*. Reports of the Ramah Project 3. Papers of the Peabody Museum of American Archaeology and Ethnology, Harvard University, Volume 40, Number 3. Cambridge: Harvard University Press.
Robinson, H. F., and Mary W. 1914. *Lens Studies of Indians*. Albuquerque: The Robinsons.
Robinson, Will H. 1928. *Under Turquoise Skies*. New York: Macmillan.
Roessel, Monty. 1991. Navajo Puberty Rites. *New Mexico Magazine* 69(8):86–95.
———. 1991. Navajos Harvest Tradition at Fair. *New Mexico Magazine* 69(9):70–77.
———. 1992. New Traditions in Navajo Pottery. *Native Peoples* 5(4):10–17.
———. 1993. A Navajo Couple Unites with Tradition. *New Mexico Magazine* 71(6):38–45.
———. 1993. The Long Walk. *New Mexico Magazine* 71(8):72–79.
———. 1995. Navajo Reactions to Historic Photography of Navajo. In *Images Across Boundaries*, W. R. Powers and Richard Hill, eds. Albuquerque: University of New Mexico.
Roessel, Robert A., Jr. 1980. *A Pictorial History of the Navajo from 1860 to 1910*. Rough Rock, AZ: Rough Rock Demonstration School Curriculum Project.
Roessel, Ruth, and Broderick Johnson, eds. 1974. *Navajo Livestock Reduction: A National Disgrace*. Tsaile, AZ: Navajo Community College Press.
Rollwagon, Jack, ed. 1988. *Anthropological Filmmaking: Anthropological Perspectives on*

Bibliography

the Production of Film and Video for General Public Audiences. New York: Harwood Academic Publishers.

Rosebrook, Jeb Stuart. 1993. Barry Goldwater. A Photographer of the Southwest. *Camera and Darkroom* 15(12):23–31.

Rosenak, Chuck, and Jan Rosenak. 1994. *The People Speak: Navajo Folk Art*. Flagstaff, AZ: Northland Publishing Company.

Rosnek, Carl, and Joseph Stacey. 1976. *Skystone and Silver*. Englewood Cliffs, NJ: Prentice Hall Publishers.

Rorty, Richard. 1980. *Philosophy and the Mirror of Nature*. Princeton: Princeton University Press.

Rubenstein, Joseph. 1981. Photographic Facts: False Realities. *Dialectical Anthropology* 5(4):341–349.

Rubenstein, Meridel. 1977. *La Gente de la Luz*. Santa Fe: Museum of New Mexico.

Ruby, Jay. 1991. Speaking For, Speaking About, Speaking With, or Speaking Alongside: An Anthropological and Documentary Dilemma. *Visual Anthropology Review* 7(2):50–67.

Rudisill, Richard, comp. 1973. *Photographers of the New Mexico Territory, 1854–1912*. Santa Fe: Museum of New Mexico Press.

Running, John. 1985. *Honor Dance*. Reno: University of Nevada Press.

Said, Edward. 1979. *Orientalism*. New York: Vintage Books.

Sandlin, Scott. 1989. Museum Settles with Navajos in Photo. *Albuquerque Journal*, 9 June 1989.

Sandner, Donald. 1979. *Navajo Symbols of Healing*. New York: Harcourt.

Sandweiss, Martha A. 1986. *Laura Gilpin: An Enduring Grace*. Fort Worth: Amon Carter Museum.

———. 1987. Laura Gilpin and the Tradition of American Landscape Photography. In *The Desert is No Lady*, Vera Norwood and Janice Monk, eds. New Haven: Yale University Press.

———. 1989. "As the Mementos of the Race" Photographs of North American Indians. In Skeet McAuley, *Sign Language. Contemporary Southwest Native America*. New York: Aperture Foundation.

Santa Fe *New Mexican*. 1964. Navajo Healing Rites Finally Recorded Upon Film. 31 May:C7–8.

———. 1988. "Madonna" Wins Round in Photo Fight. 7 October:C1.

———. 1989. Navajo Family, Museum Settle Suit Over Photo. 10 June.

Sawyer, Mark, comp. 1985. *Pictorial Photography of the Southwest*. Tucson: University of Arizona Centennial Commission.

———. 1985. *Forman Hanna, Pictorial Photographer of the Southwest*. Tucson: University of Arizona Centennial Commission.

Scherer, Joanna Cohan, with Jean Burton Walker. 1973. *Indians: The Great Photographs that Reveal North American Indian Life, 1847–1929, from the Unique Collection of the Smithsonian Institution*. New York: Crown Publishers.

Scherer, Joanna Cohan. 1978. You Can't Believe Your Eyes: Inaccuracies in Photographs of North American Indians. *exposure* 16(4):6–19.

———. 1988. The Public Faces of Sarah Winnemucca. *Cultural Anthropology* 3(2):178–204.

———. 1990. Historical Photographs as Anthropological Documents: A Retrospect. *Visual Anthropology* 3:131–155.

Scheinbaum, David. 1987. *Bisti*. Albuquerque: University of New Mexico Press.

Schiff, Stephen. 1992. Interview with Leni Riefenstahl (on the occasion of the publication of her memoirs in English). *Vanity Fair*, September, 1992.

Scruton, Roger. 1981. Photography and Representation. *Critical Inquiry* 7:577–603.

Scudder, Thayer. 1982. *No Place to Go: Effects of Compulsory Relocation on Navajos*. Philadelphia: ISHI.

Seattle Sunday Times. 1904. A Seattle Man's Triumph [Edward S. Curtis]. 22 May:Part V, pages 1–2.

Seay, Elizabeth, and Peter Rothberg. 1992. Bad Day at Black Mesa. *Lies of Our Times* 3(11):3–4.
Sekula, Allan. 1975. On the Invention of Photographic Meaning. *Artforum* 13(5):36–45.
———. 1981. The Traffic in Photographs. *Art Journal* 41(1):15–25.
———. 1986a. The Body and the Archive. *October* 39:3–64.
———. 1986b. Reading an Archive: Photography Between Labour and Capital. In *Photography/Politics Two*, Patricia Holland, Jo Spence, and Simon Watney, eds. London: Comedia/Photography Workshop, Methuen & Co.
Shaffer, Susan L. 1987. *Native Peoples of the Southwest—Diné: The Navajo.* Phoenix: Heard Museum.
Shepardson, Mary. 1986. *Fieldwork Among the Navajo.* Palo Alto, CA: BAS Press.
Shindler, A. Zeno. 1867 [1869]. Photographic Portraits of North American Indians in the Gallery of the Smithsonian Institution. Smithsonian Miscellaneous Collections 14 (216).
Simpson, Lt. James H. 1964. *Navaho Expedition: Journal of a Military Reconnaissance from Santa Fe, New Mexico to the Navaho Country Made in 1849*, ed. Frank McNitt. Norman: University of Oklahoma Press.
Singer, Andre, and Leslie Woodhead. 1988. *Disappearing Worlds: Television and Anthropology.* London: Boxtree.
Smith, Paul Chatt. 1992. Every Picture Tells a Story. In *Partial Recall*, L. Lippard, ed. New York: The New Press.
Snyder, Joel. 1981. *American Frontiers. The Photographs of Timothy H. O'Sullivan, 1867-1874.* Millerton NY: Aperture.
———. 1984. Documentary without Ontology. *Studies in Visual Communication* 8(1):78-95.
Snyder, Joel, and Neil Walsh Allen. 1975. Photography, Vision, and Representation. *Critical Inquiry* 2(1):143–169.
Soloman-Godeau, Abigail. 1985. Winning the Game When the Rules Have Been Changed: Art Photography and Postmodernism. *exposure* 23(1):5–15.
———. 1991. *Photography at the Dock.* Media & Society series, no. 4. Minneapolis: University of Minnesota Press.
Sontag, Susan. 1977. *On Photography.* New York: Dell Publishers.
Sorgenfrei, Robert, and David Peters, comps. 1985. *Marion Palfi Archive.* Guide Series Number Ten. Tucson: Center for Creative Photography, University of Arizona
Spence, Jo. 1986. The Sign as a Site of Class Struggle: Relections on Works by John Heartfield. In *Photography/Politics Two*, Patricia Holland, Jo Spence, and Simon Watney, eds. London: Comedia/Photography Workshop, Methuen & Co.
Spivak, Gayatri Chakravorty. 1990. *The Post-Colonial Critic: Interviews, Strategies, Dialogues*, S. Harasym, ed. New York: Routledge.
Squiers, Carol, ed. 1990. *The Critical Image: Essays on Contemporary Photography.* Seattle: The Bay Press.
Stewart, Rick, Joseph D. Ketner II, and Angela L. Miller. 1991. *Carl Wimar: Chronicler of the Missouri River Frontier.* Fort Worth: Amon Carter Museum.
Stewart, Susan. 1991. *Crimes of Writing: Problems in the Containment of Representation.* London: Oxford University Press.
Stirling, Betty. 1961. *Mission to the Navajo.* Mountain View, CA: Pacific Press Publishing Association.
Supplee, Charles. 1971. *Canyon de Chelly: The Story Behind the Scenery.* Tucson: KC Pubications.
Taylor, John. 1990. Mountains of Corpses. *Oppositions* 13:13–17.
Taylor, Lucien, ed. 1993. *Visualizing Theory.* New York: Routledge.
Taylor, Penny, ed. 1988. *After Two Hundred Years: Photographic Essays on Aboriginal and Islander Australia Today.* Canberra: Australian Institute of Aboriginal Studies Press.
Thompson, Hildegard. 1975. *The Navajo's Long Walk for Education: A History of Navajo Education.* Tsaile: Navajo Community College Press.
Todorov, Tzvetan. 1984. *The Conquest of America.* New York: Harper and Row.

Bibliography

Tomaselli, Keyan. 1991. The "Other" in Film: Power, Exploitation and Anthropological Responsibility. In *John Marshall Retrospective*, Werner Petermann, ed. Bonn: Trickster Verlag.

Touchette, Charleen. 1993. Brave Hearted Native American Women Artists: Breaking Through Boundaries and Shattering Stereotypes. *Signals* 2(2):6-11.

Tozzer, Alfred M. 1902. A Navajo Sand Picture of the Rain Gods and its Attendant Ceremony. In *Proceedings of the Thirteenth International Congress of Americanists*, Volume VIII (New York), pp. 147-156.

———. 1909. Notes on Religious Ceremonials of the Navaho. In *Putnam Anniversary Volume: Anthropological Essays Presented to Frederic Ward Putnam in Honor of his 70th Birthday*. New York: G. E. Stechert and Company, pp. 299-343.

Trachtenberg, Alan. 1994. Images: Indians in the Construction of American National Identity. Paper read to the 23rd Annual Meeting of the Society for Cross Cultural Research, Santa Fe, NM, 17 February 1994.

Trafzer, Clifford E. 1982. *The Kit Carson Campaign: The Last Great Navajo War*. Norman: University of Oklahoma Press.

Traugott, Joseph. 1994. Oasis in the Desert: The Mediation of Charles F. Lummis's Photographs. Paper read at the 23rd Annual Meeting of the Society for Cross Cultural Research, Santa Fe, NM, 17 February 1994.

Tremblay, Marc-Adélard, John Collier, Jr., and Tom Sasaki. 1954. Navaho Housing in Transition. *América Indigena* 14(3):187-219.

Trimble, Stephen, ed. 1986. *Our Voices, Our Land: Photographs by Stephen Trimble and Harvey Lloyd*. Phoenix: The Heard Museum.

———. 1993. *The People: Indians of the American Southwest*. Santa Fe: School of American Research Press (distributed by the University of Washington Press).

Trihn T. Minh-ha. 1989. *Woman, Native, Other*. Bloomington: Indiana University Press.

Truettner, William H., ed. 1991. *The West as American: Reinterpreting Images of the Frontier, 1820-1920*. Washington: Smithsonian Institution Press.

Tsinhnahjinnie, Hulleah J. 1993a. Proving Nothing. *Crosswinds* 5(9):13.

———. 1993b. Artist's Statement. *exposure* 29(1):27-28.

———. 1993c. Compensating Imbalances. *exposure* 29(1):29-30.

Turner, Terence. 1992. Defiant Images: The Kayapo Appropriation of Video (1992 Forman Lecture). *Anthropology Today* 8(6):5-16.

Two Bears, Davina R. 1995. *Hanoolchaad'*. Historical Textiles Chosen by Four Navajo Weavers. *Native Peoples* 8(3):62-68.

Tyler, Stephen. 1984. The Vision Quest in the West, Or What the Mind's Eye Sees. *Journal of Anthropological Research* 40(1):23-40.

Underhill, Ruth. 1953. *Here Come the Navaho!* Washington: United States Indian Service.

Van Beek, Gosewijn, and Linda Roodenberg. 1990. The Museal Gaze and Neutral Space. *Oppositions* 13:17-23.

Verplanck, James DeLancey. 1934. *A Country of Shepherds*. Boston: Ruth Hill Publishers.

Villani, John. 1991. The majestic and arid beauty of Bruce Hucko's "backyard." Santa Fe *New Mexican*, Pasatiempo, 1-7 February:12.

———. 1992. Zig Jackson is keeping his photos out of SF galleries. Santa Fe *New Mexican*, Pasatiempo, 26 June:7.

———. 1993. John Running's photos involve equal parts of respect, patience. Santa Fe *New Mexican*, Pasatiempo, 2 July:43

Viola, Herman. 1974. *North American Indians: Photographs from the National Anthropological Archives of the Smithsonian Institution*. Chicago: University of Chicago Press.

Virilio, Paul. 1994. *The Vision Machine*. Bloomington: Indiana University Press. (London: British Film Institute.)

Von Sturmer, John. 1989. Aborigines, Representation, Necrophilia. *Art & Text* 32:127-139.

Wagner, Jon ed. 1979. *Images of Information: Still Photography in the Social Sciences*.

Beverly Hills, CA: Sage Publishers.
Walton, Kendall L. 1984. Transparent Pictures: On the Nature of Photographic Realism. *Critical Inquiry* 11:246–277.
Watkins, Carleton E. 1983. *Photographer of the American West.* Albuquerque: University of New Mexico Press.
Watney, Simon. 1986. On the Institutions of Photography. In *Photography/Politics Two*, Patricia Holland, Jo Spence, and Simon Watney, eds. London: Comedia/Photography Workshop, Methuen & Co.
Weatherford, Elzabeth. 1990. Native Visions: The Growth of Indigenous Media. *Aperture* 119:58–61.
Weaver, Thomas, ed. 1974. *Indians of Arizona: A Contemporary Perspective.* Tucson: University of Arizona Press.
Webb, William, and Robert A. Weinstein. 1973 [1987]. *Dwellers at the Source: Southwestern Indian Photographs of A. C. Vroman, 1895–1904.* Albuquerque: University of New Mexico Press.
Weinberger, Eliot. 1992. The Camera People. *Transition* 55 n.s. 2(1):24–55.
Wexler, Ira. 1993. Timecatcher Art Project Winners Announced. *Smithsonian Runner* 93(4):4a (photographs).
Wexler, Laura. 1989. Photographies and Histories. Coming into Being: John Tagg's *The Burden of Representation: Essays on Photographies and Histories.* exposure 27(2):38–53.
Wheeler, George M. 1983. *Wheeler's Photographic Survey of the American West, 1871–1873.* New York: Dover.
Whiteley, Peter. 1987. Letter to the Editor [on the Navajo-Hopi land claims case]. *New York Times*, 15 June:A-16.
Willemen, Paul. 1994. *looks and frictions: Essays in cultural studies and film theory.* Bloomington: Indiana University Press.
Wilmsen Edwin N. 1991. Comments on Paul John Myburgh's People of the Great Sandface. *CVA (Commission on Visual Anthropology) Review.* Spring 1991.
Woodhead, Henry, ed. 1993. *People of the Desert.* Alexandria VA: Time-Life Books.
Worth, Sol. 1981. *Studying Visual Communication.* Philadelphia: University of Pennsylvania Press.
Worth, Sol, and John Adair. 1972. *Through Navajo Eyes: An Exploration in Film Communication and Anthropology.* Bloomington, IN: Indiana University Press.
Wyman, Leland C. 1983. The Navajo Ceremonial System. In *Handbook of North American Indians*, William C. Sturtevant, general editor; *Southwest*, Alfonso Ortiz, volume editor. Volume 10:536–557. Washington: Smithsonian Institution.
Yazzie, Ethelou, ed. 1971. *Navajo History*, Vol. 1. Many Farms, AZ: Navajo Community College Press.
Young, Robert. 1990. *White Mythologies: Writing History and the West.* London and New York: Routledge.
Zolbrod, Paul. 1995. Secrets of the Rugs. *El Palacio* 100(3):22–28. Photographs by Douglas Merriam.

Index

The Preface, Appendices, and Bibliography are not indexed. Quotation markings (for emphasis in the case of single quotes, or for title of a text or a photograph in case of double quotes), underlining, spellings, and italics are as in original reference. Illustrations are paged in italics.

Abbeloos, Glenn, 208
Abbott, Chuck, 212
Abell, Sam, 213
Aberle, David, 209
Adair, John, 209, 213, 218, 221
Adair, Peter, 221
Adams, Ansel, 213, *217*
Ad-de-sia, Nicholas, 184, *185*
Adler, Abigail, 268
Aesthetics, 15–16
Agathla AZ, 180, *181*
Allen, Tom, 194
Alvarado Hotel, 260
Amchia, *86*
American Indian Arts, 279
American Indian Film Project, 221
American Museum of Natural History, 77
Amon Carter Museum, 248–49
Anderson, Susanne. *See* Page, Susanne
Andrus, William J., 108, 114, 115, *118*, 119, 321n16
Angier, Roswell, 267, 269, 280
Antes, Mrs. Billy, *146*, 147
Anthropologists, as photographers of Navajo, 77
Anthropology, and emergence of photography, 15
Anti-aestheticists, 268
Antoineta, Sister, *126*, 127
Arizona Highways, 188
Arizona State Museum, 221
Armer, Laura, 190
Arny, H. M., 74

Bailey, Alfred, 213
Bailey, Garrick and Roberta G., 277
Barboncito, 54, 55, *56*, 57, *60*, 61
Barker, Florence, 161
Barnard, Bruce, 209
Barnett, Samuel, 221
Barthelmess, Christian, 74, 78, 82
Bartos, Stan, 208
Beals, Jesse Tarbox, *98*
Beaman, E. O., 70
Beautiful Mountain Rebellion, 186
Begay, Archie and wife, *203*
Begay, Lee H., *281*

Bell, Charles M., 74, 75
Benally, Lilly and Norman, 248
Benjamin, Walter, 13, 295
Beochito, *86*
Be-Santa-begai, *86*
Betatakin AZ, 285
Bia, Ned, 220
Bi-joshii, 162, 186, *187*
Bil'áhát'íní, 21
Bingham, Janet, 268
Black God, 159
Black Horse, *124*, 125
Black Mesa AZ, *96*, 97
Blackmore, William H., 64
Black Mountain AZ, *177*
Blackstar agency, 296
Blessingway, 269
Bluff UT, 82, *124*, 125, 260, *261*
Boas, Franz, 120, 319n4
Boltin, Lee, 247
Bonine, Elias, 75, 87
Bortell, P. Clinton, 159
Bosch, James, *207*, 208
Bosque Redondo, photographs, 53–69, 302
Bow and Arrow, *60*, *63*, *64*, *65*, *90*, *91*, *96*, *187*
Bowlero, *85*
Bowman, Arlene, 294
Bradley, Helen, 209
Breed, John, 213
Brodi, Mike, 194
Brown, Nicolas & Son, 53, 66, 67, 70, 75; attributed photographs may be by Wolfenstein, 57, *58*, *59*, *63*, *64*; posing style of, 55
Budnick, Dan, 268
Bullen, Adelaide, 209
Burciaga, Juan, 249
Bureau of Indian Affairs (BIA), 191, 236, 237
Burnett, David, 8
Byrnes, J. F., *96*, 97, 227

Calletano, 55, *60*, 61, *71*
Camera clubs, 74
Cameras: 4x5 plate, 2, 3; large view, 152. *See also* Kodak
Camp Pendleton CA, 140, *141*

Index

Candelario, John, 212
Canyon de Chelly AZ, *96, 97*, 115, 116, 157, *183, 192*, 217, 220. *See also* White House
Capitalism, 12, 15
Caplin, Harvey, 212
Carpenter, William, 162, 186, *187*
Carson, Jack, 208
Cartier-Bresson, Henri, 213
Cayetano. *See* Calletano
Chaco Canyon NM, 77, *79, 85*, 95
Chalfen, Richard, 218
Charlie (scout), *84, 85*
Chase, A. W., 95
Chase, Dana B., 75, 87, *94*, 95
Children, 64, *65, 80, 81, 94, 98, 104, 105, 155, 164, 165, 166, 167, 170–73*, 184, *185, 192*, 210, 222, 229, 261–62; avoidance of photography by, 4, *5, 80, 81*, 250–51; in cradleboard, *174*, 214–15, 217; with European-Americans, 166, *167, 174, 175*; in family photograph, 26, *95*, 124, *142, 143*, 200, 201, 214–15, 247, 250–51, 256, *265*; interest in photographer, 28, *29*, 47; Navajo taking picture of, *6, 7*; at play, *96, 97, 121*; posing for money, 8, *9*; in propaganda photographs, 132, *133, 142, 143*; in school, *50, 51, 126, 129, 142, 199, 219*
Chilocco School, 36, *37*
Chinle AZ, *118, 119*, 165
Choh, 76
Chow, Rey, 301
Churchill, Frank, 150
Ciné. *See* Motion pictures
Clarkson, Mrs. James, 4, *5*
Cly, Happy and Willie, 156, 213
Cochiti, *288*, 289
Code talkers, 140, *141*
Collier, John, 147, 237
Collier, John, Jr., *36*, 213, 218, *219*
Communism, 211
Concho collection, 208, 326–29n34
Conway, Norman and Virginia, 188
Coolidge, Dane and Mary, 190
Coolidge NM, *210*
Coors, Adolph, 276
Council of 1891, 82, *86*
Coyote Canyon Day School NM, *199*
Craig, Vinnie, *86*
Crane, Leo, 150
Crouse, J. S., 209
Crownpoint Bicentennial Project, *142, 143*
Culin, Stewart, 87, *91*, 114
Curtis, Edward S., 32, *33*, 149, 156, 208, 236, *274, 275*; compared with later photographers, 19, *190*, 241; misidentification of subject, 76, 77; modern criticism and defense of, 308, 319–20n4; Nightway photographs of, 108, *109–10*, 111, 112, *113*, 114–16, 120, 320n8, 321–22n16, 322n19; *The North American Indian*, 107, 108, 114; photograph of children, *121*; photograph types of, 116, 120; relationship with subjects, 117; use of props, staging, and posing by, 78, 108, 116, *117*, 120, 158, 240, 306; Vanishing Race image of, 107, 108, 116, 180
Curtis, Natalie Burlin, 161

Dale, Bruce, 213
Davis, Wyatt, 7, 212, *232, 233*
Day, Charles (Charlie), imitation of Navajo by, 108, *109–10*, 111; as photographer, 114, 150, 158; relation with Curtis, 114, 115, 156
Day, Mrs. Sam, Sr., *288*, 289
Day, Sam, II, 108, *109*, 158, *288*, 289
Day, Sam, III, *288*, 289
Dedera, Don, 212
Delano, Jack, 213
Dennetsosi, Hoke, 194
Dinwiddie, William, 75
Dixon, Joseph K., 149, 157, 158, *183*, 256, 257
Dodd, Theodore, 70, *71*
Dodge, Chee, 86
Donaldson, John, 86
Dry River Trading Company, 95
Dubois, Dan and Maggie, 86

East Boundary Association, 46, 47
Eiler, Terry, 213
Elanger, Woodrow, 27
Elle of Ganado, 153, 260, *261*
El Tovar Studio, *174, 175, 177*
Enemyway, *138*, 139, 290, *291*, 294
Etson, Tom, 209
Evans, Walker, 248

Fannie, 228, 229
Farabee, William C., 149
Farm Security Administration, 15, 213
Fedor, Ferenz, 268, *271*
Fetter, W. L., 87, *90, 91*
Fewkes, J. Walter, 209
Field, Katie, 188
Film: color, 150; roll, 152; slide, 364–65
Forrest, Earle R., 2, 3, 150, 159–60, 184, *185*
Forster, Elizabeth, 235, 246
Fort Defiance AZ, 82, 86, *178, 179*, 197
Fort Sumner NM. *See* Bosque Redondo
Fort Wingate NM, 77, 85, 144, *145*; photography studio in, 76, 78, 82

387

Index

Foster, Hal, 307
Foster, Kenneth, 221
Frames, framing, 12–13
Francis [Nakai], Mrs., *244*, 245
Franciscan Friars, St. Michaels. *See* St. Michaels AZ
Frank, Robert, 268, *270–71*, 280, 285
Frasher, Burton, 159, 184, *185*, 274
Friends of the Earth, 269, 273
Fringed Mouth, *109*, *238*, *288*, 289
Frisbie, Charlotte, 221
Fuller, Tim, 209

Gaede, Marc, 267, 268–69, 280
Gaige, J. G., 53, 70, 315–16n4; posing style of, 54, 55, 58, 59
Gail, Ida Mary, 202, 203
Gallup Intertribal Ceremonial, 28, *29*, *50*, 51, 158, *232*, 233
Gallup NM, 91, *136*, 137, 200, *201*; photography studios in, 78, 87, 158
Ganado AZ, 102, *103*, 151, *163*, *270–71*
Ganado Mucho, 70
Gardner, Alexander, 57, 74–75
Gates, P. G., 153, *154*, 155
Gedekoh, Clifford E., 144, *145*–46, 147, 208
Gentile, Charles, 53, 54
Gill, Delancy, 98, *99–100*, 101
Gill, Sam, 275
Gilpin, Laura, 32, 33, *250–51*, 308; compared with Curtis, 19, 120, 236, 240, 241; *The Enduring Navaho*, 223, 235, 236, 237, *238*, 246, 295; humanization of landscape by, 241, *243*; image of Navajo, 236, 237; lawsuit against estate of, 235, 248–49, 332–33n32; on McCombe, 237; photographic purpose of, 236, 237, 241; photographs of healing ceremonies, *238*, *239*, 240; relations with Navajo, 240, 246, 248; retouching of photograph, *252*, 332n31; use of props and posing, 240–41, *242*, *244–45*, *252*, 306; view of Navajo, 236–38
Gishin Biye, *232*, 233
Goldwater, Barry, 212
Goodman, Charles, 74, 78, 82, *124*, *125*, 149; photograph of weavers, *256*, 257, 260, *261*
Grand Canyon AZ, *170*, *172*, *174*, *175*, *230*, 231. *See also* El Tovar Studio
Granstaff, Congressman, 144, *145*
Grant, George, 75
Grassham, John, *231*
Green, Benny, 76
Grimes, Joel, 19, 267, 272, 277–79, 306
Guernsey, S. J., 209
Guerro, John, 188

Haile, Berard, 208
Hair brushing, *215*
Hall, E. E., 78
Hamel, F. M., 208
Hamilton, Parker, 144, *145*
Hanna, Forman, 190
Hardbelly, 241, 246
Harris, A. B., *231*
Harris, Ida, *231*
Harris, Sallie (Brewer), *142*, 143
Harrison, Mike, *288*, 289
Harvard Value Studies Project, 209, 210
Harvey, Fred, Company, 156–57, 317n19
Haske Yazzi, *232*, 233
Hatali Nez, *118*, 119
Haz pah, *170–71*
Heard Museum, 295
Hearst, Phoebe, 149
Hegemann, Elizabeth, 188, *288*, 289
Heick, William, 221
Henry, Jean and Robert, 132, *133*
Herbert, Charles, 213
Hiester, Henry T., 70, *71*, 75
Hight, George, 211
Hildebrand, J. W., 74, 75, 78, 82, 87, *88*, 89; photograph of weavers, *257*, *262*, *263*; relation with Schwemberger, 82, 158
Hill, Rick, 107, 269
Hillerman, Tony, 269
Hillers, John K., 70, *72–73*, 274
Holbrook AZ, *264*, 265
Holy People, 21–22, 121–22
Hopi, 150, 160, *161*, 273, 275
Hoskinnini, *186*
Hoskinninni Begay, *186*
Hosteen Klah, *192*
Hosteen Nez, *154*, 155, *163*, 166
Hosteen Yaga, 86
Hostine qust-gin-ayne, *155*
Hózhǫ́, 272
Hrdlicka, Ales, 75, 77, 149
Hubbell, J. L., 158, 263
Hubbell, Roman, *232*, 233
Huckel, J. F., 157
Hunter's Point Day School AZ, *130*
Hwéeldi. *See* Bosque Redondo, Long Walk

Ianbito Day School NM, *142*, 143
Indian Detours, 4

Jacka, Jerry, 212
Jackson, William Henry, 64, 74, 209
James, G. Wharton, 33, 74, 75, *80*, 81, 149, 156; photograph of weaver, 260, *261*; resented by peers, 77–78
James, Gilbert, 27
James, Harry, 144, *145*

James, H. C., 48, *49*
Jay, Bill, 307
Jeddito Springs AZ, *258, 259*
Jemez, 160
Jennings, Cyrus, 53
Jessy, Mrs., *146,* 147
Johnson, Dewayne, 278
Johnston, Philip, 140
Jones, Billy, 114, 115
Jones, Philip Miles, 149, *151*
Juanico, 86
Juanita (wife of Manuelito), 55, *62,* 71, 74, 82, *83;* as photographic subject, 75, 83, 153
Jungians, 190

Kaadt, Christian, 87, *262, 263*
Kafer, Lawrence, 218
Kaiga begai Soldow, 86
Kawano, Kenji, 279–80, *281–82,* 284
Kayenta AZ, 161, 290
Keams Canyon AZ, 77
Keedah, Wilson, Sr., *284*
Keegan, Marcia, 19, 120, 267, 272, 274–75, 306
Kemp, Edward H., 153
Kessler, Leone, 188
Kidder, A. V., 209
Kinaaldá, 221
Kirk, Mike, *232, 233*
Kirk, Tom, 188, *232, 233*
Kluckhohn, Clyde, 208, 209, 210, 211–12, 236–37, 295
Knell, C., 208
Kodak, 75, 150, 152, 269
Kolb, Emory, *230,* 231

Laboratory of Anthropology, 212
Laguna Pueblo, 160, 212, *214,* 215
Lair, Max, 221
Landgraf, John, 209
Lange, Dorothea, 213, 248
Lantern slides, 153, 188
Laughing Singer, 76, 77, 116
Law, Adelarde, 102, *103,* 161, 190
Law, Lisa, 268
Leighton, Dorthea, 209
Life magazine, 209
Lime, John, 75
Lippincott, Sally, 188, 190, *192–93*
Little Colorado River AZ, *204, 205*
Little Singer, 76, 116, *118*
Lockett, H. Clay, 194
Lomahaftewa, Gloria, 291
Long Walk, 23, 53
Lorenzen, Henry, 53, 58, *68,* 69
Lowie Museum, 221
Luce, Willard, *215*

Lummis, Charles, 78, 274

Manifest Destiny, 15
Manito, 356, 357
Manley, Alan, 212
Manley, Ray, 212–13
Manuelito, 55, 58, 60, 61, *62,* 70, *71,* 82, *83,* 86
Manuelito Segundo, 55, *62*
Mariano, Chief, 76, 91
Marmon, W. G., 86
Marshall, Karen, 268
Martin, Marie, *130,* 194
Martinez, Johnnie, 212
Mary Ann Studio, *26,* 27
Matteson, Sumner W., 74, 75, 87, 91, 95, 150
Matthews, Washington, 76, 77, 78, 82, 85, 209
Maude, Frederic, 75, 78, 87, 150, 161
Maxson, Harmon, 209
Maxwell, Delivina, *231*
Maxwell, Lucien, 231
Mays, Buddy, 212
McAuley, Skeet, 267, 280, 283, 285, 306
McCombe, Leonard, 120, 209, 211, 223, 236, 268, 280, 295; Gilpin on, 237
McKee, J., *50,* 51
McLuhan, T. C., 152
McNitt, Frank, *50,* 51
McPhee, John, *138,* 139, 208
Meadows Trading Post, 3, 184, *185*
Mearns, E. A., 75
Meguelito. *See* Miguelito
Mickle and Jones studio, 75, 76
Miguelito, 102, *103, 168,* 169, 228, *229*
Miles, Jimmie and wife, 36, *37*
Millennium project, 273
Miller, Henry, 212
Mindeleff, Cosmos, 75
Miriam, Hoskie and Howard, *142,* 143
Mitchell, Frank, *200,* 201
Mitchell, Mike, 280, 283, 285
Mohave, 158
Momaday, N. Scott, 269, 280
Monsen, Frederick, 19, 33, 74, 75, 150, 156, 236, 267; photograph of "squaw-man," *124,* 125; photograph of weaver, *258–59;* photographs of children, *96,* 97, *164, 165, 166, 167;* photo techniques of, 152–53; portraits, *155, 163*–64, *165;* posing, 78; used force to get photograph, 152
Monticello UT, *146,* 147
Monument Valley AZ/UT, 180, *181,* 207, 285; Navajo models in, 8, *9,* 156, 213, *215,* 216
Monument Valley Tribal Park AZ/UT, 285
Moon, Carl [also Karl], 19, 33, 149, 157,

389

Index

169, 172, 236, 274; deception of Navajo by, 153, 323n5; photographs of children, 170–71, 174, 175; portraits, *168*, 169, 170–71, 174, 175, *176*, 177, *179*; posing style of, 156, 158, 190
Mooney, James, 74, 75, *76*, 77
Moore, J. B., *88*, 89, 158
Moreland, J. William, 249, 253
Morgan, William, 209
Motion pictures, 218, 221
Mountain Chant, Mountainway, 175, 190, 221
Muench, David, 212
Muench, Emil, 212
Muench, Joseph, 212
Mullarky, Tom, 158, 209
Museum of the American Indian, 77
Musser, Linda, 209
Mygatt, Peter, 218

Na da Ketche, *163*
Nakai, Eddie, 147
Nakai family, 240
Nakai, Raymond and Mrs., 144, *145*
National Geographic Society, 213
Native American Church, 211, 237
Native Peoples, 296
Natonabah, Andy, 283
Navaho Material Culture, 303
Navajo: as 'borrowers,' 18, 303–4, 306; history, European-American version, 22; history, Navajo version, 21–22; photography by, 6, 7, 102, 161, 291, *293*, 291–99, 366–68; as West's Other, 12, 17; West's view of, 12, 22, 40–41
Navajo Arts and Crafts Guild, *130*
Navajo Canyon AZ, 247
Navajo code talkers, 279–80, *281–82*
Navajo impersonators, *109*, 288, 289, 290
"Navajo Madonna," 248–49
Navajo Mountain AZ/UT, *164*, 165
Navajo Mountain School UT, 219, 247
Navajo Nation Museum, 191
Navajo Office of Broadcast Service, 277
Navajo photography: Bosque Redondo, 53–69; contemporary, 267–85; denial of history and, 18–19; early twentieth century, 149–87; late nineteenth century, 70–91; list of photographers in, 339–63; need for Navajo control of, 306–7; postcard companies, 364–65; relation to texts, 19–20; resistance/reaction to, 33–34, 46–47, 48, 49–50, 51, 80, 81, 115–16, 152, 238, 248, 250–51, 305; slide companies, 364–65; stock photograph companies, 365–66; themes in, 160, 302–5; types of, 35, 38, 40–42; Western charac-

ter of, 34; West's use of, 12, 40; . *See also* Children; *under names of individual photographers and subjects*
Navajo Tribal Council, 277
Newcomb, Franc, 188, 190
New Mexico, USA, 269
New Mexico Magazine, *4*, 188, 294
Nichols, Tad, 204, *205*
Nightway, 21, 22, 82, 158, 159, 221, 289; Andrus photographs of, *118*, 119; Curtis photographs of, 108, *109–10*, 111, 112, *113*, 116–16, *118*; Gilpin photograph of, 238, *239*; Schwemberger photographs of, 114–15, 158
Nohl, Mark, 28, 218
Nordenskiold, Gustaf, 75
Northup, Steve, 213
Norton, Billy, *200*, 201
Nostalgia, 14
Nudity, 157–58; male, 157, *183*
Nusbaum, Jesse, 156, 212

O'Hara, Geoffrey, 102, *103*
Old George, *95*
Old Lady Gray Salt, 247
Old Lady Long Salt, 246, *247*
Old Washie, 82
Oljato UT, *186*
Olop, Stephen, 160–61
Olson, Marie Le Tourneau, 161
Oppen, Lucy, 194
Orchard, William C., 77, *79*, *95*, 149
O'Sullivan, Timothy, 70, 74

Pafli, Marion, 213, 218
Page, Susanne, 213, 267, 275; *A Celebration of Being*, 272, 274; *Song of the Earth Spirit*, 272, 273
Parker, G. W., *86*
Parkhurst, T. Harmon, 212, 214, 215, 264, *265*, 274
Pennington, William, 149, 158, 160, 161, 162, 186
Pepper, George H., 74, 75, 77, *85*, 149
Peri, David, 221
Peshlacoi, Clyde, *142*, 143
Peshliki, *80*, 81
Photographers: amateur, 150; coffee-table, 223; studio, 158–59
Photographs: anti-, 299; death effect of, 14; ironic, 7, 59, 280, 283, 285; power relations and, 308; racist, *136*, *137*, 218, 304; retouched, *179*, *183*, *252*, 332n31; studio, 150
Photography: candid, 75, 153; critical scholarship of, 15–17; delegation, 74; as enterprise, 11–17; exploitation by, 35, 307;

390

gazing and, 13–14; hunting metaphors in, 14; impoverished, 19; minority group, 14, 35; non-neutrality of, 301; Pueblo groups and, 18; representation and, 16; rise of anthropology and, 15; silences of, 18, 19; temporality in, 13; Westernness of, 12, 34. *See also* Navajo photography
Photography's: Other, 14, 15; vision, 12
Physical anthropology, photography in, 77, 82, *84, 85*
Pierce, Charles, 78
Pine Springs AZ, *50,* 51, 221, 238, 242, 252
Platero, Joseph K., *100, 101*
Porter, Eliot, 213
Post, Helen, *46–47,* 218, 220, 267
Postcards, 150, 158, 159, 364–65
Powell, John Wesley, 70
Price, Gene, *207,* 208
Propaganda, 209, 211; photographs by Snow, 132, *133,* 134, *135, 138,* 139, *142, 143, 199,* 204, *205–6*
Public Health Service, 134, *135*
Public Law 101-644, 297
Pueblo peoples, 18

Ramah NM, 209
Red Ant Way, 221
Redford, Robert, 269
Red Rock AZ, *235, 250, 251*
Reed, Roland W., 149, 157, *182, 183,* 190, 209
Reichard, Gladys, 208, 209
Reichard, Lillian, 209
Reid, Betty, 277
Richardson, Gladwell, 188
Richfield UT, 204, *205*
Riefenstahl, Leni, 11
Roberts, John, 209
Robinson, H. F., 160
Robinson, Mary, 160
Robinson, Will, 160
Rochester Optical Company, 3
Rock Point AZ, *203*
Roessel, Monty, 294–95
Rogers, D. A., *203*
Rose, G. L., 78
Rosenzweig, Janine, 209
Rough Rock Community School AZ, 283
Running, John, 19, 120, 267, 268, 272, 275–77
Russell, Frank, 209

St. Louis Exposition, 1904, *98*
St. Michaels AZ, *130,* 288, *289*
St. Michaels Mission AZ, 82, 128, *129,* 150, 190–91
Sandoval's camp, 184, *185*

Sandpainting, 114, 118, 238
Sandweiss, Martha, 240, 246, 248, 280, 283
Santa Barbara CA, *192*
Santa Fe Center for Photography, 269
Santa Fe NM, 55, 64, 67, 69
Santa Fe Photographic Workshops, 276
Santa Fe Railway, 206, 260, 317n19
Santistien, Billy R., 48, *49*
Sassaman, William, 188
Savage, C. R., 82
Schmuckebier, *104, 105, 136, 137*
Schofield, 82
Schwemberger, Simeon, 82, 87, *88,* 89, 149, *178, 179,* 190–91; Nightway photographs of, 114–15, 158
Scott, Julian, 75, *86*
Selective Service, *138, 139*
Shepard, Mr., 53, 57
Sherman, William T., 54
She-she-nez, 98, *99*
Shindler, Alexander (A. Zeno), 53, 64
Shipley, A. D. and Mrs., *86*
Shiprock NM, 166, 241, *243*
Sierra Club, 269
Simpson, William, 157, 180, *181*
Slim First Dancers, *239*
Smillie, Thomas W., *100, 101*
Smith, L. W., 188
Smith, Rev., *136, 137*
Smith, William A., 53
"Snake Dance," 150, 161
Snow, Milton (Jack), 28, *29,* 140, *141, 197,* 200, 201, 209, 218; career of, 191, 194; photographic classification system of, 194–96, 208; photograph of weavers/weaving, *130,* 144, *145, 264*; portraits, *198,* 202, *203*; propaganda photographs of, 132, *133,* 134, *135, 138, 139, 142,* 143, *199,* 204, *205–206*
Snyder, Elizabeth, 115
Soil Conservation Service, 191
Sombrero, 194
Southwest Native Photographers Directory Project, 291
Southwest Sheepbreeding Laboratory, 144, *145*
Spectacles, 14
'Squaw man,' *124, 125*
Staples, B., 209
Steichen, Edward, 268
Stevens, Alden, 188
Stevenson, M. C., 77
Stewart, S., 295
Strodtbeck, Fred, 209
Stryker, Roy, 213
Sumner, 139
Swinnerton, Gretchen, *104, 105*

Index

Talking God, 112, *113*, *288*, 289
Tall Chanter, 116
Tapaha, J., 194
Tapahonso, Lucy, 280, 285
Teiwes, Helga, 221, 222, 223
Texas Frontier Centennial, 228, 229
Thomas, Jim, 194
Thompson, George, 212
Tiene su se, *71*
Tin Horn, 102, *103*, 161, 292, 293
Toddy, Joe, 192, *193*
Toe-hade-len, Runs Like The Water, 184, *185*
Tozzer, Alfred, 149, 209
Traders, 188
Tschopik, Harry, 209
Tsinajinnie, Andrew, 194, 295
Tsinhnahjinne, Hulleah, 295, *295–96*, *297–98*
Tsosie-bina, *164*, 165
Tuba City AZ, 161
Turquoise Bar NM, 48, *49*

Udall, Stewart L., 269, 277
Union Carbide, 269
Updike, Lisle, 161

Van Devanter, D. W., 212
Verplanck, James, 156
Vestal, Paul, 209
Vogt, Evon, 209, 211–12, 236–37, 295
Voyeurism, 14
Vroman, Adam, 74, 75, 78, 150, 153, 274, 318n20

Wade, Bob, 177
Wagner, Sally, *288*, 289
Waite, C. B., 78
Walker, Frank, 86, 139
Walker, John G., *100*, 101
Wallace, George, 144
Wanamaker expedition, 149, 157, 314–15n1, 323–24n8
Warren, Beatrice, *126*, 127
Washington DC, 98, 101
Watchman, Louis, *178*, 179
Waterflow NM, 148, *149*
Water Sprinkler, 112, *113*
Weapons, 56, 59, 77, 82, *84*. See also Bow and Arrow
Weavers, weaving, 70, *136*, 137, 144, *145*, 215, 256–65
Weed, E. F., 53, 64, *66*, 67
Weston, Edward, 213
West's: Other, 12, 14, 15, 16, 17, 20; view of Navajo, 12, 22, 40–41
Wetherill, Ida, 102, *103*, *186*
Wetherill, John, 228, *229*
Wetherills, 77, 158

Wheeler, G. M., 70
Wheelwright, Mary C., 190, *192*
Whitegoat, Frank, *200*, 201
White House AZ, 70, *182*, 183
Whitesinger, Anna Boyd, 296
Willis, J. R., 158, 172, *173*, 209, 274
Willoughby, C. C., 209
Wimar, Charles, 53, 57
Window Rock AZ, 28, 29, 144, *145–46*, 147
Wingate Vocational High School NM, 132, *133*
Winslow AZ, 27
Wittick, Archie, 158
Wittick, Ben, 74, 75, *84*, 85, *86*, 149, 158, 275; photographic methods of, 78, 82; photographs of Manuelito, 82, *83*
Wolfenstein, Valentin (also Valentine), 53, 54–55, 59, *63*, 64, *65–66*, 67, 70; photographic style, 55; photograph of Barboncito, 55, *56*, 57, *62*; photograph of Manuelito, Barboncito, and Calletano, 55, *60*, 61; photographs attributed to Brown or Weed, 58, 67, 316n10; photographs of Juanita, *62*, 75
Woodard, 228, 229
Worth, Sol, 218
Wright, Lt., 85
Wunder, Charlie, *136*, 137, 218
Wupatki AZ, *142*, 143
Wyman, Leland H., 208, 209

Yazz, Beatin, 192
Yazzie, Alfred, 283
Yazzie, Casey F., 27
Yazzie Farm, *242*
Yeibichai (Yebitchai), *110*, 111. See also Nightway
Yé'ii: female, 111, 112, *113*; male, *110*, 111
Yellow Horse, wife of, 184, *185*
Young, Stuart M., 161, *186*

Zia, 160
Zuni, 160